Best of Baseball Prospectus 1996-2011 Volume 2

THE ESSENTIAL SYNOPSIS OF THE WORLD'S GREATEST SPORTS WEBSITE
Featuring the Best of Over 15,000 Carefully Tended Features and Articles

Featuring never-before-published material by
Tommy Bennett · Jeff Euston · Ken Funck · Gary Huckabay · Jason Parks · Colin Wyers

Ben Lindbergh, Editor
Christina Kahrl, Consulting Editor
Dave Pease, Editor at Large

Foreword by Rob Neyer
Cover by Amanda Bonner
Layout by Dave Pease

Copyright 2011 Prospectus Entertainment Ventures, LLC
ISBN 1468038354
All Rights reserved

Without limiting the rights under copyright reserved above, no part of this publication may be reproduced, stored in or introduced into a retrieval system, or transmitted, in any form, or by any means (electronic, mechanical, photocopying, recording, or otherwise), without the prior written permission of both the copyright owner and the above publisher of this book.

This book is dedicated to the memory of

Doug Pappas
1962-2004

Always our brother, always our friend

http://bbp.cx/a/6256

Thank You

Thank you to our beautiful and talented interns Charles Dahan, Clark Goble, and Daniel Rathman for fighting through the hazing and helping us produce this book. Thank you to Jay Jaffe, Tommy Bennett, everyone at Baseball Prospectus, and all the contributors to this book for your patience and assistance.

Thank you to Gary Huckabay, Clay Davenport, Christina Kahrl, Rany Jazayerli, and Joe Sheehan, both for getting the Prospectus ball rolling and for providing the structure and the backbone for the Best of book.

Thank you to our Baseball Prospectus Premium subscribers.
None of this would have been possible without your support.

Thank you for reading this.

Table of Contents

Foreword
by Rob Neyer..iv
Preface
by Ben Lindbergh..vi

PART 5 : SABERMETRICS

Introduction by Colin Wyers....................1

Introduction to the Basics
by Baseball Prospectus..............................4
Integrating Statistics and Scouting
by Dayn Perry...6
Reshaping the Debate
by Joe Sheehan...8
Statistical Consistency
by James Click...11
23 Burning Questions
by Keith Woolner..15
More Hilbert Questions
by James Click...24
A Better Way to Build a Baseball Team
by Jonah Keri..28
Flipping the Switch
by Nate Silver..36
A New Look at Aging
by Nate Silver..40
Rethinking Replacement Level
by Nate Silver..49
New Life on Different Fields
by Nate Silver..54

Look, a Navel!
by Nate Silver..60
Why Are Games So Long?
by Russell A. Carleton................................63
Replacing Replacement
by Colin Wyers..67

PART 6 : PROSPECTING

Introduction by Jason Parks..................73

The Disparate Paths of Andy Marte and Michael Brantley
by Bradford Doolittle................................78
The Draft
by Rany Jazayerli..86
The Draft, Part Two
by Rany Jazayerli..94
The Draft, Part Three
by Rany Jazayerli......................................101
The Draft, Part Four
by Rany Jazayerli......................................107
The Draft, Part Five
by Rany Jazayerli......................................112
The Draft, Part Six
by Rany Jazayerli......................................118
The Draft, Part Seven
by Rany Jazayerli......................................127
The Draft, Part Eight
by Rany Jazayerli......................................134
The Draft, Part Nine
by Rany Jazayerli......................................140

The Draft, Part Ten
by Rany Jazayerli..................144

The Draft, Part Eleven
by Rany Jazayerli..................151

The Draft, Part Twelve
by Rany Jazayerli..................156

Valuing Draft Picks
by Nate Silver..........................164

The All-Disappointment Team
by Kevin Goldstein..................170

Going Over Slot
by Kevin Goldstein..................173

Post-Draft Thoughts 2.0
by Kevin Goldstein..................179

Slotto Bonanzas, Part One
by Nate Silver..........................182

And in This Corner...
by Kevin Goldstein..................186

The Alvarez Standoff, Resolved
by Kevin Goldstein..................190

Logan White, Part 1
by David Laurila......................193

Logan White, Part 2
by David Laurila......................199

Is the Scouts vs. Statheads Argument Overblown?
by Jonah Keri...........................204

Spring Training Psychonightmare
by Jason Parks.........................209

Finding a Little Future at the Futures Game
by Jason Parks.........................214

PART 7 : POSTSEASON

Introduction by Tommy Bennett.........235

Blowing It
by Nate Silver..........................223

The Greatest Pennant Race Comebacks
by Nate Silver..........................230

Oops, They Did it Again?
by Christina Kahrl....................240

The Perils of Relying on Short-Term Memory
by Jay Jaffe.............................248

A Brief Meditation on the Power of Sabermetrics During the Postseason
by Ken Funck...........................252

Whither Runs?
by Joe Sheehan........................255

Fall Classic Memories
by Baseball Prospectus............258

Crappy Odds
by James Click.........................274

Mortal Lock or Coin Flip?
by Doug Pappas........................277

A-Rodemption?
by Joe Sheehan........................281

Are the A's Equipped to Succeed in October?
by Mark Armour.......................286

Being on the Brink
by Nate Silver..........................290

Four and No More
by Christina Kahrl....................**293**

PART 8 : BUSINESS

Introduction by Jeff Euston.................297

Player Compensation
by Doug Pappas........................301

A New Way to Rank the GMs
by Shawn Hoffman....................**304**

The Best and Worst GMs of the Aughties
by Shawn Hoffman....................308

Busting the Myth of the Salary Cap
by Shawn Hoffman....................312

The Deal Almost No One Likes
    by Joe Sheehan......................315

Salary Cap
    by Joe Sheehan......................318

Worst. Contract. Ever.
    by Rany Jazayerli...................323

Weighin' in at 19 Stone, Part One
    by Gary Huckabay...................328

Weighin' in at 19 Stone, Part Two
    by Gary Huckabay...................336

Cleaning Out the Front Office
    by Christina Kahrl..................343

A Mulligan on Guzman
    by Nate Silver......................347

One Man's Plan
    by Keith Woolner....................354

PART 9 : EXTRA INNINGS

Introduction by Ken Funck..................365

Why Edgar Allan Poe Couldn't Play Fantasy Baseball
    by Keith Woolner....................370

Casey's Random Batting Trial
    by Keith Woolner....................374

Bug Selig's Successful Testing Program
    by Will Carroll.....................377

Dr. X2
    by Will Carroll.....................380

An Open Letter to Murray Chass
    by Nate Silver......................387

When the Rains Come
    by Rany Jazayerli...................389

The Decline and Fall of Yankee Stadium
    by Jay Jaffe.......................394

Redecorating Your Glass House
    by Gary Huckabay...................399

Take Me Out of the Hall Game
    by Jay Jaffe.......................402

Fernando Perez
    by David Laurila...................408

Joe Maddon, Part One
    by David Laurila...................415

Joe Maddon, Part Two
    by David Laurila...................420

Ozzie Guillen
    by David Laurila...................424

Jack Zduriencik
    by David Laurila...................431

Learning the Game
    by Rany Jazayerli...................437

BONUS BASEBALL

Careful What You Wish For:
What it's Really Like to Work in Baseball
    by Gary Huckabay...................447

Contributor Biographies...........................455

Foreword
by Rob Neyer

If you're reading this—and I think that you are—you don't really need me to tell you that a lot of things have changed since the first print edition of *Baseball Prospectus* was published so many years ago. You don't really need me to tell you that front offices have been transformed, or that *Baseball Prospectus* has played a big role in that process, or that some *Baseball Prospectus* writers are actually working in some of those front offices today.

You also don't need me to tell you that there's still work to be done. That there will always be more work. I will tell you this, though... there are enemies out there, eager to slow or perhaps even stop the work. And those enemies might not be who you think.

Nope, not Brian Sabean. Not Murray Chass. Not Mitch Williams. Not even Joe Morgan. Those men, however talented in their chosen fields, are mere mortals. Ultimately, they will bend like tender stalks of wheat before the thresher. The real enemies of scientific progress are both insidious and eternal.

Friends, meet Messrs. Arrogance and Certainty.

Fraternal twin brothers, those two.

Look, I'm not going to tell you that Arrogance and Certainty—those bastards—have never poked their noses around *Baseball Prospectus*. It happens to the best of us. Trust me on this one.

But it happens rarely to the BP Crew. And it certainly doesn't happen often in the pages of this book, which represents the *best* of *Baseball Prospectus*. This book is what happens when Arrogance and Certainty are missing in action, cowering somewhere in abject fear, because BP's writers begin with questions, not answers.

Do they wind up with answers? Sure. But one thing you'll notice, as you read through these pages, is that these guys begin with a question rather than an answer... and even at the end, they tend to recognize that they've just begun. That there's always more work to be done. That only with more work and never-ending curiosity might those terribly destructive fraternal twins be fought off, with the Search for Knowledge living to fight another day, and another.

You want Certainty, delivered with Arrogance? You've come to the wrong place.

You want Information, delivered with Humility? Welcome. You're among friends.

 Rob Neyer began his career with legendary baseball author Bill James, and later worked for STATS, Inc. and ESPN.com, writing more words for that website than anyone else. Rob has written or co-written six baseball books, including Rob Neyer's Big Book of Baseball Legends.

Growing up in Kansas City, Rob's favorite teams were the Royals, the Minnesota Vikings and the long-lost Kansas City Kings.

Preface
by Ben Lindbergh

In August of 2011, the rock band Breaking Benjamin (or the rock band Breaking Benjamin's label) deemed it necessary to release a collection called *Shallow Bay: The Best of Breaking Benjamin*, the title of which was taken from one of the group's songs but could have just as easily have referred to its back catalog's conspicuous lack of depth. At the time, Breaking Benjamin had been a going concern for less than a decade, with all of four albums and 50 tracks to its name. A dedicated Breaking Benjamin fan (a creature whose existence I can't confirm, having been blissfully ignorant of BB's oeuvre before beginning this preface) could have run through the entirety of the band's studio output in just over three hours. It seems unlikely that such a fan would have needed a reminder of the group's "early" work so, well, early, or that those four albums contained both enough great material for a successful retrospective *and* enough filler to make segregating those standout tracks on a single disc a worthwhile pursuit. Nonetheless, *The Best of Breaking Benjamin* (also available in a two-disc, 24-track "deluxe" edition) was born. No sooner had it appeared on a torrent site near you than it was revealed that two of the group's four members had been fired: Breaking Benjamin was broken. With the band on indefinite hiatus and locked in the sort of legal battles that often accompany the dissolution of productive partnerships, it's possible that *The Best of Breaking Benjamin* will serve as the coda to the group's relatively brief career.

The arrival of a "Best Of" retrospective usually suggests that the artist it features has produced something worth reissuing and experiencing anew (Creed's *Greatest Hits* notwithstanding). However, the very act of preserving its "best" output in a crystallized package also seems to signal that whatever comes next—if anything does—won't be as good as what went before. Indeed, a decade and a half after turning pro, were Baseball Prospectus a player, we'd have left our peak long behind. Most of our founding members have moved on to other endeavors, and those who remain contribute only infrequently. In that sense, we're a bit like Breaking Benjamin. Fortunately, baseball think tanks aren't bound by the same unforgiving aging curves that cut the careers of athletes and musicians short. Unlike a band on indefinite hiatus, we're more active than ever, and the work we produce—despite some new bylines—remains recognizable as that of Baseball Prospectus. As Steven Goldman wrote in his preface to *Baseball Prospectus 2011*:

> True institutions do not survive due to the efforts of any one or two people, but because a collective of believers holds true to their animating principle, thus forming an unbroken chain from founders to inheritors. In our case, we continue

to focus on cutting through baseball's homilies—stomping the dead, whenever possible, along the way—in favor of realism and hard truths.

A year later, with a few more roster additions and subtractions behind us, Steven's observation holds true (though he might perhaps have mentioned the sense of humor with which we do some of that stomping). Two more book projects loom large on BP's horizon, including the 17th edition of our best-selling annual, which, as usual, we expect to be our best yet. Our web site features new content daily, some of which could form the foundation of a future retrospective. This collection contains more material from our most recent year than from our first few years combined, and not just because it's fresh in our minds. We've also held ourselves to a higher standard than we did in the early days, which has led to even more of the groundbreaking insight, astute analysis, and witty commentary that you'll find in the following pages.

Perhaps you've been burned by a "Best Of" before. Maybe you bought *Clapton Chronicles: The Best of Eric Clapton* expecting to hear some Cream and Derek and the Dominoes only to find that what you'd actually brought home from the store was an unplugged version of "Layla" and some soft rock unrecognizable as the work of a guitar god. Maybe you enjoy the Eagles and—like many millions before you—bought *Their Greatest Hits (1971-1975)* only to discover that *Hotel California* came out in 1976 and your collection was still incomplete. Maybe you bought *The Best of the Knack*, *Very Best of the Knack*, and *Best of the Knack* only to discover that you'd been suckered into purchasing three separate CDs that started with "My Sharona" and went downhill from there. While we crammed everything we could into *The Best of Baseball Prospectus*, I expect (and welcome) a chorus of complaints and kind-hearted suggestions from readers who wish we'd chosen a particular article that didn't make the final cut. We know how you feel—whichever article it is, we wish we'd included it, too. With an article archive that has grown well into the five figures, we could have doubled or tripled the size of this book without any significant reduction in the quality of the work. Unfortunately, we couldn't have doubled or tripled its size and produced something you could carry and still read without a magnifying glass.

I wish I could say I learned about baseball at Nate Silver's knee, but for someone who went on to work for Baseball Prospectus, I came late to objective analysis. The Yankees of my youth spared me some of the embarrassing beliefs that most BP writers and readers can recall holding during the days before they saw the sabermetric light; the teams I grew up watching were so good that there weren't a lot of empty batting averages, RBI mirages, or deceptive win totals around to mislead me. Still, once I finally rallied to BP's banner, I found I had quite an education in store. While I enjoyed creating my own curriculum, I would've preferred to have *The Best of Baseball Prospectus* as a syllabus.

At its, well, best, the "Best Of" album, book, or Blu-Ray offers a career-spanning collection that simultaneously functions as a fitting introduction for someone who's new to the material and a welcome refresher for someone who's heard, read, or seen it before. We believe this book (and its companion volume) fulfills both purposes. If you've been with us from the start, we hope you'll enjoy reminiscing about how we got here while perusing the previously unreleased material. If you're just joining us, our past work will keep while you catch up. Meanwhile, we'll be back in the studio, working on our next big hit.

Ben Lindbergh
Editor
New York, November 27, 2011

Part 5
SABERMETRICS
Introduction by Colin Wyers

When I was a kid, I was interested in science, or at least as interested as a kid can be. Of course, the sort of science that interests children is rarely the sort practiced by adults, as the sort practiced by adults can be marked by long periods of tedium, and that's not the stuff daydreams are made of. So my idea of the scientific method looked something like this:

1. Start off with some test tubes, beakers, Technicolored chemicals, Bunsen burners, electrodes, cathodes, diodes, geodes, commodes, lightning bolts, and great puffs of smoke. Y'know, science stuff.
2. Spend a few moments explaining how this latest experiment will prove your critics wrong, and how this justifies doing dangerous experiments on yourself.
3. Reverse the polarity of the neutron flow!
4. Science happens.

Yes, I realize that this is something of an indictment of my television-viewing habits as a youth. I apologize for none of it.

A somewhat more serious exposure, if not to science, then at least to electrical engineering, came in the form of electronic lab kits from Radio Shack, which were packaged in increasing levels of complexity. For the simpler kits, you'd pick a circuit diagram out of the book that came with it and assemble it by connecting a series of resistors, capacitors, and transformers pre-wired to a breadboard. (You'd stick the exposed ends of various colored wires into the little springs to complete each connection.) More complicated kits came with a bunch of loose components and a breadboard that you'd have to assemble yourself each time.

Once you built a project, you didn't have to be done right away. Say what you had built was a little oscillating siren sound. The instructions provided were vague on this (telling you just enough to encourage you to proceed with experimenting, as I recall), but you could modify the circuit board to produce different siren sounds. Not only was this fun (I mean, I recall it being fun), but it was a way to learn in a very tactile way how different electrical components interacted. This was, while still not exactly being science, a bit closer to the reality of science than the "reverse the polarity" scenario outlined above.

I tend to think of sabermetrics as, at least in some respects, baseball science. (Some aspects of sabermetrics tend more towards applications of the findings of baseball science... baseball engineering, perhaps.) And I think sabermetrics as a whole takes on some of the features of the sort of childish science I outlined above—and I don't mean this pejoratively.

First, sabermetrics often shares the same sense of enthusiasm and wonder. There is no practical call for baseball science—they don't teach it in schools, there are very few jobs in it (although many more than there used to be), nobody is clamoring for a cure for whatever it is that makes Juan Pierre a fantabulous out-making machine except for fans of whatever team Pierre ends up on that season (and their insurance won't cover it anyway).

So to end up studying baseball in depth, it essentially has to be a labor of love. And since most of us were introduced to the game as children, there is a child-like quality at times to our love of baseball. Sometimes this is detrimental—for instance, there seems to be a small but devoted group of people who publish screed after screed using tortured mathematical analysis to explain why their treasured childhood hero deserves enshrinement in the Hall of Fame. Typically, the quality of the argument resembles the quality of the player—impressive in volume and in devotion, but not in achievement. (Even so, people like Rich Lederer managed to successfully campaign for Bert Blyleven's election to the Hall, and deservedly so.) But on the whole, the passion practitioners bring to their craft is one of the things that makes sabermetrics so interesting.

The other way I think sabermetrics resembles my childhood memories of science is that it involves a lot of tinkering. Sabermetricians love to take things apart, put things back together again, and altogether figure out how they work. This is why there are roughly as many run estimation formulas as there are people interested in run estimation. (I exaggerate, and you can group over 90 percent of run estimators into three or four recognizable formulas pretty easily, but I guarantee you that right now someone out on the Internet is blithely recreating a bases per out offensive estimator.)

Of course, sabermetrics also resembles actual science. Sabermetricians rarely, if ever, conduct actual experiments, largely for practical reasons. (Everything was approved by the institutional review board, but it turns out I didn't have enough money to buy a baseball team for experimental purposes.) So the methods used in sabermetrics tend to resemble the social sciences—economics, sociology, anthropology. But you can still recognize in sabermetrics the scientific method:

1. Make observations of something (in this case, a baseball game or a series of them),
2. Form a hypothesis—a theory about the thing being observed,
3. Make predictions based on the hypothesis, and
4. Test to see if the predictions hold true.

THE LINEUP

Introduction to the Basics
by Baseball Prospectus..4

Integrating Statistics and Scouting
by Dayn Perry..6

Reshaping the Debate
by Joe Sheehan..8

Statistical Consistency
by James Click..11

23 Burning Questions
by Keith Woolner..15

More Hilbert Questions
by James Click..24

A Better Way to Build a Baseball Team
by Jonah Keri..28

Flipping the Switch
by Nate Silver...36

A New Look at Aging
by Nate Silver...40

Rethinking Replacement Level
by Nate Silver...49

New Life on Different Fields
by Nate Silver...54

Look, a Navel!
by Nate Silver...60

Why Are Games So Long?
by Russell A. Carleton...63

Replacing Replacement
by Colin Wyers...67

The scientific method is truly what distinguishes sabermetrics from the sort of "batting average during a full moon when facing a Pisces" analysis the Elias Sports Bureau made popular in the 80s (and that television broadcasters have kept alive for decades after). It's also what distinguishes sabermetrics from the mindset that views home run totals and hit records as objects of near-religious devotion; sabermetrics doesn't hold numbers as having inherent reverence, but as data points that can provide understanding when placed in proper context.

Another feature sabermetrics has in common with scientific inquiry is an emphasis on corroboration and reproducibility. To be accepted, multiple analysts should be able to come to similar findings, even starting with different data sets.

But the most important difference between sabermetrics and so-called "traditional" thinking is the emphasis on incremental gains in knowledge, combined with the understanding that there is yet more that we do not know. Just as Einstein's theories and quantum physics have superseded Newton's earlier work on physics (and as Newton's work superseded the Greeks and their natural philosophy), sabermetrics continues to evolve as new findings are made and old findings continue to be tested against new evidence.

In that spirit, I present to you these essays, largely devoted to sabermetricians discussing the field itself. Some of them present answers, but more importantly, all of them propose questions. It's my sincerest hope that someone reading this gets inspired to answer one of those questions for us all.

Enjoy.

FEBRUARY 17, 2004
http://bbp.cx/a/2563

BASEBALL PROSPECTUS BASICS
Introduction to the Basics
Baseball Prospectus

In the introduction to the "Baseball Prospectus Basics" series, the staff made the case for the value of objective analysis.

If you're not familiar with Baseball Prospectus, here's what we're all about: understanding the game better, and innovating in order to do it. Everyone at BP loves the game of baseball with a passion that most people just don't understand. We feel that this greatest of games is so compelling that we want to know everything about it. We always want to improve our understanding of the game; each player, each play, each pitch, each throw, each hit—what does it really mean? Those arguments that take place in bars about the relative merits of different players? We really want to know the definitive answer to those questions. But we don't want to kill the joy of the game while we're looking.

We want to be able to compare players on an apples-to-apples level. Most every baseball fan understands, at least on some level, that it's easier to hit .300 in Coors Field than Dodger Stadium. We calculate how much easier it is and allow you to see the players' performances without the distortion of park and league effects. It's not a very complicated idea, but it can be kind of daunting at first. There's more. What's wrong with traditional stats like wins? Are there better ways to look at a pitcher's performance? Why not use the Triple Crown stats we all grew up with to compare hitters to each other? Is there a better way? What can managers do to make better use of their bullpens? Is there a better way to evaluate defense? Does clutch hitting really exist? We're always asking these types of questions and sharing possible answers with you.

To a great extent, Major League Baseball has been insulated from many of the competitive pressures that other businesses face every day. Modern management techniques have been slow to arrive in MLB front offices. The intense pressure that drove millions of businesses to invest and focus on improvement has been absent, or at least barely noticeable in baseball circles.

Not anymore. The information revolution has finally arrived in baseball. Teams are learning better, more efficient ways to build winning rosters. They're asking many of the questions we'll be asking in Baseball Prospectus Basics, plus many more. By questioning conventional wisdom and looking for new solutions, we hope you'll develop an even greater love and appreciation for the game of baseball. As the game progresses, your favorite team will acquire a player or make a move that may not be popular in many circles; meanwhile, you'll nod your head knowingly and smile.

Will the search for new answers damage the game? Will its poetry be lost in a blizzard of derived numbers? Not in the slightest. The game is going to be better than ever before. Because better players will be playing. As defense is evaluated more and more effectively, teams will value it more highly, and you'll see better defense on the field. Teams will pass on the rickety veteran with the brand name in favor of the unknown independent league slugger, and you'll see better hitting on the field. As we learn better ways to manage pitchers, teams will experience fewer injuries and greater success, and you'll see greater pitching on the field.

And that's the way it should be. Life's supposed to get better, not worse. We want the same for baseball.

BASEBALL PROSPECTUS BASICS
Integrating Statistics and Scouting
Dayn Perry

After the publication of *Moneyball*, statistics and scouting were often portrayed as being at odds. As Dayn Perry understood, the two approaches to evaluating talent work better in tandem than in isolation.

With the rise of quantitative analysis in baseball and the prominence of Michael Lewis's bestseller *Moneyball* (which, contrary to the ruminations of Joe Morgan, was not written by Oakland GM Billy Beane) there has been cultivated a turf rivalry of sorts between traditional scouting types and their propeller-head assailants. It's my position (and the position of probably all of my colleagues here at Baseball Prospectus) that this rivalry is silly, unnecessary, and ultimately counterproductive. That's because as organizations begin to recalibrate their approach to making player personnel decisions, they don't need to be asking: Which method do we choose? Instead, it should be: How do we integrate both approaches?

You see, there's no need to replace traditional scouting with performance scouting (a term sometimes used to describe what we do here at Baseball Prospectus), and there's no need to ignore the latter completely in blind preference to the former. In a column I wrote last year, I made a "beer and tacos" metaphor out of the dilemma. It's a little like asking the question: "Which do you want, beer or tacos?" The answer, of course, is: "Both. Now, please."

I'll leave it to your druthers to decide whether beer or tacos is equated with traditional or performance dilemma, but the point is the decision to be made is one of degrees rather than one of relentless adherence to one or the other. Some organizations have cut back on their scouting staffs. While this has sent some members of the media into a moral panic, it's merely a market correction going on throughout the game. For most of baseball history, performance scouting has lurked behind the industry's dusty potted palm in the corner—devoid of influence and recognition. That's changing—and for the better, I might add. Organizations like the Red Sox, A's, Blue Jays and, now, Dodgers rely or will soon rely heavily on performance scouting. Others like the Padres, Yankees, Indians, and Mets have struck more of a balance between the two. Then there are those like the D-Rays who seem to depend primarily on treasure maps, divining rods, and magic beans.

It's perhaps useful to think of the two approaches as inputs and outputs. Traditional scouting, by focusing on things like arm strength; swing mechanics; movement on pitches; pop times; foot, bat, and pitch speed, and other physical tools, homes in on the ingredients of performance. Performance analysis tells you, on a micro level, what a player is doing with those skills and tools—how well he's bringing it all to bear on the field of play. Is that work-of-art swing actually producing an adequate number of runs? Is that jaw-dropping fastball creating enough outs? Is that fat, lumbering guy with no position quietly one of the best hitters in his circuit? Those are the kinds of things we can tell you, with advanced—yet easily absorbed—measures you won't find on any Topps card. Tools aren't worth anything unless they translate into performance on the field. Baseball is unlike many other major sports in that it requires a distinct set of athletic abilities. Plodding endomorphs like John Kruk and Cecil Fielder can become quality players at the highest level, while an athlete nonpareil like Deion Sanders flails about as a highly paid novelty act.

Things don't really get interesting when the two approaches are in agreement. Take a seasoned scout and Keith Woolner, put them in a room, and tell them to discuss, say, Vlad Guerrero. What you'll get is verbal bouquet upon verbal bouquet from both perspectives. What about when the two approaches don't agree? Well, either school of thought can point to a number of overlooked or over-hyped talents in both camps. What's different is that the performance analyst, when evaluating a certain player, is always adding to the dossier. If the tools remain the same, but the performance changes suddenly, what are we to make of this? Fluke or new level of ability? By peering deeply into the statistical record, even as it grows daily, the performance analyst can offer insight into just what's happening to a player.

Both approaches have value and are being incorporated by the most successful organizations. Which one's more useful? We no doubt have our own subjective opinions about that, but there's little doubt that the performance-analytics end of the continuum has been long neglected in baseball. That's changing, and it's changing fast. If you're fellow traveler, you already know this. If you're not, well, how about some beer to go with those tacos?

BASEBALL PROSPECTUS BASICS
Reshaping the Debate
Joe Sheehan

In a piece originally published as the introduction to *Baseball Prospectus 2000*, Joe Sheehan made the case for baseball statistics as a worthy (and non-threatening) subject of study.

The following essay appeared as an introduction to Baseball Prospectus 2000.

"Stathead."
"Stat-drunk computer nerd."
"Rotisserie geek."

You can earn a lot of derision when you look at things in a new way, and the people who have applied statistical tools to evaluate baseball players and teams have heard the above epithets and more. The work of people such as Bill James, Craig Wright, and Clay Davenport has often been dismissed as the mind-numbing analysis of people who need to put their slide rules away and get out and watch a game once in a while. Their efforts, which have been dubbed "statistical analysis," have expanded and improved the body of objective baseball knowledge, and their work is even beginning to penetrate the insular world of baseball front offices.

But the term "statistical analysis," as applied to baseball, isn't descriptive enough. Actuaries analyze statistics, and while the work pays well, it is pretty dry stuff. Life-expectancy tables and risk/benefit workups aren't going to get your average Red Sox fan excited, nor should they: baseball fans care about their teams, and the players on them, not a series of numbers.

But baseball statistics are not numbers generated for their own sake. Statistics are a record of performance of players and teams. Period. Benjamin Disraeli's oft-quoted line—"There are three types of lies: lies, damned lies, and statistics"—just doesn't apply.

Looking at statistics—looking at the record of player and team performance—helps analysts reach conclusions about players. So when Rany Jazayerli writes that Jose Rosado is one of the 10 best starting pitchers in the American League, that's not an analysis of statistics, that's an analysis of performance. In the same way that a scout watches a player run and decides whether he's fast or slow, analysts look at a player's EqA and determine how good a year he had. That's performance analysis, a more descriptive term for the work we do.

The distinction is critical in moving this type of baseball analysis from an outsider view to the mainstream, so that in the front office of a major-league team it can be as acceptable to look at a player's on-base percentage as to look at a scout's opinion of his foot speed. Organizations need to credit a pitcher for his consistently good Triple-A performance in the same way that they mark him down for his below-average fastball.

Reshaping the debate between traditional baseball people and the analyst community will give a significant push to what is currently a creeping movement. If you look at the success of the New York Yankees of the late 1990s or the 1999 Oakland A's, it's clear that some teams have embraced one of the fundamental tenets of baseball analysis: the importance of on-base percentage in scoring runs. In fact, the A's have become the first organization to emphasize plate discipline in their player-development program.

We have seen the work of Wright and Rany Jazayerli on pitcher usage, particularly young-pitcher usage, start to make inroads within the game. Teams have become increasingly aware of the workloads they put on their best pitching prospects, recognizing relationships between workload and injury and workload and ineffectiveness. Given the significant investments that organizations make in their top talent, this is a prime area in which baseball analysis can make a financial impact as well as an on-field impact.

Performance analysis does not, and should not, exist in a vacuum. First of all, it is important to understand the context of statistics, and the Davenport Translations are prima facie evidence of this. The line ".280/.350/.450" is about as informative as a George W. Bush campaign speech. At what level was this performance? How old is the player? In what park and what league does he play? What position?

And once you have all those answers, you still have half only the picture. Every player has a skill set, abilities that make him the player he is. Each player has certain strengths and weaknesses. Skills analysis—the province of scouts, managers and coaches—isn't made obsolete by performance analysis. It's enhanced by it.

Knowing that a 23-year-old right-hander has a live fastball, a middling curve and a change-up he can spot at will is essential. A pitcher's repertoire, a hitter's bat speed, a shortstop's arm... if you're going to develop a complete, accurate picture of any player, you must know these things. But you also want to know if the pitcher has an acceptable strikeout rate, because that's the best predictor of career length. You want to know if the player can drive the ball, as measured by his slugging percentage and isolated power. And if that shortstop is among the league leaders in assists and double plays, it's an excellent indication that he is great at using his arm to get outs. Isn't that what fans and general managers really want to know?

Performance analysis has limitations. Amateur baseball players, with aluminum bats, shorter schedules, and widely variable levels of competition, are best analyzed by their skills. Performance analysis of players in short-season leagues is also unreliable, both because of limited sample sizes and the adjustments that the players, usually new to professional baseball, are making. Given a choice between a scouting report and a Davenport Translation on an 18-year-old with 200 plate appearances in the Gulf Coast League, the scouting report will be a better tool.

Performance analysis paired with skills analysis is how successful teams are going to be built in the 21st century. Good organizations will accept that there's as much to be gained from looking seriously at a player's track record as there is from looking at the scouting reports on him. Successful teams will be built on principles that have developed from performance analysis. Ideas that were radical just 10 years ago will become conventional wisdom, as people like Billy Beane have success, and as other organizations imitate what made the A's successful.

Reshaping the debate continues a cycle that began with Branch Rickey's conclusions about on-base percentage and continued through Bill James's work in popularizing sabermetrics. It provides a means for the baseball mainstream to embrace the concepts of performance analysis while maintaining their established, valuable methods of skills analysis. Eventually there will be no debate, as both will be used routinely in evaluating talent and building baseball teams. A better brand of baseball for everyone will be the ultimate legacy of performance analysis.

BASEBALL PROSPECTUS BASICS
Statistical Consistency
James Click

One of the keys to understanding baseball statistics is remembering how stable they are over time. James Click produced a handy guide to which stats are the most and least stable.

February, in the baseball world, is the month of predictions. Every analyst, writer, web site, undefeatable computer program, guy with a beer, and book (some better than others) spends that month looking over the offseason wasteland and espousing conclusions. The method behind these processes varies more widely than Johnny Depp's acting roles; some are based purely on numbers, some purely on empirical data, some purely on names, and some purely on nothing. So what can you count on?

For one thing, you can count on me not offering you any spectacular predictions, guaranteed to be more accurate than anything on the market. If you want that, read up on BP's own PECOTA projection system. Instead, the aim will be to lay a basic groundwork for your expectations of the consistency of basic statistics from season to season. Surmising the volatility of various metrics, and their consistency from year to year, is the primary goal.

To accomplish this, I'm going to start with batting statistics, which are traditionally more stable than pitching statistics. To reduce outliers and the game's inherent degree of chance, only seasons in which a player accumulated at least 200 at-bats (ABs) were used. All seasons from 1991 to 2003 were considered, looking particularly for consecutive seasons of sufficient sample size. This process yielded 3066 sample seasons from which to draw data.

The variety of statistics that can be tested is understandably large, but it's important to use only rate statistics such as batting average (AVG), on-base percentage (OBP), and slugging percentage (SLG) because of the large variance in ABs and plate appearances (PAs). For the purposes of the study, 20 home runs in 300 AB is considered the same as 40 HR in 600 AB, but the difference between 20 and 40 actual home runs is irrelevant. To this end, AVG, OBP, SLG, BB% (Walk Rate, BB/PA), K% (Strikeout Rate), XBA% (Extra-Base Hit Percentage, XBA/H), HR% (Home Run Rate), and ISO (Isolated Power, SLG-AVG) were considered. Each is a rate statistic that reveals information about certain parts of a player's composition at the plate. Looking at the results both individually and in concert will yield some conclusions about year-to-year statistical consistency.

Metric	R-Squared	Standard Deviation
AVG	0.1761	0.031
OBP	0.3820	0.041
SLG	0.4171	0.080
BB %	0.5745	3.520
K %	0.6884	5.230
XBA %	0.4634	8.820
HR %	0.5751	1.730
ISO	0.5510	0.064

Before we get to the results, however, let's do some house-cleaning. To the far left we have our offensive metrics, followed by the R-Squared, as well as the Standard Deviation. For the uninitiated, R-Squared is another term for "coefficient of determination"—a measurement of correlation. The higher the R-Squared total, the greater the correlation, and thus, the more consistent the metric. Depending on how it's being used, an R-Squared of below 0.5000 is typically considered too low to justify any sort of predictive value. Standard deviation, meanwhile, is simply a measure of variance—the higher the number, the more volatile the metric.

With that being said, of these metrics, batting average has the least consistency, and thus the least predictive ability. Meanwhile, four metrics cleared the fabled 0.5000 line—Walk-Rate, K-Rate, and HR-Rate—all of which are defense-independent. This fact supports the idea that the hitters remain consistent from year-to-year, while much of the volatility of AVG and, to a lesser extent, OBP and SLG, can be attributed to the opposing defense. Removing the defense from the equation greatly increases the predictability of batting statistics, a fact that reinforces the idea that there is a significant amount of luck involved in AVG. This finding isn't really big news, but it's always nice to reconfirm something some of us might take for granted.

(As a brief aside, it's important to clarify what is meant by batting average being subject to a great deal of "luck." This is not to say that all major-league hitters are equal when it comes to AVG, or that the differences evident between them are entirely random. Rather, players have a theoretical AVG ability that varies from player-to-player, but the sample size of a season is too small to accurately reveal that every year. The high volatility of AVG from year to year—the statistical "noise," if you will—is sufficiently large enough to obscure the differences between many major-league hitters of similar ability. The book *Curve Ball*, by Jim Albert and Jay Bennett, has some excellent discussion on this topic.)

When looking at pitchers, many of the same constraints were placed on the data as batters. The minimum playing time for pitchers was set at 50 IP in any given season. This yielded 2695 sample seasons from 1991-2003. Statistics considered were, again, entirely rate metrics: starting with the mainstream ERA (Earned Run Average) and WHIP (walks plus hits, divided by innings pitched), and moving on to K/9 (Strikeouts per 9 IP), BB/9, H/9, HR/9, K/BB, and GB/FB (groundball/flyball ratio). (Data for GB/FB was available only from 1999 on, yielding a much smaller sample size of 912 seasons.) Let's see how it turned out:

Metric	R-Squared	Standard Deviation
ERA	0.1091	1.20
WHIP	0.1410	0.20
K/9	0.5627	1.82
BB/9	0.3413	1.09
H/9	0.1745	1.45
HR/9	0.1273	0.41
K/BB	0.3610	1.00
GB/FB	0.5591	0.50

If you're a regular visitor to BP, the fact that ERA is, so far, worse than any other statistic at maintaining consistency from year to year should come as no surprise. Its volatility is approaching almost total randomness due to the variety of game events it attempts to take into account: the official scorer's decisions, defense, the sequence of events, and the pitcher's actual ability, just to name a few. Interestingly, WHIP doesn't fair quite as well as expected when comparing it to H/9 and BB/9—two statistics that should map to it rather well since they take into account two of the three stats used in WHIP. Instead, by combining two inconsistent statistics, WHIP comes out worse overall. The only two metrics that seem to have any consistent value are K/9 and GB/FB—once again, statistics that do not involve the defense.

Considering the fact that much of the blame for the inconsistency of AVG, ERA, and other statistics has thus far been blamed on the defense, it would be unfair not to check and see how variable defense is. Measuring defense, though, is sticky business. It's best to read the results below with large grains of salt, constantly reminding yourself that defensive statistics don't always reflect the events on the field and that defense is inherently a team activity. Adjusting for players switching positions over the course of the year also threw a wrench into the works.

The sample group was once again drawn from the same years, but the caveats included having to accumulate at least 100 innings at any one position. Further, if players accumulated over 100 innings at more than one position, those positions were considered together only if they were similar defensively. For instance, a player who played 200 innings in right field and 200 in left field had his total defensive line added together; likewise players who played second base, shortstop, and third base. Players moving around between first base and the outfield were assigned the stats from the position they played the most in the following season. (For example, if a player played 1000 innings at first in 2002 and split time between first and the outfield in 2001, only his first-base stats from 2001 were considered. Likewise with catchers and anyone named Craig Biggio or

Chuck Knoblauch.) These conditions yielded a sample size of 5606 seasons.

The three statistics considered were again rate stats based on the (rather limited) defensive stats available. First is fielding percentage (FP, pronounced "Santangelo" if you like), which is Putouts (PO) plus Assists (A) over Total Chances (TC). Second is Total Chances per 9 Innings (TC/9), a measure that's almost the exact same stat as range factor, but with errors included. Finally, Defensive Efficiency (DE) was included because it more accurately reflects the team aspect of defense. Admittedly, this is a very small range of statistics to consider, but the current crop of available defensive statistics yields few options and instills limited confidence that the numbers are an accurate reflection of the events on the field (which, of course, is the whole point of stats).

Metric	R-Squared	Standard Deviation
FP	0.1183	0.030
TC/9	0.8056	2.580
DE	0.2767	0.011

While there is little hope for FP, TC/9 looks more impressive than any statistic sampled thus far. The only drawback to this is the fact that TC/9 doesn't reveal very much about the actual player involved. It's at least as dependent on the GB/FB and handedness of the pitchers in front of him or the quality of other defenders as it is on the ability of the player in question. Its year-to-year consistency does little more than reveal that balls put into play, for the most part, are distributed around the field in a consistent manner from season to season. The consistency of Defensive Efficiency falls towards the middle of the pack when compared with other metrics viewed so far, but its variance helps explain the high variance of H/9 and ERA, as expected. It does not, however, explain batting average, since league-wide DE stays very stable from year to year.

While the idea that defense-independent statistics are steadier than defense-dependent ones is not a new idea, it's worthwhile to clarify within those ranges which ones are the most constant. In the rather simple cases looked at here, the hierarchy would start with strikeouts, drop slightly to walks, then to home runs, and finally to anything involving balls in play. Obviously, there are ways to improve the year-to-year consistency—looking at more than the immediate previous season, adjusting for age, park, team, etc.—but for now, when various publications are predicting big things for this season based on last year's numbers, remember that things aren't quite as consistent as you might expect. That's why they play the games.

BASEBALL'S HILBERT PROBLEMS
23 Burning Questions
Keith Woolner

In an essay originally published in the 2000 annual, Keith Woolner identified 23 baseball research problems for the future, some of which have since been researched extensively.

The following essay was originally published in Baseball Prospectus 2000.

> *Who of us would not be glad to lift the veil behind which the future lies hidden, to cast a glance at the next advances of our science and at the secrets of its development during future years? What particular goals will there be toward which the leading sabermetric spirits of coming generations will strive? What new methods and new facts in the wide and rich field of sabermetric thought will the new years disclose?*

Here at Baseball Prospectus, we're not completely immune to the general fascination with the recent turn of the world's odometer. So, with this edition marking the final year of the second millennium, let's take a look forward at what the third holds for us seamheads.

Our inspiration comes from a similar effort nearly 100 years ago. In 1900, a mathematician named David Hilbert addressed the International Congress of Mathematicians in Paris and delivered what was to become history's most influential speech about mathematics. Hilbert outlined 23 major problems to be studied in the coming century. In doing so he expressed optimism about the field, sharing his feeling that unsolved problems were a sign of vitality, encouraging more people to do more research.

The above quote is, in fact, a bastardization of the opening statements of Hilbert's speech. Hilbert referred to mathematics instead of sabermetrics and spoke in terms of "centuries" instead of "years." Given the relative youth of sabermetrics and baseball analysis compared to math, it's appropriate to use a period of smaller scope than Hilbert. The quotes that appear periodically throughout this essay are similarly taken from Hilbert's speech and altered to refer to baseball analysis.

Hilbert's address was much more than a collection of problems. It outlined a philosophy of mathematics, and the problems put forth were ones relevant to that philosophy. By putting forth our own "Hilbert problems" for baseball analysts of the future, Baseball Prospectus is outlining our philosophy for how and why this kind of work ought to be done—our attempt to provide inspiration and guidance to the baseball community at large.

> *It is difficult and often impossible to judge the value of a problem correctly in advance; for the final award depends upon the gain which science obtains from the problem. Nevertheless we can ask whether there are general criteria which mark a good sabermetric problem.*

We used the following criteria to guide our selection of the baseball research problems for the future:

1. To be relevant, sabermetrics must inform a decision: data for data's sake is not useful. Bill James once defined sabermetrics as the search for objective knowledge about baseball. While this is still true, it doesn't cut to the heart of the matter. A list of players, cross-referenced by preferred breakfast cereal and astrological sign, is objective knowledge, but it isn't what anyone would call useful information. There is already too much irrelevant data clogging up the airwaves and the Web. Baseball analysis must focus on knowledge that can lead to an action or a commitment of resources (time, effort, money) by someone who wants to study the game. The decision can be anything from in-game tactical moves to judging player acquisitions. It can be prospect evaluation or an MVP or Hall of Fame ballot. It can even be some personal idiosyncratic award for things you might think are important. But, in order to produce useful information, you have to start with a relevant question that needs answering.
2. The industry of baseball encompasses more than just the action on the field. To be relevant to the sport as it's practiced today, baseball analysis must expand to explicitly consider the economic, social, technological, competitive, and governmental contexts in which the game operates.
3. The amount of potential information is larger than the amount of information that is available today. In raising some of these research questions, we acknowledge that the resources to answer them may not yet be available. It may be years or decades before there's sufficient effort, technology or understanding to create a systematic collection of observations needed to resolve some of these issues. However, by recognizing the importance of the problem itself, we can hope to guide the efforts to acquire new information in a manner that is consistent with the problems we want to solve.
4. Numbers alone are not data, and solving equations is not analysis. Some data can be expressed as numbers, and judicious use of mathematics can yield analytical insights, but we should not abandon a line of reasoning for lack of quantification or a failure to find a tidy formula.

If we would obtain an idea of the probable development of sabermetric knowledge in the immediate future, we must let the unsettled questions pass before our minds and look over the problems which the science of today sets and whose solution we expect from the future. To such a review of problems the present day, lying at the meeting of the centuries, seems to me well adapted. For the close of a great epoch not only invites us to look back into the past but also directs our thoughts to the unknown future.

Baseball Prospectus' Hilbert Problems for the Next Century

Defense

1) Separating defense into pitching and fielding.

This is one of the oldest and most vexing problems in baseball analysis. Pitching and fielding are so intertwined that they seem impossible to separate. That doesn't mean we shouldn't try.

2) Evaluating interrelationships among teammates' defensive performances.

Does having a good shortstop make the second baseman or third baseman better? Does it show up in the numbers? Does a Gold Glove center fielder cut into the apparent defensive performance of a corner outfielder? Can a poor defensive player's shortcomings be covered for by pairing him with a stellar glove man at an adjacent position?

3) Measuring the catcher's role in run prevention.

In *Baseball Prospectus 1999*, Keith Woolner presented a compelling case that catchers do not have a noticeable effect on a pitcher's performance. If there is no "game-calling" effect, what impact does a catcher have? Is it primarily controlling the running game? If so, how much of that is attributable to the pitching staff? Is it in preventing wild pitches and passed balls, thus giving the pitcher more confidence to keep the ball low? What about reading a pitcher's physical state and helping to keep his pitch count low? We've made some important first steps, but there's still a lot we don't know about evaluating catcher defense.

4) Mapping career trajectories for defensive performance.

The phenomenon of the "Age 27" peak for offensive performance is well documented. However, while we still struggle with developing a reliable assessment of defensive performance, little attention has been paid to how a player's defensive skills change as he ages. Do a player's defensive skills peak earlier in his career? Later? Do strong arms last longer than quick feet? Does defensive longevity vary by position, or by the particular mix of skills a player has? Do difficult positions such as shortstop and catcher wear a player out faster?

5) Making an assessment of relative positional difficulties.

Much is made of the "defensive spectrum," where positions are thought of as if they were laid out on a ruler, with shortstop at the high/difficult end of the spectrum and first base at the low end. This makes intuitive sense and matches well with the observed differences in offensive performance: generally, there are fewer good-hitting shortstops from which to choose, which implies a lower average offensive performance level for all shortstops. That also means that first basemen generally out-hit shortstops.

6) Quantifying the value of positional flexibility.

A player who plays two positions at a league-average level gives his manager flexibility, both in setting up the team's roster and using in-game strategies. Positional value methods that are based on playing time at a position are inadequate because they would penalize a player for time spent at the lesser position, even if a comparable offensive player who plays full-time at the more difficult position was unable to play the easier position. Because roster spots are scarce, a team gets value from a player's ability to play multiple positions, but we do not yet have an understanding of how much value there is to having a Mark Loretta or Jose Hernandez on your roster.

7) Measuring the value of non-range-based aspects of defense.

This means measuring skills like an outfielder's arm, a middle infielder's ability to hang in while turning the double play or a first baseman's ability to scoop low throws. To date, the effort spent on assessing defensive performance has focused on converting batted balls into outs, essentially measuring a player's range and sure-handedness. Fielding percentage, range factor, Sherri Nichols' Defensive Average, STATS, Inc.'s Zone Rating—these all focus on opportunities to turn batted balls into outs. While important, there are other, less-studied aspects to baseball defense.

We'd want to start measuring the impact of an outfielder's arm, both in terms of cutting down baserunners and whether an outfielder with a cannon-arm reputation intimidates runners. We'd like to establish ways to determine a middle infielder's ability to turn the double play, a first baseman's ability to handle poor throws, an outfielder's reliability in hitting the cutoff man, and a catcher's success in blocking the plate. These are all non-range-based factors in defense, they're all important skills, and they've all been ignored, for the most part.

Offense

8) Evaluating the impact on offensive performance of changing defensive positions up/down the defensive spectrum.

This is the flip side to understanding the defensive spectrum. Here, we ask whether a player's expected offensive production is influenced by the position he's asked to play, and whether changing his position would alter his performance. Would Jeff Bagwell be the same hitter had he stayed at third base? Or Matt Williams at shortstop? Ron Gant at second base? How much is a player helped by moving to an easier position?

9) Predicting the impact on career length from changing positions.

How much longer are players effective after changing positions, particularly if they're moved to an easier position? Is the trade-off in preventing an offensive decline worth the sacrifices you might be making on defense? Do you burn a productive catcher out by leaving him behind the plate and having him retire with knee problems at 32, or are you better off moving him to first base and keeping his bat on the team until he approaches 40? Mike Piazza would like to know the answer, and so would we.

Pitching

10) Projecting minor-league pitchers accurately.

One of the holy grails of sabermetrics is creating useful projections of major-league pitcher performance based on minor-league performance. While strikeout-to-walk ratios and other means of assessment can give us rough guides to good and bad young pitchers, we're nowhere near the level of certainty we want to achieve. Given the lack of progress from purely statistical approaches, this would be an ideal place to marry the analysis of player-development professionals with sabermetric methods to develop a more powerful predictor than either approach has produced alone.

11) Creating a way to better analyze mechanics.

The precision and consistency needed to be an effective major-league pitcher is exceptional. Minute variations in a pitcher's release point, arm angle, and body position make the difference between Cy Young and Matt Young. While game film and frame analysis help capture nuances in a pitcher's delivery that escape the naked eye, there's much more that could be done. Advances in data storage make it possible to record and analyze every pitch thrown in every game by a pitcher. Cataloging this information and measuring the angles, velocities, and timing of movements could open up new worlds to help instructors improve pitching. Computer-aided analysis could measure consistency in release points. You could help improve a young pitcher's consistency by having him throw 100 fastballs to the same place and measuring the variance around his optimal release point. Pitchers with greater command should see a smaller standard deviation than someone as wild as Brad Pennington. Lessons gained from biomechanics could suggest new delivery methods that improve effectiveness while reducing strain on a pitcher's arm. These kinds of approaches may help identify pitchers who should be converted to knuckleballers, submariners, or other non-traditional delivery styles.

Developmental Strategies

12) Identifying and quantifying good coaching.

Most of sabermetrics focuses on the players, and the largest portion of any remaining attention goes to managers. But a team's coaches influence the game as well, and they have rarely been studied in any systematic way. Hitting and pitching coaches affect the development of young players and may help avoid prolonged slumps for all players. Pitching coaches often influence a manager's use (or abuse) of his pitching staff. Coaches at third base make split-second calls on whether to send a runner home or hold him up. Are they doing a good job? Frankly, we have no evidence on which to base useful assessments yet. We all think Leo Mazzone is doing a great job with the Braves, but how great?

13) Assessing the "coachability" of players.

Professional baseball players, both in the majors and the minors, possess tremendous physical gifts. However, not every "five-tool" player matures into an effective ballplayer. Is the difference in the quality of his talent, his ability to learn, or both? How much patience can be taught to a free-swinger like Garret Anderson? Can you train any player with blazing speed to read pitchers well enough to become a base-stealing threat? Do draft picks who sign late diminish their peak value by missing out on a season's worth of instruction?

14) Assessing developmental strategies for minor-league pitchers.

What is the optimal strategy for developing young pitching? What kind of usage pattern and what quantity of work balances the need for experience against the possibility of physical damage? Some teams have studied the issue and come up with innovative approaches; at A-ball, the A's use eight-man rotations, where matched pairs of pitchers pitch every four days with low pitch counts. By contrast, some teams still think young pitchers need to get as many innings as possible. Should a team try to expose a prospect to as many different hitters and parks as possible? Is that good for development, or bad? Was folding the American Association into the Pacific Coast League and the International League good, because it gave Triple-A pitchers more potential opponents and parks to work in, or was it more important to hone their skills against the same seven or nine opposing teams? Are the competitive structures of the minors good for player development or not? What are some potential improvements?

Economics

15) Clarifying the win/dollar trade-off preferences for major league decision-makers.

Winning has never been the only thing in baseball. The fact that baseball is a business is not news to anyone reading this book—in fact, it hasn't been news for the last 125 years. As the ultimate decision-maker for a franchise, the owner of a team values two types of outcomes: on-field success and profitability. The relationship of one to the other isn't objectively knowable, as it comes from the personal—or professional—preferences of the owner. It's perfectly rational for an owner to refuse to risk an $80 million payroll for a 10 percent chance at a World Series, while another would spend $90 million for a seven percent chance. The second owner has a higher win-per-dollar trade-off preference than the former, or you could say he's more willing to take risks. For baseball analysis to move to the next level of relevancy for baseball teams, it must be ready to deal with varying preferences and tolerances and account for them rationally in assessing desirable trades, transactions and contracts.

16) Creating a framework for evaluating trades.

Whether a trade is a good or bad decision is something that should be assessed based on the information known (or that should have been known) at the time of the trade. Analyzing trades with any consistency is difficult, as there are always several reasons and factors that go into every trade. Salary dumps, stretch-drive pickups, overcoming key injuries, getting rid of a troublemaker or somebody the manager just can't stand, exchanging excess talent at one position to fill some other hole on the team—these have all motivated transactions of various kinds over the years. To be successful, a framework for evaluating trades must be ready to consider financial factors (including the overall health of the club), current and future expected production from the players involved, the team's current and future competitive situation, and the premium ownership places on winning.

17) Determining the value of draft picks, Rule 5 picks, player-to-be-named-later arrangements, and other non-specific forms of compensation in transactions.

The more esoteric forms of compensation in trades are usually ignored, but they must have some real value if teams continue to exchange talent for them. What does a team give up when it signs a Type-A free agent? How much is that draft pick worth? Is a typical Rule 5 pick worth the $50,000 and the roster spot? Are teams taking full advantage of the Rule 5 draft? What kinds of PTBNL deals make sense for both teams?

18) Evaluating the effect of short- and long-term competitiveness on attendance and demand elasticity.

Scholars like Andrew Zimbalist and Gerald Scully have done pioneering work in measuring the relationship between on-field success and attendance. Building on that work, we should study second-order effects in more detail, such as the impact of five or more losing seasons on long-term attendance trends. How long does it take attendance to recover from a bunch of lousy seasons in a row? How quickly will fickle fans abandon a former champion? Does fan apathy catch up with a team that consistently contends year after year but never quite wins the pennant? Is it worth overspending in the short term to build long-term fan loyalty, thus ensuring greater financial resources to devote to the team in the future?

19) Optimizing the competitive ecology of the game.

Some issues are bigger than any single team's problems. The long-term survivability of "small-market" clubs has made headlines in the past couple of years. One theory is that "small-market" teams can't hold onto their own farm-developed talent, which supposedly departs through free agency for major media markets like New York and Los Angeles. The current argument is that the Minnesotas of the world can never retain the players produced by their farm system long enough to contend. However, if we went back to making it easier for teams to retain their own players, we'd risk creating long-term dynasties like the Yankees of the 1950s, which diminishes interest in baseball in other cities. So what's the best way to achieve league-wide competitiveness?

Strategic Decisions

20) Determining optimal pitcher usage strategies.

Ideally, a manager wants his best pitchers to throw the most and most important (or highest-leverage) innings. However, he also doesn't want to abuse his pitchers' arms, risking short-term fatigue and long-term injury. There's uncertainty about when high-leverage opportunities will present themselves, yet a regular and tolerable workload is necessary to keep any pitcher sharp. Would a return to four-man rotations with stricter pitch counts lead to greater success? Should teams use a designated closer, or use their best relievers in game-critical situations even if they aren't save situations? Does Tony La Russa's ill-fated experiment with the three-inning starter warrant a longer trial? Should relievers throw fewer, longer appearances, or should they be mixed and matched as platoon differentials dictate?

21) Determining optimal roster design.

Any team's range of in-game strategic options originates with the decisions about which players are on the roster, yet the strategies for constructing a roster have undergone little scrutiny. During the season, a team has many objectives that sometimes conflict with one another. Winning the division or qualifying for the postseason is the ultimate goal, but throughout the season there are other smaller goals: seasoning a rookie, sorting out bullpen roles, assessing a player's readiness after an injury. If a team finds itself in contention, should it ignore potential future payoffs and focus on using established veterans deemed most likely to contribute this year? How would the failure to play that rookie impact the team's competitiveness next year or the year after? Is it worthwhile to carry a player whose primary talent is pinch-running? How important is a third-string catcher? Or a second left-handed specialist out of the bullpen?

Tactical Decisions

22) Quantifying the manager's impact on winning.

Bill James published his *Guide to Baseball Managers* in 1997, and in it set forth some nifty tools for estimating a manager's effectiveness based on seasonal statistics. Careful observation and recording of managerial moves (e.g., roster management, in-game tactics, pitcher usage) set the stage for a detailed assessment of a manager's impact on his team. Unifying this data into a coherent whole is a challenge, but the payoff would be a much better understanding of the value of a manager's contributions to his team.

23) Developing a game-theoretic framework for analyzing elective strategies.

In the offense-crazed world of the late 1990s, it seems quaint to concern ourselves with little-ball strategies like the sacrifice bunt and the hit-and-run. These strategies are widely derided in sabermetrics, largely on the basis of expected-run analysis. Tables, indexed by the number of outs and the location of baserunners, give an expected number of runs scored for the rest of the inning, based on the results of actual games. If expected run-scoring declines after a player bats, or given a typical success rate for a play, then the strategy is deemed to be bad. While this approach was an important and useful first step, there are two major problems with it: first, this method yields an answer for a league-average team because it's based on the results of the league as a whole; and second, it ignores the changes in shape of run-scoring that can be important for many game contexts.

To truly understand where and when to use these strategies, they must be studied not just with an expected-run analysis, but with a true assessment of how much more likely the game is to be won using such a strategy. There is a branch of mathematics called game theory which is ideally suited for studying not only the direct impact of little-ball strategies on the outcome of games, but the move-countermove nature of two managers trying to gain whatever advantages they can against one another. An in-depth treatment of little-ball strategies that recognizes the true richness of managerial decisions and counter-decisions should be welcomed.

> *The deep significance of certain problems for the advance of sabermetric science in general and the important role which they play in the work of the individual investigator are not to be denied. As long as a branch of science offers an abundance of problems, so long is it alive; a lack of problems foreshadows extinction or the cessation of independent development. Just as every human undertaking pursues certain objects, so also sabermetric research requires its problems. It is by the solution of problems that the investigator tests the temper of his steel; he finds new methods and new outlooks, and gains a wider and freer horizon.*

The range of interesting avenues of exploration is larger than a single publication—even Baseball Prospectus—can possibly hope to explore. Fortunately, the community of interested and knowledgeable baseball fans and analysts is large and getting larger, and many of these Hilbert problems will be solved by researchers nobody has even heard of yet. We look forward to seeing the solutions, and with them the posing of more interesting questions, in the century to come.

CROOKED NUMBERS
More Hilbert Questions
James Click

Several years after Keith Woolner came out with his original list, James Click added a few more questions in need of answers.

At the beginning of a new year, it's a commonly accepted practice to start thinking about things anew. Personally, I've yet to start going back to the gym, but that doesn't mean that I don't waste a lot of time thinking about unanswered baseball questions that we could potentially quantify. Many times—usually when I'm struggling for column topics—I wonder if we're beginning to run up against the limits of baseball analysis. After all, how many more ways can we quantify player performance?

Whenever I hit that wall, I pick up my copy of *Baseball Prospectus 2000*. In that edition of BP, Keith Woolner outlined some of the key questions left unanswered with regard to baseball research. Some are questions are of amazing complexity, such as #13: Assessing the "coachability" of players and #19: Optimizing the competitive ecology of the game. Others have been researched since the article's original publication: catcher defense, the relationship between wins and dollars, the value of draft picks, and game-theoretic frameworks. But there are still many great questions left unanswered.

I have a few more logs to throw on the fire. This is by no means an exhaustive list, and I'm happy to take suggestions for additional seminal questions that need answering. But this is a start. Keith listed numbers 1-23, so I'll pick up with number 24.

24) Determine the correct methodology for removing the effects of the ballpark on player performance.
Park factors have been around for a long time, and they're finally making a dent in mainstream thinking, thanks to a big push from Coors Field. However, while comparing home and road statistics to get a general idea of the way a park plays in relation to the other parks in the league is a good start, there are vast areas for improvement in the way that players are analyzed given their environments. Tom Tippett did some excellent work on this problem at the SABR convention a few years ago, discussing why using a percentage overlooks the fact that parks affect different

players in different ways.

Dayn Perry reminded us that failing to break down park factors by handedness removes key information from the analysis. The Rangers are commissioning a study on wind patterns in their ballpark, understanding that while the fences are the aspect of the park that we focus on the most, there are a wide variety of other factors that influence the game. We don't know for certain if players begin to tailor their games to their particular home park, or how that affects players stuck in Coors Field, Colorado Springs, Asheville, New Orleans, or any number of other extreme environments.

Most importantly, there is little vetting of results to determine if one methodology is correct or not. How do we determine how a player would have done in a neutral park in a given season if we cannot remove him from all those factors that influence his particular game? Does comparing the performance of players who changed parks from one year to the next reveal how accurate a park factor is? How much should we rely on previous seasons of data when parks change both in physical appearance and weather conditions every year? This problem may be one that cannot be answered with our current data; we may have to wait until more accurate ball-trajectory and weather information becomes available before a suitable solution can be identified.

25) Assessment of ideal development decisions for prospects.

As players move up through the minor leagues, their advancement or demotion can be based on any number of factors: actual performance, the mastery of a required skill, or roster need, to name a few. However, the impact of promoting a player "too soon" or demoting him has not been thoroughly explored. Recently, Nate Silver noticed that PECOTA projections change dramatically given the player's level of play, even when accounting for translations between leagues. There was a long discussion about the possible reasons behind this fact, but it highlights the concept that the impact of level of play, in the absence of performance differences, on future player performance is understudied.

Can we determine if a player will suffer long-term damage to his development if he struggles at a high level when he could have dominated at a lower one? How much do players focus on their performance if their development path is based on other factors such as mastering a new pitch or learning to hit a specific way or to control the strike zone? Is the act of keeping players in the minors longer than necessary to keep their service clocks stopped actually depriving them of needed development that will cost the team value down the road?

26) Quantifying the impact of injuries and the medical staff.

Tom Gorman, Will Carroll, Mike Groopman and others are doing some groundbreaking work in this area, but injuries and their impact are still impressively understudied. How do we determine what is a preventable injury and what is not? Can teams predict how many games a given player will likely lose to injury? How much difference does the medical staff make in player recovery and injury rate? What impact on player performance do injuries that don't require a trip to the disabled list or even missed games have?

Like the discussion of park factors, this question is more dependent on gathering the right information than anything else. Teams have real incentives to keep medical information close to the vest, and acting on incorrect data is a fault that has haunted every decision-maker since the beginning of time. If accurate information can be found and codified, we can begin to answer some of these questions. Until then, we can only speculate about what's going on in Curt Schilling's ankle and Gary Sheffield's shoulder and how those things affect their performance.

27) Valuation of player contracts, particularly options and other restrictive clauses.

There have been quite a few players signed to some interesting contracts in the past few years, contracts that include features like vesting options, multiple option years, and all sorts of no-trade clauses. Can we put a dollar figure on those options? How does a vesting option based on playing time change a player's approach to the game and the trainer's room? How do we prevent teams from benching players to prevent them from reaching those milestones in their contracts?

28) Quantification of the value of front office personnel.

One of the original Hilbert questions discussed identifying and quantifying good coaching; another discussed the impact of the manager on winning games. These questions can also be posed about front-office personnel. While the analysis of front-office performance is largely a subjective effort for the time being, there may be a way to begin to place a dollar value on decision-makers. How much is Billy Beane worth to the A's? What about John Schuerholz and the Braves? How much of a difference do they make? How much of it is actually the coaches they hired and the players they acquired? Are there people who are distinctly better at the arbitration process than others? How much do they save a team?

29) Team- and situation-specific player valuation.

As noted by many people in the performance analysis community, the process of assigning a single number value to players has been virtually exhausted. People still sometimes fight over that last little bit of accuracy, but for the most part, whether it's MLV, EqR, VORP, WARP or any of the multitude of metrics publicly available, virtually all of them are going to value most players very closely. That said, each player brings something different to the game, and matching that skill set to usage is something that teams often fail at and performance analysts sometimes overlook.

Because all players are paid in dollars and are up for the same awards, it's very handy to have a single number that contains their total value. But when constructing a roster properly—question #21—being able to deploy players of equal value in different situations increases the overall value of the team.

Additionally, most metrics involving player valuation use average run values of different events or the change in run-scoring by putting a player in an otherwise average lineup. However, inserting different players into different lineups may generate vastly different run outputs. How much does a speedster add to the plodding Boston Red Sox of 2003-04 (other than Dave Roberts and his famous steal)? Would the same player be worth more or less to a team like the 2005 White Sox or 1985 Cardinals? We have the data to determine if the Red Sox would be getting diminishing returns by signing another high-OBP, low-AVG player in 2003, and how that same player would add more to a different team. While it's easy and often highly informative to slap a single number on a player and call it his value, it's possible to quantify the value a player has specifically to his team.

This list could go on for quite some time, but considering the rate at which we've been answering the original Hilbert questions posed by Keith, it's probably best to stop here, lest we head into the 22nd century. It's a new year; let's see what other questions we can answer.

RATIONAL EXUBERANCE
A Better Way to Build a Baseball Team
Jonah Keri

Jonah Keri channeled his frustration caused by instances of inefficient roster construction into a primer on building teams properly, pointing out that the key to assembling an optimal roster was seeking several edges simultaneously.

There are some games that get me so frustrated, I want to toss my TV out the window. The hapless fifth starter not making it through the third inning. The one-out-only reliever who walks the only batter he faces, then gets yanked. The Punch and Judy utility infielder called in to pinch-hit who taps out weakly to second. The left-handed hitter with a huge platoon split predictably doing nothing against the southpaw.

Rarely does a game go by in which I don't see a player thrust into a situation in which he's overwhelmingly likely to fail. We're told that the talent pool is shallower than it used to be, that players don't have the same breadth of skills they used to have. Some say that for every strong major-league player, there are three more on the roster who barely belong there, and there's not a thing we can do about it.

I don't buy it. There's a better way to build a roster. It doesn't require a $200 million payroll or an act from above. All it takes is some common sense and a willingness to try something a little different. If done right, it can create a competitive edge for teams willing to try it and a better brand of baseball for us all to enjoy.

If you've read Baseball Prospectus long enough, you've seen us analyze roster construction in bits and pieces. Particularly notable was Rany Jazayerli's three-part series assessing the merits of a five-man rotation vs. a switch back to the old four-man format.

You've likely read plenty of other thoughts on roster construction. Joe Sheehan has written about the advantages that platooning can bring, both in simulated and real baseball games. Joe has also weighed in on the damage a bad bench can do to a team's record, particularly in the playoffs. In Bill James' most recent *Historical Abstract*, he argued against the use of one-out specialist relievers, be they lefties or righties. Not only do they help to destroy the rhythmic pace of a game,

James argues, they also do little to nothing to help a team's fortunes, especially when compared to other ways a roster spot can be filled.

All these folks, and plenty of others, have argued these points eloquently many times before. One point has been lost in all these discussions, however: to make one change effectively, you need to make them all.

Platooning requires multiple roster spots for players who'll play against one side or the other. That puts a strain on manager fetishes for third catchers and multi-position players who may not be good anywhere. Going to a four-man rotation requires being cautious with pitcher usage, such that relievers who can throw multiple innings become a must-have. That, in turn, cuts into the ability to carry a specialist pitcher who'll face no more than a batter or two a game.

To reshape a major-league roster into one that's going to produce more wins and better baseball for all involved, it's necessary to follow each and every one of these steps:

Platooning
Every team, even the richest in talent, is going to run out of star performers at some point on the roster. Sure, you want to let Alex Rodriguez and Albert Pujols and Todd Helton play every day, regardless of who's pitching. But what about Carl Everett? Adam Kennedy? In his prime, Brian Jordan? There are scads of major-league players who, given several years to prove their mettle against both lefties and righties, have consistently crapped out against one of the two. Yet whether because of their perceived status as everyday players or a reluctance to try something different, those players have had their weaknesses exposed through managerial inertia.

To address this weakness, GMs should pursue platoon players more aggressively. The list of right-handed hitters who can mash lefties—even if they're otherwise limited players on the wrong side of the defensive spectrum—is huge. Rather than chase down a no-field, no-hit wonder like Roger Cedeno for a roster spot, why not give one to Eduardo Perez or Joe Vitiello? If you have a lefty bat at a corner slot who's not getting it done against southpaws, these lefty-mashers can turn decent production at a position into very good production. Great managers ranging from Bobby Cox to Earl Weaver to Casey Stengel to George Stallings have seized on the value of platoons in the past, and there's no reason the managers of today can't do the same.

However, a manager needs to be careful in whom he opts to platoon. Young, promising hitters such as Hank Blalock and Hee-Seop Choi have struggled early in their careers against lefties. They also haven't racked up nearly enough at-bats to sentence them to a lifetime of part-time duty. Rest an up-and-coming talent against the occasional Randy Johnson, sure, but don't hold back his development by overprotecting him. For years, the knock on Eric Chavez has been his inability to hit lefties. This season, he's roasting them to the tune of .333/.434/.569.

It's worth noting that it's easier to find a player who crushes only lefty pitching than one who destroys righties alone. Righty pitchers far outnumber lefties, so there's a higher premium placed on righty-bashers. For every Matt Stairs, there are a number of Brian Buchanans.

OK, let's have a look at some platoon data. Playing the role of data genius is BP's Keith Woolner, to whom I owe my undying gratitude.

2004

Bats	Throws	PA	AB	AVG	OBP	SLG
B	L	5326	4727	.259	.331	.405
B	R	12879	11316	.266	.343	.418
L	L	9085	8016	.257	.331	.404
L	R	27402	23969	.276	.356	.455
R	L	19121	16941	.268	.339	.440
R	R	46627	41922	.263	.322	.414

2001-2003

Bats	Throws	PA	AB	AVG	OBP	SLG
B	L	20849	18632	.267	.332	.405
B	R	60744	53757	.266	.338	.413
L	L	39384	34944	.252	.323	.398
L	R	134214	117691	.273	.352	.450
R	L	81540	72208	.268	.339	.436
R	R	224051	201113	.256	.317	.408

What jumps out right away is the gap between lefty hitters vs. left-handed and right-handed pitching. So far this season, lefty swingers have hit .257/.331/.404 vs. lefties, .276/.356/.455 vs. righties. From 2001 to 2003, those totals were .252/.323/.398 vs. .273/.352/.450. Put another way, this is roughly the difference between Jamey Carroll's career line and Matt Lawton's.

Revamping the Bench

Platooning effectively does a lot of this. If three or four players are carried based largely on their platoon abilities, that's going to severely limit the possibilities for the kind of "versatile" bench Tony La Russa employs almost every year. The thesis here is that benches aren't remotely carrying their weight on most clubs, and that no third catcher, pinch-runner, or punchless utility player will match the impact that a good platoon player can bring, given 150 at-bats.

Here, we took each team dating back to 1972 and removed the batters with the most plate appearances, with the rest treated as the bench. This isn't as precise as say, constructing exact bench profiles using play-by-play data from the last 33 years, but it can still provide a reasonable estimate of bench production. (Note: OPS_PLUS = BenchOBP/LgOBP + BenchSLG/LgSLG - 1; in other words, the OPS_PLUS stat allows us to measure a bench's contributions relative to league-wide performance.)

Year	Lg	League AVG	League OBP	League SLG	League OPS	Bench AVG	Bench OBP	Bench SLG	Bench OPS	Bench OPS+
1972	AL	.239	.302	.343	.645	.222	.284	.310	.594	.843
1972	NL	.248	.311	.365	.676	.230	.297	.329	.625	.855
1973	AL	.259	.326	.381	.707	.242	.305	.346	.651	.844
1973	NL	.254	.318	.375	.693	.233	.300	.330	.630	.823
1974	AL	.258	.319	.371	.691	.236	.293	.330	.622	.804
1974	NL	.255	.321	.367	.688	.228	.295	.315	.610	.776
1975	AL	.258	.324	.379	.703	.235	.298	.339	.637	.813
1975	NL	.257	.322	.369	.691	.236	.310	.330	.639	.855
1976	AL	.256	.317	.361	.677	.228	.289	.308	.596	.765
1976	NL	.255	.316	.361	.677	.239	.306	.339	.645	.908
1977	AL	.266	.327	.405	.732	.243	.300	.351	.652	.786
1977	NL	.262	.324	.396	.721	.245	.309	.358	.667	.855
1978	AL	.261	.322	.385	.707	.236	.295	.333	.628	.781
1978	NL	.254	.316	.372	.688	.236	.305	.326	.631	.843
1979	AL	.270	.331	.408	.739	.248	.305	.362	.667	.810
1979	NL	.261	.320	.385	.705	.249	.315	.343	.658	.873
1980	AL	.269	.328	.399	.727	.244	.299	.353	.652	.797
1980	NL	.259	.316	.374	.691	.251	.312	.355	.667	.935
1981	AL	.256	.318	.373	.690	.231	.288	.329	.617	.791
1981	NL	.255	.315	.364	.679	.237	.301	.331	.632	.866
1982	AL	.264	.325	.402	.727	.240	.296	.348	.645	.778
1982	NL	.258	.315	.373	.688	.244	.307	.339	.647	.886
1983	AL	.266	.325	.401	.726	.245	.298	.351	.648	.791
1983	NL	.255	.318	.376	.694	.243	.310	.351	.661	.910
1984	AL	.264	.324	.398	.722	.238	.297	.354	.651	.808
1984	NL	.255	.315	.369	.685	.249	.310	.350	.660	.930
1985	AL	.261	.325	.406	.730	.233	.295	.350	.645	.773
1985	NL	.252	.315	.374	.689	.241	.306	.344	.650	.893
1986	AL	.262	.327	.408	.735	.237	.297	.350	.648	.768
1986	NL	.253	.318	.380	.698	.247	.315	.363	.678	.947
1987	AL	.265	.331	.425	.756	.243	.304	.370	.674	.789
1987	NL	.261	.325	.404	.728	.245	.308	.363	.672	.850
1988	AL	.259	.322	.391	.712	.230	.289	.332	.621	.749
1988	NL	.248	.306	.363	.669	.238	.300	.329	.629	.886

Year	Lg	League AVG	League OBP	League SLG	League OPS	Bench AVG	Bench OBP	Bench SLG	Bench OPS	Bench OPS+
1989	AL	.261	.323	.384	.707	.237	.292	.339	.631	.786
1989	NL	.246	.309	.365	.674	.233	.297	.335	.632	.880
1990	AL	.259	.325	.388	.712	.237	.301	.341	.642	.806
1990	NL	.256	.317	.383	.700	.242	.305	.349	.655	.874
1991	AL	.260	.326	.395	.721	.236	.300	.342	.642	.786
1991	NL	.250	.313	.373	.686	.231	.294	.332	.626	.830
1992	AL	.259	.326	.385	.711	.235	.297	.328	.625	.765
1992	NL	.252	.311	.368	.679	.240	.294	.345	.638	.881
1993	AL	.267	.335	.408	.742	.241	.307	.352	.659	.781
1993	NL	.264	.323	.399	.722	.247	.309	.376	.685	.899
1994	AL	.273	.342	.434	.776	.246	.306	.374	.680	.756
1994	NL	.267	.328	.415	.743	.257	.319	.393	.712	.920
1995	AL	.270	.342	.427	.769	.247	.312	.371	.683	.783
1995	NL	.263	.327	.408	.735	.246	.314	.371	.685	.870
1996	AL	.277	.348	.445	.793	.250	.315	.380	.694	.757
1996	NL	.262	.327	.408	.735	.242	.311	.359	.670	.833
1997	AL	.271	.338	.428	.766	.252	.316	.379	.695	.821
1997	NL	.263	.329	.410	.740	.253	.318	.382	.700	.897
1998	AL	.271	.338	.432	.769	.250	.311	.385	.696	.813
1998	NL	.262	.327	.410	.737	.245	.310	.367	.677	.843
1999	AL	.275	.345	.439	.784	.247	.309	.368	.678	.735
1999	NL	.268	.339	.429	.768	.256	.326	.386	.713	.864
2000	AL	.276	.346	.443	.790	.255	.321	.386	.707	.797
2000	NL	.266	.338	.432	.770	.249	.323	.392	.715	.865
2001	AL	.267	.331	.428	.760	.241	.301	.376	.676	.785
2001	NL	.261	.327	.425	.753	.246	.316	.387	.703	.874
2002	AL	.264	.329	.424	.753	.241	.302	.367	.669	.782
2002	NL	.259	.328	.410	.738	.246	.314	.386	.700	.900
2003	AL	.267	.331	.428	.759	.247	.306	.375	.681	.800
2003	NL	.261	.328	.417	.745	.243	.308	.375	.683	.839
2004	AL	.270	.336	.433	.769	.243	.304	.380	.683	.782
2004	NL	.263	.329	.424	.753	.248	.314	.391	.705	.875

AL bench production this year has dropped to 22 percent below league-wide levels. Note that those numbers tend to ebb and flow over time. Also note that implementing multiple platoons may be slightly easier on AL teams, which need fewer pinch-hitters to bat for pitchers. On the other hand, the DH position presents another possible platoon spot for AL rosters, and the lack of defensive requirements for the position makes the DH spot a prime candidate for platoons.

To improve the starting lineup through platooning while either improving or at least preserving current bench production, teams will need to put some thought into their reserves. I'd envision a fair number of platoon players on a typical team, say roughly three. A backup catcher would of course be a must. I'd then attempt to round out the bench with:

- An infielder who can play multiple positions, provide a decent glove, and get on base. Think Jose Oquendo in his better years.
- A solid bat who'd act as a ninth starter (or 10th in the AL). This player would have enough ability to replace an injured player for a few weeks at a time if needed without costing the team much in the way of production. Otherwise, he'd be used to give regulars occasional days off. Playing time would come to roughly 200-400 at-bats, depending on starters' injuries. Michael Cuddyer currently fills a similar role with the Twins. A player like Brendan Harris could be an option for 2005.
Like breaking a young pitching prospect in through regulated bullpen use, this method would allow a young hitter to help the club and make good use of his first year of service time, without the risk of exposing him through full-time play. A good candidate here would be a B+ prospect from the organization; impact prospects such as David Wright would still be slotted into everyday jobs as rookies.

This bench structure needn't be etched in stone, particularly since different teams will have different platoon needs. But a thoughtful, rational approach to building a bench is a must. Scrambling for Doug Glanville as a 25th-man afterthought could make the one- or two-game difference that sometimes decides a close pennant race.

Four-Man Rotation
Rany Jazayerli explains the benefits of a four-man rotation in great detail in the articles mentioned above. In a nutshell, reducing the number of starting pitchers a team must employ means chopping your worst starter out of the mix. With the way in which some lament the demise of pitching in today's game, no one would dispute that it's easier to find four good starters than it is five. A four-man staff could thus, if deployed properly, produce better starting pitching.

Here's where the issue of pitcher workload comes into play. Managers and pitching coaches have become increasingly cautious as to how they use their pitchers. The average length of a major-league start has shrunk dramatically over the last three decades. Managers may be even more cautious with starter usage in a four-man situation, potentially further limiting starters' innings pitched and thus increasing the burden on the bullpen.

The causes and suggested steps for pitching injury prevention are another topic best left for others, Dr. Glenn Fleisig of the American Sports Medicine Institute and BP's Will Carroll among them. What's worth noting here is that the elimination of the weakest link, a staff's fifth starter, also removes the pitcher responsible for the most short outings on a staff, as those pitchers typically lack either the ability or stamina to hang with the rotation's top four. Thus the increased bullpen burden caused by a more careful hand with the top four starters can be largely offset by taking out the pitcher most likely to get knocked out in the third inning by a flurry of rockets into the gap.

Here are our data measuring the average length per start by starters one through five in a rotation, by five-year intervals, 1972 to 2004.

Even subtracting the fifth starter, we're still looking at an average of just over 5 2/3 innings pitched for the fourth starter, just over 6 1/3 for the staff ace. Whether or not managers opt to be more careful with a four-man rotation, the value of a reliever who can pitch multiple, effective innings against both lefties and righties is going to increase significantly. This brings us to...

The New, Old Bullpen

Once again, we can reserve a lot of the blame for a damaging trend to Tony La Russa. When the late-'80s/early-'90s A's found success using Dennis Eckersley as a one-inning closer, other teams started emulating the practice. That Eckersley was simply a dominating reliever and not necessarily dominant only in save situations was a point lost on many within the game. From there, specialization spread to LOOGYs (Left-handed One-Out-only GuYs—thanks, John Sickels), often suspect pitchers who'd try to retire the Barry Bondses of the league in key situations. Managers increasingly refused to use their talented closers in any situation other than one defined in the rule book as worthy of a save. La Russa himself helped keep the underwhelming Tony Fossas employed through his 40th birthday, to name one LOOGY love-in.

YEAR	GSRANK	GS	IP	IP/GS
1972-1974	1	36.8	272.1	7.368
1972-1974	2	34.1	237.3	6.936
1972-1974	3	29.0	188.9	6.499
1972-1974	4	22.5	142.3	6.293
1972-1974	5	15.8	96.4	6.012
1975-1979	1	35.2	251.5	7.119
1975-1979	2	32.2	218.6	6.760
1975-1979	3	27.9	182.2	6.508
1975-1979	4	23.0	141.6	6.102
1975-1979	5	16.7	101.1	6.040
1980-1984	1	32.0	219.8	6.849
1980-1984	2	29.7	196.3	6.574
1980-1984	3	26.6	169.5	6.343
1980-1984	4	22.2	136.2	6.100
1980-1984	5	16.2	96.0	5.869
1985-1989	1	34.0	233.0	6.840
1985-1989	2	31.5	206.2	6.526
1985-1989	3	28.3	175.4	6.157
1985-1989	4	22.5	136.7	6.027
1985-1989	5	16.9	99.7	5.840
1990-1994	1	31.6	213.2	6.744
1990-1994	2	29.0	186.6	6.405
1990-1994	3	25.9	161.7	6.214
1990-1994	4	21.6	128.2	5.878
1990-1994	5	15.9	92.3	5.741
1995-1999	1	32.5	211.7	6.492
1995-1999	2	30.1	190.2	6.306
1995-1999	3	27.0	163.5	6.031
1995-1999	4	22.0	130.5	5.890
1995-1999	5	16.5	93.5	5.643
2000-2004	1	30.7	198.5	6.443
2000-2004	2	28.5	177.2	6.193
2000-2004	3	25.1	150.0	5.943
2000-2004	4	20.8	121.5	5.788
2000-2004	5	16.3	92.7	5.664

The result has been bullpen usage completely out of step with the trends of the modern game, as you'll see here (data again taken from 1972 to 2004, using five-year intervals, with average innings pitched per relief appearance included).

YEAR	AVG_RP_IP
1972-1974	1.70
1975-1979	1.74
1980-1984	1.67
1985-1989	1.52
1990-1994	1.31
1995-1999	1.19
2000-2004	1.14

You can see the problem here. The length of starts has dropped rapidly, and so too has the length of relief appearances. The easy way out is to sacrifice position players—and thus offense—for 11th, 12th, and occasionally 13th pitchers.

Of course, we're not interested in the easy way out; we want to field the best team possible. As such, I'm proposing the following for pitching staffs: four starters, one swingman, five relievers. That's it.

We need room on the roster to accommodate platoons and general offensive optimization, and one-out relievers don't deliver enough value to let them get in the way of that. The swingman can act as a sixth reliever on many days, doing long-relief duty when a starter gets knocked out early. He can slot into the rotation when a starter needs an extra day's rest to recover from a minor ailment. The five relievers must show the ability to go multiple innings at a time. As much as possible, they should be able to handle both lefty and righty hitters. Situational usage will be largely abolished, with no set closer, set-up man, or designated inning for any one pitcher.

At BP we often talk about the supposed abundance of available arms to anchor a bullpen. That theory stems from the idea that the majority of relievers are unpredictable from one year to the next, liable to put up a standout performance one year, a washout the next. With this new pitching structure, teams will need to be more aggressive in finding effective pitchers languishing in the minors or in low-leverage jobs on other teams. They'll need to devote more scouting and statistical research to finding the struggling starters around the league best suited to key relief roles. They'll need to continue their efforts to pick the cream of the crop from foreign leagues, especially in Asia.

And yes, occasionally they'll want to ante up some cash for the rare reliever who can deliver more consistent results. The money saved by going without fifth starters and eschewing one-sided name players in favor of cheaper platoons will make this happen.

The new, optimal roster will revolve around a strong offense with as few weaknesses as possible, a rotation with one less hole, and a stronger bench and a better bullpen that can control the last few innings of a game, whatever the situation. As with any strategy, it'll be up to the shrewd GM and the perceptive manager to find the right talent to make it happen and use those players in a more effective way.

AUGUST 2, 2008

http://bbp.cx/a/7743

LIES, DAMNED LIES
Flipping the Switch
Nate Silver

In the midst of the Rays' dramatic reversal of fortunes in 2008, Nate Silver explained how they'd orchestrated their jump from worst to first.

It is rare in baseball to talk about team cohesion. In contrast to the other major sports, there are relatively few interactions between players on the same club. The pitcher stands out there on the mound all by himself and throws the ball; the hitter stands there in the batters' box all by himself and hopes to hit it. There is no baseball equivalent of John Stockton passing to Karl Malone, or Peyton Manning to Reggie Wayne.

However, there is such a thing as a baseball team that is less than the sum of its parts. This is a team that would be constructed less with an eye toward winning in the near-term, and more with an eye toward stockpiling talent for the future. There are a couple ways to identify such a team. It probably has an excess of players at some positions, and a deficit at others. It probably does poorly at staffing a couple of the little luxuries that good teams get right—having a decent bullpen, for instance (nobody has much need for a closer if there are few wins to close out), or playing good defense (the effects of which are hard to quantify, and therefore, easy to give short shrift).

Until this season, the Tampa Bay Rays had been such a team, the baseball equivalent of the LA Clippers. Consider a couple of the categories I just mentioned. In 2007, the Rays were an awful defensive team, perhaps the worst defensive team in baseball history. We've tracked each team's Defensive Efficiency Rating (DER) for each season since 1959; this is simply the frequency with which teams make outs on balls hit into play. The 2007 Tampa Bay Devil Rays had the lowest DER in our entire database, making outs on just 66.2 percent of balls hit into play. There's little reason to wonder why. For large parts of the season, they had a left fielder (Delmon Young) playing center, a center fielder (B.J. Upton) playing second base, and a second baseman (Brendan Harris) playing shortstop.

The bullpen? Last season, Tampa Bay relievers combined for an unsightly 6.16 ERA, which was also among the worst figures in baseball history. Having a bullpen that bad usually makes teams do crazy things, like deciding to pay $9 million for Eric Gagne, or trading Jason Varitek and Derek Lowe for Heathcliff Slocumb. But the Rays just stood there and let their relievers take one for their team's future.

Team balance? The Devil Rays had five players who had a legitimate argument for making the All-Star team last year: Carl Crawford, B.J. Upton, Carlos Pena, Scott Kazmir, and James Shields. But they also had 28 distinct players who produced a negative VORP, collectively costing the Rays 157.9 runs below replacement level. Merely replacing those guys with passable alternatives—never mind league-average players—would have made a huge difference.

Put differently, the Rays had an awful lot of room to make additions by subtraction. The difficult part about baseball is supposed to be locking up blue-chip assets like Upton and Kazmir at below-market rates. The Rays had done plenty of that, but they hadn't really bothered to sweat the small stuff—to dump some of their dead weight, to make sure they had guys who were up to the job defensively, or to tend to their bullpen.

Until this winter, that is, because that's when the Rays decided to transform themselves from a sort of hedge fund for undervalued assets into a real, functional baseball club. The linchpin move behind that transition was trading Delmon Young for Matt Garza and Jason Bartlett. It is rare in baseball for a rebuilding team to give up the best young player in a deal, but the Rays were prepared to do just that. While Young has struggled this year, back in November he looked to most observers—including in all likelihood the Rays themselves—to be the best player in the deal. Even so, the Rays knew that if they were going to turn things around, they needed another ready-now arm, and they knew that acquiring a veteran would be prohibitively expensive. So they made a calculated risk and traded for Garza. They also knew that they were getting Bartlett in the deal, who whether or not he hit anything (and he hasn't hit much this year) would provide them with a major defensive upgrade at shortstop, a position where the Rays' defenders were a combined 25 runs below league-average last year according to our Prospectus Fielding Runs metric.

The Rays also decided to sign Troy Percival to an $8 million contract, their largest free agent deal since the Fred McGriff/Wade Boggs era. Percival has not been especially outstanding this year, probably only the third- or fourth-best reliever on his club. However, signing him took some pressure off of their young arms and demoted everyone else on the depth chart down a notch, such that some of the truly flammable arms at the back end of the bullpen would no longer have to play for them. As moves go, that's proving to be truly valuable.

PECOTA added all of this up, coupled it with the fact that the Rays' talent core was young and still on the upswing, and concluded that the club was liable to win somewhere between 88 and 90 ballgames. Not even the Rays themselves were entirely convinced by this forecast. The team executives I spoke with this winter expected—or hoped—to go .500 this year, perhaps making a serious run at the playoffs in 2009. But a quick run through their offseason checklist reveals that sometimes the best-laid plans go even better than expected:

- **Team Defense**: The Rays have gone from having one of the worst defenses in baseball history to one of the best in the league. In fact, their Defensive Efficiency Rating of .720 ranks second in baseball, just a couple ticks behind the Oakland A's. This degree of improvement is literally without precedent. The Rays have improved their DER by 58 points this year, which is the largest year-over-year improvement that we've ever tracked:

Rk	Team	Year	Current Year	Previous Year	Change
1	TBA	2008	.720	.662	.058
2	OAK	1980	.739	.690	.049
3	TEX	1981	.734	.688	.046
4	ATL	1991	.727	.688	.039
5	DET	1981	.748	.714	.034
6	SDN	1982	.739	.705	.034
7	MIL	1988	.727	.693	.034
8	SFN	1971	.735	.703	.032
9	FLO	2008	.701	.669	.032
10	CLE	1968	.754	.724	.030

- **The Bullpen**: The defensive gain has produced all sorts of subsidiary improvements too. By making it easier for their pitchers to record outs, the Rays have reduced the amount of churn in their bullpen. Instead of requiring 3.0 relief pitchers to pitch per game, as they did last season, the Rays have cut that number to 2.6 and been able to concentrate those innings among their better arms. Partly as a result of this, the Rays have cut their bullpen ERA nearly in half. Instead of the 6.16 ERA their relievers gave them a year ago, this year their mark is 3.18. The key has been the realization that you don't need a lot of flamethrowers if you have guys behind you that can catch the ball. Rays' relievers rank just seventh in the American League with 7.65 strikeouts per nine innings, but their .212 batting average allowed is the best in baseball. Percival—and Dan Wheeler, who was acquired late last year for Ty Wigginton—have been important parts of that, but the defense has made everyone look better.

- **Addition by Subtraction**: In contrast to last year, the Rays have just six players who have compiled a negative VORP in any amount of playing time, and all but Jason Bartlett have played sparingly. The combined negative VORP accumulated by those Rays has been just 12.8 this year, as opposed to their 157.9 figure from a year ago.

Is the Rays' success likely to continue in the second half? Odds are that it is. Certainly, they have had a couple of breakout performances—Dioner Navarro and Edwin Jackson and Evan Longoria, for example—but even these have come from young and talented players, to whom such things are supposed to happen occasionally. The Rays have actually had a couple of players who have underachieved, but Carlos Pena and Carl Crawford are both good bets to improve their numbers in the second half.

The whole point is that the improvements the Rays have made are structural. Yes, it is a lot of fun when you are a team like the White Sox, and you have guys like Carlos Quentin and John Danks who break out when nobody is quite expecting it. But when that happens, you also have to hope those guys aren't first-half flukes. The Rays do not really have parallel concerns.

The handful of transactions the Rays made this winter were not by any means overly complicated; in retrospect, they almost seem obvious. But they were moves made by a team that had the self-confidence to look in the mirror and like what it saw. The Rays put aside the fact that they had never won more than 70 games in a season and recognized that, on a talent-for-talent basis, they had a 40-man roster that was the envy of many clubs in baseball. They recognized that guys like Evan Longoria would be ready to start contributing immediately, and that it was not too soon to start competing.

These things are tougher than you might think, as honest self-assessment is elusive to many teams in baseball. The more commonly-seen problem is for a team to overrate the amount of talent that it has and either compromise its future for a roster that needs a lot of help rather than a little (take this year's Mariners), or fail to improve on a roster that is due to regress to the mean (this year's Rockies). There are also teams that take too long to flip the switch and make a run at competing, but the Rays turned things on at just the right time.

LIES, DAMNED LIES
A New Look at Aging
Nate Silver

When do players hit their peaks, how long does it take them to enter and exit their periods of prime performance, and how do those aging patterns vary by position? Nate Silver tackled those questions in the essay below.

This week's column was originally supposed to be a break from the usual LDL routine, inspired by Tuesday night's fantastic White Sox/Indians game, which I got to take in with *New York Sun* buddy Tim Marchman. Tim and I have some mysterious, voodoo-like power when we go to Sox games together. Earlier this year, Carl Everett, baseball's best-known proponent of intelligent design theory, came to the plate in a game against the Twins, and Tim, who might or might not have joined me in enjoying a couple of beers, screamed "Hit One For Jesus!" Everett promptly smacked a two-run homer on the next Kyle Lohse pitch.

This time around, our powers worked in reverse: Joe Crede was up against Jake Westbrook in the bottom of the third, and we were having a lively conversation about what was wrong with Crede's game, and how he had failed to live up to expectations. My famous last words were: "it's making hitters like Joe Crede look stupid that keeps pitchers like Jake Westbrook in the game." Next pitch? Boom, two-run homer. Crede followed suit with his walk-off job in the tenth, a home run that bore some eerie resemblance to the Aaron Fricking Boone shot: underachieving third baseman, first pitch of the inning against a junkballing reliever, healthy shot to left field. Boone, incidentally, also hit a home run in the game, as did Casey Blake—the two Indians I had taken special care to dis in a column earlier this season. Sadly for White Sox fans, neither positive ("hey, Mitch Williams was fun!") nor negative thoughts ("maybe Guillen really is insane") could get Bobby Jenks to throw strikes, which would apparently take Eric Gregg's being nominated to Sandra Day O'Connor's vacant seat.

In any event, it was one of those games that really reinforced the notion that, as smart as we analysts might think we can be, our science can't entirely do justice to the drama, art, and utter randomness that a September pennant race game can provide. Joe Sheehan recently riffed eloquently on this exact theme, which is why we'll be moving on to a regular LDL full of graphs and charts and database searches in a moment. But I'll conclude this detour by noting that poker theorists such as David Sklansky and Mason Malmuth have commented that poker (particularly Texas Hold 'Em) represents a perfect balance of luck and skill: enough skill to reward correct strategy over the long run, but enough luck to allow the fish to have their days and generally keep things interesting. Pretty much the same thing can be said about baseball.

###

Today's topic, then, is going to be on the differences in aging patterns by position. You'll sometimes hear one of us say things like "middle infielders don't age very well," and while I'm sure there have been studies on this subject, we haven't usually bothered to cite one of them. This article is intended to provide some simple benchmarks on the subject.

The method that I'll apply is to compare the number of Equivalent Runs (EqR) produced by players at a given position and a given age over consecutive seasons. For example, if the cohort of shortstops produces an average of 70 EqR when they're 23, but an average of 77 EqR when they've turned 24, we can say that the average improvement by a 24-year-old shortstop is 10 percent. All the numbers here were pulled out of the PECOTA major-league database, which means that everything is park- and league- adjusted, and that only post-WWII players are included. Players are classified by their primary defensive position in the first of the two consecutive seasons: for example, while Alex Rodriguez became a third baseman at age 28, the study classifies him as a shortstop for that season since that's where he played in his age-27 year.

The only real tricky part here is to figure out what to do about playing time. After some trial and error, I settled on a method that Clay Davenport employs in his league translation work, which is to weight the EqR based on the minimum number of plate appearances between the consecutive seasons. Another approach would have been to use a rate statistic like EqA and apply some minimum threshold of plate appearances. This didn't feel appropriate because it neglects the impact of a player losing playing time due to injuries or being benched because of an inability to perform substantially above replacement level, which become key concerns as a player ages. On the other hand, using a counting stat but not weighting it at all could put too much emphasis on playing time. If a rookie gets called up during August of his age-22 season, and then spends the whole year in the big leagues at age 23, his EqR total is almost certainly going to improve, even if his underlying performance really hasn't. This player remains in the study under my method, but his weighting will be dinged because he played only a partial season at age 22, so he won't figure very prominently.

Here is the typical career track for a center fielder. "Change" is the average year-over-year difference in EqR I described earlier. Note that the pattern is basically what we'd anticipate: rapid improvement through the early twenties, a peak at 26 or 27, a plateau period where the player loses just a handful of value each season, and finally some more serious deceleration after a player enters his thirties. The numbers bounce around some, particularly for the very oldest and very youngest players, which attests to the fact that we're dealing with somewhat limited sample sizes.

The "change" numbers can be extrapolated into a typical career path, which I'm calling "EqR Track." For example, we assume that the player starts off by putting up 50 EqR in his rookie season at age 21, improves on that figure by the 19 percent number given by our model to 59.5 at age 22, tacks on another 10 percent improvement at age 23, and so forth. Add in some exponential smoothing, courtesy of Microsoft Excel, and you wind up with a nice-looking graph. Note that I'm classifying everything by percentage of peak value, which I've defined here as the average of a player's EqR Track between his age-26 and age-27 seasons (it turns out under this method that player performance is essentially unchanged between ages 26 and 27, which suggests that the typical peak comes somewhere between those ages).

Age	Change	EqR Track
21	--	50.0
22	+19.0%	59.5
23	+10.3%	65.6
24	+6.9%	70.1
25	+2.2%	71.6
26	+6.3%	76.1
27	-3.2%	73.7
28	-5.0%	70.0
29	-4.7%	66.7
30	-4.5%	63.7
31	-6.3%	59.7
32	-11.0%	53.1
33	-6.5%	49.7
34	-14.4%	42.5
35	-8.6%	38.9
36	-8.9%	35.5

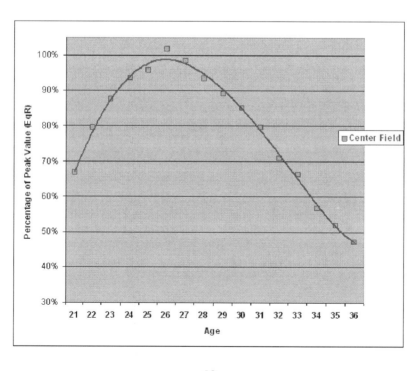

This graph isn't very useful, of course, without a comparison to players at other positions:

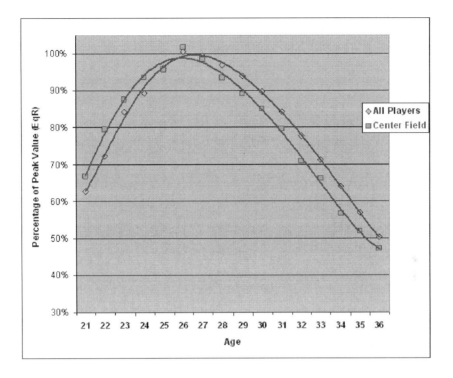

So center fielders, for example, have a rather typical looking career path, with the exception that they peak just a tiny bit earlier than players at other positions. This result came as a slight surprise; I associate center fielders with athletic, multitalented players like Jim Edmonds, Andruw Jones and Carlos Beltran, and those types of players tend to age very well. But center field is also home to lots of guys in the Willy Taveras mold—players whose games are pretty much entirely dependant on their speed. Once the speed goes—and speed evaporates more quickly than any other baseball skill—those guys become useless very quickly: they won't have the range they once did, can't do as much damage on the basepaths, and will see their batting averages drop as they can't leg out as many base hits. Center field, like shortstop, is a position that is often home to the best player on the field, and is also often home to the worst one.

Next, we'll turn to corner outfielders. I know that left field and right field are separate positions that require slightly different defensive skills, but lots of guys can play them interchangeably, and if lumping them together is good enough for Scoresheet Baseball, it's good enough for me.

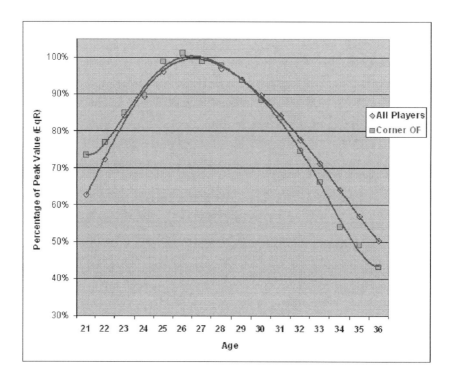

The peak comes at about the right place for the corner outfielders; for most of these guys, the primary skill is power, and power continues to develop relatively late into the twenties. On the other hand, the decline occurs somewhat quicker, probably indicating an underlying lack of athleticism and having no place on the diamond to go if defense lapses to Glenallen Hill levels. In addition, the very young (21- and 22-year-old) corner outfielders who come into the league tend to be relatively major-league-ready, which perhaps reflects the fact that teams don't tend to fool around with projects at these positions.

First basemen check in as pretty much par for the course:

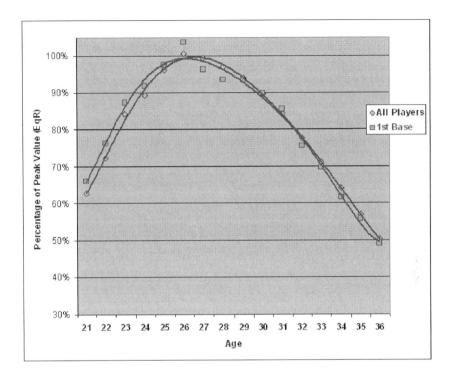

You might detect just a very slightly elongated plateau phase in the late 20s, which is mitigated by an especially sharp 12 percent drop between 31 and 32. I might have expected the first basemen to replicate the corner outfield pattern a little bit more completely. It's worth remembering, however, that first base represents the sort of alter ego of the Peter Principle at work: a player descends through the defensive spectrum until he arrives at first, a position that almost everyone can play with some bare minimum of competence. All players are subject to this erosion in defensive skill, and so it makes some sense that the aging patterns for first basemen tend to look much like the group average.

Moving violently from the right side of the defensive spectrum to the left: catcher is one of two positions—we'll get to the other in a moment—at which the divergence from normal aging patterns is unmistakable. There is no good news here; these guys take a long time to get ready and decline very quickly once they do. Some of the slow ascent may be due to teams' reluctance to give playing time to young catchers whom pitchers aren't quite comfortable working with, but the fact remains that catcher

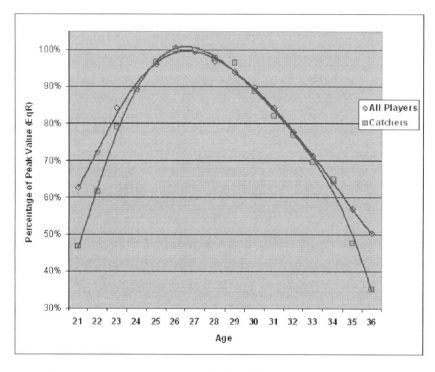

is a unique position that demands different skills and rewards a different, less athletic body type than anywhere else on the diamond. Couple that with the wear and tear that playing the position entails, and things like the Ivan Rodriguez deal begin to look very silly.

But the funkiest career track of all belongs to second basemen. You can perhaps ignore the weird blip in the graph

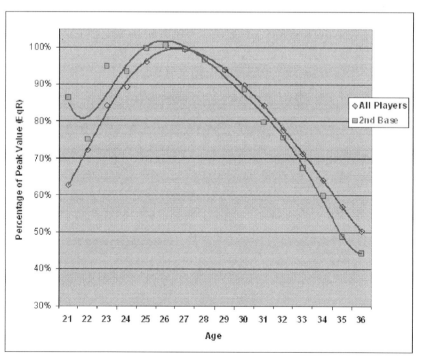

between ages 21 and 22—we're dealing with some small sample sizes there. But you can't ignore the fact that second basemen display very sluggish improvement between 23 and 26. The typical second baseman has already achieved 95 percent of his peak value by age 23—versus just 84 percent for the league as a whole. These guys just don't improve their games as much as players at other positions. And making matters worse, second basemen decline somewhat faster than normal in their thirties.

This point has been made before, but second base is something of a bastard position—it's where you wind up if you aren't athletic enough to play shortstop but don't have the bat (or the arm) for third. Almost no players are selected as second basemen in the amateur draft, and it's rare to see a second baseman on a top prospect list. That is, second base is the one position where players are selected out for their lack of a skill, rather than their possession of one; it should be no surprise that they don't tend to age well. There have been a couple of second basemen like Joe Gordon and Jeff Kent that have peaked notably late, but those guys go against type.

Analysts sometimes classify shortstops with second basemen, but the aging patterns aren't quite the same. Like second basemen, shortstops come into the league with a higher-than-usual percentage of their peak value intact. I suspect this is because, with a few obvious exceptions, shortstops are speedy, slap-hitting types, and speed and contact hitting are skills that come early. On the other hand, shortstops do tend to be good athletes, and they age perfectly well, at least up through age 32 or so.

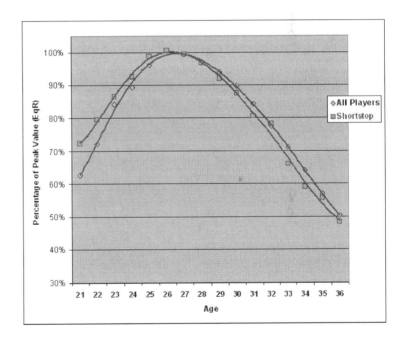

We'll complete the cycle by turning to the hot corner. Third base is the one position with a definitively late peak—the only position, for example, where a player is on average more valuable at age 29 than he is at 25. The minor trade-off is that third basemen do tend to collapse quickly at 35 or so once their nerves and reflexes are gone; that is also about the age at which many professional golfers cease to be competitive. Although third base is arguably a hard defensive position to learn—these guys don't field as many balls as players elsewhere on the field—I suspect the late peak has more to do with a typical third baseman's offensive profile. Generally, third basemen are slow and need to be bulky enough to generate arm strength, which holds down their batting averages; since 1946, third base rates as having the third-worst BA on the field, ahead of only shortstop and catcher. But third basemen are expected to make some offensive contribution, and they tend to provide it with good secondary averages. Walk rate and power peak late, and so do third basemen.

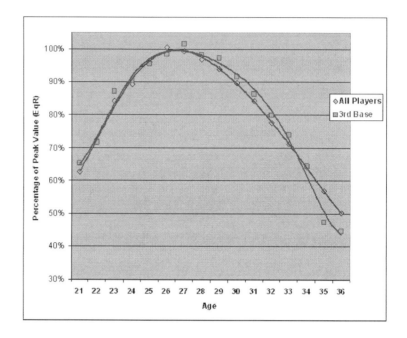

Someone like Mike Lowell or Robin Ventura fits the pattern almost perfectly. So, at least to some extent, does Joe Crede. Perhaps, just perhaps, we should have seen Tuesday night coming after all.

LIES, DAMNED LIES
Rethinking Replacement Level
Nate Silver

Critics often complain that replacement level is an abstract concept, but Nate Silver made it more concrete by looking at actual players who qualified as "freely available talent" and proposed changes to the way BP calculated its replacement level baseline.

We often interchange the phrases "freely available talent" and "replacement level player." But what does a freely available player actually look like?

To answer this simple question, I performed a search for players for all players since 1985 that met the following criteria:

1. The player was paid no more than twice the league-minimum salary
2. The player was at least 27 years old or had at least 1950 PA (three "seasons" of 650 PA) in his major-league career.

The first criterion is straightforward enough—I built in a little bit of wiggle room for players who weren't quite "free" but were certainly available very cheaply. The second requires a bit more finesse and is designed to eliminate players who were still subject to the reserve clause—Miguel Cabrera would meet the first criterion, but not the second. I've probably included a few players who were late-developing rookies, but most players who haven't had a couple of years in the show by age 27 will have become eligible for minor-league free agency or will be on their second or third organization.

The other "trick" is in figuring out how to treat playing time when evaluating these players' statistics. Say that the Mariners' Pacific Rim scout is on a flight with a pilot who has had far too much sake and happens to land in Yakutsk, Sibera instead of Sapporo, Japan. The intrepid scout can't get a flight back until the next day and decides to take in a Yakutsk Yaks game, where he discovers a set of twin left-handed pitchers, Miroslav Borscht and Radoslav Borscht, who each hit 95 on his JUGS gun. The twins are given non-roster invitations and an all-expenses paid trip to Peoria, Arizona. Miroslav turns out to be the Ozzie Canseco of the pair, with a weakness for flavored vodkas and Maricopa County's finest topless bars, and is cut a week into camp, while

Radoslav emerges as the team's second starter.

Obviously, we'd have a selective sampling issue if we gave full credit to Radoslav's performance, while forgetting about Miroslav entirely—one of the risks when signing an unknown player is that you may waste a significant number of at-bats on him before you figure out that he's not even qualified to carry Mario Mendoza's jock. The chosen solution was to "max" everyone's playing time at the rookie minimum of 130 PA. So, even if the player played a full season, his statistics were weighted as though he'd only had 130 PA. If the player had fewer than 130 PA, then his playing time was taken as is.

Here are the weighted average performances of those players based on that criterion, and their primary defensive position. These statistics are normalized to a neutral park and a .270/.340/.440 league.

Pos	AVG	OBP	SLG
C	.238	.303	.373
1B	.251	.328	.416
2B	.253	.317	.373
3B	.249	.315	.391
SS	.244	.301	.352
LF	.252	.321	.396
CF	.250	.319	.375
RF	.254	.322	.409
DH	.268	.335	.446

My first reaction when I saw these numbers was "that looks about right." That is, the numbers looked very close to what I'd have expected them to look like if we'd used another replacement level definition like VORP. However, there are some interesting differences in the relative placements of different positions, which we'll discuss in a moment. In the meantime, let's look at another part of the equation—positional defense.

These are the weighted average defensive Rate performances, measured in terms of extra runs saved or allowed per 100 games. In general, the freely available players were about average defensive performers at their respective positions—and so it would be a mistake to "double credit" a player for being better than replacement level both in the field and at the plate. But a couple of positions are exceptions. Freely available first basemen were notably above average defensive performers, probably because replacement-type first basemen are often converts from the middle infield or the outfield who have will no trouble at all handling an easier position.

Pos	D-Rate
C	99.2
1B	101.5
2B	99.7
3B	99.7
SS	96.6
LF	98.9
CF	100.1
RF	100.1
DH	N/A

Freely available shortstops, on the other hand, cost their teams 3-4 runs per 100 games with their glove. I tend to think of shortstops like NBA point guards: there are 30 NBA teams, but perhaps only 18 or 20 players in the league at any given time who can really handle the point. Similarly, there are a finite number of players who can really play a major-league average-to-plus shortstop. Why do shortstops exhibit this pattern and not, say, catchers? I suspect this is because a shortstop's defensive skills are more likely to atrophy with age, meaning that the player will already have lost a step or two by the time he becomes a freely available commodity. Catchers, while their position is very difficult, don't require much mobility and keep their throwing arm and game-calling skills intact more or less until they retire. This is why Alberto Castillo was in a major-league uniform last year.

We can combine the offensive and defensive numbers to create an overall scorecard, converting the BA/OBP/SLG numbers into runs per 162 games by means of the Marginal Lineup Value formula. For snickers and giggles, I've also added basestealing to the mix. We'll abbreviate this method FAT, for Freely Available Talent.

Pos	Hitting	SB/CS	Defense	TOTAL
C	-28.6	-0.3	-1.3	-30.1
1B	-10.8	-0.3	2.4	-8.7
2B	-22.9	0.4	-0.5	-22.9
3B	-20.1	-0.2	-0.5	-20.7
SS	-33.0	0.0	-5.5	-38.5
LF	-16.9	0.2	-1.8	-18.5
CF	-22.2	1.0	0.2	-21.0
RF	-13.6	0.2	0.2	-13.3
DH	-0.4	-0.2		-0.5

So, a shortstop who hits and fields at the league average should be credited with 38.5 runs above replacement under this method, and a league-average first baseman 8.7 runs. How does the FAT approach compare to VORP, or the implicit positional ratings embedded in our WARP rankings? Here are the replacement level thresholds produced by the three metrics, taken as runs below average per 162 games. (Note: the VORP numbers change from year to year, depending on league-average performances in a particular year. The figures included here represent the cumulative league averages across both leagues from 1996-2005).

Pos	FAT	VORP	WARP
SS	-38.5	-32.9	-33.0
C	-30.1	-27.4	-39.0
2B	-22.9	-28.3	-29.0
CF	-21.0	-22.0	-24.0
3B	-20.7	-21.6	-22.0
LF	-18.5	-12.2	-14.0
RF	-13.3	-10.0	-14.0
1B	-8.7	-10.6	-10.0
DH	-0.5	-20.2	0.0

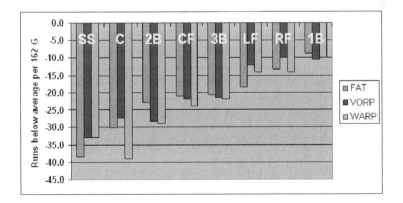

As I've said, the three metrics are in almost perfect agreement in the aggregate (although WARP may be subject to the double-counting phenomenon that I described before when Batting Runs Above Replacement are added to the mix). But the relative values of the positions are quite different.

FAT sees shortstop as far and away the most difficult position on the diamond, mainly because it's able to recognize that freely available shortstops usually give something up with their gloves as well as with their bats. VORP still has shortstops in front, but by a smaller margin. WARP goes in the other direction and gives much more credit to catchers.

FAT, however, is considerably more skeptical than the other two metrics about second basemen. Whereas VORP and WARP posit a four-run difference between shortstops and second basemen, FAT puts the gap at about 15 runs. Remember when I suggested that it seemed strange that so many second basemen rated so highly in the PECOTA prospect rankings? Those rankings were derived based on offshoots of VORP and WARP, and so this may be the reason why.

At the risk of starting a firestorm within the authors group, let me argue that FAT gets it right on this particular question. Although the original formulation of VORP was based on looking explicitly at the performances of reserve players (very similar to the FAT approach), the version that we use more commonly takes the slight shortcut of backing into replacement level based on a comparison to league positional averages. The problem is that shortstop tends to be a feast-or-famine position: the shortstop is usually one of the very best players in the everyday lineup (Derek Jeter, Michael Young), or perhaps the very worst (Neifi Perez, Angel Berroa). Second basemen, on the other hand, tend to cluster around league average—you have your Placido Polancos and your Aaron Hills. The overall positional averages may not be that different, since the Jeters and Youngs lift the numbers, but they understate just how much easier it is to find a credible second baseman than a credible shortstop.

Psychologists talk about something called g, or General Intelligence Factor, the notion that abilities in certain seemingly unrelated mental fields are positively correlated. It seems probable that there is baseball analog to this, which we might call General Athletic Ability. That is, although the specific skills and motor abilities required to field a good defensive shortstop are quite different than those required to hit a curveball, a truly elite overall athlete will be able to do both things well. I suspect that major-league shortstops, as a group, have quite a bit more g than major-league second basemen. You could put Miguel Tejada at second base if you wanted to, and he'd still outhit pretty much everyone at the position, but there's no reason to since his defense is more valuable at short. You couldn't put Jeff Kent at shortstop, however, without your pitching staff chipping in on a bounty against you.

The three metrics are in strong agreement in their treatment of center fielders and third basemen. However, FAT sees more separation between first basemen and corner outfielders than its counterparts. Once again, I suspect this has to do with the practicalities of finding a freely-available player who can handle a given defensive position: virtually any outfielder can play a decent first base, but not the other way around. FAT does posit a fairly large difference between left fielders and right fielders, with LF rating as the more difficult position. This is a bit strange, since I can't think of any reason why LF should be more difficult than RF, and is probably a sample size fluke. I'm open to hearing explanations to the contrary, however.

Finally, FAT works around any issues with designated hitters. DHs have been outhit as a group by outfielders and first basemen at most points in the recent past, and so a strict league-average-based notion of replacement level will actually give more credit to a DH than a LF or RF with the same statistics. But it's very rare to see a truly awful regular DH, since teams have so much flexibility at the position.

If it sounds like I'm suggesting that we reinvent the replacement level wheel—well, I guess that I am. We're fighting over table scraps and percentage points, but replacement level is so vital to what we do that the fight may be worth having.

LIES, DAMNED LIES
New Life on Different Fields
Nate Silver

Nate Silver identified the 10 biggest mistakes teams were continuing to make in 2007 despite sabermetric advances in understanding the game.

This piece was originally intended as a response to Gary Huckabay's column of last week, the idea being to contradict his assertion that baseball analysis is dead by counting down 10 points of decision that at least a significant minority of baseball franchises get wrong. But after reading through my article—I generally write my introductions last—as well as re-reading Gary's piece, I am not so sure it is orthogonal to it at all. I agree with Gary that there is relatively little to be gained from what he describes as "the rigorous review of player performance data." Relatively little does not mean "nothing," however, and I have isolated some of the exceptions below. Most of the items on my list, however, have to do with questions that run outside the scope of the GM or the field manager. They have more to do with the guy sitting in the owner's box, and those places on a baseball team's org chart where the names stop becoming familiar.

10. Inappropriate Leadoff Hitters: We start with one of those minor exceptions that takes place at the field level. There are very few in-game strategic decisions that amount to a hill of beans, and lineup order—within reasonable boundaries of sanity—is no exception. Most teams, save perhaps for three or four outliers like the Dodgers, have no trouble understanding the value of on-base percentage.

Still, for fully one-third of the teams in baseball, the most frequently-used leadoff hitter this season has a lower OBP than that of the team in general. The ten culprits are these.

By contrast, 29 of the 30 primary leadoff hitters are on pace to finish with double-digit stolen base totals; the lone exception is Craig Biggio, which can readily be explained by the fact that the Astros came into the season apparently thinking they were getting the 1997

Team	Hitter	Hitter OBP	Team OBP
BOS	Lugo	.296	.362
NYY	Damon	.350	.364
CHW	Owens	.307	.317
PHI	Rollins	.346	.356
WAS	Lopez	.307	.321
CHC	Soriano	.329	.332
CIN	Freel	.308	.336
HOU	Biggio	.283	.326
ARI	Young	.293	.316
SDP	M. Giles	.306	.321

version of the former star. Generally speaking, the conceit of using a Brian Downing or Wade Boggs type as a leadoff hitter never really caught on.

What's funny is that there are several analysis-friendly teams on the list, like the Red Sox, Padres, and Diamondbacks. It would appear that this is a battle that our SABRCat Superfriend GMs have concluded is not worth fighting; there is just too much inertial momentum going the other way, and too little marginal gain to be had.

9. Underaccounting for Injury Risk: I have only anecdotal evidence to present here: Randy Wolf. Jason Schmidt. Nomar Garciaparra. Wait, all of those guys are Dodgers? There is ample room for improving analysis of injury risk and its concomitant effects on performance, feeding off the head start that Will Carroll and Sig Mejdal have given us. But for the time being, there are a number of clubs that could stand to develop a respect for the Inertial Law of Injuries: what's healthy tends to stay healthy, and what's injured tends to stay injured.

8. Focusing Too Much on Year N-1 and other small sample sizes: now we start to get into the more serious sins. My analysis of the free agent market indicates that the player's performance in his most recent season generally accounts for about 65 percent of the salary package he eventually receives, when statistically speaking the proper fraction for a mid-career player is closer to 50 percent. This is especially problematic if, as Dayn Perry found in *Baseball Between the Numbers*, players tend to perform especially well in contract drive seasons (and even more so if my further speculation is correct that baseball players are more likely to use PEDs when they're angling for a new contract).

7. Failure to Understand Pitcher Peripherals, Especially for Relief Pitchers: Stop me if you've heard this one before. Baseball seems to have experienced some improvement in downplaying the importance of W-L record, but it still treats ERA as the holy grail. Yet ERA is not much more reliable; the year-over-year correlation for ERA is just .38 for starting pitchers, and a fair bit lower than that for relievers. Key peripheral statistics like walk rate, strikeout rate, and groundball percentage, on the other hand, all check in with correlations between .68 and .81. The failure to heed the importance of peripheral statistics can lead to disasters like the White Sox middle relief corps of the past two seasons.

A related adage is the old piece of Bill James wisdom about power pitchers holding up better than finesse pitchers over the longer run. But after seeing the difference in the value of the recent contract extensions signed by Mark Buehrle and Carlos Zambrano, I am not so sure that teams haven't started to price this into the market.

6. Failure to Adjust Strategy Based on Position on the Wins Curve: This is a tricky one, because it requires both a solid understanding of baseball economics and a capacity for intellectual honesty.

Because of the substantial increase in marginal revenues associated with making the playoffs, proper strategy differs rather radically based on where a team falls on the wins curve; a free agent who might be a good buy for an 88-win club could be an awful investment for a 73-win club. The problem is that a baseball team may not be honest with itself about just where it stands. Most people that establish a high degree of authority in a people business like baseball tend to be optimists, and optimists tend to exaggerate their lot in life. If you surveyed the 30 major-league GMs about how many games they expected their team to win next season (and were somehow able to get an honest answer) I would guess that the average would come out to something like 88. This fact alone begets substantial irrationality in the free agent market

5. Lack of Objective Analysis of Marginal Returns: and this issue facilitates those problems. Most teams don't seem to be conducting objective analysis of how much extra wins or extra championships will actually improve revenues in their market. Rather, teams tend to spend the money they have, and market prices are dictated by a monkey-see, monkey-do approach. How else to explain how 27 of 30 teams lost money on their marginal spending on payroll last year? Or that in spite of that, prices for free agent talent in this winter's market increased by nearly 50 percent because of an influx of cash from sources like MLBAM and national TV rights, neither of which is responsive to marginal changes in team quality?

4. Lack of Coordination between Baseball Ops and Ownership: I was talking recently with Aaron Schatz about the differences in ownership structures between baseball and football. In football, for whatever reason, there are a large number of franchises owned by families; by my quick count 11 of the 32 current NFL owners fall under the category of legacy hires. In contrast, this is relatively rare in baseball; baseball teams tend to be owned by corporations, investment conglomerates, or Very Rich Dudes. You would think that this breakdown would tend to be favorable to baseball, since family legacy teams tend to make nepotistic hires, leading to occasional disasters like the pre-Carson Palmer Cincinnati Bengals.

In fact, however, Aaron theorizes that all this nepotism tended to breed less tension into the NFL's culture of ownership-management relations. In the NFL, the owner was some rich guy wearing argyle socks, and the general manager was probably also some rich guy wearing argyle socks, who happened to share half the owner's DNA. In baseball, on the other hand, the owner was some guy wearing argyle socks, and the GM was some ex-jock who had come up in a different culture.

Sure, the argyle-sock guys might authorize the trade of John Elway for an offensive lineman and a six-pack of Schlitz, but at least they knew where one another was coming from. Baseball, on the other hand, seems to be in a perpetual state of ownership-management tension, damned if they do and damned if they don't. On the one hand, you have the Drayton McLanes of the universe, who interfere with their GM's ability to do his job. On the other hand, you have cases like the Cubs, where ownership changes its payroll requirements willy-nilly from year to year based on balancing the corporate bottom line, rather than trying to maximize the profits from the baseball team itself. The few franchises where ownership and management seem to see eye-to-eye, like the Red Sox and the Angels, stick out like a sore thumb, and they almost always do well in the standings column.

3. Misuse of the Closer: Gary touched on this one—optimizing the use of the bullpen is perhaps the one in-game managerial decision that has the most impact on a team's ultimate place in the standings. Unfortunately, it is also the one that teams routinely get wrong. We are not talking about using a closer by committee; most teams will have an alpha dog in their bullpen, and he deserves to get the most important opportunities. But those opportunities are not particularly strongly related to the definition of the save.

This is a cultural thing, not an analysis thing. The theory behind it is not particularly hard to understand, and yet almost every team is giving away a couple of wins a season by succumbing to the groupthink that the save rule has engendered. With the notable exception of NFL coaches' irrational disdain for going for it on fourth down, this might be the most reliably botched strategic protocol in American sports.

2. Failure to Appreciate the Value of Draft Picks and Pre-Free Agent Players: I am not necessarily talking about the signing bonuses paid to draft picks. Although teams are generally rewarded when they go over slot for a special player, there are also some incentives toward collective action that keeps prices down overall. Nevertheless, baseball teams fail to appreciate that essentially the only reliable way to make money at the margins in the industry is to employ quality talent at below-market prices. The expected savings on a premium prospect like Jarrod Saltalamacchia can approach $50 million before he hits his first cycle of free agency. There is almost no reasonable combination of veteran talent, and no reasonable discount rate, that could justify trading away such an asset.

But at least the guy the Braves got for Saltalamacchia is a good player. How to explain a trade like Scott Moore and Rocky Cherry for Steve Trachsel? Nobody noticed this one, but it might be the worst trade in several seasons, and it required a violation of at least half of the ten principles that you see in this column to come to fruition. Trachsel is a liability rather than an asset; he is not worth his prorated salary. In fact, provided that you understand #7 above, he is worth less than nothing. His QERA at the time the Cubs acquired him from the Orioles was 6.47, largely because he had walked 50 percent more batters than he'd struck out. Nevertheless, the Cubs gave away a prospect in Moore whom PECOTA thinks could produce about $30 million in value before he becomes a free agent, and a decent reliever who would cost at least a million or two each season in the free agent market to replace. It makes absolutely no sense, nor does the rationalization that the Cubs traded for Trachsel to keep him away from the Brewers and Cardinals; the Cubs should actively seek to have Trachsel pitching for their rivals. You can't tell me that the arbitrage opportunities in baseball are anywhere near exhausted when you see a trade like that, which barely got a shrug from the analysis community.

1. Too-Long Contracts (and Too-Short Time Horizons): How many contracts of at least four years in length turn out to produce a positive return on investment for the club? I've given an off-the-cuff estimate of between 20 and 30 percent when asked this question. People like David Regan who have studied this issue more systematically would tend to support that conclusion. By the third year of his contract, a free agent hitter has generally lost about 40 percent of his value from his contract-year season, and a free agent pitcher has generally lost 60 percent of his value. Yet teams give out extra years on their contracts like they're Halloween candy. It's very common to hear of a team that is considering signing a particular player to a three-year, $30 million deal, and before you know it, that contract has become four years and $40 million (or worse still, the extra year might be a player option).

Now, overall, a great number of these problems—certainly #1 and #2, but also to some extent #4, #5, #6, and #8—stem from the fact that teams are exceptionally focused on the near-term. Vince Gennaro in *Diamond Dollars* suggests that the discount rate applied by baseball teams approaches 35 percent—you'll trade 1.35 wins next season for one win today. Such a discount rate would be unconscionable in any other mature industry, but it should not be entirely surprising, given the principal-agent problems that baseball teams face. The median tenure of current major-league managers is between two and three years, GMs between four and five years, and principal team owners last about seven years. Why should the Cubs care about giving too much money to Alfonso Soriano if neither Lou Piniella nor Jim Hendry (and certainly not the Tribune Corp.) is going to be around when that deal expires?

Of course, the Tribune should care about Soriano's contract if the potential new ownership groups are smart enough to recognize that it represents a liability, but they have some reasonable hope that it will be written off as rounding error by whoever purchases the franchise. The market for baseball franchises is not particularly liquid, nor are the prospective owners necessarily evaluating the investment as rigorously; they might understand finance, but not baseball economics. The owners may be willing to pay substantially more than the price that the P&L justifies because they think they'll be able to pass the franchise off to a greater fool.

The next revolution in baseball will not take place at the field level, and it will probably not take place at the general manager level; it will take place at the ownership level, and it will not be led by statheads, but by investment bankers. Like a lot of revolutions, it might be precipitated by hardship. I believe there is at least a 60:40 chance that that franchise valuations for baseball are presently in a bubble, and that the bubble will burst at some point within the next decade. If the credit crunch has legs, such that leveraged buys of baseball teams become harder to execute, the collapse could come toward the beginning of that cycle.

If baseball's existing owners want to protect their investments, they ought to change their practices for vetting potential new owners, focusing not so much on those owners who are likely to perpetuate the collective groupthink, but rather on those who come with business plans in hand and have a demonstrated ability to shepherd long-term investments. In contrast to the perception that everything is just ducky, I believe that the industry is in a fairly dangerous place. That's what I have to conclude when I see discount rates of 35 percent, or the market price for free agent talent jumping by 50 percent with little underlying economic rationale, or the Cubs throwing away $30 million in future value to trade for a player like Steve Trachsel.

LIES, DAMNED LIES
Look, a Navel!
Nate Silver

In 2004, Nate Silver took a break from statistical analysis to offer some insights into the progress made by the sabermetric movement and the shape it would take in the future.

Perhaps because the presidential campaign is now in full swing—Zell Miller, incidentally, is a good comparable for Larry Bowa—I've been thinking a lot lately about the politics of what we do. If you place hard-core sabermetric orthodoxy on the left and reactionary traditionalism on the right (perhaps this reveals too much about my political leanings), I'd like to think that Baseball Prospectus belongs somewhere in the area of Bill Clinton or maybe John Edwards; a centrist Democrat, so to speak.

It wasn't long ago that we were Ralph Nader. Two things have happened: we have moved to the right, and the center has moved to the left. Most of the chapters in our annual book are improved by discussions with scouts and other team officials. Most of the articles that appear on our site fall into the category of hard-hitting but even-handed baseball analysis, using our statistical methods and metrics for support but not drowning in them. Baseball Prospectus writers have been known to share beers with *Baseball America* writers.

Meanwhile, *The New York Times* is running a column every Sunday on baseball analysis (a very good one, I might add), and shock jocks like Max Kellerman are as likely to belt out the phrase "OPS" as they are "clubhouse chemistry." There are analytically friendly administrations in Boston and Los Angeles—two of the flagship franchises in the game—as well in the other places that you folks are familiar with. Perhaps an even more important indication of the progress of the movement is that, in the darker corners of the world, decision-makers are often making "analytically correct" decisions without even realizing it. We might gripe about pitch counts now and then, for example, but they are down radically across the league from where they were even 10 years ago.

Does that mean that the battle has been won? Hardly; it is likely to take a while, perhaps a whole generation, before analysis crosses the chasm between the early adopters and the mainstream. Baseball executives, with some notable exceptions, are older men with backgrounds in scouting and player development. Beat writers, by and large, are a worn lot and neither particularly well-versed in analysis nor particularly interested in learning about it. While the internet and other forms of new media provide fans with greater discretion in just how they take their baseball, there is also an increasing tendency within the media (this means you, ESPN) to take a Paparazzi-like approach toward their sports coverage, with a focus on personalities and storylines rather than numbers and nuance. It will be a quiet revolution, and those tend to be slower than the bloody ones.

In the meantime, I think we are likely to see the emergence of what might be called analytical post-modernism. Sabermetrics, from the very start, has been a remarkably positivist movement: the answers are out there, it is within our capacity to discover them, and their application will provide us with a better world, or at least a better baseball team. There are two things that I think will characterize this post-modern period.

The first of these will be a greater willingness to accept and discuss openly the limitations of analysis. Many of the Hilbert Problems that Keith Woolner describes are likely to be resolved in some way, shape or form. In fact, substantial progress has been made on many fronts, such as the separation of run prevention into pitching and fielding since Keith's essay first ran four years ago. Others, like quantifying the impact of the field manager, are likely never to be solved. PECOTA, I'd like to think, is a post-modern forecasting engine. It uses all of the information available to come up with the best forecast but also admits freely that a certain amount of uncertainty is intrinsic to the process of forecasting human performance.

This first tendency, by and large, should be helpful to the analytical movement. Being willing to admit when you are wrong, or at least when your knowledge is limited, tends to help one's credibility when pressing the really important points. This is a little piece of psychology that all good politicians (and all good poker players) recognize. There is, in fact, a sort of feedback mechanism at work here: as sabermetrics moves more comfortably toward the orthodoxy, it can acknowledge more freely those places where it performs imperfectly, just as a standing president with a high popularity rating can withstand a scandal that would kill the careers of a thousand lesser-knowns in the party primaries. That admission, in turn, should help to increase the sympathy that traditionalists have for analysis, enhancing dialogue and pushing both sides toward the center.

The other thing that tends to characterize post-modern thinking, however, is a sort of navel-gazing that is useless at best and outright destructive at worst. By that I mean analysts fighting with one another for territory, usually over issues that are ultimately trivial to the movement as a whole. I would like to think, for example, that much of the discourse on the competing methods to evaluate offensive performance boil down to a lot of hot air; the difference between a very good metric and a pretty good one might boil down to a couple of runs over the course of a whole season.

Movements, whether social, political or intellectual, tend to be unified when they have a lot of work to do and when there is a lot to accomplish, and fractionalized when there is not. If sabermetric thinkers come to believe prematurely that their mission has been accomplished, the infighting is likely to increase, and the movement could set its progress back. It is also probably true that the pace of discovery within sabermetric circles will slow as more and more data is analyzed and more and more conclusions have been proclaimed. Baseball, while a wonderfully complex game, is nevertheless a closed system, and the returns on further research efforts are likely to diminish.

I am not going to try and boil all of this down into some nice, meaty conclusion; think of this week's column as an Etch-A-Sketch rather than rather than a painting hanging on the wall of the Louvre. I am not even certain that the characterization of sabermetrics as political movement is correct; it may be more proper to think of it as technology, and technology has a way of marching along, ignorant of the desires of its inventors.

I will now go back to doing something useful, like watching Chris Matthews.

BASEBALL THERAPY
Why Are Games So Long?
Russell A. Carleton

Amidst complaints about interminable Yankees-Red Sox matchups, Russell Carleton determined what factors were most responsible for lengthening games, and what—if anything—could be done to counteract the trend toward three-plus-hour contests.

A few weeks ago, umpire Joe West caused a stir when he publicly called out the New York Yankees and Boston Red Sox for doing what they do best: playing games that take forever to finish. He's certainly not the first person (nor will he be the last) to wonder aloud why it is that baseball games last so long (particularly between those two teams). Is there a way to shorten the great American game? If there was, should we try?

In 2009, the average MLB game lasted 175.38 minutes, or just short of the three-hour mark. Contrary to popular belief, games played in National League stadia (that is, without the DH, unless it's the All-Star Game) were slightly longer (by a couple of seconds) than games in American League stadia. Throwing out extra-inning (and rain-shortened) games, the mark drops to 171.79 minutes, this time with AL games lasting a minute longer (172.31 to 171.32).

The quickest nine-inning game of 2009 was an inter-league tilt between the White Sox (2) and Pirates (0) on May 22. It lasted 111 minutes (Gavin Floyd vs. Zach Duke, go figure). On April 25, two teams needed 4:21 to play an 8 ½-inning game (that ended 16-11). Anyone want to guess which the two teams were? As it happens, four of the 15 longest nine-inning games of 2009 were between the Yankees and Red Sox, and five of the other games in that group involved one of the two teams. In fairness, the Blue Jays, Indians, Mets, and Rays also made multiple appearances on that list as well. Perhaps some teams are simply built to be slowpokes?

During these discussions about shortening the game, the same set of culprits is identified over and over. Do managers really need to bring a reliever into the game mid-inning? Why don't the umpires call the strike zone the way that it's supposed to be called? What's with all the throws to first? A few folks have floated proposals intended to shorten the game, but I have to wonder whether some of them are misguided. Leaving aside the counter-argument from addiction (a four-hour game is great because it's *baseball for four hours!*), nerdiness (all the stuff that takes so long is the mental side of the game, and that's fascinating!) or sentimentality (it's not often I get to spend much time with my dad, and I'd rather have four hours than two-and-a-half), there are a few logical counter-arguments to be made.

I'd argue that the much-maligned mid-inning pitching change might actually serve to shorten games. Consider that a reliever is generally brought into the middle of an inning for one of two reasons: to replace an ineffective pitcher or to gain a handedness advantage. The way that you make the clock move in baseball is to get batters to make outs like nervous seventh-graders at their first co-ed party. An ineffective pitcher isn't recording outs, whether through fatigue or through just plain being awful. Managers try to play left-right match-ups because the platoon advantage is worth about 30 points of on-base percentage, also known as the "Did you make an out or not?" stat.

What about throws to first? It's true that it's rare that a pitcher actually picks a runner off, but while a throw to first doesn't make a runner less likely to try to steal, it does make him less likely to be successful when he does try. That means a greater chance of an out, and the greater chance that you'll get home quicker.

But let's see what the data say. I took all games from 2009 and ran a regression to predict the length of the game in minutes. I entered the following variables into the regression to see what shook out.

- The number of times a reliever was brought into the middle of an inning. A reliever brought into the game between innings can slip in and do his warming up during the usual time set aside for that, and the PA announcer can wait until after the fans are done singing "Sweet Caroline" to announce him.
- The number of throws to first made
- The number of pitches thrown
- The number of plate appearances for both teams
- The number of two-strike foul balls
- The number of stolen-base attempts by both teams. After all, this is more than just an average pitch. There's probably a throw down to second afterward, and that all takes time.
- The number of walks (intentional and unintentional considered separately), strikeouts, home runs, and balls in play hit by both teams
- Whether the DH was used (1 = yes, 0 = no)
- The percentage of pitches not swung at which were called strikes. This is a (very) rough estimate of the size of the strike zone but obviously is conflated with the wildness of the pitchers involved in the game

- The number of between-inning breaks. Most of the time, that's 16 or 17 for a nine-inning game, but of course in extra innings, there are more.

I ran the regression as a stepwise regression. For those not familiar, a stepwise regression looks first for which variable is the best predictor of the dependent variable (in this case, length of the game) and then runs the regression again looking for the next-best predictor, and so on.

The variable most associated with the length of the game was the number of pitches thrown. No surprise there. In fact, it picked up the first 82.3 percent of the variance. The next variable that entered was the number of mid-inning pitching changes, followed by the number of throws to first. Combined, those two picked up another 4.8 percent of the variance. *Mid-inning pitching changes and throws to first really are a big driving force behind games being longer!*

Several other variables entered the regression, although combined they added only another 2.1 percent to the R-squared. The final equation (for time of game, in minutes), for the morbidly curious, was:

```
.430 * pitches + 3.084 * mid-inning relief + .673 * throws to first +
2.264 * IBB + .604 * plate appearances + .878 * SB attempts + .742 *
inning breaks - .628 * HR — 1.362 * presence of DH - .154 * balls in play
— 11.729.
```

The average mid-inning change of pitchers adds about three minutes to the game, while each throw to first adds about 40 seconds. In fairness, the average MLB game featured 2.06 mid-inning pitching changes and 7.28 throws to first. Even if they all disappeared, we're talking about 10-12 minutes off the average game.

Other things of note included how much time intentional walks and stolen-base attempts added to the game. Stolen bases, in addition to taking extra time beyond the average pitch, also indicate that the pitcher hasn't been doing such a good job keeping runners off base. Intentional walks are apparently time-intensive, probably because they occur during situations in which there's a lot of "button-pushing" going on and everyone seems to be out of the dugout gesturing to each other. Then there are the events that apparently take negative amounts of time, including home runs and balls in play. The careful reader will notice that walks and strikeouts did not enter the equation, so what happens here is that each additional ball in play or home run probably comes at the expense of an additional walk or strikeout, both of which take more pitches to complete, on average. So, home runs and balls in play are a sign of a game where players are getting things over and done with.

There's one variable that I can't account for that probably has some influence. Some pitchers like to work quickly, while others take their sweet time. Rafael Betancourt, during his time with the Indians, earned the nickname Señor Slow Mo for his... reluctance... to throw the ball toward home plate. There may be some teams that either coach their pitchers to be slow (or fast) or simply just happen to employ a bunch of pitchers who work slowly (or quickly). However, there's another lesson to be gained here. The main driver of the length of a game is how many pitches are thrown. More pitches means longer games, and teams that have batters who stretch out the count will play longer games.

Looking at the top 50 players in pitches per plate appearance for 2009 (minimum of 250 PA), we find Kevin Youkilis, Nick Swisher, David Ortiz, J.D. Drew, Brett Gardner, and Johnny Damon, all of whom played for either the Red Sox or Yankees last year. Also in the top 50 were Nick Johnson, Jeremy Hermida, and Marco Scutaro, now members of the Yankees and/or Red Sox. It looks like the Yankees and Red Sox have put their teams together and coached their players, intentionally or unintentionally, to try to win games by a war of attrition. (I should note that I'm not the first person to notice this.) It's not really a bad strategy. If you can tire the starter out before the sixth inning, you often get to see the soft underbelly of the other team's bullpen. Even within an inning, even at the same pitch count, there's probably a difference between throwing my 70th pitch when it's the 20th of the inning versus it being thrown after I've had a few minutes to sit and rest in the dugout between frames (although I've not seen any research addressing the topic.) The problem with this war of attrition strategy is that it produces games that take three-and-a-half hours.

So if baseball really wants to shorten up games, it could cut 15 minutes out per game if it cut out two pitches of each half inning. How to encourage that? Well, consider the circumstances under which the war of attrition strategy has flourished. Pitchers go out to the mound with a sign around their neck that says "I'm leaving after 100 pitches." Teams also appear to unflinchingly stick to an inning-based usage schedule for relievers. If it's the sixth inning, then Smith is going to be the guy to get the call, never mind that Smith is awful and the game is tied. He's our sixth-inning guy. Given that, it makes sense to try to stretch the starter out a little bit in the hope that you can exploit this quirk of what is loosely called "strategy."

Baseball has inflicted this situation on itself. The merits of the 100-pitches-and-out guideline can be debated, but it's silly to expect that as it has become more emphasized, the game wouldn't have evolved along with it. If baseball wants shorter contests, it can toy with little rule changes, but what it's really fighting is the natural evolution of the game, and that's hard to do.

MANUFACTURED RUNS
Replacing Replacement
Colin Wyers

In order to refine replacement level further, Colin Wyers went back to the empirical data to see who exactly the "replacements" have been in baseball's past.

This is something of a culmination of work I've been doing over the past few months—taking a menagerie of stats available here at Baseball Prospectus and merging them together under the heading of "Wins Above Replacement Level." We've had WARP for quite a while—and its close sibling, VORP, as well—but it has been rather distinct from the rest of our offerings. That's coming to an end.

We will, of course, still carry a number of baseball statistics not concerned with directly measuring a player's value—there are a number of stats both descriptive and predictive that aren't going away. But in terms of value measures, we're going to consolidate down to one view.

And that view will not be identical to similar measures of wins above replacement found at other websites. It will obviously bear some similarities (they all should agree more often than they disagree, I would think) but it's not the goal of the enterprise. A while back, Rob Neyer quoted a letter that sums up a growing point of view:

> *Instead of competing on WAR, Tango, Forman, BP and anyone else relevant should try to come to some consensus. Maybe you can serve as the summit leader? Otherwise, the sabermetric viewpoint will drown in its own contradictions.*

Let me tell you why I disagree—and let's start off with the definition of sabermetrics proffered by Bill James, who after all coined the word to start with: "the search for objective knowledge about baseball." I think you can restate that definition simply as "baseball science," or the study of baseball using the scientific method.

And what I've been coming to grips with is how little of the field of sabermetric endeavor that definition covers (not all of what follows is necessarily going to be science, although it is definitely informed by what I would term a scientific study of baseball). Once you know things, you still need to interpret them—facts in isolation do not necessarily carry meaning.

So in coming to a reckoning of a player's value, science is only going to take us so far. And two reasonable people can disagree over the assumptions one starts out from. I've talked before about why I find the systemic approach valuable—in short, I find it more useful to start off with assumptions and move to conclusions than vice versa. But that doesn't mean our assumptions are perfect.

I think it's tempting for some people to make the perfect the enemy of the good—what cannot be done perfectly is dismissed outright. And when it comes to replacement level metrics, where that's most tempting is in the definition of replacement itself.

Average Joes
The case against replacement level, I think, can be summed up like so:

1. It is a hypothetical construct—one perfect embodiment of replacement level doesn't exist,
2. It is difficult to define—different people have different conceptions of replacement level, and
3. It doesn't convey any additional meaning.

The first two of those I feel are correct but don't detract from the usage of replacement level—because the third point is clearly wrong.

The most frequently cited alternative to replacement level is average. On the first point, it fails to improve upon replacement level—an "average" baseball player does not exist any more or less than a replacement player. It's an abstraction, designed to help us visualize a player's value relative to something else. It does improve on the second point, as "average" (if we take that to signify the arithmetic mean) has a consistent definition; in other words, everyone understands it to mean the same thing.

There is one question that average is deeply unsuited to answer, except circularly—what is the value of an average ballplayer? What it will tell you is simply this—the same as every other average ballplayer. Often this will serve, but just as often, it really won't.

The biggest point of breakage is in determining the value of playing time. Again—average is equal to average, be it in 150 plate appearances or 650 plate appearances. But realistically, we know that the player who manages to sustain an average level of performance is more valuable than the player who does so for only 150 plate appearances. It is possible that the 150 PA player could, given an additional 500 PA (assuming he was capable of playing an additional 500 PA at all), put up the same level of performance. But that's irrelevant to measuring what has happened.

Or take the example of a player who has produced 20 runs below average. That is, again, very different if it occurs in 150 PA or 650 PA—roughly the difference between a .150 TAv and a .230 TAv.

And while above we extolled the virtues of the average player with more playing time, nobody would find a "true" .150 TAv hitter (that is to say, one who will hit .150 TAv regardless of playing time, not a hitter who hits .150 TAv over a cold streak) more valuable the more he plays—there's an opportunity cost to deploying that hitter, in that he's taking at-bats from a player who can do more to help his team. He's actually hurting his team more the more he plays.

And this is why we find replacement level useful—we are trying to find the point at which a player starts to contribute to his team by playing more, as opposed to detracting from his team. And this is something that is difficult to measure, as the critics of replacement level say—but the difficulty doesn't make it any less important for us to know.

Baseball fans have always known intuitively that there is such a point, of course—they even have a name for it, the Mendoza line. But it may be helpful to know why it exists. Consider the distribution of MLB batting performance, by TAv, in 2010 (with an idealized normal distribution fit to the data, for illustration purposes):

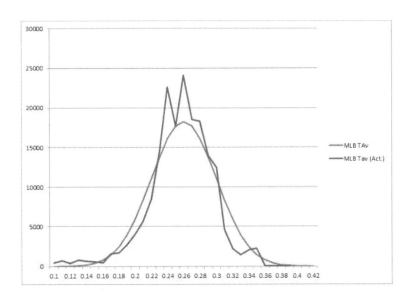

What you see is the majority of plate appearances at the average of .260, with outliers becoming less common the further you get from the average. The normal distribution seems to be a very good (although not perfect) approximation for the data.

That is, again, in terms of plate appearances. If you consider players, on the other hand, it becomes a very different story. Looking at the area of the graph between 1 and 4 standard deviations above the average, we see that those plate appearances came from 78 players. Looking at 1 to 4 SDs below the average, we instead see 305 players.

What the graph seems to suggest, at first blush, is that below-average players are just as rare as above-average players. But this simply isn't the case—below-average players are much, much more common than above-average players (and this isn't even considering the number of those players available in a club's minor-league system). What's limited is the number of opportunities for below-average players—baseball teams have a limited amount of playing time available to them, and they strive mightily to make sure the lion's share of that playing time goes to their better players.

The break-even point (that is, our platonic "ideal" replacement level) is the point where the number of available players at that level of talent (note—at that level of talent) exceeds the available playing time. Where this gets tricky is that there are transactional costs to acquiring baseball players—making trades, adding players to the 40-man roster, etc.—that impose a limit on how flexible teams can be with their replacements. In other words, the supply of talent isn't totally liquid. So the practical replacement level may be a bit lower than our platonic "ideal" replacement level—which is fine, as typically we define replacement level as it exists in practice, not in terms of the distribution of talent.

Defining replacement level
So in order to come up with a baseline of what a replacement player is, we need to define a population of replacement players and take the average of that (This is important to note—50 percent of our replacements will be above our baseline, and 50 percent of them will be below it. So in practice, we fully expect to see submarginal performance—that is, some level of performance below replacement).

I had two main objectives in picking my replacement-level pool. On one hand, I wanted to make sure I was picking my pool of replacements independently of how well they performed—using a player's observed level of performance to set replacement level runs the risk of leading yourself around by the nose, leading you to a lower replacement level than you really should find.

On the other hand, I wanted to avoid something like Nate Silver's study of freely available talent, which relies on salary data that goes back only to the mid-'80s. And I wanted to ensure that I had a sizable pool of replacements at which to look.

What I came upon was the notion of looking at a team's Opening Day roster and calling anyone who replaces a player on it, well, a replacement. Not finding a ready source of Opening Day rosters, I did my best to reconstruct estimates of every team's Opening Day roster from the play-by-play accounts provided by Retrosheet.

Now, this may differ in theory from other definitions of replacement—these players obviously aren't "freely-available" in all cases, in that some of them are either players returning from injury or top prospects. In practice, this matters very little.

What it does give us is a far more sensitive indicator of replacement level than we've had previously, allowing us to track changes in replacement level over time. Looking at replacement-level TAv+, by year:

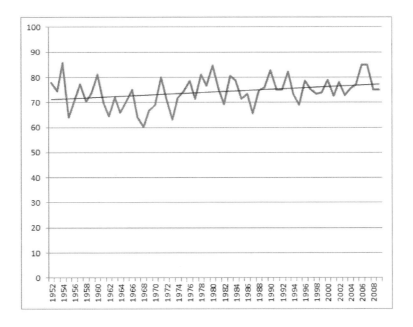

These are not smooth values, so you can see the magnitude of the noise in the measurement (the values will be smoothed out when applied to what you see on the site). But you can see the replacement level shifting gradually over time. What this means is that any particular replacement metric's baseline is set by the period of study; by taking a closer look, we can use a different replacement level for the '50s than the aughts, better suiting our metric to a wide range of time frames.

Combined with our positional adjustments, runs above average derived from linear weights, and park factors, we now have the elements necessary to compute a new VORP, one which meshes with TAv, our preferred rate stat for measuring offense. We can go further and combine that with our estimates of a player's contributions on defense and baserunning (EqBRR and its component stats will be undergoing slight changes, mostly so that they draw upon the same run expectancy tables used to generate our offensive stats) to come up with something like what Nate used to call SuperVORP. Running those figures through Pythagenpat converts runs to wins, and we have WARP.

Part 6
PROSPECTING
Introduction by Jason Parks

The Origin of Magic and the Search for Martin Perez

It was late Summer 2008, and I was involved in a heated message board standoff with a virtual entity that fashioned a cartoon character as an avatar. I was slowly sinking to the level of ad hominem and conceptual consternation, unable to keep my thoughts to myself and unable to find perspective in the growing animosity. At the time, I was 30 years old, and I earned a paycheck in the private sector. I had been writing about the Texas Rangers farm system since the beginning of the 2008 season for a boutique blog with the traffic of a ghost town. I was on the outermost periphery of the baseball landscape. There I was, sitting comfortably in my own adulthood, fighting an adolescent battle in the abstract construct of a minor-league message board, whose indigenous population was only casually aware of my existence. My chest reached full expansion and I was wearing the fire that I was breathing with every clever retort. My BP subscription was my library card.

The argument was easy to enter and difficult to leave, as I knew (intrinsically) that I was fighting from a sturdy foundation, but the cartoon character I was engaged with continued to disrupt my belief in the strength of that foundation. I was getting pulled in. The debate started innocuously enough, as most cyber battles do, with a few innocent, yet pompous pontifications that soon found company with didactic instructions followed by passive-aggressive swoons, followed shortly by "I know you are but what am I" attacks, followed by more passive-aggressive swoons and then more personal attacks. I'm a 30-year-old having an internet battle of knowledge with a guy who thought it would be an awesome idea to use a cartoon character as a visual representation of his identity. The love of baseball is a powerful drug.

The battle centered on a 17-year-old Venezuelan southpaw named Martin Perez. At the time, Perez wasn't a ubiquitous presence in the prospect world, even among the Rangers-specific message board brethren that made a point to know the specifics of the system. I was relatively new to the prospect game myself, but I was very aware of the who/what/how of Perez thanks to online sources like Kevin Goldstein, just as I was aware of how unfortunate it was to spend hours of my time arguing with a Disney character.

I started to think: Does the person who is attempting to destroy my arguments digest the same information I was chewing on? Does Disney put in the wrench work at the fields? Does he scroll thousands of words of prospect gold from the aforementioned (and fedora'd) Goldstein? Does he extract every ounce of statistical analysis from the Nate Silvers and Rany Jazayerlis of the world?

Does his appetite for prospects run so deep that he anxiously awaits front office interviews by David Laurila, just to pick apart the nuggets of information that might add to the overall equation? Does the passion for prospects consume him? Based on his casual knowledge, I'd wager that the answer is "no."

The more I studied, the more prospect knowledge I craved. It moved beyond wanting to be ahead of the message board curve and started to feel more like a vision quest. I wanted to see what my favorite writers were seeing. I wanted to participate in the process. I wanted to know more about Martin Perez than my contemporaries. The lights were starting to turn on, but I was still very much in the dark.

My Journey into Baseball: Sunstrokes and Scouting Tips
I arrived in Surprise, Arizona two weeks into the month of September. The year was still 2008, and I was still in my early 30s. As a virgin to the backfields, I was still somewhat unaware of how to go about extracting the prospect meat from the large carcass of players assembled on the field. I was attending the Fall Instructional League; a league created for instruction and evaluation opportunity that runs for a month after the minor-league season fades into the shadows. The rosters were constructed using the youngest talent in the organization, talent that would either be making its stateside debut the following spring, or had a brief taste during the previous season. It's an instructional league. You get the idea.

It was well over 105 degrees outside, and my head was on a swivel. My thirst for prospect knowledge was growing at the same rate as my fear of dehydration and/or sunstroke in that oppressive environment. Somebody lend me a clue and I'll lend you my ear. I'm braving the elements to learn as much as I can. The light is starting to turn on. I'm hungry to learn.

My first official morning on the backfields of the Rangers' facility in Surprise changed my life forever. I arrived early and found the fields abandoned, save for a few employees who were grooming the field itself, wearing matching shirts with a purple hue and big floppy hats that were closer to sombreros than to anything else. I had a notebook in hand, and a bottle of water whose chill decided to hang itself upon contact with the sun. Just when I thought about heading back to the car and then back to the air-conditioned room of the Days Inn, two players and two coaches started their journey from the clubhouse to field number one, located in the back fields section of the facility. It was 17 year-old Martin Perez, set to throw a controlled bullpen in front of an audience of three: two coaches, and one message board know-it-all who was about unearth his long-standing but still unrealized passion for the game.

I stood just feet away from the segregated bullpen area; an area wedged between fields one and two, guarded somewhat by a chain-link fence and a seating area designed for coaches and players and not random fans. I was the only one in the world at this point. Perez took to the mound and

THE LINEUP

The Disparate Paths of Andy Marte and Michael Brantley
by Bradford Doolittle..................78

The Draft
by Rany Jazayerli..........................86

The Draft, Part Two
by Rany Jazayerli..........................94

The Draft, Part Three
by Rany Jazayerli.........................101

The Draft, Part Four
by Rany Jazayerli.........................107

The Draft, Part Five
by Rany Jazayerli.........................112

The Draft, Part Six
by Rany Jazayerli.........................118

The Draft, Part Seven
by Rany Jazayerli.........................127

The Draft, Part Eight
by Rany Jazayerli.........................134

The Draft, Part Nine
by Rany Jazayerli.........................140

The Draft, Part Ten
by Rany Jazayerli.........................144

The Draft, Part Eleven
by Rany Jazayerli.........................151

The Draft, Part Twelve
by Rany Jazayerli.........................156

Valuing Draft Picks
by Nate Silver..............................164

The All-Disappointment Team
by Kevin Goldstein......................170

Going Over Slot
by Kevin Goldstein......................173

Post-Draft Thoughts 2.0
by Kevin Goldstein......................179

Slotto Bonanzas, Part One
by Nate Silver..............................182

And in This Corner...
by Kevin Goldstein......................186

The Alvarez Standoff, Resolved
by Kevin Goldstein......................190

Logan White, Part 1
by David Laurila..........................193

Logan White, Part 2
by David Laurila..........................199

Is the Scouts vs. Statheads Argument Overblown?
by Jonah Keri..............................204

Spring Training Psychonightmare
by Jason Parks.............................209

Finding a Little Future at the Futures Game
by Jason Parks.............................214

---

delivered approximately 30 pitches, receiving instruction along the way. With every pop of the mitt, I became more smitten with the idea that baseball can be more than just a mere hobby; a mere distraction from the banality associated with working a standard day of 9-to-5 operation. The room was aglow, although it could have been the first stages of sunstroke coming on. It was too early to tell.

The following morning firmly took both of its hands and shoved me in the back towards my future. I once again arrived early, hoping to catch another bullpen, or perhaps some fundamental instruction. The minutes grew to hours, and it was almost 10 AM before I saw the first signs of life at the facility. The players slowly made their way from the clubhouse to the 100-yard patch of grass behind field two, where calisthenics and sprints would be on the menu. As the roster for the visiting Cleveland Indians made their way from the parking lot to the field, I spotted a familiar face approaching the bleachers associated with field one. It was Jamey Newberg, a central cog in the Internet fan relationship with the Rangers' organization. Little did he realize that a debate on his very own message board sparked my journey to the land of the 1000 sunstrokes. We shook hands and made small talk. Jamey was the face of Rangers fandom. I was writing for a blog that popped champagne when 200 people put their eyes on the work. Different worlds.

A few minutes before the Rangers fired the opening salvo, Jamey introduced me to a man who has forever changed the way I view the game. The man had an interesting combination of a staggered gait and a culturally displaced Guayabera, both of which played well with the wisdom he carried with his presence. We shook hands and spent the entire game sharing the same angle to the field. His name was Don Welke, and he was a senior advisor to Texas Rangers general manager, Jon Daniels.

Over the next few days, "Coach," as Welke is affectionately referred, had my undivided attention, as every question I asked was met with a lifetime of knowledge condensed into snapshots for my consumption. Coach was teaching me how to scout. I can honestly say that I've never felt more incomplete or insignificant (in relation to the game) as I did over those three days. I had always been a fan of the game, and I always fancied myself someone who could articulate my thoughts on a player based on his actions on the field. But I was blind to the realities of the process, and the rush of information I was presently receiving was making it hard to breathe.

During those hours of education, I discovered that my happiness existed in a world within in a world; a world where you get to start with raw material and watch it reach definition through the developmental process; a world that allows the imagination to function in a controlled state, yet allows color to penetrate the binary, black and white, dud or stud observations that form the skeleton of most fan debate. I had found my calling, if you want to call it that.

The vacation away from the realities of my life in Brooklyn turned out to be the first steps in a new direction. My passion for the game had found its focus, as I now realized that I could no longer avoid the bait being dangled near my open mouth. I was hooked. I didn't want the trip to end.

Since those fateful days in Arizona, I've devoted most of my life to developing my evaluation skills, landing back on the soil of Surprise for more education with Coach whenever possible. I've made every concession to push forward with this dream; a dream that was born out of a pompous insecurity, enhanced by the wealth of information previously discussed, nurtured by a few mentors along the way, and finally released to test the boundaries of what was possible using my own senses.

It's now 2011, and I write about prospects for Baseball Prospectus. My net is now national, and my passion for the game is stronger than ever. Even as I type this, I'm reminded of the gravitational pull minor-league baseball had on me before I got close enough to the hook to realize it was too late to resist. There is something about prospects and the evaluation of those prospects that brings a certain type of person out of the shadows and into the subsequent discussions and debate. There is something pure about it. It's difficult to articulate, but minor-league baseball allows people to indulge in the abstract nature of the game itself. In the minors, dreams are always possible, even if they are unlikely to occur. The dream itself, whether you call it projection or possibility, is the backbone of the sport. The minor leagues are the origin of the magic.

That's great, Jason, cool story. But what if I can't devote my free time to flying to Arizona in order to get blood from Don Welke's scouting stone? Here's the thing: the magic of the minor leagues exists on many planes. You don't have to live in the shadows of the field in order to acquire knowledge on a player. We are fortunate enough to live in a world where publications such as Baseball Prospectus (cheap plug) offer substance over sparkle. If the passion for prospects is taking a trek through your veins, you can start building your own fire by reading the words of those that share and appreciate the passion. Who knows, maybe that fire will push you beyond general consumption and throw you out into the great baseball unknown.

APRIL 11, 2010 http://bbp.cx/a/10525

INSIDE THE PARK
The Disparate Paths of Andy Marte and Michael Brantley
Bradford Doolittle

Bradford Doolittle caught up with high-profile prospect bust Andy Marte during his last gasp in the big leagues, as Michael Brantley, who had never enjoyed the same prospect buzz, surpassed him in potential. As Doolittle observed, Marte's disappointing career trajectory reveals how inexact the art of scouting often proves to be.

Andy Marte is a forgotten man at 26. Just a few years ago, Marte was a darling of the prospect hounds, including those of Baseball Prospectus. He was compared favorably to players like Adrian Beltre (at his best) and Miguel Cabrera. He posted mouth-watering power numbers at precocious ages in his respective leagues. He even displayed improving strike-zone command, with gradually rising walk rates and gradually decreasing strikeout totals. There was nothing not to like.

In 2005, BP declared Marte the top prospect in the game, after ranking him third in 2004. Ours wasn't the lone voice praising him in the prospect-rating wilderness. *Baseball America* rated him as the Braves' top prospect in 2004 and as Boston's great minor-league hope in 2006. (The rankings were put together before Marte was flipped to Cleveland.) He was *BA*'s ninth-ranked overall prospect in 2005. Even after Marte was traded twice in a 45-day span in late 2005 and early 2006, he seemed like as sure a bet to become a big-league fixture as a young player possibly can be.

Now, Marte enters his 10th professional season as the Indians' primary backup at the infield corners. The job is as precarious as it sounds. When Russell Branyan, one of Cleveland's off-season acquisitions, returns from a back injury, Marte might be out of a job. He almost found himself without a team last spring, when Cleveland designated him for assignment in early March. The Indians needed the roster spot after acquiring slow-developing power reliever Juan Salas from the Rays. The one-time consensus top third-base prospect in the game went unclaimed, so the Indians brought him back to camp and then assigned him to Triple-A Columbus. It was the eighth season in which Marte spent significant time in the minor leagues.

What happened? It might be easier to point out what didn't happen. By definition, baseball prospects aren't finished products. Bodies change as athletes mature, often for the worse. For young hitters, every increase in level is a new challenge, with the biggest leap being the last: the transition to the major leagues. In Marte's case, what looked like a rapidly-improving approach at the plate crumbled when he was confronted by the nasty repertoires of big-league pitchers. Marte's approach at the dish now is almost the polar opposite of Cleveland's Opening Day left fielder, Michael Brantley. Ironically, if the advanced command of the strike zone Brantley displayed as a minor-leaguer pays off in real big-league production, it could have a direct effect on Marte's destiny. Reportedly, the Indians would have preferred Brantley get a little more minor-league time to gain some experience and hold off the service-time clock. His performance in spring training, along with Branyan's injury, forced the team's hand. Now, if he struggles at the season's outset, he may get that time in Columbus after all. But if he succeeds, then someone else will go.

That someone could be Marte.

The New Skipper
First-year Indians manager Manny Acta, like Marte, is from the Dominican Republic, but he didn't know the former phenom well until he took the job in Cleveland. Acta is an engaging man, a baseball lifer who loves to spin yarns about his many days in the minor leagues.

"This is a team trying to win a division, and they don't have time to be experimenting with guys," Acta said before a recent game against the White Sox. "You play the guys that can help you win." Acta spins a bat in his hands as he talks. He pauses, considering his words before speaking, comfortable in the silence. He's a stark contrast to Ozzie Guillen, the opposing skipper that night, but in his own way, he's just as funny. It's a cold, rainy night at U.S. Cellular Field, the second game of the season. It's April in Chicago, and Acta relates a tale from the previous afternoon, when he was walking along State Street downtown. He was enjoying a warm breeze from the north, when all of a sudden a frigid gale blew in off Lake Michigan from the east. With the snap of a finger, early spring turned back into late winter. Acta shakes his head and laughs at the recollection.

Batting practice has been canceled, but some of Acta's players have made their way out into right field to loosen up and play a little catch. Acta holds court in the Indians' dugout, watching the rain fall on the red tarp spread across the infield with a small group of writers. When Acta speaks about Marte, he tries to be complimentary, but the glowing rhetoric that once drove critiques of Marte is notably absent.

"It's about consistency, whether you get 10 at-bats or 100 or 200, you have to take advantage," Acta says. "(His struggles) have been consistently at the plate, basically. Everybody knows that he's a very good defender. You can put him with the glove at first or third base."

When Marte was attempting to break in with the Braves, his path was blocked by franchise stalwart Chipper Jones. At the time, Atlanta needed a shortstop, so Marte was traded to Boston for Edgar Renteria during the winter meetings in 2005. That trade was engineered by then-Red Sox honcho Bill Lajoie, who headed the small committee that ran Boston's front office during Theo Epstein's time away from the team. Boston already had an established third baseman—Mike Lowell.

"This is a throwback-type of third baseman," Lajoie told reporters at the time. "This is the power corner that you hope will hit 25 homers when he does play in the majors. We want to keep that player. He's ready to have a good year. He would be one of the five players you would want to start a ballclub with."

Seven weeks later, Lajoie flipped Marte to Cleveland, along with Guillermo Mota, Kelly Shoppach, Randy Newsom, and cash in exchange for Josh Bard, Coco Crisp, and David Riske. Not exactly the kind of haul you'd expect for one of the game's five most-valued assets, if indeed that's what Marte was. Last year, Lajoie, now with the Pirates, shed some light on his Marte scheme.

"We got him to trade him," Lajoie told reporters. "We knew Tampa (Bay) or Cleveland wanted him. So Crisp was the guy we wanted, and they wanted Marte. That deal had started well before we got Marte, because they indicated they wanted him, and that was the guy they were looking for. You get him, and you say, 'Well, he might play left field, and we'll get him some at-bats,' but truthfully we were going to trade him."

Waiting For A Chance

Back in the Cleveland clubhouse, Marte is relaxing in front of his locker, dressed for a batting practice session that is never going to happen. He lockers next to Jhonny Peralta, the latest third baseman to stand in Marte's way. There always seems to be somebody. Peralta was shifted to the hot corner full-time last season, while Marte was in Columbus, just beginning the process of winning back some of the club's confidence in him. Mark DeRosa opened the season as Cleveland's everyday third baseman. Prior to that, it was Casey Blake.

"There are a lot of things that once you get up here, you can't control," Acta says, still holding the bat, just in case one of the hovering writers gets out of line. "Even if you have a good year in Triple-A, if you have somebody in front of you, they're not going to move someone just to see if you can do it here. A lot of it is being in the right place in the right time. He's had Blake here, now Jhonny. He's going to have to take advantage of the opportunities he gets and open some eyes."

By now, Marte has accumulated about the number of big-league plate appearances that Jimmy Rollins gets in a full season. It's taken Marte over five years to get there. His pseudo-season line reads: .215/.272/.351. He's hit 15 home runs in 737 plate appearances and struck out nearly three times as often as he's walked. This is not the path that PECOTA foresaw. In 2006, when Marte was still in the good graces of the prospect hounds, PECOTA's mean projection for Marte that campaign was .254/.335/.445, with 20 home runs. His most-similar comps included Rico Petrocelli,

Manny Ramirez, and Ron Santo. Yeah, he was *that* kind of prospect. Now, Marte is still battling to learn the lessons he would have learned years ago, if it were ever going to happen.

"(I need) to be more consistent," Marte says, echoing the sentiments of his manager. "I know I can hit up here. I need to be more selective at the plate and get better pitches. Everything comes from there. If I do that, I'll have good success."

He makes it sound so simple, but of course it's not.

The New Left Fielder
The lessons that have been so hard for Marte to learn seem to have been hard-wired into Michael Brantley at birth.

Brantley, who turns 23 next month, is good-looking and affable. Despite his age, he seems right at home in the Indians clubhouse, the most animated figure at a table full of ballplayers engaged in a friendly card game while the rain falls outside. He grew up around ballplayers. His father, Mickey, played four seasons for the Mariners in the 1980s. The younger Brantley's favorite player growing up was Ken Griffey Jr., whose arrival in 1989 may have helped to hasten his father's departure from the majors. Brantley was not yet two years old when Griffey made his big-league debut for the Mariners on April 3, 1989. Now, with Griffey back in Seattle and near the end of a Hall of Fame career, Brantley is bubbling with the excitement of youth, the kind which used to define his hero.

"It's what you dream of as a kid," a smiling Brantley said in the hours before his first Opening Day start. "Opening Day, left field, in front of however many thousands of people. That's what you dream of, to get to experience it first hand."

Unlike Marte, Brantley isn't an uberstar in the prospect guides. He's merely solid, clocking in at fifth among Cleveland prospects at *Baseball America*. BP's Kevin Goldstein had Brantley 10th in Cleveland's system in his "Top 11" series from last season, writing:

> The Good: Brantley profiles as a classic leadoff hitter. He works the count well, rarely strikes out, and combines plus-plus speed with outstanding instincts on the bases, as he stole 46 bases at Triple-A Columbus in 51 attempts. He's a very good outfielder at all three positions.
>
> The Bad: Brantley will need to hit for a high batting average to play every day in the big leagues, as he has below-average power, although his six home runs this year matched his career total entering the year. His arm is weak.

On Opening Day, it was Marte sitting in front of his locker, wondering if he was going to get into the game, while Brantley was bouncing around preparing to face Chicago's Mark Buehrle.

"I like to use my speed and create havoc on the basepaths," Brantley said, describing his strengths as player. "At the same time, I feel like I'm a pretty good all-around ballplayer."

Brantley was part of Cleveland's haul when it dealt CC Sabathia to the Brewers in July, 2008. The initial deal was Sabathia for a player to be named later, Rob Bryson, Zach Jackson, and Matt LaPorta. Brantley turned out to be the fourth player. When this season began, Brantley was perched in left field, while LaPorta manned the first-base bag for the Indians. Brantley advanced quickly, first through Milwaukee's system, then through Cleveland's, after being taken in the seventh round of the 2005 draft. Like Marte, he was always young for his level, hitting the Triple-A International League last season at 22.

His advanced approach at the plate manifested itself right away in the pros and has never wavered. In five minor-league seasons, he walked more than he struck out in each campaign. While Brantley's walk rates have always been merely solid, his ability to get the bat on the ball consistently has kept his batting averages high and propped up his on-base percentages. He did suffer a drop in average at Columbus, but his excellent walk-to-strikeout ratio remained intact. That may indicate that his dip in average was merely due to the mischievousness of balls in play. Or it may not—with prospects, you can never quite be sure about anything. In fact, after drawing about 1.4 walks for every strikeout in the minors, Brantley now has nine walks against 23 strikeouts in the early stages of his big-league career. The transition is something Marte can appreciate.

"Pitching (in the majors) and in the minor leagues is not the same," Marte said. "The pitchers here don't make mistakes like they do in the minor leagues. It's just different."

However, Marte is working from a very different innate set of traits. In his first two professional seasons, at the ages of 17 and 18, he struck out 2.6 times for every walk. At 18, Brantley had 28 walks and 17 strikeouts in 241 plate appearances. These are two very different starting points for two very different kind of ballplayers.

"When I was growing up as a kid, I was the same way," Brantley said. "I didn't try to swing at too many balls (out of the zone). I was (always) a very patient hitter. Then in my professional career, I just tried to stay focused on swinging at good pitches."

That approach proved to be consistent during his time with the Brewers, and the Indians weren't about to change a style of play that they, as an organization, hold so dear.

"When I was traded over here, they just told me to be the same player," Brantley said. "They liked what I was doing. I didn't try to do too much or change too much. I just tried to stay on an even keel."

As for Marte, he was reared in an Atlanta organization whose philosophy has always been to encourage and develop the natural traits of its young hitters. Royals general manager Dayton Moore, who was with the Braves during the time of Marte's rearing and refers to Marte as "a son," has always preached about the importance of "not taking away that natural aggressiveness" from young hitters. It's easy to point at Marte and other Atlanta products like Jeff Francoeur and call that philosophy cock-eyed, but you can't do so without acknowledging that not so long ago, the Braves won 14 division titles in 15 years.

"(The Braves) let you play. You're more free," Marte said, referring to organizational approaches. "They let you be you. Here (in the Cleveland organization), it's a little different. It's 'do it this way and do it that way.'"

There Is No Magic Bean
You can't really say that Marte has more natural ability than Brantley. In fact, he probably has less. Brantley is an exceptional athlete and, despite being deft with the glove, Marte looks—for lack of a better term—a little lumpy. However, Marte's power potential still dwarfs that of Brantley, who is trying to develop his power stroke at the game's highest level.

"I believe so," Brantley said when asked if he expected to generate more power in the future. "I think you'll see a little more in 2010. I make no guarantees, but I feel a lot stronger and, mentally, I'm tougher than I've ever been in my life."

PECOTA has cooled considerably on Marte, as you would expect given his big-league totals. His mean projection is for a line of .261/.316/.437, less than that which was predicted for him at age 22. His top comps are now Tracy Woodson, Willis Otanez, and German Rivera, but Aramis Ramirez still crops up. Brantley, meanwhile, is at .275/.348/.368, with notable similarity to Coco Crisp, the player for whom Marte was once traded.

Because Marte's fatal flaw has been strike-zone command, which happens to be Brantley's strength, it's easy to see the ratio of walks-to-strikeouts as some sort of prospect mining panacea. But of course, it's not. There is no magic bean. If there were, somebody would have discovered it and planted it long ago.

There were 53 different position players who appeared in BP's Top 50 Prospects list in the 2004 and 2005 annuals, when Marte's stock was at its apex. Two of those players—Eric Duncan and Mitch Einertson—have never played in the big leagues. On that list of one-time prospects, 12 have posted a higher major-league OPS than they did in the minors.

The players that have most outperformed their minor-league OPS are some of baseball's brightest young stars—Hanley Ramirez, Grady Sizemore, Joe Mauer, Brian McCann, and David Wright. Mauer, of course, has exceptional strike-zone command, while Sizemore and Wright are very good in that area. However, neither Ramirez or McCann had very good walk-to-strikeouts ratios in the minors. Both have improved, particularly McCann, at the big-league level, but there was little in their minor-league records to suggest this would happen.

For what it's worth, one believer in the predictive power of strike-zone command is Manny Acta. The Indians skipper says of young hitters, "(Command of the strike zone) helps them become better. The strike zone up here is better, the pitchers are more consistently around the plate. Guys that are usually good in the minor leagues at knowing the strike zone become better at the big-league level. That doesn't mean it's going to translate into hitting the ball, but it helps. (Plate discipline) helps everybody, if you have it. (Marte) had a good year in Triple-A last year, so he must have been doing something right. But baseball up here, it's completely different."

On the list of 2004 and 2005 prospects, there is one name that stands out. There is one player who has seen the biggest decline in OPS from the minors to the majors. As it happens, that player, despite scouting reports to the contrary, did not display a great statistical command of the strike zone over the course of eight minor-league seasons. That player's name is Andy Marte.

Again, there is no magic bean. A favorable ratio of a player's walks to strikeouts doesn't ensure anything, nor do the rates at which those outcomes occur. Nevertheless, all things being equal, players who demonstrate strike-zone command, and the ability to maintain that command as they advance up the baseball ladder, are safer bets than players who see those indicators erode in the face of superior pitching. These indicators might not give us the bottom line on whether a player will succeed or fail, but they can help guide teams in projecting how well a player's overall performance is going to translate to the higher levels.

We don't know what will happen with Marte and Brantley. Marte has been the top name on the hot list, while Brantley has jetted to a regular big-league job while skirting the edge of it. Now it's Brantley's time to shine. You can contrast Acta's careful words about Marte—about needing to "take advantage of the opportunities he's given"—with shining platitudes about Brantley's potential.

"He's very good all-around, man, despite his age," Acta said. "He's honed his skills very well. He can take pitches, he can run, he plays good defense. It didn't hurt him growing up around his dad. He's mature beyond his years. He's going to be a very good player very soon."

Last Chance, First Chance
On Opening Day, the Mark-Buehrle-flip-between-the-legs game, the hits are few and far between for the Tribe. Brantley manages to poke a single through the hole at shortstop off Sox reliever J.J. Putz once Buehrle has left the game. Marte doesn't play. The Indians are shut out.

In the second game, the cold, rainy contest, Brantley steps to the plate in the fourth inning, with Cleveland down 3-0. The bases are loaded. He works the count against Sox starter Jake Peavy, then bloops a single off the end of the bat into shallow center field. Brantley's single plates Cleveland's first run of the season. The Indians go on to erase the deficit in the inning, then go ahead on a LaPorta double in the seventh. With the late-inning lead, Marte is summoned to employ his superior glove at first base.

In the bottom of the ninth inning, with the tying run on base and two outs, Marte moves into the hole and makes a nice stab of a hard A.J. Pierzynski grounder. He flips to Cleveland closer Chris Perez for the game's final out. Afterward, the Indians' clubhouse is decidedly upbeat, if not jubilant. Rap is blaring from one end of the room to the other, while the players pile their post-game plates high with pasta, ribs, and corn on the cob.

Marte dresses quickly, then walks around the clubhouse, chatting and pounding fists with teammates, happy to have contributed to the cause. When you catch up to him and ask for a chat, he actually seems glad to see you. You ask how cold it was out there. He offers a mock shiver and smiles.

"Yeah, it was hard to get loose," Marte says. "About the sixth inning, we started drinking coffee, trying to get warm. You do everything you have to do so when they need you, you're ready."

That's Marte's job these days. Being ready. It's not how we thought his career would go and probably not what he anticipated, either. But it's the big leagues, and for now at least, it's a job. Tomorrow, the story may be different. Russell Branyan is healing, and Cleveland gave him $2 million to return to the organization during the offseason. When he's ready, someone's got to go. Marte is out of options. This may be his last chance.

On the other hand, Brantley looks like a professional, not just because of the way he carries himself off the field, but more so because of the approach he takes with him each and every time he steps up to home plate. For Brantley, it's only his first chance, and to watch him goof and play with his veteran teammates, you get the feeling it's the only chance he's ever going to need.

If not, it's no big deal. There will be others.

DOCTORING THE NUMBERS
The Draft
Rany Jazayerli

After painstakingly compiling decades of draft data, Rany Jazayerli examined the returns teams have seen from the first 100 picks and formulated his first two "draft rules."

For most teams, the most important day of the year isn't Opening Day, or a day in October that ends in a dogpile, or the November day that marks the start of free-agent season. No, for most teams, the red-letter day falls on the first Tuesday of June, a day that involves sitting around a telephone, on a conference call with 29 other teams and the Commissioner's office, a day on which, if you're really, really lucky, you get to say something like this: "the Chicago Cubs select Redraft Number two-six-four-one, Mark William Prior, University of Southern California."

Sexy, it's not. Neither is it all that telegenic, although it certainly could be if MLB ditched the conference call for an amphitheater with good lighting and tried to make a production out of it. There's no denying its importance, though. There is no source of talent that comes close to matching what's available in what is officially called the Rule 4 Draft. Moreover, there is almost no way to build a successful ballclub without some measure of success in the draft. (The Yankees are trying to prove that last sentence incorrect. They are not succeeding.)

It's one thing for the media to treat the baseball draft with far less reverence than its football counterpart. Historically, it has been taken far less seriously by the participants. Some football teams were using sophisticated, computer-aided analysis of potential draft picks as far back as the early 1970s. For the first 20 years of the baseball draft, so little effort was made by teams to hone their draft strategies that it was revolutionary when Bill James discovered, as he wrote in the *1985 Baseball Abstract*, that "not only is there no basis for the prejudice against the drafting of college players, but in fact the reverse is true." He went on to state that "the rate of return on players drafted out of college is essentially twice that of high-school players."

Keep in mind, in the early years of the draft, it was an inviolable concept that the best way to create a superstar was to find an athletic 18-year-old with the good face and mold him into one. Take 1971, for instance, in which every first-round pick was drafted out of high school. All those picks yielded just two stars (Jim Rice and Frank Tanana) and two more quality players (Rick

Rhoden and Craig Reynolds). Take 1977, when 21 of the 26 first-round picks were high schoolers. The five college players included Paul Molitor, Bob Welch and Terry Kennedy. Of the high-school players, aside from Harold Baines and Bill Gullickson—the first two picks in the draft—the only picks that had any kind of substantial major-league careers were Rich Dotson, Wally Backman, and Dave Henderson.

Teams finally started to catch on in the early 1980s. In 1981, more college players than high schoolers were taken in the first round, the first time that had occurred. For their efforts, teams selecting from the college ranks were rewarded with Mike Moore, Joe Carter, and Ron Darling; the best high-school players picked that year were Dick Schofield and Daryl Boston.

Nevertheless, the inefficiencies in the baseball draft continued to vastly exceed the inefficiencies in every other method of talent acquisition, in large part because no team seemed willing or able to exploit those inefficiencies at all. They were all drafting with one eye closed. (The A's may be the exception to the rule; they started focusing on college talent soon after Charlie Finley sold the team in 1980.) Even as it became acceptable to select college players in the early rounds of the draft, the notion that teams ought to pay attention to the production of those players while in college—the idea that college statistics matter—is a remarkably recent innovation, as chronicled in *Moneyball*.

Still, draft patterns have changed over the years, making it unlikely that James' original study, as groundbreaking as it was in its time, still paints an accurate portrait of the draft two decades later. In particular, the age-old question of high-school vs. college players is being continually revisited, and more than one expert has arrived at the conclusion that there is no longer any substantial advantage in selecting college players over high-school players early in the draft. Two years ago, Jim Callis of *Baseball America* wrote the following regarding a study of the 10 ten rounds of the draft from 1991 to 1997:

> "We find that 90 college players (8.8 percent) and 77 high-school players (8.4 percent) became at least major-league regulars for a few seasons. Though colleges produced slightly more regulars, high schools won the race for above-average players. They came out ahead in terms of good regulars (3.2 percent vs. 1.5 percent) and stars (1.1 percent vs. 0.9 percent). Once again putting that in terms of 250 draft picks, collegians generally would yield four above-average regulars and two stars. The prep ranks would generate eight above-average regulars and three stars."

BA's study produced interesting results, but I wanted to take a look at the data myself. I couldn't do it all, so I recruited an army of one, also known as BP intern John Erhardt. This study would not have been possible without the efforts of John, who entered almost all of the data involved into a spreadsheet, mostly by hand.

This study includes the first 100 picks—roughly equivalent to the first three rounds—in every draft from 1984 to 1999. (Going forward, as shorthand I will refer to picks one through 30 as "first-round picks"; picks 31 through 70 as "second-round picks"—this would include the supplemental first round; and picks 71 through 100 as "third-round picks.")

I selected these endpoints for a couple of reasons. The 1984 draft was the first one in which college players really took center stage; the accomplishments of the U.S. Olympic Team gave college talent a national audience for the first time. Guys like Cory Snyder, Mark McGwire, Shane Mack, and Oddibe McDowell were drafted that year, though they were just an appetizer for the following year, when the first six picks of the draft featured B.J. Surhoff, Will Clark, Bobby Witt, Barry Larkin, and Barry Bonds. (The only high-school player selected in the top six, catcher Kurt Brown, never reached the majors.)

Also, the draft process was streamlined in the mid-1980s with the abolishment of the "supplemental" draft in January, leaving just one draft to analyze.

I end the study in 1999 because, for one, not enough time has elapsed to adequately judge more recent drafts. Also, the 2000 and 2001 drafts appear to be unusual; the 2000 draft was historically barren, the 2001 draft was historically fruitful. Consider this: the first five picks in 2000 were Adrian Gonzalez, Adam Johnson, Luis Montanez, Mike Stodolka and Justin Wayne. The first five picks in 2001 were Joe Mauer, Mark Prior, Dewon Brazelton, Gavin Floyd, and Mark Teixeira. Slight difference there.

So we have 16 seasons of data, which will become handy when I break up the data into eight-year chunks to see whether draft patterns have changed over time.

I eliminated from the study all the players who did not sign with the team that drafted them. This includes players who went back into a future draft, as well as "draft loophole" players like Travis Lee and John Patterson. There are enough variables that determine the value of a draft pick without having to account for whether he was signed or not. I also didn't want players selected twice, like J.D. Drew, mucking up the data.

(It's a lot harder than you might think to determine, 20 years after the fact, which players signed and which didn't. We think we located every player, but I wouldn't be surprised if we missed a few. In a study of this size, I don't think an omission or two alters the data significantly.) Out of 1,600 draft picks, that left us with 1,526 players.

Once we had every player in our database, the next thing we—OK, John—did was to enter WARP data for every year of that player's career. WARP stands for Wins Above Replacement Player, and is an overall measure of a player's worth in the only currency that really matters, wins. The data was categorized by how many years it had been since the player was drafted. In other words, for a player drafted in 1984, "Y0" refers to the player's WARP number in 1984, "Y5" refers to his value in 1989, etc. If a player didn't play in the majors in that year, the cell was left blank. (Obviously, only about a dozen players of the 1,526 played in the majors in Y0.)

The one tweak we made to the data was that a player who managed a negative WARP value in any given year had his value zeroed out instead. Given that we're evaluating a set of players who may or may not have even reached the major leagues, I felt it was inappropriate to penalize a player for being a bad major leaguer—even a woefully bad major leaguer—relative to another player who may have peaked in A ball. (This didn't affect many players, because it's awfully difficult to muster a negative WARP. David Howard, who spent most of the 1990s driving me to the edge of homicidal rage, never had a negative WARP as a member of the Royals.)

Finally, we only looked at the first 15 years of a player's career, ending the columns at "Y15." For one thing, just six draft classes (1984 through 1989) even had completed data for Y15, and extending the data any further would have rendered sample sizes of dubious significance. Also, anyone who drafts a player based on what he does 16 years later needs to take a refresher course in baseball labor relations over the past 35 years, with a special emphasis on the abolishment of the Reserve Clause and the establishment of free agency.

Enough prologue: let's look at the data. Before we break the data down into subsets, let's start by looking at the overall numbers. After all, before you can decide whether a certain set of players make for a good pick, you have to know what those picks are worth.

First, let's look at the percentage of players selected who reached the majors, even for a Moonlight Graham appearance, based on their draft position. The data has been aggregated in groups of five to minimize random variation from one draft slot to the next.

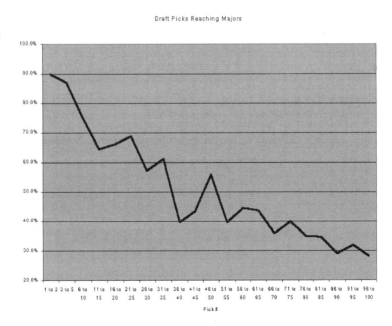

As you would expect, the probability of reaching the majors drops in a fairly linear fashion from the first pick to the 100th. There is a big dropoff after pick 35, but there's also a spike upward between picks 45 and 50, which suggests random variation. Overall, the probability of reaching the majors starts at 90 percent, drops by about 0.9 percent per draft spot for the first 50 spots, then drops by about 0.3 percent per spot from picks 50 through 100.

I was curious as to whether teams became any more savvy in making draft picks as the years went on, so I decided to break the data up into 1984-91 and 1992-99. Here's the chart comparing each set of eight years.

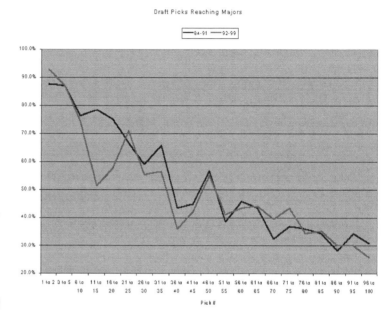

The lines are similar throughout, although the more recent drafts, surprisingly, have seen fewer major leaguers identified in the middle of the first round. They have done a slightly better job between picks 65 and 75—the early third round, basically—but not enough to compensate. Overall, 386 of 760 players taken in the first 100 picks from 1984 to 1991 reached the majors, or 50.8 percent. The numbers from 1992 to 1999 are 366 of 768, or 47.7 percent. The difference is almost entirely the result of the fact that players from the more recent drafts have had less time to reach the majors; with the benefit of a few more years, the more recent drafts should equal, if not exceed, the success rate of the earlier set.

(There is also the question of how much major-league talent is available in the draft at all, as more and more major-league players are signed as international free agents. I don't have the data to answer that question, but intuitively it would seem that as international talent occupies more roster space, the relative amount of talent available in the draft has gone down. In other words, relative to the total amount of value available in the draft, it is possible that teams are doing a better job of identifying that talent and selecting it in the first three rounds.)

Of course, the goal of the draft isn't simply to find a player who will get a pinch-hit appearance in the majors a decade later; any draft measure which labels Alan Zinter a "success" is obviously incomplete. So let's look at a different and much more telling set of data, which is the average

WARP accumulated by a draft pick in the first 15 years after he was drafted (in other words, his Y0 through Y15 cells added together).

For this exercise, if a player didn't play in the majors that year, he was treated as if he had zero WARP for that season—which, of course, is true. But if a player had not yet reached that year in his career, then he was not counted in that year of the study. For instance, since 1999 draft picks have only reached Y5 in their career, any data analysis involving Y6 onward eliminated these players from the study. In this way, we are able to get an accurate measurement of value in each year of a player's career, without penalizing recent draft picks because they haven't reached that point in their career yet.

So in the following chart, keep in mind that "Total WARP" means that the average WARP for all players in Y15 who played in that season were added to the average WARP for all players in Y14 who played in that season, etc. Years Y0 through Y5 include every player in the study, as it has been more than five years since the last players in the study were drafted.

Here's the 15-year WARP data for every draft position from 1 through 100.

In this case, because I didn't aggregate the data into groups of five, the data looks significantly more erratic as the smaller sample sizes introduce more randomness into the study.

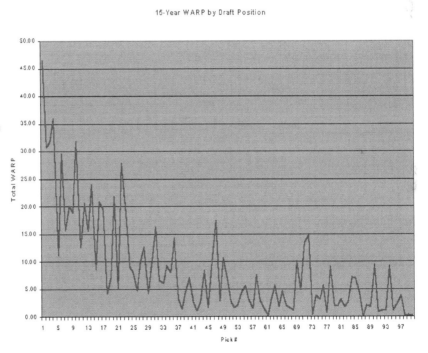

So in this next chart, I've clumped the data into groups of five again, with the exception that the #1 overall selection is divorced from picks 2 through 5.

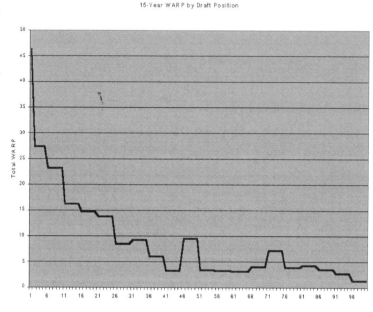

The first thing that stands out is that the #1 overall selection is significantly more valuable than the picks that come after it, even the picks that come immediately after it.

This isn't just the result of smoothing out the data; here's another chart that looks only at the first 25 picks.

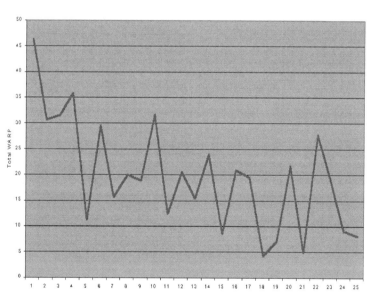

The typical #1 overall pick is worth more than 46 WARP in the first 15 years of his career; no other draft slot comes within even 10 wins of that total. Just as importantly, the benefits of the #1 overall pick do not extend to the #2 pick; in fact, historically, the #2 pick has been worth slightly less than the #3 and #4 picks, and from that point random variation kicks in and strongly influences the downward progression for the rest of the first round. This leads me to coin the first of many draft rules from this study:

Draft Rule #1: The greatest difference in value between consecutive draft picks is the difference between the first and second picks in a draft.

(Naturally, this is the year that Major League Baseball decided to stop arbitrarily assigning the first pick in the draft to a specific league—it would have been the AL's turn this year—and simply have all teams draft in inverse order of their winning percentage from the year before. So my Royals are picking #2 instead of #1.)

Getting back to the previous chart, you will notice that the value of a draft pick drops off rather steeply and consistently for the first 40 picks—and then flatlines. There are a pair of weird plateaus in the data, at picks 46-50 and again at 71-75, but otherwise the value of a draft pick seems to hold steady until pick 90, at which point it starts to tail off again. In fact, the average WARP for picks 86-90 (3.55) is actually greater than the average WARP for picks 41-45 (3.26).

This is in contrast to the chart which looked only at whether draft picks reached the majors. While draft picks are less likely to reach the majors when picked in the third round than in the second, in terms of real value the classes are almost identical. Overall, picks 41-65 had an average WARP of 4.51; picks 66-90 had an average WARP of 4.56. Which leads to the next rule:

> **Draft Rule #2: There is surprisingly little difference in value between second-round and third-round draft picks.**

As an interesting sidenote, in James' original study, he wrote that "players drafted #1 have produced about 8.5 times the major-league approximate value of those drafted #50." In our study, the value of a player drafted #1 (46.37 WARP) was 7.2 times the average value of players drafted from #46 through #55 (6.44 WARP). The eras may have changed, and the metrics certainly have (the difference between Approximate Value and WARP is sort of like the difference between logarithm tables and Nate Silver's supercomputer), but the relative numbers have remained reassuringly stable.

Next week, we'll answer the age-old question: on the whole, do college players or high-school players make better picks?

DOCTORING THE NUMBERS
The Draft, Part Two
Rany Jazayerli

In the second part of his draft study, Rany Jazayerli tackled the age-old question of whether it's better to draft high school or college players.

Before we continue our study, Jim Callis of *Baseball America* chimes in with this interesting fact about the draft's early days:

> While teams did prefer to get their hands on guys out of high school and mold them themselves in the early days of the draft, the draft rules also led to the high number of high-school picks in the first rounds. If a player had been taken out of high school, then he wasn't eligible for the June regular draft (which most closely parallels the single draft of today). He would go into the secondary phase of the January or June draft. In 1971, which you cite, Pete Broberg, Burt Hooton and Rob Ellis (all college guys who shot to the majors) were the top three prospects and went 1-2-3 in the delayed phase of the June secondary draft. Steve Rogers and Steve Busby also were part of that draft. Steve Garvey and Dave Kingman are two examples of previous years.
>
> After 1971, baseball changed the rules, and all college guys not taken within the past 13 months were eligible for the regular phase. Teams did prefer the young guys, and it wasn't until 1981 that colleges had a majority in the first round.

The existence of multiple drafts through 1986 greatly complicates the analysis of draft reviews from that period, and is all the more reason why draft research from that era, such as the work done by Bill James, is essentially obsolete. (That's not to say James' conclusions are obsolete—we'll find out soon enough.)

In this series' first article, we established the general value of each draft pick in their first 15 years, ranging from more than 45 WARP for the #1 overall pick to about four WARP for a second- or third-round pick.

That's the average value of all picks. What happens if we separate out the picks based on whether the player was drafted out of college or high school?

Of the 1526 players in our study, 749 were drafted out of high school and 715 were drafted from college. (The remaining 62 were junior college players—we'll address them later.)

The first place to start would be to compare the percentage of players from high school and from college who eventually reached the majors. Once again, players were broken down into five-pick segments—picks 11-15, 16-20, 21-25, etc. were grouped together—except that #1 and #2 overall picks were separated from picks 3-5. Here's a chart comparing the major-league matriculation rate of both segments of players.

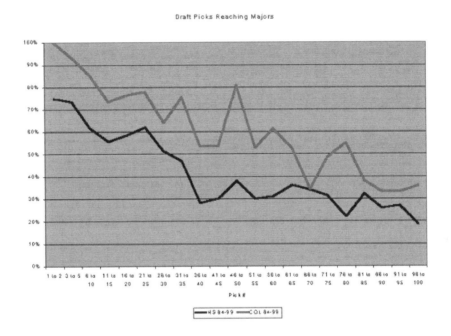

As you can see, the edge in favor of college players reaching the major leagues is substantial and sustained. At one point the lines touch, but they never cross; in every subset of draft picks, a higher percentage of college players reached the majors than high-school players. I calculated a weighted average for all players in the study from picks 1 through 100, and found that 41 percent of high-school players reached the majors, compared to 59 percent of college picks.

What if we break the study down into two eight-year chunks and look at the data from 1984-91 separately from the data from 1992-99? Here's the same chart, but broken down into four different groups.

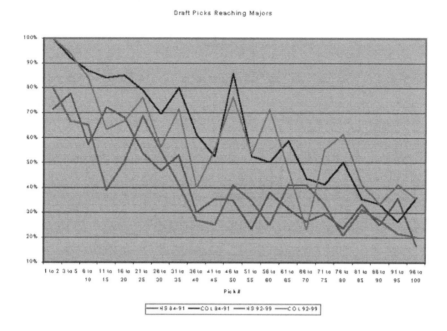

The chart looks pretty messy, but the important thing to take from this is that the blue lines—representing college players—are a lot higher than the red lines, which represent high-school picks. As you would expect, the lines representing player groups from the earlier era (1984-91) are generally higher than their counterparts from the more recent era, as players from 1992-99 have had less time to reach the majors and some eventual major leaguers have yet to debut.

Even so, the baby-blue line—the more recent cohort of college players—is consistently higher than the burgundy line representing the older cohort of high schoolers. At only two points (11-15 and 66-70) are high-school players from 1984-91 more successful at reaching the majors than college players from 1992-99. This, even though the high schoolers have all had a full opportunity to reach the majors (the youngest of them is about 32 years old.)

In chart form, the weighted averages of these groups are:

High School, 1984-1991	41 percent
High School, 1992-1999	39 percent
College, 1984-1991	60 percent
College, 1992-1999	57 percent

The gap between college picks and high-school picks reaching the majors, which was 19 percent in the earlier era, has shrunk all the way to—18 percent.

Which leads to Draft Rule #3:

> **Draft Rule #3: College players are roughly 50 percent more likely to reach the major leagues than high-school players of equal draft caliber. This advantage has not changed over time.**

This is not a revelation, mind you. Even those studies, like the one done by Jim Callis, which argue that high-school picks are of essentially equal value to college picks, have shown that college players are more likely to reach the majors. The argument has been that the extra advantage in college players is primarily in getting more marginal players up to the majors for a brief cup of coffee. In terms of quality players and stars—in other words, in terms of real value extracted from the draft—the groups are not substantially different.

So let's compare these two groups again, only this time we'll look at 15-year WARP, the same metric we used to determine the value of draft picks in the first place. For this study, let me introduce a row of numbers you're going to see more of in future articles:

Y0	Y1	Y2	Y3	Y4	Y5	Y6	Y7	Y8	Y9	Y10	Y11	Y12	Y13	Y14	Y15	WARP
	0.00	0.73	3.10	2.57	3.27	4.72	5.00	5.14	5.78	5.76	5.24	4.05	3.53	2.63	0.55	52.07

This set of data represents the year-by-year WARP data for all #1 picks out of high school. Some explanations are in order:

- The blank space under "Y0" means that no player in this group played in the major leagues in year 0, i.e. the year he was drafted. We haven't seen a high-school player reach the major leagues in his draft year since 1978, when gimmicks like Mike Morgan, Tim Conroy and Brian Milner were essentially escorted directly from their high-school graduation to a major-league stadium.
- The numbers are the average WARP value accumulated by all players who have had the opportunity to play in that year. There are six high-school players drafted #1 overall in the study: Shawn Abner, Ken Griffey Jr., Chipper Jones, Brien Taylor, Alex Rodriguez, and Josh Hamilton. Those six players combined for 19.6 WARP in their Y5 years, which averages out to 3.27 WARP. Just three of those players—Abner, Griffey and Jones—have reached their Y14 season, so the total WARP accumulated by those players (7.9) is divided by three, not six. True, we can say with some certainty that Taylor is not going to amass any WARP this year, which is his Y14 season, but then again there's a good chance that Rodriguez will add to that total in 2007.

The final WARP figure is the sum of all the totals from Y0 through Y15, which is our estimate for the overall worth of a draft slot. Certainly, most players will reach free agency before Y15, but I wanted to design the study in such a way that high-school players would not be unfairly penalized by virtue of the fact that they require longer to develop. If I had looked at only a draft pick's first 10 years, say, most high-school players are just 28 at that point, and unless they established themselves in the majors very quickly, they were probably still short of free agency. In an ideal world, we would figure out the point at which every single player reached free agency, or was released, or picked in a Rule 5 draft—this isn't an ideal world, and there are only so many hours in the day. This data should suffice for most of our conclusions.

Let me relist the data above with a second line, the 15-year WARP data for all college players taken #1 overall:

	Y0	Y1	Y2	Y3	Y4	Y5	Y6	Y7	Y8	Y9	Y10	Y11	Y12	Y13	Y14	Y15	WARP
HS		0.00	0.73	3.10	2.57	3.27	4.72	5.00	5.14	5.78	5.76	5.24	4.05	3.53	2.63	0.55	52.07
Col	0.00	0.94	1.86	3.10	3.84	2.93	2.65	4.23	3.71	3.86	3.75	2.88	3.48	1.30	2.38	0.78	41.69

Here, we see that while the college players taken #1 overall reach the majors faster and are more valuable than their high-school counterparts in the first four years after the draft, they tail off quicker (understandable, as they're about three years older on average), and overall they fall far short of the value of high-school players. Their average 15-year WARP is a full 10 wins less than the average WARP of high-school picks.

(For the record, the college players are: B.J. Surhoff, Jeff King, Andy Benes, Ben McDonald, Phil Nevin, Paul Wilson, Darin Erstad, Kris Benson, Matt Anderson and Pat Burrell.)

So with the #1 overall pick, at least, high-school picks seem to be worth more valuable than college players. Of course, this is an extremely small sample size, which makes the conclusion suspect. The evidence that high-school players are more valuable really comes down to three data points—Griffey, Rodriguez, and Jones—as two of the other three didn't even reach the majors, and Shawn Abner had 3.3 WARP for his career.

Still, exactly one-half of the #1 overall picks out of high school went on to become superstars. That's a pretty good ratio. If we look back further in time, four high-school players were picked #1 overall from 1974 to 1983: Harold Baines, Al Chambers, Darryl Strawberry, and Shawon Dunston. So out of 10 players, three may end up in the Hall of Fame, one fell just short, one had a Hall of Fame start to his career, and one spent a remarkable 18 years in the major leagues without ever taking a called strike.

So I'm comfortable making this rule:

> **Draft Rule #4: In a year where there is a clear superstar talent available in the high-school ranks, it is a perfectly acceptable draft strategy to select that player with the #1 overall pick.**

I qualify this rule because there are some years where, going into the draft, no high-school player stands out as a can't-miss superstar. That's happened twice in the last five years; it was pretty clear on draft day that Adrian Gonzalez and Matt Bush were #1 picks by default, and not out of any clear conviction that they were future Hall of Famers. The two players in the last five years who did fit that profile, Joe Mauer and Delmon Young, are coming along rather nicely.

Why am I separating the #1 overall pick from the rest of the draft? That will become clear when we look at the rest of the data. The following chart once again uses five-player groupings, with the #1 overall pick removed from the study, and compares the 15-year WARP value between high-school and college picks.

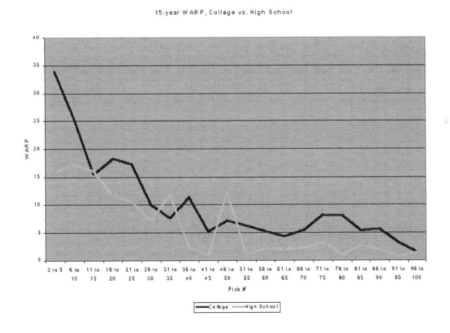

The edge for college players on this chart may not be quite as dramatic as it was in this article's first chart, but it's equally as significant. With the exception of two small spikes at 31-35 and 46-40, there is no cohort of high-school players that outplays its college counterpart. The gap is particularly striking in the first half of the first round; high-school players picked from #2 to #10 average just 16.70 WARP, while college players drafted in the same spots average 29.16 WARP—nearly double the career value.

If we break it down round by round, here's what we get:

Round	HS	Col	% Diff
1st (#1-30)	14.31	20.32	42.0%
2nd (#31-70)	4.37	6.59	50.6%
3rd (#71-100)	1.88	5.34	183.8%
Overall	6.68	10.33	54.5%

College players taken in the first round have, on average, 42 percent more overall value than their high-school counterparts—and the gap (in relative terms) only widens from there. Third-round picks out of college have almost triple the value of picks out of high school. (Remember Draft Rule #2, which states that there isn't much difference between second and third-round picks? Apparently, that really only applies to collegiate players.)

What's particularly interesting is that earlier, we saw that college players were more likely to reach the majors than high-school players, by a margin of 59 percent to 40 percent, which works out to a 48.6 percent increase in the likelihood of reaching the majors. But college players have 54.5 percent more WARP than high-school players. In other words, if you do the math, not only are college players more likely to reach the majors, but the ones who do reach the majors have more career value than the high-school players who reach the majors. The advantage college picks enjoy in terms of reaching the majors is not simply because of the added bulk of a bunch of marginal draft picks.

Which leads us to Draft Rule #5, which is pretty much the most important draft rule of them all:

> **Draft Rule #5: In the first three rounds, not only are college players about 50 percent more likely to reach the major leagues than high-school players drafted in the same slot, they produce approximately 55 percent more value over the course of their careers. This advantage is persistent at every point after the #1 pick.**

Twenty years ago, Bill James wrote that "the rate of return on players drafted out of college is essentially twice that of high-school players." If you simply change "twice" to "55 percent more," that statement still holds true today.

Next time, we'll look at whether the advantage enjoyed by college players has diminished in the more recent set of draft picks.

DOCTORING THE NUMBERS
The Draft, Part Three
Rany Jazayerli

Having established that college players tend to be safer bets in the draft, Rany Jazayerli investigated whether their advantage over high-school draftees had diminished in recent years.

Before we move on to a discussion of whether the balance of power between high-school and college players has changed over time, I want to clear up some loose ends. The two salient conclusions from the last article were that:

1. College players taken in the first three rounds are about 50 percent more likely to reach the majors than high-school players;
2. College players, on average, yield about 55 percent more value than high-school players drafted with the same pick.

The shorthand for this is that college players are both more likely to reach the majors and more likely to develop into star-caliber players once they reach the majors. However, a number of readers questioned this final summation, wondering whether, even though they trailed in both their matriculation rate and their overall value, it was possible that high-school players were more likely to achieve true stardom than their college counterparts.

The best way to tackle this question is to break down each group, college and high-school players, by their 15-year WARP tally.

Despite the fact that slightly fewer players were drafted out of high school than out of college, there are more players on the college side of the ledger in every row of players that reached the major leagues. If anything, the gap widens as we look at the truly elite players: Of the 65 players who amassed 40 or more WARP, 47 of them (72

Career Result	High School	College
Never reached majors	459	281
WARP Between 0 and 1	58	66
WARP Between 1 and 5	63	101
WARP Between 5 and 10	30	47
WARP Between 10 and 20	41	56
WARP Between 20 and 30	27	43
WARP Between 30 and 40	16	23
WARP Between 40 and 50	6	15
WARP Between 50 and 60	2	8
WARP Between 60 and 80	6	11
WARP Greater than 80	4	13
Total	749	715

percent) were college draftees. Of the players who reached the majors but failed to reach 40 WARP, "only" 336 of 571 (59 percent) were from the college ranks.

Or think of it another way: if we come up with PECOTA-like "percentile ranks" for how much WARP you could expect from a player drafted out of college vs. high school, here's what we end up with. Keep in mind that the mean value for each set of players is 10.33 WARP for college players, 6.68 for high-school players.

Percentile	High School	College
90th %	18.3	29.3
75th %	1.1	8.6
50th %	N/A	0.3
25th %	N/A	N/A
10th %	N/A	N/A

Since less than 50 percent of high-school draftees made the majors, their 50th-percentile projection (i.e. the median) is zero. This is why it's important to differentiate between the median and the mean; the presence of a few superstars in each group increases the mean WARP value, but overall the majority of draft picks in either group are near worthless.

If we run this same chart but exclude all the players who didn't reach the majors at all—an exclusion which definitely favors the high-school draftees, since so many more of them failed to reach the majors—here's what we get.

Percentile	High School	College
90th %	33.4	42.0
75th %	15.2	20.7
50th %	3.6	4.9
25th %	0.4	0.8
10th %	0.0	0.0

Even in this study, college players make out better. So, at least from 1984 to 1999 as a whole, not only are college players more likely to reach the majors than high-school players, but among those who reach the majors, college players are more likely to fashion a valuable career than high schoolers.

But the question arises: Has this advantage in favor of college players changed over time? Sixteen years is a long time, after all. Jim Callis' study for *Baseball America* looked at players drafted from 1991 to 1997; it is certainly possible that the advantage enjoyed by collegiate players in our study is just a residual artifact left over from the 1980s.

We can break down the data into chunks, looking at the high-school vs. college data from 1984 to 1991 separately from the data from 1992 to 1999. There is one problem with this approach, however: the players in the more recent data set do not have as many years of data to analyze. Extending the data in the more recent group to Y15 is impossible because none of the players has reached Y15.

We'll work around this problem. First, here are the 15-year WARP charts for both groups:

	Y0	Y1	Y2	Y3	Y4	Y5	Y6	Y7	Y8	Y9	Y10	Y11	Y12	Y13	Y14	Y15	Total
HS	0.00	0.02	0.15	0.31	0.46	0.61	0.69	0.74	0.71	0.73	0.66	0.51	0.52	0.34	0.24		6.68
Col	0.01	0.11	0.36	0.62	0.84	0.91	1.00	0.98	0.98	0.84	0.76	0.73	0.64	0.59	0.53	0.44	10.33

A couple of points about this comparison. One possible objection to this study's methodology is that, even looking 15 years out, the study is biased against high-school players because, being younger than college players, they would still have more good years left in them at the conclusion of the study.

What I find interesting is that, even in the last few years of this study, the college players are still kicking the high-school guys all over the playground—even though you would think the three-year gap in age would become a particularly large advantage for the high-school draftees at that point. At Y15, the college players are about 36 years old, the high-school guys are only 33—and yet the college guys have nearly twice as much value. It seems to me that if we ran the study out until every player had retired, the advantage enjoyed by college players might increase even more. Hell, just including Barry Bonds' last few years would move the needle.

However, even though college players seem to do better at the far right end of the chart, they still derive more of their value (as you would expect) in the early years after the draft. College players tend to peak at Y6, high-school players between Y8 and Y10 (which fits comfortably with the old canard that most players tend to peak around age 27.)

Let's look at when a typical college vs. high-school draft pick accumulates most of his value. Not only do collegiate players return 55 percent more value than high-school players, but they produce twice the fraction of that value within five years of being drafted.

Career Segment	High School	College
Y0 through Y5:	0.94 (14%)	2.85 (28%)
Y6 through Y10:	3.47 (52%)	4.56 (44%)
Y11 through Y15:	2.28 (34%)	2.93 (28%)

Without getting into economic details like the discount rate of future earnings, it's obvious that if you have the choice between two players of equal overall value, you'd rather have the one that will produce all that value now than one who will produce that value a decade from now. The farther off in the future a player's value is, the less likely the team that drafted him will reap that value; he might get released in the interim, file for free agency, get claimed on waivers, get traded for pennies on the dollar, whatever. Al Leiter has had more career value than Steve Avery, but I know which one I'd want my team to draft.

So that's another point in favor of college players.

But back to the original question. Have the scales that have historically favored college players tipped the other direction in more recent times?

To answer that, I'll start by reproducing the 15-year chart comparing high-school and college players above, but using data from 1984 to 1991 only:

	Y0	Y1	Y2	Y3	Y4	Y5	Y6	Y7	Y8	Y9	Y10	Y11	Y12	Y13	Y14	Y15	Total
HS		0.00	0.02	0.13	0.26	0.38	0.56	0.57	0.66	0.66	0.68	0.58	0.48	0.52	0.34	0.24	6.08
COL	0.01	0.16	0.47	0.71	0.92	0.99	1.05	1.05	1.04	0.87	0.81	0.83	0.68	0.59	0.53	0.44	11.15

Relative to our entire group of players, college players drafted from 1984 to 1991 amassed more value (11.15 to 10.33 overall), while high-school players amassed less (6.08 to 6.68 overall). Between 1984 to 1991, collegiate players were worth 83 percent more than high-school players, compared to a figure of just 55 percent more for the entire period from 1984 to 1999.

But if the gap between collegiate and high-school players was larger in the first half of the study... you see where I'm going with this.

Here's the same chart, this time using data from 1992 to 1999. In this case I'm taking the data out to only Y10, as only three draft years (1992-94) have even reached Y10.

	Y0	Y1	Y2	Y3	Y4	Y5	Y6	Y7	Y8	Y9	Y10	Total
HS		0.00	0.02	0.13	0.26	0.38	0.56	0.57	0.66	0.66	0.68	5.22
COL	0.01	0.16	0.47	0.71	0.92	0.99	1.05	1.05	1.04	0.87	0.81	6.33

This is what Alan Dershowitz might call Reversal of Data. The gap between collegiate and high-school players has narrowed to just over one WARP; after rolling up 83 percent more WARP than high schoolers from 1984 to 1991, collegiate players have only maintained a 21 percent edge from 1992 to 1999.

Actually, it's even smaller than that. As you can see from the numbers, while high-school players lag their collegiate counterparts in the first six years after the draft, the lines cross at Y7 (when collegiate players are about 28 and high schoolers are only 25), and then high-school players have more value from Y8 through Y10, when our study runs out of numbers to crunch. It stands to reason that with the benefit of more years of data, the gap between high-school and college players would narrow further.

We can estimate what the final numbers might look like by extrapolating the data from our older set of players. As we showed above, about 28 percent of a college player's value comes between

Y11 and Y15, compared to 34 percent for high-school players. Those are the figures for the entire data set; if we look only at players from 1984 to 1991, the numbers are 27.5 percent and 35.5 percent, respectively.

If we assume that the more recent set of players will also derive about 27.5 percent and 35.5 percent of their 15-year WARP value between Y11 and Y15, we can fill in the numbers with a little algebra.

Value	High School	College
through Y10 (Actual)	5.22	6.33
Y11 - Y15 (Estimated)	2.87	2.40
Total	8.09	8.73

I wouldn't take these numbers as pure gospel; there are a lot of reasons why these data may prove to be inaccurate in the long run. These players are all still in the middle of their careers, so the numbers could change. And by using only eight years of data, we've cut our sample size in half. In particular, the numbers for Y9 and Y10 involve very few draft classes, and a few more years of data might change the numbers significantly.

But let's not beat around the bush here: according to the data, the advantage between college and high-school players has shrunk from 83 percent to all of 8 percent. That's not just significant—it's mind-blowing.

Mind you, it's not mind-blowing simply because the gap has evaporated. When I first started compiling these data two months ago, I actually suspected that the gap between high-school and college players had closed over the years. But my rationale was that in the 1990s, teams were more and more inclined to take college players in the early rounds of the draft. After all, almost no college players were taken in the first round in the early 1970s; by the early 1980s, nearly half the players being taken in the first round were out of college. I assumed that trend had continued.

And if it had, it would certainly explain why the gap has closed: namely, teams had sensed the overwhelming advantage enjoyed by college players in the 1970s and 1980s and had changed their draft strategies to accommodate. In other words, they had identified the inefficiencies in the market, and by taking advantage of them as a group, they had worked to remove them.

But that's not the case. Here's how the distribution of college vs. high-school players breaks down:

Draft Position	1984-1991			1992-1999		
	High School	College	%Col	High School	College	%Col
First round	95	131	58%	109	118	52%
Second round	150	135	47%	167	125	43%
Third round	102	112	52%	126	94	43%
Overall	347	378	52%	402	337	46%

I'm man enough to admit it: I'm completely befuddled by these results. Not only did the gap between the value of college and high-school players shrink to almost nothing in the 1990s; this has occurred even though the pendulum swung back towards taking more high-school players.

In my 10 years of writing for Baseball Prospectus, this is the most surprising conclusion I have ever reached in an analytical study. I suspected that the advantage enjoyed by collegiate players had diminished, but I didn't anticipate the degree to which it has. And I certainly did not suspect that high-school players would jump in value relative to college picks even as teams were drafting more high-school players, not less. This seems to violate the basic principles of economics. Prices don't drop when demand goes up, but in this case the "price" of high-school talent—the difference between the value of the draft pick and the return on the player drafted—has gone down even though the demand for high-school players has also increased.

Bill James was right. But it appears that Jim Callis is also right, more or less. Meanwhile, we need a couple new draft rules:

> **Draft Rule #6: Draft Rule #5 appears to be obsolete when looking at data from after 1991. The advantage enjoyed by college players over high-school players has dropped to eight percent, a margin of dubious statistical significance.**

> **Draft Rule #7: The value of high-school players relative to their college counterparts has shot up, even though teams were more likely to use top draft picks on high-school players in the 1990s than in the 1980s.**

What can explain this paradox? One factor that can cause prices on a commodity to drop even as demand increases is the advent of technology that makes the production of that commodity more efficient, and therefore increases the supply of the commodity to keep up with demand. Applying that analogy to the baseball draft, if teams somehow became more efficient at identifying high-school talent—if they somehow managed to weed out the worst mistakes of years past—they could increase their yield even as they drafted more high-school players.

It's a good theory. Of course, my last theory blew up in my face. Next time, we'll delve into this topic a little deeper.

DOCTORING THE NUMBERS
The Draft, Part Four
Rany Jazayerli

After discovering that the superior returns generated by college players in the draft had declined over time, Rany Jazayerli attempted to determine why.

The people have spoken. When I ended my last article with the conclusion that the gap between high-school and college players in the draft has almost completely evaporated, I expected to spend the next few days figuring out for myself the reasons for the change. Fortunately, you did that for me.

Reader after reader responded with their own theories as to what could cause teams to do a significantly better job of drafting high-school talent, even as they drafted more high-school players. And each response looked frighteningly liked the last: it's the signing bonuses, stupid.

In 1988, #1 overall pick Andy Benes received the highest signing bonus for an amateur player in baseball history, breaking Rick Reichart's 24-year-old record. Benes signed for $235,000.

By 1991, the #1 overall pick—the ill-fated Brien Taylor—signed for $1.55 million.

That, in a nutshell, is what changed the equation of the draft. Signing bonuses exploded in the late '80s and early '90s. The average first-round signing bonus nearly tripled between 1989 and 1992 and went up more than 10 times between 1989 and 1999, from an average of $176,000 to $1.81 million.

Why bonuses went up so much, so fast is not something I can adequately answer in a paragraph, but a variety of factors were in play. The general increase in revenues that made baseball owners flush with cash meant they were more willing to spend more money to make more money. Aided by the emergence of super-agents, drafted players were more aware of their leverage and were more than willing to use it. Once Taylor and Todd Van Poppel had shown that teams were willing to shell out seven-figure bonuses, the dam broke.

Teams were willing to pay for the best talent, because they began to realize that even at inflated prices, it was still far more cost-effective to sign amateur players than to throw money at free agents. Whereas, 10 years ago, teams were perfectly willing to let high-school players walk away over a small disagreement over compensation, now those teams became willing to shell out the dough. After all, many of the players that headlined the historic college crops of the mid-'80s—Barry Larkin, Will Clark, Barry Bonds, etc.—were very highly regarded high-school players but chose to go to college because the money wasn't there. Bonds, famously, was a second-round pick by his hometown Giants in 1982 but didn't sign over a difference of six thousand dollars.

Of course, many top high-school players didn't go to college because of a spat over money—many of them went to college because they wanted a college education. When they were leaving a five-figure sum on the table—a dollar figure that was barely worth more than their college scholarship—it was an easy choice. When the '90s dawned and top players were being offered million-dollar bonuses to sign—suddenly the resolve of even the most college-committed player was tested.

So it might not be that major-league organizations started doing a better job of identifying high-school talent. They simply were doing a better job of convincing those players to sign. Not only did this increase the pool of high-school players in the professional ranks, but it meant that college programs had less talent to draw on, and the pool of collegiate talent that was draftable three years later was thinned out.

That seems to be, by far, the most compelling and significant reason for the swing of the pendulum. Just to be sure, though, I spoke with Jim Callis of *Baseball America* for more insight; frankly, after my discovery that Callis had been right all along, I pulled an Anakin and got down on bended knee to swear my allegiance and beg for his knowledge of the dark side. (Yes, Anakin turns to the dark side. Palpatine turns out to be the Sith Lord, Padme gives birth to twins, and all the Jedi except Yoda and Obi-Wan get offed. Hope I didn't ruin the movie for anyone.)

Here are a couple of other factors that are much less significant than the signing bonus issue, but as Callis said, were all pulling in the same direction:

1. MLB instituted the college scholarship plan in the 1980s, in which players signed out of high school were guaranteed to have their college tuition paid for should their pro careers not pan out and they choose to go on to college later. In reality, the plan is more bark than bite—it's a lot harder for a 26-year-old with a wife and kid to go back to college than it is for an unattached 18-year-old, and of course it's a lot harder to get admitted to a quality school when you can no longer offer your services on the diamond. But it may have helped tipped the scales for a few high-school picks.

2. The NCAA made drastic reforms around the same time, cutting scholarships by 10 percent (from 13 to 11.7 scholarships per school) and preventing teams from scheduling more than 56 games a year (some schools played 70 or more games prior to the reforms). The NCAA also limited the hours spent coaching, preventing college coaches from working with their players in the summer, and also eliminating a formal fall schedule. These reforms allowed pro teams an opening, making it possible to convince a prospect that he wouldn't get nearly as much time to refine his skills in college as he would in the pros.

3. The emergence of regional showcases for high-school talent—events like the Area Code Games—has given high-school players an opportunity to play against the best high-school players in the country—and given scouts the opportunity to see how those players fare against top-line talent. This has been particularly beneficial in helping scouts get a read on players from cold-weather areas like the upper Midwest and New England.

These factors explain perfectly the existence of our paradox—the fact that high-school players yielded more value even though teams were drafting more of them. It's precisely because teams were drafting more high-school players that their value went up. Teams were drafting the very best players available, and not simply the best ones who would sign.

(Note that there's still room for improvement here. Even today, some high draft picks out of high school don't sign—remember, Mark Prior was a supplemental first round pick of the Yankees—and others announce their intentions to go to college in advance and are all but ignored in the draft. Of course, money still talks: Grady Sizemore promised he wouldn't sign out of high school, then got an enormous bonus from the Expos (!) that changed his mind.)

The only problem with the theory, frankly, is that I know of no way to test its validity one way or the other. This is one of those theories that we'll just have to take on faith.

Having settled the reasons behind the change in the draft, I want to tweak my final conclusion from Part Three a little. I ended the last article by stating that the difference in value between college and high-school players had dropped to a mere eight percent. The exact figure, however, depends on the assumptions you make.

In particular, the assumption I made that we should measure a draft pick's value over 15 years has come under some fire from readers, who (correctly) wonder why a team should care what their draft pick does 15 years from now, since there is no reasonable chance that said player would not have reached free agency by that point. It's a fair question. Remember, the eight percent figure was derived by extrapolating data from 10 years out (which is all we have at this point); if we use the 10-year data, college players have a much more comfortable 21 percent cushion.

What should the cutoff be? Theoretically, a team can hold the rights to a high-school player through Y12; a high-school player doesn't have to be added to the 40-man roster until after Y3, then can be optioned to the minors for three more years (Y4 through Y6), and then the service time clock starts ticking at Y7. College-signed players have to be added to the 40-man roster after Y2, which puts a theoretical cap at Y11 for them.

Realistically, Y10 is a pretty fair estimate of how long we should count a player's value towards the team that originally drafted him. If we use Y10 as our cutoff, then, college players are still 21 percent more valuable than high-school players on average.

But high-school players are younger, and take longer to develop, than college players. Is it fair to make the cutoff the same for both groups? College players reach the majors 18-24 months quicker than high-school players, so it stands to reason that they would declare for free agency 18-24 months quicker as well. If we then use two different cutoffs, two years apart—Y8 for college players, Y10 for high-school players:

Average Y8 value (college players)	5.03
Average Y10 value (high-school players)	5.22

We can make the argument that high-school players are more valuable to the teams that drafted them than college picks.

But there's also the issue of discounting. "Discounting" is an economic principle that refers to the fact that a dollar today is worth more than a dollar 10 years from now. You can invest that dollar today and have more than a dollar in 10 years, or you can spend that dollar today and derive value from it that you can't do with the dollar you have to wait 10 years on. Similarly, a draft pick that has value immediately is more valuable than a draft pick that will develop in five years. The Al Leiter/Steve Avery comparison holds here—Al Leiter has had significantly more career value than Avery, but it took so long for him to realize his value that the Yankees got rid of him for pennies on the dollar, while Avery's peak occurred early in his career, when he was able to do the most good for the team that drafted him.

The exact "discount rate" that applies to baseball players is impossible to state definitively, but given the rapid attrition of ballplayers and the likelihood that they'll be traded or released if they don't develop quickly, we can say it's rather high, on the order of 10-15 percent. Which is to say, a player worth one WARP today is as valuable as a player worth 1.15 WARP next year.

By this token, a college player will have more value than a high-school player, other things equal, simply because he develops faster. For instance, a team gets more present value out of a college player's Y3 year (when he creates 0.52 WARP) than it does out of a high-school player's Y10 year (when he creates 0.87 WARP) because the discount rate knocks more value off of the more distant timeframe.

If we use the data we arrived at in the last segment and discount future years' WARP data into Y0 WARP equivalents, we find the following. Using a 10 percent discount rate:

Average Y8 value (college players)	2.84
Average Y10 value (high-school players)	2.47

Using a 15 percent discount rate:

Average Y8 value (college players)	2.13
Average Y10 value (high-school players)	1.68

And suddenly, the college players once again enjoy an advantage of 15 percent in the first example, 27 percent in the second.

There are a lot of different ways to massage the data. I'm not smart enough to know which methods are the most valid, but then I'm not deathly interested in knowing whether the advantage enjoyed by college players is 12 percent or 13 percent. In terms of the general brushstrokes, I'm comfortable in saying that college players are worth, on average, somewhere between 10 and 20 percent more than an equivalent high-school draftee. It's enough of a disparity that you need to be aware of it, but not so much that you need to obsess over it.

Whether a player is drafted out of high school or out of college is a factor that must be considered, but it's only one factor of many, and unlike 20 or even 10 years ago, it's no longer the dominant factor.

Next time, we'll break down the data into pitchers and hitters and see whether some of our other time-honored principles—like Thou Shalt Not Draft a High-School Pitcher in the First Round—still hold true.

DOCTORING THE NUMBERS
The Draft, Part Five
Rany Jazayerli

In part five of his draft study, Rany Jazayerli investigated the relative virtues of drafting pitchers and position players.

I had hoped to complete my series on the draft before, you know... the draft. That didn't happen, but that doesn't mean we can't soldier on. Enough with the whole high school/college thing. Let's just jump into the pitcher vs. hitter angle, shall we?

Here are the 15-year WARP lines for all pitchers and all hitters, from 1984 through 1999:

Player	Y0	Y1	Y2	Y3	Y4	Y5	Y6	Y7	Y8	Y9	Y10	Y11	Y12	Y13	Y14	Y15	Total
Hitters	0.00	0.04	0.16	0.33	0.51	0.68	0.84	0.89	0.99	0.92	0.83	0.81	0.63	0.65	0.48	0.38	9.13
Pitchers	0.01	0.08	0.24	0.48	0.65	0.71	0.76	0.74	0.68	0.62	0.64	0.55	0.49	0.43	0.40	0.34	7.83

As you can see, for all years and all players, hitters do enjoy a modest advantage of about 17 percent over pitchers drafted in the same slot. (Although, if you look at the data through Y10 only, the advantage is just 10 percent.) This is not surprising; TNSTAAPP didn't come out of nowhere, after all. If anything, the advantage was a little smaller than I would have suspected.
Let's break the data down into early (1984-91) and late (1992-99) groups:

Player	Y0	Y1	Y2	Y3	Y4	Y5	Y6	Y7	Y8	Y9	Y10	Y11	Y12	Y13	Y14	Y15	Total
H, pre-91	0.00	0.07	0.23	0.37	0.51	0.67	0.82	0.91	0.98	0.86	0.83	0.80	0.61	0.65	0.48	0.38	9.15
P, pre-91	0.01	0.11	0.32	0.56	0.73	0.78	0.86	0.75	0.71	0.68	0.64	0.59	0.53	0.43	0.40	0.34	8.45

Player	Y0	Y1	Y2	Y3	Y4	Y5	Y6	Y7	Y8	Y9	Y10	Total
H, 92+	0.00	0.02	0.08	0.27	0.51	0.69	0.88	0.88	1.00	1.05	0.83	6.21
P, 92+	0.00	0.05	0.16	0.41	0.57	0.65	0.63	0.74	0.62	0.49	0.63	4.95

The advantage enjoyed by hitters of all stripes, which was a mere eight percent in the early half of our study, increased to 25 percent in the second half of the study, even though the later subset of player is missing years 11 through 15, which significantly favored the hitters in the early group.

This certainly would lend some credence to TNSTAAPP theory; teams may have gotten better at drafting high-school talent in the 1990s, but they showed no signs at cracking the code for how to identify which pitchers will go on to stardom and which ones will break down.

Let's break the data down into its four component groups, separating players into high-school pitchers, high-school hitters, college pitchers and college hitters. First, the composite data:

Player	Y0	Y1	Y2	Y3	Y4	Y5	Y6	Y7	Y8	Y9	Y10	Y11	Y12	Y13	Y14	Y15	Total
HSH	0.00	0.00	0.02	0.12	0.24	0.42	0.59	0.69	0.75	0.76	0.77	0.70	0.52	0.53	0.26	0.17	6.54
HSP	0.00	0.00	0.01	0.20	0.40	0.51	0.58	0.64	0.67	0.55	0.57	0.60	0.48	0.49	0.43	0.34	6.47
COLH	0.00	0.10	0.33	0.60	0.90	1.04	1.20	1.17	1.31	1.11	0.90	0.98	0.79	0.83	0.79	0.68	12.75
COLP	0.01	0.12	0.37	0.63	0.79	0.81	0.85	0.84	0.69	0.62	0.67	0.52	0.49	0.36	0.33	0.27	8.37

The first thing that jumps out is the huge difference in value between college and high-school picks; remember, this data looks at all players drafted from 1984 to 1999. But while hitters are, on the whole, significantly more valuable than pitchers when looking at the collegiate pool, there's essentially no difference whatsoever in the value of high-school hitters vs. high-school pitchers.

Before we jump to any conclusions, though, I'm going to break the data down into rounds: Round 1 refers to the first 30 picks in the draft, Round 2 refers to picks 31-70, and Round 3 refers to picks 71-100. Furthermore, I'm going to break the data up to look at 1984-91 separately from 1992-99. Here's how the numbers shook out between 1984 and 1991:

Player	1st Rd	2nd Rd	3rd Rd	Average
HS H, 84-91	16.13	2.11	1.03	5.99
HS P, 84-91	7.74	6.98	2.51	5.87
COL H, 84-91	26.24	5.91	9.94	13.22
COL P, 84-91	18.48	6.79	4.14	9.50

College hitters taken in the first three rounds are significantly better values than college pitchers, who are significantly better values than either species of high-school talent. Look at the data round by round, though, and a much more interesting pattern emerges.

First off, it's pretty easy to see why the mantra of Thou Shalt Not Draft A High-School Pitcher in the First Round came to pass. The 15-year WARP value of high-school pitchers taken in the first round is less than half that of any other subset of draft picks. That is an enormously valuable piece of information to know. The spectacular failure of high-school pitchers almost entirely explains the disparity between college and high-school players in the first round; as you can see, high-school hitters were almost exactly as valuable as college pitchers.

It's in the second round where the rules are turned upside down. High-school pitchers have the most value of any group of players drafted in the second round. That's shocking. For every Kurt Miller or Dan Opperman who goes bust as an early first-round pick, there's a second-round gem like Greg Maddux, Tom Glavine, Arthur Rhodes, or Al Leiter.

Overall, high-school pitchers drafted in the second round are almost as valuable as their counterparts in the first round. Compare this to college players, where first-round picks were worth between three and five times as much as second-round picks. Or better still, compare that to high-school hitters:

Player	1st Rd	2nd Rd	Ratio
HS Hitters	16.13	2.11	7.64
HS Pitchers	7.74	6.98	1.11

Slight difference there.

Overall in the second round, high-school pitchers, college pitchers, and college hitters all yielded roughly equal amounts of value, while high-school hitters averaged just a third as much value as the other three groups. It's not an exaggeration to say that between 1984 and 1991, the only pick worse than taking a high-school pitcher in the first round was taking a high-school hitter in the second.

Theoretically, if you took high-school hitters in the first round and high-school pitchers in the second round, you could beat the overwhelming odds in favor of collegiate hitters of that period. But your luck ran out in the third round; both cohorts of high-school players got smoked by both college groups. In fact, while it's almost certainly a reflection of small sample size, college hitters were better values in the third round than they were in the second. Guys like John Olerud, Ken Caminiti, David Justice, and Luis Gonzalez all used the third round as a springboard to stardom (although Olerud fell to the third round in part because he wasn't considered signable.)

To put it in stark terms: on average, the typical college hitter selected in the third round was more valuable than the typical high-school pitcher taken in the first round.

Of course, that's all ancient history. Here's the data from 1992 to 1999. Keep in mind we're looking only at the performance for the first 10 years after each player was drafted, compared to the first 15 years above, so the overall value of these picks is lower.

Player	1st Rd	2nd Rd	3rd Rd	Average
HS H, 92-99	10.72	3.14	1.76	5.00
HS P, 92-99	9.40	3.20	1.61	4.52
COL H, 92-99	17.28	6.07	3.07	8.53
COL P, 92-99	10.95	4.11	1.11	5.26

Once again, college hitters rule the roost. Between 1984 and 1991, the average college hitter had 39 percent more value than the average college pitcher, which was the next most valuable commodity. Between 1992 and 1999, that edge actually rose slightly to 62 percent.

Which leads to Draft Rule #8:

> **Draft Rule #8: Even though the traditional collegiate edge nearly evaporated in the 1990s, collegiate hitters remain far and away the most valuable draft picks on average, enjoying a substantial edge on every other class of draft pick for the entire duration of our study.**

You will note, though, that the reason college hitters increased their edge on college pitchers was not because college hitters became better draft picks, but because college pitchers fell back to the pack. Between 1984 and 1991, collegiate pitchers were between 59 and 62 percent more valuable than high-school hitters and pitchers, respectively. Between 1992 and 1999, those edges dropped all the way to five percent and 16 percent, respectively.

We can isolate the reasons for why the gap closed by directly comparing the 1984-91 data to the 1992-99 data. For this comparison, we need to look at the Y10 data for the early group as well as the late group, so that we're comparing apples to apples.

Player	1984-91	1992-99	% Change
HS Hitters	4.31	5.00	+16%
HS Pitchers	3.43	4.52	+32%
COL Hitters	9.53	8.53	-10%
COL Pitchers	7.63	5.26	-31%

Both sets of college players lost value from the early years to the later years, and both sets of high-school players gained value. However in both cases, the talent drain from college to high school affected hitters less than it did pitchers. As a result, high-school pitchers no longer present the unacceptable risk they posed in the 1980s, while college pitchers are not significantly more valuable than high-school players of any stripe.

If we look solely at first-round data, the change in draft values becomes even more apparent:

Player	1984-91	1992-99	% Change
HS Hitters	10.82	10.72	-1%
HS Pitchers	4.62	9.40	+103%
COL Hitters	17.82	17.28	-3%
COL Pitchers	14.39	10.95	-24%

Both college and high-school hitters are almost exactly as valuable in the 1990s as they were in the 1980s. College pitchers, who in the 1980s enjoyed a comfortable advantage over high-school hitters, lost a quarter of their value and are now essentially tied with high-school hitters when it comes to first-round value.

The most striking change has been with high-school pitchers. Once upon a time, these were disastrous picks, earning less than half the value of any other subset of first-round pick. High-school pitchers more than doubled their value in the later set of drafts. From 1992 to 1999, while they were still the riskiest picks overall, high-school pitchers were just 12-14 percent less valuable than high-school hitters or college pitchers.

The old mantra is dead. Thou Probably Should Not Draft a High-School Pitcher in the First Round, but Thou Can.

Here's the second-round data, again comparing Y10 data:

Player	1984-91	1992-99	% Change
HS Hitters	1.42	3.14	+121%
HS Pitchers	4.17	3.20	-23%
COL Hitters	4.01	6.07	+51%
COL Pitchers	5.29	4.11	-22%

In the second round, college hitters continue to dominate, amassing 48 percent more WARP than college pitchers and nearly double the value of high-school players. Notice how the values of high-school hitters and pitchers converge. Whereas in the early group, high-school pitchers were nearly three times as valuable as high-school hitters, now the two groups are essentially equal. The most likely explanation I have for this is simply the vagaries of small sample size; we've broken down the data into so many parts that a few outliers in a single group can skew the data one way or the other.

Certainly, the newer data set is smoother and seems more intuitively correct. Yet once again, it appears that the time-honored criticism of high-school pitchers is no longer relevant. High-school players do appear to be riskier than college players in the second round, but the blame for that is shared equally among hitters and pitchers.

Finally, the third-round data:

Player	1984-91	1992-99	% Change
HS Hitters	0.69	1.76	+155%
HS Pitchers	1.50	1.61	+7%
COL Hitters	6.75	3.07	-55%
COL Pitchers	3.22	1.11	-66%

The third round is where the gains made by high-school players are most obvious. High-school hitters, who were almost worthless in the early group, more than doubled in value, while both collegiate cohorts dropped in value by over half. While college hitters are still the most valuable subset overall, college pitchers were actually the least valuable of the four groups. This is the only instance in the entire study in which one of the college groups was the least valuable of the four.

That's a lot of numbers to throw at you. Let's sum up the important findings here:

1. No matter how you slice the data, college hitters come up on top every time, usually by a wide margin;
2. High-school pitchers are still the riskiest selections in the first round, but the margin is much, much less than it used to be. It is no longer appropriate to make a blanket statement that it is always a mistake to take a high-school pitcher in the first round;
3. With the exception of the first round, high-school pitchers are almost exactly as valuable as high-school hitters.
4. College pitchers are, generally speaking, not significantly more valuable than high-school players in any round.

If I wanted to sum all five articles into 40 words or less, I could do it like this:

> You're going to get about 50 percent more value from a college hitter than from any other draft pick. High-school pitchers are somewhat riskier than other picks in the first round.

That's all you need to know.

So after poring over the musty archives of draft history in the search of some piercing wisdom, what we have found is—there isn't that much wisdom to be had. Teams have done a pretty good job of ferreting out the inefficiencies in the market on their own.

Then again, we're not done searching. Next time, we'll go position by position and see whether there are any inefficiencies to be exploited on a smaller scale. Are high-school catchers really as bad a selection as their reputation suggests? Do college left-handers pan out more often than their less genetically deviant brethren? Stay tuned.

DOCTORING THE NUMBERS
The Draft, Part Six
Rany Jazayerli

AUGUST 2, 2005

http://bbp.cx/a/4291

In part six of his draft study, Rany recalibrated his system to adjust for the fact that players who produce early in their careers are more valuable to the teams that drafted them, then identifies the best picks ever and the most talent-rich drafts.

It's been a long time since we spoke. Since my last article on the draft, I've suffered two emotionally draining events: the big 3-0, and the birth of my second daughter, Jenna. (Mother and daughters are doing fine. Father is trying to figure out how to squeeze in baseball highlights between diaper changings and viewings of *Dora the Explorer*.)

I'm back now, and I promise to get the next installment of this series out well in advance of the big 4-0.

The time off wasn't entirely wasted—I did have an epiphany of sorts while trying to figure out different ways to extract useful information from a veritable mountain of data.

Up until now, I had tried to calculate the value of draft picks by aggregating them into large groups —like all college players drafted in the first round—and then determining the average value that each of those picks had in Year 1, Year 2, Year 3, etc. after each player was drafted.

That was a very useful method for looking at large groups, but there were problems in extrapolating that method to look at other issues. For instance, an issue as simple as asking "Which teams have done the best job of drafting?" would be poorly-served by this approach. Comparing, say, the average value of every first-round pick by the Atlanta Braves with the first-round picks of the Tampa Bay Devil Rays would be useless, because—as tradition dictates—they draft on opposite sides of the round. You simply can't compare the value of the third overall pick with the 30th overall pick. And if you break the individual groups down into smaller parts—say, looking at top-10 picks only—you quickly end up with sample sizes so small that they're essentially meaningless.

So I had to look for another way. Which meant I had to get over my hang-up over using discounted values.

By that, I mean the best way to compare one pick to another is to assign a precise value for each pick—to determine, as accurately as possible, what the fourth pick in 1992 was "worth" going into the draft, i.e. its expected value. But to come up with an accurate measure to determine expected values, I first had to try to determine the actual values of previous draft picks.

Until now, I had used the simple approach of summing up a player's WARP value for the first 15 years after he was drafted. It was a quick-and-dirty method that yielded quick-and-dirty results. To get a more precise answer, we need a metric that, like 15-year WARP values, distilled a player's contribution into one tidy figure, but unlike 15-year WARP values only measured the value that player generated while still under the control of the team that drafted him.

The ideal method would have been to figure out the exact date at which every player was released or declared free agency for the first time and count only his value to that point. Players who were traded would have the players they were traded for tacked on to their value, and so on. The problem with this method is that it would have taken, approximately speaking, forever.

So I tried to come up with a system that sacrificed a minimum of accuracy in exchange for a maximum of usability. The formula I came up with also had to account for the fact that high-school players tend to spend more time in the minor leagues and therefore tend to spend more years with their original team before hitting free agency. Here's the formula:

For collegiate draftees: Full value for years Y0 through Y8, plus two-thirds of their value for Y9, plus one-third of their value for Y10.

For high-school picks: Full value for years Y0 through Y9, plus three-quarters of their value for Y10, plus half their value for Y11, plus one-quarter of their value for Y12.

Are there college players who don't reach the major leagues until five years after they were drafted and don't reach free agency until after Y11? Sure. Are there high-school players who are in the major leagues 18 months after they were drafted and say goodbye to their original club (hello, A-Rod) after Y7? Absolutely. This formula is going to be inaccurate on the margins. But for large groups of players, or even small ones, it's accurate enough.

(Incidentally, we haven't addressed Junior College players up until now—that's one of the goals of this new system. For Junior College players, I decided to compromise, figuring out their value using each formula and then averaging the two.)

The other adjustment I had to make was to discount future value relative to present value. All things considered, you'd much rather prefer an All-Star season this year than an All-Star season five years from now. And when drafting a player, you'd much rather have a player who can contribute right away than one who won't have an impact for years. For one thing, the longer you have to wait for a player to contribute, the more likely you are to have given up on his future and let him go for a fraction of his value.

In previous articles, I had suggested a fairly steep 10-15 percent discount rate as appropriate. I have heard from several readers with a slightly more impressive economics background than mine —at least if you consider "University Professor of Economics" to be an impressive background— who intimated that such a discount rate was too high. Among other reasons, baseball players are not as liquid as, say, Microsoft stock. You can't cash in a ballplayer at any time and get his exact fair market value in return.

If you have a thousand dollars in the bank that you don't really need, you can put that in a money market and withdraw it—with interest—at any time. If your farm system develops a terrific shortstop and you've already got Miguel Tejada under contract for the next five years, you're either going to move that shortstop prospect to another position—and lose some of his value—or put him on the trade market, where you may or may not find a good fit for another player who 1) has equal value and 2) fills a need position.

So in the end, I used a discount rate of eight percent. Which means that a player's WARP value in year Y0 is counted in full; his value in year Y1 is counted at 92 percent, in year Y2 at (92 percent)^2 or 84.6 percent, etc. Because future value is always worth less than present value, this means that a player's "discounted value" is always going to be less than his original 15-year WARP value, which was not discounted.

Let's take a look at two college pitchers to give you an idea of how the new system differs from the old one:

Player	Y0	Y1	Y2	Y3	Y4	Y5	Y6	Y7	Y8	Y9	Y10	Y11	Y12	Y13	Y14	Y15	Total	DisVal
Kevin Brown	0.20		0.20	6.00	4.70	4.10	8.50	7.50	3.70	6.60	11.30	8.80	10.20	8.00	8.30	4.60	92.70	26.06
Ben McDonald	0.00	4.80	2.10	5.00	8.10	5.50	2.30	7.50	3.70								39.00	26.99

Using the old system of simply summing up each player's value for the first 15 years of his career, Kevin Brown has more than twice as much value as Ben McDonald. But if we look at the year-by-year breakdown of each player's career, it's clear that much of Brown's value came late in his career—he was 31 when he had his breakthrough season with the Marlins—which was of no value whatsoever to the team that drafted him, the Rangers. For the period of time when both pitchers were under the control of their original teams, they had essentially equal value. In fact, McDonald comes out slightly ahead, largely because he had a fine rookie season just one year after he was drafted.

On average, a player's Discounted Value works out to about 46 percent of his 15-Year Value, but for players who flamed out quickly, the ratio is much higher, whereas for players who were late bloomers the ratio is much lower. Here's a list of the five most extreme players on each end of the spectrum:

Player	15-Year WARP	DisVal	Ratio	Player	15-Year WARP	DisVal	Ratio
Ariel Prieto	7.9	7.07	0.895	Mike Remlinger	23.7	1.42	0.060
Jim Parque	11.3	9.39	0.831	Paul Abbott	10.2	0.67	0.065
Matt Anderson	7.1	5.71	0.804	Anthony Telford	14.6	1.23	0.085
Dave Fleming	14.8	11.86	0.801	Rudy Seanez	8.4	0.96	0.115
Brian Barnes	7.6	5.97	0.785	David Weathers	22.2	2.65	0.119

Ariel Prieto, the one player in our draft study who didn't fall into the "high school," "college," or "junior college" camps, was drafted in 1995 and made nine starts for the A's that year, hung around as a .500 pitcher for two more years, then fell off the face of the earth. He wasn't a particularly good draft pick, but he did provide an immediate return for the A's. Compare him to Mike Remlinger, who has appeared in nearly 600 major-league games—but only eight of those came for the team that drafted him, the Giants; he didn't permanently stick in the major leagues until 10 years after he was drafted.

So—now that we have a method to determine the Discounted Value (henceforth called the DV) of every drafted player, we can come up with a formula to calculate how much DV a team can expect from a specific draft pick. Only one adjustment had to be made, which is that the value of more recent picks had to be adjusted to account for the fact that a player drafted in, say, 1999 hasn't had an opportunity to achieve his full DV. The adjustment I made was to figure out what proportion of a player's DV was earned through Y5, since a player drafted in 1999 has only played through Y5, and then give all 1999 draftees credit for future performance by assuming they would continue to amass DV at a typical rate. For 1998 draftees, I looked at the average proportion of DV earned through Y6, and so on. (Keep in mind that these proportions differ for high-school vs. college picks, as college picks tend to reach the majors sooner and earn more of their DV early in their careers.)

That adjustment having been made, the chart below plots the average DV of every draft pick from the #1 through the #100 pick in each draft:

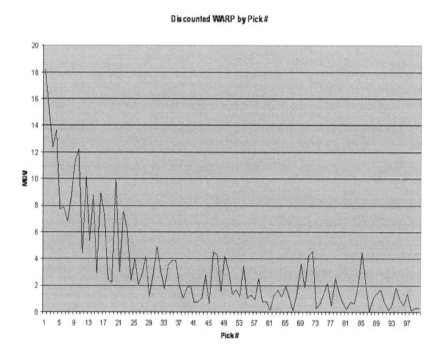

The shape of this chart looks very similar to the 15-Year WARP chart that was run in the first article. The key now was to construct a best-fit curve that would smooth out the random spikes and troughs in this chart. The first thing to notice was that the drop in value was not linear, but rather logarithmic; the value of a draft picks comes closer and closer to zero as we move later in the draft, but it never crosses zero—it's impossible for a draft pick to have negative value. (Though some have tried.)

Without getting into the mathematical details here (in large part because my methods would mortify the mathematicians in the audience), what I found was that the best way to approximate the values in the chart above was to assume there was an inflection point around pick 38 or so. Up until that pick, the value of each pick dropped by about 4.5 percent from the preceding pick; after pick 38, the depreciation rate fell to about 1.2 percent.

Here's the same chart, with the best-fit curve overlaying the actual data:

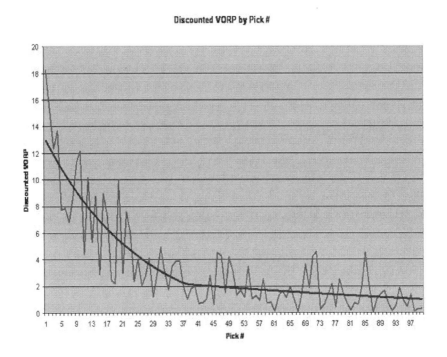

Now we have a tool to measure the expected value of every draft pick in our study. I can say, for instance, that the average DV of the #1 overall pick is 12.96 WARP; the average DV of the #100 overall pick is only 1.01. Again, an adjustment has to be made for more recent draft picks; the #1 overall pick in 1999 is worth only 3.97 WARP. This figure—the average DV—can also be called the Expected Value of that draft pick, or XV.

Armed with this knowledge, it becomes a cinch to answer a question like, who were the five best draft picks in our study?

Player	DV	XV	Diff
Barry Bonds	56.34	10.40	45.93
Mike Mussina	43.09	5.47	37.62
Frank Thomas	46.24	9.95	36.28
John Olerud	36.78	1.35	35.43
Will Clark	46.75	12.40	34.35

Bonds is an easy #1, but Will Clark, who had the second-highest DV of any player in the study, falls to fifth by this measure because the as second overall pick, he could have been expected to have more value than Frank Thomas (#7), Mike Mussina (#20), and especially John Olerud (#78).

How about another question: Which draft class (at least among the first 100 picks) had the most talent? What the following chart shows is the DV, the XV, and then the margin by which the DV exceeds or lags the XV in percentage terms. So, for instance, the players selected in 1984 combined to produce 5.6 percent less discounted value than they should have, had they all been "average" draft picks.

Year	DV	XV	Margin
1984	299.2	317.0	-5.6%
1985	433.5	317.6	+36.5%
1986	309.2	322.5	-4.1%
1987	419.2	321.6	+30.4%
1988	363.0	323.8	+12.1%
1989	313.9	306.2	+2.5%
1990	297.9	331.1	-10.0%
1991	298.5	309.4	-3.5%
1992	289.6	322.6	-10.2%
1993	328.7	324.7	+1.3%
1994	212.4	321.1	-33.8%
1995	322.5	300.8	+7.2%
1996	223.6	242.4	-7.7%
1997	167.6	221.7	-24.4%
1998	228.4	189.8	+20.3%
1999	136.4	135.2	+0.9%

The 1985 draft has long held serve as the strongest draft of all time, and as this study shows, with good reason—players drafted that year include Bonds, Clark, Barry Larkin, Rafael Palmeiro, and Randy Johnson. The 1987 draft doesn't receive as much attention but was nearly as fruitful, with Craig Biggio, Ken Griffey Jr., Kevin Appier, Ray Lankford, and Albert Belle leading the pack.

The 1994 draft? The first five picks were Paul Wilson, Ben Grieve, Dustin Hermanson, Antone Williamson, and Josh Booty. The scary thing is that Hermanson was actually the fifth-best pick among the top 100; only Nomar Garciaparra, Aaron Boone, A.J. Pierzynski, and Brian Meadows (Brian Meadows?!) were better.

(Keep in mind, even the 1994 draft looks like a gold mine compared to the 2000 affair. Five years later, only two first-round picks from that season are even marginal major leaguers: Rocco Baldelli and Chase Utley.)

Now let's see what this new draft tool has to say about the issue that consumed most of the past five articles in this series: the debate between high-school and college picks.

First, the comparison of the overall data from 1984 to 1999:

Class	Players	DV	XV	Margin
COL	715	2965.6	2455.7	+20.8%
HS	749	1479.5	2003.4	-26.2%
JuCo	62	191.5	137.7	+39.1%

As we would expect, college players hold a significant edge on high-school players. If we compare the two groups to each other, a draft pick spent on a collegiate player is worth 64 percent more than the same draft pick spent on a high-school player. This figure isn't far off from the 55-percent edge that we calculated using the older method in Part 2.

What is interesting is that Junior College players—an admittedly small group of draftees—have yielded significantly more value than the players taken from four-year institutions.

Looking at the data from 1984 to 1991 only:

Class	Players	DV	XV	Margin
COL	378	1837.1	1349.6	+36.1%
HS	347	755.4	1113.9	-32.2%
JuCo	35	141.8	85.9	+65.1%

Again, as we would expect, the differences between college and high-school players are accentuated during this period. College players were worth almost exactly double (101% more, to be exact) what high-school picks were worth. What also stands out is that Junior College players from this period were VERY valuable. Only 35 players were signed out of JuCo in those eight drafts, but among those 35 were Appier, Alex Fernandez, Ray Lankford, and Jaime Navarro. Take those four players out, and Junior College players would perform under expectations, an example of how only a few players can make a difference when you're looking at small groups.

From 1992 to 1999, the data stacks up like this:

Class	Players	DV	XV	Margin
COL	337	1128.5	1106.1	+2.0%
HS	402	724.1	889.6	-18.6%
JuCo	27	49.7	51.8	-4.0%

Just as we discovered in Part Three, the disparity between collegiate and high-school picks has been compressed dramatically. College players were 25 percent more valuable than high-school players during this period. This number is significantly higher than the eight percent figure that we arrived at in Part Three, but keep in mind that the assumptions have changed quite a bit. For instance, in Part Four we pointed out that if we simply ignored a player's value after Y10 (instead of after Y15) the advantage enjoyed by college players increased to 21 percent. This is a reasonable assumption, one that is employed by our new formula. (Actually, high-school picks do get a little credit for what they produced in Y11 and Y12, while college picks don't.)

Essentially, what I am saying is that simply using 15-Year WARP data probably understated the value of college picks a little. In each of the three charts above, college players have a more pronounced edge over high-school players than they did using our original method. It's not an enormous difference, and it does not undercut our conclusion that the collegiate edge shrunk dramatically in the 1990s. But there are differences in the conclusions reached by the two methods, and I strongly feel that the newer method yields a more accurate result. I am comfortable stating, then, that for the most recent years in our study, collegiate draft picks yielded approximately 25 percent more value than high-school players.

The value of junior college picks normalized during this period, but there is certainly no evidence to indicate that junior college players are a bad value; it's safe to say that they are at least as good a value as regular college players.

Finally, it's interesting to note that as a whole, players selected from 1992 to 1999 appear to be less valuable than picks from 1984 to 1991. I suggested this as a possibility earlier, but this data strongly supports the notion that the increasing internationalization of Major League Baseball has made the draft a less fruitful source of talent than in years past. Overall, draft picks from 1984 to 1991 were worth 15.6 percent more than picks from 1992 to 1999.

Next time—whenever that is—I'll use this new method to examine the value of draft picks at different positions on the diamond and then wrap up by examining which teams have done the best (and worst) jobs of drafting talent over the last 20 years.

DOCTORING THE NUMBERS
The Draft, Part Seven
Rany Jazayerli

In part seven of his series on the draft, Rany Jazayerli went position-by-position in search of inefficiencies in teams' typical draft patterns for high-school players.

Welcome back to my periodic series of articles—"periodic" in the sense that Halley's Comet is visible periodically—on the draft. This time around, I want to break the data down into tiny chunks to see whether certain positions make for better draft picks than others.

Using the technique described in the last part of this draft series, here's a breakdown of draft-pick value for college and high-school players, separated into pitchers and regulars, from 1984 through 1999:

Class	1st Rd	2nd Rd	3rd Rd	Overall
COL H	+31.2%	+28.2%	+110.0%	+37.6%
JUCO H	-100.0%*	-22.0%	+162.8%*	+4.6%
HS H	-18.4%	-33.6%	-58.3%	-27.0%
JUCO P	+104.8%*	-18.6%	+61.7%	+53.9%
COL P	-1.0%	+34.3%	+12.5%	+7.4%
HS P	-36.5%	-2.4%	-19.3%	-24.6%

In this table, each value represents the degree to which that subset of draft picks exceeded or underperformed expectations. For instance, collegiate hitters selected in the first round produced 31.2 percent more value than draft picks taken in those same slots in the draft would be expected to provide.

Asterisks are listed where the sample size was extremely small, fewer than 10 players. As the data for junior-college hitters can show, you can get some wacky data in small sample sizes. The data set for first-round juco hitters is made up of exactly three players, none of whom reached the majors. From now on, we won't even bother to list data for groups of five players or less.

As this data is for the entire period from 1984 to 1999, the conclusions—that college players are better than high-school players across-the-board—is not surprising. Perhaps the most interesting new conclusion is that junior-college pitchers are significantly more valuable than juco hitters, although both returned good value.

Here's the same data, but stripped to its relevant core, from 1992 to 1999:

Class	1st Rd	2nd Rd	3rd Rd	Overall
COL H	+21.3%	+50.7%	+30.4%	+28.2%
HS H	-22.3%	-6.8%	-49.7%	-20.9%
JUCO H	SSS	SSS	SSS	-34.9%
JUCO P	SSS	SSS	SSS	+4.1%
COL P	-19.6%	+14.3%	-36.9%	-14.6%
HS P	-15.4%	-15.0%	-13.1%	-14.9%

(SSS = Small Sample Size, less than five players; from this point on, we won't break down juco players by round—there aren't enough data points.)

The first thing that stands out is that almost every group of draft picks is underperforming expectations. There's a simple reason for that—as pointed out in Part Six, draft picks as a whole from 1992 to 1999 were worth about 15 percent less than picks from 1984 to 1991. Over time, more and more major-league talent comes from outside the confines of the draft, and that in turn reduces the value of the draft as a method for talent procurement.

We could normalize the data to account for this, but since the point of this exercise is to compare one set of draft picks to another, it really doesn't matter. Normalizing the data isn't going to change the fact that collegiate hitters outclass every other set of draft picks, in every round.

From 1992 onward, the margin between collegiate and high-school pitchers is essentially a rounding error; there is no evidence whatsoever that high-school pitchers are any riskier than collegiate pitchers, whether in the first round specifically or for the first three rounds as a whole.

Finally, it's interesting to see that high-school hitters actually turn out worse than either set of pitchers. In Part Five, using a different study method, high-school hitters were worth about 10 percent more than high-school pitchers overall; by our new method, they're worth about five percent less. Since the main difference between the two methods is that we've added discounting to the new method, my guess is that the reason for the discrepancy is that high-school pitchers render more of their value early in their careers—before they get hurt?—than high-school hitters.

Junior-college hitters turn out the worst of the six groups, but in a sample of just six players overall... ignore that. That's the last we'll talk about junior-college players; there simply aren't enough players taken out of junior college to break the data down any further.

Next, we'll look at how players drafted at different positions fare. For instance, here's the data for every high-school catcher taken from 1984 to 1999:

Pos	Years	1st Rd	2nd Rd	3rd Rd	Overall
HS C	84-91	-78.2%*	-55.2%	-73.7%	-71.8%
HS C	92-99	+18.8%*	-43.1%	+136.1%*	+17.2%
HS C	84-99	-42.9%	-51.3%	-18.9%	-41.5%

Years	Biggest Bargains	Biggest Busts
84-91	Todd Hundley, Greg Myers	Tyler Houston, Kurt Brown
92-99	Jason Kendall, A.J. Pierzynski	Joe Lawrence, Ben Davis

Biggest bargains and biggest busts are simply the players who most outperformed or underperformed the expected value of their draft slot.

In the 1980s and early 1990s, high-school catchers developed a reputation for being the place where draft picks go to die, and with good reason—they returned less than 30 cents on the dollar. Or to put it another way, over that time frame they were about half as valuable as high-school pitchers, themselves no bargain.

Something changed in the 1990s. Not one catcher selected in the first three rounds from 1984 to 1991 developed into anything remotely resembling a star, but in 1992, the Pirates took Jason Kendall with the #23 overall pick. Paul Konerko has had his moments, and Justin Morneau is climbing the charts—both no doubt helped by a position change—but the fact remains that all three players will almost certainly end up with better careers than any catcher taken between 1984 and 1991.

Moving on to first base:

Pos	Years	1st Rd	2nd Rd	3rd Rd	Overall
HS 1B	84-91	SSS	-98.6%*	-42.4%	-56.6%
HS 1B	92-99	-30.8%*	-100.0%*	-36.4%*	-52.9%
HS 1B	84-99	-29.0%*	-99.3%	-39.4%	-54.5%

Years	Biggest Bargains	Biggest Busts
84-91	Rico Brogna, Reggie Jefferson	Drew Denson, Lee Stevens
92-99	Derrek Lee, Nick Johnson	Matt Smith, J.J. Davis

Wow. High-school catchers get all the bad publicity, but high-school first basemen have actually been a worse value for the dollar over the entire 16-year draft study, and whereas teams seem to have learned how to avoid making mistakes behind the plate, they have shown no improvement here.

In total, 39 high-school first basemen have been drafted in the first 100 picks from 1984 to 1999. Just one of them—Derrek Lee—achieved stardom. The results of the second round are particularly grisly—of the 16 first basemen drafted in the second round, the most valuable proved to be the immortal Tim Hyers. Let's put it this way: Chris Weinke was one of the data points.

Why the terrible performance? It's pure speculation, but if you're playing first base on your high-school team, you're probably not the most athletic player in the world. No doubt almost all of these players were drafted for their bats, but athleticism has a lot to do with whether that bat develops, particularly since even the best high-school hitters need a lot of refinement before they're ready for the major leagues. It's not a surprise that Lee, the best player in this group, is a remarkably good athlete for a first baseman, what with his Gold Glove defense and 15 steals a year. It's that athleticism that has helped him continue to improve as a player into his late 20s.

But most high-school first basemen, by definition, have "old players' skills." It's a well-established point of baseball analysis that players with old players' skills—players who take 'n' rake but lack speed or defensive aptitude—peak earlier and decline faster than other players. An 18-year-old with old players' skills is generally not a winning combination. (The picture is very different at the college level. Very, very different. More on that later.)

Continuing the theme of high-school hitters at less-athletic positions, let's take a look at the comic relief that is second base:

Pos	Years	1st Rd	2nd Rd	3rd Rd	Overall
HS 2B	84-91	NSS	-58.2%*	SSS	-70.6%
HS 2B	92-99	NSS	-87.2%	-100.0%*	-89.7%
HS 2B	84-99	NSS	-79.5%	-99.4%*	-84.0%

Years	Biggest Bargains	Biggest Busts
84-91	Uhh...Alex Arias	Mike Hardge, Glen McNabb
92-99	Uhh...Brent Abernathy	Victor Rodriguez, Cleatus Davidson

If SSS stands for Small Sample Size, NSS stands for No Sample Size—no high-school second baseman was ever taken in the first round. Victor Rodriguez, the #39 pick in the 1994 draft by the Marlins, comes closest. The reason for this, and the reason why high-school second basemen make such awful draft picks, is pretty obvious. At least at the high-school level, second base is a position by exclusion. Shortstops, center fielders, catchers… these are all skill positions, and the guys who man those positions for their high-school teams are there because they're the most skilled players available. Players stationed at first base or in the outfield corners tend to be bigger, slower guys who are drafted for their bats. Third basemen are guys with good defensive skills—the ones who are drafted high probably could have played shortstop in high school—but end up at third base, in all probability, because they're considered "too big" to man shortstop.

Second basemen? The skills required to play second base are the exact same skills required to play shortstop, so if you're playing second base, it's because there's someone else on your team that can play shortstop better than you. If you're not the best shortstop on your high-school team, then unless you played with Alex Rodriguez, that's a pretty good sign that you don't have the skills to make it to the major leagues.

That is exactly what the data says. Twenty-seven high-school second basemen were drafted in the first three rounds from 1984 to 1999; Alex Arias and Brent Abernathy are the only two to have exceeded their expected value. As a group, they returned just 16 cents on the dollar, easily the worst value of any class and position.

Compare that with their partners across the diamond:

Pos	Years	1st Rd	2nd Rd	3rd Rd	Overall
HS SS	84-91	+21.1%	-88.5%	-94.6%	-0.3%
HS SS	92-99	-7.4%	-41.2%	SSS	-16.3%
HS SS	84-99	+9.9%	-64.5%	-95.8%	-6.7%

Years	Biggest Bargains	Biggest Busts
84-91	Travis Fryman, Gregg Jefferies	Patrick Lennon, Austin Manahan
92-99	Alex Rodriguez, Derek Jeter	Matt Brunson, Mark Farris

Relative to other high-school position players, shortstops have been a pretty good value. Obviously, the inclusion of Rodriguez and Derek Jeter has a strong impact on the numbers, but that's just it: there are superstars to be had out there. It makes sense that as high-school teams are wont to put their best overall athletes at shortstop, guys drafted from that position have more ways to make it—with their bats (Gregg Jefferies, Gary Sheffield), their gloves (Royce Clayton, Pokey Reese), or in the case of Rodriguez, both.

Two interesting things come out of the data. One is the fact that in the 1980s, the best high-school shortstops almost all found success at points much further south on the defensive spectrum. Travis Fryman made it as a shortstop but found most of his success at third base. In retrospect, it's borderline astonishing that Jefferies played shortstop in the minors and Sheffield played 94 games there for the Brewers in 1988-89. Chipper Jones, like Sheffield, also quickly slid from shortstop to third base, then made a much slower transition to the outfield. Jay Bell was the only draft success from this period to spend most of his career at shortstop.

The best high-school shortstops of the '90s, on the other hand, tended to stay at the position—Rodriguez, Jeter, Jimmy Rollins and Reese. (The other high-school shortstop from this era who found success? Michael Barrett.) It may just be a sample-size fluke, but I thought it was interesting.

The other interesting piece of data is that almost all of the success garnered by high-school shortstops comes from the first round. Second- and third-round draft picks were almost uniformly awful. Forty-two high-school shortstops were selected from the #31 pick on in our study; Rollins was the only one who exceeded his expected value by even half a (discounted) win. Most of the success was clustered not just in the first round, but in the first 10 picks. Seven high-school shortstops have been taken in the first six picks of the draft. Five of them are Rodriguez, Jeter, Sheffield, Jones, and Dmitri Young. Corey Myers was inexplicably taken with the #4 overall pick by the Diamondbacks in 1999, a pick that was mocked openly at the time. The only real bust was Mark Lewis, whom the Indians selected #2 overall in 1988.

All of the sample sizes are small when we break down the draft by position, so I don't want to read too much into the data. But it appears that while it's a good idea to invest in a high-school shortstop if he's a truly elite prospect, getting the third- or fourth-best high school shortstop available is usually a losing proposition.

Pos	Years	1st Rd	2nd Rd	3rd Rd	Overall
HS 3B	84-91	SSS	-26.3%*	-100.0%*	-67.3%
HS 3B	92-99	-20.8%*	+266.0%*	-72.4%	+31.1%
HS 3B	84-99	-34.5%	+114.3%	-86.6%	-1.7%

Years	Bargains	Busts
84-91	Scott Cooper, Dave Hansen	Greg David, Gordon Powell
92-99	Scott Rolen, Eric Chavez	Josh Booty, Kevin Witt

In the 1980s, high-school third basemen were nearly as bad a gamble as high-school catchers—Scott Cooper and Dave Hansen were the only two high-school third basemen (out of 15) who even reached the majors. As with catchers, third basemen taken in the 1990s have provided a much healthier return. That's almost entirely the work of Scott Rolen and Eric Chavez. Brad Fullmer is the only other draftee to return more than a discounted win above expectations. In a sample size of just 27 players, two potential Hall of Famers can have an enormous impact on the rate of return.

The difference between the two eras is probably just noise, but contemplating Rolen and Chavez —and David Wright, a 2001 draftee who fits the same profile—I wonder if the increased rate of return is a function of high-school teams making third basemen out of guys who might have played shortstop in an earlier era. Certainly, judging from their defensive prowess in the majors, all three could have easily played shortstop in high school. When deciding whether to draft a third baseman out of high school, that question—"could he have played shortstop?"—seems like a good litmus test.

Pos	Years	1st Rd	2nd Rd	3rd Rd	Overall
HS OF	84-91	-15.3%	-68.7%	-40.3%	-31.2%
HS OF	92-99	-44.6%	+19.2%	-82.0%	-31.8%
HS OF	84-99	-26.9%	-31.6%	-55.7%	-31.4%

Years	Bargains	Busts
84-91	Ken Griffey Jr, Manny Ramirez	Mark Merchant, Jeff Jackson
92-99	Carlos Beltran, Johnny Damon	McKay Christensen, Jaime Jones

There's precious little to say here. Outfielders rank around the middle of the pack among high-school hitters, and there's little variation in the data across years or rounds. It would be nice if we could break down outfielders by where they played, but the data we have is very inconsistent about listing a specific outfield position for each player. I find it personally interesting that the two best draft picks from 1992 to 1999 were made by the Royals; finding toolsy outfielders is apparently one of the team's only strengths. Then again, they also made first-round picks out of Juan LeBron and Dee Brown...

Let's run a chart ranking high-school hitters by their overall value from 1984 to 1999, and again just for the 1992-99 period.

In essence: left side of infield is good. Right side of infield is very, very bad. And high-school catchers, relative to other high-school hitters, are a much better value than conventional wisdom suggests.

1984 - 1999		1992 - 1999	
Pos	Overall	Pos	Overall
HS 3B	-1.7%	HS 3B	+31.1%
HS SS	-6.7%	HS C	+17.2%
HS OF	-31.4%	HS SS	-16.3%
HS C	-41.5%	HS OF	-31.8%
HS 1B	-54.5%	HS 1B	-52.9%
HS 2B	-84.0%	HS 2B	-89.7%

We'll look at a breakdown of college hitters next time.

DOCTORING THE NUMBERS
The Draft, Part Eight
Rany Jazayerli

After coming up with some positional guidelines for drafting high school hitters, Rany Jazayerli turned to comparing college picks by position.

Before we pick up the draft study where we left off, let's make a deal: I'll agree not to bring up the fact that it's been six months since Part Seven if you do. Deal.

Last time, we looked at the relative merits of high-school players by position, ending with this chart.

	1984 - 1999		1992 - 1999
Pos	Overall	Pos	Overall
HS 3B	-1.7%	HS 3B	+31.1%
HS SS	-6.7%	HS C	+17.2%
HS OF	-31.4%	HS SS	-16.3%
HS C	-41.5%	HS OF	-31.8%
HS 1B	-54.5%	HS 1B	-52.9%
HS 2B	-84.0%	HS 2B	-89.7%

Generally speaking, players on the left side of the infield graded out best, players on the right side of the infield were (by far) the worst picks, and guys in the middle—outfielders and catchers—stayed in the middle in terms of their draft returns. The most surprising finding may have been the fact that, at least in the 1990s, high-school catchers were better-than-average risks among prep talent, belying their reputation as the riskiest of draft picks.

Now for the analysis of college position players, where the calculus is significantly different.

Pos	Years	1st Rd	2nd Rd	3rd Rd	Overall
COL C	84-91	-10.9%	+6.1%	+99.2%*	+1.1%
COL C	92-99	SSS	-10.5%*	+63.9%*	+88.0%
COL C	84-99	+18.1%	+1.5%	+83.6%	+18.9%

Years	Biggest Bargains	Biggest Busts
84-91	Craig Biggio, Mike MacFarlane	Bob Caffrey, Scott Hemond
92-99	Charles Johnson, Jason Varitek	Tommy Davis, Sammy Serrano

Much like their high-school counterparts, collegiate catchers improved their relative value significantly from the first half of the study to the second. Craig Biggio may be a Hall of Famer, but the quality falls off quickly—Kirt Manwaring was the third-best draftee of that era. Still, a large number of draftees enjoyed long, if not particularly distinguished, careers, including Dan Wilson (the only college catcher in the whole study who was a top-10 draft pick), Jorge Fabregas, Scott Hatteberg, Brent Mayne, and Scott Servais. Eric Wedge deserves a special mention, I suppose.

Since 1992, teams have become far more selective about picking college catchers, with far better results. There were 33 catchers taken among the top 100 picks between 1984 and 1991; that number dropped to just 16 between 1992 and 1999. Only two college catchers were taken in the first 40 picks—Charles Johnson and Jason Varitek, the two biggest bargains of the era. You can question the data here if you want—Brandon Inge is categorized as a catcher, but he had minimal experience at the position until the Tigers drafted him and put him behind the plate. I guess you could argue that Matt LeCroy has yet to play the position. But that would be cruel.

Pos	Years	1st Rd	2nd Rd	3rd Rd	Overall
COL 1B	84-91	+162.9%*	+49.1%*	+573.2%*	+174.3%
COL 1B	92-99	+104.7%*	SSS	-78.3%*	+87.1%
COL 1B	84-99	+144.2%	+97.0%*	+204.8%	+144.3%

Years	Biggest Bargains	Biggest Busts
84-91	See below	Dave McCarty, Joe Vitiello
92-99	See below	Eric Munson, Danny Peoples

I was at first reluctant to break down the draft by individual positions, thinking that the sample sizes might be so small as to render the data meaningless. But the chart above single-handedly justifies it. Hell, it justifies the whole draft study. If there's one piece of advice for GMs to take away from this entire study, it's this: college first basemen make GREAT draft picks.

Between 1984 and 1991, nine college first basemen were drafted in the first round. Two of them rank as the biggest busts in this era, Dave McCarty and Joe Vitiello. Scott Stahoviak was the Doug Mientkiewicz of his day, a great defensive first baseman (he played 41 games at third base in the majors, with an average fielding rating according to our DTs) who could get on base but had no pop and was finished at age 28.

The other six players, in increasing order of draft value: Tino Martinez, Mo Vaughn, Mark McGwire, Rafael Palmeiro, Will Clark, and Frank Thomas.

It's a very small sample size, but if you were drafting a first baseman out of college in the first round, you had a two-in-three chance of drafting a perennial All-Star, and a four-in-nine chance of drafting a Hall of Famer or near-HoFer. Throw in John Olerud, who was a third-round pick because no one thought he was signable, and your odds of getting a star/superstar player out of the first round was 50-50.

The returns on first basemen dropped in the 90s, but they still ranked as one of the most underpriced commodities in the draft. Only 15 college first basemen were selected in the top 100 picks from 1992 to 1999, but they included Todd Helton, Lance Berkman, Sean Casey, and Carlos Pena. Helton and Berkman were both first-round picks, along with Pena and three washouts (Peoples, Munson—who was really more of a catcher in college—and Jeff Liefer). Taken as a whole there were 15 college first-rounders from 1984 to 1999, 16 if you count Olerud. If you ignore the voting implications of steroid or alleged steroid use, five of those 16 are likely Hall of Famers, three more (Vaughn, Olerud, Clark) had a case for being the best first baseman in the game at some point in time, and three more (Martinez, Casey, Pena) were average or above-average first basemen in their prime.

That's a hell of a return.

Because the sample size was so small—only 35 first basemen in the whole study—I decided to take a look at the first basemen drafted in the last five years to see whether the trend shows signs of holding up or not. Here are the first basemen taken in the top 100 picks between 2000 and 2005:

2000: None
2001: None (well, unless you count John Van Benschoten, Pittsburgh, #8)
2002: Larry Broadway, Montreal, #77; David Jensen, Kansas City, #78
2003: Michael Aubrey, Cleveland, #11; Vince Sinisi, Texas, #46
2004: Mike Ferris, St. Louis, #60; Adam Lind, Toronto, #82
2005: Stephen Head, Cleveland, #62

Gee, that wasn't very useful. In the last six years, only seven college first basemen have gone in the top 100 picks, and only one—Michael Aubrey—went in the first round. Aubrey's career got off on the right track—he was our #17 prospect a year ago—but he threw out his back last season, which is among the worst chronic injuries you can have if you're a first baseman.

Actually, there is one college first baseman who was selected even higher than Aubrey in the last six years. Unfortunately, the Pirates chose to send John Van Benschoten to the mound, even though the consensus throughout baseball was that he was a better hitting prospect than pitching prospect. Given the returns on college first basemen in the first round, you could argue that the Pirates made one of the most foolish draft-day decisions of all time. Especially now that it's his shoulder that's benschoten. (Thank you. I'll be here all week.)

Why have college first basemen proven to be such great investments, when their high-school counterparts have been among the worst investments? I think it has to do with two things:

1. A player who mans first base in high school is, almost by definition, unathletic. The increased quality of competition at the college level, particularly the elite conferences, means that it is possible to be quite athletic and still be "relegated" to playing first base.
2. Even the best high-school first basemen still require several years of refinement before they're ready for the majors, years in which their lack of athleticism inhibits their development. The best college first basemen, on the other hand, are essentially ready for the majors on draft day.

Of all the high-school first basemen in our study, the one who probably had the most initial success as a pro was Jack Cust, who hit .334/.452/.651 as 20-year-old in the California League. Cust's downfall has been the fact that he has not improved one whit as a player since he was 20. (This does not bode well for Prince Fielder, incidentally.)

Contrast Cust with Will Clark, the highest-drafted college first baseman (#2 overall) in our study. Clark was considerably more athletic than Cust, capable of winning a Gold Glove at the position and a good baserunner, if not a good basestealer. Moreover, he needed all of 71 minor-league games before he was called to The Show; he was one of the best first basemen in the game two years after he was drafted.

To put it succinctly: college first basemen are not only considerably further along in their offensive development than high-school first baseman, but they are considerably more athletic as well, giving them more potential for improvement after they have signed. The ones who are not athletic, like Thomas or Vaughn, are such prodigious mashers that it really doesn't make any difference. Yeah, it's a shame that Frank Thomas essentially reached his peak as a 22-year-old rookie. But a 22-year-old rookie with a .345 EqA needs no improvement to produce a Hall of Fame career.

Mind you, the first baseman that mashes the ball so thoroughly in college that he's considered worthy of a first-round pick despite his limited positional value is rare indeed; in recent years, at least, no such player existed. The best college hitters in recent years have also had the athleticism to play other positions, such as third base (Mark Teixeira and Alex Gordon), shortstop (Stephen Drew), or even second base (Rickie Weeks).

This year's draft, which is considered to be particularly weak in college hitters, may be no different. But keep your eye on Matt LaPorta, who plays first base at Florida and whom *Baseball America* states "is the draft's premier college power hitter." If history is any guide, he's going to make the team that selects him very happy indeed.

Pos	Years	1st Rd	2nd Rd	3rd Rd	Overall
COL 2B	84-91	SSS	-80.0%*	SSS	+30.4%
COL 2B	92-99	SSS	+44.2%*	SSS	+55.6%
COL 2B	84-99	+91.0%*	-21.5%	-69.6%	+41.0%

Years	Biggest Bargains	Biggest Busts
84-91	Chuck Knoblauch, Luis Alicea	Ty Griffin, Mike Watters
92-99	Adam Kennedy, Marlon Anderson	Charles Abbott, Dan Cey

The story at second base is the story at first base, writ small. Just like first basemen, second basemen drafted out of college make excellent investments even though their high-school counterparts have had the absolute worst returns of any position.

The reasoning is similar. Whereas playing second base at the high-school level is a major red flag—how good a prospect can you be if you're not even the best middle infielder on your high-school team?—that stigma is not there at the college level, where the standards are much higher. And as with first basemen, second basemen at the college level have had three additional years to develop their batting skills, which is relevant because most second basemen are drafted as offense-first players. (This makes sense; if these guys were considered great defensive second basemen, they would have been playing at shortstop.)

Yes, Chuck Knoblauch won a Gold Glove at second base, but 1) he wasn't considered a great defensive player coming out of college, and 2) according to our defensive metrics, he was a below-average player defensively for the bulk of his career. Of the other guys above, only Adam Kennedy has a strong defensive reputation. (And the two other players who have provided the most returns are legendary iron gloves Mark Bellhorn and Todd Walker.) If you're drafting a collegiate second baseman with a high draft pick, you're probably drafting him because you think he can hit well enough to carry his glove—and by and large, that has been a wise and successful strategy. (Cub fans are permitted to disagree; I think Will Carroll is still holding out hope that Ty Griffin can make a comeback. And bring Gary Scott back with him.)

As at the high-school level, relatively few second basemen in college make for elite draft picks—only 21 players were selected in the 16 years of our study. Let's look at the years from 2000 to 2005 again; this time, there's some useful insight to be gleaned here:

2000: Chase Utley, Philadelphia, #15; Dominic Rich, Toronto, #58
2001: Chris Burke, Houston, #10; Mike Fontenot, Baltimore, #19; Michael Woods, Detroit, #32; Richard Lewis, Atlanta, #40
2002: None
2003: Rickie Weeks, Milwaukee, #2; Tim Moss, Philadelphia, #85
2004: None
2005: Jed Lowrie, Boston, #45

That's a pretty impressive list. Not only has Chase Utley emerged as an elite player, but he did so coming out of the 2000 draft that ranks as probably the weakest draft in the last 25 years. (The only other established major leaguer out of the first round that year is Rocco Baldelli.) Rickie Weeks, by far the highest-drafted second baseman ever, is a trendy breakout pick this year. Chris Burke—who is listed in the *Baseball America* database as a 2B/SS in college—was a disappointment last season after being touted as a Rookie of the Year candidate, but there's still time.

These recent draft picks confirm the notion that collegiate second basemen are drafted for their bats—none of these guys was considered a stellar glove man in college. Interestingly, most of them have stayed at second base as pros; having already spent a draft pick on the players, the teams that drafted them have already accepted the fact that their defense is going to be a liability, and are not as eager to move them down the defensive spectrum as you might expect.

The other thing that stands out is that almost every one of these draft picks, even failed picks like Woods and Lewis, possess secondary skills in abundance. For the most part, none of them hit for a good average, but they all draw a bunch of walks, and most of them have above-average power and speed. I don't know if it's a coincidence or a reflection of the type of player that teams are looking for at the position.

This year, there may not be a college second baseman drafted in the first 100 picks; the top-rated player, Adam Davis, is ranked by *Baseball America* as the 32nd-best college hitter available. Coincidentally, Davis is teammates with Matt LaPorta at Florida. He definitely fits the mold—he hit only .306 as a sophomore, but with 12 homers in 294 AB (despite checking in at 5'9"), 40 walks, and 24 steals.

Back next week—I promise—with the rest of the college hitters.

DOCTORING THE NUMBERS
The Draft, Part Nine
Rany Jazayerli

Wrapping up his study of college draft picks by position, Rany Jazayerli found that the positions to target and avoid among collegiate players are much different than they are among high-school players.

Two quick things before we move on with the rest of the college position players:

1. After giving it more thought, I have decided that in the case of a player who played one position in college but was immediately moved to another position as a pro—like Eric Munson, who was a collegiate catcher but a first baseman as a pro, or Brandon Inge, who was drafted as a catcher even though he had only played shortstop in college—the player should be classified according to his collegiate position. Even if he didn't play there professionally, it is on campus that a player is evaluated for the draft, and it stands to reason that we should evaluate the merits of a draft pick based on the position he plays when he is being evaluated for the draft.

   So I've gone back and re-run the numbers, moving Munson and Inge to their appropriate positions. This has the impact of making college first basemen look even better—Munson was one of the few first-round busts—while making college catchers look a little worse, as they are now saddled with Munson while losing Inge, who has produced good value after a shaky start. At the end of this piece we'll run the numbers for every position; just be aware that the numbers at catcher and first base differ from those presented in Part Eight.

2. I wrote last week that the top-rated collegiate second baseman was Adam Davis at the University of Florida. An intrepid reader checked and found that Davis has played exclusively shortstop for the Gators this season after playing mostly second base in 2005.

Speaking of shortstops...

Pos	Years	1st Rd	2nd Rd	3rd Rd	Overall
COL SS	84-91	+51.5%*	+16.2%	-79.3%*	+34.5%
COL SS	92-99	+17.6%*	+41.5%*	SSS	+45.1%
COL SS	84-99	+39.9%	+22.7%	+54.3%	+37.9%

Years	Biggest Bargains	Biggest Busts
84-91	Barry Larkin, Matt Williams	Monty Fariss, Gary Green
92-99	Nomar Garciaparra, Chris Gomez	Jason Dellaero, Brandon Larson

Nothing really pithy to say here; college shortstops are a good bet overall but pretty much in the middle of the pack as far as college hitters go. The nice thing about this position is that you have a lot of positional leeway if your draftee can't handle shortstop as a pro. While a few draft picks have the leather to carry a sub-optimal bat (Walt Weiss, Adam Everett), far more college shortstops have major-league bats but are forced to move down the defensive spectrum pretty quickly. Some still have the glove to shine at another key position, like second base (Brian Roberts, Alex Cora) or third base (Matt Williams). Others make you wonder how they ever played shortstop in the first place (Cory Snyder, Michael Tucker). If you draft the guy who can do both, as with Barry Larkin or an early-career Nomar Garciaparra, you've hit the jackpot.

The positional flexibility of shortstops stands in stark contrast to catchers, who with rare exceptions move to either first base—where the offensive demands are much greater—or third base, where the defensive demands are such that if you can't hack it behind the plate (and if you're being considered for a position switch, it's because of your defense), you probably aren't going to be a stud at the hot corner either. Think Todd Zeile.

The interesting case here is Inge, who was a shortstop in college and was made a catcher immediately after signing. Inge actually took to his new position extremely well, but his bat never came around, and it was only after he moved to third base that his offense perked up to the point where he has become a valuable player. If the Tigers had cut out the middleman and just moved him to third base from the start, he might have developed quicker.

Pos	Years	1st Rd	2nd Rd	3rd Rd	Overall
COL 3B	84-91	+5.1%*	-57.0%*	+133.1%*	+4.1%
COL 3B	92-99	+13.4%*	+171.3%*	SSS	+55.2%
COL 3B	84-99	+8.7%	+20.9%	+186.4%*	+24.4%

Years	Biggest Bargains	Biggest Busts
84-91	Robin Ventura, Ken Caminiti	Tim Costo, Stan Royer
92-99	Jason Giambi, Aaron Boone	Antone Williamson, Gabe Alvarez

Troy Glaus and Pat Burrell would almost certainly surpass Aaron Boone on the list of recent bargains if 2005 data were included. Like catcher, third base is a position whose return on investment has increased markedly over the years. While Ventura and Caminiti were great draft picks, the return on third basemen from the 1980s was hit hard by five first-round busts from 1987-91. In chronological order: Chris Donnels, Royer, Eddie Zosky, Costo, and Eduardo Perez.

Only 12 college third basemen were selected in the top 100 from 1992 to 1999, but the dozen included Giambi, Boone, Glaus, and Burrell. Phil Nevin was a #1 overall selection who has almost earned his expected value, but with a career arc so delayed that the Astros received essentially nothing for him. As at second base and first base, the key to success at the hot corner seems to be to draft for the bat, and if the glove is a plus, that's a bonus. So while Ryan Zimmerman got off to a great start, chances are Alex Gordon will still prove to be the more valuable draft pick.

Pos	Years	1st Rd	2nd Rd	3rd Rd	Overall
COL OF	84-91	-0.3%	+103.7%	+168.9%	+31.0%
COL OF	92-99	-12.8%	+34.0%	-44.8%	-5.3%
COL OF	84-99	-6.4%	+60.3%	+75.5%	+12.5%

Years	Biggest Bargains	Biggest Busts
84-91	Barry Bonds, Marquis Grissom	Donald Harris, Mike Kelly
92-99	J.D. Drew, Mark Kotsay	Chad Mottola, Chad Green

The "bargains" only scrape the tip of the iceberg; other guys drafted from 1984 to 1991 include Albert Belle, Tim Salmon, and Luis Gonzalez. From 1992 on, you can add Darin Erstad, Jacque Jones, and Brad Wilkerson to the list. It's interesting that the system tabs J.D. Drew as the best draft pick among college outfielders in the 1990s, given that a half-dozen teams passed on him in the draft solely because of his contract demands.

But the only reason there are so many bargains is that there are so many draft picks from the outfield ranks—outfielders have actually returned less value than any other college position. The four busts listed above give you a pretty strong clue as to why: while Chad Mottola was a well-regarded hitter who didn't hit, the other three were legendary tools guys who never converted their tools into production. Harris and Green in particular weren't impressive hitters in college, and more than a few heads were scratched when they were each drafted in the top 10.

Other college tools goofs who famously washed out as pros include Calvin Murray, the #7 overall pick in 1992; Ken Felder, the #12 pick the same year; Dante Powell (#22 in 1994). Shea Morenz (#27 in 1995). Keith Reed (#33 in 1999). And, of course, Jason Tyner (#21 in 1998). That's just a sampling. There have been a LOT of draft picks, particularly high first-rounders, that have been wasted on college outfielders. Chris Gwynn. Steve Hosey. Someone stop me...

The converse side of that is that the best draft picks out of college have been the guys who were already elite hitters; by and large, they didn't need a whole lot of projection to see them as quality major-league hitters. No one was complaining about Barry Bonds' performance at Arizona State, or Albert Belle back when he was still known as Joey. Mark Kotsay's performance at Cal State-Fullerton was so impressive that he ended up being drafted #9 overall even though scouts were extremely lukewarm on his skills. Geoff Jenkins was a world-class masher at USC, and to this day Pete Incaviglia is one of the most legendary power hitters in NCAA history.

Not to belabor the point, but it's an important one to make: among college hitters, performance matters. The ability to hit against a strong level of collegiate competition is a very good indicator of one's ability to hit and be successful as a pro. The player whose tools have not translated into production at the college level is unlikely to learn how to turn the trick later on in life. Historically, most of the college players who have been drafted high on the basis of their "tools" have been outfielders, and not surprisingly, outfielders have provided the least return on investment among all college hitters.

At the high-school level, outfielders are pretty middle-of-the-pack in terms of value. This gets to the heart of the Scouts vs. Stats issue: you can't weigh scouting vs. statistical comparisons the same with an 18-year-old that you would with a 21-year-old. An 18-year-old who has tremendous athletic gifts but a questionable bat can reasonably be expected to learn how to hit as he matures. (Though it's still a gamble; hello, Reggie Taylor.) If you're still expecting a player to convert his tools into hitting ability when he's 21, you're just setting yourself up for disappointment.

The preseason favorite to be the first college hitter selected this year, Drew Stubbs from the University of Texas, may fit this profile. He has world-class speed and is considered a potential Gold Glover, but as one scouting director told *Baseball America*, "Stubbs can't hit. He never could hit, and he never will hit." While his .338/.449/.563 line to date is nothing to be ashamed of, neither is it the line of a player who is likely to go in the top half of the first round. (Especially since it's still an improvement over his .311/.384/.527 line as a sophomore.)

To sum up—here's a chart comparing the relative values of college hitters. Overall, this is a very different picture from the one we saw with high-school hitters. At the high-school level, you want to avoid first and second basemen like the plague; at the college level, they are the two most fruitful positions to draft from. High-school outfielders are a reasonable risk overall, but at the college level they are clearly the riskiest position to draft from. Back soon with a look at pitchers.

1984 - 1999		1992 - 1999	
Pos	Overall	Pos	Overall
COL 1B	+155.3%	COL 1B	+113.1%
COL 2B	+41.0%	COL 2B	+55.6%
COL SS	+37.9%	COL 3B	+55.2%
COL 3B	+24.4%	COL C	+49.8%
COL C	+12.5%	COL SS	+45.1%
COL OF	+12.5%	COL OF	-5.3%

DOCTORING THE NUMBERS
The Draft, Part Ten
Rany Jazayerli

In the 10th installment of his draft study, Rany Jazayerli found that hard-and-fast rules about drafting pitchers are difficult to identify.

We complete our tour of the diamond with a stop at the mound, where we'll compare left-handers to right-handers and starters to relievers and see what the data shows.

Pos	Years	1st Rd	2nd Rd	3rd Rd	Overall
COL LHP	84-91	-4.4%	+54.7%	+133.4%	+21.5%
COL LHP	92-99	-7.3%	+61.1%	+15.0%	+8.0%
COL LHP	84-99	-5.8%	+57.8%	+82.4%	+15.2%

```
Years      Biggest Bargains            Biggest Busts
84-91      Jim Abbott, Greg Swindell   Drew Hall, Kyle Abbott
92-99      Barry Zito, Randy Wolf      B.J. Wallace, Jeff Granger
```

Note that the two most valuable draft picks from 1984 to 1991 are not Randy Johnson, who was third on the list. Johnson is a future Hall of Famer, but was not a full-time starting pitcher in the major leagues until four years after he was drafted, and didn't become RANDY JOHNSON until 1993. And of course, along the way he was traded by the team that drafted him, the Montreal Expos, essentially for four months of Mark Langston. The point bears repeating: the sooner a draft pick renders his value, the less likely the team that drafted him will have already given him up for pennies on the dollar.

By way of comparison, Jim Abbott had his last good year at age 27 but returned instantaneous value to the Angels. Abbott signed too late to pitch in his draft year of 1988, then made the Angels' rotation the following spring without any minor-league experience and won 12 games, the most major-league wins of any pitcher in his first pro season in nearly a century.

In consecutive years, the A's made the best draft selection on a college left-hander (Barry Zito in 1999) and the third-best selection (Mark Mulder in 1998). Drafting wisely is still the best way to arbitrage talent.

Overall, college left-handers have yielded good value in both eras, although the value seems to be far more concentrated in the second and third rounds. Whether this is signal or noise is debatable. A quick perusal of college southpaws taken in the first round reveal quite a few guys who were selected because they could throw hard but didn't particularly know how to pitch (Wallace, Granger, Hall). Ryan Mills blew out his arm almost from the moment he signed. Some of the second- and third-rounders who panned out were guys who didn't throw all that hard but changed speeds and pitched to spots, like Denny Neagle, Jarrod Washburn, and Mike Maroth. On the other hand, Johnson threw harder than anyone, and he wasn't picked until the #36 overall selection.

Pos	Years	1st Rd	2nd Rd	3rd Rd	Overall
COL RHP	84-91	+27.4%	+52.3%	+21.2%	+32.0%
COL RHP	92-99	-23.9%	-1.7%	-55.2%	-22.5%
COL RHP	84-99	+0.9%	+26.1%	-13.4%	+4.5%

Years	Biggest Bargains	Biggest Busts
84-91	Mike Mussina, Jack McDowell	Bill Bene, Pat Pacillo
92-99	Jeff Weaver, Jon Lieber	Steve Soderstrom, Pete Janicki

That's the long-forgotten third wheel in the Alternatively Spelled William Beans, the one who is neither in the A's front office nor out of the closet. David Schoenfield ranked Bene #53 on his list of the worst draft picks in sports history.

Bene ranks among the two or three wildest minor-league pitchers of the last 25 years. In 1989, his first full pro season, Bene had 18 walks in 27 innings. No, wait—he had 18 wild pitches in 27 innings; he walked 56 batters. In 445 career minor-league innings, Bene walked 489 batters, hit 31, and threw 140 to the backstop. His main competition for wildest first-round draft pick ever would probably be Jacob Shumate, the Braves' first-round pick out of high school in 1994, who walked 265 batters in 211 innings before retiring. (Jason Neighborgall, selected by the Diamondbacks last year, could one day surpass both of them—he walked 113 batters in 101 college innings, then got his pro career off to a rousing start with 45 walks and 23 wild pitches in 23 innings. But at least Neighborgall was a third-rounder.)

There isn't much of a trend here. The four bargains listed above were successful college pitchers who were known more for their polish than their pure stuff, but you can easily come up with just as many exceptions to that rule. In 1995, the first college right-hander taken was Jonathan Johnson, a highly polished pitcher from Florida State who barely sniffed the majors after Texas took him with the #7 pick. The Cardinals took advantage of the Rangers' gaffe by taking a comparatively less ready starter with a better arm out of Seton Hall with the #12 pick, got him to start throwing strikes, and ended up with Matt Morris. And while he's outside the scope of our study, Justin Verlander was a so-so college pitcher at Old Dominion despite electric stuff, and the

Tigers wisely calculated that they could translate his stuff into results as a pro.

Pos	Years	1st Rd	2nd Rd	3rd Rd	Overall
HS LHP	84-91	-36.6%	+135.3%	+90.5%	+14.7%
HS LHP	92-99	-48.6%	-72.0%	-3.0%	-45.2%
HS LHP	84-99	-40.4%	+55.0%	+21.3%	-8.4%

Years	Biggest Bargains	Biggest Busts
84-91	Tom Glavine, Justin Thompson	Brien Taylor, Chris Myers
92-99	C.C. Sabathia, Jeremy Affeldt	Doug Million, Geoff Goetz

I wouldn't have guessed that Justin Thompson would rank as highly as he did, but he reached the majors quickly and had a pair of very good seasons at the height of the offensive explosion—his 3.02 ERA in 1997 was worth nearly nine WARP. Steve Avery ranks ahead of him in terms of overall value but was the #3 overall pick compared to Thompson's #32, so more was expected.

High-school left-handers from the 1980s are almost shockingly successful, coming in the era that gave high-school pitchers a bad name. As you can see, the value of high-school southpaws plunged dramatically in the 1990s, for reasons that are unclear.

And yes, that's Jeremy Affeldt on the list of bargains. If you think listing Affeldt second is bad, consider that fourth on the list of bargains from that era is Jimmy Gobble. And Chris George is fifth. Swear to God. (Rick Ankiel is third.)

Doug Million is excused from approbation; for those of you not familiar with him, he died from an asthmatic attack during Instructional League in 1997, a story which is as tragic and unfathomable now as it was then.

Pos	Years	1st Rd	2nd Rd	3rd Rd	Overall
HS RHP	84-91	-64.0%	-40.1%	-58.4%	-55.6%
HS RHP	92-99	-7.1%	+1.3%	-17.1%	-6.4%
HS RHP	84-99	-34.9%	-21.4%	-32.7%	-30.7%

Years	Biggest Bargains	Biggest Busts
84-91	Greg Maddux, Roger Pavlik	Kurt Miller, Roger Salkeld
92-99	Jeff Suppan, Roy Halladay	Kirk Presley, Matt Drews

Yes, Roger Pavlik. Of 86 high-school pitchers taken between 1984 and 1991, a total of nine of them rendered positive value. Here's all you need to know: of those 86 pitchers, Todd Van Poppel ranked 11th. That means that nearly 90 percent of high school right-handers taken from 1984 to 1991 were worse draft picks than Todd. Van. Poppel.

It is not a stretch to say that over an eight-year span, Greg Maddux was the only high-school right-hander taken in the first three rounds that fulfilled the expectations placed on him on Draft Day.

As we've documented before, high-school pitchers were much better values after 1991. As with college right-handers, there does not seem to be a trend towards or away from "stuff" pitchers. Jeff Suppan was about as polished a high-school right-hander as you'll ever find; he was in the majors at age 20, and while it took a few years for him to stick, by age 24 he was a decent #3/#4 starter—and he really hasn't improved a whit since then. Roy Halladay, on the other hand, was a scouts' favorite despite terrible strikeout-to-walk ratios in the minors, crashed and burned in 2000, then had his motion completely rebuilt in one of the most impressive reconstructions of a pitcher ever. Among the 10 best picks from this era are Kerry Wood and Matt Clement, as well as Jon Garland and Brian Meadows.

A look at the failures isn't any more instructive; some of the guys weren't particularly good to begin with, and most of them got hurt along the way.

So what can we take from this?

1984 - 1999		1992 - 1999	
Pos	Overall	Pos	Overall
COL LHP	+15.2%	COL LHP	+8.0%
COL RHP	+4.5%	HS RHP	-6.4%
HS LHP	-8.4%	COL RHP	-22.5%
HS RHP	-30.7%	HS LHP	-45.2%

From 1984 to 1999 as a whole, there is a small but clear trend favoring left-handed pitchers at both the college and high-school ranks. That trend disappears into complete randomness if we just focus on pitchers since 1992, albeit in a smaller sample size. If we break things down by round, the data gets a little more interesting—and a little more confusing.

First Round

In the first round, at least, it looks like right-handers have a small advantage for the data as a whole, although in the 1990s the edge only holds at the high-school ranks.

1984 - 1999		1992 - 1999	
Pos	Overall	Pos	Overall
COL RHP	+0.9%	HS RHP	-7.1%
COL LHP	-5.8%	COL LHP	-7.3%
HS RHP	-34.9%	COL RHP	-23.9%
HS LHP	-40.4%	HS LHP	-48.6%

Second and Third Round

1984 - 1999		1992 - 1999	
Pos	Overall	Pos	Overall
COL LHP	+66.5%	COL LHP	+45.9%
HS LHP	+45.1%	HS RHP	-5.5%
COL RHP	+12.7%	COL RHP	-19.0%
HS RHP	-24.8%	HS LHP	-41.5%

After the first 30 picks, left-handers have an enormous advantage over the course of the entire study, but again, the trend doesn't hold in the 1990s, as high-school right-handers gain the upper hand.

I'm leery of coming to any conclusions based on data that is this inconsistent, but I'll try to make inappropriate inferences anyway. At the college level, left-handed pitchers have a persistent edge over right-handers, an edge which primarily manifests itself after the first round. It could be that once teams have gone through the elite collegiate pitchers, they start looking for pitchers who "know how to pitch" despite the lack of top-shelf stuff. As it is far easier for a left-hander to succeed in the majors with average velocity, a left-hander who has a strong collegiate track record and makes the most of his 87-mph fastball is far more likely to maintain that success in the pros than his right-handed counterpart. Washburn was a second-round pick in 1995. Maroth went in the third round in 1998, as did Scott Schoeneweis two years earlier.

At the high-school level, I'm reluctant to make any generalizations, for the simple reason that the data swings so violently between eras: between 1984 and 1991, left-handers returned more than twice as much value as right-handers, but between 1992 and 1999 right-handers were about 80 percent more valuable. The only static data point is that right-handers have a persistent advantage in the first round. I suspect this is because at the high-school level, right-handed pitchers tend to have a lot of projection left in them, whereas left-handers are frequently drafted as relatively finished products. Even while they count as "successes" in our system, George and Gobble are good examples of high-school lefties who looked like they were ready for the majors before their 21st birthday and haven't really progressed at all since then.

This may be a case of grasping for conclusions that aren't in the numbers. If Ryan Anderson doesn't get hurt, that first-round advantage for right-handers may completely disappear. The data may be trying to tell us something, but it's not entirely clear what.

Let's see if the data can be any more articulate on the subject of relievers. For this portion of the study, we only looked at college pitchers (high-school relievers don't exactly make for high draft picks), and only since 1992. While college relievers were occasionally drafted high before that (notably Gregg Olson, who was taken #4 overall by the Orioles in 1988 and was a huge part of their "Why Not?" season the following year), it was a rarity.

Kevin Goldstein graciously did the legwork for me in coming up with the names of every Top 100 draft pick who was used in relief during his final college season. He gave me a list of 37 pitchers from 1992 to 1999. He might well have missed a few players; it's surprisingly difficult to check the day-by-day game logs for Southwest Texas State's 1997 season. And not every pitcher was drafted with the intention of being used in relief—Darren Dreifort, for instance, was used as a sort of uber-reliever his junior year at Wichita State but was certainly considered a future major-league starter when the Dodgers took him #2 overall in 1993. But it's close enough.

Pos	Years	1st Rd	2nd Rd	3rd Rd	Overall
COL R	92-99	-32.4%	+35.4%	-7.1%	-18.7%
COL S	92-99	-0.4%	+28.3%	-12.3%	+4.5%

Years	Biggest Bargains	Biggest Busts
92-99	Scott Sullivan, Mike Maroth	Rick Greene, Al Shepard

Al Shepard is one of the most mystifying first-round picks of recent times; the Orioles took him even though he had a 6.57 ERA his junior season at Nebraska. Kevin is correct when he writes that great college numbers sometimes mean nothing when it comes to a player's major-league chances, but terrible college numbers in a player with great stuff is usually a red flag that something's wrong. Speaking of things going wrong, Matt Anderson ranks third on the list of disappointments.

The data here isn't compelling one way or the other; as a whole, relievers returned value below college starters, but that's likely because 31 of the 37 relievers were right-handed. Relievers actually returned more value than college right-handers in the same era. But relievers in the first round did particularly poorly, a result which can be traced to this run of picks from 1992 to 1997:

1992: Paul Shuey, #2
1993: Darren Dreifort, #2; Wayne Gomes, #4
1996: Braden Looper, #4
1997: Matt Anderson, #1

In total, five college relievers were taken in the top four picks in a six-year span, culminating with Matt Anderson at #1. Looper has returned about 13 percent more value than expected, Dreifort and Shuey didn't reach expectations but weren't terrible, whereas Gomes and Anderson were unreserved busts. But none of these relievers ever came close to achieving the kind of dominance you would expect from a Top Five pick. It's worth noting that no reliever has been taken in the top five since.

If there is a sweet spot in the draft for relievers, it would appear to be in the late second/early third rounds. Scott Sullivan was a #62 pick; Tim Crabtree went #63; Danny Wright went #64.

The trend of teams drafting college relievers early in the draft, and the trend of college teams putting their best arms in the bullpen, has accelerated over the last decade, so these results may not be relevant. Both Chad Cordero (#20, 2003) and Huston Street (#40, 2005) figure to join Olson on the list of college relievers who went on to have sterling major-league careers. David Bush (#55, 2002) has also proven to be a wise pick, although Bush is interesting in that most teams—not just the Blue Jays—thought of him as a starter in the pros even though he came out of the bullpen in college.

Then again, Ryan Wagner (#14, 2003) and Royce Ring (#18, 2002) have been disappointments, and Bill Bray (#13, 2004) has yet to reach the majors. Craig Hansen (#26, 2005) might live up to the hype, but it's early. Joey Devine (#27, 2005) has so far demonstrated only an impressive knack for giving up grand slams and season-ending home runs.

As much as we'd like to have some hard-and-fast rules about drafting pitchers, there don't seem to be any. The best we can do is make a few suggestions. At the college level, left-handed pitchers tend to be a slightly better value than right-handers, at least in the second and third rounds. At the high-school level, right-handers tend to be slightly better values than left-handers, at least in the first round. And you better have a damn good reason to draft a reliever in the top five picks. That's about it.

Next time, we'll start tying up some loose ends by summarizing the "rules" of the draft, as well as looking at whether recent changes in draft strategies have altered the draft equation.

DOCTORING THE NUMBERS
The Draft, Part Eleven
Rany Jazayerli

In the penultimate installment of his draft study, Rany Jazayerli summarized his findings and produced a "pocket guide to the draft."

When this draft series started over a year ago (gulp), I tried to summarize my findings as handy Draft Rules, capitalized, that every team should obey. At least until it turned out that the calculus of the draft changed from the 1980s to the 1990s, and the new rules contradicted the old rules. Suddenly the Draft Rules were made to quietly disappear.

Now that we're done, it's safe to bring them out again. Starting from scratch, here is a summary of everything we've covered in the first 10 parts of this series. Consider this your pocket guide to the draft, especially if you happen to be on a conference call next Tuesday afternoon. Feel free to print out, laminate, and place in an attractive wood frame with gold trim.

> **Draft Rule #1: The greatest difference in value between consecutive draft picks is the difference between the first and second picks in a draft.**

Historically, the #1 overall pick has returned at least 40 percent more value than any other draft slot. After the first pick, the typical return on a draft pick falls four-five percent per slot until approximately the 40th pick and then drops by a little over one percent per slot until pick #100.

> **Draft Rule #2: College players are roughly 50 percent more likely to reach the major leagues than high-school players of equal draft caliber. This advantage has not changed over time.**

Among players taken in the first 100 picks between 1984 and 1991, 60 percent of college players drafted reached the majors, compared to 41 percent of high-school players. Between 1992 and 1999, college players had a roughly equal edge, 57 percent to 39 percent.

> **Draft Rule #3: In a year where there is a clear superstar talent available in the ranks of high school hitters, it is a perfectly acceptable—if not mandatory—draft strategy to select that player with the #1 overall pick.**

High-school players selected #1 overall since 1984 include Ken Griffey Jr., Chipper Jones, Alex Rodriguez, and more recently, Joe Mauer. The best college player selected #1 overall since 1984 is probably Pat Burrell, although you could make a case for B.J. Surhoff or Andy Benes.

> **Draft Rule #4: While college players returned almost exactly double the return on investment that high-school players did between 1984 and 1991, that advantage dropped dramatically, to approximately 25 percent, between 1992 and 1999.**

> **Draft Rule #5: The increase in value of high-school players relative to their college counterparts occurred even though teams were more likely to use top draft picks on high-school players in the 1990s than in the 1980s.**

The era of the mid-to-late-1980s was marked by an unusually large number of elite college players who were highly coveted as high-school players but were not signed out of the draft. The massive increase in signing bonuses which occurred in the early 1990s meant that virtually all of the top high-school players in any given year signed pro contracts, bolstering the crop of high-school signees while simultaneously depleting the college ranks. This appears to be the primary reason why college players no longer enjoy the enormous advantage they once did. The improved quality of competition for elite high-school players, who now frequently compete in tournaments against the best players from all over the country, has likely had an impact as well.

> **Draft Rule #6: The overall value of draft picks dropped about 15 percent from the 1984-1991 era to the 1992-1999 era.**

This is almost certainly a reflection of the increasing importance of talent procurement from outside the draft. The percentage of major league players who were born in the Caribbean continues to increase, and since Hideo Nomo debuted in 1995, the majors have welcomed a not-insubstantial number of players from Japan, Korea, and other countries along the Pacific Rim. A few undrafted players have even emerged from the independent leagues, although this has had a very small impact.

> **Draft Rule #7: College hitters enjoy a sizeable advantage over every other class of draft pick, in both eras, and in every round.**

Even from 1992 to 1999, collegiate hitters were anywhere from 51 percent to 62 percent more valuable than any other draft group. The gap was at least 32 percent in each of the first three rounds.

> **Draft Rule #8: There is virtually no difference in the value of the other three groups of draft picks. In particular, it is no longer apparent that high-school pitchers, even in the first round, are significantly riskier than either high-school hitters or college pitchers.**

From 1992 to 1999, pitchers out of college returned 14.6 percent less value than expected. Pitchers drafted out of high school were at -14.9 percent. High-school hitters checked in at -20.9 percent.

> **Draft Rule #9: There is no evidence either way to suggest that Junior College draft picks fare better or worse than traditional college or high-school picks.**

For the draft study as a whole, JuCo hitters were +4.6, ranking comfortably between college and high-school hitters. JuCo pitchers actually returned the highest value of any group of players at +53.9 percent, albeit in a very small sample size.

> **Draft Rule #10: The long-held bias against high-school catchers is no longer appropriate.**

While high-school catchers were terrible picks (-72 percent) from 1984 to 1991, since 1992 they actually return positive value at +17 percent, better than any other high-school position other than third base.

> **Draft Rule #11: Among high-school hitters, players on the left side of the infield are the most valuable selections, and players on the right side of the infield are—by far—the least valuable selections, with outfielders and catchers ranking in the middle.**

Here's a chart listing all high-school positions:

	1984 - 1999		1992 - 1999
Pos	Overall	Pos	Overall
HS 3B	-1.7%	HS 3B	+31.1%
HS SS	-6.7%	HS C	+17.2%
HS OF	-31.4%	HS SS	-16.3%
HS C	-41.5%	HS OF	-31.8%
HS 1B	-54.5%	HS 1B	-52.9%
HS 2B	-84.0%	HS 2B	-89.7%

Draft Rule #12: College first basemen are the most valuable group of draft picks by an enormous margin. College first basemen selected in the first round have gone on to have Hall of Fame-caliber careers approximately one-third of the time.

Over the course of the entire draft study, college first basemen have returned a ridiculous +144 percent in draft value. Thirteen first basemen were selected in the first 30 picks between 1984 and 1999, including Frank Thomas, Mark McGwire, Will Clark, Todd Helton, and Lance Berkman. John Olerud was a first-round talent who slipped to the third round because he was considered a tough sign.

Draft Rule #13: Among college hitters, after first basemen there is almost no difference between the other infield positions, including catcher. Collegiate outfielders trail all other positions by a significant margin, probably because of an overemphasis on "tools" guys with great athleticism but underdeveloped bats.

Here's the chart for college position players:

	1984 - 1999		1992 - 1999
Pos	Overall	Pos	Overall
COL 1B	+155.3%	COL 1B	+113.1%
COL 2B	+41.0%	COL 2B	+55.6%
COL SS	+37.9%	COL 3B	+55.2%
COL 3B	+24.4%	COL C	+49.8%
COL C	+12.5%	COL SS	+45.1%
COL OF	+12.5%	COL OF	-5.3%

Draft Rule #14: There are minimal differences in the value of left-handed vs. right-handed pitching. Left-handed pitching may be slightly more valuable at the college level, particularly in the second and third round. Right-handed pitching may be slightly more valuable at the high-school level, particularly in the first round. The differences are so slight that they're best ignored.

Draft Rule #15: It is too soon to tell whether the strategy of drafting college relievers is a wise strategy or not. Drafting one in the first five picks of the draft is probably a bad idea.

College relievers selected in the first five picks include Gregg Olson, but after him it goes Paul Shuey, Darren Dreifort, Braden Looper, Wayne Gomes, and Matt Anderson.

And—cue Tony Kornheiser—that's it! That's the whole list!

Except for one thing—every data point that we have looked at in the entire study has stopped after the 1999 season. While it's simply too early to analyze players drafted in the 2000s, are there any trends in the way teams have drafted over the past several years that we can use to extrapolate an analysis of which draft picks are the most valuable today?

There are. And before Tuesday's draft, in the final (thank God) installment of the Draft Series, we will.

DOCTORING THE NUMBERS
The Draft, Part Twelve
Rany Jazayerli

In the final edition of "The Draft," Rany looked into the future, attempting to forecast future draft value based on recent trends and discovering that the pendulum may have swung too far in favor of college players.

If there's one indisputable fact about our draft study, it's that the dynamics of the draft change over time; the calculus of the draft from 1992 to 1999 is much, much different than it was from 1984 to 1991.

Well, there's no reason to think that change suddenly ground to a halt in 1999, and the data from a decade ago may hold little bearing on the decisions that will be made next Tuesday.

On the other hand, it's too early to analyze more recent drafts, and some data is better than none. The question is, can we extrapolate what the trends of the draft might have been based on how teams' drafting tendencies have changed?

With an assist from John Erhardt, here's a chart comparing the number of (signed) high-school players vs. college players selected in the first 100 picks.

The chart is a little too spiky for my tastes—let's look at a moving three-year average to smooth out some of the random variation from year to year.

The mid-'80s represented the Golden Age for college draft picks, both in terms of quantity and quality—the era of Will Clark and Barry Bonds and Barry Larkin and Mark McGwire. As we've mentioned before, one of the biggest reasons for that bountiful crop was that so many of these players were allowed to slip off to college despite being highly regarded in high school.

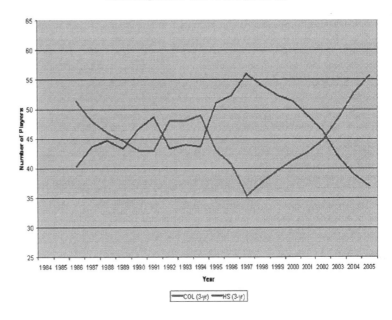

The emphasis on drafting collegians quieted down by 1990, and both groups were equally likely to be drafted through about 1995, when high-school players suddenly spiked upwards—at around the same time that the return on high-school players increased dramatically. But starting with the 2001 draft, teams have gone after college players by an ever-increasing amount. Here are the year-by-year breakdowns since 1995.

Year	COL Players	HS Players
1995	36	56
1996	35	57
1997	35	55
1998	43	50
1999	41	52
2000	40	52
2001	47	43
2002	49	44
2003	51	39
2004	60	34
2005	56	38

More high-school players were drafted in the Top 100 than college players for six straight years from 1995 to 2000, but the numbers reversed in 2001 and have not looked back. The 60 college signees in 2004 was even more than the 57 college players signed in 1984, and represents the greatest emphasis on college talent (in the first 100 picks) ever.

The "Moneyball" draft was 2002. More importantly, the book came out in the spring of 2003. It would be naive to think that the timing was just a coincidence. Several organizations—notably the Red Sox and Blue Jays, but also less-heralded teams like the Diamondbacks and Royals—started focusing overwhelmingly on college talent at that point.

So here's the question: Does the sudden emphasis on college talent change the return on draft picks? We know that college hitters returned about 25 percent more value than high-school hitters from 1992 to 1999. But in that eight-year span, there were 130 college hitters signed in the top 100 picks, compared to 227 hitters. From 2000 to 2005, there were more college hitters (138) than high-school hitters (129) taken. In the 1990s, the 10th-best college hitter was being drafted, on average, after the 17th-best high school hitter. In the 2000s, when the 10th-best college hitter gets selected, more often than not the 10th-best high school hitter is still on the board. That has to mean something, doesn't it?

The answer is more complicated than you think, because such a relationship did not exist between the 1980s and 1990s. More high-school players were drafted in the 1990s relative to college players, but the return on investment also increased. We've already recounted some of the reasons for this, but to recap the two biggies:

1. Signing bonuses had reached a level in the 1990s that made it highly unusual for a top high-school prospect to bypass the pros in favor of college;

In 1984, 10 of the top 100 draft picks did not sign; in 1985, nine did not. I don't have precise data on previous years, but in the early '80s the number of top-100 picks that failed to sign was likely much higher. But in 1986, there were only three unsigned players, which was the start of a trend: the most unsigned players in any draft since is just six.

Which is to say, the trend that has funneled the best high-school talent into the pros instead of to the college ranks has not suddenly reversed course. In 2003, for the first time ever, every single player drafted in the first two rounds signed. (The first two players selected who didn't sign? Andrew Miller—possibly the #1 pick this year—and Drew Stubbs, who should go in the top 10.)

In the 1990s, teams could afford to select more high-school talent, because the college talent had been weakened by the siphoning off of the best high-school talent three years prior. In the 2000s, teams are selecting more college players even though the ranks of collegiate talent have not suddenly swelled with an influx of top high-school players who dissed the pros.

2. The level of competition for elite high-school talent had increased dramatically as a result of the development of traveling teams, the Area Code Games, etc, which made it considerably easier for scouts to evaluate the best high-school players against each other.

The trend towards more competitions pitting the best high-school players from around the country has continued, if not accelerated. Travel baseball teams for top players as young as 12 years old are commonplace, and by the time many high schoolers are available in the draft they've been playing against their best peers from around the country for up to six years. Showcase events in the offseason are a tremendous opportunity for scouts to observe the best incoming high-school juniors and seniors in the country, and the preseason draft hype for a player is frequently dictated by his performance there.

Meanwhile, the format for the NCAA has changed only slightly with the expansion of the tournament to 64 teams and the advent of "Super-Regionals." The typical college player might pick up a few extra games over the course of his career, generally not a meaningful impact from a scouting perspective. The best collegiate players do get to tour with Team USA in the summer (although some high-school players get to play on junior national squads themselves), and wooden bat summer leagues—i.e. the Cape Cod League—are definitely useful for both players and scouts.

But overall, the trends that made high-school players easier to scout (relative to college players) in the 1990s vs. the 1980s have continued into the 2000s.

So while there was good reason for teams to load up on high-school players in the 1990s (even though high-school players were such a bad bet in the 1980s), there has been little reason for teams to load up on college players in the 2000s except for the obvious one: in the 1990s, college hitters (not pitchers) were undervalued in the draft.

Are there any other baseball trends that have emerged over the past five-10 years which might tilt the balance of draft strategies one way or the other? I can think of one significant one: as recently as 10 years ago, if you were a 19-year-old with a howitzer for an arm, you had no safe haven. Go to college and you would be slagged by the likes of Gene Stephenson and Cliff Gustafson; go pro and you had to watch your back for Dallas Green. You were going to throw a lot of pitches no matter who you pitched for.

Today, while college teams sensibly make winning their top priority, every single major-league team monitors pitch counts and has implemented pitch limits in the minor leagues. The argument has been made for years that organizations would rather direct the development of an 18-year-old kid than take the risk that the 21-year-old they just signed has a ticking time bomb in his shoulder. It's hard to argue with that logic when Tim Lincecum, who's likely to go at the top of the first round this year and stands 5'11" in cleats, throws 146 pitches in a start for the Washington Huskies.

So chalk up another advantage for high-school pitchers over their collegiate brethren.

Here's a chart breaking down draft picks not only by their class, but by position—again, these are three-year averages.

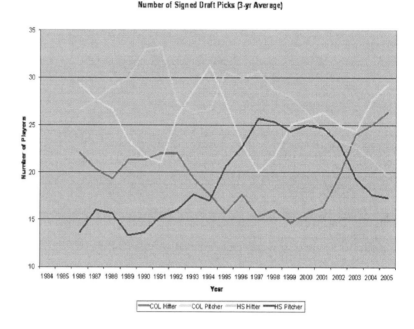

Since 2000, the number of college hitters taken in the top 100 has increased by over 50 percent, while the number of college pitchers has increased only slightly. The number of high-school pitchers has dropped from its high in the late 1990s, but they are still more popular picks than they were 20 years ago. High-school hitters, meanwhile, have been trending downward since the late 1980s. In 1989 there were 40 high-school hitters signed from the top 100; there were just 37 signed in 2004 and 2005 combined.

Looking at this chart, it's clear that most teams have been doing their homework. College hitters were the most valuable subset of draft picks in both the 1980s and 1990s—as a result, since 2000, teams have become much more aggressive about drafting them.

But it's also clear that in trying to address one inefficiency, teams may be creating others. After a span in the late 1990s where college and high-school pitchers were selected with equal frequency, college pitchers have once again become much more popular—by a margin of 88 to 52 in the last three drafts. This, even though both groups returned almost identical value from 1992 to 1999. This would suggest that high-school pitchers are now a better investment than college pitchers. Plus, the decline in selections from the ranks of high-school hitters has been so steep, and sustained for so long, that they may no longer be the overpriced commodities they once were.

Let's see if we can describe this numerically. From 1992 to 1999, here is the amount of value (relative to expectations) squeezed out of the typical player drafted out of each of the four main player groups.

Group	Value
COL H	1.282
COL P	0.854
HS P	0.851
HS H	0.791

And here's a chart comparing the average number of players selected in each group in the 1992-99 era to the 2001-05 era.

Group	Avg # (92-99)	Avg # (01-05)	Ratio
COL H	16.250	24.4	0.666
COL P	25.875	27.8	0.931
HS H	28.375	21.0	1.351
HS P	21.875	18.6	1.176

Now, here's the controversial part. In order to get a ballpark measure of how each group should be valued today, we can simply multiply the value of each group from 1992-99 with the ratio of how the desirability of that group has changed over the last five drafts. I make no claims that this method is mathematically rigorous or even particularly accurate, but it's the best we can do. Here's what the new value chart would look like from 2001 to 2005, if these assumptions are accurate.

Group	Old Value	Ratio	New Value
HS H	0.791	1.351	1.069
HS P	0.851	1.176	1.001
COL H	1.282	0.666	0.854
COL P	0.854	0.931	0.795

The numbers get turned on their head. Now, for perhaps the first time in draft history, a compelling argument can be made that high-school players are underrated. According to these admittedly fuzzy numbers, high-school players render nearly 25 percent more value than college players—the exact opposite conclusion we reached from the 1992-99 data.

If we used the draft trends just since *Moneyball* was published in 2003, the discrepancy is even larger:

Group	Old Value	Ratio	New Value
HS H	0.791	1.443	1.141
HS P	0.851	1.262	1.074
COL H	1.282	0.617	0.791
COL P	0.854	0.882	0.753

Using this data, over the past three drafts high-school hitters were worth approximately 40 percent more than college players—an advantage which, if not quite as sizable as the one college players enjoyed in the 1980s, is still incredibly significant.

That's the simplistic method. A more complicated method goes like this:

Between 1992 and 1999, an average of 16.25 college hitters were signed out of the Top 100, or roughly one every six picks. If we assume a random distribution of those hitters in the Top 100, the 10th college hitter selected would be drafted around pick #58.

Between 2003 and 2005, an average of 26.33 college hitters were signed out of the Top 100, meaning the 10th college hitter selected would be drafted around pick #36.

If we make one assumption—that the 10th college hitter selected in one draft is just as good as the 10th college hitter selected in the other—then we can give the 10th college hitter selected between 2003 and 2005 the "expected value" of the 10th college hitter selected between 1992-99. In other words, a college hitter selected with the #36 pick between 2003-05 is comparable to a college hitter selected #58 between 1992-99 (since they were both selected 10th among their cohorts), and so we should expect the the college hitter selected #36 today to be only as valuable as a college hitter selected #58 in the 1990s.

The opposite is true—the 10th high-school pitcher selected from 2003-05 would be drafted around pick #55; the same pitcher would have been selected around pick #43 between 1992-99.

From our previous work, we found that the average value of each draft pick drops around 4.5 percent per pick for the first 38 picks, then around 1.2 percent per pick after that. Using this information, we can say that the 10th college hitter selected between 2003-05 provides a return on investment that is 28.5 percent less than the 10th college hitter selected from 1992-99, simply because he was drafted so much higher. The 10th high-school pitcher, on the other hand, is 14.5 percent more valuable than before, because he was drafted considerably later than before.

If we run these numbers for all four groups, and look at how this affects the fifth, 10th, and 15th player in each cohort, here's what we come up with.

Player	COL H	COL P	HS H	HS P
5th	-38.6%	-9.1%	+36.2%	+26.9%
10th	-28.5%	-18.0%	+38.0%	+14.5%
15th	-33.8%	-7.7%	+31.0%	+23.0%
Average	-33.6%	-11.6%	+35.1%	+21.5%

While our method changed, the results are the same: the value of college players declines precipitously, while high-school players are much more valuable than before.

If we take these numbers and combine them with our value matrix from 1992 to 1999, the results look like this. The gap between high-school and college players has shrunk, but by a very small margin—the advantage enjoyed by high-school players ranges between 26 percent for hitters and 37 percent for pitchers.

Group	Old Value	Ratio	New Value
HS H	0.791	1.351	1.069
HS P	0.851	1.215	1.034
COL H	1.282	0.664	0.851
COL P	0.854	0.884	0.755

Any way you look at it, the pendulum has swung too far. Based on the data at hand, we can estimate what the ideal breakdown of draft picks should be that would make all four groups of players equally valuable in a typical year. After accounting for the fact that in a typical draft, eight of the first 100 picks are either JuCo picks or do not sign, here's what the ideal breakdown of the other 92 looks like.

High School Hitters	24.6
High School Pitchers	20.4
College Pitchers	24.2
College Hitters	22.8

Or in percentage form:

% College Players	51.1%
% High-School Players	48.9%
% Pitchers	48.5%
% Hitters	51.5%

This isn't particularly groundbreaking: the platonic ideal is about a 50/50 breakdown between college and high-school talent, and a 50/50 breakdown between pitchers and hitters. But in recent years, the breakdown has, well, broken down. Over the last three drafts, the distribution was tilted 60/40 towards college players.

Last year, the Oakland Athletics surprised casual observers by snapping up three high-school pitchers in a row—Craig Italiano, Jared Lansford (Carney's son), and Vincent Mazzaro—after selecting college hitters with their first two picks. Some people speculated that this was a repudiation of their "Moneyball" philosophy, an acknowledgment that their earlier methods were not working.

But *Moneyball* was never about a specific philosophy of valuing production over potential, or statistics over scouts. It was a philosophy of identifying inefficiencies in the market—whatever they are—and exploiting them. As the inefficiencies change, so do the tactics. The sudden change in the A's drafting tactics doesn't invalidate their philosophy; it simply proves that they were doing their homework and noticed the trends in other teams' draft strategies. When everyone else was zigging, they were zagging. Now that everyone else is zagging...

The A's figured out a long time ago that flexibility and adaptability are the keys to staying ahead of the market. Because if there's one overarching Golden Draft Rule that governs everything else, it is this:

The only rule that isn't subject to change over time is that all the other rules are.

LIES, DAMNED LIES
Valuing Draft Picks
Nate Silver

Using Wins Above Replacement Player (WARP), Nate Silver estimated the monetary value of each pick in the draft and discovered that early selections are extremely valuable assets.

Three weeks ago, I prepared an analysis of the ill-fated Manny Ramirez-to-the-Mets deal. The workup applied some standard valuation techniques in an attempt to put a price on something that is notoriously difficult to quantify: the value achieved by dumping a big, backloaded contract. That article triggered about as much response as anything I've written in the past year. Most of the responses focused on complementary applications of the framework—those other difficult economic questions that both sabermetrics and traditional analysis have largely avoided.

For example: What is the value of a first-round draft pick? This is an essential thing for a baseball club to have a handle on. Under baseball's compensation rules, a team signing a Type-A free agent must sacrifice its first-round draft pick (or its second-round pick, if it picks in the top half of the first round), while a team losing the same free agent acquires that first-round pick, as well as a sandwich pick between the first and second rounds. If the value of these picks is material—above and beyond the signing bonus that would typically be paid to a draft pick—that ought to have a corresponding impact on a team's behavior in the free-agent market.

The economic value of a prospect or a draft pick is in his potential to provide on-field value to his club before he accumulates six years of service time. This period incorporates both his first two years of service—when he has little to no negotiating leverage—and his subsequent four years of service time, when he is subject to arbitration, a process through which teams generally get to pay desirable players well below market price.

After I published my previous article, BP up-and-comer Tom Gorman was kind enough to forward me a paper written by John D. Burger and Stephen J.K. Walters, from Loyola College in Maryland, which quantifies the arbitration discount more precisely. Burger and Walters concluded that:

- A typical, arbitration-eligible player entering his third year of service time is priced at about 31 percent of his market value;

- An arbitration-eligible player entering his fourth year of service time is priced at 44 percent of his market value;
- An arbitration-eligible player entering his fifth year of service time is priced at 61 percent of his market value;
- An arbitration-eligible player entering his sixth year of service time is priced at 64 percent of his market value.

These figures imply a somewhat larger discount relative to market than the guesstimates I had made before. But my figures weren't based on any evidence, and since a player has limited flexibility under the arbitration system—a player who doesn't like his arbitration result can hold out but can't sign with another team—it makes sense that the discount is substantial.

What about a player's first and second years of service time? For the purposes of this article, I am going to assign a marginal cost of $500,000 for a player's first major-league service year and $750,000 for his second major-league service year. These figures are intended to represent a player's marginal salary above the major-league minimum in his first two service years, as well as some attendant costs, such as his salaries and benefits in the minor leagues, the allocation of developmental resources toward that player, and the possibility that he will be subject to arbitration early if he is a "Super Two" player (16.7 percent of players with between two and three years of service time can go to arbitration). It is not meant to incorporate his signing bonus, which we will discuss later.

We also, of course, need to have an estimate of a draft pick's value. In the spirit of Rany Jazayerli's recent series of articles, I looked at each of the six major-league drafts from 1989-1994 and attempted to evaluate a typical first-round draft pick's WARP score for each of his first six years of service time. Since precise records of service time are hard to come by, I instead applied a quick-and-dirty estimate of service time years using the following criteria:

- A player's first year of service time consists of all seasons up to and including the first in which the player accumulates 200 career at-bats or 50 career innings pitched.
- Subsequent years of service time accumulate after each season, or set of seasons, in which a player has at least 150 AB or 35 IP (e.g., if a player has 121 AB in 1996 and 85 AB in 1997, this counts as one service-time year rather than two).
- A player ceases to accumulate value in the 11th season after his draft class. For example, a player drafted in 1991 can accumulate value in the years 1991-2001, but not in 2002 or any year thereafter. This is meant to account for players who become subject to minor-league free agency before their arbitration eligibility expires, accumulate unaccounted-for service time while sitting on the major-league bench or the major-league disabled list, or

take so long to develop that their original owners find it suitable to dispose of them to clear a spot on the roster.

This is not a perfect set of rules—it gives Alex Rodriguez one too many years of arbitration time, for example—but should provide a good approximation in the vast majority of cases.

I broke down the first-round draft picks into four sub-classes: Tier 1 (picks 1-7), Tier 2 (picks 8-15), Tier 3 (picks 16-25) and Tier 4 (26 and higher, including first-round sandwich picks). The divisions among the tiers are necessarily somewhat arbitrary, although Tiers 3 and 4 are intended to represent the typical draft picks that a team gives up when it signs a free agent. I excluded those players I identified as not having signed with the clubs that drafted them.

Applying that method, here are the average WARP scores for 1st Tier draft picks (selections 1-7 overall):

Service Time	WARP
Year 1	2.11
Year 2	2.37
Year 3	2.44
Year 4	2.99
Year 5	2.56
Year 6	1.94

There are a couple of things to keep in mind. First, these figures are averages from draft picks who achieve all sorts of different outcomes. Many prominent draft picks never reach the majors, and many more never make a significant contribution at the big-league level. On the other hand, we have folks like Rodriguez and Chipper Jones, and one A-Rod makes up for an awful lot of Antone Williamsons.

Second, a considerable majority of draft picks, including many who make some contribution in the major leagues, never reach six years of service time. Indeed, it is quite a feat to accumulate six years of service time; there are many more fringe players than there are major-league regulars. This is why the WARP scores tail off in years five and six: there are more zeroes to average in. One upshot of this is that some players who are widely perceived as disappointments may nevertheless give their clubs a reasonable return on their money. Willie Greene, for example, contributed about 14 wins to his clubs, far less than what was expected of him, but decent value for a player who never achieved his free-agent payday.

With these considerations in mind, we can plug in our estimates of a draft pick's cost and value into our net present value framework. As before, I'm using a figure of $2.14 million for the marginal cost of a win in the free-agent market, as derived from this study. These are the results for the Tier 1 draft picks:

Tier 1 (1-7)	Y1	Y2	Y3	Y4	Y5	Y6	Total
WARP	2.11	2.37	2.42	2.99	2.56	1.94	14.38
Market Value ($M)	$4.51	$5.08	$5.17	$6.39	$5.48	$4.14	$30.78
Marginal Cost ($M)	$0.50	$0.75	$1.60	$2.81	$3.34	$2.65	$11.66
Net Value ($M)	$4.01	$4.33	$3.57	$3.58	$2.14	$1.49	$19.12
Gross Present Value ($M)	$3.55	$3.65	$2.87	$2.74	$1.56	$1.03	$15.39
Signing Bonus							$3.00
Net Present Value ($M)							$12.39

I've described this methodology in some detail before, so I'll discuss it just briefly now. Market Value is a player's WARP score translated into dollars, using the $2.14 million/win estimate. Marginal Cost represents the salary and related costs to be paid to that player, which we estimate as a fixed sum of $500,000 in his first service year, $750,000 in his second, 31 percent of his Market Value in Year Three, 44 percent of his Market Value in Year Four, and 61 percent and 64 percent of his Market Value in Years Five and Six, respectively.

Net Value is simply the player's Market Value less his Marginal Cost. The next row, Gross Present Value, takes his Net Value and discounts it at a rate of five percent a year, assuming that his first year of service time begins 2 1/2 years after he is drafted.

The "Total" column at the right is the key. We figure that the Gross Present Value of a Tier 1 draft pick—a player who goes between first and seventh overall in the amateur draft—is about $15.4 million. Keep in mind that, even though this analysis is derived from the results of players who were selected from 1989-1994, it is calibrated to present-day market rates and so would represent the value of a player selected in the 2005 draft.

Let's pause for a moment and consider that number. MLB bigwigs are fond of complaining about the escalating cost of signing bonuses paid to amateur draft picks (and have done a remarkably good job of controlling them), but a typical top-tier draft pick can be expected to contribute about $15 million worth of value to his club above and beyond what comparable production would cost in the free-agent market. That is a large margin of error to cover for the Williamsons and Brien Taylors of the world, and a team that punts on a first-round pick for the sake of saving a few bucks of signing bonus is almost certainly making a large mistake.

We can, of course, consider the signing bonus if we want to do so. Over the past year or two, a typical signing bonus for a Tier 1 draft pick has run at about $3 million. If we subtract that number to come up with the Net Present Value associated with a top draft pick, we are left with about

$12.4 million of profit for the club. If amateur draft picks were tradeable, this is about what they ought to be worth in the market.

Here are the results for the Tier 2 picks:

Tier 2 (8-15)	Y1	Y2	Y3	Y4	Y5	Y6	Total
WARP	1.53	1.94	2.44	1.94	2.73	1.80	12.37
Market Value ($M)	$3.28	$4.15	$5.22	$4.15	$5.83	$3.85	$26.48
Marginal Cost ($M)	$0.50	$0.75	$1.62	$1.82	$3.56	$2.46	$10.71
Net Value ($M)	$2.78	$3.40	$3.60	$2.32	$2.28	$1.39	$15.77
Gross Present Value ($M)	$2.46	$2.87	$2.89	$1.77	$1.66	$0.96	$12.61
Signing Bonus							$1.90
Net Present Value ($M)							$10.71

The years 1989-1994 were a fruitful time in this range of the amateur draft, as players like Nomar Garciaparra, Manny Ramirez and Billy Wagner were nabbed between picks eight and 15. The drop-off might have been slightly larger if we'd considered a wider range of years; nevertheless, it's clear that these picks are plenty valuable too.

Tier 3 (16-25)	Y1	Y2	Y3	Y4	Y5	Y6	Total
WARP	1.37	1.92	1.85	1.67	1.70	1.32	9.84
Market Value ($M)	$2.93	$4.10	$3.96	$3.58	$3.64	$2.83	$21.05
Marginal Cost ($M)	$0.50	$0.75	$1.23	$1.58	$2.22	$1.81	$8.09
Net Value ($M)	$2.43	$3.35	$2.74	$2.01	$1.42	$1.02	$12.96
Gross Present Value ($M)	$2.15	$2.82	$2.20	$1.53	$1.03	$0.71	$10.45
Signing Bonus							$1.50
Net Present Value ($M)							$8.95

Tier 3 is significant since it represents the draft pick that an upper-division club would sacrifice when signing a Type-A free agent. That sacrifice amounts to about $9 million—the chance to pick up a player like Mike Mussina, Chuck Knoblauch, or Jason Kendall, all of whom were selected in this phase.

Tier 4 (26+)	Y1	Y2	Y3	Y4	Y5	Y6	Total
WARP	0.87	0.90	0.80	0.63	0.53	0.35	4.08
Market Value ($M)	$1.87	$1.93	$1.72	$1.34	$1.13	$0.74	$8.73
Marginal Cost ($M)	$0.50	$0.75	$0.53	$0.59	$0.69	$0.47	$3.54
Net Value ($M)	$1.37	$1.18	$1.19	$0.75	$0.44	$0.27	$5.19
Gross Present Value ($M)	$1.21	$0.99	$0.95	$0.57	$0.32	$0.19	$4.24
Signing Bonus							$1.00
Net Present Value ($M)							$3.24

There do appear to be some diminishing returns once we reach the sandwich pick stage. Still, we figure that a team losing a Type-A free agent is compensated with about $12 million in draft picks ($9 million for the Tier 3 pick and $3 million for the Tier 4 pick); it's well worth it to offer arbitration to your veterans if there's any material chance that they'll sign somewhere else.

It's also worth considering very briefly the perverse incentives that the draft compensation system creates. A team seeking to sign a Type-A free agent from another club starts off about $9 million in the hole, the cost of the first-round draft pick it would give up by signing that player. But the team seeking to re-sign its player has an even bigger disincentive—it is giving up the opportunity to acquire both a first-round pick and the sandwich pick, total value about $12 million. Thus, the compensation system is ill-designed as a way to keep potential free agents at home; it's no surprise that someone like Billy Beane wasn't willing to go the last dollar with stars like Jason Giambi and Miguel Tejada.

Of course, the real intention of the draft compensation system isn't to balance incentives, but to hold the salaries paid to premium free agents down by acting as a tax on whichever club winds up with the player. The mechanism ought to work in that regard—sacrificing a draft pick worth $9 million is significant. My guess, however, is that the compensation system fails here as well, because I doubt that major-league teams are adequately accounting for the value of their draft picks. Certainly, Major League Baseball is within its rights to act as a cartel in an effort to hold signing bonuses down. Nevertheless, a significant and increasing number of draft picks have gone unsigned each year, even when a rational analysis reveals that draft picks provide very good value on the money. It's possible that teams like the Cincinnati Reds are taking one for the team in steadfastly refusing to pay a draft pick above his slot value, but it's more likely that these teams are behaving in both a self-interested and a short-sighted manner.

NBA and NFL teams intuitively recognize the value of high draft picks, probably because players take less time to develop in those sports, making the gratification more instantaneous. But high draft picks are very probably just as valuable in MLB. If baseball draft picks are a little bit more difficult to project, the sport's economic structure more than makes up for this by allowing a club to hold a player essentially free of charge in the minor leagues until he's ready, and then providing him at a deep discount for six full seasons of performance.

FUTURE SHOCK
The All-Disappointment Team
Kevin Goldstein

By popular request, Kevin Goldstein picked the top prospect busts at each position. As a few of his inclusions suggest, early disappointment isn't always insurmountable.

One of the highlights of my job (and there are many) comes in the chats with our readers. They're always fun, I hope entertaining, and as a bit of gravy, they're good for column ideas. One topic that came up in my last chat was the concept of an all-disappointment team. You asked for it, and here it is. Some positions were much harder than others, and I tried my best to avoid injury problems. We're looking for players who haven't lived up to expectations... as opposed to those who simply haven't played.

Catcher: Jeff Mathis, Angels. Once one of the brightest catching prospects in the game, Mathis crapped the bed when he earned a big-league job out of spring training last year, and he's gone nowhere but backwards since. Now 24, he's hitting a miserable .240/.293/.372 in the friendly confines of Triple-A Salt Lake, and on the road he drops to .202/.250/.298. The only good news is that he remains an excellent defender, nailing 40 percent of attempted base stealers.

Backup: Max Sapp, Astros. Last year's first-round pick was seen as an offense-first catcher whose best tool was his power, but he's homerless in 181 at-bats for Low-A Lexington, hitting just .260/.369/.337.

First Base: Eric Duncan, Yankees. With no obvious candidate, we offer up a lifetime achievement award to Duncan, a first-round pick in 2003. Duncan seemed to be turning it around following an MVP campaign in 2005's Arizona Fall League, but he did nothing last year and is doing even less this season at Triple-A Scranton/Wilkes-Barre, batting just .224/.315/.351.

Backup: Travis Ishikawa, Giants. The swing sure is pretty, but the results are horrible. Batting just .214/.292/.295 for Double-A Connecticut, Ishikawa is on the DL after slicing open his knee while making a diving catch, and the organization is talking about sending him down to the Cal League when he's healthy.

Second Base: Elliot Johnson, Devil Rays. Last year at Double-A Montgomery, Johnson did a little bit of everything, reaching double-digits in all three extra-base categories and swiping 20 bases. With 10 doubles, four triples and seven home runs at Triple-A Durham, Johnson has a good shot at repeating the feat this year, but a profound lack of singles has him hitting just .204/.277/.347.

Backup: Hernan Iribarran, Brewers. The Venezuelan native seemed ready for the big test at Double-A Huntsville with a career batting average of .330, but he needs to maintain averages like that because of his lack of secondary skills. Instead Iribarran is hitting just .257/.334/.325.

Third Base: Andy LaRoche, Dodgers. While LaRoche was given a shot to fill the team's big-league opening at the hot corner, it wasn't exactly because he was tearing up Triple-A Las Vegas, as he's hit the DL with more shoulder problems with a batting line of just .244/.336/.366.

Backup: Ronnie Borquin, Tigers. A second-round pick last year after leading the Big Ten in batting average, Bourquin hit just .192/.326/.218 in 26 games for High-A Lakeland and now finds himself back in the New York-Penn League.

Shortstop: Reid Brignac, Devil Rays. After winning California League MVP honors last year, Brignac looked like a sure-fire elite prospect with a .302/.340/.500 mark for Double-A Montgomery in April, but following a homerless May and a .229 June, his total line sits at a well-below-expectations mark of .246/.298/.399.

Backup: Elvis Andrus, Braves. Everyone is still waiting for the much-ballyhooed tools to turn into some kind of baseball production, as Andrus is hitting just .236/.321/.329 for High-A Myrtle Beach to go with 19 errors.

Outfield: Trevor Crowe, Indians; Carlos Gonzalez, Diamondbacks; Andrew McCutchen, Pirates. Crowe is likely the anti-MVP of this team, though a recent streak has him finally over the Mendoza line at .207/.303/.258. Gonzalez had a brief hot streak when Justin Upton joined him at Double-A Mobile, but now he's in the midst of a 5-for-33 slump and hitting just .252/.278/.418 overall. After showing power, speed and plate discipline in his full-season debut last year, McCutchen almost made the big-league squad out of spring training but was instead jumped to Double-A, and the 20-year-old hasn't done much, sitting at .234/.296/.350 in 74 games.

Backups: Cedric Hunter, Padres; Daryl Jones, Cardinals. A third-round pick last year, Hunter opened eyes with a .364/.458/.469 pro debut, but the Midwest League has proven to be much tougher, as a lack of power and walks have him at just .276/.330/.346 for Low-A Fort Wayne. Jones seemed to be finally tapping into his tools last year in the Appalachian League, but like

Hunter, the Midwest League has proven a far greater challenge, as Jones has looked lost at times—hitting just .199/.297/.282.

Left-handed starter: Donald Veal, Cubs. Veal still has control problems, but the fact that he's suddenly giving up hits (76 in 75 innings) has his ERA at 5.64 as he's hasn't shown the breaking ball that he made such sizable progress with last year. Good news: he had his best start of the year on Wednesday, striking out 11 while giving up just two hits in five innings.

Right-handed starter: Jeff Samardzija, Cubs. A disturbing double-dip for the North Side. After giving him a record deal to buy him away from an NFL career, the big right-hander from Notre Dame has been far worse than his 5.22 ERA would indicate—allowing 93 hits in 69 innings with a ridiculously low 25 strikeouts. He could be on the way to being one of the biggest bonus mistakes in draft history.

Closer: Zech Zinicola, Nationals. Zinicola looked like a sixth-round steal last year when he reached the Eastern League in his pro debut and had a 1.65 ERA in 27 appearances. Back at Double-A Harrisburg, his control has abandoned him, as he has more walks (23) than strikeouts (19) in 29 innings to go with a 6.21 ERA.

Backup: Craig Hansen, Red Sox. It's time to face the facts and wonder if the former first-rounder will ever live up to expectations, or have any kind of significant big-league career at all. Back at Triple-A Pawtucket, the former St. John's star is floundering with a 6.04 ERA in 24 games while allowing more than two base runners per inning.

FUTURE SHOCK
Going Over Slot
Kevin Goldstein

As the 2007 signing deadline approached, Kevin Goldstein surveyed where we stood with the draft and discussed the advantages of going over-slot.

"Broken."
"Dysfunctional."
"Goofy."
"A Charade."

The quotes from above are from a scout, scouting director, and an agent, and made in reference to what is going on with signings in this year's draft class. If both sides are agreeing on this level, something very wrong is happening here. Let's delve deeper into what's going on in the form of questions and answers.

Question: So where are we at right now in terms of the 2007 draft?
With 10 days to go before the newly-implemented signing deadline of August 15, 13 of the 30 first-round picks, including eight of the first 12 picks, are still without a deal. In addition, there are 26 players between the supplemental first round and the fifth round who are also officially unsigned.

Question: Wait a second—what do you mean by "official?"
There appear to be plenty of deals where all the terms have been agreed upon but not signed and announced yet. All of these deals include bonuses that are far greater than the slot recommended by MLB. For example, Detroit has signed fifth-round pick Casey Crosby for what is believed to be $750,000; rumors abound that Atlanta has agreed to terms with first-rounder Jason Heyward for approximately $1.7 million, and the Yankees have agreed on several above-slot deals, including around $1 million for fourth-round pick Brad Suttle, and somewhere between $750-900,000 for 10th-round pick Carmen Angelini.

Question: So why aren't these deals announced yet?
On the surface, because MLB doesn't want the over-slot deals being used in negotiations to raise the bonus demands of the legitimately unsigned picks. That said, it's an exercise in futility. "Once a deal is done, everyone knows it's out there," said one scouting director; teams talk to each other, and agents quickly let their good deals be known. As another scouting director put it, "I really don't know who they think they are fooling."

Question: So what is this slotting system? Is it like the NBA?
No, not at all. MLB simply recommends a bonus for each selection. Teams do not have to adhere to the recommendation. In addition, the recommended bonuses this year are 10 percent lower than last year.

Question: Why are most teams adhering to the slotting recommendations?
For a multitude of reasons. The simple answer is because they can, but opinions vary as to whether or not they should. "There is a real belief, from both ownership and the union, that the draft is an area that could stand some cost control," said one scouting director. "Ownership sees bonuses as getting out of hand when compared to the money spent on proven talents, while at the same time, there's a finite amount of money being spent, and the union knows that money saved in the draft is going to be redistributed to a union member, so they're fine with it as well." Another scouting director saw the lower recommendations as bad for the development of the unsigned players. "Every other aspect of the game—revenue, free agency, arbitration—they're all up, but the draft is now 10 percent less?" he asked. "And now we miss a summer of development on guys, and for what?"

Needless to say, agents are far from thrilled with the system. "I have no idea why teams are going with this," questioned one agent. "Why give MLB that kind of power? They can't control arbitration, and free agency is an open market, but the draft is in limbo. MLB can tell you this is collectively bargained, but it's not—the system for compensation picks is, but this slotting system is not." A scouting director came back wondering why player representatives would be so upset. "The big agents—Boras, the Hendricks brothers, CAA, SFX—they don't make their money on the draft, they make their money after the draft."

In addition, there are some teams and/or individuals within teams that might feel like they have to adhere to the recommendations. "I'm not going to name names here, but you can figure it out just by looking," said one scouting director. "There are some teams that MLB seems to have leverage with when related to other things that have nothing to do with this process, and they hold it over their head. So if they toe the line, my question is what MLB is going to do for those teams when they're sitting in the bottom half of their division because they couldn't take the player they really wanted."

A second agent talked about how the process that is put in place for teams that want to pay over slot actually keeps bonus figures down. "This is producing a chilling effect on clubs because the process goes through ownership," said the agent. "You can only ask ownership for so many favors, and you don't want to burn your bridges with the money people." The agent noted that signing players for over-slot bonuses also puts scouting directors in a spotlight they might otherwise want to avoid. "Anytime a scouting director asks for more money and that player doesn't pan out, it produces more accountability," he explained. "How many of these guys are going to spend their entire career with one organization? What happens when they want to go somewhere else? Those other clubs are going to look at how he spent his money." He added that the end result does little for getting the best players to the best teams. "So now these teams say that they are passing on and losing the best players because they can't afford them. In the bigger picture, what they really can't afford is not to sign them."

Question: You said the process for going over slot involves ownership, but what is the process exactly?
In many ways the process for exceeding the slot bonus seems solely designed to make it as inconvenient as possible, as MLB has no real recourse when a team decides to hand out the big dollars it feels it has to spend to land a particular pick.

"The only thing MLB can do is fine you if you don't call them first," said one scouting director, who then went into detail about the process, the annoyance in his voice coming through perfectly. "You call MLB and say you want to go over slot, and they tell you not to, and that they've worked so hard to put this system in place and that you are blowing everything up." From there, things get uglier. "Now, the process can't continue until MLB talks not to your GM, but to your ownership, where they will once again yell about your team messing everything up but also often telling them that their own scouting director is doing the wrong thing here," he added. "Unfortunately, there are owners who listen."

The key to getting an over-slot deal done seems to then rely on having a supportive internal management structure. "In the end, you have to have a strong enough ownership where you can tell him that signing this player for big money is in the best interest of the organization," he continued. "When that happens, the owner has to call MLB back and let them know that their message has been heard and considered, but we're doing it anyway. Then after MLB yells at you one more time, you sign the guy. It's a bad process."

Question: Why is MLB so concerned about this? In the bigger scheme of things, how much is being saved?
This issue seems to baffle both teams and agents. "The way some teams are spending in the international amateur market is far more damaging to any kind of parity than the draft or free agent signings," said one scouting director, and another agreed. "On July 2nd, the Yankees spent

$3.9 million dollars on international players. That's in one day. Did they have to call anyone to do that?" he questioned.

Even an agent agreed that there are other places where even if minimally successful, cost-cutting measures might be more successful. "They [MLB] have tried to do the same thing in the arbitration market and it's met with less success," he said. "But it's kind of goofy that they are focusing on this so much—saving less than six figures here and there—especially when they are making so much money from television revenue and other sources." The agent added that the recommended slotting system and (perhaps surprisingly) the teams that go against it, both currently serve MLB's purposes. "Most clubs have been in lockstep with the slotting, and that's good for MLB," he stated. "But as always, there will be a few teams that step outside the box and pay more. That's good for them too, because that way there's no collusion, and MLB can say it's not a fixed market."

Question: So what teams are going over slot?
There seem to be two types of organizations that are consistently going over slot: smart ones and rich ones, not that the two are mutually exclusive. Four teams that immediately come to mind are the Tigers, the Angels, the Red Sox, and the Yankees. Go look at the standings, and then go look at the amount of elite-level young talent in each system. It's not a coincidence.

"Look, MLB can yell and scream, and they can use their scare tactics and their peer pressure, but in the end, teams are going to go over slot anyway," said one scouting director. "When MLB tells the Yankees that going over-slot on all these guys is a bad idea, they're going to look at their system and see Joba Chamberlain and Ian Kennedy from 2006, and other guys they've gone over slot for and say to themselves, 'Well gee, it's working pretty good for us.'"

One scouting director said he can't blame the Yankees for doing things this way, but he was worried that credit would go in the wrong direction. "I don't blame or fault other teams for taking advantage of the system or begrudge them for what they're doing under the current rules," he stated. "However, if a team has five-million-dollar bullets to shoot, and you have one-million-dollar bullet, they're going to get more credit for their 'scouting' when it's the dollars doing the work."

And then there are the Tigers, who have used their first-round picks to grab top talent as it has fallen to them because of real or perceived bonus demands. This philosophy has allowed them to add Justin Verlander, Cameron Maybin, Andrew Miller, and potentially Rick Porcello to their organization. The Tigers have selected them all at positions well below where their talent merited. Clearly, it's working in Detroit, and one would think others would learn their lesson.

One amateur scout who admires the Tigers' approach said the philosophy is obviously paying dividends. "It should be pretty clear that a bigger draft budget saves more money in the long run," he said. One agent agreed completely: "Any team that passes on some guy over 200 grand is killing themselves," he observed. "If you're not taking the best player on the board because you 'can't,' you're just hurting yourself."

One scouting director insisted that money still isn't everything. "You can still succeed as it is right now without spending $10 million every June to sign your picks," he asserted. "Look at the Twins, for example. You just have to be good at it, and you can get talent."

Beyond just the Tiger trio (perhaps eventually a quartet), there is empirical evidence supporting this philosophy as well. A recent study by *Baseball America*'s Jim Callis showed an overwhelming success rate for players who received well-above-slot bonuses.

Question: So the system is completely broken right now, right?
Yes and no. Yes, in the sense that unlike drafts in the other major sports that have a legitimate and enforceable slotting system, the talent in the baseball draft does not go off the board in order of talent. In fact, the gap between where guys should go based on talent and where they do go in actually seems to increase annually.

At the same time, it's not like the above-slot teams are doing anything unethical in any way. If anything, the teams getting the top talent in lower rounds should be appreciated by fans of the business side of things as well as believers in the "Moneyball" ethos of exploiting market inefficiencies.

There are no rules preventing other teams from going Detroit's route. Consider the overall expense of doing so. It's high when compared to what other teams are spending on amateur talent, yet still well below the kind of cash that gets thrown around for even mediocre free agents. It's surprising that more teams aren't jumping on the talent bandwagon and gunning for players who drop in the draft.

That said, both team officials and agents had ideas on how to get the draft going in a better direction in order to have the best talent at the top. While everyone agrees that a real slot system would solve the problem of talent dropping, everyone also understands that even discussing the concept is moot, as the players union would never concede to it. "Look, everybody knows who the top players are, it's not a big secret," said one agent. "Let the teams trade picks. The best players should get more money—these guys are free agents, it's a free agent draft, if you can't take the best guy because of money, you should be able to trade the pick to get value back that way. It would be a much cleaner system, and the top players might go more in order."

A scouting director insisted that trading picks is something he's always been in support of, not just for better balance on draft day, but for some additional benefits as well. "Draft picks have value for teams at the trade deadline who might not have existing minor-league talent to trade," he said, while adding that such a system add a positive challenge to teams. "It takes away excuses. You always hear about Team A liking Player B so much, but he goes two picks ahead of them. [Now, if] (y)ou like him so much, now you can trade for him."

Question: Why did it get this far? Why weren't these problems addressed earlier?
This is the cause for most of the anger over the current system, although one scouting director remained optimistic that it will get better. "No, this is not a perfect system right now," he said, "but the intent is good and the aim is true. The problem is at the CBA they take care of everything else and then at the 11th hour they say, 'Oh wait, what about the draft?'" Another scouting director was not so positive. "Look, MLB had their chance to fix it and they didn't," he insisted. "They missed a golden opportunity in the last CBA, and they just blew it. They got this pick compensation piece in there, but who wants that? If you pick in the top 15, you have to take the right guy and sign him. The price doesn't matter, and the pick I get next year if I don't sign him doesn't do me any good."

Question: OK, so lets get back to the here and now—what will happen with all of these unsigned picks over the next 12 days?
Even though nearly half of the first-round picks are unsigned, when posed the question of how many will sign by the deadline, the overwhelming majority of industry people contacted for this article believed that all 30 will sign. However, the game of chicken with nobody going over-slot continues, as seemingly no team wants to be the bad guy and be the first to do it, in what one scouting director characterized as, "pulling the finger out of the dike." He goes on to add with frustration, "Again, there's no true slotting system—it's a de facto system, it's recommendations, and it's yelling and it's arm-twisting. In the end, we're heading for a collision, and there are plenty of teams that are going to pay over-slot to get their guy and as soon as one guy goes, they're all going to go." Another scouting director agreed completely. "Once the dam breaks, people start feeling empowered on both sides, and the feeding frenzy begins."

A third scouting director agreed that this is the likely scenario, but at the same time, he explained the potential nightmare. "What if it doesn't blow up? Then what happens? Has anyone said they'll be first? If everybody says I won't be first, then logic says that you have no first."

With exactly one player in the first 10 rounds signing in the last 10 days, the finger remains in the dike, at least for now.

FUTURE SHOCK
Post-Draft Thoughts 2.0
Kevin Goldstein

Following the 2008 signing deadline, Kevin Goldstein asserted that the deadline itself wasn't working.

The New Deadline Is An Absolute Failure In Every Way Imaginable

When Major League Baseball instituted the new draft rules beginning in 2007, the most consequential change it made was setting the deadline of August 15 for signing that year's draft picks, giving teams roughly nine weeks to sign their players. Team officials frankly weren't sure what it would ultimately mean to the draft, but they surely understood the intentions. The goal was to end the 11-month holdouts that were becoming all too common and to provide more leverage to the teams during negotiations. Over the course of the first two years, the exact opposite has happened.

If anything, 2007 was the test case, and there was one clear conclusion to be drawn from the results—those who waited, got paid. Players and agents took notice, and this year more of them than ever followed suit. What MLB really did was to make it more expedient to hold out, since two idle months are much easier to cope with on the player's side than the possibility of nearly a full year away from the game.

In addition, MLB has only added to the problem by mandating additional holdouts behind the scenes. There is a truckload of evidence that several seven-figure deals for non first-round picks were agreed upon—at least the terms—well before the signing deadline, and that the powers-that-be coerced the teams into delaying announcements of those deals out of fear that they'd create greater inflation in the market. Unfortunately, that inflation is more organic than they'd like to believe, and holding those signings back only resulted in more players deciding to wait and simply steered that inflation down an alternate road.

As long as there's a slotting system that is merely "suggested," the players will always have the upper hand in terms of leverage, because teams need talent, and they need to sign their draft picks. That said, many are suggesting another move of the deadline to July 15. The purpose of this would not be to gain any additional leverage in negotiations, as that's simply not going to happen, but rather to get the players playing baseball. The value of 30-50 games in a complex or short-season league should not be discounted. It takes care of the acclimation period to the professional game and gives teams some valuable early information on how and where to slot the talent into their system the following year. That "head start" has meant a big difference in the development of many players, and with the current situation allowing for players to simply sit around and wait to negotiate until the last minute, why not just concede that the bonuses are going to be what they are no matter what and move that last minute to a point where players would still be able to get six weeks' worth of games in?

Such a deadline was discussed at this week's scouting meetings in Arizona, and the response was generally favorable. It would require a modification of the current CBA, but there is reason to believe that the union might be open to such a change. The only real obstacle seems to be that some general managers fear that there could be time-management conflicts with the trading deadline. Still, the two-week window between the proposed July 15 signing deadline and the July 31 trading deadline would be no different than the time between the two current deadlines.

Let's hope that this gets done. Stop worrying about bonuses that in the grand scheme of the baseball economy add up to a pittance, and start worrying more about getting guys onto the playing field.

Unfair Bashing Of Coonelly
I just don't get this one. Both before and after the negotiations with top pick Pedro Alvarez, story after story came out discussing the irony of Pirates president Frank Coonelly, once charged with enforcing MLB's toothless slotting system, now negotiating a deal with the second overall pick in the draft, Pedro Alvarez, who required a well-over-slot bonus in order to ensure his signing.

Is there really any irony here? Some even went as far as to classify Coonelly as something of a hypocrite, which is downright ridiculous. Before taking his position with the Pirates, Coonelly was a senior vice president and a chief labor negotiator in the commissioner's office. One of his many responsibilities was overseeing the slotting system, which meant that he was the man whom teams dreaded to call when they intended to go over the recommended slot. He was the man who called the general managers, and even team owners, to try to convince them to do otherwise, and to explain to them that what they were doing was bad for baseball. While it's interesting to see Coonelly now on the other side of the negotiating table, I don't understand how anyone can find any contradiction in the situation.

When he was in the commissioner's office, enforcing the slotting system was Coonelly's job, and that's all it was. He was by all accounts highly competent, and one of the most powerful and influential people in the league's executive offices. In other words, he was really, really good at his job. Now then, think about your job; I imagine that you may be faced with situations and charged with performing tasks that are not completely to your liking. I personally know that I have what many would characterize as a dream job—hell, I'd characterize it that way myself—but even I have to do things that I don't necessarily agree with, and I'm expected to do them well. Frank Coonelly was not some kind of evangelist, he had simply been assigned the role of an enforcer, and that's a responsibility that absolutely cannot be fulfilled without ruffling some feathers along the way. That doesn't mean he necessarily liked it, and that doesn't necessarily mean he agreed with everything he was being asked to do. What he was doing was what was considered (rightly or wrongly) to be in the best interest of Major League Baseball.

Coonelly now no longer works for MLB; he works for the Pittsburgh Pirates. Signing Pedro Alvarez, for whatever it took, was certainly in the best interest of the Pirates, who now sign his paycheck. We shouldn't concern ourselves with the irony in that situation; we should concern ourselves far more with the fact that the best interests of baseball—as seen by the commissioner's office—and the best interests of the individual teams have become two completely different things when it comes to the draft.

LIES, DAMNED LIES
Slotto Bonanzas, Part One
Nate Silver

Nate Silver examined MLB's slotting structure and found that a system designed to protect small-market teams was actually having the opposite effect.

Maybe you've had this experience. Your wife's annoying cousin is in town, and you've managed to get him out of the house for the evening. Eventually, he walks back in and states emphatically, "I just paid 20 dollars for a steak dinner!" You are at a complete loss for how to react. Is he telling you this because he thinks $20 for a steak dinner is really expensive? Or because he thinks it's really cheap? If you guess wrong about his intentions, you will either make him feel like a cheapskate, or some kind of country bumpkin. So, you shrug your shoulders and just say "huh."

That's sort of how baseball fans tend to react when they hear about draft signing bonuses. So the Tigers just committed $7 million and change to Rick Porcello. Is that a rip-off or a bargain? Well, we don't know; clearly it's a rip-off if he turns out like Brien Taylor and a bargain if he turns out like Josh Beckett. But are above-slot signing bonuses generally a good deal for the club?

I've long asserted that the answer to this question is yes, simply because we've established elsewhere that draft picks usually provide a very good return on investment to their clubs. It does not necessarily follow that paying extra for draft picks produces sufficient extra reward. By definition, draft picks go for below-market value because the player has limited bargaining power; that's why compensation scales up so much when a player becomes a free agent on a technicality or can make a credible threat to play another sport. However, teams might not be discerning enough about just whom they give that extra money to. Among others, players receiving bonuses way above their slot include Gavin Floyd, Michael Garciaparra, Eric Munson, and Mike Gosling. It is hardly a guarantor of success.

If for any reason you haven't read Kevin Goldstein's outstanding background piece on the subject of draft slots and signing bonuses, please take a moment to do so. Basically, the draft slots are quasi-official numbers (though not binding) provided to each club by MLB. In 2006, for example, it was recommended that the first pick make $4 million and the second pick make $3.25 million. All teams follow the draft slot recommendations much of the time, and some of them follow them all of the time. In any given draft, there are perhaps a dozen or a half-dozen players out of the first 100 picks that come in materially above slot.

Teams have two ways to ignore the slotting bonuses if they so desire. First, they can simply give the player the bonus they want to give him and brush off the angry phone call from Park Avenue. Alternatively, they can guarantee a major-league contract to the player, which has much the same effect but can preserve the appearance that they've respected the slot system. The Royals, for example, gave Luke Hochevar a $3.5 million bonus last year, which was under MLB's recommendation of $4 million. But they also guaranteed him $1.8 million in major-league money, bringing the total value of the package to $5.3 million.

As far as Luke Hochevar is concerned, that was an above-slot offer, because for all intents and purposes, guaranteed major-league money is just as valuable to the player as a signing bonus. The typical major-league package will guarantee a salary over a period of four or five seasons, including the season in which the player was drafted. He does not actually have to be in the majors to receive this money. A typical sequence for a player with a five-year guaranteed contract might be:

- Year 1: Drafted by MLB club. Joins minor-league club in August, does not reach majors.
- Year 2: Player gets recalled to majors after September 1, which doesn't count against his service-time clock.
- Year 3: Player begins the year in the majors and spends the season there. At its conclusion, he's accumulated 1.0 years of service time.
- Year 4: Player's sophomore season in majors. He's accumulated 2.0 years of service time by year's end.
- Year 5: Player's third season in the majors. He doesn't have quite enough service time to qualify for arbitration under "Super Two" status, so he continues to be paid under the reserve clause.
- Year 6: Player is finally eligible for arbitration. However, at this point his original deal has expired, and the team needs to come up with some fresh money.

In other words, the way that these deals are structured, the guaranteed seasons almost never overlap with a player's arbitration years, when he can actually begin to earn some real money. Since pre-arbitration players are generally paid close to the league minimum, all the team is doing is making a down payment on a couple years' worth of the minimum salary, and that's if the player reaches the majors in the first place. Between 1998 and 2001, for example, there were 11 draft picks who received guaranteed major-league packages. Only one of those players (Mark Prior) reached an arbitration season while still under the terms of his original contract, and he had a clause to opt out of his deal once he did (which he exercised).

The chart below presents several different conceptions of slot value for the first 100 picks in the draft. The green line indicates the actual slotting bonuses as recommended by MLB in 2006. The blue line represents the average amount that the players in each draft slot were actually paid between 1998 and 2006, including any guaranteed major-league money. As you can see, this number generally follows the recommended slot money, but it's noticeably higher in the case of the first four or five draft picks. This is even more apparent if we look at the orange line, which sorts the players not by where they were drafted, but by how much they were paid. So Mark Prior rates as the #1 pick in 2001 rather than Joe Mauer, for example, since he was given $10,250,000 in guaranteed money to Mauer's $5,150,000.

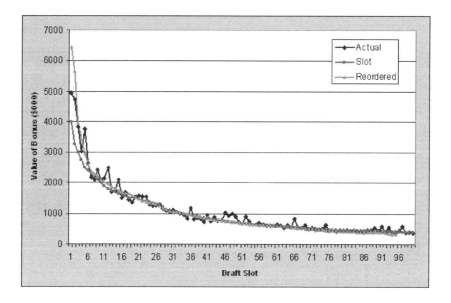

It is this orange line that represents the truest conception of how MLB teams value their draft picks. As you can see, the teams are fairly well-behaved in general, but they will go well above slot for roughly the five most talented players in a given draft, and especially for the best one or two players—the highest-paid player in each year's draft class can expect about $6.5 million in guaranteed money, well above MLB's recommendation of $4 million for the #1 pick.

Teams are doing this for a simple reason: it's much more proportionate to what these elite players are actually worth. The next graph presents a comparison of the de facto and de jure slot values to lifetime WARP scores of players in particular draft slots as calculated by Rany Jazayerli.

The most noticeable difference is that the first five picks in the draft, and particularly the #1 overall pick, are worth considerably more than the MLB slotting system provides for:

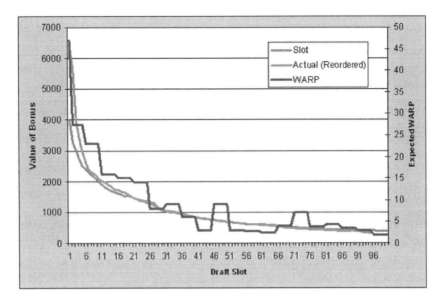

If I were running Major League Baseball, I might provide a range of acceptable bonuses for the first dozen or so picks in the draft, rather than simply one number. Something like this would work pretty well.

Now, you can argue that if you provide teams with a range, they're naturally going to gravitate toward the upper end of that range. But all drafts are not created equal, particularly toward the top of the spectrum; Justin Upton was a substantially better prospect than Luke Hochevar, and everyone knew it. More importantly, teams are already ignoring the slotting system where the talent is strong enough to warrant it, usually by "hiding" bonuses in the form of guaranteed MLB money. If you got the teams to abandon the practice of providing major-league contracts to draft picks, you could go up to the top of these ranges without creating any inflation in the draft system.

Pick	Range (in $100K)
#1	$4,000-7,000
#2	$3,500-6,000
#3	$3,000-5,000
#4	$2,750-4,000
#5	$2,500-3,500
#6	$2,250-3,250
#7	$2,100-3,000
#8	$2,000-2,750
#9	$1,900-2,500
#10	$1,800-2,225
#11	$1,750-2,000
#12	$1,700-1,850
#13	$1,650
#14	$1,600
#15	$1,550
...	

Frankly, all that the rigid slot structure is doing is impeding the talent from being distributed to those that most need it, because the teams that refuse to go above slot are usually the teams that are—how can I put this nicely—economically illiterate. It's bad for the competitive ecology of the sport when the Pirates draft a mid-first round talent with the #2 pick because they want to ensure they have a prime seat at Bob DuPuy's Christmas Gala. Some clubs need protection from themselves.

FUTURE SHOCK
And in This Corner...
Kevin Goldstein

As agent Scott Boras faced off with the Pirates (and the MLBPA took on the Commissioner's Office), Kevin Goldstein dissected the contentious signing of prospect Pedro Alvarez at the 2008 deadline.

It really was the statement heard 'round the world, as from the time of its release until the end of the day, my phone has been burning in non-stop discussions with teams, agents, players, and other members of the media all looking to talk about the Pedro Alvarez situation. The statement issued by the Pirates is very strong in tone and tells us quite a bit in only 575 words. We all know that Pittsburgh team president Frank Coonelly has a close relationship with the commissioner's office, and the document almost sounds as if it came straight from New York. Let's take a word-by-word look at it and talk about what is actually known, what is merely rumored, and what may eventually happen.

> At the Pirates' request, the Office of the Commissioner today placed Pedro Alvarez on Major League Baseball's Restricted List. The Pirates were forced to request that Pedro be placed on the Restricted List because we were informed by his agent, Scott Boras, that Pedro will not sign the contract to which he agreed on August 15. Boras further informed us that Pedro will not report to the Club unless we renegotiate his contract and agree to pay him more than the $6 million signing bonus to which he agreed.

The first sentence simply describes a legal maneuver meant to protect the Pirates' best interests. It's important to note here that Pedro Alvarez has not signed a contract. That's not unique. As we get to the final hours of the deadline, teams are in one place, agents in another, and players are often in a third. All a team has to do is to notify the Commissioner's Office that the terms to a deal have been reached. This is an important point that we'll get back to later on, when we attempt to figure out what Scott Boras is trying to achieve. Having Alvarez put on the restricted list is the way that the Pirates make a claim to their control of the player; it prevents anyone else from talking to him and also gives them a legal leg to stand on should the Alvarez camp try going the independent-ball route. This is also the first of several mentions that Boras wants to renegotiate the deal, and it's one of the main sticking points here. If one follows the letter of the rule, Alvarez has either signed and is a Pirate, or he hasn't signed and the deadline has passed, which now forces him to wait a year to re-enter the draft. But that's not what Boras is looking for—he's looking for a renegotiation, and believe it or not, these aren't totally uncharted waters.

> *The Major League Rules provide that a player who refuses to sign a Uniform Player Contract to which he has agreed and report to the signing Club shall, upon a report of the signing Club, be placed on the Restricted List until he signs a contract reflecting the terms to which he has agreed. Such a player may not sign a contract with or play for any other Club. While demanding that we renegotiate his contract and pay Pedro more than the $6 million signing bonus to which Pedro agreed, Mr. Boras has contended that the contract we reached with Pedro was consummated after the August 15 deadline. This claim was not raised on the evening of the 15th when we informed Mr. Boras that Major League Baseball had confirmed that the contract was submitted in a timely fashion. Mr. Boras asserted this claim several days later, after all of the draft signings had become publicized.*

Note the term "timely fashion"—how it avoids saying anything about the midnight deadline. We'll come back to that one as well after we really set this candle to burning.

> *The Pirates are confident that the contract reached with Pedro Alvarez was agreed to and submitted to Major League Baseball in a timely fashion and properly accepted by Major League Baseball. In fact, the contract between the Kansas City Royals and Eric Hosmer, another Boras client, was submitted to the Office of the Commissioner after our contract with Pedro was submitted. Mr. Boras is apparently satisfied with the $6 million bonus that he secured for Mr. Hosmer and has not challenged the validity of that contract. Mr. Boras has been informed that if he pursues a claim that our contract with Pedro was not timely he puts Eric Hosmer's contract with Kansas City in jeopardy.*

Wow. This is a huge power play for so early in the process. This is sitting down at the World Series of Poker and going all-in on your first hand before the flop. Hosmer is suddenly hit by shrapnel—at risk of becoming collateral damage in a war that went from skirmish to blitzkrieg in about three seconds flat (or more literally, 12 days). Also a Scott Boras client, Hosmer got his $6 million and is already playing, going 3-for-6 with a pair of doubles in his first two games for Idaho Falls in the Pioneer League. But once again, we see the term "timely fashion." Not the midnight deadline, simply a timely fashion. According to multiple sources, Hosmer did not come to terms with the Royals until after the midnight deadline. He turned down $5.5 million just minutes before and agreed to the $6 million offer after midnight. With the deadline approaching, the Royals seemingly contacted Major League Baseball and asked for some kind of window in which they could finish negotiations, and that request was granted. In multiple discussions with industry insiders, nobody whom I spoke with had ever been through such a process themselves, but they universally believed that baseball would likely allow such a thing in some cases, since an extension window would be in the best interests of both sides in the negotiation.

This creates a number of open questions. First, is the deadline real or not? Hosmer and the Royals clearly received an extension, and there have been industry rumors concerning an extension for the Nationals and Aaron Crow as well—an extension that did not result in a deal. Not insisting that the deadline really means The Deadline only further breaks this broken process. The second question involves whether or not the Pirates were also granted an extension to complete negotiations with Alvarez. If they were, they could be in a bit of a pickle, as either the deadline was the deadline and Alvarez is unsigned because he came in late, or he's signed to a deal for which Boras has found another loophole.

The Players Association has now stepped into the fray and filed a grievance, issuing a statement that says the action "was not filed on behalf of any particular player." Their statement further confirms the information regarding extensions being granted, saying in part, "Within hours after this year's August 15 midnight deadline passed, the Players Association learned from several sources that the Commissioner's Office had extended the deadline for negotiating and reporting signings with drafted players. This was done without notice or consultation with the Players Association, despite a firm deadline having been established though collective bargaining."

The statement does not define what kind of relief they will seek from the grievance—that would come from an arbitration panel—but this could take us to the most aggressive of all legal arguments that could be made in Alvarez' favor, as one could legally claim that the rules of the process were not followed in Alvarez' case, therefore making Alvarez completely exempt from the process and thus a free agent. It should be noted that, at least initially, this is not what Boras is looking for; the Pirates' statement seems to solely indicate a desire for a new negotiating window. However, as with most issues of this nature, the further down the line it goes, the more both parties can become entrenched.

Now, back to Hosmer for a moment. If Alvarez' deal is ruled illegal on the basis of timing alone, then logic would dictate that Hosmer's deal could meet the same fate. It's important to note that Boras has not in any way contested the Hosmer contract, but the agent's tactics with his other client have put this one within the blast zone. Which again takes us back to the legality of a window extension, and whether or not the Pirates received one. As an additional note, Hosmer has already signed an actual contract, has already played, and has likely already received a significant amount of money. There is no way he'd have NCAA eligibility should his deal be voided.

> The Pirates made several attempts to commence negotiations immediately following the draft and were willing and ready to agree to pay Pedro a $6 million signing bonus from the very outset. Predictably, however, Mr. Boras refused to engage in any negotiations at all until shortly before the August 15 deadline and even then an agreement was reached only

> *after Pedro took control of the negotiations.*

This paragraph really comes to the core of the Boras problem, which in many ways appears to be an ego thing. Boras did not agree to Pittsburgh's offer, but Alvarez did. Six million dollars is a lot of money for a kid from modest upbringings whose father drives a taxi as the main bread-winner for a family living in New York's tough Washington Heights neighborhood.

> *Regrettably, we are not surprised that Mr. Boras would attempt to raise a meritless legal claim in an effort to compel us to renegotiate Pedro's contract to one more to his liking. We are, however, disappointed that Pedro would allow his agent to pursue this claim on his behalf. Pedro showed tremendous fortitude and independent thinking when he agreed to his contract on August 15.*

Indications all along were that Alvarez wanted to play; that eventually he seemed to have had enough of the protracted negotiations and agreed to a very rich deal. However, Boras thought he could get him more and has obviously convinced Alvarez of just that in the past two weeks. Another factor is that Boras did not technically "win" this draft; CAA did when then got $6.2 million for their client, Buster Posey. Don't discount this measly $200,000 as possibly playing a huge role in this maneuver—Boras' ego is sizable, and he does not like to be bruised with also-ran laurels. Boras has always owned the draft, and now someone has done a better job for their client, and he's not going to take that quietly.

> *The Office of the Commissioner has assured us that we have a valid contract with Pedro and that it will vigorously defend any claim to the contrary. Despite our disappointment, we continue to believe in Pedro Alvarez the person and the baseball player and remain excited to add Pedro to our system. We will sit down with Pedro and his family as soon as Mr. Boras' claim is rejected to chart a new and much more productive start to Pedro's career with the Pittsburgh Pirates.*

The Pirates wrap up with a carefully constructed ending and a fine PR move. The Pirates believe that in the end Alvarez will begin his career with the organization, and they want him to come up as the young exciting superstar, not as public enemy number one.

So where do we do from here? The battle between the MLBPA and the Commissioner's Office will begin as early as September 10, and the statement from the MLBPA made references to "inaccuracies" in the statement released by Coonelly and the Pirates without going into specifics. There are certainly some half-truths in the statement, especially in terms of the "timely fashion" in which the contract was submitted. MLB broke the rules in granting extension windows for later negotiations. They did so with the best intentions for both the team and the player at the time, but they didn't see the bigger picture, and now they just might have to pay a large price.

FUTURE SHOCK
The Alvarez Standoff, Resolved
Kevin Goldstein

After Pedro Alvarez signed with the Pirates, Kevin Goldstein described how the deal went down.

Late Sunday night, the Pedro Alvarez drama took a turn toward a surprising conclusion when the second overall pick in this year's draft agreed to terms on a major-league deal that could pay him close to $8 million over the next four years.

There is still much to be done here. Alvarez has yet to actually sign a contract. There is still a physical that needs to happen, and there are still items to be worked out, including the salary guarantee provisions and injury protections that agent Scott Boras routinely appends to the deals that he negotiates. In addition, the union and Major League Baseball have to agree to additional settlements around the grievance in order to put this all to bed. As a result, this week's grievance hearings will not take place, but for now, the grievance is officially on hold, as opposed to dropped. All indications are that this will all be taken care of over the next week or so, and all sides are working diligently to end this. This conclusion will also release Royals first-round pick Eric Hosmer from his "pending active" purgatory.

Conversations with multiple sources indicate that the Pirates and the Alvarez camp re-opened discussions on or around the first day of the hearing two weeks ago. These discussions took place with the knowledge and bilateral agreement of the union and Major League Baseball, and arbitrator Shyam Das also approved of the talks.

Sources indicate that the first day of testimony, which featured Commissioner Bud Selig and Dan Halem, MLB's number-two labor attorney, did not go well in any way for Major League Baseball. The feeling among many is that MLB informed the Pirates to work out the best deal possible, as some worst-case scenarios were suddenly looking very possible, primarily the one that included the initial deal being voided and the Pirates being punished by losing their compensation pick for not signing him.

From a previous article on possible outcomes, this is most related to the second scenario I suggested, in which an additional negotiating window was provided. In theory, this provided

Alvarez with a normalized negotiating arena, one that he did not have once the extensions were granted. As discussed in that piece, such an allowance would create some understandably hard feelings among other draftees and agents who feel that this arrangement allowed both the Pirates and Alvarez more negotiating time, as well as more knowledge than either they or their clients received in their own negotiations. In order to avoid this from becoming an issue, both sides will hold their noses and work together to insist that this is no longer a draft contract. If you look at the details of the new deal, one aspect of it is very important with regard to this subject: the bonus has not changed. It remains $6 million, so that both sides can say that this is the draft deal initially agreed to, and that all of the things on top of it (the major-league deal and all of its advantages, the guaranteed salaries, etc.) represent the settlement in this case.

As for the settlement of the grievance, there are still details to be worked out, and most of them revolve around the undocumented reporting process. The current system shuts the union out, as communications are solely between teams and MLB's offices. That helped create confusion as to the precise timing of the Alvarez and Hosmer situations, and some believe this might be addressed by no longer requiring an agreement of terms, but rather an executed contract by the deadline, with, of course, no more extensions granted. This would eliminate much of the gray area, and many teams hope that it would also end Major League Baseball's ongoing practice of delaying the acceptance and announcements of many over-slot bonuses until the last week before the draft, a policy that delays teams from getting their highly-paid players on the field.

Let's make no mistake here—Scott Boras won this one. It's not a massive, blowout victory, but it's a win; he got his player more money and benefits. That wasn't necessarily the ultimate goal, but it counts for something. Beyond that, Boras ensured that this situation will not happen again, and on a grander scale, Pirates president Frank Coonelly took him on directly and looks foolish for his troubles. As one front-office staffer with another team assessed the Pirates' performance, "they went into a gun fight with a water pistol and ran away before shots were fired."

There's no doubt that the Pirates lost this one. Yes, they got their player, a potential middle-of-the-order run producer who instantly becomes the top prospect in the system, but at the same time, the negative image hit both externally and within baseball is massive. Polls taken by local media had most fans blaming the Pirates for this situation. Coonelly looks like a paper tiger after making a strongly-worded statement at the beginning of this situation, only to fold up like a cheap suit in the end and give Boras and Alvarez that extra negotiating window—the concept that he was so against in the first place.

Now we can start looking forward to next year's draft. Going into 2008, the Pirates' new administration was under considerable pressure to take a potential superstar, no matter the cost, and avoid the cheap tactics that had the previous administration selecting Daniel Moskos over Matt Wieters in 2007. If the season ended today, the Pirates would select fourth overall in the draft behind the Mariners, Nationals, and Padres. As usual, many of the top talents in the draft are being advised by Boras. This year's actions simply refocus the pressure on next year's draft, as the Pirates once more could be placed in the position of being forced to select a Boras player or again be accused of playing it cheap after going without a winning year since George W. Bush's father was president.

When the Pirates had a press conference to announce the initial signing of Alvarez in August, owner Bob Nutting called the new administration, led by Coonelly and general manager Neal Huntington, "the single best management team in all of baseball, maybe all of sports." Much like Coonelly's opening statement which began this battle, so far, that's all talk.

PROSPECTUS Q&A
Logan White, Part 1
David Laurila

David Laurila talked to Dodgers Assistant General Manager Logan White about draft data and his drafting philosophy.

Few teams draft as well as the Dodgers, and even fewer do so with a data-driven approach that melds risk aversion with a gunslinger's bravado. Logan White and company aren't shy about taking high-school pitchers in the first round, nor are they unwilling to take a calculated gamble that a highly-prized sleeper will fall into their laps in a later round. The results have been impressive, with the likes of Clayton Kershaw, Matt Kemp, James Loney, and Russell Martin already in Dodger blue, and Dee Gordon, Chris Withrow, and Ethan Martin soon to follow. White, the club's assistant general manager in charge of scouting, sat down with Baseball Prospectus to talk about his approach to the amateur draft and why "The Dodgers Way" has been so successful.

David Laurila: Scouting directors have reputations. How do you think people around the game view you?

Logan White: That's a great question, because I've never been asked about it and have never really thought about it. My concern is that my staff respects me, so I would hope that if I have a reputation it is that people respect the job I do and that I have the knowledge base and a plan.

DL: Taking the best player available is a mantra among scouting directors, but it really isn't that simple, is it?

LW: You're right; it's not that simple. We always say we want the best available talent when we're picking, but I like to think that I'm a little bit more of a strategist. Sometimes you might take a player who is a little lesser than another player if you think you can flip them and get both, whereas if you don't do it that way, you won't. There is strategy involved, and we're not afraid to use it. When I first started, a lot of the major-league teams weren't drafting as many high-school players and were strictly college-oriented. That was in 2002 and 2003, particularly teams like

Toronto, and knowing that we were certainly going to be more high-school-oriented. So, I like to think that we're strategy-based and that we pay attention to the trends, but at the end of the day, you still want to draft the guy who is going to have the best major-league career.

DL: To what extent do you analyze draft data and trends?

LW: I believe that we were ahead of the curve back when I started, because everybody was focused in on the individual statistics of the players. At the major-league level that is certainly very valuable, and even in the minor leagues it's going to show you trends, but I think it is less applicable in the amateur draft. What we focused on was the use of statistical data and analysis of what the draft has produced. One of the first things I did when I came here was look at the history of the Dodgers drafts. I looked at how many players they produced and I broke it down by the decade. They produced roughly 30 per decade up until the 1990s and then it was about 12. I found out by looking at that that the key to success—at least getting to the World Series and having championship teams—is that you need to produce about 30 major-league players. And when I say 30, what I mean is that they need to have five years of major-league service time or better. Guys who just a got a cup of coffee don't count.

We also look at where we're picking in the draft. Every year we're picking late. A lot of teams have a pretty good idea of what they're doing out there, so what I found by researching past data is that if you're picking 26th, a lot of time the quality college players have been taken. I'm not saying there isn't an occasional guy that is there, or an exception to the rule, but as a history you had Jimmy Rollins, Scott Rolen—all of these guys were second-round picks, whereas if you say, "I'm going to get Barry Zito" or "I'm going to get Mark Mulder," well, those guys were taken by the time we picked. Prince Fielder, Zack Greinke—you can go on and on. These guys were taken fifth, eighth, ninth, and in slots like that, so what I did was pay attention specifically to what the draft has produced where we're usually picking, and I let that trend lead us.

Another thing I did was take trends, from the entire history of the draft, breaking it down as to how many players made it to the big leagues versus how many signed out of each area. So, I knew how many players came from which state, and which region of the country, and I also knew the success rate that each position had. Not surprisingly, left-handed college pitching had the highest success rate—by a little bit of a margin, not a lot. That's the type of stuff that we utilize. I like to think that we use statistics and probabilities an awful lot.

DL: Is there anything else that maybe differentiates you?

LW: A lot of teams get caught up in making sure that they turn in every player that is going to get drafted. If you do that, you have 1,500 players. What I want our scouts to focus on is, "Let's really know the 600 that we're going to turn in." I don't want every player; I want them to be more selective and more discerning and be able to eliminate guys who aren't going to be major-league players. If we do a better job of scouting we should be able to pick the roughly 150 that the draft will usually produce—that's from cup-of-coffee guys to all-stars to whatever. I figure that if your scouts are good enough to analyze and break it down to 600—and maybe they miss two dozen cup-of-coffee guys—it is easier to figure 150 out of 600 than 150 out of 1,500. Those are things we look at.

Another thing we do—and we're probably one of the few teams that do it—is that we work the draft board backwards. In all my years of being in draft rooms, we'd go in and we're already tired because we've been traveling all spring, and we'd rank the top players right away. We'd rank our top 60, we'd rank our top 100, and whatever. But then—my experience has been—later on, guys would kind of get put on the board randomly at times. I felt that if we go in and rank the board backwards, starting with the senior-sign guys and down-the-line guys, and try to pick guys out of that group and work our board backwards, we'd have more success in the later rounds. Closer to draft day is when we actually put our rank board together. We already have a pretty good idea of who our first- and second-round guys are, or who we are focused in on. We've taken a number of kids down the line who have played in the major leagues. We took Russell Martin in the 17th round, Eric Stults 15th, James McDonald 11th—you can see our track record on that. We got Travis Denker around the 20th round.

DL: When do names first begin going up on your board?

LW: Our guys turn in reports, and we have all the lists in our computer, but we don't begin putting them on the board until around the end of March. Now, I don't pay any attention to it until we get in there for the draft and really start working it. One of the things that we're trying to do this year, and I don't know how it will work because we're doing it differently than we ever have in the past, is that we had a meeting here in February with our cross checkers and supervisors, and we went over all of our scouts top-12 players—who they had going into the spring. We watched video film of them, we talked about them—what we need to know more about them, what we need to see more of, if there is someone we need to eliminate already. Things like that. I think it may actually give us a better direction to start the season.

The fact that video is better than it ever used to be is a help, although that's just a tool, like anything. You certainly can't draft on it. I've tried that and made my mistakes in the past, drafting off of video. It's a tool, just like the radar gun. You can't draft off of it, but you certainly want to utilize it.

Another thing I do is keep a private log of certain types of arm actions—the success rates of them. Certain types of deliveries—their success and failure rates. The same with hitters. There are certain things that we will either like or stay away from based on our own statistics of how those have been working over the past 10 or 15 years. I've kept these since I was an area scout. Let's say for example that a guy is a slinger or he has a bad wrist wrap. How many guys have that who have been drafted and signed, that I've seen, and have actually made it? And how far? Things like that. I've kept pretty good records and I haven't publicized them, not even to my own staff, but I do utilize that kind of stuff.

DL: Did you use that type of data when assessing Chris Withrow?

LW: Absolutely. And for us, the thing with Chris is that in terms of athleticism he was off the charts. In terms of arm action and delivery, he was at the top of the chart with everything we see. Obviously, the physical stuff is there. He was 90-94 in high school and he's throwing harder than that now. He's got real good rotation on the breaking ball. He has all of those things, and he has a father who played at the University of Texas, and minor-league baseball, so he has some history with professional baseball in his background. He scored really well on all of the things that we look at, even the psychological matrix that we use. And I want to make sure that this is understood: You can have all of those factors working, saying that someone is really good, or even off the chart, and they still fail. There are two things that happen to pitchers, and I talk to our pitchers in camp here—there are two things that keep pitchers with major-league stuff from making it. That's injury and choices. More specifically, bad choices, whether it's off-field, work habits, whatever. If they have the stuff, it's usually injury or choices, so that's one of our outlooks.

Pitching is the one position that you draft where guys are going to get taken out through no control of your own. By that I mean the injury factor. With position players you don't really have that come up. It comes up occasionally on a knee, or something like that, but it's pretty rare that a position player gets taken out by an injury.

DL: To what extent can you quantify injury risk in young pitchers?

LW: I've done studies on it, and you have to look at what I call the two-four rule. I've told people this in the past, and basically what I'm saying is that 50 percent of the time you're going to have an injury of some form or another where they have to have a surgery. Then you have the risk of how many of those 50 percent that break down are going to come back. About 20 or 30 percent aren't going to come back to the same level, so you have to factor in that maybe 30 percent of your pitchers are going to get wiped out by an injury that you have no control over. That is one reason that we draft a lot of pitching and why you have to draft a lot of pitching.

Maybe it's a bad analogy, but say you're looking at automobiles and you're looking at a top-of-the-line Mercedes Benz. It has the best engineering and everybody says that the aerodynamics are great and it has the smoothest ride. It's the top car on the market. Even that car might sometimes be a lemon. You're going to end up with some lemons, but if you end up buying that car over a

Kia, or something like that, you're probably going to have more longer-term success than you would with the Kia. It's kind of like that with pitching. You know you're going to have some factors, but you still have to work off the ideal.

DL: What constitutes an ideal?

LW: We have what we consider the ideal pitcher and the ideal hitter, and we work off of ideals. We haven't found a perfect pitcher yet, nor a perfect hitter, but that's what we work off of. We try to get that person. We're looking for Roger Clemens; we're looking for Pedro Martinez; we're looking for Curt Schilling—guys who had those types of deliveries or arm actions that allowed them to be successful for a long time. Nolan Ryan. And then we have a similar thing we look for with hitters. We try to teach our scouts what to look for—here is the ideal; here are some of the key points we're looking for.

I think, too, that one of our biggest successes is that while we haven't given psychological tests, we do have a psychological matrix that I've come up with over my years of scouting. I got a minor in psychology, in college, and I utilize that. There are certain things we ask the scouts to find out about the players that we have to know. Examples are GPA and SAT scores. We find out if their parents are married or not; we find out their birth order. We find out all of that stuff and put it together in a matrix, and it gives me a composite score that tells me an order of makeup. When we go into a draft, we know where guys rank from a makeup standpoint.

DL: Do you use standardized tests or only your own?

LW: We don't do the standardized testing at all. I don't want to disparage all psychological tests, but I've had too many in the past, with teams that I've worked for, that have been totally wrong. To me, it was a lot like reading a horoscope—it was hit-and-miss and too generic. I never had one rank the players, whereas this one is different. It's based on a lot of different factors that I don't think they look at. It has a lot to do with past history and not just the player—it could be his family and things like that. Believe it or not, it has been pretty key in helping us make decisions on some players, and I think that's part of why we've had some success. Plus, it helps our scouts realize: "Do you know what? Our butts are on the line." It tells them: "I've got to know. I need to know what kind of student this guy is. I need to know if he has a job after school. Has he ever worked in his life? Are his parents together or are they divorced? Maybe one of them has passed away." We want them to find out all of those things.

Going back to what I was saying about 1,500 players, we have 17 area scouts and there are maybe 100 players on their lists. No way can these area scouts get into 100 homes and talk to 100 families and do a thorough job of it. That's one of my reasons for getting my guys to really focus in on the talent—who they think are the real players—and let's really know them. I'd rather have my area scout have 40 guys and really know them, rather than have 100 guys. We'll take a chance that we might miss a guy, but I'll promise you that of the 40, he's going to know them better than the other scouts in his area because of how much data they have to gather and know. It's a process that I think is important, and it also gives us the ability to sign players because most of the time the parents know us from our talking to them. That's unless it's a case where we're trying to lay low in the weeds and not tip our hand or something.

PROSPECTUS Q&A
Logan White, Part 2
David Laurila

In the second part of his discussion with Dodgers AGM Logan White, David Laurila talked about Dodgers prospects, Dodgers executives, and other scouts and front offices around the game.

David Laurila: You're in charge of scouting, but you also employ an amateur scouting director. How does Tim Hallgren's role differ from your own in regard to the draft?

Logan White: You know what? We do it just like we did. When I was promoted to assistant GM, the only thing that changed significantly was my international work and level of involvement with the major-league team. The one element that [general manager] Ned [Colletti] requested was that I make sure to stay very focused on the amateur draft, because we'd had success. Tim and I had worked together as a scouting director and a national cross checker, so it was an easy process for us after he was promoted. We still collaborate and work together. The final say is obviously mine—who we take and don't take—but we work the draft board together like we have since I've been here.

DL: You draft more high-school pitchers than do most scouting directors. Why?

LW: Number one, we trust our development people. We think our development staff is outstanding. We think that when [pitchers] come here, we can take care of their arms better than the college game. And with the coaching staff that we have, we think that we have better instruction than the college game. We have great confidence that these guys are going to make major-league pitchers out of the talent that we hand them. We think they have fewer flaws. Plus, if you notice the talent quicker, you can get it quicker. By waiting until he goes to college, you might not get that player down the line. For example, we took James McDonald out of high school. To me, he's the perfect example of being able to get a pitcher who has some ceiling that you might do something with. But there are a lot of good college pitchers who make the big leagues—we took Aaron Miller last year and Josh Lindbloom—so we are definitely not opposed to taking college pitchers.

I guess, to me, it's kind of a weird question. It's kind of like saying, "You guys sign more players of one nationality than another." To me, nationality doesn't play into it any more than the high school-college thing does. I think that if we evaluate the player right, the high-school player has just as good a chance of success as the college player, and a lot of times better. They may have a better secondary pitch, they may have a better delivery, and they may have better size. In today's game, with the showcases and the exposure these kids get—like when we took Chad Billingsley. He was arguably the ace of the Junior Olympics team that won the gold medal. So there is a track record there already. He's pitched against great competition. It's not like you're taking some raw high-school kid from Iowa that you're guessing on. Clayton Kershaw is the same way. [Jonathan] Broxton is from Georgia, albeit from a small town, but we loved his delivery. He was 90-93 [mph] with a good arm, and he had an excellent breaking ball. If they've got quality secondary pitches to go with a plus fastball, and they've got size, it doesn't really matter if they're high-school or college.

I do think that college is easier to go evaluate. They're closer, and it's easy to drive to a college ballpark and get involved in the atmosphere and see them in that environment. It's darn tough to go out to Defiance, Ohio and freeze your butt off and try to determine what someone is. But if you have the courage to do it, you can have success with it. I actually wish that all teams would just draft college players and leave us the high-school guys. That would be fine by me.

DL: You drafted Dee Gordon in the fourth round, in 2008. At the time, did you have any idea that he would become the top-rated prospect in your organization?

LW: I don't know if I would have expected him to be ranked as our top player, but I will tell you that when he came to us… [Dodgers farm director} De Jon Watson had roomed with his father in pro ball at one time, and De Jon said, "Hey, I have this kid, Flash's kid." I said, "Yeah, let's bring him down to Vero Beach." We brought him down and he was outstanding in his workout for me, but De Jon and I both kind of cold-shouldered him. You can ask the kid and he'll tell you the same thing. We kind of acted like, "Hey, thanks for coming" and we didn't bother him for the rest of the year, until late, because we did not want to tip our hand in any way, shape, form, or fashion. But once you know the player and see his desire and his tool set, his skills, it's not surprising. When we drafted him, and I think that our scouts—Tim and everybody—would agree, I was his biggest fan. I'd had a lot of looks at him. But to say that he'd be our number-one prospect? No, but after he's been here, and knowing what kind of makeup he's got, it doesn't surprise me.

DL: You mentioned having an ideal-hitter prototype. How would you describe your third-round pick in 2008, Kyle Russell?

LW: Well, Kyle Russell was a little bit different from how we normally draft, because generally we like to draft guys who are quality hitters first and then the power comes. I believe that you have to hit to get to your power. But Kyle Russell's makeup as a person is outstanding, and he's got tremendous raw power. And in our opinion, he can play center field. We're probably going to play him in center field this year. He can run, he can throw, and we figured that if the guy can hit .280, and hit 20-plus [home runs], and play center field, we don't care if he strikes out 150 times; he's going to be a pretty decent major-league player.

One of my scouts that I trust is very much a Kyle Russell fan, and there's that yin and yang where you look at all that other stuff and then you also look at your scouts and piece it all together. When we got to the third round, we just felt that the tools—being able to play defense and hit for that kind of power—were too much to pass up. Plus, we had Billy Mueller, who was a good hitter, in the draft room, and I asked him, "What do you think? Can we help him with that uphill swing he's got? Can we improve it?" He seemed to think that we could. Sometimes you have to have trust in people that they can help with things like that, and I think that if Kyle Russell makes those improvements, he's got a chance to be a pretty special hitter. I know it's rare, because there were guys like [Reggie] Abercrombie and different people in the past that I wasn't big on because it's tough, when you strike out that much, to get to the power. But I think that Kyle will, and I think that he'll be able to play center field. He's really smart and a hard worker with some pretty good aptitude.

DL: How closely do you work with De Jon Watson?

LW: I've been the most fortunate man in scouting, in my opinion, in that I've had really good development people. It started with Bill Bavasi and went to Terry Collins, and now De Jon. We've all been on the same page since I got here. I ask for their input, and they ask for mine. One thing about De Jon is that he's scouted. He was the scouting director for Cincinnati, so he knows how tough it is. There's a lot of collaboration that goes on between us, and we have a very good friendship. We help each other all the time and pick each other up on things. We share a lot of things together, and that's important. If you're not going to have one person running both departments, you better have the two on the same page or it could become a disaster.

DL: Does De Jon weigh in on players like Kyle Russell leading up to the draft?

LW: He sits in the draft room, but he doesn't come in and say, "Draft this guy and that guy." Not by any stretch. I'm pretty particular about that. I believe that the scouts scout, and I trust them. It's no more than I allow my scouts to go down to the bullpen and instruct the pitchers. You need to know where to draw the line on what your job is. That doesn't mean you're not going to have input, but you have to go through the right channels. I have no problem if De Jon comes up to me and says, "Hey." It's like with Dee Gordon—I give De Jon credit all the time for being the first person to bring the name to us. That was awesome. But he was never a factor in going, "You have to draft this guy" or "Don't draft this guy." By the same token, I never tell him, "You have to hire this coach." We have a lot of respect for each other that way.

DL: I've heard it said that there are no secrets in scouting, that if someone can play, everyone knows it within five minutes. Do you agree with that?

LW: The people that say that there are no secrets in baseball... I'd say that 90 percent of the time... it's probably like a relationship. With my wife and me, our friends know who we are and everything, but there's maybe 10 percent of our relationship that nobody knows. When you think that everything is an open book, that's when you're going to get beat on a Dee Gordon or a Matt Kemp. You can go look at the Scouting Bureau and see if they had Dee Gordon. If there are no secrets, how can we get Dee Gordon in the fourth round and have him become our top-rated prospect? There are definitely secrets.

I come from the old-school way of thinking, and granted, the internet and everything else makes it harder today, but... and another thing: when I first started scouting, people talked about finding a sleeper. That's what they called them, sleepers. I train my scouts that most of the time the sleeper is right under your nose. What I mean by that is, in my first year of scouting, Arizona State had Mike Kelly, who was the second pick in the draft. They also had a second baseman/shortstop named Fernando Vina who went in the ninth round. Well, Vina turned out to be the best player in a highly-heralded class of players there. And that's what I try to teach scouts. I don't care how the industry drafts them. I don't care where the publications have them. I want our scouts to get the best guy right, because the sleeper might be right under your nose. Yeah, everybody may know about him, but it's how you rank him.

I'm pretty private, and maybe that hasn't always helped me, because I'm not open about sharing draft information with anybody. Your peers probably wonder why you don't want to share with them, but I also don't want to lie to anybody. And I don't want to tell anybody that I like James Loney as a hitter instead of a pitcher. That was a secret. Every team in baseball wasn't thinking that way. There are things that you want to keep in-house, for sure. You don't want to promote that you want to take Russell Martin, this kid at Chipola Junior College, and convert him into a catcher. The minute you do that—there are too many good baseball people. If about eight of these other teams that I know would have known about Dee Gordon, we probably would have had to take him higher than the fourth round. There are too many good scouts out there, and too many good directors who know what they're doing, so the more you can keep information to yourself, the better off you are. In my mind, there's proof. There are definitely secrets, and when I say secrets, probably a few teams may know about someone. And with the 90 percent that we all know about, beauty is still in the eye of the beholder. Only time will tell if you ranked them right.

DL: Having a good staff is obviously crucial. Do you look around the game and say to yourself, "This guy is a great scout; I wish we could bring him on board?"

LW: Let's face it, baseball is very much a good-old-boy-network sport. That's one of the things that they wrote about in the book *Moneyball*, and I think it's true. I think that you have scouts, and other baseball people, who have jobs year to year to year just because of who they know and not because of ability. In a lot of industries that wouldn't fly, but in baseball it does. But I think that if you're objective, and you really research and watch, you learn some things. I learned a lot from some veteran people who helped me along the way. And I look at my peers and see who works and who doesn't, and how they think and how they draft, and I have a lot of respect for a lot of people out there. It's not easy to draft well.

Going back to the 30 per decade I was talking about, we try to get six major-league players out of every draft. That's our goal. And you can look at one person's draft and see that only three guys made it, and another guy had five, but you have to look at more than one year. You have to look at multiple years and at a combination of what they did, including where they were picking in the draft. I've done the research, and if you're picking in the top 15, in the first round, your odds of getting a quality big-league player are far greater. That's just the way the numbers play out. That's partially why we have the mindset of having to be really diligent after the first 15 picks, and more than likely it's going to be a high-school player. There are so many good scouting directors. Say [the Twins'] Mike Radcliffe misses someone. Well, if he does, [the Cubs'] Tim Wilken probably won't, or [the Padres'] Jason McLeod won't. There are a lot of people out there who know how to evaluate. Maybe someone didn't even have a first-round pick and they still got some guys down lower. You say to yourself, "They're doing something right."

DL: Any final thoughts?

LW: Oh, man. I love talking about scouting. I could talk all day about the different aspects of scouting. One thing I will say is that I love that much more attention is being paid to scouting, and that there is an accountability factor with so many people going back and looking at past drafts. That's great. With the internet, and people like yourself, doing this—but don't get me wrong, not every blogger or media outlet is unbiased. Some have a certain way they want to paint something. But a lot of them are open and fair, and it adds to the accountability. We put a high premium on our scouts, on their experience and their wisdom. We put a lot of trust in them. We don't consider our guys to be just information gatherers; we consider them evaluators as well. That's maybe a little different philosophy than some other teams might have.

I come from the old-school way of scouting, but I also like to think that I'm educated enough, and smart and modern enough, to know where a lot of the younger, progressive people are thinking. I admire what the guys in Boston have been doing, like Jason McLeod and Theo Epstein and those guys. They're very progressive. They use a lot of avenues and aren't stuck in just one way of thinking. I like to believe that I'm the same way.

SCOUTING THE DEBATE
Is the Scouts vs. Statheads Argument Overblown?

Jonah Keri

In the spirit of Dayn Perry's "beer and tacos" treatise on the importance of both stats and scouting, Jonah Keri tried his hand at scouting High-A players and discovered that even statheads can be deceived by tools in small samples of performance.

Michael Lewis' *Moneyball* and the fallout from the best-selling book have given rise to what some have deemed the great statheads vs. scouts debate. While some reactionary members of each camp have assumed their battle stations, by and large it's a false argument.

"The goal is the same in either case—identify players who'll help you win at the big-league level," said Joe Bohringer, amateur scout for the Seattle Mariners. "Both methods will help you make your evaluation."

Every team relies on scouting of some kind. Scouting budgets and tie-breaking decisions may vary from team to team, but every club relies on scouts, in some form, to evaluate talent. Likewise, every team uses performance analysis to shape its decisions. Statistics are simply a record of a player's performance. Even the most tools-informed scout on the planet won't throw out results entirely.

Bohringer takes a holistic approach to his work. Just as general managers like Theo Epstein and J.P. Ricciardi have combined scouting backgrounds with analytical approaches to run their ballclubs, so too has Bohringer wedded scouting and analytical principles in his work for the Mariners.

An MIT graduate with a B.S. in Management, Bohringer started his professional life armed with a knowledge and hunger for objective analysis. He hoped to parlay his business acumen into a career in baseball. After several stops, Bohringer landed at Triple-A Ottawa. From there, the parent Expos sent him to the Major League Scouting Bureau—scout school. Bohringer had already cut his teeth keeping pitching charts. He'd also worked on the administrative side, acting as a liaison between the farm director and the big-league club.

But scout school, he said, changed everything. "It was an entirely different way to watch the game. We were taught to observe the mechanics, as opposed to the final results."

Despite that lesson, Bohringer has also immersed himself in statistical research. He's read Bill James, *Moneyball*, *Baseball Prospectus*, and other analytical tomes. He's just as comfortable at a Pizza Feed as is he working closely with Mariners' Amateur Scouting Director Bob Fontaine.

Recently, I took in a game between the homestanding Lake Elsinore Storm (Padres affiliate) and the visiting High Desert Mavericks (Brewers affiliate) with Bohringer, Cleveland Indians scout and long-time baseball man Dave Malpass, and the world's best baseball wife, Angele. Being untrained in scouting, I planned on asking questions between Bohringer's radar gun clockings and recorded throw and run times. No way would I get caught up in admiring a great catch or a burst of speed—I was going to let the larger body of performance guide my evaluations... or at least that's what I told myself. Here's what transpired.

- Speedy High Desert outfielder Kennard Bibbs leads off the game and draws a walk. He gets a great jump off starter Chris Tierney and steals second. Big deal, I say, the guy's a pop-gun hitter (.095 Isolated Slugging through Monday's games). He sure looked fast, though, I think to myself.

    The rest of the inning goes strikeout, walk, double, fielder's choice, groundout to second, as the Mavericks push across one run. How can a scout get a read on a player so quickly, I ask, when you may only see a swing or two per at-bat, three or four times a game?

    "Batting practice is very important," Bohringer says. "You can look for a line-drive or uppercut swing, or if the guy's beating the ball into the ground. You can see it in infield and outfield practice too, whether a player shows soft hands when taking groundballs, if he can throw from the hole at short, if he's fluid chasing down a flyball."

    Turns out minor-league coaches will actually lay out what they want to see during warmups from players in A-ball, which helps the scout a lot; each time he watches infield and outfield practice, he knows the players will give it their all, running through a regimented set of drills. Don't tell Larry Bowa.

- Bottom of the first, and Paul McAnulty steps to the plate. Listed at 5'10", 220 lbs., McAnulty was a 12th-round pick out of Long Beach State in 2002. He's showing moderate power and solid plate discipline, with a decent .293/.396/.473 line. Needing to protect work product, Bohringer isn't tipping his hand about McAnulty or anyone else. He does disclose a scouting truism, though:

"The less physical projection you have, the more polished your skills have to be. If you see a pitcher who throws 85, you may be able to look at him and see a body that will only go 85. If it's a tall, lean guy, it may be different—a more projectable player may be able to improve."

McAnulty is the Storm's #3 hitter and looks like one of the bigger threats on the team. Still, already 23, showing decent but not great power in a hitter's haven while DHing, the scouting and performance analysis views seem to agree here.

- Bohringer brings up another challenge of melding stats with scouting. The further you get from the majors, the less reliable the stats become, and the more scouting reports become necessary. Funny, that sounds exactly like Joe Sheehan talking.

  Both scouts and analysts liked Michael Johnson, a .636 slugger in four years at Clemson. The Padres picked the big first baseman in the second round in '02, but thus far he's disappointed. Turning 24 this week, Johnson has posted a line of .241/.345/.460, striking out about once every three at-bats. He failed to impress in this game, and the clock is ticking.

- I told myself I wouldn't get worked up over any individual plays... but who is this Kervin Jacobo guy, and when did he get possessed by the spirit of Brooks Robinson? I'm cataloguing the Dominican third baseman's plays as the game goes on:

  2nd inning: Charges weak grounder, bare-hand, rocket throw to first for the out
  3rd inning: Ditto
  5th inning: Fields cut-off throw, wheels and fires strike to second, nailing runner trying to advance
  6th inning: Backhand stop on screamer to third as he hits the ground; fast runner beats the throw, still a laser

  I'm mesmerized by this guy.

  Jacobo (pronounced Ha-ko-bo) laces a solid single to center in the fourth, flying out of the box after contact. I turn to Angele and ask how she'd feel about naming our first-born Kervin Jacobo Keri.

  "Your boy runs OK too," says Bohringer, as he and fellow scout Dave Malpass snicker quietly. Something's amiss. I pull open the stats. Through Monday, the 21-year-old Jacobo is hitting .227/.288/.367.

I've let my eyes deceive me. Huckabay will be coming any minute now to claim my BP badge. Huckabay and Jacobo, by the way: distant cousins. True story.

- Chris Tierney, a tall lefty with a funky delivery, isn't showing much. He's throwing only fastballs, topping out at 87 to 89 mph, and from my vantage point behind home plate, looks like he's throwing them dead straight. A High Desert hitter lines one up the middle for a two-run single, nearly knocking Tierney off the mound. And the stats say...42.1 IP, 6.96 ERA, 56 H, 18 Ks, 19 BBs. Ouch.

    It's another case of the scouting report agreeing with the numbers. "A guy like Vladimir Guerrero, the scout and the analyst will both have positive things to say, obviously," Bohringer says as Tierney goes to ball three again. "Most guys are in the 40-60 scouting range, in the middle of the pack, unlike Vlad, who's going to be up there in the 70-80 range. We're paid to spot the subtle differences between the 50 and 55 guys, the 55s and 60s."

    Bohringer's job is essentially the same as any performance-oriented analyst or general manager's. A superstar is a superstar, no matter your philosophy. The trick is to find that hidden gem whose skills get overlooked by the masses. In the late rounds of the amateur draft, an analysis-focused team like the A's or Blue Jays may go after an unknown player with a body unloved by scouts, if the numbers are there. Meanwhile, a tools-oriented team like the Twins or Braves might pursue a raw athlete who's either played little baseball or struggled on the field. Both offer degrees of risk and reward, just in different ways.

- I'm struck by the difficulties of relying on personal observation. Looking over my scorecard, it looks like every player has gone a generic 1-for-3 with a single, without doing anything extraordinary. And what to make of the player who works the count and draws walks? It's tough to find a player with a great batting eye who jumps out at you, Bohringer concedes, as opposed to one who slams a triple off the center-field wall. Plate discipline can be a tie-breaker between two players with similar tools, but it's tough to base a scouting report on it.

    Sample size can be a significant problem with scouting as well, just as it can with statistical analysis. Thirty at-bats beats four at-bats, but you'd always like to have more. Pitchers can be especially tough. A scout may write up a pitcher after a couple starts, noting that he's wild, only to see him strike out eight and walk none the next time he sees him. As with analysis, context must be considered: Does the other team swing at everything? Did the pitcher make a mechanical adjustment? Did he simply have a great day? Learning to spot relevant conditions is a huge part of his job, Bohringer says.

As the game winds down, we see Marcus Nettles, in his third tour of duty at Lake Elsinore this season, fly around the bases for a triple. We see more dazzling plays—a few even of the non-Jacobo variety. We watch players with bodies scouts love and players with the patience that statheads love. Malpass, who's seen all types in his career as a scout, coach and instructor for the Indians, Expos, Long Beach State and elsewhere, waves a hand dismissively.

"Most of what you've seen is irrelevant," he says. At the end of the day, Malpass—like Bohringer, or Billy Beane, or anyone else who follows baseball—goes by one simple, all-encompassing theory:

"No hittee...no playee."

PROSPECTS WILL BREAK YOUR HEART
Spring Training Psychonightmare
Jason Parks

As he recovered from spending 35 straight days watching baseball, Jason Parks captured what spring training is like for a scout.

Detox

The spring training detoxification process started when I received my boarding pass from the obnoxiously attractive boarding pass czar at the JetBue terminal at Phoenix's Sky Harbor International Airport. Her name was "Katie." It was 10:30 p.m. on a Thursday night, and my mental state closely resembled Nick Nolte's liver. As I approached "Katie," my eyes were stinging from the Arizona scene and my skin was rocking this half Guatemalan/half English-countryside tone that made me look slightly dangerous and unkempt. I'd been living in Surprise for five weeks. I started talking to myself at some point during the second week.

"Will you be checking any bags?" She obviously wanted to know my darkest secrets. "Mr. Parks? Will you be checking any bags?"

Playing along with her game, I reluctantly answered, and our relationship took a step forward.

"You look like you've been out in the sun." Katie didn't miss much. "New York? I've always wanted to visit New York." Chuck Woolery would offer to pay for the date at this point. "You are all set, Mr. Parks. Have a great flight."

Just like that, Katie and I parted ways. She passed me a folded piece of heavy stock paper, which I assumed had her cell phone number and a list of her personal likes and dislikes. I played it cool, gave her a wink (I can't wink, so it probably looked a little suspect [read: palsy]) and drifted into the night. The piece of paper in my hand turned out to be the credit card receipt for the second checked bag. Take it easy, "Katie." Thanks for the memories.

I was three hours deep into my five-hour flight, and I had never felt more isolated. I spent 60 percent of the first three hours staring into space and the other 40 percent thinking about what I'd like to think about in the last two hours of the flight. I tried to find solace in my television-viewing options, but you can only watch original Bravo programming so many times before you start to hate your own life and wish harm upon one or all of the Housewives. I reached into my hipster-approved messenger bag to find the contraband alcohol I smuggled onto the plane and stumbled upon the three scouting journals I kept during my tour of duty. I was quickly transported back to Surprise, where I lived a strange *Groundhog Day*-like adventure for an amazing and terrible 35 days. Two hours until wheels-down at JFK. I might as well ask for a club soda, open up the alcoholic stowaway living under the seat in front of me, take a quick drink (or two) while the stewards tend to the snack needs of the other passengers, and reconstruct the formula my daily life followed. The sun will be up shortly.

A Day in the Life...
I rented a furnished apartment at The Cliffs at Sun Ridge, which housed more suspect personnel than any complex I've ever had the privilege of visiting. I didn't do an official poll, but I'm pretty sure 90 percent of the occupants had substantial criminal records, and at least 75 percent had starring roles on *COPS*. If you enjoy smoking meth, making meth, wearing Rude Dog t-shirts, watching television with your front door open, smoking more meth, smoking Misty cigarettes, digging through the trash for treasure, or drinking hard liquor from plastic bottles in front of your shoeless children, this apartment might be what you're looking for. Tell them Jason sent you. Ask for Kent.

Most days saw me up by 7:30 a.m., but I did manage to sleep until 8:30 a few times. I cherished those days like Cristiano Ronaldo cherishes his bone structure. After a quick up-and-at-'em shower, I would normally devour a Clif Bar and a banana, but the granola bar experience was always a letdown because the chewy texture I had grown to expect was replaced by the stale, sawdust-like taste of food purchased at a Wal-Mart. Aside from a few mornings when time was on my side and Starbucks was an easy in-and-out, this was my morning meal.

Before leaving the apartment to head to the fields, I went through my checklist: radar gun, notebooks, two pens (Zebra Orbitz Gel Retractable 0.7 mm—I'm very particular about the pens), bottle of water, stopwatch(es), media credential, messenger bag, sunscreen, handy wipes, gum, cell phone, comfortable shoes, and a hat (just in case).

Most back-field workouts start with stretching, which is lame to watch, but not lame to participate in, especially when your yoga instructor happens to be from Sweden. When the players were stretching, I usually found myself wandering aimlessly around the complex, looking for coffee in the media area or coming up with unusual scenarios in my head in which my "talents" for scouting were appreciated and rewarded by full-time employment. After stretching, pitchers head to throw on the field before taking their spot in the line for bullpens. At this point, I'm usually still staring off into space.

The pen line typically has anywhere from five to eight pitchers throwing to five to eight catchers, while coaches and front-office personnel stand behind and/or to the side of them. I like watching bullpens, but eight at a time is hard to focus on—I'm sure a porn joke can be inferred without further comment. When I'm watching a bullpen, I pay attention to mechanics and how frequently the pitcher is hitting his spots. At this time I'll make note of his arm slot (assuming I have a good angle), arm action, and any idiosyncrasies to his delivery. Again, I don't go crazy with the 'pens, but they are a good source for mechanical info, so I treat them as such.

As the 'pen rotations proceed, position players find their way onto the field for live batting practice, usually in rotating groups of five or six. In the cages, hitters aren't always swinging, so you can't sit back, watch for hard contact, and judge it accordingly. In situational drills, hitters are often asked to move a runner with contact, plate a runner with a fly ball, or go to the opposite field with a pitch out over the plate so you can see which players can execute on command. I like watching batting practice, but after a few weeks it gets old, especially when you can watch the same players hit in game action later in the day. After the shine of batting practice wore off, I spent a great deal of time staring at the sun, waiting for a sun god to descend from the sky, take the form of a scouting director, and offer me a contract for my services.

After batting practice, groups rotate from fields with live-action (coach throwing) to fields with machine-action (machine) infield/outfield fielding drills. This is chaotic, because watching two coaches hit balls to a group of infielders while a coach hits balls to a group of outfielders is like watching a giant live-action pinball game, except it's not really interesting and there are no flashing lights or cute monophonic sounds. I find my focus when the drills become more isolated and specific. I take some notes. Nothing crazy. I stare off into space.

Food consumption during commonly recognized lunch times rarely occurred. I was running on the fumes of stale granola by 12:30 P.M., but with minor-league games set to commence at 1 P.M., I was able to placate my hunger with bottled water and a promise to hit In-N-Out if I didn't pass out. At this point I would head over to the benches where the players tasked with charting would set up shop. I'd get the rosters and decide which game to focus on. As the players took the field, my gun parts were out and assembled, my notebook of choice was in my opposite hand, my Zebra Orbitz Gel Retractable 0.7 mm was in my breast pocket, and my stopwatch was wrapped around my right wrist, with the watch itself cupped in my palm. It's time.

During the game I spent most of my time charting pitches and taking notes in my journal. Here is a sample of what my pitch charts look like:

First Inning of Work:
vs. (LH): 87 (FB) b; 87 (FB) ground out (weakly hit)
vs. (LH): 88 (FB) b; 75 (CB) k/looking; 87 (FB) fly out
vs. (RH): 74 (CB) k/foul; 74 (CB) fly out

Second Inning of Work:
vs. (RH): 88 (FB) b; 87 (FB) b; 88 (FB) fly out
vs. (RH): 88 (FB) k/foul; 75 (CB) b; 75 (CB) E6 (Thrown out trying to steal 2B)
vs. (LH): 88 (FB) b; 81 (CU) b; 88 (FB) b; 88 (FB) BB
vs. (RH): 89 (FB) k/foul; 89 (FB) k/foul; 89 (FB) b; 81 (CU) b; 88 (FB) b; 88 (FB) BB
vs. (RH): 83 (CU) k/foul; 75 (CB) k/swinging; 76 (CB) k/looking

Basic stuff. Along with the charts, I used my watch to collect home-to-first times, first-to-third times, pitch delivery times, catcher pop times, and times when I could actually feel my skin cooking in the sun. After roughly 2 1/2 hours of note-taking and general observation, the games end and the back fields become ghost towns. I'm starving as I reach the parking lot. To fulfill my duty as an American, I feed at the trough until the mastication process exhausts me. I attacked In-N-Out burgers like John Belushi attacked cocaine and In-N-Out burgers. I felt ashamed and triumphant at the same time. I conquered the Double Double with ketchup and cheese like Aroldis Chapman would conquer a matchup with Helen Keller. Question: Are Helen Keller jokes funny? For whatever reason, I've always enjoyed making them. I'm a bad person.

After my embarrassing display of gluttonous consumption, the time is 4 P.M. I'm exhausted from the onslaught of the sun and the half-pound of beef and bun that my body is struggling to process. I really need to nap, but I've never been able to nap. I've tried for most of my adult life, but the ability to sleep for 45 minutes and wake up with a charged battery has eluded me. I usually end up sleeping for two hours and wake up confused, cranky, and unable to function as a human. Basically, I go to sleep as Jason and wake up as my grandmother.

With notebooks full of work waiting for me, I remove an attempted nap from the agenda and press on with the tasks at hand. For the next three hours, I will go over my notes for the day and attempt to recreate the action from the text. For the first few weeks of camp, I attended a series of college games in the evening hours, not to mention the occasional "A" game that would start at 6 P.M. This pushed the note reconciliation and second feeding back several hours. These days were obnoxiously long.

As many of you know, I also write for a Texas Rangers-specific prospect site called "Texas Farm Review." Depending on what I saw that day, I would extract all Rangers-related information and produce a camp notes article for my site. After publishing my daily update, I would usually Google my name for a few minutes and then stare into space until my appetite returned and informed me that it was 8 o'clock and time for my second feeding.

Feeding number two is more controlled, with less violence in the attack and more chewing. Because chain restaurants that were flanked by chain restaurants that were flanked by shopping malls surrounded me, my choices were slim and unappealing. Almost without exception, I was joined at feeding number two by my good friend alcohol, which made eating at Chili's slightly more appealing, although pounding drinks at Chili's presented a whole new set of problems. I'd finish my salt and butter nightmare, slam another drink or six, pay my bill with a "please bring me a rope so I can hang myself at the table" smile on my face, then return to my palatial apartment, buzzed from the fat content of the food and ready for the final phase of my day at 10 P.M.

After taking yet another look at my notes from the day's action, I put the baseball away and find sanctuary in my bedroom, which I convinced myself was a room at the Waldorf rather than a room with "To Catch a Predator" written on its face. Some nights I read, but some nights my eyes don't really work, so I stare into space. I downloaded a few shows from iTunes, which help pass the time and don't require much participation on my end. That's the beauty of the television medium: you don't have to participate in the process; even if the show sucks or the aesthetic is cheap, you aren't invested, so it doesn't have a true effect either way. I watched all three seasons of *Sons of Anarchy* while in Arizona. Ron Perlman, who plays the patriarch of the biker gang the show is centered around, has an incredibly large face, so that helped me relax and find comfort in my surroundings. I'm a sucker for a large face. It's like a pacifier or a mother's heartbeat to me. I'm fast asleep by 2 A.M.

The spring training detoxification process is still ongoing: my diet has been regulated, but my appetite for baseball is too salacious for the simple meal provided by MLB.tv. As lonely and depressing as my journey was, it might have been the happiest five weeks of my adult life. I was spread thin and deposited in a cultural wasteland, but can you think of anything better than watching baseball in person, for six to eight hours per day for 35 straight days? I really can't. I miss it already. See you soon, "Katie."

PROSPECTS WILL BREAK YOUR HEART
Finding a Little Future at the Futures Game
Jason Parks

Jason Parks' credentialed trip to the Futures Game gave him a look at some of baseball's best young players, but it also helped him realized how far he'd come.

I've been in Arizona for a week, and my eyes have been privileged enough to witness a remarkable amount of questionable baseball; sometimes calling it baseball is too generous, as the refinement level of the talent often leaves a lot to be desired. Of course, I will continue to refer to the experience as a privilege because, let's face it, being at the back fields of a complex league park is better (for me) than being in a cubicle watching the countdown to closing time, and most people aren't fortunate enough to get to participate in their passion on a daily basis. This is going somewhere, I promise.

My days have been spent standing in triple-digit heat, starting with the afternoon workouts, where the sun rains showers of pure hell, and concluding in the evening, when I find myself standing behind a back-field fence for three-plus hours at a clip, saved from the intense vengeance of the sun but still subject to the oven-like temperatures that pack a punch deep into the night. By the time I return to my hotel, I feel like a slice of leftover pizza, something edible that was once fresh but gets exposed to the elements and reheated to the point that it loses its molecular identity, transforming the overall appeal from appetizing to agonizing. I'm inedible by the time July 10 rolls around. Arizona failed to offer the necessary chill to keep my structure established, and my texture isn't pleasant to the senses.

I didn't know what to expect when I made the journey into Phoenix (proper) to attend the Futures Game, the annual event where prospects get to stand on the biggest stage and dress up like big-leaguers as active participants in the All-Star weekend pageantry. My surreal experience starts almost immediately, as I'm in the media line waiting to claim my credential for the event and am engulfed by the very industry that I've been trying so hard to become engulfed by. Up to this point in my life, I've been credentialed in many a minor-league situation, ranging from the max capacity games of spring training to the lonely bullpens that begin the day. I'm not new to the pass itself or the access granted with said pass, but like the minor leaguers chosen for the Futures Game, I was about to step onto a bigger stage and get to dress up like a bigger kid.

As I make my way to the front of the media line, I am greeted by a friendly smile from an attractive face and am asked for my confirmation e-mail from the league, which I don't have. Great start. I say I'm with Baseball Prospectus and flash a smile that's a cross between innocuous flirtation and a creepy, "Hey, you might not be that safe in my presence" vibe, which I felt awkward about almost immediately. Looking confused at the coquetry but satisfied with the organizational affiliation, the media line lady disappears from view and quickly returns with a packet clearly marked "Jason Parks: Baseball Prospectus." Housed in the manila packet is a lamented all-access credential with my name and affiliation displayed on a printed transparent sticker, and a commemorative All-Star weekend pin, which I think is a nice touch, even though I don't have any designs for its utility. I give her my ID and apologize with the same smile that no doubt crossed a few ethical boundaries earlier, and after signing her confirmation slip, I set off to explore the vast wilderness of the industry's hierarchy. I'm already nervous.

The stadium seems bigger than I remember stadiums being, with walls the size of office buildings and more designated concession areas than consumers. Ticket holders are forced to stand in the heat outside for another hour-plus, so I gleefully play in my new playground, free from any distraction a general crowd might present. I feel like a middle-school student walking the halls of an empty high school, wide-eyed over the sheer enormity of my surroundings, playing salesman to convince myself that I'm ready for this level.

I make my way to the press box to pick up the game notes and rosters, running into friends along the way, most notably Christina Kahrl, my former editor here at Baseball Prospectus and good friend. We play a quick game of catch-up and I'm on my way, but it's positive reinforcement for me; sometimes a friendly face is the push in the back you need when you feel isolated and overwhelmed. After making my way back up to the main concourse area, I stand on the third-base side of the stadium, taking in my first detailed look at the field itself, once again drinking in the enormity of the scene.

The field is set up for batting practice; the World Team had already taken its rips, and Team USA players (Mac from South Philly: "USA! USA! USA!") are milling about waiting for their turn in the cage. The media presence on the field is reminiscent of the lobby at the Winter Meetings, as the heavy hitters hold court in the center of the universe with satellite cliques orbiting nearby. From my view on the main concourse level, third-base side, the field looks alive.

Just as I'm starting to question my next move, my phone vibrates, and the name Mike Ferrin appears on the digital display. For those that haven't heard the name, well, you must not try in life, because if you follow baseball, you know of Ferrin's work on SiriusXM radio. Anyway, Mike is 1) Finding out if I'm in the park, 2) Asking where I am in the park, and 3) Coercing me to meet up with him on the field. Panic washes over me at the thought of stepping onto a major-league field for the purpose of representing Baseball Prospectus. Am I ready for this?

Here's the thing: I fancy myself a scout; I prefer to sit in the stands, watch in hand, evaluating talent from the shadows of the game. I have never considered myself much of a writer, and I'm certainly not comfortable being a part of the media machine, so the escalation of my role in that world is overwhelming for me. I'm not as anxiety-ridden and socially awkward as I often present myself to be, but I do have certain limitations and hang-ups, and to be honest, the thought of navigating the social environment of the field terrifies me. I'm off to join a satellite clique on the field and my anxiety just snorted an eight-ball of cocaine, but I'm determined to put on my grown-up pants to properly represent Baseball Prospectus at the Futures Game. This is a big step for me.

My heartbeat feels like it's playing over the public address system as I travel in the tunnel leading up to the field level; each step is accompanied with the concussion kick of John Bonham's right foot. Not to get sappy, but I'm a little shaken as I take the final steps from the tunnel's shade into the lights and energy of the field. It reminds me of the first time my eyes ever caught a glimpse of a major-league field. I must have been five years old at the time, and I remember holding my mother's hand as we walked from the shade of the bustling concourse into the glowing openness of this brand new world, a world where everything was so big and so magnificent, especially for a relatively poor kid from a smallish town. At the time, the stadium was the biggest thing I had ever seen. I was hooked at first glance, and I gripped my mother's hand with a physical acknowledgment of that excitement. It's a moment I share with many, but one I hold in my mind every time I see the dirt of an infield or catch the aroma of freshly cut and watered outfield grass.

I approach the padded gate and prepare to take my first steps onto the field. I'm once again gripping my mother's hand, this time searching for the physical contact that will comfort my fears. My mother lost her life when I was 16 and never had the opportunity to see her son find his way, but she is standing behind me as I climb these steps and walk out into that world. I'm not exactly an emotional person; in fact, I often exhibit limited sentiment when delivering a response, whether it is one of glee or gloom. But I'm a little emotional as my boots touch the soft ground of field level and the hands of my beginnings firmly shove me into my future. Sometimes memories can be enough.

I'm gaining strength as I spot XMFerrin and start making my way toward the familiar face. Before I arrive, I (basically) walk right into Mike Piazza, who is freakishly handsome in person and understanding of our collision. After staring into Piazza's eyes for a little longer than what is normally considered comfortable [read: acceptable], I find an audience with my first satellite clique, joining Ferrin for a front-row seat for a few rounds of Bryce Harper's batting practice. My life is good. My life is fun.

I'm on the field for what feels like 10 minutes but is actually well over an hour, talking with friends, watching batting practice just feet from the cage, sneaking glimpses at Piazza's face, and even doing an interview with the great Grant Paulsen. I'm still overwhelmed by the depth of the water I'm in, but I'm making it work and finding my footing. Fans are starting to flood into the stadium, and my face is on the JumbroTron for all to see because I'm carelessly located in the middle of an interview with Devin Mesoraco. I think it's about time to get back to where I belong, in the scout section with my watch and my confidence, where I won't be tempted to stare at Piazza's bone structure like it holds the answers to all of life's problems, which I believe it might.

As a scout, or someone who certainly fancies himself one, the Futures Game is the celebration of our chosen craft, a gathering of all the top-of-the-line talent you are tasked with finding and evaluating. Originally, I wanted to provide you with my first-hand observations, detailing what I saw, what I didn't see, and even offering up an indictment on all the sofa scouts out there who take a small sample size performance and vomit reactions because people like giving opinions. I charted every pitcher, clocked every time to first, made notes on the physical tools, and documented every nuance of the game, but when I sat down to write about the game, those developments didn't develop on the page. It wasn't what I took away from the event.

For me the Futures Game wasn't about the future of the players on the field as much as it was about my own future in the game. As solipsistic as this will read—and frankly I don't care if it comes off as such—July 10, 2011 was the best day of my brief baseball career. It was the first day where I felt like I belonged, like I had a seat at the table—regardless of the fact that that seat was still very much in the shadows of the scene. I was still the same little kid who gripped his mother's hand after catching that first glimpse of the exceptional world on the field below. Only this time, I was the one standing on it.

Part 7
POSTSEASON
Introduction by **Tommy Bennett**

On August 22, 2010, Cody Ross was a solid but unspectacular major-league ballplayer. In two seasons as an everyday player and two others as a fourth outfielder, his batting averages (.265 career to that point) and on-base percentages (.321 career) had never strayed far from league average. That he could play a passable center field (he was almost exactly average as a defender) and hit for a decent amount of power (.466 career slugging percentage) were his most attractive attributes. They were ones teams would be happy to have if the price wasn't too high.

On that day in August—the Florida Marlins having decided that Ross's $4.45 million salary was in fact too high and placed him on waivers—he became a member of the San Francisco Giants. As a Giant, Ross's numbers were better than his career averages: he hit .288/.354/.466 in 33 games. But it wasn't until the playoffs began that Cody Ross started to hit like Willie Mays. In 15 playoff games, he hit five home runs and posted a batting line of .294/.390/.686. In the NLCS against the Phillies, Ross had seven hits—only one of them was a single. Bill Richardson, the governor of Ross's home state of New Mexico, declared October 27th Cody Ross Day. On the field after the Giants defeated the Texas Rangers in the World Series, Ross was asked by ESPN's Boog Sciambi what enabled him to be so successful in the playoffs. Ross's response: "Heart."

In the offseason, the Giants re-signed Ross to a one-year, $6.3 million deal. Through his first 265 plate appearances of that contract, Ross was hitting just .267/.355/.427 and had only seven home runs. In other words, he was more or less back to being the same old Cody Ross he was on August 22, 2010 (albeit with a few more walks and a bit less power). The suddenness and serendipity of Ross's remarkable two months ache for explanation. If it was heart, what happened to it? If it was talent, why hadn't it shown up before or since? And if it was the team, why didn't his success continue with the 2011 club, which was almost identical to the championship roster?

At the same time, it is inescapable that the Giants identified a need, filled it with Ross (and, to a lesser extent, Pat Burrell), and it turned out famously. Other teams had every opportunity to acquire Ross, and none of them did. Even if the Giants would have been content to pick up the player Ross had been his entire career, they must have seen something in him that made them think, that's our guy. No account of playoff success would be complete if it did not at least offer an explanation for Cody Ross and other unlikely October phenomena. But before we declare that Brian Sabean's shit works in the playoffs, as it were, we should be clear what we are talking about when we say a general manager has "shit" in the first place.

The most enduring line of the 2004 feature-length comedy *Dodgeball: A True Underdog Story* comes when ESPN8 ("The Ocho!") announcer Cotton McKnight shouts, "Do you believe in unlikelihoods?" Playoff sports, and baseball in particular, have the ability to beatify improbability. What a computer simulation might have said was a one-in-a-thousand longshot before the fact is rewritten as destiny simply because it really happened that way. It's the sainted truth that resonates every time Ron from accounting yells "Scoreboard!" at you from the dugout of the softball diamond. It's this kind of knee-jerk post facto explanation that Baseball Prospectus has tended to argue against, because that kind of talk is cheap.

At the other end of the spectrum, it would be a mistake to assume that every aspect of the playoffs is just a crapshoot. That belief effectively models a seven-game series as a zero-game series. It's no less a mistake than assuming that the best team is always victorious. Surely the truth lies in between. Doug Pappas found that, from 1903 through 2002, the team with the better record had a .550 winning percentage in seven- or nine-game series and just a .532 winning percentage in five-game series. And while James Click was sober about how common it is for upsets to take place in a short series, he found that even in five-game series, a favorite might hold a 75 percent chance of victory. There isn't a craps table in Vegas that would offer you those odds. "Something more than luck but less than destiny" could just as easily describe the role of team quality in the playoffs as it could be the title of the new Sting album. For many statistically minded baseball fans, Ken Funck's contribution leads the way by encouraging relaxation as the unpredictability of the playoffs unfold.

Not everyone lets go so easily, and general managers are the last to do so. There are as many clichés and talismans of success in the playoffs as there are games in the regular season. Some elevate experience, others consistency, others pitching and defense, and others still clutch hitting. For some, these properties become the sole determinant of playoff success. Baseball Prospectus has preferred a standard at once both more abstract and more easily tested: predictability. It sounds absurd to rally around a banner that, by all accounts, utterly fails to describe what happens in the playoffs. But to paraphrase Winston Churchill, relying only on statistics with predictive value is the worst way to analyze the baseball playoffs except for everything Tim McCarver says from time to time.

In other words, to the degree that the playoffs are predictable, they are predictable only by those numbers that have been proven to have predictive value. If this smacks of circular logic, I assure you that is only because of the simplicity of the proposition. On a fundamental level, if a feature of playoff performance is to be of any use in analyzing an upcoming series, it must have some measurable and predictable impact on the outcome of that series. Stated in the negative, if a factor does not impact the number of runs a team scores and allows, or the number of games it wins, it is not relevant to understanding a series that has not yet taken place.

THE LINEUP

Blowing It
by Nate Silver..223

The Greatest Pennant Race Comebacks
by Nate Silver..230

Oops, They Did it Again?
by Christina Kahrl..240

The Perils of Relying on Short-Term Memory
by Jay Jaffe..248

A Brief Meditation on the Power of Sabermetrics During the Postseason
by Ken Funck...252

Whither Runs?
by Joe Sheehan..255

Fall Classic Memories
by Baseball Prospectus...................................258

Crappy Odds
by James Click...274

Mortal Lock or Coin Flip?
by Doug Pappas...277

A-Rodemption?
by Joe Sheehan..281

Are the A's Equipped to Succeed in October?
by Mark Armour...286

Being on the Brink
by Nate Silver..290

Four and No More
by Christina Kahrl..293

This kind of rigor is not easy. It requires you to be very clear and detailed about what you are saying. For example, if you want to argue that faster teams win more playoff series, you first need to define "fast." Mark Armour's answer was to use regular-season stolen base totals as a proxy for team speed. When he looked at postseason series in which running teams played teams that had not stolen many bases, he found that the running teams lost more series than they won. His conclusion was that a running game was not strictly necessary to win in the playoffs, and therefore that the relatively one-dimensional offense of the 2003 Oakland Athletics was not doomed to an early exit. And while the A's lost to the Red Sox in the ALDS, it wasn't because they were outrun: both teams stole exactly three bases all series.

This kind of playoff skepticism, limited only to those factors of the game that persist over time, is most satisfying when other superstitions come crashing down to earth. Joe Sheehan took great delight when Alex Rodriguez finally proved that he was not a "choker," because not only was there little evidence that Rodriguez himself was a choker, there was little evidence that any individual player is a choker. Over the course of his career in the playoffs, Rodriguez proved statistically minded patience to be the prudent path.

Here's what it would take to say the Giants saw Cody Ross's playoff outburst coming. First, we would have to believe that there existed some discrete, identifiable aspect of Ross's game above and beyond what shows up on the back of his baseball card. Second, we would have to say the Giants identified that factor as the sort of thing that could cause Ross to become the walking ghost of Willie McCovey for a few weeks. Finally, we would have to be confident that this feature really does cause players to help their team score more runs and win more games. It's that last factor that kills almost every traditionalist talisman.

The ultimate challenge is to put your money where your mouth is. If you think consistency breeds playoff success, come up with a list of players you think are consistent before the playoffs start and see if they outperform their season stat lines more than the players you think are inconsistent. Do the same for players who do the little things, for players who don't overthink things, or for players who have playoff experience. That's all we are asking for: just beat the field. If you can't do that, then exactly what kind of analysis are you doing?

If you'll humor us that far, then you'll find that playoff skepticism becomes the embrace of playoff unpredictability. It may seem backwards to say that faith in predictability leads to appreciation of unpredictability. But once you realize how little of what happens in an individual series is determined by immutable truths, unpredictability is all that is left. Baseball in October is just as unpredictable as baseball in April, and for exactly the same reason. They might play the games in front of bigger crowds and with higher shares of the television audience in October, but a ground ball with eyes is just as likely to sneak through, and Cody Ross is just as likely to play, if only for a few weeks, like a Hall of Famer. That's not the genius of any one GM, that's not collecting a team full of dirtbags, that's just the nature of the game. If it were all so predictable, what would be the fun in watching?

LIES, DAMNED LIES
Blowing It
Nate Silver

A few years before the implosions of the 2011 Braves and Red Sox, Nate Silver used Clay Davenport's playoff odds to determine the biggest late-season collapses of all time.

Today's article represents an update of a Clay Davenport piece from two years ago that described the biggest collapses in playoff chase history (spoiler alert!), as defined by the teams that had the highest percentage chance to reach the playoffs at some point during the regular season who then failed to do so. I have a comprehensive set of playoff odds reports that Clay prepared for us in connection with *It Ain't Over* and was therefore able to identify a couple of races that Clay had missed during his spot-checking. In addition, I will be looking all the way back to the start of the season, rather than limiting things to August 1st as Clay did; it's surprisingly easy for teams to establish a stranglehold on a playoff spot relatively early in the season in the wild-card era, and if they're a bit less dramatic as narratives go, those collapses still deserve discussion. In addition, Clay has made some improvements to his methodology since the time his article was originally published, so all of that goodness is incorporated herein.

Thirteen is an appropriately unlucky number, so let's count down that many of the worst collapses in baseball history.

13. **1921 Pittsburgh Pirates**
Peak Playoff Probability: 94.57 percent after games of August 22nd
Odds of Collapse at Peak: 17-to-1 against
Record at Peak: 76-40, 7.5 games ahead of the New York Giants
Record after Peak: 14-23

The Pirates' hitting completely fell apart, as they averaged just 2.75 runs per game from August 23rd onward in a league that scored about as many runs as are scored today. It was a five-game series against the Giants from August 24-27 that marked the beginning of the end—the Pirates were swept, scoring six runs over the five games, and their playoff probability dropped from 93.9 percent to 72.9 in the process. Although the Giants played exceptionally well—they managed to put together eight- and 10-game winning streaks within a stretch of about three weeks—this one was probably attributable to true talent levels coming to the forefront, as the Giants would go on to win the pennant four years running. In Bill Simmons' terminology, it was a Princeton Principle collapse.

12. **1908 New York Giants**
Peak Playoff Probability: 95.46 percent after games of September 18th
Odds of Collapse at Peak: 21-to-1 against
Record at Peak: 87-46, 4.5 games ahead of the Cubs
Record after Peak: 11-10

This was the "Merkle's Boner" team, as beautifully chronicled by Steve Goldman in *It Ain't Over*. Unlike many teams on this list, the Giants' peak was not sustained for a particularly long time. This was the season that all three of the nineteen-hundred-and- aught dynasties were on a collision course, as the Giants traded places with the Pirates and the Cubs all season long; their September 18th peak date marked the end of a stretch in which they'd won 18 games in 19 tries. They looked to be in good shape heading into the final couple weeks of the season, as 17 of their remaining 21 games were to be played at home, whereas the Cubs were in the midst of a period of 24 consecutive road games but nevertheless managed to finish out the season at 14-2 to overtake the John McGraw's club. Of some note is the sheer number of games that the Giants played during this stretch—during the period of September 18-October 1, just 14 days on the calendar, the Giants played in 18 baseball games, including six doubleheaders.

11. **2002 Boston Red Sox**
Peak Playoff Probability: 95.84 percent after games of June 6th
Odds of Collapse at Peak: 23-to-1 against
Record at Peak: 40-17, 3.5 games ahead of the Yankees in the AL East; 6.0 games ahead of the Anaheim Angels for the wild card
Record after Peak: 53-52

It might seem odd that a team can establish this much of a probability of reaching the playoffs so early in the season, but consider the mechanics of the wild card. What it does is to effectively eliminate the 1942 Brooklyn Dodgers scenario, which is when a team plays fairly good baseball but is overtaken by a team that plays really great baseball. Nowadays, when that happens both teams still make the playoffs, one of them as the wild card. At their peak, for example, the Red Sox were projected to win their division less than 70 percent of the time, but the wild card made up most of the difference and provided them with a huge landing pad. The 2000 Red Sox (93.36 percent playoff probability at peak) and 2001 Red Sox (92.50 percent) also nearly made this list, which might help everyone outside of New England understand if it seems that Sox fans are a little paranoid.

10. 1964 Philadelphia Phillies

Peak Playoff Probability: 96.15 percent after games of September 17th
Odds of Collapse at Peak: 25-to-1-against
Record at Peak: 89-58, 6.5 games ahead of the Cardinals
Record after Peak: 3-12

This collapse is particularly famous because of just how badly the Phillies played down the stretch, and just how poorly Gene Mauch managed his pitching staff. However, it was not quite as bad as it might seem at first glance because of the disparity in the schedules. From September 18th onward, the Phillies played teams with an average winning percentage of .548, as opposed to .470 for the Cardinals, which was enough to wipe the equivalent of a game or two off of their lead.

9. 1983 Atlanta Braves

Peak Playoff Probability: 96.39 percent after games of August 10th
Odds of Collapse at Peak: 27-to-1 against
Record at Peak: 69-45, 6.5 games ahead of the Dodgers
Record after Peak: 19-29

The Braves nearly blew this big a lead a year earlier, in 1982. That club had a 90.9 percent chance to reach the playoffs as of July 29th, and then proceeded to lose 15 of their next 16 ballgames; at one point, their playoff probability was down to less than five percent before they recovered. This time around, they were not so fortunate. A huge part of the problem was losing Bob Horner for the season to injury on August 15th. Whereas Horner was hitting .303/.383/.528 at the time he went down, his replacements at the position, Jerry Royster and Randy "Not the Pitcher" Johnson, combined to hit just .202/.269/.225 the rest of the way out; that batting line represents a total of two extra-base hits in 193 total plate appearances.

8. 2005 Cleveland Indians

Peak Playoff Probability: 96.50 percent after games of September 24th
Odds of Collapse at Peak: 28-to-1 against
Record at Peak: 92-63, 1.5 games behind the White Sox in the AL Central; 1.5 games ahead of the Yankees and Red Sox for the wild card
Record after Peak: 1-6

The neat trick that the Indians pulled off was to fall behind both the Red Sox and the Yankees when those teams had to play one another in the final series of the season. The Indians, meanwhile, were set to finish their series against the Royals before going home to face Tampa Bay. They did have to conclude their season against the White Sox, but at that point the White Sox had already clinched.

7. 1978 Boston Red Sox

Peak Playoff Probability: 96.54 percent after games of August 12th
Odds of Collapse at Peak: 28-to-1 against
Record at Peak: 73-42, 8.0 games ahead of the Yankees
Record after Peak: 26-22

The '78 Red Sox had a couple of points that might have represented their peak; they were still as high as 95.5 percent to win their division on August 28th. However, the '78 Yankees played exceptionally well, finishing out their season at 35-13, and although that season is remembered for the blowouts of the Boston Massacre, it was the Yankees' play in closer contests that counted, as they went 14-4 from August 12th onward in games decided by two runs or less.

6. 1942 Brooklyn Dodgers

Peak Playoff Probability: 96.90 percent after games of August 15th
Odds of Collapse at Peak: 31-to-1 against
Record at Peak: 79-33, 9.5 games ahead of the Cardinals
Record after Peak: 25-17

Although the National League's star talent was relatively intact in 1942 in spite of the increasing migration of players into the armed services, it was nevertheless a boom-or-bust league with a very weak bottom; the Phillies went 42-109 that year. So it was like the Dodgers were engaged in a leisurely carriage race and then suddenly saw Secretariat coming around the bend. The Cardinals finished their season at 38-6, which according to David Smith at Retrosheet is tied for the second-best record over a 44-game stretch in baseball history.

5. 1969 Chicago Cubs

Peak Playoff Probability: 97.90 percent after games of August 19th
Odds of Collapse at Peak: 47-to-1 against
Record at Peak: 77-45, 8.0 games ahead of the Mets
Record after Peak: 15-25

I was chatting with my neighbor after the Cubs lost yesterday and said something to the effect that if the Cubs blow this to Milwaukee, this might really be the one that proves the existence of the curse. He quickly reminded me that 2007 would be at most a low-magnitude star in the constellation of Cubs agony, well behind 2003, 1969, and 1984 (probably in that order). What was remarkable about the 1969 team was that they not only lost a substantial lead, but that they wound up getting absolutely thrashed in the process, finishing eight full games behind the Mets at the end of the season, a 17-game swing over about six weeks worth of competition.

Who was most responsible for the '69 Cubs' collapse? There was plenty of blame to go around (see table below), but most of the damage was done by the pitching staff, or by players like Randy Hundley and Don Kessinger who played premium defensive positions. That would tend to validate the hypothesis that the Cubs were just exhausted, since those are the positions that take the most wear-and-tear during the season.

Player	Pre-Peak	Post-Peak
Don Kessinger, SS	.291/.350/.385	.207/.268/.297
Glenn Beckert, 2B	.298/.330/.347	.272/.313/.325
Billy Williams, LF	.301/.368/.469	.269/.314/.488
Ron Santo, 3B	.300/.394/.519	.250/.354/.371
Ernie Banks, 1B	.257/.315/.406	.243/.290/.444
Randy Hundley, C	.284/.361/.441	.153/.237/.220
Jim Hickman, RF	.229/.312/.433	.248/.348/.518
Don Young, CF	.230/.342/.348	.286/.348/.500

Player	Pre-Peak	Post-Peak
Fergie Jenkins, SP	17-10, 2.72 ERA	4-5, 4.91 ERA
Bill Hands, SP	15-9, 2.46 ERA	5-5, 2.57 ERA
Ken Holtzman, SP	14-7, 3.12 ERA	3-6, 4.84 ERA
Dick Selma, SP	12-4, 3.12 ERA	0-6, 6.17 ERA
Phil Regan, RP	12-5, 3.00 ERA	1-1, 6.98 ERA

4. 2003 Seattle Mariners

Peak Playoff Probability: 97.91 percent after games of June 18th

Odds of Collapse at Peak: 47-to-1 against

Record at Peak: 48-22, 7.5 games ahead of the A's in the AL West; 8.0 games ahead of the Red Sox for the wild card

Record after Peak: 45-47

Whenever you produce a list of the best or worst of something, those Mariner teams from 1995-2003 have a habit of showing up. This team got off to nearly as good a start as the 2001 club, who achieved 90 percent playoff probability as early as May 3 but finally surrendered their lead to the A's on August 25th. Worth nothing is that this had become a pretty old team—the average age of the positional regulars was 32.2—so fatigue might once again have been the decisive factor.

3. 1993 San Francisco Giants

Peak Playoff Probability: 98.25 percent after games of August 7th

Odds of Collapse at Peak: 56-to-1 against

Record at Peak: 74-47, 9.5 games ahead of the Braves

Record after Peak: 29-22

The last truly great two-team pennant race somewhat mirrored the 1942 season, because although these Giants were incredibly streaky, they didn't exactly play badly. It's just that the Braves played better, winning 39 of their final 50 games. As Clay pointed out two years ago, this Giants team was particularly heartbreaking because they had something of a second wind—after seeing their playoff probability fall to 6.4 percent on September 16th, they reeled off 14 wins in 16 games to tie the Braves in the division, only to succumb to the Dodgers on the last day of the season.

2. 1951 Brooklyn Dodgers

Peak Playoff Probability: 99.74 percent after games of August 12th
Odds of Collapse at Peak: 384-to-1 against
Record at Peak: 72-36, 12.5 games ahead of the New York Giants
Record after Peak: 25-24

As Roger Kahn wrote, and as Kevin Baker quoted in *It Ain't Over*, "Summarizing the 1951 race is akin to summarizing King Lear. Before anything else, your effort will diminish majesty." Kevin succeeded in proving Kahn wrong in 19 pages; I'm not going to attempt the same in a paragraph. The only thing I'll point out is how the odds against a collapse have increased exponentially from the previous teams on this list. While 99.74 percent doesn't sound all that different from 98.25, the former represents a 56-to-1 shot, and the latter is a much more unlikely 384-to-1 shot.

1. 1995 California Angels

Peak Playoff Probability: 99.988 percent after games of August 20th
Odds of Collapse at Peak: 8,332-to-1 against
Record at Peak: 66-41, 9.5 games ahead of the Rangers and 12.5 Games ahead of the Mariners in the AL West; 12.0 games ahead of the Yankees for the wild card
Record after Peak: 12-26

I posed this in the form of a trivia question to our internal mailing list: Which team had the worst playoff chase collapse of all-time? I got one guess for the 1964 Phillies, one for the 1978 Red Sox, one for the 1962 Dodgers (who rank 17th), and three for the 1951 Dodgers. Only Rany suggested the 1995 Angels, and that is because he has the best memory of anyone in our group (Christina Kahrl being a close second) and recalled Clay's original article.

But in fact the answer isn't even close. The 1951 Dodgers' odds were 384-to-1 against missing the playoffs, while the Angels were more than 8000-to-1 against. In fact, even if you ignored the wild-card possibility and looked only at the divisional race, this would still rank as the worst collapse of all time. With 38 games left to play, the Angels were a combined 24.5 games ahead of the Mariners and Yankees, the two teams that would eventually pass them in making the playoffs. It took a perfect storm of events to knock the Halos out of the race—two distinct losing streaks of nine games apiece, plus the Yankees and Mariners each winning two-thirds of their games—and even then they still had the chance to redeem themselves in a one-game playoff against the Mariners. It's also interesting to note that if the Mariners had blown that playoff game, because the Angels played so badly that the M's opened up a three-game lead at one point, the '95 Mariners would rank 13th on this list.

A Quick Note on This Year's Collapses
The Tigers (93.51 percent on July 20th), who only a few days ago looked like they would certainly own the worst collapse of the season, presently rank 16th on the all-time list after having "clinched" their elimination yesterday.

Naturally, most of the action is now in the National League. There are five NL teams that have at some point during this regular season had at least an 80 percent chance of reaching the playoffs, and there are only four playoff spots to be had, so at least one and possibly as many as three teams are going to wind up with a place on this list of all-time infamy:

- The Padres (83.37 percent to make the playoffs after games of September 20th) would rank 50th all-time if they miss;
- The Brewers (86.65 percent on July 2nd) would rank 40th if they miss;
- The Cubs (95.58 percent on September 23rd) would rank 12th if they miss;
- The Diamondbacks (96.64 percent on September 24th) would rank seventh if they miss;
- The Mets (99.80 percent on September 12th) would rank second all-time if they miss, making good on a 500-to-1 shot against.

It's easier to make this list in the wild-card era, simply because there are more playoff spots available, and the number of teams that reach a certain threshold of probability and miss the playoffs is directly proportionate to the number that make it. However, the notion that this year's playoff races have turned into something very special is absolutely correct.

LIES, DAMNED LIES
The Greatest Pennant Race Comebacks
Nate Silver

Determined not to be a total downer, Nate Silver also turned a statistical eye toward identifying the greatest comebacks to qualify for the playoffs.

I've had kind of a lucky year. The PECOTA projection I made in the offseason that gained the most notoriety is that the White Sox would finish 72-90; that turned out to be their actual finish. After that, the next-most controversial projection was that Dustin Pedroia was going to have a very good year; now he looks like a shoo-in for the Rookie of the Year Award. And in a July article for *Sports Illustrated*, we noted that the Secret Sauce predicted that the Red Sox would meet the Cubs in the World Series, an outcome that now looks entirely possible (though incrementally less so after the Cubs' loss last night).

That doesn't mean we've gotten everything right. PECOTA missed high on a lot of rookie hitters. We thought the Devil Rays would somehow win 78 or 79 ballgames. We thought big breakouts were coming for Jeremy Bonderman and Daniel Cabrera. Overall, it was a pretty normal year for PECOTA; our philosophy is if we get six hits for every five misses, we've done pretty well. But those bad predictions didn't generate a lot of press hits, and the good ones did.

So it was kind of fortuitous that I wrote an article last week about the greatest pennant race collapses in baseball history. At the time that I wrote that piece, the Mets still had a 96 percent shot at making the playoffs. By the time we published it, they were down to 85 percent, but still looked relatively safe. Then a terrible thing happened, and the Mets joined the ranks of the rich and infamous. The topic got a lot of coverage; I did an update for SI, and Clay did another take over here. As you might guess, I'm pretty tired of this subject by now, but I got so many reader requests to do the opposite of that topic—the greatest pennant race comebacks in baseball history—that I'm going to aim to please.

As it happens, most of the greatest comebacks conceived of strictly as the longest odds overcome begin toward the middle of the season rather than toward the end. This is the result of a sort of statistical quirk—if we're looking at those teams that had the longest odds against coming back, what we want are the closest numbers to zero that aren't exactly zero; basically, those numbers that are between 0.001 and one percent. In the middle of the season, a team cannot really be "mathematically" eliminated; they could always win their last 72 games in a row or whatever and make the playoffs. You might have to run 100 simulations before they made the playoffs, or 10,000, or one million, or 100 million.

So the middle of the season is when it's easiest to achieve these small, but nonzero numbers. At the end of the season, on the other hand, the function is a bit less continuous. With four games left to play, you either have a somewhat tangible chance to make the playoffs, or you are at exactly zero and no combination of wins and losses will get you in. Maybe you wake up in the morning with a percent percent chance to make the postseason—low but not that low—and if you win it goes up to 10 percent, and if you lose it goes to exactly zero.

Therefore, we're going to break these rankings down into three categories:

- Early-Season Comebacks: Teams that came back from the longest odds to make the playoffs with more than 60 games left to play.
- Stretch-Run Comebacks: Teams that came back from the longest odds with more than 20 but no more than 60 games left to play.
- Buzzer-Beater Comebacks: Teams that came back from the longest odds with 20 or fewer games to play.

First, those early birds that overslept but eventually caught the worm:

Greatest Early-Season Comebacks (more than 60 games yet to play)

Team	W-L	YTP	Play%	Odds
1914 Braves	10-24	$119	<.01%	>10000:1
1963 Cardinals	47-48	$67	.18%	549:1
1906 White Sox	15-20	$116	.26%	391:1
1973 Mets	33-43	$85	.28%	356:1
1964 Cardinals	40-41	$81	.30%	338:1
2006 Twins	25-33	$104	.31%	327:1
1978 Yankees	47-42	$74	.41%	245:1
2005 Astros	21-34	$107	.41%	242:1
1984 Royals	40-51	$71	.43%	231:1
2003 Marlins	19-29	$114	.79%	126:1
1988 Red Sox	25-26	$111	.81%	123:1
1973 Reds	39-37	$86	.86%	116:1
1936 Giants	40-40	$74	.87%	114:1
2002 A's	28-30	$104	.97%	102:1

YTP stands for "yet to play," the number of games that a team had remaining on its schedule, excluding any ties or tiebreaker games. One team is the unchallenged king of this list—the 1914 Boston Braves. In fact, there were two separate occasions on which they failed to make the playoffs in any of Clay's simulations, the latter of which came on June 1, when they were already 12.5 games behind both the Cincinnati Reds and New York Giants. Now, this isn't quite as impressive as it sounds, because for his historical simulations Clay ran the seasons through only 10,000 times each rather than one million. Nevertheless, they went 0-for-10,000 on two separate occasions and at the very least had what might be described as a couple of near-death experiences.

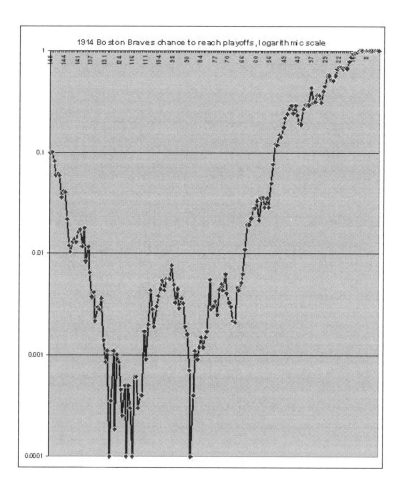

Here's the Braves' record by month. I haven't looked this up, but I would guess that they are the only team in baseball history to improve their winning percentage in five consecutive months. Even more remarkable is that the Boston Braves not only won the pennant, they did so by a commanding 10.5 games. Instead of being 10-24 on June 1, they could have started out 0-34 and still made the postseason. That is one hell of a comeback.

Month	W	L	Pct
April	2	7	.222
May	8	15	.348
June	16	13	.552
July	18	10	.643
August	19	6	.760
September	26	5	.839
October	5	3	.625

The other teams on this list generally fall into one of two categories—teams that are paired with a single opponent that suffered a great collapse (like the 1978 Yankees), and those that weren't so far behind any one team but instead were pretty far behind several different teams (like the 1984 Royals). Being 10 games out of first place with nobody in between is vastly different from being 10 games out with five or six teams in between, because you can expect that at least one of those teams is going to get hot, especially since they have to play one another. In some cases, both of these things were true—the 1964 Cardinals were not only 10 games behind the Phillies with about half their season left to play but also 9.5 behind the Giants and 3.5 behind the Reds, both of which were excellent clubs.

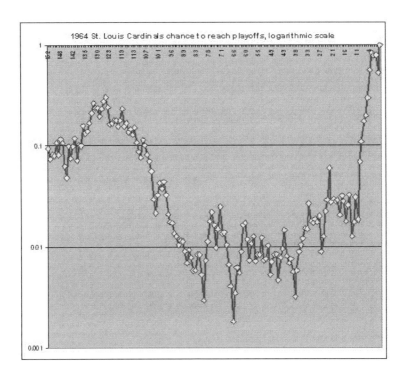

Greatest Stretch-Run Comebacks (21 to 60 games yet to play)

Team	W-L	YTP	Play%	Odds
1973 Mets	48-60	53	.17%	600:1
1951 Giants	62-51	44	.25%	407:1
1964 Cardinals	65-58	39	.32%	314:1
2004 Astros	64-63	35	.41%	243:1
1930 Cardinals	61-56	37	.51%	195:1
1974 Orioles	63-65	34	.75%	132:1
1906 White Sox	50-43	58	.77%	128:1
1969 Mets	62-51	49	.97%	102:1
1934 Cardinals	77-53	23	1.11%	89:1
1993 Braves	65-47	50	1.71%	58:1

We see the '64 Cardinals again, and also the 1951 Giants, with whom we should already be familiar. For a closer look at the latter:

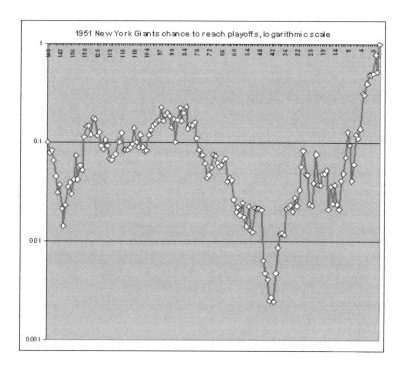

However, the greatest stretch-run comeback belongs to neither of those two teams but to the 1973 Mets, who upended even their 1969 brethren for miraculousness. After losing both games of a doubleheader on August 5th, the Mets were 11.5 games back with five teams in front of them. And then, suddenly, the Mets turned into a .642 team while nobody else in the division compiled a winning record the rest of the way out, and thus they snuck into the playoffs at 82-79.

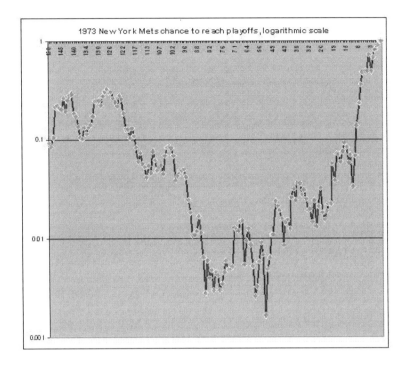

More recently, we have the 2004 Astros, who had it hard because they could rely only on the wild card to reach the playoffs, as they were as many as 20.5 games behind the division-leading Cardinals at one point in the season. Their longest odds came on August 26th, just before they ran off a 12-game winning streak. They needed every one of those victories, beating out the Giants for the wild card by just one game.

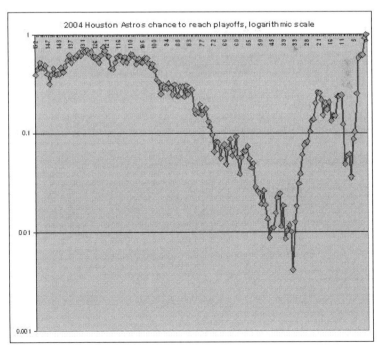

Greatest Buzzer-Beater Comebacks (20 or fewer games yet to play)

Team	W-L	YTP	Play%	Odds
1934 Cardinals	82-56	15	1.16%	85:1
1964 Cardinals	83-66	13	1.26%	79:1
2007 Rockies	77-72	14	1.82%	54:1
1951 Giants	82-55	20	2.09%	47:1
1908 Cubs	85-53	16	2.21%	44:1
1965 Dodgers	82-64	16	2.88%	34:1
1973 Mets	73-77	11	3.35%	29:1
2004 Astros	85-70	7	3.59%	27:1
1982 Braves	82-70	10	4.80%	20:1
1959 Dodgers	75-63	18	5.76%	16:1
1962 Giants	96-59	10	6.60%	14:1

Do these teams look familiar? They probably should, because four of the top five made the pennant race book. The only exception is the 2007 Rockies, who surely will merit their own chapter if we do a second edition of *It Ain't Over*.

The 1934 Cardinals were 5.5 games back with 15 games yet to play. Fortunately (for them, if not for the hapless New York Giants), they were one of the streakiest teams in history, usually based on the mood and effort of the Brothers Dean. They caught a hot streak at the end, going 13-2 over the season's final stretch to take the pennant:

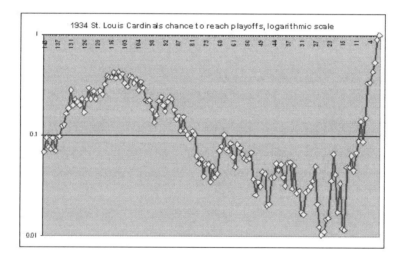

As for this year's Rockies, what's impressive about them is that they came back from the dead essentially three distinct times. On May 21, the Rockies bottomed out at 18-27 and had only a 1.46 percent chance to make the playoffs, almost enough to qualify for the early-season comeback list. They gradually started playing better baseball but had fallen back down to 1.8 percent just before they began their 14-1 stretch. And even within that 14-1 stretch, their one stumble nearly killed them; they temporarily were back down to 4.4 percent after last Friday's loss:

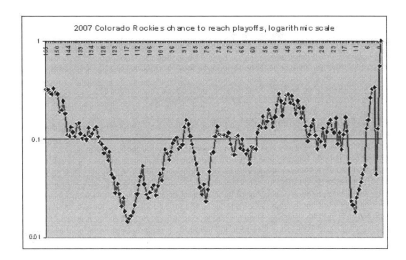

But you want to know what was most impressive about these Rockies? They were never, not for one day, greater than even-money to make the playoffs until they actually did. Actually, this conclusion is debatable, because they might have been the favorite in Monday night's playoff, although I didn't have them that way with Jake Peavy on the mound. But they certainly were not as high as 50 percent to make the playoffs at any time before late Sunday afternoon; in fact, they were never higher than 34 percent.

We can also form the best comebacks question in a slightly different way, which is this: Which team made the greatest comeback with X number of games left to play?

Greatest Comebacks with Given Number of Games Yet to Play

The Rockies hold the records for one, two, eight, nine, 10, and 14 games to go (and remember, the YTP total does not include tiebreaker games). The early part of the list is dominated by those 1914 Braves, with several teams weaving in and out in the middle.

YTP	Team	W-L	Play%	Odds
1	2007 Rockies	88-73	12.83%	7:1
2	2007 Rockies	87-73	4.40%	22:1
3	1967 Red Sox	90-69	18.97%	4:1
4	1949 Dodgers	94-56	11.91%	7:1
5	2004 Astros	87-70	10.34%	9:1
6	2004 Astros	86-70	8.67%	11:1
7	2004 Astros	85-70	3.59%	27:1
8	2007 Rockies	82-72	4.41%	22:1
9	2007 Rockies	81-72	3.61%	27:1
10	2007 Rockies	80-72	3.11%	31:1
11	1964 Cardinals	84-67	1.85%	53:1
12	1951 Giants	85-57	2.11%	46:1
13	1964 Cardinals	83-66	1.26%	79:1
14	2007 Rockies	76-72	2.33%	42:1
15	1934 Cardinals	82-56	1.16%	85:1
16	1964 Cardinals	82-64	1.80%	55:1
17	1934 Cardinals	81-55	1.76%	56:1
18	1934 Cardinals	81-54	4.10%	23:1
19	1964 Cardinals	80-63	2.05%	48:1
20	1964 Cardinals	79-63	2.80%	35:1
25	1934 Cardinals	75-53	1.23%	80:1
30	1934 Cardinals	72-51	1.67%	59:1
35	2004 Astros	64-63	.41%	243:1
40	1951 Giants	63-51	.48%	208:1
45	1951 Giants	59-50	.41%	246:1
50	1964 Cardinals	59-53	.52%	190:1
55	1973 Mets	48-58	.68%	147:1
60	1973 Mets	44-57	.26%	385:1
70	1914 Braves	39-44	.40%	248:1
80	1914 Braves	32-41	.17%	587:1
90	1914 Braves	26-37	.16%	624:1
100	2006 Twins	28-34	.53%	188:1
110	1914 Braves	15-28	.09%	1110:1
120	1914 Braves	10-23	.03%	3999:1
130	1914 Braves	5-18	.09%	1175:1
140	1951 Giants	2-12	1.42%	69:1
150	1974 Pirates	2-10	2.80%	35:1

The Greatest Comeback Team Ever: A Foolishly Objective Approach

Finally, we might want to come up with an objective answer to the question of the best comeback team of all time. We want to reward teams like the 1914 Braves that battled back from extremely long odds early in the season but also those like the 2007 Rockies that kept the beat writers busy late into September. After some trial and error, I came up with the following "Comeback Credibility Score" (CCS) based on Clay's historic odds reports:

$$CCS = -\log_{10}(Pr(P)) * (GP/GT)$$

That is, the base-10 logarithm of a team's playoff probability, multiplied by the fraction of the teams total games (GT) that had been played to date. I then summed this number across all days of the regular season to come up with the total CCS. The leaders in this category are as follows:

Year	Team	Score
1964	Cardinals	137
1973	Mets	120
1951	Giants	109
1914	Braves	103
2007	Rockies	93
1934	Cardinals	91
1978	Yankees	90
1984	Royals	87
2004	Astros	84
2003	Marlins	82

That seems like a pretty good list. The 2007 Rockies rate as the fifth-greatest comeback of all time, with the 1964 Cardinals, who spent nearly a quarter of their season with less than a one-percent chance to make the playoffs, holding the top spot by a fairly wide margin.

IT AIN'T OVER 'TIL IT'S OVER
Oops, They Did it Again?
Christina Kahrl

As an intended addendum to *It Ain't Over 'Til It's Over: The Baseball Prospectus Pennant Race Book*, Christina Kahrl wrote about where the 2007 playoff races ranked in the all-time accounting.

Given the peril the Tigers' season is in, it seems appropriate for us to bring this back to provide a sense of the history of epic collapses. This was the new chapter that was supposed to go into the paperback edition of It Ain't Over, but for reasons only the publisher can adequately explain, it didn't get inserted. Given that we've got a great race in play once again, here's what you missed.

Last year we did a book on the subject of the best pennant races, in which we revisited some of the game's great stories and its most celebrated seasons. But as Francis Fukuyama learned, perhaps to his regret, history is not dead but instead has a way of being made again year after year. No sooner did we publish the first edition of this book than we found ourselves enjoying not just one really entertaining race but a full spread of exciting possibilities for all four playoff spots in the 2007 National League. When the dust cleared, not only did the senior circuit deliver an entirely different slate of playoff teams from the year before, but all four races—the division races and the wild card—involved their own dramatic reversals of fortune and well-timed bursts of excellence. If, in sabermetric circles, "clutch" is not a skill, it certainly remains an appropriate adjective to describe how so many teams fought for their shot at October glory.

Perhaps the least dramatic but still compelling race was in the National League Central, where the Cubs passed by the Brewers in August and then fought to hold onto that lead over the next six frantic weeks. The two teams made for a study in contrasts. The Cubs were trying to bounce back from their hangover after coming up short in the infamous 2003 National League Championship Series (best known for Steve Bartman's star turn in Wrigley's seats near the left-field corner). By 2007, the team had long since been disappointed by homegrown talents like Kerry Wood, Mark Prior, and Corey Patterson, and it had also finally severed its longtime association with slugger Sammy Sosa. General manager Jim Hendry—perhaps with an eye towards his future under new ownership—needed to change gears and field a winner quickly. He did so by entering the free agent market and spending aggressively—$288 million to put Alfonso Soriano's power and speed in the lineup, add Cliff Floyd to the outfield mix as well, shore up the rotation with Ted Lilly and Jason Marquis, plug in Mark DeRosa at second base, and keep third baseman Aramis Ramirez at the hot corner for years to come. With a group of nearly-ready hurlers and position-playing prospects down on the farm, Hendry was willing to go for broke in the present. Finally, he brought in veteran Lou Piniella to skipper the club. Waiting 'til next year was something that Hendry was no longer willing to do.

In contrast, the Brewers were the product of a long-term, more traditional player development plan executed by GM Doug Melvin and fueled in large part by the products of scouting director Jack Zduriencik's pickups in the amateur draft; from 2001-05, Zduriencik picked shortstop J.J. Hardy, first baseman Prince Fielder, second baseman Rickie Weeks, top pitching prospect Yovani Gallardo, and third baseman Ryan Braun. If the 2007 edition of the Brew Crew had a signature weakness, it's wasn't their relative inexperience but their execrable defense. As talented as this group of young infielders were that Zduriencik and the rest of the organization's scouts had assembled with such remarkable speed, they were not an exceptional group of talented glovemen, and the team's Park-Adjusted Defensive Efficiency rated next to last in the NL and 28th overall. That inability to turn balls in play into outs contributed to the collapse of first the Brewers' bullpen and then their rotation, and the team managed to blow an 8 1/2-game lead it had built up in June. They would make life interesting for the Cubs almost until the very end, even reclaiming first place for one day on September 18, but Milwaukee then lost four of their next five and saw their hopes finally killed off with two games to go by an equally desperate Padres club.

Most years, we take one such reversal of fortune as an exciting development. In 2007, though, that was the boring division race. Within that last weekend of regular-season baseball in Milwaukee, we got to witness additional drama, as the Brewers would repay the favor by dropping the Padres into a tie for the wild card by winning those last two games. By doing so, Milwaukee had done their own small part to help produce what might be the most stunning turnaround yet in exploiting baseball's four-team playoff format. That's because with little more than two weeks left, the Colorado Rockies bounded back from virtual elimination to pass the rest of a crowded field by winning 14 of their last 15 games, earning a one-game playoff against the Padres to determine the NL wild card team. As Nate Silver explained, the Rockies are one of the five best buzzer-beating comebacks of all time—so slender was their margin for success that even their one loss on the last Friday of the season dropped their shot at the playoffs to 4.4 percent.

What was truly remarkable about the Rockies? As Silver pointed out, "They were never, not for one day, greater than even-money to make the playoffs until they actually did," and they "were not as high as 50 percent to make the playoffs at any time before late Sunday afternoon [on the final day of the season]; in fact, they were never higher than 34 percent." Looking at it from the perspective of how unlikely they were to come back with 10 games or less remaining in the season, the Rockies proved to be the least-likely team to make it with one, two, eight, nine, and 10 games left to play. (See Table One.)

Table One: Greatest Comebacks with a Given Number of Games to Play

GTP	Team	W-L	Playoff%	Odds
1	2007 Rockies	88-73	12.83%	7:1
2	2007 Rockies	87-73	4.40%	22:1
3	1967 Red Sox	90-69	18.97%	4:1
4	1949 Dodgers	94-56	11.91%	7:1
5	2004 Astros	87-70	10.34%	9:1
6	2004 Astros	86-70	8.67%	11:1
7	2004 Astros	85-70	3.59%	27:1
8	2007 Rockies	82-72	4.41%	22:1
9	2007 Rockies	81-72	3.61%	27:1
10	2007 Rockies	80-72	3.11%	31:1

The math is dizzying enough for the numerically inclined, but what might get overlooked in the future about Colorado's late-season heroics is that they'd also managed to put themselves into the NL West's playoff picture, trying to come up from behind to almost catch the equally surprising Arizona Diamondbacks, not to mention leave both the defending division champion Padres and a strong, heavily-favored Dodgers squad in their wake. In this, perhaps the strength of the competition was what was needed to help forge an astonishing comeback team, as keeping up with the Joneses is as much incentive as any team requires.

Although some were quick to credit Rockies GM Dan O'Dowd for picking up bit parts like center fielder Willy Taveras or second baseman Kazuo Matsui in minor deals, these sorts of add-ons hardly proved critical to the Rockies' fortunes. Instead, where the team really made progress wasn't in the areas of quick-fixes through free agency or picking through the waiver wire for any choice bits, it was in the development of its core talent, in assembling an exceptional defense, and in supporting those reliable everyday elements with a quality bullpen—one place where a manager and GM can make an outsized impact without automatically breaking the bank.

The assembly of a talented, relatively young, and effectively homegrown team core was essentially a new proposition for the Rockies. For years, the franchise had invested too much time chasing down first one notion and then another as far as what kind of talent might be able to win at altitude without addressing the more basic issue of fielding a team that could win anywhere. The team's offense ranked sixth in the National League in Equivalent Average in 2007, still far from rating with the best teams, but its .264 EqA mark was an all-time high and the first time the club had ever finished above the base average of .260. Despite past talk about trying to field a faster team, they weren't especially fast and were in the middle of the pack in stolen bases; losing the speedy Taveras for an extended period of time didn't help.

Although they slugged a modest .395 on the road, what they did do was draw walks, finishing first in the league in unintentional freebies. That's a skill that carries over, whatever environment you're playing in, and it made for a lineup that generated all-time franchise highs in OBP (.336) and runs scored per nine (4.7) away from Coors Field, which turned into another high-water mark—a franchise-best 39-42 on the road. It's fair to say that the greatest Rockies lineup wasn't the Blake Street Bombers of the over-inflated high-offense '90s, it was this team, a unit built around Rockies stars like Matt Holliday and Todd Helton, solid second-tier sluggers like Brad Hawpe and Garrett Atkins, and rookie shortstop Troy Tulowitzki.

Tulo's play at short was a big part of another plays-everywhere asset of a new-and-improved Rockies club—its exceptional defense. In terms of overall Defensive Efficiency, the Rockies ranked a solid eighth in the majors and sixth in the senior circuit. Modest-sounding enough, those marks represent all-time bests in franchise history, and they do the talent of the Rox D a disservice—with Coors Field's massive outfield pasture, playing defense at altitude isn't any easier than pitching, and Colorado's leather legion traditionally rates near the very bottom. Adjusting for the park's effect on Defensive Efficiency, we find that the Rockies were actually the second-best defensive unit in baseball, rating just a hair behind the eventual AL pennant-winners, the Red Sox. Players like Helton, Holliday, and Tulo rated among the best at their positions, and it was here that veteran add-ons like Taveras, Matsui, and catcher Yorvit Torrealba made an impact. That spread of top-tier defensive talent provided the additional offensive boon of allowing the Rockies to carry two less glovely players in the corners that many teams might have long since moved to first base; right fielder Hawpe and third baseman Atkins.

The final element that Rockies manager Clint Hurdle employed to good effect was a bullpen that, if short of being outright dominant, boasted both depth and talent. The Rockies have always had to compensate for rotations handicapped by the challenges of their environment, and beyond the contributions of a solid starter like lefty Jeff Francis, their rotation was not one of their assets. This was less a problem than an excuse to turn to a better pen, as the Rockies got more than a third of their overall innings thrown from a relief unit that posted a Fair Runs Allowed mark of 4.18, the ninth-best mark in the majors; in contrast, the rotation ranked 18th with a 4.96 rate and an equally modest rotation-wide Support-Neutral Value Above Replacement mark of 17.0, rotation achievements that were better than those of only one other playoff team—but more on the Phillies in a bit.

The Rockies created drama over the course of the season—they didn't ebb and flow, they careened. The offense struggled in the early going, helping to deliver a weak 18-27 opening run. Then they snapped off one of the happier streaks for which they subsequently became famous, racking up 20 wins in their next 27 games to move back above .500; during this stretch, they started dumping some of their worst veterans (Steve Finley, John Mabry) and turning to their own system to provide better, fresh-legged alternatives (Ryan Spilborghs, Cory Sullivan). They followed this up with another pratfall, losing eight straight at one point, handicapped by closer Brian Fuentes' four consecutive blown saves at the end of June. Down to 39-43 after their July 1 game, they rallied again, winning five of six to even things out at the All-Star break and going 37-29 through September 15. Only four games over, they put together their 13-1 run and then handily beat a listing Padres club in the one-game playoff against eventual Cy Young winner Jake Peavy. They did this despite the breakdowns of several rotation members (notably Rodrigo Lopez, Aaron Cook, and Jason Hirsh), and in no small part because of the defense and the pen. Fuentes' late-June setback turned into an opportunity for the equally talented Manny Corpas to close. Tulowitzki's bat came alive, and rotation patches Ubaldo Jimenez and Franklin Morales came up from the minors to fulfill the promise that both prospects held.

What might get blurred in all those shifting fortunes is that when you look at the league's playoff picture in the aggregate, the Rockies really were supposed to win. Take a look at the NL West's straightforward Pythagorean projection and Clay Davenport's more involved "third-order" projection that adjusts for strength of schedule and the quality of the opposition:

Table Two: As it Was, Oughta Be, and Really Oughta Be

Actual Standings	Pythagorean Projection	Third-Order Projection
D'backs 90-72	Rockies 91.4-71.7	Rockies 90.2-72.8
Rockies 90-73	Padres 89.5-73.5	Dodgers 87.3-74.7
Padres 89-74	Dodgers 81.8-80.2	Padres 84.6-78.4
Dodgers 82-89	D'backs 78.9-83.1	Giants 78.2-83.8
Giants 71-91	Giants 77.1-84.9	D'backs 77.8-84.2

The upset that we enjoyed in reality wasn't nearly as surprising from a statistical perspective—the Rockies were the best team in the division, and you can probably forgive them for taking their time in making that discovery, since it was as unexpected in analytical circles as it was within baseball. The real surprise teams in this context were the Snakes and the Padres, with the Dodgers representing the division's big underachiever. That Arizona ran out to such an early lead, five games up by August 18 and ahead by three on the day that the Rockies launched their late-season run, sapped the race of much of its drama, and a cooperative late-season schedule that had them face the already-dead Dodgers and two of the worst teams in the league (the Giants and Pirates) made the outcome of that last weekend's series against the Rockies meaningless to them, while representing everything for Colorado. This was synchronous with the Padres' dying drive running up against the equally desperate Brewers; the two team's split of that four-game set made necessary the one-game playoff, launching the Rockies' next seemingly improbable stretch, running riot in the NL playoffs en route to their own eventual rout at the hands of the Red Sox.

The simple fact of having four good teams in the NL West mounting their individual runs at the division title—with the wild card as their consolation prize—in turn created the backdrop for the year's truly surprising winner-take-all division race over in the NL East. Up until the Padres managed to blow their lead in the final weekend and then lose the one-game playoff against the Rockies, the Mets briefly held the record for the fastest-ever fold, going from having a 90 percent shot or better of making the playoffs to simply not making it at all, falling that far in only five days. The Mets are also arguably the second-most-unlikely "miss" from the playoff picture in major-league history, managing to drop from a 99.8 percent shot on September 12, when they were seven games up on the Phillies with only 16 games left to play. Using the same methodology as used in Table Two, they should have won the division by three or four games, while the Phillies weren't necessarily all that likely to finish second ahead of the Braves. How did this happen?

The tragedy wasn't the product of the Mets' lineup taking a powder; the hitters delivered their best months as a unit at the very end, averaging 5.7 runs per game in August and September after putting up 4.6 per in the four months before. The real problem at that point was a pitching staff that saw its ERA go up in every month over the course of the season; a staff that was allowing only 3.5 runs per game in April was hemorrhaging 5.7 by September, making the club's 14-14 record in that last month not at all surprising. Even there, though, this was a team that had obvious problems much earlier in the season that were being masked by the club's overall record. A good first couple of months put them at 34-18 and ahead of the Braves by 4 1/2 games; the Phillies were 8 1/2 back with their pitching a shambles. But the Mets' offense had started off badly and got worse in June and July. This was a team that literally never had a stretch where it was firing on all cylinders.

As a result, the questions that can be asked as far as "why" should be directed at the club's problem-solvers: general manager Omar Minaya, and manager Willie Randolph. Whether a matter of the overly sunny optimism about the virtues of aging journeymen Jose Valentin and Shawn Green, and unduly sanguine faith that Moises Alou could remain healthy over a full season, or the misplaced belief that catcher Paul Lo Duca was an offensive asset, the lineup had problems beyond its star talent, problems that were fixed—by trading for speedster Luis Castillo, and by benching Green once Alou came back from the DL—later in the day than proved wise.

The rotation was an even worse problem, where a similar Godot-like patience with injured ace Pedro Martinez exacerbated matters. The in-house alternatives all failed, as first prospect Mike Pelfrey failed to overawe the league with an arsenal short of solid off-speed stuff, and then journeyman Jorge Sosa provided a reminder about why he's moved around. Tom Glavine proved to be something less than an ace at the age of 41, and the playoff-minded pickup of el Duque, Orlando Hernandez, predictably involved yet another injury for the infrequently-healthy postseason legend. Perhaps relying on the virtue of their good early start and blinded by the star power of their own roster, the Mets ignored the problem. By the time September had rolled around, Martinez was back but couldn't go deep into games, Glavine and John Maine were spent, Hernandez wasn't available, and spotting drubbable alternatives like Brian Lawrence and rookie Phil Humber against the Nationals only led to beatings that the club couldn't really afford.

In contrast, the Phillies were nothing but active in fixing their problems. They recognized things were going terribly amiss early on, but perhaps having learned their lesson in 2006, they never gave up on their year. As what had initially looked like a well-stocked rotation came to pieces, they added Kyle Kendrick, a strike-throwing rookie from within their system. When they needed more, they traded for the Reds' Kyle Lohse. When the bullpen came apart early, they flipped struggling starter Brett Myers to the pen and then shored it up even further in-season by rescuing rubber-armed lefty J.C. Romero from the waiver wire. When the lineup suffered the potentially crippling blow of losing star second baseman Chase Utley for more than a month, they made a quick swap with the White Sox to patch the hole with Tadahito Iguchi, a regular on the Sox's 2005 championship team. The absence of a solid third baseman was papered over with a three-headed platoon that involved one guy to face lefties, another for righties, and a third to field because the other two were defensive liabilities. When Rod Barajas, their expensive free agent catcher, struggled early on and then got hurt, they leaned on another ready rookie, Carlos Ruiz.

These improvisations were all built around the basic proposition that the core of this team's lineup —Utley, shortstop Jimmy Rollins (the eventual NL MVP), center fielder Aaron Rowand, first baseman Ryan Howard, and left fielder Pat Burrell—could deliver runs in heaps. They provided, and GM Pat Gillick and manager Charlie Manuel helped employ the right kind of backfill to be just good enough to catch up to and then pass the Mets in the season's last two weeks. If the season had been a shorter 150 games or a longer 200, the Mets might have won, either because they'd have been able to truly rest on the merits of their hot start, or because the extra time would have encouraged them to fix their problems more aggressively. Instead, the questions of time, a limited number of games, and the superior virtue of several discrete assets had all allowed the Phillies to build their monument to in-season problem solving.

Now, if you're Bud Selig, this sort of excitement is a reflection of the four-team playoff format at its best. The wild card is perhaps the commissioner's signature achievement, something that when it works, generates late-season enthusiasm in multiple markets and might help boost season ticket sales throughout the industry, since the number of franchises truly without hope and faith in any given season can almost be counted on only one hand.

The question is where so much on-field excitement rates in the context of *It Ain't Over 'Til It's Over*, and whether we have to revisit any of our listings. Using the same methodology as Clay's first pass and the same methods as you'll find in his Playoff Odds Report, the NL East race in 2007 rates only 16th, while the NL West winds up at a distant 61st. However, when he measured the 2007 season with his more time-sensitive third list's methodology, while the NL West and the escape valve of the wild card still only rates 51st, the Phillies' exceptional finish winds up deserving the second spot all-time, ranking behind only the "Impossible Dream" in Boston back in 1967. So, as unlikely a proposition as the Phillies' triumph this past season making everyone forget 1964 is, you can congratulate them for doing unto somebody else as had been done to them 43 years before. We'll see if Mets fans can bear the indignity any better, or if Willie Randolph might wind up being the manager who makes people forget—or perhaps even worse yet, remember—Gene Mauch.

PROSPECTUS HIT AND RUN
The Perils of Relying on Short-Term Memory
Jay Jaffe

Many pundits insist that how a team does during the last leg of the regular season tells us something about its postseason prognosis, but Jay Jaffe did the research and determined that whether you go into October hot or cold has no bearing on playoff success.

Against long odds, the final week of the 2009 regular season wound up producing down-to-the-wire excitement in both leagues, though for the most part, that excitement had nothing to do with stellar play. The Dodgers used a season-high five-game losing streak to keep the suspense regarding the NL West flag and home-field advantage building for an entire week, with the Phillies and Cardinals failing to capitalize, and the Rockies falling just short of overcoming a lackluster two-week stretch prior to their final sprint. Meanwhile, the AL Central has produced its second consecutive Game 163 play-in, this time due to a mad rush by the Twins and a collapse by the Tigers that may yet prove to be historic.

Against this backdrop, viewers have been treated to writers, broadcasters, and in-studio pundits admonishing such slumping teams to pull themselves together as they pontificated on the importance of heading into the playoffs with momentum. The oft-cited example remains the 2007 Rockies, who won 13 of their final 14 regularly scheduled games, then a play-in, and ultimately the NL pennant. Forget the fact that just one year prior, the Cardinals dumped nine of their final 12 before becoming the team with the lowest victory total ever to win the World Series—these experts certainly did. The question obviously arises as to whether there's truth to such conventional wisdom about whether late-season performance carries over into the playoffs. The answer is a fairly resounding no.

Interval	Corr162	Corr163
Final 7	.019	.016
Final 14	-.020	-.021
Final 21	-.042	-.043
Final Month	-.028	-.028

With the help of Eric Seidman, I pulled late-season records for every playoff team of the wild-card era from 1995 through 2008, 112 teams in all. We recorded each team's record over the final seven, 14, and 21 games, as well for September and whatever fragment of October remained. The results of Game 163 play-ins initially weren't included in either the "week" records (which didn't always coincide to weeks, but which were somewhat easier to gather) or the "month" records; including them didn't change the results substantially. Here are the correlations between the interval's winning percentage and first-round success:

That, folks, is a whole lot of nothing, an essentially random relationship between recent performance and first-round success. None of the correlations even reached .05 in either direction, and six of the eight were actually negative.

Okay, so those few week intervals don't tell us much about the outcome of those five-game series. They tell us only slightly more about the entire postseason. Here are the correlations between those winning percentages and overall playoff success as measured by the number of series won:

Interval	Corr162	Corr163
Final 7	-.043	-.049
Final 14	-.097	-.101
Final 21	-.119	-.121
Final Month	-.112	-.115

That's still nothing to write home about, and the slate is now uniformly negative, suggesting that, if anything, there's an ever-so slight inverse relationship between success in the final weeks and in the postseason. Perhaps that's because some of these playoff-bound teams are resting their regulars more often, or simply regressing to the mean after a summer of beating up on opponents. Even if we create a points system, doubling the value of winning the League Championship Series and quadrupling that of the World Series such that the same number of points are awarded per round, the magnitude of the largest correlation—for the final month, 163-game version—still doesn't get any bigger than .137, and it's negative at that. It's still essentially nothing.

By and large, these teams that made the playoffs did well over the various intervals in question, winning at a .595 to .601 clip and serving to remind that there's a selection bias at work here: the teams that did very poorly likely missed the postseason, relegating themselves to the dustbin of history. Indeed, just 13 of these 112 teams put up sub-.500 records from September 1 onward, and only two of them, the 1998 Padres and 2008 Brewers, were more than five games below .500 during that stretch run. Even so, six of those 13 teams won their first-round matchups, all six of them won their respective League Championship Series, and three of them won the World Series (the 1997 Marlins, 2000 Yankees, and 2006 Cardinals). Recall those 2000 Yanks lost 15 of their final 18 games prior to the postseason while being outscored 148-59, exhuming the memory of the 1899 Cleveland Spiders in the process before flipping the switch and trampling everything in their path to a third straight World Championship.

As well as those teams did over these short stretches, it's noteworthy that the recent records of the teams that won in the Division Series and the teams that lost are virtually indistinguishable.

Over the seven-game split, the two teams' aggregate records differ by one win across a sample of 784 games, and over the month-long split, the difference is a net of four games. The split between the two grows as the pool of teams decreases in the Championship Series and World Series rounds, but not in the direction we'd expect:

Interval	DS W	DS L	CS W	CS L	WS W	WS L
Final 7	.594	.592	.571	.621	.551	.592
Final 14	.597	.600	.581	.612	.541	.622
Final 21	.598	.604	.578	.617	.558	.599
Final Month	.599	.601	.579	.619	.570	.589

Every single split but the seven-game/Division Series one—the only one from among the first two tables with a positive correlation—shows that the teams that lost the series had a better aggregate record over the recent intervals than the teams that won, again suggesting that there might be some effect of resting the regulars or otherwise regressing down the stretch.

On a team level, recent performance as measured by wins and losses simply isn't predictive. For further evidence of this, consider a quick-and-dirty study I did in the service of the Hit List this summer in response to the suggestion of making recent performance a stronger factor in the rankings, thus conforming to some readers' perceptions that the hottest teams at the moment were thus the strongest teams overall.

Using the 2008 Hit List, I broke the season up into four-week chunks ("months," for the purposes of this study) and tested the correlation between each team's "monthly" actual, first-order, second-order, and third-order winning percentages, as well as its Hit List Factor (the average of those four percentages), against the following "month's" actual record. I used these four-week splits because they were easily created from my master Hit List spreadsheet, as I only save the adjusted standings for the days I use to compile the list.

The correlations for "monthly" _____ winning percentage to next "month's" actual winning percentage:

Indicator	Corr
Actual	.21
First-order	.24
Second-order	.18
Third-order	.17
Hit List Factor	.22

Not much to hang onto there.

I then tested the correlation between the various year-to-date winning percentages from those increments and the next month's actual winning percentage.

Indicator	Corr
Actual	.304
First-order	.289
Second-order	.298
Third-order	.296
Hit List Factor	.312

Though it's hardly a robust effect, this admittedly slapdash study does support the none-too-controversial idea that a larger sample size such as a year-to-date performance is more useful than a recent incremental performance in predicting wins and losses going forward. Even so, as I found last year, when it comes to the playoffs, actual records over the full season aren't as helpful as Pythagorean ones, which are based on the underlying performances that tend to even out across even larger sample sizes.

As the postseason unfolds over the next few weeks, you're going to hear a lot about momentum and its importance to a ballclub, and while it's undoubtedly a good idea to bear Earl Weaver's famous maxim in mind, the take-home message is that the conventional wisdom that a team's recent performances foreshadows its playoff fate is generally wrong. The fact that there are no shortage of pundits who elevate the 2007 Rockies as their evidence while forgetting the 2006 Cardinals underscores either how little attention some talking heads pay to actual results, or how short their attention spans are.

In any given series, there may well be reasons to predict one team having the upper hand in a given series due to the strengths and weaknesses of the various matchups; things like the Phillies' closer situation and the Dodgers' rotation jumble will have a very real impact who gets to play, and what might arise from that. Even so, the differences between any two teams who make it to the October crapshoot are small enough that the range of outcomes in a short series is almost unlimited, and the effect of recent performance shouldn't be overemphasized.

CHANGING SPEEDS
A Brief Meditation on the Power of Sabermetrics During the Postseason
Ken Funck

As Ken Funck explained, the short-series format that determine winners in October forces us to accept that sabermetrics can help us only a little in picking favorites and helps us learn to love small-sample-size baseball.

My apologies for giving this piece a title more suited to a Sufjan Stevens song than a baseball article, but I'm a little bit hyper today. Like many of you, I'm struggling through this two-day break before the playoffs begin again on Friday night, featuring an ALCS showdown between the Texas Rangers, coming off their first playoff series victory in franchise history, and the New York Yankees, who've won 28 playoff series and nine world championships since the Senators/Rangers franchise came into existence in 1961. Over in the senior circuit, the Giants and Phillies tee it up on Saturday night with one of the more compelling pitching matchups of recent vintage: Tim Lincecum vs. Roy Halladay, who in their two playoff starts have combined for two complete games, one no-hitter, four baserunners allowed, 23 punchouts, and 48 instances of a broadcaster saying "that pitch just wasn't fair." I can't wait, because this is going to be good—in fact, given how exciting (if sloppy) the playoffs have been so far, I'm more excited about them than I've been in years.

To me, this two-day gap feels like a deep breath before the plunge, as the arrival of a "real" (i.e., best-of-seven) series means the playoffs have become serious—I've never quite understood why a divisional series is best-of-five, since the loser is just as fully required to go home as if it were a full seven, but that's a discussion for another day. To fill this short breathing space, the interwebs are teeming with series previews, player profiles, predictions, and occasional pablum. Sometimes this analysis will give heavy weight to things like clubhouse chemistry, clutch hitting, veteran steadiness, and other factors that are difficult to quantify. Since you're reading this at BP, however, you're probably interested in a more sabermetric take on each series, and I'm here to help. Here's the best, most informed, most statistically advanced analysis of each series I can give you:

(cue crickets chirping)

OK, that's not completely true. Colin Wyers, Eric Seidman, and Matt Swartz, our resident Navajo Stat Speakers, have done yeoman's work putting together game-day PECOTA projections and pitcher previews, and their output has been interesting, entertaining, and informative. But if there's one overriding principle everyone interested in baseball analysis should always keep in mind, it's that nearly anything can happen given a small sample. In a series that lasts four-to-seven games, most any batter can produce like Mickey Mantle or Tony Gwynn for a short period of time, just as he can during any given week in June. Even the worst teams in baseball can be world-beaters for a short stretch—as an example, on five different occasions this season, the Pirates won four out of five games.

This holds true for in-game strategies as well. Over the course of a season, a manager prone to calling for a sacrifice bunt in situations where it almost certainly lowers his team's run expectancy is going to cost that team wins, as will a manager who structures his lineup inefficiently or doesn't maximize his bullpen usage. Baseball writers are right to point these errors out. Over the course of a week, however, these small inefficiencies have much less opportunity to accumulate and therefore play less of a role in determining who wins a series, as compared to their effect on winning enough games to make the playoffs.

You already know this to be true, of course, as do I, as does Billy Beane, who famously said "my sh*t doesn't work in the playoffs." There are those who read that statement and take it to mean that the methods used by more saber-friendly organizations are "tricks" that have value only during the regular season and are doomed to fail against the best teams in the league once the playoffs start. Rarely do those folks remember, or understand, that the rest of the quote is this: "My job is to get us to the playoffs. What happens after that is… luck." While "luck" was perhaps an unfortunate choice of words, since it makes it sound like there's no advantage to being the better team (something that's patently untrue), Beane's point was that the market inefficiencies he was trying to exploit could help him leverage enough small advantages over the course of a season to get him into the dance, but once the playoffs start the teams are too evenly matched and the time horizon too short for those things to make a difference. The best teams almost always make the playoffs, but the better team frequently doesn't win a short series. Dayn Perry and Nate Silver wrote this in *Baseball Between The Numbers*, after cribbing Beane's quote for a chapter heading: "That there is a great deal of luck involved in the playoffs is an incontrovertible mathematical fact." Their attempts to determine the factors that lead to playoff success formed the basis of our Secret Sauce calculation, but even that noble effort hasn't show any great predictive power.

As I said, everyone reading these words probably know this, since we've all been using advanced metrics to help us stay competitive in our fantasy leagues for years now—leagues that usually depend on a full season of baseball, where there's enough time to apply this knowledge. It's an easy thing for us to reconcile, despite what may be said by those who are not only disinterested in the statistical side of baseball but can be actively hostile towards it: sabermetrics (for want of a better term) can go a long way towards helping your team's GM put together a consistent winner over the long haul, and the fact that we may have difficulty predicting the outcome of a single game or a single short series in no way invalidates that fact, regardless of what may be said by those who not only aren't interested in sabermetrics but are downright hostile to it.

Once the playoffs start, it's easy for me to just sit back, relax, and let the games wash over me, to revel in their beauty and drama, their heroes and goats, their nail-biting personal confrontations and otherworldly athletic displays, and everything else that makes baseball such a wonderful game. I can take pleasure in watching the Buddy Biancalanas of the world enjoy their unexpected moments in the sun just as much as (or even more than) I can enjoy watching superstars like Halladay and Lincecum shred opposing lineups, regardless of their respective PECOTA projections. This makes me no different than anyone else reading this, and no different than any other baseball fan. As for my in-depth ALCS and NLCS analysis, I'm picking the Yankees and the Phillies, the teams I thought were the most talented in each league back in March, and nothing since then has changed that opinion. When all is said and done, though talent doesn't make you a lock, it's what matters most.

OCTOBER 19, 2001 — http://bbp.cx/a/1251

THE DAILY PROSPECTUS
Whither Runs?
Joe Sheehan

During the memorable 2001 playoffs, Joe Sheehan explained that at times, low-scoring playoff series require a different strategic mindset than the one we're used to during the regular season.

One of my friends made an offhand comment to me Wednesday, something about how he thought that evening's game would be a 3-2 contest, "just like all the other ones."

The line was a throwaway one, but I thought it was a good observation. It certainly has seemed to me that the postseason has been distinctly different from the regular season. It seemed as if runs were very hard to come by, there'd been very few home runs, and in particular, very few walks, as compared to the regular season. It also seemed to me that last year had been similar, but again, I didn't have a lot of data to support the notion.

So I decided to work through the problem, as much to satisfy my curiosity as anything else. My gut tells me that the popular notion that "pitching and defense wins in the playoffs" is just so much conventional hooey, but what I'm seeing on the field tells me that maybe there's something to it.

We'll start at the top. The average major-league baseball game in 2001 saw 9.55 runs scored. So far in the playoffs, there have been 6.18 runs per game.

Case closed, enjoy the weekend.

OK, it's not that simple. For one, there are no playoff games in Denver, and none that involve the Rangers pitching staff. Only the top halves of pitching staffs are being used, for the most part, and some of the best pitchers in the game are accounting for a huge chunk of the innings being thrown.

Let's run at this from a different angle. The following chart lists the average runs per regular-season team game for each of the eight playoff teams, followed by the runs per game in their playoff games:

Team	R/G Season	R/G Playoffs	Decline
Mariners	9.59	7.57	-21%
Yankees	9.48	5.86	-38%
A's	9.44	6.00	-36%
Indians	10.60	8.40	-21%

Team	R/G Season	R/G Playoffs	Decline
Braves	8.47	6.20	-27%
Diamondbacks	9.23	4.71	-49%
Astros	9.98	6.67	-33%
Cardinals	9.25	4.40	-52%

In every case, these teams are seeing at least 20 percent fewer runs scored in their games than they did in the regular season. In an era in which we expect scores of 11-6 and 9-8, where multi-homer games are commonplace, the postseason looks like two weeks out of 1966.

That's important for everyone involved. With runs more scarce, tactics that should normally be reserved for late-inning situations—sacrifice bunts, for example—become more acceptable earlier in the game. All one-run strategies have a more prominent place, with fewer long innings and almost no crooked numbers on the board. Risks on the basepaths, usually anathema when the threat of the multi-run jack is present, look a lot better when the best you can hope for is a sacrifice fly (sorry, Mr. Tejada; you shoulda gone).

This is important to opinionated guys writing baseball columns, too. Watching Thursday's ALCS game, I cringed when Derek Jeter bunted following a leadoff single by Chuck Knoblauch in the first inning. That's the kind of thing that causes us to want to hang Don Baylor in effigy, but when games are all ending 3-1 and 4-3, getting ahead, getting a run on the board, is a valuable thing. (Especially when, as David Schoenfield's excellent ESPN.com piece illustrated, the Yankees' dynasty is all about the work they get from their pitchers, particularly their bullpen.)

We're not used to this, a function of seven years of inflated offense. It's hard to recalibrate on the fly, but it's something we have to do, the same way we have to watch games in pitchers' parks and hitters' parks with different mindsets. That's the difference between regular-season and playoff baseball right now: the difference between a game in Dodger Stadium and a game in Enron Field.

Why are there fewer runs being scored? Well, there's the obvious point that a disproportionate number of innings are being thrown by future Hall of Famers. Breaking it down, we see that all the elements of offense—batting average, walks, and power—are way down

For the eight playoff teams:

Statistic	Season	Playoffs
Batting Average	.271	.234
AB/Walk	9.8	12.4
AB/HR	28.3	36.7
AB/XBH	10.7	13.8

(Aside: Exactly how hard do you have to hit a ball to go yard at Safeco Field? Yeah, I know Stan Javier did it, but it sure seems to me like a lot of well-struck balls the last few days have ended up as F7.)

None of this is going to change the world, and I know there are a lot of problems with the analysis, small sample size foremost among them. But I now think, looking at this, that the conventional wisdom about the playoffs being a different game has merit and that the playoffs we've been watching over the past couple of years don't really bear much resemblance to baseball we watch during the regular season.

Year	Season R/G	Playoffs R/G
2000	10.28	8.29
1999	10.17	10.52
1998	9.58	7.23
1997	9.53	8.41

Only in 1999 did scoring not drop by at least a run per game in the postseason. (That was the year of the Indians/Red Sox Division Series, during which the teams combined for 79 runs in five games.) Generally, though, the run environment of the regular season looks nothing like the run environment in October.

Keep that in mind as you watch Alfonso Soriano try to steal third base in the second inning this weekend.

WORLD SERIES PROSPECTUS
Fall Classic Memories
Baseball Prospectus

On the eve of the 2010 World Series, BP staff members shared their memories of special Fall Classics from years past.

Every baseball fan has a special World Series memory, whether it's Willie Mays' catch, Bill Mazeroski's home run, Brooks Robinson's defense, Kirk Gibson's limp around the bases, or Derek Jeter becoming the first-ever Mr. November. With the World Series opening tonight at AT&T Park in San Francisco with the Giants facing the Texas Rangers, many of our writers, editors, and interns share their favorite memories of the Fall Classic.

Stephani Bee: 1999
In my 21 years growing up a Yankee fan, I have had the great fortune of celebrating a World Series title with my father five times. My dad grew up loving Yogi and Mickey, Joe D. and Whitey, Howard and Bauer. I grew up loving the stories he shared about them, and in 1999, I finally had the opportunity to see the greatness of those players personified with the unveiling of the All-Century Team.

It was the bridging of a generation gap. There were Yogi and Ruth, Stan the Man and Hammerin' Hank, the Big Train and the Iron Horse. As each name was called out, my skin prickled with goosebumps. I finally started to understand why my dad got starry-eyed talking about these men and their accomplishments. This was what baseball was all about.

The day after the All-Century team was unveiled, my favorite game in the '99 World Series was played—Game Three. Andy Pettitte, one of my childhood favorites, matched up against Tom Glavine, and the Bravos knocked him around for five runs. But I didn't need to worry—these were the Yankees. "Have faith in the Yankees, my son," Ernest Hemingway had written in *The Old Man and the Sea*. I had faith. The Yankees would pull this out.

Glavine started to tire. The Bombers were down by a deuce. Up stepped Chuck Knoblauch with a man on. With one swing, it was knotted up. I had no doubts. This was the Yankees' game.

Mariano Rivera came on to pitch and did what he has always done—shut the opposition down. It was the bottom of the 10th, and the Yankees were at home. Playoff magic was knocking on the door.

Chad Curtis, who had already homered against Glavine, came up to face Mike Remlinger. His bat must have been blessed that night. He belted a homer to left field. At home in front of the TV, my dad and I were hugging and cheering. As my dad and I high-fived and jumped around for the rest of the night, I started to realize how much a sport could bond a family.

I spent the offseason looking up every man on the All-Century squad and learning more about his life and on-field feats. Now my dad and I banter endlessly about which player had the better career, who will end up in the Hall of Fame and who deserves enshrinement, and what lies ahead for baseball. I pepper him with questions about players from the past. Dad always has stories to share, and the importance of those stories and the father-daughter connection that baseball fosters was magnified for me during the '99 World Series.

Charles Dahan: 1989

The odds of any two teams meeting in the World Series in 1989 (when MLB consisted of only 26 teams)? 1:162. Odds of a major northern California earthquake occurring on a given day? Considering three earthquakes over 7.0 occurred over the past 150 years, a completely unscientific assumption would be that one occurs every 18,000 days. Odds a World Series game is played on a given day in a year? Generously, 7:365. The odds of each of these events occurring on the same day? 1 in six billion.

Memories are sparse prior to 1989, when I turned five years old—the field behind our house, our dog Maggie, my first tee-ball team (the Braves), and a few selections from pre-school. The 1989 baseball season is the first sporting experience I remember in full. I grew up in Mountain View, California, at the time a town dominated by a military base, a few technology companies, and a few Asian restaurants; the blue collar neighbor to the ultra-wealthy suburbs populated by San Francisco elite—this, of course, prior to the influx of tech millionaires and, later, Google. The Giants (and 49ers) were their teams—we rooted for the A's. The players—despite the stereotypes of the aloof and arrogant team—were accessible and generous. After games, Tony La Russa set up autograph sessions in the parking lot of Oakland-Alameda Coliseum for his animal rescue charity, and every star participated. That said, there weren't many "non-stars" on that roster, and even those—specifically, Billy Beane—did all right for themselves in baseball.

I remember driving home with my mom to watch Game Three, waiting for Big Mac and Jose and Rickey and Eck and Walt Weiss (hey, he'd just won ROY and, more importantly for the family, was a University of North Carolina graduate) drop the hammer on the Giants. We were stopped at a light on El Camino when everything started shaking; minimally at first, then being thrown around the front seat of the car. The street lamp to my right looked like it was going to come loose from its bearings and crash on the hood of the car. We were directly between San Francisco and the epicenter, 50 percent closer than what the folks saw on TV.

The 1989 World Series is the only championship a professional team to which I gave my allegiance won in the past 26 years. The A's absolutely pummeled the Giants, outscoring San Francisco 32-14 during the four-game sweep, pouring on 13 runs in Game Three when the series resumed 10 days after the quake. The team that should have been a dynasty managed to be foiled by Kirk Gibson, Mother Nature, and Jose Rijo.

The memories of the moment the team won are complicated. Early promotional material dubbed it as the "Bay Bridge Series," yet during the earthquake the Bay Bridge had collapsed. Like most successes, the payoff of a championship never lived up to the expectation, even for the most improbable of World Series.

Jeff Euston: 1985

Every World Series has a lasting image, and 1985's is The Denkinger Call. The Cardinals, three outs away from a championship, thought they had retired the Royals' Jorge Orta leading off the ninth inning of Game Six. Even those of us sitting down the left-field line could see the ball had beaten Orta to the bag. But Denkinger missed the call and ruled Orta safe, setting the stage for a game-winning Kansas City rally and a Game Seven victory the next night.

But the fallout from the call obscures the fact that the Cardinals—baseball's best team that season with 101 victories—were out-hit and out-pitched by the Royals throughout the Series. The Royals could have won Game One, should have won Game Two, and decisively won games Three and Five before coasting to an 11-0 rout in Game Seven.

Despite building a 3-1 series lead, St. Louis looked nothing like the Runnin' Redbirds who had led the league in runs and stolen bases. One problem was the Cardinals' loss of leadoff man Vince Coleman to a freak accident with the automated tarp at Busch Stadium. A more immediate problem was the Royals' pitching staff, which allowed just 13 earned runs in 62 innings. A baby-faced Bret Saberhagen shut down St. Louis twice and welcomed into the world a baby of his own between starts. Danny Jackson was electric, and Charlie Leibrandt was quietly dominant.

The Series featured several other signature moments: Frank White's long blast in Game Three at Busch Stadium. Coach Lee May catching a flying George Brett as the third baseman careened into the KC dugout chasing a foul pop in Game Five. Darryl Motley hitting a long drive—foul—in the second inning of Game Seven, then hitting the next pitch from St. Louis ace John Tudor deep—and fair—into the left-field seats. And, poignantly, Dick Howser finally finding post-season success and winning "the whole enchilada" just months before his cancer diagnosis.

My favorite memory was the aftermath of Saturday night's Game Six. When the Cards scratched out a run in the eighth, the game and the Series seemed lost for the Royals, and the mood in the ballpark was impending heartbreak. Then, in a half inning, everything changed. Orta reached on Denkinger's Call, and St. Louis imploded. Dane Iorg got the hit to score Jim Sundberg with the winning run, and the ballpark shook. Another fan in my row—who will remain nameless—fell into the row in front of us and promptly jumped up and continued cheering.

Now, 25 years later, World Series appearances are nearly a birthright in St. Louis. In Kansas City, post-season play is something of an urban myth, like the $30 face value for tickets to the '85 Series. Missouri, always a swing state politically, has gone decidedly red—in its baseball rooting interests, anyway. But in one October, the upstart Royals turned the state blue.

Ken Funck: 1994

Due to a series of events involving the settlement decisions of my German immigrant forebears, and the almost pathologically stubborn loyalty which I inherited from them, I've been a Cubs fan my whole life. Thus, I don't have any happy World Series stories to share involving triumph, tears, and multi-generational group hugs—though I remain convinced that they're out there waiting to be told, and the sooner I get to tell them, the better. For many years, the pleasure I got from watching the World Series was tempered by a deep-seated longing to be that guy in the stands beaming with delight as he watches his favorite team's dugout empty to celebrate a hard-won championship. Envy isn't the most dignified of human emotions, but it's certainly a common one, as evidenced by its placement among the Seven Deadly Sins—and for many years, envy was a feeling I could never entirely shake come the end of October.

That ended in the fall of 1994, when the men who run baseball conspired to cheat us all out of a World Series. I didn't claim then, and I don't claim now, to know who was in the right—and frankly, I didn't (and don't) care. What mattered is that in their attempts to ensure that their side was allotted an appropriately large piece of an already massive pie, the owners and players engaged in a game of economic chicken that ended with neither side willing to swerve, and the aftershocks of that head-on collision continue to be felt today. You don't need the uncanny navigational skills of William Bligh to plot a course from the 1994 labor stoppage through the decreased attendance of 1995 and into the fan-pleasing run environment of the late '90s, an era that fans continue to argue whenever a player of the "Steroid Era" is discussed.

In 1994 I didn't have a team to root for in the World Series, but that was nothing new. Instead, regret was a pebble that wiggled its way into every fan's shoe, not just mine. Expos fans, of course, were the most cheated, as the NL's best team by far was unable to play on the ultimate stage—perhaps a world championship would have kept baseball in Montreal to this day. The Yankees would have been a solid bet to represent the AL that year for the first time since 1981, setting up a terrific matchup between the team that had never been there and the team everyone loves to hate. I like to think we missed out on some fantastic moments: young Pedro Martinez striking out Don Mattingly to finish his Game Two shutout; Luis Polonia's unexpectedly dazzling catch to save the Yankees' bacon in Game Five; Wil Cordero's three-run shot off Jimmy Key in Game Seven. But we'll never know. The 1994 World Series That Wasn't taught me that misery doesn't love company, and as much as I'm a fan of a certain team, I'm even more a fan of baseball itself—and the Fall Classic has been more important to me ever since.

Chase Gharrity: 2001
Let's set the scene. It's Halloween night in 2001 and, while children across the country are dressing up and asking for candy, I was sitting in my living room with my family learning about the power of rooting for the underdog and watching the epic tragedy that was Byung-Hyun Kim's playoff experience. It was a night and series filled with classic names like Tino Martinez and Orlando Hernandez, as well as soon-to-be-great ones like Jorge Posada and Alfonso Soriano, playing alongside a Matt Williams who was manning third instead of coaching first and a Mike Stanton who was known more for his arm than his monster home runs.

Yes, the 2001 World Series matchup between the then-teal Diamondbacks and the dynastic Yankees was memorable for many reasons. Perhaps it was the fact that I was able to see a game that featured both Curt Shilling and Randy Johnson on the same team and pitching on the same night or maybe it was because I, a lifelong Chicago Cubs fan, could root for a team that could win a World Series. Whatever the reason, it is clear that, while this duel was memorable to me for things that I saw, it was important for the things that I learned. I'd like to share a few of those lessons here.

The first lesson this series taught me was that no matter how hard you can throw or how far you can bend a breaking ball, if you don't have control of your pitches, you can get hit. Hard. We'll credit that lesson to Professor Kim and his 13.50 ERA, 18 H/9, and three homers allowed.

The second lesson I learned from this series: in the playoffs, nothing is off-limits. This lesson was demonstrated by Bob Brenly's move to have Randy Johnson appear in relief during Game Seven instead of their surely-frazzled closer. The Big Unit would throw 1 1/3 hitless innings, K'ing one and earning the win. It was at this moment that I realized that being in the playoffs can change the entire dynamic of the game, causing managers to go against traditional, regular-season strategies and letting pitchers show what they can do in less than 24 hours of rest.

The final lesson I learned from this series is that anything can happen. In a world that was shocked by the seemingly impossible in 2001, baseball was ready to answer back with a shock of its own. After all, this was the season of baseball beyond October, "Mr. November," and a championship not won by the Yankees. Even that series-winning hit, though whacked by the most probable hitter, was set up by some of the most improbable weapons. Starting with a single from Mark

Grace, players like Damian Miller, Jay Bell, and Tony Womack all had meaningful contributions to the final inning. It's games like this that remind us that no matter how small, worn down or unassuming one is, anything, and everything, can happen.

Steven Goldman: 1996

The years 1995 and 1996 were intense ones for my future wife and I. I got my first professional writing published and encountered the bane of every writer, the underfinanced entrepreneur who can get you a ton of money if you just consent to write a hundred or so items for free, while she was trying to get established in her PhD program, which required that she become fluent in German, pass several exams with should-I-stay-or-should-I-go consequences, and figure out a course of research that would sustain her for the rest of her working life. In the midst of this, we also had to cope with unexpected heartbreak: in 1995, my wife's mother was diagnosed with an advanced case of lung cancer, and at Christmas, she died.

My wife and I had bonded, among other things, over baseball. She was a Braves fan. I had grown up a Yankees fan. The Braves had known recent success, including winning the 1995 championship. The Yankees had been repeat World Series winners when I was a child, but the first World Series I experienced with any kind of mature understanding was the heartbreaking 1981 World Series in which they went up two games to none and then proceeded to lose four in a row. And then, nothing. Though the Yankees were the most successful team of the 1980s in terms of piling up regular-season wins, they could never get to the playoffs. To quote William Shatner in one of the films of the era, "Like a poor marksman [they] just kept missing the target."

By 1996, I had been waiting 15 years for the Yankees to win, which is the blink of an eye to a Cubs fan but nonetheless represented three-fifths of my entire existence and 100 percent of my maturity. They had been lost in the late '80s and early '90s. Bud Selig destroyed their chances in 1994. Edgar Martinez and Buck Showalter helped hurry them out of the playoffs in 1995. The World Series against the Braves was their first real chance since the debacle of 1981. In the event, they went down two games to none, and then, in shocking, emotional fashion, they won four straight to win it—1981 in reverse.

As the Yankees celebrated, I looked over at my wife. She was crying. Now, I'm a supportive husband, or partner, or whatever I was at that time. Yet, I have to confess that I was more than a little put out. The Braves had won the year before. She knew I had been waiting. Couldn't she just have been happy for me? Summoning up all the compassion I could muster at that moment, I asked, "Are you crying because of the Braves?"

"No," she sobbed.

"Then why?"

"My mother."

Fellow males, put yourselves in my shoes. I knew it wasn't that her mother (who, parenthetically, I greatly cared for) was a huge Braves fan, or that my wife was flashing back on memories of going to the ballpark with a pennant-waving, foam-fingered mommy in matching Dale Murphy T-shirts. It was simply that, as often happens to people who are grieving, an unrelated emotional moment lowered her barriers enough that all the sadness she had been coping with for the previous nine months spilled forth. What would you do? Celebrate or sympathize?

I chose sympathy; I knew this was my life-mate, and some things are more important and lasting than a transient feeling of euphoria resulting from watching a bunch of guys in their pajamas win a game. A funny thing happened after. The Yankees won again in 1998, and this time my wife didn't cry, but I didn't feel a thing. They took another in 1999, from the Braves again, and this time my wife was congratulatory, but I was mostly numb. By the next year, I had begun writing about the Yankees professionally and getting to see how things worked behind the scenes, and quickly almost all fannish enthusiasm was gone. It is not hard for me to be objective now, because I am objective. But, when I look back at the 1996 Series, I do have a feeling, an odd, unresolved feeling, a gap in memory where I know a good feeling is supposed to be but isn't. All these years later, I haven't quite forgiven my wife for stealing that moment from me, however innocently, but I also know that if that was the price I had to pay to keep her, I would gladly pay it a thousand times over.

Kevin Goldstein: 1986

1986 was a good year. I was an independent adult for the first time, and after living through the Nino Espinosa/Craig Swan eras, the Mets were finally good. The future seemed limitless. Unless one was a Met fan, the team was impossible to like, filled with enough arrogance, cockiness, and hubris to make cast members of *Jersey Shore* blush. Luckily, they backed it up with an almost boring regular season that saw them run away with the National League East by winning 44 of their first 60 games to open up an 11 1/2-game lead by early June. The Astros, thanks almost solely to the presence of Mike Scott (that year's postseason of Cliff Lee) gave the Mets an unexpected challenge in the playoffs, but all alone, the World Series title was, if anything, seen as a fait accompli.

Everyone remembers what happened after that, with the Red Sox winning the first two games in New York to create a panic in the city, followed by the most famous first-base error in the history of baseball that cost Boston its first title since 1918. Millions of words have been written about Mookie Wilson's ground ball and what followed, but what I remember most about Game Six is how I felt.

Growing up a Mets fan, I hated the Cubs, as they had a strange, almost irrational rivalry based on which team was really worse, but as I got into the business I'm in now, those kinds of feelings went away. When you talk to people who work for a team, it's hard to demonize them based on location or logos, but the inverse is true as well, as on a pure team basis, my ability to live and die with each loss is gone to the point where I'm not sure I even have a favorite team as much as I simply just love the game itself. On October 25, 1986, during the 10th inning of Game Six, I punched a wall with anger and cried tears of joy within the span of about 15 minutes. I know far more about baseball now than I did then, but at the same time, I know the game will never make me feel that way again.

Jay Jaffe: 1981
For the third time in five years and the 11th time in 40, the Dodgers faced their all-too-familiar foes, the Yankees, in the 1981 World Series. The Yankees had won eight of the previous 10 battles, including the most recent ones in 1977 and 1978, with the latter marking the first Fall Classic in which I truly grasped the proceedings. The Dodgers lost that year in six games, dipped below .500 in 1979, and lost a Game 163 play-in to the Astros in 1980. To an 11-year-old third-generation Dodgers fan, it seemed like forever until they'd get another chance to win.

To a familiar cast of holdovers—the "Longest Running Infield" of Steve Garvey, Davey Lopes, Bill Russell, and Ron Cey, as well as Dusty Baker, Rick Monday, Burt Hooton, and manager Tommy Lasorda—the 1981 Dodgers added a new weapon: Fernando Valenzuela. After debuting as a reliever late in 1980, the chubby 20-year-old screwball-tossing lefty from Etchohuaquila, Mexico took the mound on Opening Day in place of injured Jerry Reuss, blanking the Astros to spark a brilliant eight-start stretch: 8-0 with an 0.50 ERA, seven complete games, and five shutouts. Fernandomania was born via a transcendent superstar who could pack stadiums but couldn't speak a lick of English. As a baseball geek, I'd tape box scores of Valenzuela's starts into a notebook, compute his microscopic ERA on my mom's calculator, and trace pictures of him out of *Sports Illustrated*. No other player ever inspired such fandom in me.

Though a seven-week strike would mar the 1981 season, the Dodgers made the three-tiered playoffs on the strength of their Valenzuela-led burst from the gate. Quickly pushed to the brink of elimination against the Astros in the ad hoc Division Series and again in the NLCS against the Expos, they nonetheless won five straight elimination games to return to the World Series and face an all-too-familiar cast of Yankees, including Graig Nettles, Lou Piniella, Willie Randolph, Goose Gossage, Ron Guidry, and most notably, Reggie Jackson.

The Dodgers fell behind two games to none on the road, but Valenzuela proved the stopper in Game Three, weathering the slings and arrows of nine hits and seven walks while throwing 147 pitches over nine innings; the Dodgers won 5-4. Aided by a Jay Johnstone pinch-homer and a late rally against the Yankee bullpen, they overcame a 6-3 deficit the next day to win 8-7, then squeaked by in Game Five via back-to-back solo shots by Pedro Guerrero and Steve Yeager against Guidry—the game which preceded Yankee owner George Steinbrenner's phantom elevator fight with two Dodgers fans. Returning to the Bronx, they broke open a 1-1 tie in Game Six once Yankee manager Bob Lemon pulled Tommy John for a pinch-hitter in the fourth inning, with Guerrero and company pummeling a parade of relievers to run the score to 9-2. When Bob Watson's lazy fly ball settled into the glove of center fielder Kenny Landreaux for the last out, my brother and I jumped gleefully: finally our team was on top.

Christina Kahrl: 1988

A fan's experiences vary—despair and joy are our lot. You invest years of your life awaiting a payoff, the expectation of some great reward; sometimes, you actually get one. But sometimes you first get dealt deep-dish agony, which you have to eat entire, because Emily Post teaches us that it's rude not to at least make the attempt.

I became an A's fan as a matter of local duty, but even so it was hard to get excited about the Gary Alexander A's, the Bobby Winkles A's, the pointless A's of the late '70s, followed by Billyball's false promise. Then Dave Kingman's '84 re-fired my enthusiasm, probably making me the first and last person whose love of the game depended upon the performance of one of the most unloved and apparently unlovable figures of the day. Rickey got traded, Jose arrived, I left for Chicago and college, but Sandy Alderson won a power struggle to become the man in charge. Then Hawk Harrelson did something (else) spectacularly stupid, canning Tony La Russa. Within weeks, La Russa was skippering the A's, and on his first day he started journeyman Dave Stewart against Roger Clemens, a sure loss—except that everything changed that day. The hard-throwing badass pitched well enough to beat Boston, to beat the Rocket. A new destiny seemed to start right there, one in which Alderson's canny pickups of innumerable discards, La Russa's thoughtful skippering, and a good farm system combined to produce a team that had direction.

Anticipating that team's arrival in the postseason seemed to be a matter of inevitability, something that would make everything that preceded it worthwhile, even Dave Collins, even Shooty Babbitt, even Chris Codiroli. The comfortable romp of 1988 had me going to classes listening to ballgames with a portable radio tucked into an inside coat pocket, sitting to the side so that one professor or another couldn't see the old-school earpiece's thin connection snaking from my left ear. That was how I listened to the A's drub Mike Boddicker in the ALCS, months after I had derisively, confidently snorted to friends over his deadline pickup, "'We own that guy.'"

It all seemed so very certain.

So on October 15, I popped by my best friend's place off campus with a couple of friends from LA with a couple of cases of beer to watch the first game of the Series, expectant that "my" guys would come through. Heading into the bottom of the ninth, all seemed fine. Stew had pitched eight, the A's were up by a run, Eck was on the mound. The Dodgers had made a fine accounting of themselves, but now it was time to play their part and lose, like they were the Mariners. This was what I'd been waiting for, after all, and the A's were supposed to win this thing, going away. One out, two outs... wait a minute, a Mike Davis walk? Is that even possible? That's OK, it's just Dave Anderson on deck, no, wait... it's Gibby. Well, hell, the man can't even walk to the plate, so no problem...

Oh, problem.

There was a stupefied moment of silence in that living room, at which point the two Angelenos and my friend Al erupted from their seats with shouts and yells and expletives and exultations, because they had seen something wonderful and amazing. Then they paused, looking my way to the room's quiet corner. I remained rooted in my chair, staring at the TV, through the TV, seeing nothing and saying less for a long moment. Then I stood, mumbling that, right now this instant, I needed a shot of something stronger, and left without another word. I trekked back downstairs to the Falcon Inn, ordered and downed a row of shots from Daik, the ageless Asian barkeep, and then set off in the darkness for the long walk back to the dorm, alone in my thoughts to ponder the necessary death of certainty.

So in 1988 the World Series re-taught me the lesson that nothing is guaranteed, that no foe is beaten and no victory won until the very end, on the diamond as in life. Perhaps I also learned a little bit about how unnecessarily, ludicrously serious about the whole thing I'd been. Unfortunately, that maturity didn't come all at once, and I still had the balance of a bitter cup to drink in the World Series games to come, an experience for me that wound up being just like that of my father watching "his" '54 Indians go down in flames. But where that outcome drove him away from baseball and straight into the orbit of Paul Brown and Woody Hayes, I figured if I'd made it this far, I'd stick it out. This was my team, and their time would come. I mean, c'mon, I wasn't rooting for the Cubs, right?

So, as we step into this Series, that's the thing I always remind myself of, that this is the flip side of every moment in sports history, however glorious—for every win, there is a loss.

Only that is certain.

David Laurila: 1968
For a fan, the importance of any World Series is directly related to the impact that it has on his/her life. For me, the 2004 Fall Classic stands as the most meaningful, but the most formative came in 1968 when the Detroit Tigers defeated the St. Louis Cardinals. It helped trigger my love affair with baseball.

Game Seven of the 1968 Series was played on a weekday afternoon, and as a grade-school student in Upper Michigan I was immersed in reading, writing, and (pre-sabermetric) arithmetic when Mickey Lolich took the mound against Bob Gibson. Baseball had recently begun to appear on my radar screen, and I learned a valuable lesson about the importance of America's pastime when a radio was turned on for the final hour of the school day. A lasting memory is hearing the call of Mike Shannon's ninth-inning home run as I left to board a school bus for the ride home.

The next summer I began to collect baseball cards, which is how I learned that Gibson had logged a 1.12 ERA in 1968 and that Denny McLain had won 31 games. Unlike the people in my hometown, they were larger than life.

Preteens lack perspective, but 40 years later it is easy to recognize the historical importance of the 1968 World Series.

The championship came one year after the 1967 Detroit race riots, which included Tigers outfielder Willie Horton, a hometown hero, venturing into the mayhem in full uniform to implore rioters to cease and desist. Less than 15 months later, Horton and his teammates helped to heal a city.

The Tigers and Cardinals squared off in what would be the last "pure" World Series. In 1969, divisional play was introduced, making it possible for a team like the 2006 Cardinals to win a title despite finishing the regular season with just 83 wins and the fifth-best record in their league. The 1968 Series was also the last played with a 15-inch mound. Following a season in which American and National League batters hit a combined .237, it was lowered to 10 inches.

When Lolich bested Gibson in Game Seven, on two days' rest, it was his third win, and third complete game, of the Series. Gibson, who struck out a record 17 batters in Game One, allowed only one baserunner through six innings of Game Seven. After retiring the first two hitters in the seventh, he allowed a pair of singles followed by a Jim Northrup triple that broke a scoreless tie. The ball was misplayed by Curt Flood, a seven-time Gold-Glove winner. The final score was 4-1.

In what might be the boldest move ever made in the Fall Classic, Tigers manager Mayo Smith benched Ray Oyler, who had hit just .135 in the regular season, in favor of Mickey Stanley. Stanley, a center fielder, started all seven games at shortstop, a position he had never played as a professional. It was a remarkable stratagem in a most memorable World Series.

Ben Lindbergh: 2001

I can't write the book on the 2001 World Series; for one thing, it has already been written. For another, I'm on a strict word limit (which I'm about to break). That's just as well, since I'm more easily captivated by the reassuring slog of the six-month regular season than the small-sample dramatics of the playoffs. Like a whiff of perfume that tantalizes from afar but becomes cloying when unleashed on the unsuspecting occupants of an elevator, the concentrated agony and ecstasy of October often leaves me longing for a less heady sensation. Still, my memories of one particular series refuse to fade.

I was 14 in the fall of 2001, and a high school freshman at the Manhattan BP talent mill that produced Joe Sheehan, Derek Jacques, and Jon Sciambi before me. To humanize a Yankees fan may prove an impossible task, but put yourself in my privileged place: I'd come of age with the '96 team and known little but ultimate victory in the intervening years, leaving me almost totally unprepared for an outcome that didn't end with a pinstriped pile-up. Yes, I can hear the ensemble of world's smallest violins sounding from your fingertips, but remember—every dynasty's end elicits some sadness from the parties ousted from power.

On some level, I knew that teams just didn't do this, as the 2010 model's recently aborted attempt to repeat illustrates. But as the Bombers recovered from a two-game deficit in the Division Series and trounced the 116-win Mariners in the ALCS, a sense of destiny seemed to envelop them. Recall that this Fall Classic was played less than two months after the September 11 attacks. As a New Yorker, I suppose I should have felt more affected, but my world didn't collapse along with the Twin Towers; whether out of naiveté or premature disillusionment, I felt no less safe than I had on September 10. Still, the team's playoff run—as well as baseball's continued presence—acquired a significance to many that was hard to ignore, setting this series apart.

The match-up produced several moments so memorable that I hardly need recount them. For Game Four's—Tino Martinez's game-tying blast and Derek Jeter's "Mr. November" heroics—I stood at the Stadium, adding a personal perspective to the televised vantages in my mental highlight reel. As Game Five drew to a close, I huddled in bed with a radio, unwilling to watch what I expected to be a bitter end, but unable to tune out completely. Say what you will about John Sterling (remember, there may be children present), but his call of Scott Brosius' game-tying homer forged an indelible memory for me that night. In both games, the Yankees clung to a single-digit chance of victory when down to their final out (though at 14, I wasn't yet thinking in terms of win expectancy), prompting Joe Buck to call their comebacks "surreal."

The Stadium's serenade of Paul O'Neill just before the latter blow amplified the series' *Abbey Road*-esque vibe of a band on the verge of dissolution attempting to go out on a high note: O'Neill, Martinez, Brosius, and Chuck Knoblauch would all move on after the final out. I didn't bother to watch the blooper off the bat of Luiz Gonzalez land, having seen enough Rivera cutters morph into dying quails to know that this one would not be caught by a drawn-in infield. Scanning the list of contributors to this article, it looks like most of us chose to recall a series from our respective youths. That's probably not a coincidence. I could easily make this series an important element of my bildungsroman—a further loss of innocence as I embarked on my teen years armed with the unsettling knowledge that even Mo couldn't always be counted on. If I'm being honest, though, it was really just a snippet of spectacular baseball, in which a collection of players whom I'd grown up watching nearly vanquished an opponent that nearly tripled their run total.

A well-meaning relative gave me the 2001 Series DVD set for my 15th birthday. I still own those discs, but I've left them sealed in their original packaging. I'm not quite ready to revisit those seven special games, but I haven't let them go.

John Perrotto: 1979

Those under the age of 25 may find this hard to believe, but the Pirates were once one of the premier franchises in baseball. They won six division titles in the 1970s, the decade in which I grew up about 40 miles northwest of Pittsburgh in the rural community of Ohioville, Pennsylvania.

The last time the Pirates played in the World Series was 1979. Like most baseball-playing 15-year-olds in Western Pennsylvania, I idolized Chuck Tanner's Pirates—Chuck's Bucs—who had such great players as Willie Stargell, Dave Parker, Bill Madlock, Bert Blyleven, and Kent Tekulve. Also like most 15-year-old in Western Pennsylvania, I was the son of a steelworker. While our family wasn't poor, we also couldn't afford the best box-seat tickets to the World Series that year as the Pirates faced the Orioles.

Thus, on a Sunday afternoon, with the Pirates down 3-1 in the series and facing elimination, my father and I decided to drive to Pittsburgh and pay $10 each for standing-room tickets at Three Rivers Stadium. Little did I know it would be one of the most fortuitous and memorable days of my life.

Hoping against hope, my father and I tried to negotiate with the various scalpers outside Gate A, thinking that maybe we might strike a good deal. Suddenly, a kindly older gentleman approached and asked if I needed two tickets and showed me a pair that were in Section 75, Row E, five rows off the field just beyond third base.

I figured he would want a small fortune for them, or at least a heckuva lot more than the face value of $35 each. Much to my amazement, he looked at me, smiled, and said, "If you don't mind sitting with some Orioles fans, they're yours for free." I was so stunned that I could barely get the words "thank you" out of my mouth.

It turned out the Good Samaritan was the owner of the Hilton in downtown Baltimore, the hotel that then hosted most of the visiting American League teams. Thus, my father and I sat in the Orioles' family section and cheered under our breaths as the Pirates won Game Five, which started them on their way to a stunning comeback victory in the series.

Dad will have been gone 19 years next month, and I've been beyond blessed to have covered the last 15 World Series, which would tickle him to no end if he were still with us. Yet I'll never have a Fall Classic memory to match that crisp autumn late afternoon 31 years ago.

Mark Smith: 1995

1995 was the year I became a baseball fan. I was seven years old, and I had finally realized that baseball went beyond tee-ball. My brother, Adam, was an Atlanta Braves fan, and similar to most little brothers, I wanted to be just like him and chose to be a Braves fan as well. As it turns out, I had excellent timing.

Chipper Jones arrived as a rookie and became my favorite player, and the Braves made the World Series against the Cleveland Indians. The World Series even had excellent timing that year. Game Six landed on October 28, and October 28 just happened to be Adam's birthday. Most of you realize what happened next—the Braves, behind Tom Glavine and David Justice, won the World Series. Making the situation all the sweeter, an uncle of mine lived in Canton and was an Indians fan. Once the game ended Adam ran to the nearest phone and dialed my uncle, and when my uncle didn't answer (for reasons still unknown), Adam left him a celebratory voicemail that sparked a family rivalry. It was the happiest I had ever seen young Adam. I don't think I fully realized what had happened in that moment, but my interest was irrevocably sparked. The Yankees, unfortunately, ruined my first truly cognizant World Series the next October, and I still yearn for that moment of pure childish ecstasy my brother had that night. It's what we all hope for every spring.

Matt Swartz: 2008

In 2008, I went to Citizens Bank Park in Philadelphia to see the Phillies five times in one week even though they only played three games at home that series. That was because Bud Selig and Mother Nature gave birth to a two-part miniseries for Game Five which, when completed, sent me back to the park a fifth time to watch a parade.

The Phillies came into the game as underdogs against the young Tampa Bay Rays, but they split the first two games on the road. They won Game Three on a walk-off dribbler in the bottom of the ninth and won Game Four in a convincing 10-2 blowout. Philadelphia started to believe; a pre-parade broke out spontaneously in the middle of Broad Street at midnight upon the Phillies' victory, three miles north of the stadium, as the city's mouths watered for the first championship of any kind in 25 years. Fans also filled South Philadelphia in anticipation of a win on Monday night, in hopes of being near a celebration that a pessimistic city suddenly felt was inevitable. The Phillies led 2-1 through five innings as rain began falling harder, but the umpires were hesitant to call a rain delay in fear that the World Series would be clinched on the technicality of a shortened ballgame.

Ultimately, the Rays scored to tie it at 2-2 going into the bottom of the sixth, and the umpires quickly suspended the game. As if 25 years without a championship—28 years in baseball—were not long enough to wait, it rained through Tuesday night too, so the series resumed Wednesday. Geoff Jenkins had been relegated to pinch-hitting duties, but when the game began again, he was given the opportunity to get the biggest pinch-hit of his life and launched a double off the top of the right-center field wall, scoring two batters later. However, the Rays tied it up in the top of the seventh. Luckily, Pat Burrell led off the bottom of the seventh. He had spent a decade with the Phillies as they worked their way up from last place to first but had been hitless upon finally reaching the World Series. Burrell launched a double to deep left-center field that ultimately led to the winning run.

Brad Lidge may have been perfect all year, completing 47 saves in 47 tries going into Game Five of the series, but he had narrowly missed blown saves all year. His 48th try looked like it might become his first blown save, as a runner reached second base with one out, but a lineout later, Lidge struck out Eric Hinske to give the Phillies a world championship for the first time since 1980. The stadium shook as the Phillies ended their drought. Fans filled the aisles, attempting to get closer to the celebration on the field. The Phillies team understood how long the fans had waited and celebrated on the field for hours after the game ended.

Brandon Warne: 1991
Five one-run games. Four walk-off wins. Three extra-inning games. Two 1990 last-place finishers. Number one on ESPN's "World Series 100th Anniversary" countdown. Zero road-team victories.

Umpire Steve Palermo threw out the first pitch; he had been shot three months earlier while helping a robbery victim in Dallas and was forced into early retirement. From that moment until a game-winning Gene Larkin single in Game Seven, there was plenty of excitement in this Fall Classic.

Game One was the first of two nondescript games in the series; the Twins won 5-2 on the power of home runs from Greg Gagne and Bloomington native Kent Hrbek. Game Two was far more controversial, as Kevin Tapani and NL Cy Young winner Tom Glavine squared off. The Twins jumped out to an early 2-0 lead as Chili Davis socked a two-run homer to take advantage of defensive miscommunication that allowed Dan Gladden to reach.

The controversy emerged as Ron Gant stoked a single into left in the second. Lonnie Smith, who made numerous gaffes in the series, attempted to gain third. Tapani, backing up the throw from Gladden, scrambled to recover the errant toss and fired to first to catch a napping Gant. Eyewitness accounts vary, but Hrbek received the throw and toppled backward, carrying Gant back with him. Umpire Drew Coble ruled Gant out, later explaining he felt Gant was off balance and fell with Hrbek. Hrbek still maintains his innocence and bristles when asked. The Braves were held to one run in the inning and fell by the score of 3-2 as the Twins took a 2-0 series lead.

Game Three was billed as the first World Series game played south of the Mason-Dixon line, and after four-plus hours, it did not disappoint. Braves hurler Steve Avery pitched brilliantly for seven innings but gave way to closer Alejandro Pena, who promptly gave up Davis' second home run of the series to tie the game. After a litany of double-switches, one Twins relief pitcher (Rick Aguilera) pinch-hitting for another (Mark Guthrie), and the Twins running out of bench players, Mark Lemke singled home the winning run in the bottom of the 12th. Lemke played the role of hero again in Game Four as he scored on a Jerry Willard sacrifice fly for the series-evening victory. The Braves pummeled Tapani in Game Five 14-5 to send the Twins back home, trailing 3-2.

Game Six will forever be known as the game in which Kirby Puckett told his teammates to "jump on his back" and let him carry them to victory. Puckett made a sensational extra-base-hit-robbing catch off Gant in the third and homered off Charlie Leibrandt in walk-off fashion to send the series to a decisive seventh game.

Jack Buck's famous call of "We'll see you tomorrow night!" rang true for Game Seven. Smoltz and Morris exchanged scoreless innings, with Smoltz departing after 7 1/3. Morris, however, refused to be removed from the game and retired the Braves quietly in the 10th inning. Gladden led off the inning with a bloop double, was sacrificed to third by Chuck Knoblauch, and scored on Larkin's base hit. In a modern age where pitchers never go more than nine innings and rarely much further than 100 pitches, Morris' 10-inning, 126-pitch MVP-clinching effort capped what was a World Series for the ages.

CROOKED NUMBERS
Crappy Odds
James Click

As James Click explained, the playoffs may mostly be a crapshoot, but that doesn't mean that underlying talent plays no role in the proceedings.

It's a crapshoot.

That's the easy way to explain the playoffs, but more so since the advent of divisional play and Billy Beane's now-famous line, "My [means of building a baseball team by continually taking advantage of tiny inefficiencies in the market] doesn't work in the playoffs." Saying that the playoffs are a crapshoot is the easy way of saying that small sample sizes render the minute differences between playoffs teams largely moot. But largely does not equal entirely.

Take the Cardinals and Padres series. Assuming that each team's true probability of winning a baseball game is its winning percentage for the season, that gives the Cardinals a .617 percentage and the Padres a .506 chance. Matching those two teams, we can estimate the Cardinals' chances of winning the game by a shorthand version of the log5 method as .500 + .617 - .506 = .611. Conversely, the Padres' odds of winning a single game between the two teams are .389. However, this doesn't mean that the Cardinals have a 61 percent chance of winning the series, for several reasons.

The primary reason is that it's not a one-game playoff, but rather a five game series. To estimate the chance of the Cardinals winning the series, we can use a method similar to Pascal's Triangle or Khayyam-Pascal's Triangle or n choose k. However, because the series ends as soon as one team wins three games, we'll use a slightly different arrangement. Assuming that the Cardinals have the same odds of winning each game, the odds of them sweeping the Padres before the series begins are $(.611)^3$ = 22.8 percent. Because there are three ways for them to win three of four (win-win-loss-win, win-loss-win-win, loss-win-win-win), the odds that they will win three of four are $3 * (.611)^3 * (1-.611)$ = 26.6 percent. The odds of winning in five games are similar: $6 * (.611)^3 * (1-.611)^2$ = 20.7 percent. Adding those three numbers up gives the Cardinals a 70.1 percent chance of winning the series. While their chances of winning a five-game series are higher than their chances of winning a single game over the Padres, the Redbirds will still lose nearly three of every ten times they play a five-games series.

The second reason the Cardinals likely don't have a 70 percent chance of winning each game is home field advantage. Home teams win about 54 percent of their games over the course of the season, so that gives the Cardinals a .660 winning percentage at home and a .562 clip on the road. The calculation to determine the Cardinals' odds of winning the series gets rather complicated now because there are both home winning percentages and road winning percentages, but in the end, St. Louis comes out with a 71.8 percent chance to take the series, compared to their 70.1 percent chance when ignoring home field advantage. Intuitively, this seems about right, since the Cards only get a single extra game at home. Assuming that additional 1.7 percent chance to win the series is similar in other series—we'll get to those in a minute—all the hand-wringing going on in the AL over Buck Showalter pulling his starters against the Angels in the last game of the season seems a little silly. That's not to say that a 1.7 percent chance is worthless, but only once in every 59 series will that make the difference.

Finally, there is one other factor that can alter a team's winning percentage: the starting pitcher. In particular, teams typically only start their top three or four starters in the postseason, so instead of using a team's actual winning percentage as its odds of winning each game, we can use its winning percentage when its top three or four starters take the mound. Here's how teams have done behind their top three starting pitchers as measured by SNLVAR:

Team	W	L	W%	Full W%	Diff
SLN	66	31	.680	.617	.063
ATL	54	28	.659	.556	.103
NYA	48	28	.632	.586	.046
ANA	59	36	.621	.586	.035
BOS	59	36	.621	.586	.035
CHA	60	38	.612	.611	.001
HOU	57	43	.570	.549	.021
SDN	47	38	.553	.506	.047

Amazingly, the Astros' top three starters, who are the third-best Big Three since 1972 by SNLVAR, only increase their team's winning percentage by 21 points. Given the rather poor W-L record of Roger Clemens and, to a smaller extent, Andy Pettitte, that low percentage isn't terribly surprising, but the Astros' inability to turn over 675 innings of 2.43 ERA pitching into more than a .570 winning percentage is astounding. Certainly there are some problems with assuming that the winning percentages above are the true winning percentages of the playoff teams—most notably, some teams are using a four-man rotation—but they give us a decent idea of which teams benefit from dropping the back of their rotation.

Plugging those winning percentages into the equations (and of course keeping the home field advantage adjustments), the Cardinals now come out as a 74.6 percent favorite to win the series. Obviously, one Jake Peavy start and two Peavy ribs later this isn't still the case, but going into the series, even considering their regular-season record, home field advantage, and an increased advantage based on a shorter rotation, the Cardinals still come out as only a 74.6 percent favorite to win a five-game series.

As for the other matchups, the Braves come out as a startlingly high 68.1 percent favorite over the Astros, due mostly to Houston's low winning percentage when the Big Three pitches. It's hard to see that kind of trend keeping up, but the Astros have shown an impressive ability to squander those games all season long. In the AL, the Yankees come out as a 50.6 percent favorite, and the Red Sox enjoy a healthy 50.2 percent chance to win their series.

If those numbers are a little too close for comfort, consider just how little things would change in a seven-game series. Here are the four playoff matchups and the odds of the "favorite" winning a five-game series versus a seven-game series:

Matchup	5-game Series	7-game Series
SLN-SDN	74.6%	77.5%
ATL-HOU	68.1%	70.3%
NYA-ANA	50.6%	51.2%
BOS-CHA	50.2%	50.7%

Expanding the division series to seven games does little to increase the odds of the true favorites, clearly not enough to justify beginning to expand the playoffs towards an NHL-style season-long second season.

When the games actually take place, there are many other factors in play—the strength of lineups, injuries, availability of bullpen pitchers—that affect the odds of a team winning a game. Perceived upsets in short series are explained as a favorite running into a "hot team" or a few "bad bounces." But even without considering if teams are truly under- or over-playing their seasonal winning percentages, the favorite in any postseason series isn't likely to exceed the 74.6 percent chance the Cardinals have to win just their first series, not to mention two more after that against stiffer competition. And when it comes to teams as evenly matched as those in the two AL series, the postseason is, to a large extent, a crapshoot. Which is, of course, why it's so much fun to watch.

PREDICTING THE PLAYOFFS
Mortal Lock or Coin Flip?
Doug Pappas

How substantial an advantage does the superior regular-season team have in a relatively brief playoff series? Doug Pappas showed that the playoffs aren't quite random, though they do involve a large element of unpredictability.

After the 2003 regular season ended, the time before the divisional series was filled by "experts" forecasting the outcome of the four divisional series. This phenomenon will be repeated before the League Championship Series, and again before the World Series. These same pundits will look back after each series to pat themselves on the back, make excuses or explain how they went wrong. They believe, or at least pretend, that postseason results can be accurately predicted.

Others believe that the postseason is essentially a crapshoot, that any club can win a succession of short series among eight clubs which all finished within 10-15 games of one another during the regular season. This group includes Billy Beane, quoted in *Moneyball* as saying: "My s*** doesn't work in the playoffs. My job is to get us to the playoffs. What happens after that is f****** luck." Those in the first group have criticized Beane's Oakland A's and Bobby Cox's Atlanta Braves as teams that "can't win the big ones"; those in the second think "clutch postseason performance" is as real as "clutch hitting," or the Easter Bunny.

Who's right? Let's look at the past century of postseason play. Since 1903, there have been exactly 200 postseason series of best-of-five or longer. This includes 94 best-of-seven World Series, four best-of-nine World Series (1903, 1919-21), 34 best-of-seven League Championship Series (LCS), 32 best-of-five LCS, 32 best-of-five divisional series, and four best-of-five divisional playoff series following the 1981 strike-induced split season. That's a sizable data set.

Absent an easily accessible, generally accepted way to compare clubs in different leagues all the way back to the deadball era, I'll define the "better team" as the one with the better regular-season record. Four of these 200 series matched clubs with identical records, leaving 196 with a "better team" that, at least in theory, "should have won." The better team has won 106 of these series and lost 90, for a .541 winning percentage. These 196 series break down as follows:

- World Series: Better teams are 52-44 (.542), with two evenly matched Series.
- Seven-game LCS: Better teams are 19-14 (.576), with one evenly matched Series.
- All best-of-seven or -nine series: Better teams are 71-58 (.550).
- Five-game LCS and divisional series: Better teams are 35-32 (.532), with one evenly matched series.

As the tables below show, the better club is more likely to win blowout series and less likely to win those decided by a single game. Better clubs lose more deciding fifth or seventh games than they win.

Results for Team with Better Record, World Series

Win by 4 (10)	1907 1927 1928 1932 1939 1950 1966 1976 1989 1998
Win by 3 (14)	1905 1908 1910 1915 1920 1929 1937 1938 1941 1942 1961 1970 1983 1984
Win by 2 (13)	1903 1911 1917 1919* 1923 1930 1936 1944 1948 1951 1977 1978 1981
Win by 1 (15)	1909 1912 1925 1940 1947 1955 1956 1967 1968 1973 1975 1986 1991 1997 2002
Lose by 1 (19)	1924 1926 1931 1934 1945 1946 1952 1957 1960 1962 1964 1965 1971 1972 1979 1982 1985 1987 2001
Lose by 2 (11)	1906 1918 1921 1935 1953 1959 1980 1992 1993 1995 1996
Lose by 3 (8)	1913 1916 1933 1943 1969 1974 1988 2000
Lose by 4 (6)	1914 1922 1954 1963 1990 1999

Note: In 1949 and 1958, the World Series opponents had the same regular-season record.
* - The 1919 Reds may well have won even a non-fixed World Series. Their .686 regular-season winning percentage is the NL's second-highest since 1910.

The 4-0 losses include three of the biggest World Series surprises: the 1914 Braves over Philadelphia, Dusty Rhodes and the 1954 Giants over the 111-43 Indians, and the 1990 Reds sweep of Oakland, which I won't discuss further because a crying Gary Huckabay is not a pretty sight. The four recognized "miracle" pennant winners, the 1914 Braves, 1961 Reds, 1967 Red Sox, and 1969 Mets, went 2-2 in the World Series, suggesting that "magic" loses its strength when confronted by Bob Gibson or Mickey Mantle and Roger Maris.

Note that the 1999 and 2000 Yankees, Exhibit A to Commissioner Selig's competitive balance laments, both beat clubs with better regular-season records. In fact, the 2000 Yankees had only the ninth-best record in the majors and fifth-best in the American League. That's the same as the

1987 Twins, who won the World Series despite being outscored during the regular season. At the other end of the spectrum, the 4-0 wins include six Yankee demolitions of inferior opponents and one humbling of the Yankees at the hands of the Big Red Machine.

Results for Team with Better Record, Best-of-7 LCS

Win by 4 (3)	1988A 1990A 1995N
Win by 3 (6)	1989A 1991A 1996A 1999A 2001N 2002A
Win by 2 (6)	1985N 1986N 1993N 1995N 1998A 1999N
Win by 1 (4)	1986A 1987N 1992N 1996N
Lose by 1 (3)	1985A 1988N 1991N
Lose by 2 (6)	1990N 1993N 1997A 1997N 1998N 2000A
Lose by 3 (5)	1987A 1989N 2000N 2001A 2002N
Lose by 4 (0)	

Note: In 1992, both ALCS opponents had the same record.

Compared to the World Series, the seven-game LCS is significantly less likely to end up as a four-game sweep—but in non-swept series, the club with the better record holds only a 16-14 edge. The big surprises here include easy wins by the 1987 Twins over the Tigers and the 2001 Yankees over the 116-46 Mariners. The late-'80s Oakland juggernaut barely broke a sweat, going 12-1 in three consecutive LCS.

Results for Team with Better Record, Best-of-5 LCS and Division Series

Win by 3 (19)	1969A 1969N 1970A 1970N 1971A 1975N 1976N 1979N 1981AE 1982N 1984A 1995A1 1995N2 1996N1 1997N1 1997N2 1998A1 1998N1 1999A1
Win by 2 (9)	1971N 1974N 1978A 1978N 1979A 1995N1 1996A1 1997A1 1999N2
Win by 1 (7)	1972A 1976A 1981NE 1981NW 1981N 1982A 2001A1
Lose by 1 (15)	1972N 1973A 1973N 1977A 1980N 1981AE 1984N 1995A2 1997A2 1999A2 2000A1 2001A2 2001N2 2002A1 2002N2
Lose by 2 (10)	1974A 1977N 1983A 1983N 1996A2 1998A2 1998N2 1999N1 2000N2 2002A2
Lose by 3 (7)	1975A 1980N 1981A 1996N2 2000A2 2001N1 2002N1

Note: In 2000, one of the NL divisional series matched opponents with identical records.

In all best-of-five postseason series, the team with the better record is 19-7 in sweeps and 16-25 in 3-1 or 3-2 series. In divisional series since 1995, the team with the better record is just 13-18. Since 2000, 10 of 11 divisional series have been won by the team with the worse record.

Does this foretell wins by the Red Sox, Twins, Marlins, and Cubs? No. Overall, as one would expect from series between relatively evenly matched teams, the teams with the better record hold a small but consistent edge. But while the playoffs aren't quite random, when the better team can be expected to win just 54 percent of the time, anyone who claims to know what will happen is only fooling himself.

PROSPECTUS TODAY
A-Rodemption?
Joe Sheehan

Alex Rodriguez became known as a postseason failure early in his tenure with the Yankees, but as Joe Sheehan noted, making a case for Rodriguez as a "choker" required an especially selective memory. Considering A-Rod's elite regular-season performance and earlier October outbursts, his 2009 playoff success shouldn't have come as a surprise.

Maybe this will be the stake in the heart, the straw that breaks the camel's back, the end of an era. Maybe the RBI double that tore up a thousand game stories will wreak its havoc on millions more to come. Maybe, just maybe, Alex Rodriguez did not only himself a favor, but did one for hundreds upon hundreds of baseball players to follow him.

With a late-night, two-out line drive to left field, Rodriguez broke a ninth-inning tie in Game Four of the World Series. His overall statistics in the Series remain poor—.143/.333/.429—but he's made his hits count, with a two-run home run that turned Game Three around and his game-winning double last night. The overall postseason line remains staggering, .348/.483/.804 with six home runs. It's not just that he's put up statistics; Rodriguez has had big hit after big hit in this postseason, so many that there's no longer any way to argue that he has some ineffable quality that makes him a great player for six months and a poor one after that. He is a great player all the time.

This has always been obvious to anyone willing to take a reasoned look at Rodriguez's work in the playoffs or, for that matter, to anyone sensible enough to understand baseball's complexity. We can train all the cameras we want on a playoff game, but it's still baseball. Failure is more common than success, at least for hitters. Outcomes swing wildly over the span of a few games, and just as players do in the regular season, they have good stretches and bad in the postseason. Few get enough opportunities for their postseason statistics to acquire significance, so we inflate or deflate the reputations of some based on tiny amounts of evidence; not enough evidence, just data, data that doesn't carry nearly enough weight for the conclusions drawn from it. Sometimes, and this is the insidious part, data gets carved up to reach preconceived notions. Both contributed to the narrative of Alex Rodriguez.

Through October 16, 2004, Rodriguez had played in 22 postseason games, stretching back to some cameos with the 1995 Mariners and through Game Three of the 2004 ALCS. In those games, he batted 94 times, hitting .372/.419/.640. This included a monster series in the 2000 ALCS against the Yankees, and a carry-the-team performance, clutch hits included, in the 2004 ALDS against the Twins. In his next 15 postseason games, from the Yankees' collapse in the ALCS that year through the first two games of the 2007 Division Series, Rodriguez batted 67 times and was awful: .096/.299/.173. Most famously, he was 1-for-14 against the Tigers in the 2006 Division Series and was dropped by Joe Torre to the eighth slot in the batting order for the fourth game. It was in this period that the legend of Rodriguez was formed but, in fact, that legend was the product of variance and viciousness. His performance, while terrible, was out of context not just with his career, but his postseason career. To decide that Alex Rodriguez had a fatal flaw, you had to ignore 60 percent of his postseason plate appearances, including a series-dominating performance in 2004 against the Twins. You had to want it.

By the end of that second stretch, Rodriguez had 161 career plate appearances, about a quarter of a season, and a line of .268/.369/.464. That's below his career numbers, of course, but given top postseason competition well within a reasonable range of performance.

Starting with the last two games of the 2007 Division Series, Rodriguez has gone crazy, batting .364/.478/.800 in 69 plate appearances. His career postseason line now stands at .295/.400/.560 in 230 plate appearances. Compare that to his regular season rates of .305/.390/.576, adjust for competition and weather, and realize that Rodriguez, on the whole, has perhaps been a better player in the playoffs than he has in the regular season. He now has 163 plate appearances outside of the 15-game slump in which he's hit like Babe Ruth's little brother, and those appearances count for about 70 percent of his postseason career. Broken down by series, and tossing 1995 (two PAs in two rounds), you find that Rodriguez has had four great series, three good ones, four middling ones, and that disastrous ALDS in 2006. That's a track record any player would take.

It's not enough, though, for the story around Rodriguez to change. The lesson here shouldn't be that maybe people were wrong to destroy Rodriguez for having 15 bad games at the wrong time. (Not that it will be; the narrative is now about how he's changed, relaxed, matured. God love the mainstream media.) No, the lesson here should be that it's wrong to reach conclusions about a person's character based on his postseason performance. Hits are clutch. Pitches are clutch. Great double-play turns are clutch. Baseball players are just people, and they're subject to the ups and downs of a baseball season even when, maybe especially when, they get to play into October. A three- or four-game stretch in which a player does nothing—or does everything—isn't that unusual in any season. It happens, in fact, all the time without notice. The problem when a player does the very baseball thing in October isn't him; it's the observers, desperate to divine meaning, airtime, column inches from something that is actually quite mundane.

The lesson of the 2009 postseason isn't that Alex Rodriguez really is clutch. It's that over a week or two or three of baseball, performance varies so wildly that the results tell you nothing about the players. Given enough time, Alex Rodriguez has played in the postseason as he does during the regular season. For any of these guys, given enough playing time, they'll perform in the postseason as they do in the regular season. That's the takeaway.

I hope.

- Remember the movie *Superman*, when Lois Lane is clinging to a helicopter dangling from a rooftop, and Superman flies through the air to catch her just as she loses her grip and begins to plummet to her death?

  That was what Rodriguez did for Girardi last night. Girardi's use of Mariano Rivera has been one of the only redeeming qualities of an otherwise poorly managed postseason, but the manager lost an eighth-inning lead last night without getting either of his best two relievers into the game. With four outs standing between him and a step-on-their-throats 3-1 Series lead over the Phillies, Girardi went with Joba Chamberlain rather than Rivera or Phil Hughes, continuing his month-long infatuation with using Chamberlain to do Hughes' job. That's beside the point, however; the point is that Girardi had a one-run lead, Mariano Rivera at his disposal, and didn't use him. It was managerial failure on an epic scale, and but for a miraculous rescue by Rodriguez, Girardi could be getting absolutely destroyed today. Winning, not sunshine, is the best disinfectant, and Girardi's charges are winning so frequently that he comes out squeaky clean.

  There is no justification for holding back Rivera. He'd thrown just a handful of pitches the night before, and if overwork is a concern, you address that the next night, when you're facing a guy who may make the use of Rivera a non-issue anyway. You address it up 3-1, not up 2-1 with some outs left to get. What's worse is that If the Yankees had failed to score in the top of the ninth, Girardi was going to use Phil Coke, rather than Rivera, so Rodriguez not only erased one egregious mistake, he saved Girardi from making a second.

  I'll say it again: the Yankees are one win away from a title in spite of their manager.

- I'll cop to this: when I saw Johnny Damon break for third in the ninth inning, having stolen second base and spotted an undefended bag in front of him, I thought he'd lost his mind. I even exclaimed, which is something of a no-no when you're wearing a lanyard and sitting in section 235. I never saw the undefended bag. Damon did, and he immediately figured out that not only would no one beat him there, but that Pedro Feliz couldn't catch him if he ran for it. It was fantastic baseball awareness, but it also took an enormous amount of courage; no one was going to criticize Damon if he hadn't gone, but if he goes and gets caught, if he falls down or gets beaten to the bag by Lidge or if he doesn't but gets called out because, well, it's the 2009 postseason, he's going to wear that for a long time.

Damon's nine-pitch at-bat ending in a single and the subsequent baserunning adventure will be remembered now more than his defense was. He got a terrible jump on Shane Victorino's "double" in the first, and his terrible arm allowed Ryan Howard to score in the fourth, tying the game. For a player who still has good wheels, Damon is a pretty bad outfielder, a flaw that limits his attractiveness as a free agent. Even in left field, his arm cripples you, and he still occasionally takes poor routes to the ball. We'll be seeing that break for third base for a long time, but teams evaluating Damon need to be realistic about what he actually brings as a free agent.

- It wasn't terribly surprising to see Brad Lidge allow runs. Although he's posted a clean sheet in the playoffs, it was only his final couple of outings that were actually impressive. He's still got the same location issues that plagued him throughout the season, and they bit him badly last night.

   Charlie Manuel may have misused his pen to get to that situation. Perhaps he's being careful with Chan Ho Park and not using him for multiple innings, but taking out Ryan Madson after just one frame in a tied game was wasteful. Manuel went through the two pitchers without needing to hit for either, and by chance had the Phillies gotten through the ninth unscathed, they would have been hitting for Lidge to start the inning and perhaps heading into extras with Chad Durbin or Brett Myers. Down one and then tied, Madson was the right call for a two-inning appearance.

- I think Joe Blanton has slimmed down considerably from when he was in Oakland. Not only does he just look thinner, he's pretty mobile, getting to first base from the mound with ease when necessary. His stats last night aren't great, but he was victimized by a number of balls that found holes. His approach was solid: pound the strike zone to take walks away, and make the Yankees beat him by swinging. The Yankees countered by going after him the way they went after Cole Hamels in the fourth and fifth innings, and while they didn't hit Blanton nearly as hard, they had some good fortune.

- Speaking of slimming down, Ryan Howard is now making his biggest contributions on the bases and in the field. He stole a base that led directly to a run last night and showed improved speed scoring—if not exactly touching the plate—on Pedro Feliz' single. He also made a number of plays in the field that I'm not sure he would have made before this season. It's been impressive to see him develop as a player, which bodes well for him arresting his deficiencies against southpaws—ones killing him in this Series—next year and beyond.

- Phillies fans were criticizing Yankee fans for their early departures from Game One. It should be noted that once the Yankees scored their sixth and seventh runs last night, people at Citizens Bank Park started streaming for the exits, an exodus that continued throughout the very quick bottom of the ninth.

LITTLEBALL
Are the A's Equipped to Succeed in October?
Mark Armour

The plodding Moneyball Athletics' perennial early exits from the playoffs led some to allege that they weren't a team built for October, but Mark Armour looked at the playoff pasts of speedier teams and found little evidence to support that position.

As one might expect, the success of Michael Lewis's great new book, *Moneyball*, has led to a number of criticisms of Oakland Athletics' GM Billy Beane, his staff, and their entire organizational philosophy. These criticisms should not have come as a surprise: Lewis presents Beane as a brilliant visionary operating in an antiquated system peopled, for the most part, with morons. There may be a great deal of truth to this, but the idea that some of Beane's competitors would be defensive is understandable.

The most interesting criticism of the Athletics' success is that as impressive as their regular-season results have been, their style of play cannot succeed in the playoffs against quality competition. Sure, the Athletics win 100 games every year with one of the lowest payrolls in the game, but if they can't win in the postseason, what good is it? This turns out to be a convenient critique, since the A's have lost in the first round of the playoffs for the past three seasons.

This criticism is not new, of course. Joe Morgan has been saying similar things for the last year or so: the A's offense, which has relied mainly on reaching base and hitting home runs, is not effective in the postseason facing quality pitching. A team needs to be able to "manufacture runs"—steal bases, bunt, hit behind the runner, etc. The A's do not, or cannot, do these things, so they are doomed to fall short in the playoffs. Or so the argument goes.

The 2002 Athletics had essentially a league-average offense, scoring 4.94 runs per game in a league that averaged 4.81. Yes, the Coliseum is normally a pitcher's park (though it did not play like one last year), but this is offset by the fact that the A's did not have to face their own great pitchers. The team finished fourth in the league in home runs and third in walks, yet ninth in batting average, 13th in sacrifice bunts, 13th in sacrifice flies, and 14th (last) in stolen bases.

When the A's dropped a five-game series to the Twins, heck, even while the series was still going on, Joe Morgan was telling viewers that the Athletics' brand of offense was at a disadvantage against post-season pitching staffs.

There are a few holes in this theory.

First of all, the Athletics scored 26 runs in the series, 5.2 per game, slightly more than they did during the regular season. Unfortunately, their vaunted pitchers allowed 27, 5.4 per game, versus a season average of just over four. The problem was not the hitting, it was the pitching, specifically Tim Hudson, who got hammered in games One and Four.

In addition, the Athletics finished 21-17 in regular-season games against the Yankees, Twins, and Angels, the other three AL playoff teams. Unless Morgan is claiming that the A's offense cannot win against these teams in the postseason specifically, these 38 games are better evidence of the team's ability against quality pitchers than the five they played against the Twins in October. As further evidence that it was pitching that let them down, Oakland played Minnesota six times in nine days around Labor Day. The A's scored 25 runs, just 4.2 per game, a much worse performance than they would manage a month later, yet the team still won five of the six contests.

Analysts tend to shy away from post-season studies, and for good reason. In order to examine any sort of baseball strategy, you really want a large sample of games to be able to make a convincing case. There is a lot of luck involved in a baseball game, and it does not even out over five or seven games. This fact is unsatisfying to a lot of people, but it is nonetheless true. Additionally, such a study does not lend itself to looking at other periods in history, because different run environments change the way the game is played.

About the best we can do is look at all of the post-season series in the wild-card era.

Since 1995, when baseball began inviting eight teams into the playoffs, there have been a total of 56 post-season matchups. A supposition, which is far from perfect, is that teams that steal more bases (keeping in mind that these are all good teams) are also more able to play for one run when needed late in a close game. (We could use sacrifice hits as a proxy instead, but bunting is likely more a reflection of the manager than the talents of the players.) The team with the higher number of regular-season stolen bases has won 28 times, exactly half.

Since many of these series pitted teams with very similar regular-season steal totals, let's instead examine only the matchups in which one team stole at least 40 more (regular-season) bases than the other. This narrows the study down to just 23 series.

Year	Series	Fast Team	SB	Slow Team	SB	Result
1995	ALDS	Seattle	110	NY Yankees	50	W 3-2
1995	NLDS	Cincinnati	190	Los Angeles	127	W 3-0
1995	NLDS	Colorado	125	Atlanta	73	L 1-3
1995	NLCS	Cincinnati	190	Atlanta	73	L 0-4
1995	WS	Cleveland	132	Atlanta	73	L 2-4
1996	ALDS	Cleveland	160	Baltimore	76	L 1-3
1996	NLDS	Los Angeles	124	Atlanta	83	L 0-3
1996	NLDS	St. Louis	149	San Diego	109	W 3-0
1996	NLCS	St. Louis	149	Atlanta	83	L 3-4
1997	NLDS	Houston	171	Atlanta	108	L 0-3
1997	ALCS	Cleveland	118	Baltimore	63	W 4-2
1998	ALDS	NY Yankees	153	Texas	82	W 3-0
1998	ALDS	Cleveland	143	Boston	72	W 3-1
1998	NLDS	Houston	155	San Diego	79	L 1-3
1998	WS	NY Yankees	153	San Diego	79	W 4-0
1999	ALDS	Cleveland	147	Boston	67	L 2-3
1999	WS	Atlanta	148	NY Yankees	104	L 0-4
2000	ALDS	NY Yankees	99	Oakland	40	W 3-2
2000	NLDS	Atlanta	148	St. Louis	87	L 0-3
2001	ALDS	NY Yankees	161	Oakland	68	W 3-2
2001	ALDS	Seattle	174	Cleveland	79	W 3-2
2001	WS	NY Yankees	161	Arizona	71	L 3-4
2002	WS	Anaheim	117	San Francisco	74	W 4-3

The running team won 11 series, just less than half, and finished 49-55 in games. The biggest mismatch occurred when the speedy 1995 Cincinnati Reds (a league-leading 190 steals) reached the NLCS against the plodding Atlanta Braves (73 steals) and were summarily swept, "manufacturing" just five runs in the four games. Does this prove that the makeup of a post-season offense is irrelevant? No, of course not—it's still a ridiculously small sample, further skewed because many of the same teams are involved for multiple seasons.

What we can say is that there is quite a bit of recent evidence that a team constructed like the Athletics can win in the postseason. The 1995 Atlanta Braves finished 13th (of 14) in the NL in stolen bases and 10th in sacrifice hits, yet beat three much more aggressive base-running teams to win the World Series. The next season, the Braves finished dead last in steals and won two post-season series before bowing to the Yankees. The 2001 Diamondbacks were built on pitching and home runs, yet defeated three teams in the postseason, all of whom were better at "manufacturing" runs.

Again, there is nowhere near sufficient data to draw any firm conclusions.

Joe Morgan is a smart guy, one of the smarter players I ever had the pleasure to watch. If you want to know why Joe believes that offenses need to be broad-based, take a look at his great Cincinnati teams. The 1975-76 Big Red Machine likely had the best offense ever assembled. They didn't merely lead the NL in runs, they led by 105 and 87, respectively. In '76, they paced the circuit in doubles, triples, home runs, walks, batting average, slugging average, on-base percentage, stolen bases, stolen base percentage, and fewest GIDP. What's not to like? In 17 post-season games, of which the Reds won 14, they out-stole their opponents 32 to one.

Morgan epitomized this diversity in '76, smashing 27 home runs, walking 114 times, swiping 60 bases (against nine caught stealing), and leading the league with 12 sacrifice flies. Although you can't blame Morgan for wanting an offense to do all of this, we might never see its likes again.

Morgan ought to know about the vagaries of the postseason. His 1973 Reds also featured fine pitching and an excellent well-rounded offense, finishing second in the league in runs and pacing the circuit in stolen bases, yet they lost a five-game series to a vastly inferior Mets team that they had handled eight out of 12 times in the regular season. Did this series expose a flaw in the Reds' makeup? Of course not. Anything can happen in five games, and much of it did in that series.

I loved the baseball of the 1970s and 1980s. The different parks and playing surfaces, coupled with the lower run totals of the era, resulted in a wide variety of viewing experiences. Each game seemed not simply a battle between the players, but a contest to decide the proper way to play. The 1972 Athletics defeated the Reds despite scoring just 16 runs in a seven-game World Series. After three years of doing this, Oakland was finally toppled in 1975 by the Boston Red Sox, a slow team that hit home runs. And then the Red Sox were felled, by the thinnest of margins, by the Big Red Machine, a club that did essentially everything well.

The point everyone seems to have missed about Lewis' portrayal of the A's philosophy is that Beane knows that he can't have it all. If Scott Hatteberg could steal 60 bases and play great defense, like Joe Morgan, he would be making $10 million a year and playing somewhere else. I suspect that Beane would gladly take a team that could steal 210 bases with a high success rate (like the 1976 Reds) if he could afford it. He's looking for players whose performance exceeds their perceived value.

It's not easy. The 2000 Athletics scored 947 runs (second in the league) but then slipped to 884 (fourth) in 2001 and 800 (eighth) in 2002. This year they are on a pace for 744 (10th). It is not a great offense and has not been for a few years, but there is no evidence that this type of offense has caused any problems in the postseason, or that it will in the future. They have placed a high burden on their great starting pitchers, and that is not likely to change.

That is, of course, unless the A's start listening to Joe Morgan.

LIES, DAMNED LIES
Being on the Brink
Nate Silver

After the Red Sox came back from a three-game deficit to beat the Yankees in the 2004 ALCS, Nate Silver crunched the numbers to establish how improbable their victory was.

For all intents and purposes, the World Series is over. No team has ever come back from a 3-0 deficit—

Scratch that. It was less than a week ago that David Ortiz busted about a 250-pound hole through that particular argument. But to hear the pundits talk, you'd think that the Red Sox had pulled off a one-in-a-million feat.

Cardinals fans can rest assured that their odds of pulling off a similar miracle are substantially better than that. A naive model, which simply assigns each team a 50 percent probability of winning each game, would conclude the odds of a Cardinal comeback are 15-to-1 against, or exactly the same as having a coin come up tails four times in a row. Clay Davenport's model, which is anything but naive and takes into account relative team strength (and regards the Cardinals as the better team), puts the odds at a more palatable 12-to-1 against.

Neither of those estimates would seem to take history into account. The Sox, after all, were the first team ever to come back from a 3-0 deficit to go on to win the series. How amazing is that?

Actually, it's not all that amazing. The Red Sox might have been the first team to pull off the feat, but only 25 teams before them had had the opportunity. If the team leading the series and the team trailing were of equal strength—meaning a team trailing 3-0 has a 1-in-16 chance of going on to victory—we'd expect the trailing team to have come back to win the series 1.625 tries in 26. Instead, they've come back one time out of 26. We can't draw any conclusions from that.

In fact, there's no reason to think that the teams ought to be of equal strength. That a team has won the first three games of a series provides some prima facie evidence that it is, in fact, the stronger club. For example, suppose that, if the two teams played one another an infinite number of times, Springfield would win 55 percent of the time, and Shelbyville would win the other 45 percent. Shelbyville will jump out to a 3-0 lead in a seven-game series approximately nine percent of the time (figured as .55^3), while the Isotopes will manage the feat around 17 percent of the time, or almost twice as often.

Similarly, if a team trailing 3-0 in a series is at an intrinsic 45-55 disadvantage, we'd expect it to go on to sweep the last four games and win the series about 4.1 percent of the time, or one try in 24. Instead, the trailing team has gone 1-for-26. The empirical results have been exactly what we'd expect them to be.

I should point out that I'm not going to consider data from other sports. I realize that we have a lot more trials to work with if we include NBA and NHL results—and basketball and hockey teams have done remarkably poorly when facing 3-0 deficits—but I don't think that it tells us anything. The difference between two "good" basketball teams is a couple of orders of magnitude greater than the difference between two good baseball teams. If you pitted the 2002 Lakers against the 2002 Nets, say, 100 times, I'd expect the Lakers to win something like 75 of those games. If you did the same thing with the 1989 A's and the 1989 Giants, it's hard to imagine the A's emerging with more than 60 victories. It's also my belief that momentum plays a greater role in basketball, though I'm sure someone like John Hollinger could shoot a few holes in that theory. As for hockey, I don't know the sport as well, but I do know that it places intense physical demands upon its combatants, and it's easy enough to imagine a team trailing 3-0 collapsing from exhaustion.

We do, however, have some additional baseball-specific data to work with. Let's look at the 26 post-season series in which a team has trailed 3-0 in a little bit more detail.

Year	Series	Ahead	Behind	Game 4 Result	Series Result
1907	WS	Cubs	Tigers	2-0	4-0
1910	WS	A's	Cubs	3-4	4-1
1914	WS	Braves	A's	3-1	4-0
1922	WS	Giants	Yankees	5-3	4-0
1927	WS	Yankees	Pirates	4-3	4-0
1928	WS	Yankees	Cardinals	7-3	4-0
1932	WS	Yankees	Cubs	13-6	4-0
1937	WS	Yankees	Giants	3-7	4-1
1938	WS	Yankees	Cubs	8-3	4-0
1939	WS	Yankees	Reds	7-4	4-0
1950	WS	Yankees	Phillies	5-2	4-0
1954	WS	Giants	Indians	7-4	4-0
1963	WS	Dodgers	Yankees	2-1	4-0
1966	WS	Orioles	Dodgers	1-0	4-0
1970	WS	Orioles	Reds	5-6	4-1
1976	WS	Reds	Yankees	7-2	4-0
1988	ALDS	A's	Red Sox	4-1	4-0
1989	WS	A's	Giants	9-6	4-0
1990	ALDS	A's	Red Sox	3-1	4-0
1990	WS	Reds	A's	2-1	4-0
1995	NLDS	Braves	Reds	6-0	4-0
1998	NLDS	Padres	Braves	3-8	4-2
1998	WS	Yankees	Padres	3-0	4-0
1999	NLDS	Braves	Mets	2-3	4-2
1999	WS	Yankees	Braves	4-1	4-0
2004	ALDS	Yankees	Red Sox	4-6	3-4

What stands out is the number of sweeps. The team with a 3-0 lead has gone on to win Game Four and bring out the brooms on 20 of 26 occasions. The series has been extended to five games just six times, and six games just three times. The 2004 Red Sox, of course, are the only team to force a Game Seven and the only team to win it.

All told, teams trailing 3-0 in a postseason series have managed an 11-25 record in the games that follows. That seems, at first glance, to be a non-random result. Is it?

Once again, the answer depends on the skill advantage of the team that holds the lead. If you take two teams of equal strength, Team A will win 25 or more times in 36 games about 1.4 percent of the time (this is estimated using a binomial distribution. If instead Team A has a 55-45 skill advantage—a much more realistic assumption—it will go 25-11 or better about 5.6 percent of the time.

The latter figure is just on the cusp of statistical significance. But it's also worth looking at the scores of Game Fours when a team trails 3-0:

- 1 run: four times
- 2 runs: four times
- 3 runs: seven times
- 4+ runs: four times
- Lost game: six times

In 14 of 26 Game Fours, the leading team has won by one run or two runs, or has lost the game. If the trailing team were laying down and setting its golf schedule for the winter, you'd expect a lot of blowouts. Instead, the games have been quite competitive: just four times has the game been decided by more than three runs.

None of this is likely to provide much comfort to Cardinal fans. St. Louis has to win four games in a row, and that's no easy feat in baseball, especially against a team a good as the Red Sox. But history provides no compelling evidence that the feat is any more difficult than that.

PROSPECTUS PERSPECTIVES
Four and No More
Christina Kahrl

Her plea may have fallen on deaf ears at the Commissioner's office, but Christina Kahrl made a strong case for limiting the number of playoff teams per league to four. The second wild card will indeed make its appearance in 2012, but the announcement of a subsequent realignment of divisions and leagues in the following season should make its arrival more palatable.

It was a glorious World Series to cap a glorious October, and detracting from it in any way would be difficult. Sadly, baseball managed it.

With his usual knack, Bud Selig could not help but find a way to leave something floating in the punch bowl where the postseason was concerned, because on Sunday, with the 2010 campaign cresting with a matchup reflecting a decade almost as glorious as the '80s as evidence of a dynamic, healthy competitive balance, Selig couldn't help but fidget. He could not help but suggest that maybe what baseball needed was two more playoff teams.

There's something appropriate about the fact that Selig spoke diffidently about his "pragmatic" appetite for extra post-season action on Halloween. Where this past postseason was concerned, while we all got to overindulge from an overstuffed October goodie bag, there's always that one kid who couldn't settle on having just that one last Milk Dud. To his shame, Selig was the one glutton who 'fessed up to wanting more.

So the Commissioner talks of being pragmatic about this, which is just as well, because the logistical challenges to adding two more wild-card teams for one-game play-ins or best-of-three miniseries are considerable. Does it really make sense to have six teams standing around while two wild-card clubs play their parts in the near-total trivialization of the regular season?

Selig might repeatedly and plaintively mention his horror for November baseball, but he's the man who created its near-unavoidability, certainly as long as post-season scheduling is tethered to network preference.* Inviting the addition of another short series or a scripted one-game death match hardly helps MLB avoid this ever-present threat. Admittedly, other antidotes to a November dogpile are being kicked around, as Selig commented at the All-Star Game: moving Opening Day (or Night) forward from Sunday/Monday (the 2011 season will start on Thursday/Friday), as well as deleting the odd day off or two during the LDS round.

That's all just embroidery, because the 162-game schedule is considered safe, and it isn't like the new generation of Lordlings of the Realm operating franchises these days are going to dip into their in-pocket profits from television, radio, ticket sales, and ancillary revenue streams by old-school scheduling or even day/night doubleheaders. The sixth-month slog might scoot up by a weekend, but it's still the unavoidably huge commitment, the game's greatest logistical feat as well as its handicap, simultaneously making a ballgame a ubiquitous pleasure while reducing it to seasonal wallpaper on a few too many local sports pages and national sports sites. Adding pre-scheduled baseball-as-bloodsport wild-card miniseries doesn't resolve that, while simply adding some new scheduling difficulties when it comes to avoiding trophy-hoisting in November.

Perhaps the man's disappointment is a product of our first play-in-free October since 2006. That was the last time we didn't need a one-game playoff to determine the identity of the eighth team on the slate, with the NL West doing the honors in 2007, and the AL Central generating sudden-death entertainment in 2008 and 2009. But as with so much else about the game, I'd argue that such pleasures are best savored when they occur by accident. As is, we got a contact high for this particular thrill's possibilities from the Braves, Padres, and Giants, right up until the regular season's last day.

That it didn't happen, that we did not get the Padres and Giants stepping out into the street for one last duel, or that we didn't get a three-way tie that left us having to determine the identities of both the NL West winner and the NL's wild-card club, is not an oversight to be corrected. Instead, it's an endorsement of how healthy what BP alum Keith Woolner referred to as the game's competitive ecology is.

Beyond the NL's near-miss for procuring this season's one-game playoff, the bunching up of today's contenders reflects an increasingly desperate scramble. In the American League, setting aside division alignments for the moment, the argument over who might have been the fourth-best team in the circuit had three teams—the Rangers, Red Sox, and White Sox—separated by just two games. The heavies from the AL East didn't just get beaten twice over by the upstart Rangers, they very nearly lost home-field advantage to the Twins. Look at third-order Adjusted Standings (here), and you find the AL tightly grouped, with a half-dozen clubs knocking around in a range of 88-92 wins.

Now, you can say that thick pack of possibles makes the actual outcome of which four clubs finish in the postseason too much of a toss-up, especially when you have an unbalanced schedule and the conceits of interleague action helping determine who lives and who golfs at season's end. And I'd collaboratively quibble over these and other complaints. But scheduling a play-in series strikes me as that last bit of bastardization too far.

Perhaps you cannot blame the man overmuch. As a matter of personal destiny, some by design, but by accident as well, Selig has had to preside over some of the most humiliating moments in the history of the sport. There are the matters of his guilt for 1994 as one of the leading architects of the first season sans World Series since 1904, or the embarrassment of an All-Star Game sloppily managed into a unresolvable tie, or his testimony on Capitol Hill that should place him with Rafael Palmeiro among the list of targets should already officious Congressmen decide to take up again their sense of slow-news-cycle outrage.

Where other sports seem to armor themselves with one Teflon-coated corporate dullard or another, for better and for worse, Selig is transparently a fan of the game and not merely his own initiatives. But he's also no simple traditionalist, since he has presided over and achieved more change than any Czar has or perhaps ever will. In this, he has had the advantage of being of the game as well as above it. Maybe, to achieve change within the industry, its idiosyncrasies required an equally idiosyncratic, in-bred solution. Dropping the pantomime of the past and dispensing with the dopey naivete that the Commissioner was some impartial elective monarch died a necessary death after the brief tyranny of Fay Vincent, baseball absolutism's last fantasy manager.

Instead, we have Selig, mogul and fan, a figure out of history nevertheless willing to thumb his nose at it and tinker. That's admirable in some ways. After all, who among us doesn't have his or her own agenda "were I Czar/ina for a day." My own two cents, worth even less than the zinc wasted to mint them, is that I'd want us to go back to the two-division alignment for both leagues and accept two wild-card clubs, which might in the worst-case scenarios help limit any one season's October slate to just one geographical accident per league. Admittedly, there's some lingering nostalgia for the alignment of my youth, but then again, I find the lopsided divisional alignments that give us the NL Central's six-pack and the AL West's short stack a bit ridiculous. However, I'm not so far gone as a hard-line historicist to insist we come down from four playoff teams per league back down to two.

But if Selig's willingness to break with history has its highlights and its uses, it also risks teetering into gimmickry, as it has with the "meaningful" All-Star Game. Here's hoping he doesn't go too far looking for some new, scheduled gewgaw. Let's take our one-game playoffs where and when we get them, delight in the game's stronger competitive dynamic while hoping the mechanisms that help achieve it either remain in place or get additional aid, and stick with four invitations to the dance per league.

And effectively that alone, because of one of the great triumphs of Czar Bud the Builder, since one of the basic benefits of the baseball-only facilities almost every franchise enjoys today is there's little need to worry about anyone else's uses for the venues.

Part 8: BUSINESS
Introduction by Jeff Euston

It was 1925 when Calvin Coolidge famously said, "The chief business of the American people is business." So it really should come as no surprise that America's pastime is a business, as well.

But the myth persists that baseball—even at the highest level—is just a game. The myth is born in the minds of children who fall in love with baseball at an age too young to realize that players can earn millions of dollars, communities pay millions for ballparks, owners pay multi-millions for franchises, and networks pay billions for broadcast rights. It is reinforced each time a fan complains about the salary a lackadaisical player earns for playing a game. The public pays good money to hear Springsteen play, DiCaprio act, and the Kardashians do whatever it is the Kardashians do. Few begrudge them their money or even know how much they earn. But when it comes to ballplayers, the usual rules are suspended in the minds of many fans. Supply and demand? No. Our American belief that everyone is entitled to earn as much as he can? Not here. Greed is good? Forget it. They're just playing a kid's game, after all.

In 1922, three years before Silent Cal's observation, the myth that baseball is not a business was established as the official policy of the federal government when no less an authority than the United States Supreme Court declared Major League Baseball to be exempt from the country's antitrust laws. Fifty years later, when Cardinals center fielder Curt Flood challenged the reserve clause, the Court again upheld that principle, though cracks in the idea had begun to show. In dissent, Justice William O. Douglas declared the notion that baseball is not interstate commerce to be a "derelict in the stream of the law."

Now, 90 years later, the jig is up. Baseball's anti-trust exemption no longer extends to employment practices, and free agency has been established since the mid-1970s. But more broadly, any pretense that baseball is not a business has left and gone away. During his annual visits to major-league cities, Commissioner Bud Selig never misses an opportunity to tell fans that the game has never been more healthy, a talking point he hits so repeatedly and with such fervor that he takes on the air of a children's doll who speaks when you pull the string. The commissioner is especially fond of reminding fans that since he took the top job, the sport's gross revenues have seen remarkable growth, from $1.2 billion in 1992 to a figure approaching $7 billion in 2011.

So if there was ever any doubt, there should be none now. Baseball is a business, and now more than ever, the race goes to the swift. Yes, at the game's core, on the field, players still play. But the almighty dollar informs and explains decisions throughout the sport, from small details in collective bargaining to the financial costs of a big mid-season trade, ballpark renovations, or franchise sales.

With the stakes so high, those business decisions are now scrutinized almost as closely as a manager's strategies or the play on the field. For at least a century, the lords of baseball's realm treated the game's financial information as proprietary, preferring to have fans focus on the game itself, not the proprietor's books or players' salaries. But that has changed, giving armchair general managers and talk-show callers an endless supply of opportunities to second-guess the brain trust in charge of their favorite team. Unfortunately, transparency tends to complicate, not clarify, the decision-making process for those calling the shots.

"Keep making our lives challenging by providing quality information to the rest of the world!" one general manager told me upon learning I had started Cot's Baseball Contracts, a web site listing breakdowns of each club's payroll and contract information. (I'm still not exactly sure whether he was endorsing the site or criticizing its existence.)

But much more than just contract information is now publicly available. Anyone with a smart phone or an internet connection can read the Major League Constitution, the Major League Rules, and the Collective Bargaining Agreement between the owners and players. MLB itself made unprecedented—if limited—financial disclosures to Congress in late 2001 in an effort to buttress its case for a plan to eliminate two clubs because the industry was losing so much money ($232 million in 2001, or $519 million including interest payments and depreciation). The financial numbers were met with skepticism at a Capitol Hill hearing convened after Congress responded to the contraction plan by threatening to eliminate baseball's antitrust exemption as it applies to franchise movement and elimination.

Less than a decade later, in 2010, a leak of actual financial documents from six clubs showed that the doubts from politicians in Washington in 2001 had not been unfounded. Many of the worst teams on the field, the new documents showed, nevertheless had managed to make money. To take the most notorious example, the Florida Marlins had received nearly $92 million in revenue sharing in 2008 and 2009 and reported $33 million in profits. Meanwhile, the club's combined 2008 and 2009 Opening Day payrolls totaled just $58.6 million.

Owners of clubs paying into baseball's revenue-sharing system had long suspected that some clubs were pocketing the checks rather than using the money to improve their teams. Now, for the first time, owners of high-revenue payor teams had concrete financial numbers confirming their suspicions, and they were not amused. Nor were many taxpayers in South Florida, who had just approved $350 million in public financing for a new $515 million ballpark without any access to such detailed information regarding the profitability of the payee Marlins.

THE LINEUP

Player Compensation
  by Doug Pappas..................................301

A New Way to Rank the GMs
  by Shawn Hoffman..............................304

The Best and Worst GMs of the Aughties
  by Shawn Hoffman..............................308

Busting the Myth of the Salary Cap
  by Shawn Hoffman..............................312

The Deal Almost No One Likes
  by Joe Sheehan....................................315

Salary Cap
  by Joe Sheehan....................................318

Worst. Contract. Ever.
  by Rany Jazayerli................................323

Weighin' in at 19 Stone, Part One
  by Gary Huckabay...............................328

Weighin' in at 19 Stone, Part Two
  by Gary Huckabay...............................336

Cleaning Out the Front Office
  by Christina Kahrl..............................343

A Mulligan on Guzman
  by Nate Silver.....................................347

One Man's Plan
  by Keith Woolner...............................354

From the formation of the players association in the late Sixties until the 1994 strike that cost baseball a World Series, the game's long, twilight labor relations struggle was a bipolar war of attrition, a contest to determine which side—the owners or the players—had the leverage to impose its will on the other. Led by United Steelworkers veteran Marvin Miller, the players won.

"If anyone does not believe that we had our ass kicked in this labor matter, they are dead wrong," Cardinals owner August Busch Jr. grumbled in 1976, after approval of the game's first labor deal to include free agency. "We have lost the war, and the only question is, can we live with the surrender terms."

Busch was right. The owners lost the fights over the reserve clause, arbitration, and free agency. But, now that a relative labor peace has broken out, it turns out both the owners and players can coexist and live quite comfortably in financial partnership with each other. In the decade since the contraction controversy, baseball has enjoyed unprecedented growth in revenue streams from the game's internet presence (MLB Advanced Media), a lucrative new national television contract, record-setting attendance figures, and eight new ballparks, extending the building boom that began in 1992 with Oriole Park at Camden Yards. All that money has helped forge something almost unimaginable in 1994: a partnership between the owners and players. Baseball's last four collective bargaining agreements (1997, 2003, 2007, and 2011) were brokered without work stoppages. Today's collective bargaining process is less a traditional tug-of-war between management and labor than a collegial trilateral negotiation among high-revenue owners, low-revenue owners and the players. And everybody has a share.

But even in an era of partnership and relative prosperity and goodwill, myriad issues remain. Who will replace Selig when his contract expires after the 2012 season? What is the right amount of revenue sharing between clubs? What is the appropriate threshold for the competitive balance tax, more popularly known as the luxury tax? What can be done to broker agreements for new ballparks for the franchises in Tampa Bay and Oakland? Should the post-season format be changed? What is the future of interleague play and realignment? Will changes in post-season format, interleague play, and divisional alignment pay off? What is the ideal time and place for the World Baseball Classic? What will be the shape of the media landscape when baseball's national television contracts with Fox, TBS, ESPN, DirecTV, and iN Demand (Extra Innings) expire after the 2013 season? What is the future of MLB Advanced Media and the MLB Network?

Over the last 10 years, the authors at Baseball Prospectus have weighed in on many important business issues confronting the game, and some of their best work is reproduced in the pages that follow.

- Shawn Hoffman dispels the myth of the salary cap and proposes a new yardstick for measuring general managers, Payroll Efficiency Rating. He then applies his work to rank the best and worst GMs of the decade of the Aughts, with a result that should not surprise anyone who has seen the latest Brad Pitt film.
- Joe Sheehan props up one idea no one seemed to like, MLB's exclusive Extra Innings broadcast contract with DirecTV, then skewers another idea many fans love, a salary cap.
- Rany Jazayerli examines Boston's recurring contract with knuckleballer Tim Wakefield, a deal he ranks as the worst ever, at least from a player's perspective.
- Gary Huckabay conducts a roundtable with two team executives who hold forth on everything from agents and evaluating their front-office peers to the difficulty of landing a job in the game and the long hours their work demands.
- Christina Kahrl reacts to the firing of Dodgers general manager Paul DePodesta and the implications for anyone who might dare employ the next generation of management techniques, with a healthy and prescient dose of scorn for team owner Frank McCourt, whose problems in Los Angeles only got worse.
- Doug Pappas provides perspective on player compensation and, using Marginal Dollars per Marginal Win, lays a foundation for evaluating how efficiently teams spend money.
- Nate Silver asks for a mulligan on his pronouncement that shortstop Cristian Guzman was the best free-agent signing of the 2004-05 offseason. In the process, he discovers that there is a hidden cost to players substantially below championship caliber for teams with aspirations of championship-caliber performance.
- Keith Woolner creates a revenue-sharing plan that provides incentives to small-market clubs to field more competitive teams.

Taken together, the pieces are both wide and varied in scope, providing the sort of sharp insight that's at a premium in an era when the business of America's pastime is business.

THE NUMBERS (PART FOUR)
Player Compensation
Doug Pappas

When determining how efficiently a team spends its money, one can't simply divide its total payroll by its wins. As Doug Papas explained, marginal dollars per marginal win provides a much clearer picture of a team's financial success or failure.

As the longtime owner of an unsuccessful small-market team, Commissioner Bud Selig has 30 years of practice arguing that "small markets can't compete." (The Brewers' mediocrity surely couldn't be management's fault.) Inevitably, Exhibit A in this argument is a table similar to the first two columns below, which show some teams spending two or three times as much as their rivals on player salaries.

Salaries tell only part of the story. Two of the three most expensive teams in 2001 missed the playoffs. The A's, with the majors' second-best record, ranked #26 in payroll. More fundamentally, "small market" is often mistakenly used as a synonym for "low revenue." A team's revenue, and the payroll it can support, is more a function of the team's recent success than of the size of its market. As the population data here shows, metropolitan Minneapolis is larger than Cleveland, Miami is larger than Seattle, and Philadelphia is larger than Phoenix and St. Louis combined.

Player salaries are investments. A team that spends its money wisely wins more games, and in any market, a winning team means higher attendance and more public interest, which ultimately translates into larger media contracts and more money for the owner. Conversely, a team perceived as too cheap to sign quality players will alienate its fans and have less to spend. A team that spends poorly, like the Orioles or Devil Rays, has the worst of both worlds: higher expenses without higher revenues.

Here's how the 2001 payrolls break down:

Team	Player Compensation (in thousands)	Adj Player Compensation (in thousands)	Win Pct	Marginal $/ Marginal Win
Boston Red Sox	$118,471	$118,471	.509	$3,115,000
New York Yankees	$117,936	$101,936	.594	$1,867,000
Los Angeles Dodgers	$116,077	$116,077	.531	$2,754,000
Cleveland Indians	$102,491	$100,491	.562	$2,061,000
Atlanta Braves	$99,671	$97,042	.543	$2,135,000
Arizona Diamondbacks	$99,434	$86,434	.568	$1,691,000
New York Mets	$99,144	$99,144	.506	$2,581,000
Texas Rangers	$92,793	$92,793	.451	$3,262,000
Seattle Mariners	$83,946	$76,409	.716	$941,000
Toronto Blue Jays	$83,801	$83,801	.494	$2,253,000
St. Louis Cardinals	$80,148	$78,660	.574	$1,479,000
Baltimore Orioles	$79,783	$79,783	.391	$4,530,000
Chicago Cubs	$78,091	$78,091	.543	$1,653,483
San Francisco Giants	$72,185	$72,185	.556	$1,427,000
Houston Astros	$71,577	$71,058	.574	$1,308,000
Colorado Rockies	$69,983	$69,983	.451	$2,329,000
Chicago White Sox	$66,721	$66,721	.512	$1,564,000
Detroit Tigers	$57,184	$57,184	.407	$2,549,000
Tampa Bay Devil Rays	$57,000	$57,000	.383	$3,272,000
Pittsburgh Pirates	$53,227	$53,227	.383	$2,992,000
Anaheim Angels	$52,239	$52,239	.463	$1,486,000
Milwaukee Brewers	$51,164	$51,164	.420	$1,963,000
Philadelphia Phillies	$49,384	$49,384	.531	$972,000
San Diego Padres	$46,089	$46,089	.488	$1,086,000
Cincinnati Reds	$45,410	$45,410	.407	$1,870,000

Marginal salary per marginal win = (Adjusted player compensation - $13,000,000) / ((Winning percentage - .300) x 162)

The first column of data is each club's total 2001 player compensation, as reported by MLB. These figures are higher than those generally published: they include salaries for everyone on the 40-man roster, plus bonuses, termination pay received by players whose options aren't exercised, and $6 million per team for pensions, insurance, benefits, and related expenses.

The easiest comparison would be simply to divide a club's payroll by its wins to come up with "dollars per win," but neither side of this equation reflects reality. The worst team a club can field won't go 0-162, and despite Carl Pohlad's best efforts, it's impossible to spend $0 on a team. This simple formula also errs by ignoring the postseason: it suggests that the 2000 Cleveland Indians, who missed the playoffs despite a 90-72 record, had a better year than the 87-74 Yankees who won the World Series.

A better measure is to look at marginal dollars per marginal win. Using MLB's accounting, the cheapest possible team would cost its owner about $13,000,000: $5,000,000 for 25 players making the major league minimum of $200,000; another $800,000 for four minimum-salaried players on the DL; $1.2 million for the remaining 11 men on the 40-man roster; and $6 million for benefits. I estimate that such a team would win 30 percent of its games, roughly a 49-113 record, 13 games worse than the 2001 Devil Rays and five games behind the 1998 "fire sale" Marlins. (The exact number used doesn't matter when comparing teams from the same season.)

A team's marginal spending per marginal win thus equals its payroll, minus postseason revenues and minus the $13 million minimum, divided by its winning percentage minus .300, times 162 games. Using the Yankees for an example: ($118,000,000 payroll - $16,000,000 postseason money - $13 million minimum) / ((.594 - .300) * 162), or $89 million/47.6 wins, or about $1.87 million per marginal win. That's the same as the Cincinnati Reds spent to finish 66-96.

The average club spent just under $2 million per marginal win. The four most efficient clubs—the Twins, A's, and Phillies, who won most of their games despite very low payrolls, and the 116-win Mariners—spent about half as much. At the other end of the spectrum, the four members of the $3-million-per-win club illustrated four different types of bad management. The Orioles paid top dollar to hold onto the remnants of a 1993 All-Star team; the Devil Rays wasted money on free agents instead of developing a farm system; the Rangers bid against themselves for Alex Rodriguez and had no money left for pitching; and the Red Sox' bench earned more than the entire Twins team.

THE BIZ BEAT
A New Way to Rank the GMs
Shawn Hoffman

Building on Doug Pappas' original marginal dollars per marginal win formula, Shawn Hoffman introduced a new-and-improved approach that also factored in individualized marginal revenue curves instead of penalizing big-market teams for throwing their financial weight around.

Back in 2004, the late Doug Pappas came up with a simple way to evaluate how well each team was spending its money: marginal payroll per marginal win. Here's Doug's original formula:

```
(club payroll - (28 x major league minimum)) /
        ((winning percentage - .300) x 162)
```

Simple enough, and it managed to give us yet another way to show how great Billy Beane and the A's were. But while it was a decent first step, it failed even the simplest laugh tests: Were the Yankees really one of the bottom 10 teams, even when they were running away with their division every year? Are the Marlins consistently one of the best-run teams, just by virtue of not spending much beyond the minimum on payroll? Probably not.

Looking at it now, the biggest problems are fairly obvious. First off, not all wins are created equal—as Nate Silver touched on in *Baseball Between the Numbers*, a team's 90th win creates significantly more marginal revenue than its 70th (see chart below). Also, each team has its own marginal revenue curve—the Yankees' ninetieth win is much more valuable than the Marlins' ninetieth win, at least in terms of pure revenue potential.

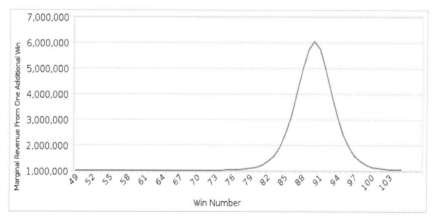

So while Doug's original formula punished large-market teams for spending significant sums on payroll, the reality is that the Yankees would have to have a brain lapse to cut their payroll below $100 million. The question really should be: How well are they spending their $200 million, and is that the right number, given their competitive position and market size?

Neil deMause was on the right track two years ago when he added Nate's marginal-revenue-per-win curve to Doug's method. But we need to go a couple steps further. Here's how we'll do it:

1. First, we need to know how much marginal revenue each team is likely to bring in, based on its win total and market size. To do this, we'll use Nate's MR/MW curve, updated for 2009 revenues. We'll then assign each team a market-size factor based on its 2007-2008 gate receipts. (We already know that this is the only short-term revenue source that significantly impacts a team's payroll spending). The Red Sox won 95 games last year, which should generally lead to $108 million in marginal revenue. Multiply that figure by Boston's market-size factor (2.48), and we get expected revenue of $267 million.

2. Next, we'll use a regression equation (MW = 0.1106*MP + 22.538) to determine how many games a team should win—and, therefore, how much revenue it should bring in—based solely on its payroll. For example, Boston's $133 million payroll in 2008 should have led to 86 wins. According the win curve, multiplied by the team's market-size factor, that would create $165 million in marginal revenue.

3. Then we just divide these numbers: 267 / 165 = 1.61. In other words, given their payroll and revenue potential, the Red Sox performed about 61 percent better than average in 2008.

Let's compare the top and bottom teams from 2008, first using Doug's approach, and then using our new one.

Of the top five teams, only one —the Rays—actually made the playoffs, and of the other four, only the Twins should have even been close. The Marlins, D-Backs, and A's performed reasonably well given their small payrolls but still averaged only 80 wins.

Team	Marginal Payroll	Marginal Wins	MP / MW
Marlins	$10,636,500	36	$300,466
Rays	$32,620,598	49	$673,979
Twins	$50,982,767	40	$1,293,979
Athletics	$36,767,126	27	$1,392,694
Diamondbacks	$55,002,713	34	$1,646,788
...			
Nationals	$43,761,000	11	$4,207,788
Padres	$62,477,617	15	$4,338,723
Yankees	$197,881,579	41	$4,898,059
Tigers	$127,485,197	26	$5,019,102
Mariners	$106,793,982	13	$8,612,418

The results of our new method seem a lot closer to reality. The Rays run away from the pack, with the 100-win Angels and 97-win Cubs coming in a distant second and third, respectively. Instead of punishing large-market teams, the system accounts for their inherent advantage and judges them on how well they actually use it. The Yankees remain in the bottom five —which is actually identical to the previous list, just with a different order—but it's no longer their fait accompli, as they would have finished in the top half had they played up to expectations. The Red Sox, for example, finish nineteenth on the old list despite winning 95 games, as compared to fifth on the new list.

Team	Marginal Revenue	Expected MR	MR / ExpMR
Rays	$51,461,633	$23,524,473	2.19
Angels	$115,533,623	$64,051,489	1.80
Cubs	$185,744,330	$106,445,281	1.74
Phillies	$132,870,709	$78,183,106	1.70
Red Sox	$267,185,811	$165,780,654	1.61
...			
Yankees	$228,824,384	$302,239,343	0.76
Tigers	$46,166,722	$67,111,767	0.69
Padres	$26,758,423	$53,501,930	0.68
Nationals	$26,758,423	$42,507,738	0.63
Mariners	$32,245,120	$55,863,187	0.58

If we want to make it even more meritocratic, we can use third-order wins instead of actual wins, in order to strip out some of the luck involved.

The Rays remain in front, while the Red Sox, Blue Jays, and Dodgers all move up a few spots.

Here's the same chart for 2009, assuming each team's current third-order winning percentage holds.

If there's still a piece missing, it's the value that comes with finishing last. The first pick in the draft is worth a lot more than the fifth or the 10th or the 15th, so a team that wins 59 games, as the Nationals did last year, should have that factored into its marginal revenue figures. But we'll leave that for another day.

Team	3rd-Order MR	Exp MR	MR3 / ExpMR
Rays	$51,461,633	$23,524,473	2.19
Red Sox	$290,486,158	$165,780,654	1.75
Blue Jays	$66,790,624	$39,300,599	1.70
Cubs	$175,942,093	$106,445,281	1.65
Dodgers	$128,566,277	$100,454,854	1.28
...			
Padres	$41,255,570	$53,501,930	0.77
Tigers	$51,211,783	$67,111,767	0.76
Nationals	$30,054,408	$42,507,738	0.71
Pirates	$14,483,537	$20,635,720	0.70
Mariners	$35,986,509	$55,863,187	0.64

Team	3rd-Order MR	Exp MR	MR3 / ExpMR
Rays	$50,733,695	$24,508,966	2.07
Dodgers	$181,196,617	$91,143,942	1.99
Rockies	$58,385,603	$38,702,035	1.51
Rangers	$41,117,147	$28,721,444	1.43
Red Sox	$217,262,599	$152,072,010	1.43
...			
Royals	$15,701,747	$19,530,582	0.80
Mets	$94,833,032	$124,697,984	0.76
Pirates	$15,300,110	$20,216,344	0.76
Astros	$49,817,523	$66,058,454	0.75
Reds	$24,847,828	$33,316,875	0.75

For now, some other notes on the data we do have:

- Andrew Friedman and the Rays are clearly the class of Major League Baseball right now. Ignore their actual 2009 record; first-, second-, and third-order wins have them as the second-best team in the American League, and they're trailing only a team that will spend three and a half times as much on payroll. Combine that with a runaway victory in 2008 in both actual and third-order MR/ExpMR, and it's hard to argue they're not the best around right now.

- The Yankees are currently 12th in MR3/ExpMR (we seriously need a name for this, if anyone has any ideas), but only 27th in the classic MP/MW, despite being on pace to win 101 games. I think the new method is a pretty fair approximation; the marginal returns clearly diminish very quickly after about $120-$130 million (which is where the Red Sox usually are), and the Yankees could obviously win a lot of games with a $150 million payroll, if managed correctly. That they're about average seems right—when you spend fifty percent more than anybody else, you probably should win 101 games.

- The Mets are a disaster.

- The Pirates, Royals, Orioles, and Nationals would definitely benefit if we included the value of their ensuing draft picks. Of those teams, I'd guess that the Pirates are the only one that actually understood this coming into the season.

It doesn't surprise me that the Nationals aren't in the bottom five—they've tracked well ahead of their actual record all year, and they actually aren't that far behind the Mets in the adjusted standings.

Now, about that name...

SQUAWKING BASEBALL
The Best and Worst GMs of the Aughties
Shawn Hoffman

Having introduced his "Payroll Efficiency Rating," or PER, system for assessing the spending of major-league teams, Shawn Hoffman applied it to determine the most- and least-efficient general managers of the 21st century's first decade.

For me, this is a lot of fun, but as a refresher, here's how these rankings are calculated. First, we find each team's expected revenue, based on its third-order winning percentage and how big its market is. Then, we divide that by what each team's marginal revenue should have been, had it won exactly as many games as its payroll would have predicted. (Draft pick value is also factored in, so the worst teams get slightly more credit than the vanilla mediocre teams.) The end result is PER—Payroll Efficiency Rating—which tells us how well each team spent its payroll dollars.

To run through a quick example, the Rockies spent $75 million on payroll last year, a bit below average. That should have led to around 79 wins, which, given their local market, would have created around $41 million in marginal revenue. But the Rockies actually had 90 third-order wins, which likely created somewhere around $58 million. Divide the two, and you get a 1.43 PER. Since 1.00 is average, we can say the Rockies' front office performed 43 percent better than average in 2009.

On to the lists. Starting with the bottom ten, among all general managers with at least three years on the job this past decade. Smith gets credit for 2002—he was fired a week in—which keeps John Hart out of the bottom ten by the skin of his teeth.

Rank	GM	Years	PER
10	Randy Smith	2000-02	.976
9	Dave Littlefield	2002-07	.970
8	Wayne Krivsky	2006-08	.966
7	Doug Melvin	2000-01, 2003-09	.954
6	Mike Flanagan/Jim Beattie	2003-07	.954

Hart had the misfortune of leading the Rangers through the last two years of the A-Rod era, which, along with Melvin's last year in Texas, were three of the worst years in the entire database. Melvin has been better since moving to Milwaukee, but Branch Rickey couldn't have made up for those last couple of years with the Rangers.

Unlike Hart and Melvin, the other three didn't have any years that were overly terrible—they just didn't have any really good ones either. Flanagan/Beattie, Krivsky, and Littlefield averaged 71, 73, and 78 third-order wins, respectively, right in that dead zone where it's impossible to make the playoffs and extremely hard to get the first overall pick.

The only name that doesn't fit here is Cashman. The Yankees made a lot of mistakes this past decade, and it's not totally clear which of those were his and which were George Steinbrenner's. But it's pretty easy to look at that list and pick the one that

Rank	GM	Years	PER
5	Chuck LaMar	2000-05	.935
4	Brian Cashman	2000-09	.869
3	Syd Thrift	2000-02	.807
2	Bill Bavasi	2004-08	.786
1	Steve Phillips	2000-03	.670

doesn't go with all the others. We'll probably have to wait another five years to really judge him on his merits, but there's already been significant progress—the Yankees are spending much less now than they did earlier in the decade (after you adjust for baseball inflation), and they just fielded their best team since 1998.

As for the rest, I'm not sure the system could have done any better. Phillips, Bavasi, Thrift, and LaMar were all pretty abysmal and would have made just about anybody's bottom ten list (objective, subjective, or otherwise). If there's a surprise, it's how badly Phillips lapped the field despite having a World Series team in 2000, but his 2001-03 stretch is even worse than the A-Rod-era Rangers.

Now, for the best. Let's get the obvious ones out of the way first. Shapiro has had some really tough breaks, particularly in 2006 and 2008, but the third-order standings see through that and reward him for building some very good teams on

Rank	GM	Years	PER
10	Terry Ryan	2000-07	1.154
9	Brian Sabean	2000-09	1.162
8	Ned Colletti	2006-09	1.195
7	J.P. Ricciardi	2002-09	1.216
6	Mark Shapiro	2002-09	1.228

limited budgets. Ryan led four division winners on miniscule payrolls and was generally considered one of the best at drafting and developing young talent right up until his retirement in 2007.

The other three took less obvious paths. J.P. Ricciardi has been torn apart on this site and others, but had the Blue Jays been in any other division, his record could look very different—the 2006-2008 Blue Jays were very good teams, but were simply in the wrong place at the wrong time. Colletti has also taken his lumps, but he had an outstanding year in 2009—the Dodgers had 99 third-order wins—which pushed him up to number eight despite three middling seasons from '06-'08. As for Sabean, if that doesn't get Barry Bonds into the Hall of Fame...

If we had taken a poll on BP, there's a pretty good chance that Beane and Friedman would have been the top two. Beane dominated the first half of the decade, Friedman the second half. Together, they accounted for six of the top 10 individual seasons of the decade (see below), with the Moneyball-era A's taking the first, third, and fifth spots.

Rank	GM	Years	PER
5	Walt Jocketty	2000-07, 2009	1.232
4	Gerry Hunsicker	2000-04	1.292
3	Pat Gillick	2000-03, 2006-08	1.386
2	Andrew Friedman	2006-09	1.428
1	Billy Beane	2000-09	1.518

The other three aren't exactly sabermetric favorites, but they were all very successful nonetheless. Jocketty's Cardinals tallied 90 or more third-order wins five times and won the World Series in one of the years that they didn't. Gillick led one of the best teams of all-time—the 2001 Mariners—as well as the world champion 2008 Phillies. Hunsicker just missed the Astros' World Series run in 2005 but put together several teams that were actually better before leaving in 2004.

How about the best and worst single-season performances:

Rank	GM	Year	PER
1	Billy Beane	2001	2.10
2	Mark Shapiro	2005	2.06
3	Billy Beane	2002	2.06
4	Bill Stoneman	2002	2.01
5	Billy Beane	2003	1.97
6	Andrew Friedman	2008	1.90
7	Andrew Friedman	2009	1.88
8	Billy Beane	2000	1.88
9	Brian Sabean	2000	1.85
10	Ned Colletti	2009	1.84
...			
296	Syd Thrift	2000	0.61
297	Dan Duquette	2001	0.59
298	John Hart	2002	0.59
299	Dave Dombrowski	2008	0.58
300	Steve Phillips	2003	0.53

It's a bit surprising that Gillick's '01 Mariners just missed (they were 12th), but the marginal gain for each win over 100 is minuscule, and several of these teams were within a few games of the Mariners' 109 third-order wins. The 2001 A's, for one, had 105 third-order wins, despite spending less than half what the Mariners did.

Finally, the best- and worst-run teams of the decade:

Rank	Team	General Manager(s)	PER
1	Oakland Athletics	Billy Beane (2000-09)	1.52
2	St. Louis Cardinals	Walt Jocketty (2000-07), John Mozeliak (2008-09)	1.25
3	Cleveland Indians	John Hart (2000-01), Mark Shapiro (2002-09)	1.18
4	San Francisco Giants	Brian Sabean (2000-09)	1.16
5	Toronto Blue Jays	Gord Ash (2000-01), J.P. Ricciardi (2002-09)	1.16
...			
26	Pittsburgh Pirates	Cam Bonifay (2000-01), Dave Littlefield (2002-07), Neal Huntington (2008-09)	0.97
27	Los Angeles Dodgers	Kevin Malone (2000-01), Dan Evans (2002-03), Paul DePodesta (2004-05), Ned Colletti (2006-09)	0.95
28	Baltimore Orioles	Syd Thrift (2000-02), Mike Flanagan/Jim Beattie (2003-07), Andy MacPhail (2008-09)	0.92
29	New York Yankees	Brian Cashman (2000-09)	0.87
30	New York Mets	Steve Phillips (2000-03), Jim Duquette (2004), Omar Minaya (2005-09)	0.81

With that, on to the debate about the results.

LET FREEDOM RING
Busting the Myth of the Salary Cap
Shawn Hoffman

Small-market teams often clamor for a salary cap, but as Shawn Hoffman explained, introducing one would only cause problems in a prosperous era for baseball.

Small-market teams love salary caps. Or rather, they think they do. At least on paper, caps stop teams in New York, Boston, and Chicago from oligopolizing the free-agent market and should therefore help level the economic playing field. And, to a certain extent, they do; a small-market team in a capped league is more likely to acquire or retain top-tier talent. But there's a catch. That same small-market team will need to win, and keep winning, just to stay financially viable. And sometimes, winning might not even be enough.

Let's say, in some far-off universe, MLB owners and players actually did agree on a salary cap. With it would come the normal provisions: a salary floor at around 75-85 percent of the cap, and a guaranteed percentage of total industry revenues for the players. Since the players have been taking in about 45 percent of revenues the past few years, we'll keep it at that figure (the other three major sports leagues, which are all capped, each pay out over 50 percent).

Using 2008 as an example, the 30 teams took in about $6 billion (not including MLB Advanced Media revenue), for an average of $200 million per team. Forty-five percent of that (the players' share) is $90 million, which we'll use as the midpoint between our floor and cap. If we want to make the floor 75 percent of the cap (a low-end figure, relative to the other leagues), we can use $77 million and $103 million, respectively.

With a $103 million cap, nine teams would have been affected last year, and a total of about $286 million would have had to be skimmed off the top. Since total salaries have to remain at existing levels, the bottom 21 teams would have had to take on this burden, which had previously been placed on the Yankees, Red Sox, et al. On the other end, 14 teams would have been under the payroll floor, by a total of $251 million. Even discounting the Marlins' $22 million payroll, the other 13 teams would have had to spend an average of $15 million more just to meet the minimum. Some of those teams might be able to afford it; most wouldn't.

Imagine being Frank Coonelly in this situation. Coonelly, the Pirates' team president, has publicly supported a cap. Had our fictional cap/floor arrangement been instituted last year, the Pirates would have needed to increase their Opening Day payroll by $28 million. Not only would the team have taken a big loss, but Neal Huntington's long-term strategy would have been sabotaged, since the team would have had to sign a number of veterans just to meet the minimum payroll.

Now fast forward to 2009. Let's say the Pirates' sales staff runs into major headwinds, with the team struggling and the economy sinking. The team's top line takes a hit, falling $10 million from 2008. The Mets and Yankees, meanwhile, open their new ballparks, and each team increases its local revenue by $50 million. If the 27 other teams are flat, total industry revenues rise by $90 million (not including any appreciation in national media revenue). Forty-five percent of that, of course, goes to the players. So even as the Pirates' purchasing power decreases, the payroll floor actually rises.

In other words, without a more egalitarian distribution of income, the system crumbles.

Until recently, the NFL has been uniquely fit for this type of model, since most of its revenues have come from national television contracts. But now, with local revenues rising, small-market teams are feeling the pinch. This past May, the owners unanimously voted to opt out of their CBA, which was supposed to run through 2012. Some blamed the players' share of revenues. Others, including Dan Rooney of the Steelers, cited the need for more local revenue sharing.

But sharing local revenue has a major drawback: it is a tax, which inevitably lowers incentives and decreases output. If the NFL shared all (or even most) local intake, why would an individual team ever look to maximize revenues at its own cost (i.e. by hiring a sales staff or cleaning its own stadium)?

The NHL, which also has a hard cap, does very little revenue sharing, partly thanks to an overly convoluted system. On a league-wide level, the results have been very positive; the NHL has had record revenues every year since its lockout, and Gary Bettman has been very positive about this season as well. But the NHL is a great example of why caps and capitalism don't mix: as the league grows, it ends up leaving teams behind. Small-market clubs like the Columbus Blue Jackets and the Nashville Predators are forced to spend almost two-thirds of their revenue on player payroll. And the Phoenix Coyotes, after years of hemorrhaging money, are on the verge of going bankrupt.

So what's the best solution? Certainly not the NBA's soft-cap system, which has too many problems even to count—imagine having to take on Luis Castillo or Carl Pavano every time you wanted to unload a high-priced veteran.

So instead of these models, what if there was an uncapped league, with limited local revenue sharing to support small-market teams and a post-season system that naturally created tremendous parity? Does this sound familiar? It should. It's what MLB has had in place for over a decade, leading to record growth in both attendance and revenue.

The expanded postseason is key. More than any other sport, MLB's playoff system acts as an equalizer. Fair or not, in broad strokes, a team that wins 83 games in a bad division has as much chance of winning the World Series as the Yankees or the Red Sox. Seemingly, no matter how much those teams spend over the winter, that competitive advantage is neutralized come October.

So while the capped leagues all struggle to find the right balance between capitalism and socialism, baseball continues to prosper operating within a much more free-market system. Teams in big markets and small markets alike are making money, and everyone has a chance to win it all.

If it ain't broke, don't fix it. And right now, baseball is anything but broke.

Note: All salary data taken from the Lahman Database.

PROSPECTUS TODAY
The Deal Almost No One Likes
Joe Sheehan

The news that Major League Baseball was on the verge of awarding exclusive broadcast rights to its Extra Innings package of out-of-market games to DirecTV prompted Joe Sheehan to explain that a deal that threatened to infuriate fans might still be in MLB's best interests.

> Hi, Joe. Long time reader here. You may be aware that MLB just gave exclusive broadcasting rights for MLB Extra Innings to DirecTV. This completely screws thousands of displaced fans who don't have satellite TV as an option and don't want to sit at their desk watching a small, grainy picture on MLB.TV.
>
> There may not be anything that can be done about this, but I'm worried the national media won't really say anything. I think it might be fodder for a nice op-ed piece either on BP or perhaps some other forum. There are a lot of people who are pretty angry about being deprived of watching their favorite team for what amounts to about $1,000,000 per team per year. Myself included. Just a thought.
>
> —Michael Newman

I sent Michael a note privately to tell him that I would write about this for today, although I did warn him that this would not be the piece he was looking for.

Michael is correct about a number of things. Yes, Major League Baseball appears ready to assign exclusive rights to its Extra Innings (EI) package of out-of-market televised baseball games—as well as the exclusive rights to an MLB Channel—to News Corp.'s DirecTV satellite service. DirecTV is paying a whopping $100 million a year over seven years for these rights. Based on the information in the *Sports Business Journal*, that represents a five-fold increase over what inDemand was paying for the rights to EI. This is a considerable boost to MLB's bottom line, although the marginal gain isn't necessarily over the $20 million or so they were making under the previous deal, but over the reported $70 million a year *SBJ* claims inDemand offered. Even at that, $30 million a year is nothing to sneeze at.

Michael is also correct in his statements about the deal's effect on fans. This has been the talk of the town over the weekend, both on Internet message boards and on BP's internal mailing list. The majority of expressed opinions resemble Michael's: frustration among those who do not have DirecTV that they will now be denied an opportunity to purchase what many of us call simply "the package." Is it worth, as Michael puts it, alienating a segment of your fan base for a million bucks per team per year?

Here's the problem: the answer to that question is "yes."

Before I go any further, let me make something clear: I am a DirecTV subscriber who would normally not be affected by this decision. However, I will almost certainly be in new housing by Opening Day, and the area to which I'm moving is not always amenable to satellite dishes. Whether by rule or by circumstance, I may well be unable to have the package for this upcoming season. At the least, it's another factor complicating the housing search. I would personally prefer not to be in this situation.

Back up a second and consider what Extra Innings is: 1200 or so baseball games a year beamed into your house. Some nights, there are 15 games to be watched, and the only nights during the season when you're not getting something are over the All-Star break. That is, by even the standards of a lifelong fanatic, a lot of baseball. It's a product aimed at the very top of the pyramid; 750,000 subscriptions were sold last season, a bit more than a third of the number that bought the NFL equivalent.

MLB is going to tick off a subset of that group: EI subscribers who either have Dish Network or cable. However, it's not going to lose that group of people as baseball fans. Some of those people will switch to DirecTV, others will make do with MLB.tv, still others will not purchase a package and live without the extra games. The number of fans that MLB will lose because of this decision, however, could fit in my living room. You simply don't go from being such a big fan of baseball that you would purchase 1200 games a year on satellite to a non-fan based on one decision.

This also goes to the point that Maury Brown chose to emphasize today, that this decision goes against the idea of growing the game's popularity. In fact, it is completely orthogonal to that notion. New fans of baseball aren't created by having them consume the game from a firehose, but by having them attend games, or watch the local team on local channels, or perhaps catch highlights on the news or on "Baseball Tonight." EI is a non-factor in that process. It is a niche product for extreme users, not a gateway drug.

I don't mean to dismiss the concerns of the disenfranchised. Remember, the frustration that's being expressed is largely among those people who will not even have the opportunity to purchase the package at any price. Even this, however, may work in MLB's favor. The largest clusters of these users are likely to be in large urban areas, where renters may struggle against either rules that ban dishes or a lack of the famous "view of the southern sky." These people, however, are likely to turn to one of two sources for their fix: the local team's games on cable, or MLB.tv. If the former, those teams will see a rise in ratings that should eventually lead to higher rights fees and ad rates. It is this factor, actually, that I see as the biggest hidden benefit in this deal. When you consider how many teams are now either wholly or partially co-owned (or vice versa) with their broadcast outlets, the idea of pushing hardcore fans to watch the local nine seems to be a genius move.

The other landing point for the EI refugees will be MLB.tv, the online source for all televised games. For $80, you get roughly what EI offered, although on your computer screen without the ability to rapidly flip between games with online-video quality. This is not a comparable product. I used MLB.tv this year as an adjunct to, not a replacement for, Extra Innings. It was helpful when I was on the road or as a marriage saver, but it is not any kind of substitute for watching games on a television. Besides, from an aesthetic standpoint, who wants to relax at the end of the day while watching their monitor?

Nevertheless, MLB.tv will likely see a nice boost this year from people who cannot purchase the package. That's more direct revenue as a result of the new deal.

When you break it down, this decision is clearly the right one for MLB, which makes more money up front. The people it affects negatively have a series of options, albeit aggravating or inferior ones, and their pursuit of those options is likely to create additional revenue. The far-left-end users who will be hurt by DirecTV's exclusivity will also be the most vocal about their unhappiness, but at the same time, they are the ones least likely to be completely turned off of baseball.

Make no mistake: this is a fairly fan-hostile decision. However, MLB has proven that it will alienate a segment of the population in the short term to make more money in any term. This is comparable to the way in which teams have rushed to move their telecasts to new channels that they own. By doing so, they've instigated public pressure on cable companies to add that channel to their lineups, even when said channel has just three hours of valuable programming a day.

DirecTV is essentially going to be calling the same play. They will not only get a boost in dish ownership and subscriptions to EI, but there should be some benefit in the resulting demand for dish penetration in areas where regulations have kept the units out, a move likely to be led by disenfranchised baseball fanatics.

Michael, I'm sorry. This is a pretty good move for MLB across the board, with more hidden benefits than hidden costs. I sure hope I get to use channels 734-748 this year, but if I can't, I'm not going to be able to argue against the deal with anything but self-interest.

THE DAILY PROSPECTUS
Salary Cap
Joe Sheehan

The idea of a salary cap has become popular with many fans who believe it would bring lower ticket prices and greater competitive balance, but as Joe Sheehan contended, the only people who would stand to benefit from such a measure are the owners.

It has taken me three weeks to put together a coherent salary-cap column, because there are so many issues that come into play when trying to write about it. There's a mythology that surrounds the salary cap, one so ingrained in any discussion of the topic that to get through the layers of misconceptions takes the work off on a half-dozen tangents, all of which are informative and entertaining but which make for a difficult read.

So let's start with the basics about the salary cap, and actually, the term itself. The so-called "salary cap" is actually a payroll cap, or a labor-cost cap. Salaries are not limited on an individual basis, but by team, so the restriction is not on the players, but on the teams.

That's an important distinction. Were the more accurate term "payroll cap" used, the effects and intent of the tool would be more clear: to restrict the amount of money management can spend on labor. It's an agreement among competitors to inhibit the labor market, lowering salaries.

A salary cap transfers wealth from labor to management.

That's all it does, and that's all it's supposed to do. The nominally fan-friendly effects of a salary cap are either fictional, or secondary, weak ones. A salary cap merely keeps teams from bidding on labor past a certain point, regardless of the value of the available labor or the team's resources, with the effect of lowering salaries across the board.

The salary cap is a popular concept among many fans, for as best as I can tell, two reasons, both the result of heavy league and media proselytizing:

- The idea that a salary cap will lower the costs associated with attending games.
- The idea that a salary cap will lead to better competitive balance.
- Neither is true. The first case is probably the most important one, because it's the one that the leagues and its respective owners have spent years promoting.

The price of tickets is not set to recoup costs, but to maximize revenue.

If you take nothing else from this column; if you think I'm a blithering idiot unfit to spend time in the company of humans; if you'd rather I be carved up and sold for pennies a pound... believe the above statement. Send it to two friends. It's the single misconception most damaging to the public discourse on sports economics.

Prices are set by teams to maximize revenue and are based on anticipated demand. They are not set to "make up" whatever rise in payroll is anticipated, no matter how many teams send out letters to season-ticket holders claiming this to be the case. Rising player salaries do not drive ticket-price increases.

There are countless examples that show this, but the two I like best are major college sports—where the players are "paid" with scholarships and stipends, yet ticket prices are comparable to those in their professional counterparts—and the NBA and NFL, where a salary cap hasn't stopped a steady rise in ticket prices over the last 15 years. Baseball ticket prices are high because lots of people are going to baseball games. (I know corporate purchases, and the tax laws that drive them, are part of this equation. It's a topic for another day.)

For a salary cap to impact the price of tickets, you'd need something along the lines of a "revenue cap" to balance the scales. This would be a completely irrational solution, in part because implementation would be difficult, and in part because the market would correct for the lowered prices. There would be a huge secondary market in which tickets are priced according to demand, with the revenues going not to the teams themselves, but to the brokers in that market. There's no reason to implement a system that encourages this.

A salary cap isn't going to put money back in fans' pockets.

The notional impact of a salary cap on competitive balance comes from two places. One is the idea that a team's success is tied to its payroll. It's a wrong-headed one, driven by a number of factors, including the Yankees' success over the past seven years with a high payroll, the willingness of some teams at the low end of the revenue and payroll scales to suck up revenue-sharing dollars, and a whole host of convoluted statistics cooked up by the Blue Ribbon Panel of Experts Picked by Bud Selig to Produce a Report That Supported His Ideas With as Little Input From Unfriendlies as Possible.

There is no clear relationship between success and payroll, particularly at the high end of the scale. Spending gobs of money on baseball players doesn't guarantee success, even in the wild-card era, as recent performances by the Orioles, Mets, Dodgers, and Red Sox show. It is possible—if more difficult—to win while having a low payroll. The success of the A's and, at least in 2001, the Twins is evidence that even a vanishingly low payroll isn't an absolute barrier to success.

The interactions among payroll and success and market size and revenue and capitalization are complex. When you look at the big picture, at all the reasons why some teams are successful and some aren't, why some are high-revenue and some aren't, there's just no way to pick one solution—a salary cap—from the ether and say "this will make everything right."

Well, to some people there is: the NFL. The blessed NFL is held up as an example of a wildly successful league with a salary cap. The truth is that the NFL's nominal "competitive balance" is a function of a number of factors, including the shorter season, larger playoffs, fixed scheduling, and the greater impact of a reverse-order draft in a sport where players can make a more significant initial impact.

To the extent that the salary cap contributes to competitive balance, I would say that it works negatively: it punishes success, forcing well-built, winning teams to shed talent on a near-constant basis. It also makes it virtually impossible to trade, increasing the impact of a single catastrophic event in a league where teams cannot make adjustments on the fly. A system that punishes success rather than rewards it seems an odd construct for any endeavor, and it's one I have difficulty supporting.

The NFL is successful, and the NFL has a salary cap. Unless you're an owner, though, the case that the latter has been a cause of the former is awfully weak.

I'm really going to need to do an entire column on MLB v. NFL, because surface comparisons of the two don't advance the discussion much. Suffice to say that, "because the NFL has one" is a lousy reason to support a salary cap. The two entities share little more than green fields and space on the national stage.

What would the actual effects of a salary cap be, if one were implemented in Major League Baseball? Well, because the cap is generally tied to a specific percentage of revenue, the first thing you'd have to do is get MLB owners to be honest about their finances. That alone could take us into the 2020 season.

After I wrote my article on revenue sharing, a number of people made the claim that the money going from high-revenue to low-revenue teams would cause the low-revenue teams to become more active in player acquisition, increasing demand for lower-tier free agents and essentially keeping the amount of money going to the players constant. It's a nice theory, and it's popular among those who want to believe that 1) teams are aching to give players money and 2) the MLBPA actually has something to gain from a payroll restraint.

It's not likely to be the case, though, and in fact, this is why all salary cap plans come with a salary floor. There are plenty of team owners who don't want to spend more on players than they absolutely have to pay them. This would be especially true if revenue sharing increased enough to guarantee a profit for every team in the league.

Remember what we know about the distribution of talent in MLB: it's the right end of a bell curve, with a few great players at the extreme, more players with good talent towards the middle, and a near-endless supply of free, or replacement-level, talent. It's taken some time, but teams are beginning to recognize this, as we saw this winter.

Put another way, there is no "middle class" in baseball. You start young and cheap, and you either become older and expensive, or just older. Changing the distribution of revenue in baseball isn't going to change these things. If Jason Giambi makes $12 million per year instead of $17 million, Tino Martinez isn't still going to make $8 million just because the Reds, Devil Rays, and Royals all have some of the Yankees' money. The entire scale slides down; no "middle class" emerges just because the revenue is distributed differently. None should, because the salary scale should match the distribution of talent.

Any "demand effect" of the extra money going to lower-revenue teams is not going to cancel out the impact of what is happening at the top of the salary scale.

There are other reasons to oppose a salary cap, not the least of which is that it will make being a fan tedious. For an example of life under a cap, check out Bill Simmons's latest ESPN.com column. Baseball fans may complain about money now, but there is simply no way to talk trade in the NBA without retaining all kinds of ridiculous information, as well as the knowledge of cap rules that are, to understate the case, intricate.

The salary cap is the Holy Grail of sports ownership. If you can get one in your league, you lock in ungodly profits while eliminating risk. That is a perfectly good business plan, and it's hard to fault MLB and its member owners for doing everything they can to force one on the players.

Recognize, though, that the only people who gain anything from a salary cap are those member owners. A salary cap doesn't benefit fans, it doesn't benefit the game as a whole, and it doesn't do anything for competitive balance. It reduces the financial incentives to improve and innovate and succeed. Moreover, the pursuit of a salary cap has caused the leadership of MLB to relentlessly trash its product in an attempt to reach the ultimate goal. The anti-marketing of baseball, which has done more actual damage to the game than any economic system ever could, has one goal: get a salary cap.

DOCTORING THE NUMBERS
Worst. Contract. Ever.
Rany Jazayerli

After recounting some of the least favorable contracts signed by players over the years, Rany Jazayerli concluded that the worst player contract ever went to knuckleballer Tim Wakefield, and not just because he didn't negotiate a sufficiently high annual salary.

As sports fans, we love to make lists. They're easy to devise, they're always good for hours of heated debate, and they can be constantly revised and updated as current events dictate. Fans who wouldn't know Jose Tabata from Jose Cuervo nonetheless will argue whether, at #22, he's too high or too low on our Top 100 Prospects list.

And few lists are more fun to break out than the list of the worst free-agent contracts of all time. We love any excuse to mock owners for their reckless decisions; plus, as fans, we have a morbid sense of pride in having been forced to taste the bitter fruit of those moves. Darren Dreifort, Mike Hampton, Russ Ortiz, Barry Zito... okay, I guess we can reserve judgment on the last one for now. (Says the fan of the team who signed Gil Meche.)

But all of these lists are utterly one-sided—they look at the question only from the team's point of view. What about the reverse—the worst contract ever signed by the player? What player has screwed himself out of the most money by signing a deal that vastly underpaid him relative to what he was worth?

To answer this question, we have to define it a little better. Miguel Cabrera delivered an MVP performance last year for $472,000—obviously, he was underpaid, and just as obviously, he didn't sign a "bad" contract—he signed the only contract he could get with the leverage that he had. Which, as a zero-to-three player, was none. When we talk about a bad contract, we mean one that was signed when a player had other options at his disposal, such as signing with another team, or waiting another year until free agency.

(Also, I'm talking about terrible contracts that a player did sign. We'll have to save the list of players who turned down good contract offers because of an inflated sense of self-worth, then settled for an NRI offer two months later, for another day. So Jody Reed is safe.)

In general, contract negotiations are a zero-sum game; a good deal for the player is bad for the team, and vice versa. So we could start our search for the worst player contract by looking at the contracts that have been considered the model for teams to pursue, i.e. the John Hart model of signing players at the beginning of their arbitration years to long-term deals that buy out their first year or two of free agency, ideally with a team option year or two tacked onto the end.

Certainly, some of these deals have worked out very well for the teams, and the players that signed them have wound up with far less money than had they simply signed one-year deals every year. But in this case a good deal for the team doesn't have to be a bad deal for the player. Some contracts really are win-win. Travis Hafner, to pick a random example, will make $3.95 million this year, and $4.95 million next, per the terms of a four-year contract he signed before the 2005 season. Had Hafner not signed a long-term deal and was arb-eligible over the next two seasons, he likely would stand to make about twice as much money each year.

But was this really a terrible deal for Pronk? At the time he signed it, he had already agreed to a contract for 2005 that paid him $377,400, after making less than that the previous two years. Good money for you and me, but not nearly enough to guarantee a lifetime of financial security in the event of a career-ending injury or other worst-case scenario. By signing the contract, Hafner was guaranteed a minimum of $7 million over three years—enough money to insure that whatever post-baseball career he chose for himself wouldn't be for the money.

This is a form of what is called the St. Petersburg Paradox—people will sometimes make the rational decision to take a smaller amount of money that is guaranteed over a larger expectation of money that involves some risk. If I offered you the choice between one million dollars, or a 50/50 chance of winning 2.2 million dollars (and a 50/50 chance of winning nothing), most of you would take the guaranteed million. Why? Because that first million dollars would do a lot more to change your life (marginal utility) than the second million.

(Before you flood me with e-mails, I know that's not precisely what the St. Petersburg Paradox is about. Humor me here; I'm trying to make a point about baseball, not economic theory.)

Signing a long-term deal early in one's career not only can guarantee financial security, it sometimes can turn out to be a way for a player to cash in at the moment his perceived value peaks. Take Angel Berroa. (Please?)

So how would we define a baseball contract that was truly a terrible deal for the player? It would be signed by the player when he was a free agent, and so had complete leverage. It would be a deal signed at below-market value. And it would give the team that signed him the ability to keep the player at below-market rates for a long time, while not giving the player any security in return.

The first contract usually mentioned in the discussion of bad player contracts is the one Andruw Jones is about to complete. Not that I would turn my nose down if Prospectus Entertainment Ventures offered me a six-year, $75 million contract, but there's a good reason why the players union put up a mild ruckus when Jones signed the deal over the pleas of his agent, one Scott Boras. Jones was a year away from free agency when he signed before the 2002 season; he would have been, at age 25, the second-youngest major-league free agent (behind only Alex Rodriguez) in history; and he was the pre-eminent center fielder in the game at the time, at an age where he was still getting better. He probably left somewhere between 15 and 30 million dollars on the table he signed the contract on.

But even Jones' contract had mitigating circumstances. For one thing, he was young enough at the time that he has a chance to make amends when his contract expires next winter, when he will still be just 30 years old. He's made it clear that this time there will be no hometown discount.

So I have a new favorite candidate for title of "worst contract signed by a player." This one has no mitigating circumstances. It was signed less than two years ago, on April 19th, 2005, by a veteran pitcher who had already made his millions and who was a free agent at the time. This pitcher, who was about to complete a three-year deal that paid him a little north of $13 million, agreed to a one-year extension worth $4 million—a one-year deal, and a pay-cut, even though said pitcher had just gone 12-10 with a league-average ERA the year before. At the time he signed the extension, he had started the new season 2-0 with a 1.37 ERA; he would finish 16-12 with a 4.15 ERA.

That information alone is enough to place this contract among the worst ever. Then keep in mind that this pitcher had gone 22-12 the two years before that, with ERAs of 4.09 and 2.81 (the latter was fourth-best in the league). This pitcher was in his 13th major-league season and had never suffered a significant arm injury.

So let's see—an above-average major-league starting pitcher, showing no signs of decline, with a stellar health record, signs a one-year, $4 million deal. About the only good thing we can say is that he only had to wait another year to sign a better contract.

Oh, but if only Tim Wakefield's contract were that. If he had signed a one-year extension in 2005, he would have hit the market again this winter, and even though he went 7-11 with a 4.63 ERA and suffered an oblique injury that limited him to 140 innings, he undoubtedly would have taken advantage of the wacky market for pitchers this winter, possibly even doubling his salary. Whom would you rather have over the next three years: Wakefield or Miguel Batista?

(Wakefield is 40 years old, but in non-knuckleballer years that's about 35. Charlie Hough threw over 200 innings of league-average ball when he was 45; Phil Niekro was an All-Star at age 45.)

But Wakefield not only signed a 1-year, $4 million deal (with a little over $1 million in incentives), he gave the Red Sox a perpetual option on the contract. I can't overemphasize how astonishing that is. The Red Sox can keep renewing Wakefield's contract, one year at a time, for the same salary, from now until forever. In return, Wakefield gets—um, absolutely nothing. The moment he loses it, the Red Sox can cut him, with no buyout and no future contract obligations.

In effect, Wakefield has bonded himself to the Red Sox franchise for the remainder of his career, without being compensated one iota for his allegiance. We used to have a term for this type of contract in the annals of baseball history. What was it... oh yeah, we called it the Reserve Clause.

Wakefield has essentially turned back 35 years of bitterly-fought labor victories by the players union. He has signed a one-year contract with a perpetual option to renew. To the best of my knowledge, since the dawn of free agency, no player has signed a comparable contract. (The Royals dished out "lifetime contracts" to players like George Brett and Dan Quisenberry in the early 1980s, but those contracts were less like the Reserve Clause and more like business partnerships—the players became real estate investment partners with then part-owner Avron Fogelman.)

I understand the stated reasons why Wakefield signed the contract: he loved Boston, he loved the team, and he wanted to pitch for them for the remainder of his career. So he made the team an offer they couldn't refuse.

I understand that Wakefield's contract was an expression of loyalty to his team. But what about the team's expression of loyalty to him? If Wakefield had signed the same one-year contract and made it clear to the Red Sox that he would be interested in continuing his employment under the same terms indefinitely, he would have shown the exact same amount of loyalty, while keeping his options open for a worst-case scenario.

Walter Alston is in the Hall of Fame, and deservedly so, with four world championships and seven NL pennants dotting his resume. He never worked with a multi-year contract, having famously signed 23 one-year contracts in a row to serve as manager of the Dodgers. Alston was famous for his loyalty to the team and to owner Walter O'Malley, but he showed that loyalty in part because O'Malley was equally loyal to him.

If O'Malley had sold the team to George Steinbrenner's meaner, more penurious brother, Alston could have bolted at any time. But if kind old John Henry sells his stake in the team to, say, Larry Dolan, Wakefield is just going to have to suck it up and do whatever new manager Isiah Thomas tells him to.

(Let's hope that Wakefield at least received a no-trade clause in return, so that he can't be forced to show his loyalty to the Nationals instead. But if there is a no-trade clause, we haven't heard about it.)

Loyalty is a two-way street. Wakefield's decision to give the Red Sox ownership of his baseball career isn't loyalty, it's capitulation.

Still, as irrational as Wakefield appears to be for signing this deal, I have to admit there's something oddly endearing about it. Sports are, in a purely utilitarian sense, irrational. Love is irrational. It's hard not to be at least a little impressed when a sports figure professes his love for his team, his teammates, and his fans by making such an irrational decision.

If nothing else, the next time someone bemoans the state of modern sports, spouting off the usual nonsense about how today's players are mercenaries whose only loyalty is to Ben Franklin, let them know that out in New England, there's a player who has offered his fan base one of the purest and most expensive forms of loyalty ever seen from a professional athlete.

Everyone knows that the Red Sox are blessed to have revenue streams that non-Yankee teams can only dream about, one that allows them to go to war every year with a nine-figure payroll. But in employing the services of one of the most underrated starting pitchers of our generation at 50 cents to the dollar—with no downside risk to speak of—they have another sizeable, if unseen, advantage.

As an analyst, I think Tim Wakefield is nuts. As a fan, I just wished he pitched for my team.

SIX-FOUR-THREE
Weighin' in at 19 Stone, Part One
Gary Huckabay

In the first part of a rambling discussion with two team executives, Gary Huckabay discussed the smartest teams, the life of a front office employee, and how to break into the game.

I recently sat down to talk with two executives, one from an AL club, and one from a NL club. They agreed to the interview only if their identities were protected. Also, in the interests of full disclosure, the executives had final edits of their statements in this two-part interview. To answer the inevitable questions, no, I won't tell you who these guys are, nor are you the only person to email in, either asking for their names, or certain you know who they are.

GH: Okay, let's get this out of the way at the very beginning. The two of you have been kind enough to agree to sit down and talk with us, and we really appreciate it. Our readers enjoy these conversations a great deal, and I always get a bunch of emails trying to find out the identities of the front office execs who sit down with us. So, just to set the record straight, has either of you ever worked, in any capacity for Baseball Prospectus?

NL Exec: No, I've never made that kind of money.

AL Exec: No, so your posse is safe.

GH: Excellent. Okay, let's get started. I'd like your opinion on the front offices that have done the best job this year, and why. And don't be falsely modest.

NL Exec: Believe it or not, I think the Oakland team's done very well.

AL Exec: Oh, come on.

NL Exec: No, I'm serious. They've been destroyed by injuries, and they're within breathing distance of .500. They're not going to win the World Series, but Forst and Beane have done great. They lost Loaiza, the Harden kid, Crosby, Chavez, Street, and they keep finding guys like Gaudin, Hannahan, and Buck. That's good work, no matter what the results end up being. And Jack Cust has worked out great for them.

AL Exec: I see it another way. Two ways, really. They were in trouble because of some really bad contracts. Kendall was a total disaster, and if they'd done their homework there, they wouldn't have gotten him. I know the perception's different, but Beane's hurt himself with some pretty bad contracts. Remember Terrence Long?

GH: What's the other way?

AL Exec: Not valuing durability highly enough. It's a good thing to have a bunch of talent, but you've got to have dependability, too. It's not surprising to see Crosby, Harden, and Chavez out with injuries, is it? If you have a portfolio of six guys that are very good but fragile, that might be enough, but it might not. Everyone knows Chris Snelling can play if he's healthy. And everyone knows he'll never be healthy. He's just not.

GH: So who'd you nominate for best 2007 front office work?

AL Exec: Maybe Arizona, Milwaukee, or Cleveland.

GH: Why?

AL Exec: It's not a fluke that Arizona's way outperforming what they should be doing in terms of runs scored and allowed. Having a real outlier bullpen, one way or another, will distort the team's performance relative to expectations. That should be obvious, but it's not talked about enough in the blogs. The reason is simple. If you have great relievers, you can control their tactical deployment, and use them in higher-leverage situations. You can't control when your sluggers will hit home runs. You can't know, in advance, when your number one starter is going to have his dominant stuff. But you always know the score of the game. And the Snakes have shown they know how to do that.

GH: Okay, so the D-Backs understand the value of leverage and have multiplied the amplitude of their strength. What about Cleveland and Milwaukee?

AL Exec: Look at the young talent Milwaukee has. It's not 2007 front office work, really, but it's pretty impressive—that's some serious scouting. Cleveland took a bunch of good gambles. Two of them, Dellucci and Nixon, haven't worked out, but that's really just bad luck. And not many teams could survive having their core offensive guy just totally tanking for the year. Hafner's not a much different hitter than Pujols, and where would the Cardinals be if he [Pujols] fell off the face of the earth for a year?

NL Exec: I think they re-upped him to a deal that will look cheap a year from now, too.

AL Exec: If he was just hiding a one-year injury. If not, it's going to hurt.

GH: Let's talk about Barry Bonds.

NL Exec: Do we have to?

AL Exec: He'll play 110 games next year, start 65 as a DH.

GH: Where?

AL Exec: Won't step over the line on anything close to tampering. Uh-uh.

NL Exec: Sorry, you're the press.

GH: You'll have total anonymity!

NL Exec: We'd only be guessing anyway.

AL Exec: Next question.

GH: Hmph. What do you think would surprise our readers the most about your jobs?

NL Exec: Probably the hours. I don't know how it is everywhere else, but I work pretty much around the clock. Always have, since I've been in the game. And as you move up to higher positions than mine, it only gets worse. I know that policemen have problems keeping their families together because of the stress, but the same goes for our [jobs]. I don't know too many people whose marriage can stand the hours of the jobs. We've always got tons of stuff to work on, and we never have enough people to do the work. Never. Not even close. You talk about scientific decision-making a lot, and that's kind of your thing, but a lot of times, you don't have the time necessary to do that kind of studying on something. You have to move, and everything's always a fire drill.

AL Exec: I agree. I think everyone knows we work a lot of hours, but when we say 'A lot of hours,' we're not talking about 50 hours a week. Things kind of come and go. There are weeks where I actually sleep in the office with a duffel bag of clothes. We really can work 90, 100 hours a week, and that's out of 168 in a week to do everything, including eat, sleep, and go to the bathroom. But there are quiet times, too. Most of those are during the season.

GH: How do the decisions about players get made in your office?

AL Exec: In our office, guys like me respond to requests that can come at any time when we're considering a tender or a pickup or something. I put together an information packet, which gets passed up the line. Usually, the decisions are discussed by several people above my pay grade. It gets kind of complicated, because it's never a question of "should we get this particular guy?" It's usually picking the best available option out of a whole bunch, and I haven't been privy to most of those discussions. The ones I have been involved in have been pretty thorough, and the money usually complicates things.

GH: Always does.

NL Exec: I think it's a little bit different for us—the money doesn't enter into it as much. Not because we're the Yankees or anything, but because there's a pretty close relationship between the baseball up-or-down guy [*GH Note: that's a decision maker*] and the finance people. I've seen other teams have to make decisions all the time where they have to decide on, say, a second baseman, and they're looking at four possible candidates, and they don't know how much two of them will cost, or for how long. That would be hard, and I've seen that from the outside.

AL Exec: And that's one of the big differences between baseball, or really any entertainment, and other businesses. Can you imagine buying a house where you've narrowed it down to three houses, and you knew two of their locations, and two of their prices, leaving certainty for only one house, and then having someone point a gun to your head to decide on which one to buy? It's messed up, but it's the way things are.

NL Exec: The agents make it that way.

AL Exec: They certainly don't make it easier.

GH: How much contact do you have with agents?

AL Exec: I don't have much. I talk with them occasionally, and it's usually one of the people in the office, rather than the specific agent.

NL Exec: I have some, but it's usually on behalf of someone who has been DFA'd and is scrambling for a job somewhere. There's a pretty substantial network of friends and people you just talk to more. Some are agents, some are GMs, some are scouts. That's probably true anywhere, though. I mean, if you have 20 people at Baseball Prospectus, how many do you talk to on a very regular basis, and how do you learn about things? So the people in the agency that know me, they talk to me, and I talk to them.

GH: Come to think of it, those kind of informal networks do track exceptionally well with communication patterns. And to answer your question, the people I talk most with at BP are Nate Silver, Joe Sheehan, Dave Pease, and Will Carroll. And there's about 40 people total, I think. Interesting.

AL Exec: One big difference is that you're paid more than we are.

NL Exec: Stone.

GH: Stone?

NL Exec: I agree completely. You're old.

GH: I may be old, but I've never heard that expression.

AL Exec: I haven't, either. But I'll use it from now on.

GH: I've heard salary horror stories and had an offer that I couldn't come close to accepting, but is there really a massive difference compared to what you could make elsewhere?

AL Exec: Yes, absolutely. But I have fewer expenses, too. Since I have no time, I don't spend any money. And I can't remember the last time I paid for food at lunch or dinner. But I'd easily give up the extra $50,000 a year I could make somewhere else for the life I have now. You just can't beat it. No way. It's as cool and fun as people dream it is, and there's thousands of qualified people who would take my job at half the salary I make now. Which is why I don't get paid much.

NL Exec: For me, there's not that much of a difference. I never considered doing anything else, so I really don't know what I could make elsewhere.

GH: I still get probably 50 emails a month from people wanting to break into the game. Most of them have perseverance to offer over qualifications. Is that enough?

NL Exec: If they have an 'in,' and a reference that someone will actually read, then it might be enough in the right circumstances. But they've got to know that if they can do that, so can everyone else, and we get people that dedicated with college degrees from MIT every week. So that guy's going to get a look first. But there's also just not that many job openings.

AL Exec: I can only say that for us, it's not enough. We get at least a hundred unsolicited resumes a month, in a slow month. If it didn't get handed to us by someone we trust who's willing to vouch for the guy, it won't get a serious look.

GH: Is it always guys?

AL Exec: I don't remember a woman's resume showing up this year, but there were a couple last year.

NL Exec: We get a lot from women—maybe five, 10 a month.

GH: Hired any?

NL Exec: No, but no men either, at least recently.

GH: I'll ask this, knowing I won't get an answer.

AL Exec: You already destroyed our consulting budget. No, we don't want your study.

GH: Darn. My question is about discrimination. Do you see it, at your club or others?

AL Exec: I really don't. I'll grant you that there's a lot of white guys in the game and that hiring tends to go that way. But I don't see it as racist, or sexist, or discriminatory. The hiring and promotion is so much based on relationships and comfort. Loyalty is everything in this game. I'm loyal to the guy that hired me, and the guys I've worked with, so if I move on and have hiring authority, I'm going to want to bring someone in who I know does work well, and who I'm comfortable with.

NL Exec: That's part of the hours thing. If you're working as much as we are, in close quarters, you absolutely have to get along with your friends on the team. Otherwise, work becomes a bad place to be, and you can't do that if you're spending more than half your life at work.

AL Exec: Exactly. And so if someone moves, they try to bring in the people they know, which is one reason you see movement of people, rather than an influx of new people. It's all driven by connections.

NL Exec: How many calls and emails have you made on behalf of your guys, trying to introduce them to people and singing their praises?

GH: I don't know. Probably a hundred.

NL Exec: Why?

GH: Because I want to help.

AL Exec: See? There you go. How many of those people have been African-American or female?

GH: None.

AL Exec: That's all part of it. And let me ask you this: How many of the people you've made calls for are highly skilled?

GH: All of them. Wouldn't make the calls otherwise.

AL Exec: Because your reputation is on the line.

GH: Sure. If I recommend or introduce a bozo, then I take a credibility hit. The communication network is more complex than that, too, as you know.

AL Exec: So the team adds someone great, but the diversity isn't there.

NL Exec: And think of how many people there are like you, making those calls, passing on resumes, IMing about how great someone is. You're not even an insider, but you can get an ear of someone. Think of how many people there are in your shoes. We get calls and resumes and lunches out with agents, sports information directors, people from other teams, broadcasting teams, local sportscasters, radio guys—it never stops. And most of the time, they're pushing a pretty well-qualified white guy.

AL Exec: Almost always. So if I get a resume and a note from you for some 22-year-old kid who just graduated Pepperdine, where he played ball, and worked as an intern for you on research projects, I'm going to read his resume. But if it arrives in a stack, no chance.

NL Exec: You're just more likely to be pushing someone who's white and male. You just are. There's no grand plot, it just works out that way.

GH: Do you think clubs need to do more in terms of building a more diverse management mix, in terms of race and gender?

AL Exec: I think that if there's going to be progress made on that, it's going to take a considered, planned effort, really. We really do try, but as I said earlier, that takes time, and it makes it more likely that you'll make a bad hire, because you won't necessarily have someone vouching for someone.

GH: Whoa, whoa, whoa—I want to clarify this, so you don't get pilloried because of a lack of context. You're not suggesting that a woman or a minority is more likely to be a bad hire, right? You're suggesting that anyone, regardless of race, gender, sexual preference, religious affiliation, political affiliation, or affiliation affiliation who doesn't come with a trusted recommendation is more likely to be a bad hire?

AL Exec: Yes, that's right. And we're not going to edit that out or ever release my name, right?

GH: Absolutely.

NL Exec: It's all about the networking. True everywhere.

SIX-FOUR-THREE
Weighin' in at 19 Stone, Part Two
Gary Huckabay

In the second part of a far-reaching discussion with two team executives, Gary Huckabay discussed baseball's standing relative to other sports, the relationships between teams and agents, and what aspects of the game were and were not working.

I recently sat down to talk with executives from an AL Club and an NL Club. They agreed to the interview only if their identities were protected. In the interest of full disclosure, the executives had final edits of their statements in this two-part interview. To answer the inevitable questions, yes, this is an easy way for me to generate content, but readers seem to like it, and no, I won't tell you who these guys are, nor are you the only person to email in, either asking for their names, or letting me know how certain you are about who they are.

GH: I'd like to talk a little bit about the overarching trends in baseball.

AL Exec: Like what?

GH: Let's talk about baseball's standing in the public relative to other sports. I first kind of revived my interest in this during a phone call with Gary Gillette about five years ago. Before that, I didn't worry about it. Since then, it's been clawing at me some. So I'd like your opinions on the subject. Does baseball have a problem of eroding support, with the rise of the NFL, NASCAR, and all the other sporting enterprises that have been filling the ever-increasing media? If so, what would you suggest be done about it?

AL Exec: That's not something that I should be focusing on in my job.

NL Exec: I don't think there's a problem. I know that's a minority opinion, but I don't think there's anything to worry about. Like you said, there's more and more new outlets for media all the time. Before the internet, there was cable TV, which started sucking viewers away from the big networks. Now, there's literally hundreds of channels, more coming, an infinite number of channels on the web, XM Radio, and even more live events and competing baseball leagues. I think Major League Baseball is still a very big dog and will continue to be so. Maybe there's a problem coming, but if that's true, it's not unique to baseball. Everyone's seeing the effects of it.

AL Exec: It could be a lot worse—we could be the record companies.

NL Exec: Sons of Napster have killed them.

AL Exec: As I've heard someone say, it used to be the job of the record companies to completely screw over artists. Now the general public has taken over that job, and the record companies are pissed.

GH: Is there a similar threat to baseball?

AL Exec: I really don't think so. No matter what else is true, people's eyes light up when they learn they're going to a ballgame. They can be any age, root for any team, and they still want to go to the game, get a hot dog and a beer. And if you think about, baseball is the original and best reality show. It's unscripted, the outcome is truly in doubt, there's a kind of long drama to it that you can't get from a movie, play, or TV, and there's a natural pull on people's emotions. I still go to as many games as I can, and I still bitch and moan about trades my team should make, even when I know why they don't happen.

GH: That's cool. It leads me to another question: Are either of you working for your boyhood favorite team?

NL Exec: No.

AL Exec: No.

GH: So how long did the transition take to start rooting, in your heart of hearts, for the teams you work for now, even when playing your favorite team?

AL Exec: I still haven't.

NL Exec: No way!

AL Exec: No, I'm serious. I don't wear the colors anymore, since I don't want to lose my job or any teeth, but deep down, I still root for my boyhood team, even against us.

NL Exec: Dude, that's not normal! For me, it took about a week, until I started to meet everyone at my office. Normal friendships develop, and my hometown team is just as much a target as everyone else. It kind of feels like they're a girlfriend that dumped me. In a lot of ways, I like beating them more than anybody else.

AL Exec: You might want to edit that, right? It's going to read like you enjoy beating your girlfriend.

GH: Um, I'll just leave in that sentence, that way we're covered. And besides, what woman in their right mind would date him?

NL Exec: I never had much luck with women in their right mind anyway.

GH: Moving on, one common thing I hear is a kind of disparagement of agents. Is that just a kind of "Us versus Them" foxhole mentality, or is there a basis for those sentiments? Or am I just misreading it, and that attitude isn't pervasive?

NL Exec: I think it's a little of both. I don't usually deal directly with an agent, but they definitely have an agenda. That's their job—they may be friendly, but if they're friendly, they're friendly with a purpose, you know what I mean? I think they're all pretty ethical, really, but there are some exceptions. Based on their behavior, there are some agencies that I personally wouldn't deal with. Even if I could get Alex Rodriguez for the league minimum.

AL Exec: I think there's absolutely a basis for those sentiments, and at least with me, those feelings are very real. There are some good eggs, but I've been lied to on multiple occasions. And when you call them on it, they treat it like it's all just part of the game. It's not. We are playing a kid's game here, but outright lying to make a few extra bucks is fraud. And maybe there are some clubs that do that, but I've never seen it from a club, and I have seen it from agencies, both from the agents and the assistants. I can say that my boss incurs a real cost from that kind of shitty behavior.

GH: Can you explain the cost?

AL Exec: Can't take what they say at face value, so everything has to be verified. Which means that unless there's some extreme reason we have to deal with that group, we don't.

NL Exec: Which only really screws that agent's clients. Because there's always more than one option.

GH: Are there a lot of agents you won't deal with? And who are the bad apples?

AL Exec: Just one group for me, but no way in hell you get their name.

NL Exec: More than that for me, but I won't name names. Everyone knows the bad ones.

GH: So why not share the name with our readers?

AL Exec: If your readers can figure out who I am, find my home, clean my gutters, paint my house, wax my car, wash the dog, unclutter my garage, and stock my fridge with Dr. Brown's, I'll tell them.

GH: So let's go the other way: If you had a son who was coming out of college, who would you want him to sign with?

NL Exec: Scott Boras.

AL Exec: Scott Boras.

GH: OK, I'll admit to being surprised by that, since I assumed he was someone on your 'bad guy' list.

NL Exec: I think there are some clubs that it'd hurt you with, and he certainly makes some strategy blunders, but I've never run into a client of his that's been unhappy.

GH: A lot of people have left him, though, right?

AL Exec: I think Barry Bonds did, but I'm not sure. I do know that those guys are on top of everything. Great chess players want to play Kasparov or young Bobby Fischer, right?

GH: I suppose. Is Boras that much better than everyone else?

NL Exec: I don't know everybody else for sure, but... well, yes.

AL Exec: I think so. Part of it is that whoever you deal with from that office, they're always prepared. Always. Always.

GH: OK, running out of time a little bit—can I get some thoughts on one thing in the game you absolutely think is working well, and one thing that you'd like to change?

NL Exec: Slotting guidelines for the draft completely and totally suck the big one. Completely and totally stupid, unnecessary, counterproductive, and ultimately expensive.

GH: Why, and why can't you just ignore the guidelines?

NL Exec: Because they operate under the assumption that all draft classes are created equal. In years where there's just no talent, why should I pay the same for the #18 pick who's never going to be a starter as in a year where I can grab some fireballer that late? It's also insulting. It implies that we're too dumb to do the homework on our own. We have great scouts. Great. We can tell when a guy is worth the money or when he's not.

GH: So can't you just ignore them?

NL Exec: You're talking to the wrong guy. I think we absolutely should ignore them, completely.

AL Exec: There's an awful lot of pressure to adhere to the guidelines.

GH: In what form?

AL Exec: I'm saving my time to talk about my pet peeve.

GH: OK, fire away.

AL Exec: Umpiring.

GH: Seriously?

AL Exec: Absolutely. Ball- and strike-calling sucks, and umpires are way too in-your-face. They also hold grudges like you wouldn't believe. It's OK for them to always have the last word, or change the strike zone depending on whether or not they have dinner reservations, but if one of the players goes the same place, that guy's going to pay, with all the umpires, for a long time.

GH: You don't think it's better than it used to be?

AL Exec: I don't know about longer than I've been in the game, but I think it's getting worse, not better. The exceptions among the umpires are the good ones, not the bad ones, at least in terms of calling balls and strikes. There's also some that are real professionals whom you can have respect for. Kerwin Danley. Gary Cederstrom.

NL Exec: I think you're overstating it. Most of them are outstanding and professional in how they go about their work.

AL Exec: No way. They've been more and more mouthy, which is exactly the opposite of their jobs.

NL Exec: No. Their job, first, is to make sure no one gets hurt because of unsafe conditions, then to be consistent in dealing with both clubs.

AL Exec: No! That's not their job, and that's part of the problem—we accept bad performance as a good job! Being consistent, if you suck, isn't a good thing!

NL Exec: That's completely unreasonable! When some tool ballplayer starts insulting you personally, and you take it for 30 weeks a year, day in and day out, you can't expect guys not to push back! And they should push back! Throw more guys out, and there'll be less of that crap! Ask the pitchers and hitters! All they want from the umps is a consistent strike zone and that they be in position!

AL Exec: Umps don't get their own personal strike zone! We've got a dominant number-one starter, and depending entirely on whether a particular ump is pitching, I can absolutely tell you whether or not he's going to get shelled or kick ass! That's wrong! The rulebook has a defined strike zone—it should be called!

NL Exec: It is called! They can't be 100 percent perfect!

AL Exec: Then get Questec rolled out as fast as possible, so we can move a couple generations down the road and get the zone actually called, rather than just be a f—-ing suggestion!

NL Exec: You must be kidding! Questec sucks! The way it's set up, it'll never work, because it can't! The hitter and catcher will always be in the way, or will manage to beat the system.

AL Exec: As opposed to the home plate ump, whose view is blocked, and whose eyes are off anyway? Can you tell how fast a car is going by standing directly in front of it? So what makes you think you can track a pitch that way?

GH: This is great, but I'd like to hear what's working.

AL Exec: Interleague play. More lame-ass NL teams on our schedule, please. Can't get enough of those easy wins.

GH: Um, OK. That's what we're going with?

AL Exec: I'll stand by it. The NL was dominant in the Sixties and Seventies. Big Red Machine and all that. Right now, the yawner AL teams would be in contention in the NL, and teams like the Red Sox and Yankees might win 110 games.

NL Exec: First, I want to thank you publicly, as I promised I would, for exposing me to King's X. I now own all their CDs and will be attending my first live show when they come around next year.

GH: You are welcome, and a gentleman of your word. What's working, and what's your favorite King's X album?

NL Exec: *Dogman*, and what's working is Advanced Media. MLB.com is doing great stuff, and it's promising enough that there's peace among the clubs and among the players. I like not having to worry about fallout from that stuff.

GH: Guys, thanks very much for the time, the insight, and the excellent musical taste. From one of you anyway. Creed, really? That just ain't right.

AL Exec: Hey, I'm man enough to stand up for good music.

GH: I'll print that without comment, as none would be sufficient. You're the type of person who adds an umlaut to Hanson to look cool.

AL Exec: Hope you're enjoying that job at, what is it, a bank?

TRANSACTION ANALYSIS
Cleaning Out the Front Office
Christina Kahrl

When Paul DePodesta was fired by the Dodgers and Theo Epstein appeared (for the first time) to be leaving Boston, Christina Kahrl took stock of where the sabermetric revolution stood inside the game.

BOSTON RED SOX
Announced a failure to reach an agreement with General Manager Theo Epstein, making him a free agent executive. [10/31]

LOS ANGELES DODGERS
Fired General Manager Paul DePodesta. [10/29]

The revolution is dead, long live the revolution.... now wait a minute, what the hell is going on here, and since when? If you thought it was Turn Back the Clock Day at the Congress of Vienna, when Old Europe tried to pretend that revolutions hadn't happened, then you'll be even more impressed by this new trend in ignorance on the diamond. But in this, baseball is only imitating the days in which it is played.

In case you've missed the events of the last 72 hours, counterrevolution is the fashion, and as our own Will Carroll has put it, the weapon of choice is the White Sox. Skip however smug and frequently fact-free interpretations of why the White Sox won are—maybe it's just me, but "pitching, defense and the three-run home run" was Earl Weaver's formula, not Gene Mauch's. However much Ozzieball is a put-up job, it's manna from heaven for the industry's old guard, a generation of men grown jealous in recent years over the credit heaped upon the game's up-and-coming wave of general managers.

However unnecessary the "rivalry" between old-school baseball and the next generation of management techniques could and should have been, that struggle has taken on a life of its own. In this sort of contest, the scorecard is not one that counts whether DePo and Theo were both general managers of teams in the postseason in 2004, or one that records that Epstein's Red Sox did something that Gorman's or Duquette's did not. Success is apparently not the measure of success, it is instead what the now-unfashionable smart kids were damned well supposed to deliver, and the moment that they didn't, they were there to be scapegoated.

These are not the same stories, this particular tale of two cities, but I would suggest that both team's decisions to make changes at the top reflect a battle over fundamentals, not just over the way the game is operated, but how it is supposed to be remembered, and more basically, who is supposed to be remembered. In Beantown, the capacity for jealousy is what poisoned what was supposed to be a model for success in contemporary front office management. Sadly, a team president seems unusually insecure over his place in history. But when America was treated to the bizarre spectacle of Tom Werner, the man who Huizenganated San Diego baseball, suddenly sharing in the credit for Boston's victory in 2004, we were reminded of the truth in the adage that victory has many fathers, while defeat is an orphan.

In Larry Lucchino, we have a man who long ago cultivated the legend that he's somehow solely responsible for Camden Yards, and devil take those who remember otherwise. Especially those who might recall his stated desire from the time, which was to tear down the warehouse that today is the signature feature of Baltimore's ballpark. Such a man is jealous of his place in history, coveting the past and the present as comfortably as he feigns disinterest in taking up Czar Bud's scepter the day after the car salesman steps down. In his need to portray himself as the father of victory, he has instead become like Cronus, so jealous of his prerogatives that he would rather consume the future than truly shepherd it. He came to Boston with a reputation for self-promotion, and this latest incident makes it plain that in Lucchino's world, he's the star of his own show.

As for events in L.A., whether you're a boomer on the beat or a frustrated fan of the boys in blue, it's an easy exercise to gleefully blame these newfangled ideas for this past season's failures. We've already had to endure a season's worth of uncomprehending screeching from the likes of Bill Plaschke, but Plaschke was merely the point man in a media crowd ready to blame failure on a willingness to take risks. Such a racket seemed to overlook that DePodesta's willingness to take risks is what helped the Dodgers win their division in 2004. For whatever reason, some people never got over trading Paul Lo Duca or Guillermo Mota and were only too ready to blame DePo's willingness to upgrade his ballclub as some sort of shortcoming.

But in letting those complaints make him wonder about what was going on with his ballclub and then subsequently taking too seriously the counsels of men like Tommy Lasorda, team owner Frank McCourt betrayed the quality that has been feared from the start as his stewardship's symbolic signature: weakness. But where before his shallow pockets were supposed to be the source of his problems, McCourt has added a more basic weakness of character. By gutlessly catering to the local media harpies, McCourt ignored the unhappy accidents that reduced the Dodgers to also-rans and fudged his commitment to a sharp GM with the ability to build a winner.

McCourt has instead chosen to kowtow to the memory of the Pastaman, but all he will get for his troubles is a mouthful of wet noodle. That, and the canny wisdom of the man who dumped Paul Konerko and then tried to cover his tracks by making up a career-ending injury that, last I checked, never did end up keeping Konerko off of the diamond. And did I mention Pedro Martinez, a fact which has left Pedro bitter to this day?

The poisonous synergy between baseball's old guard and media figures only too ready to rely upon them for the peculiarly dopey "inside dope" is a significant component of this backlash. Both are motivated by careerism, and both stand to lose a lot to what will inevitably be characterized as the "Moneyball" generation of GMs. Again, baseball reflects the times in which we live, an age where the historical actors and the fourth estate interact in such a way that each simultaneously perverts and supports the purposes of the other. Journalists consider their jobs to be no more than the regurgitation of the information they're handed, either from every baseball club's increasingly polished media relations department, or courtesy of some unnamed inside source.

It doesn't matter that such sourcing is transparent, whether it's Bob Nightengale's reliance on tales told by two owners named Jerry or Dan Shaughnessy playing Howdy Doody to fulfill the desire of a Larry To Be Named Later to play "who's your daddy." The '90s showed us that careers involving hopping up and dancing on laps were lucrative; little did we know it was journalism that was the real growth industry on that score. Face it, whether you're a columnist or you're on the beat, once you've settled in, it's not only easy to settle for repeating what you're told, it spares you a lot of the lame daily exercise that goes with chasing down stale pre- and post-game quotes. Nobody thinks of affording themselves the opportunity to pursue actual storylines, like the events of a game (you know, the news event), or assessing a team's performance using facts. Such things simply are not done.

But however bad that content, or however transparent its craven quality, however standard-issue the bilge may be, that bilge possesses an addictive quality all its own to the subjects of such attention. Insulated within their profession, baseball management, on the field or off, is notoriously tin-eared. It's this that links these two decisions, whether it is Lucchino's jealousy of the credit given to his one-time protege, or McCourt's fear of being singled out for not being a good "baseball guy" for hiring one of those damned kids. In both cases, the elder man has betrayed his responsibilities to the future to hoard the worthless kudos of fickle friends. In each case, I would suggest they have made life easier for their division rivals in the long term. In the short term, whoever inherits the Dodgers has a great chance to look good for a year before being forced to rely on his own judgement. As for the immediate future for whoever goes to Boston, I think it's much less rosy: whoever goes in is going to have to have plenty of Blistex on hand to keep the Bossling happy, while having very little actual control over the franchise.

And what of the so-called revolution? It won't go away, in the same way that I'd argue that it never did in the first place. The game's mechanics just aren't that complicated once you've mastered the waiver rules and built up the contacts to be able to assemble a management and player development team that can run an entire organization. What the current disappearances of figures like Epstein and DePodesta from the stage represent is the object lesson that in the future it's going to be better to be the stathead in scout's clothing, someone who walks the old-school walk but whose actions will be an informed blend of Moneyball sensibilities and traditional player evaluation. The next-gen GM who can do that is the one who will slip under the radar long enough to build, win, and stay, no differently than the original artifact, Billy Beane, has in Oakland.

LIES, DAMNED LIES
A Mulligan on Guzman
Nate Silver

Nate Silver's discovery that teams were willing to pay a premium for star talent, spurred by a bad call on Cristian Guzman, prompted him to create a new framework for evaluating player earnings called "Market Value Over Replacement Player," or MORP.

You folks have long memories. I've already gotten several sarcastic comments about an article of mine that made the claim that Cristian Guzman was the best free-agent signing of the past winter. Although it will be nice to receive that Christmas card from the Bowdens, this obviously doesn't rank among the highlights of my analytical career. At least the Phillies almost made the playoffs this year.

I do try to be accountable when I get an aberrant result like this one, to see if there is anything wrong with the method that produced it. Guzman, certainly, had a worse season than most anyone might have anticipated. His .219/.260/.314 batting line was a dead match for PECOTA's .226/.260/.315 10th-percentile projection. The real problem, however, was in the field, where he lost a Kevin Garnett-sized step, going from a +14 FRAA player to a -11. Nobody was claiming that Guzman would have a breakout season—on the contrary, PECOTA gave him a 31 percent collapse rate. But a premium glove at shortstop is worth something, and his deal looked comparatively better than the likes of Orlando Cabrera's, who got twice as much money for being essentially the same player.

To be frank, however, that result also looked pretty aberrant before the season even began. Coming into the year, Guzman was a flag-bearer for what might be called the "sub-premium" group of players—those players who are notionally better than replacement level but no better than average in a good season. (If Guzman were a beer, he'd be Miller High Life). A lot of Guzman's fellow sub-premium players fared well in my free agent analysis—Corey Koskie, David Eckstein, Damian Miller, and so forth. It would seem that either the market is undervaluing these players, or my analysis is overvaluing them.

I decided to re-run my analysis with a couple of new wrinkles:

- In order to get a better sense of how things look on the wrong side of the tracks, all free agent signings of the past winter were considered, and not just those that met some minimum salary threshold. The only exceptions were minor-league deals.

- Rather than use PECOTA to project performance, I reverted to a "naive" projection system. This system establishes a player's baseline WARP projection based on a simple weighted average of his WARP scores over the past three seasons, with 2004 weighted at 50 percent, 2003 at 30 percent, and 2002 at 20 percent. We then knock five percent off a player's baseline for each year past the age of 29, and an additional five percent for each year past the age of 32. Here's Adrian Beltre's projection, for example:

2005 (26)	6.6 WARP
2006 (27)	6.6 WARP
2007 (28)	6.6 WARP
2008 (29)	6.3 WARP (-5%)
2009 (30)	5.9 WARP (-5%)

    This projection system isn't going to be as accurate as PECOTA, but it isn't intended to be. Rather, it's meant to be a representation of how typical major-league teams actually value players in the market; they assume the player is going to do pretty much what he's done in the recent past, unless maybe he's really old.

- Everything was translated to an annual basis by dividing the total WARP and the net present value of the contract by the number of contract years. So Carlos Beltran's deal looks like: $14.5 million per year for 6.4 WARP per year.

This is what we get:

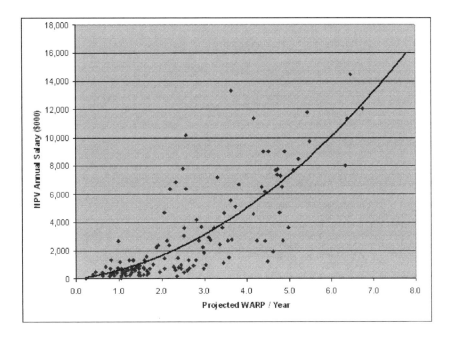

The pattern here is non-linear. Teams are willing to pay a premium for star talent, above and beyond the number of wins that they can be expected to contribute; signing one six-win player is more costly than signing two three-win players. The equation here, so that you can play along at home, is:

$$\text{Salary} = (\text{WARP}^2 * \$212{,}730) + (\text{WARP} * \$402{,}530)$$

This new formula results in a substantially more sensible salary projection for Cristian Guzman, who now rates as only a $2.8 million "bargain" for the life of his deal, rather than the $17 million implied by the original analysis. But does this non-linearity reflect rational behavior on the part of baseball clubs? Or are they overpaying for superstar talent?

I suspect that it's probably the former, for a couple of reasons. Firstly, the distribution of talent in baseball is highly uneven: a relatively small group of players is responsible for providing a relatively large portion of value. We can get some sense of this by looking at a Lorenz Curve that compares the percentage of value, as measured by VORP, against the percentage of playing time for all position players in 2005 (players with negative VORPs have their scores treated as zeroes).

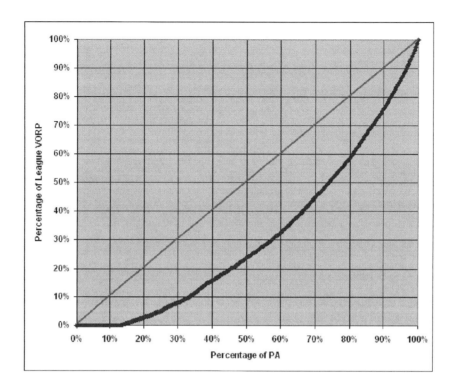

The top 10 percent of players were responsible for about 25 percent of all VORP in 2005, and the top 25 percent of players were responsible for about 50 percent of all VORP. Of course, we wouldn't expect talent to be evenly distributed. But the distribution here is particularly skewed; there are a lot of David Ecksteins, and not very many Albert Pujolses. Lorenz Curves are traditionally used to evaluate income distribution within an economy; if baseball were an economy, it would be the United States, and not Sweden.

The second reason is that, while salaries are non-linear with respect to marginal wins, so too are revenues. There is a very substantial economic benefit that comes from making the playoffs, and most teams enter the baseball season with one of two goals—either be competitive enough to reach the postseason (a 90-win club), or save costs and write off the season as a rebuilding year (a 65-win club).

It's easy enough to see what happens when we put these two things together. Teams have every incentive to try to reach the playoffs. Reaching the playoffs requires the presence of a number of above-average players, and probably a couple of superstars. But there are relatively few above-average players to go around, and even fewer superstars. Ergo, top players demand and receive a premium. (It's also worth referencing Michael Wolverton's work in our 2002 annual. Michael examined the relationship between wins above replacement and pennants added and discovered that it is not linear; a player who contributes one 10-win season will provide more than twice as many pennants than he would with two five-win seasons.)

Conversely, sub-premium players like Guzman become less valuable. It's very hard to punt on a position and still expect to reach the playoffs, because that's just one more really good player that you'll have to find to make up for his lack of contribution. Even Billy Beane would find it hard to stomach the presence of a truly replacement-level player in his lineup. The A's have had a few Scott Hattebergs—players who perform slightly below-average and are paid well below average—and a few mistakes like Terrence Long, but they won't call up an underqualified rookie from Sacramento, pay him the league minimum, play him every day, and sit around patiently while he posts a .235 EqA. That would turn Beane's job from being difficult into outright impossible.

Put differently, there is a hidden cost to fielding players who are substantially below championship caliber if you have aspirations of being a championship-caliber ballclub. A championship-caliber team generally needs to get about 35 wins out of its position players, accounting for both their offensive and defensive contributions; the average position player WARP for the 24 playoff clubs since 2003 has been 33.1. We could get there by fielding a uniformly above-average lineup like this one. That lineup would cost us about $43.2 million to put on the field, according to the market data that I presented above.

Pos	WARP	Salary
C	4.0	$5,013,800
1B	4.0	$5,013,800
2B	4.0	$5,013,800
3B	4.0	$5,013,800
SS	4.0	$5,013,800
LF	4.0	$5,013,800
CF	4.0	$5,013,800
RF	4.0	$5,013,800
DH	3.0	$3,122,160
Total	35.0	$43,232,560

Now, suppose that our second baseman is a free agent; we decide that he'll be too expensive, and that we're going to play a replacement-level player there instead, making up his contribution elsewhere on the field. If we take the four wins we were expecting out of him and distribute them evenly among the other eight positions, we wind up with this.

That lineup will be no better and no worse than the one that we fielded previously, but it will be about $3.5 million more expensive, since we have to move farther up the salary curve at the other positions to make up for his loss.

Pos	WARP	Salary
C	4.5	$6,119,168
1B	4.5	$6,119,168
2B	0.0	$0
3B	4.5	$6,119,168
SS	4.5	$6,119,168
LF	4.5	$6,119,168
CF	4.5	$6,119,168
RF	4.5	$6,119,168
DH	3.5	$4,014,798
Total	35.0	$46,848,970

Alternatively, and more realistically, we could make up for our replacement-level second baseman by signing a superstar, eight-win third baseman.

Pos	WARP	Salary
C	4.0	$5,013,800
1B	4.0	$5,013,800
2B	0.0	$0
3B	8.0	$16,834,960
SS	4.0	$5,013,800
LF	4.0	$5,013,800
CF	4.0	$5,013,800
RF	4.0	$5,013,800
DH	3.0	$3,122,160
Total	35.0	$50,039,920

But that is even worse; now we're paying nearly $7 million more for the same talent. Call it opportunity cost, scarcity, or the Tony Womack Effect, but that "free" guy we're playing at second base comes at a fairly substantial price.

Even Guzman, of course, wasn't projected to be a replacement-level player, merely a below-average one. Still, the effect exists to some extent any time that we lock in a "sub-premium" player, and the problems are compounded if we sign him to a multi-year deal, as the Nats did with Guzman. Too many baseball clubs are fixated on cost certainty, when the vast majority of them are capital-rich enough that they don't really need to be, and too many statheads go gaga when a team locks up its young players with multi-year contract extensions, when these extensions don't usually represent a material discount below market price.

I prefer the concept of flexibility: avoiding long-term commitments at enough positions that you can properly take advantage of arbitrage opportunities in the market. Let's look for example at this winter's Phillies, who aren't very flexible. They might well have both the cashflow and the desire to upgrade their offense, but they don't really have the position at which to do it:

- Catcher. Mike Lieberthal under multi-year contract (option vested);
- First Base. Jim Thome under multi-year contract; Ryan Howard good and cheap;
- Second Base. Chase Utley is good and cheap;
- Third Base. David Bell under multi-year contract;
- Shortstop. Jimmy Rollins under multi-year contract (signed in June).
- Left Field. Pat Burrell under multi-year contract.
- Right Field. Bobby Abreu under multi-year contract.

That leaves center field. Johnny Damon might well be a good fit, but with the Red Sox, Yankees, and Cubs all likely to take a long look at him, the bidding could get fast and furious. If Lieberthal's option hadn't vested, they could make a play for Ramon Hernandez; if they weren't overzealous to sign Burrell to an extension three winters ago, they could give a deal to Brian Giles; if they hadn't signed Bell for so long, they could take a flier on Nomar Garciaparra at third. Say what you want about sunk costs; the market for baseball players isn't terribly liquid, and trades aren't as easy to make as they are in Baseball Mogul. The Phillies either overpay for Damon, or they give up on materially upgrading their group of position players and lose to the Braves by three games again. That's the kind of opportunity cost I'm talking about.

Ultimately, we may need a more flexible understanding of replacement level. I've felt for some time that we've set the bar a bit too low if the goal is not describing how baseball teams win games but, rather, how they win championships. One option might be to use the salary equation that I described above; instead of talking about a player's WARP or VORP, we'd talk about his MORP—Market Value Over Replacement Player. A player would get some credit for being better than replacement level in the literal sense of the term—as bad as Angel Berroa has been, he's probably better than a guy you could find on the waiver wire. But he'd receive relatively more credit for being above-average, and extra credit still for being an elite player who facilitates championships. The 2005 AL shortstops would look like this:

Player	WARP	MORP
Peralta	9.2	$21,708,743
Jeter	8.8	$20,016,075
Tejada	7.6	$15,346,513
Lugo	7.0	$13,241,480
Young	6.2	$10,673,027
Uribe	4.5	$6,119,168
Crosby	4.2	$5,443,183
Cabrera	4.1	$5,226,364
Guillen	3.3	$3,644,979
Bartlett	2.5	$2,335,888
Renteria	1.8	$1,413,799
Berroa	1.8	$1,413,799
Adams	0.9	$534,588
Betancourt	0.7	$386,009

That, to me, is a more accurate rendering of the player's relative values. Salary considerations aside, I don't think you'd trade Derek Jeter for Juan Uribe plus Cabrera, which WARP suggests would be a fair swap. And I don't think you'd trade Jeter for a team full of Cristian Guzmans.

SENSIBLE REVENUE SHARING
One Man's Plan
Keith Woolner

Big-market teams have a competitive edge over small-market teams, but it's difficult to identify a solution, short of a radical restructuring of the United States population. Keith Woolner attempted to solve the problem by proposing a revenue-sharing plan that wouldn't simply perpetuate the wealthy teams' institutional advantages.

One of the most complex and bedeviling problems in baseball today is understanding to what extent large-market teams have a competitive advantage over small-market teams. Many people have proffered solutions despite not analyzing the problem thoroughly, with most of the plans featuring some sharing of revenues between large- and small-market teams. These plans have generally suffered from one or more problems:

- Revenue sharing that simply puts money into a small-market owner's pocket without a guarantee that the money will be used to field a more competitive team.
- Revenue contributions that are tied solely to expenditures, not actual inherent market advantages.
- Revenue sharing designed simply to put a drag on salary inflation.
- Confusing on-field success and off-field marketing savvy with market size.

I've attempted to define what "large" and "small" markets should mean, to understand how a large-market team might have a systematic advantage over small-market teams, and to construct an alternate revenue sharing plan that addresses these issues.

Assessing Market Size

To begin, we need a clear understanding of what we mean when we discuss market size. Market size is not attendance, winning percentage, or payroll. Those are all variables that are intertwined, and are heavily dependent on the decisions of management. A revenue-sharing plan shouldn't insure against having a poorly-run team. It should instead compensate for the inherent factors that result from operating a team in a given location.

Markets should be measured by their revenue potential. How well a team does in marketing its product and extracting that potential should not play into the evaluation of a market. Clearly, population will be one major factor in determining market size. In addition to having a larger pool from which to draw attendance, more people means more TV viewers, greater reach for commercials aired during televised games, and thus correspondingly higher valuations for TV packages.

The average affluence, or wealth distribution, in the area may also have an effect on revenue potential. A city heavily reliant on a declining industry may have the same population as a city with a broader economic base, but the revenue potential of the two are not the same, and that's not a function of team's management.

A more controversial idea is that certain areas of the country may have a greater cultural affinity for baseball than others. Does a team with a hundred-year history of rabid fandom (say, Boston) have an advantage in being more culturally invested in baseball than a city of comparable size with a team of more recent vintage and less history (Anaheim)? This is a dangerous area in which to draw conclusions, however, because there is a strong interaction between the long-term success and competitiveness of a franchise and how much support it draws even in down years. Because competitiveness is controlled to a large degree by the team's decision-makers and managers, the team exerts an influence on the market affinity for baseball. Separating background cultural affinity from the team's influence may be nearly impossible.

Dividing markets that have multiple teams also presents a possible problem. On one hand, the simplest approach is to divide the market equally. However, it's possible that the presence of more than one team causes a higher consumption of baseball per fan than in single-team markets, which makes those markets even larger by virtue of having multiple baseball options.

Another problem is that teams within the same market have different local competitive advantages and disadvantages. The age of a ballpark, cultural identification, attractiveness of the location where it plays, and differences in wealth distribution in the area around the park can cause an uneven division of the market between the two teams in ways that are difficult or impossible to counteract in the short term.

Ultimately, the entire issue of assessing market size is something that would have to be negotiated among the teams as part of an overall revenue-sharing agreement. (Sadly, this would probably end up being something as illogical as the free-agent rating system.) Factors that could be counted in such a system include market size, affinity, presence of a public/privately funded stadium, and so on. The key is to get it away from associating current revenues or team success with market size.

Potential Competitive Problems Resulting From Market Size

One of the assumptions in the debate is that some revenue sharing is required to level the field. There's a sizable contingent in the sabermetric community, including a large portion of the Baseball Prospectus staff, who do not think that there is a problem here to be solved, or certainly not one of the magnitude that is it is believed to be.

It seems relatively clear that in the current game, there's enough variation in the quality of team management and player-development programs to overcome any actual market advantage. Neither the Athletics nor Mariners are large-market teams, yet both are enjoying extraordinary success. Therefore, I do not believe that there is a critical need for revenue sharing.

However, that's a far cry from saying there's no possibility for market size to become a significant issue, and I think it's worth exploring what market-related advantages could exist. One real and under-explored possibility is that rational differences exist in risk tolerance according to the revenue potential of the market. In other words, large-market teams have a cushion of profitability that allows them to take more high-cost, high-upside risks than small-market teams can.

For example, consider two teams, one large-market (L), the other small-market (S). At the moment, L is operating at a $20 million profit, and S is operating at a $3 million profit. We'll assume, for simplicity's sake, that those profits are certain.

Each team faces the same possible investment in a development program. The program has risks, and it carries a 50 percent chance of making a $20 million profit and a 50 percent chance of a $10 million loss. Team L then has a 50/50 chance of either a $40MM or a $10MM profit outcome. Team S, in contrast, is looking at an equal shot at a $23MM profit or a $7MM loss. These teams are not in the same situation, even though the expected value of gambling on the development program in both cases is $5MM larger than the guaranteed value of operating the club without it.

Teams in markets with high-revenue potential have greater flexibility to bounce back from high-cost errors. This is a competitive advantage, though how large this is in practice in unclear. This phenomenon is not limited to baseball. Larger-revenue entities in any industry can generally afford more risk tolerance than smaller firms can in the same business. The financial flexibility to bounce back from poor outcomes on an investment is an ongoing advantage in high-revenue-potential markets.

This leads into the concept of a baseball team as an investment and brings up the issue of capitalization. There's no reason, a priori, why owners worth hundreds of millions or billions of dollars (such as Carl Pohlad) can't invest capital in the product during periods in which revenue is expected to be lower in the hopes of gaining revenue down the road. Having well-capitalized ownership is important because it relieves some of the short-term cash-flow pressures that would otherwise exist, ones that could cause the team to make less desirable competitive decisions based on short-term financial necessities. Capitalization allows ownership to ride out the inevitable down cycles and economic recessions to retain and fund a long-term profitable investment in the team.

That suggests that conglomerate ownership has advantages over a hypothetical owner who relies on the team to operate as a standalone business. Conglomerates that have a baseball component should be less risk-averse than a standalone owner with less overall wealth. But unless all conglomerates have the same risk preference, or if the range of differences is sufficiently small over the range of possible baseball-related cash flows, risk preferences do not go away as a potential issue, though they can offset some of the market-specific risk. If the conglomerate is run such that each sub-entity is evaluated as a standalone business, then we're back to square one, as business decisions for the baseball team will be made as if it must be self-funding in the short term.

Provided that the expected cash flow over time turns out to be positive, it's an entirely reasonable thing to expect that well-capitalized owners will ride out the fluctuations in business. However, financing a baseball operation through personal wealth or redirected revenues from other businesses without an expected net financial gain over some reasonable time horizon (including tax benefits to other holdings) shouldn't be a requirement or expectation of ownership. This is not to say that a one-year cash-flow deficit should be seen as a disaster. Rather, as long as teams do not freely enter and leave the market, I think it's reasonable to expect a decently-run team to be profitable and self-funding over the long haul, while fielding a competitive product with some reasonable frequency.

Competitive Ecology
Another important aspect to evaluating the appropriateness of a revenue-sharing plan is an issue that I refer to as the "competitive ecology" of the game. These are issues facing game as a whole, rather than a specific team. For example, how often does a franchise have to be competitive to be self-sustaining in the long term? Is once every five years the minimum? Every three years? Every 10 years? Does a streak of five playoff appearances have a lasting effect on marketability that five years with the same number of wins but multiple failures to reach the postseason times doesn't? How long does the bump in demand last following a World Series win? Is any of this dependent on market size? If the Dodgers can afford to compete in 80 percent of seasons over the long term, and the Royals can afford to compete only 20 percent of the time, can they be equally healthy businesses? Does it matter if they are?

Suppose a small market has a maximum revenue potential of $100 million, and a large market has a maximum revenue potential of $180 million. The latter is going to be willing to invest more to tap the market to the greatest possible extent, assuming that it continues to be marginally profitable to do so as costs increase.

If this investment is directed to payroll (as opposed to marketing, promotion, stadium renovations, or other items that improve the team's marketability without impacting the caliber of the on-field product) then it improves the caliber of team the large-market franchise can field on an ongoing basis. Because baseball is a zero-sum game, if one team wins more, other teams must lose more.

A sustainable payroll advantage given to a smart management team allows them to field a better team than they could if they had a smaller budget. This then lowers the expectations of competitiveness for markets with lower revenue potential, which makes it even harder to extract the revenue they could get, since competitiveness is recognized as a key requirement for maximizing market revenues. Sustained success in one (or a few) markets drives down interest in other markets if the local team is perceived as not being competitive (such as the effect the Yankees/Dodgers dominance in the 1950s had on the rest of the sport).

The Fatal Flaw
The single largest problem with most of the revenue-sharing plans that have been put forth to date is that they have failed to address the basic fact that the best way to encourage a desired behavior is to create incentives that reward it. Teams are governed primarily by self-interest, and management makes decisions according to expected risks and rewards. If true small-market teams aren't investing in a competitive on-field product, it is likely because they do not receive the benefits proportional to the risks they take (at least in their own minds), whether that be from lack of revenue or risk aversion.

Revenue sharing that simply puts money in a small-market owner's pocket is a handout that may help increase the capitalization and cash position from which he can operate a team but does not create any direct incentive to actually invest the money to field a more competitive team. Revenue sharing that is tied solely to expenditures (i.e., payroll) taxes large- and small-market teams at the same expenditure level equally, despite the fact that the small-market team is likely incurring greater risks with its investments. Lastly, tying revenue sharing to actual revenues generated confuses on-field success and off-field marketing savvy with the actual revenue potential of the market.

The Solution

All of this would be just so much hot air unless there's something substantive proposed to solve the problems I've raised. Therefore, I've attempted to construct an alternate revenue-sharing plan that addresses these issues. If revenue sharing is going to happen, it's important that it be done well.

The basic idea is to create a revenue-sharing plan that would actually give incentives to the small-market teams to field more competitive teams. At the plan's core is an incentive pool into which teams would contribute a fraction of their payroll, where that fraction is determined by market size. Teams in larger markets would be taxed at a higher rate.

The pool would be divided among small-market teams who compete with each other for a share of the pool. The competition for the dollars available is among fewer teams, with a narrower gap in market size separating them, giving each a legitimate shot to earn additional revenue and ensuring that all of the money will go to small-market teams. In addition, one of the criteria to be used will be the team competing against its own record, meaning that any small-market team can earn revenue sharing dollars simply by improving from year to year. This accomplishes a few things:

- Large-market teams contribute proportionally more but can still control how much they have to pay according to their total payroll.
- Small-market teams can win a substantial amount of additional money, but only by either improving their own team or by competing successfully against other small-market teams.
- Small-market teams that continue to do poorly do not get much, if any, of the shared pool.
- Thus, there is increased financial incentive for the small-market teams to field a competitive team.

The Plan

I will illustrate how such a plan might be structured, and how it would have been implemented for the 2001 season.

Market size will be determined by a combination of two factors. One is the relative market size based on Nielsen TV markets, as determined by a study by Mike Jones. The other factor is market affinity for baseball, though I reiterate the caveats about using this as an inherent attribute of a market. The source for this factor is a study by Scarborough Research showing the affinity for baseball in each market. In particular, they measured the percentage of total adults who are avid fans (defined as "very interested in major league baseball") in the designated market area.

The sample plan has the following characteristics:

- The teams in the bottom 40 percent by market size are eligible for a piece of the pool.
- Small-market teams are exempt from payroll contributions to the pool.
- The team in a market equal to the average market size of all taxed teams (thus excluding the small markets from the average) will contribute five percent of payroll to the pool.
- The minimum a contributing team will be taxed is one percent of payroll.
- The revenue-sharing percentage is determined by the formula:
- Contribution % = 1% + 4% * SQRT[(S-MinS)/(AvgS-MinS)]
  —where S is the team's market size
  —the average market size of all contributing teams is AvgS
  —the market size of the smallest contributing team is MinS
- The bottom 40 percent of teams will compete for the shared revenue pool. Each team can earn shares according to the following schedule:
    - Team earns one share for every game of improvement from the prior year. For example, in 2001 the Padres improved from 76 wins to 79 wins and earn three shares.
    - A team gets shares for the number of total wins in the most recently completed season, rewarding overall excellence.

Wins	Shares
90+	10
85-89	8
80-84	6
75-79	4
70-74	2

    - 15 shares for having the best three-year record among the small-market teams.
    - Ten shares for having the second-best three-year record.
    - Five shares for having the third-best three-year record.
    - Five shares for winning the division.
    - Three shares for finishing second in the division.
    - One share for winning the wild card.
- Each small-market team gets a percentage of the shared pool equal to the percentage of shares it has of the total shares earned by all small-market teams that season.

The shares for winning the division/wildcard or finishing second may seem small compared to the other rewards, but consider that those teams have already earned shares for the number of overall wins, have likely improved from year to year, and probably rank well among all small-market teams.

An Example

Using 2001 as an example, I used the 2001 total payroll figures found on ESPN.com. Calculating each team's market size, 12 teams qualify as belonging to small markets. The market sizes and contributions are in the following table:

Team	Market Size	Small Market?	Contribution Rate	Total Payroll	Contribution
New York Yankees	342	No	8.92%	$109,791,893	$9,798,427
New York Mets	318	No	8.57%	$93,174,428	$7,985,902
Cleveland Indians	188	No	6.18%	$91,974,979	$5,687,952
Los Angeles Dodgers	163	No	5.59%	$108,980,952	$6,094,903
Atlanta Braves	158	No	5.47%	$91,851,587	$5,026,761
Boston Red Sox	154	No	5.36%	$109,558,908	$5,869,930
Baltimore Orioles	146	No	5.15%	$72,426,328	$3,727,357
Anaheim Angels	137	No	4.87%	$46,568,180	$2,269,487
Seattle Mariners	125	No	4.50%	$75,652,500	$3,405,870
Philadelphia Phillies	113	No	4.07%	$41,664,167	$1,695,580
St. Louis Cardinals	108	No	3.86%	$77,270,855	$2,986,079
Florida Marlins	94	No	3.25%	$35,504,167	$1,154,772
Texas Rangers	90	No	2.99%	$88,504,421	$2,642,480
Toronto Blue Jays	89	No	2.98%	$75,798,500	$2,257,575
Houston Astros	85	No	2.73%	$60,382,667	$1,647,287
Chicago Cubs	85	No	2.68%	$64,015,833	$1,716,462
San Francisco Giants	73	No	1.29%	$63,332,667	$820,108
Chicago White Sox	73	No	1.00%	$62,363,000	$623,630
Tampa Bay Devil Rays	70	Yes	0.00%	$54,951,602	$0
San Diego Padres	67	Yes	0.00%	$38,333,117	$0
Arizona Diamondbacks	64	Yes	0.00%	$81,206,513	$0
Colorado Rockies	62	Yes	0.00%	$71,068,000	$0
Cincinnati Reds	56	Yes	0.00%	$45,227,882	$0
Oakland Athletics	53	Yes	0.00%	$33,810,750	$0
Montreal Expos	44	Yes	0.00%	$34,774,500	$0
Detroit Tigers	35	Yes	0.00%	$49,831,167	$0
Minnesota Twins	34	Yes	0.00%	$24,350,000	$0
Pittsburgh Pirates	34	Yes	0.00%	$52,698,333	$0
Milwaukee Brewers	29	Yes	0.00%	$43,089,333	$0
Kansas City Royals	21	Yes	0.00%	$35,643,000	$0

A total of $65,410,561 in incentive revenue would have been collected last year.

How many shares did each small-market team earn in 2001?

Scenario	ARI	CIN	COL	DET	KCA	MIL	MIN	MON	OAK	PIT	SDN	TBA
Wins, 2001:	92	66	73	66	65	68	85	68	102	62	79	62
Wins, 2000:	85	85	82	79	77	73	69	67	91	69	76	69
Wins, 1999:	100	96	72	69	64	74	63	68	87	78	74	69
Win Division	1	0	0	0	0	0	0	0	0	0	0	0
Finish 2nd	0	0	0	0	0	0	1	0	1	0	0	0
Wild card	0	0	0	0	0	0	0	0	1	0	0	0
3Yr Avg Wins*	92	82	76	71	69	72	72	68	93	70	76	67
3-Year Rank	2	3	5	8	10	7	6	11	1	9	4	12
Improvement	7	0	0	0	0	0	16	1	11	0	3	0
70-74 Wins	0	0	1	0	0	0	0	0	0	0	0	0
75-79 Wins	0	0	0	0	0	0	0	0	0	0	1	0
80-84 Wins	0	0	0	0	0	0	0	0	0	0	0	0

* rounded

Lastly, how much do those shares amount to?

Here we have a system that rewards small-market teams for being successful, with Oakland, Arizona, and Minnesota earning the lion's share of the incentive pool. A modestly improving team like the Padres would have earned over $4 million in incentives. Even the Expos earned almost $600,000. A team can always earn money by competing against itself but can do even better by outdoing other small-market teams.

Team	Incentive Share
TBA	$0
SDN	$4,016,438
ARI	$18,360,859
COL	$1,147,554
CIN	$2,868,884
OAK	$22,951,074
MON	$573,777
DET	$0
MIN	$15,491,975
PIT	$0
MIL	$0
KCA	$0

Teams that refuse to invest in talent or player development won't share in the benefits, as they will continue to be outplayed even by their small-market brethren. The Pirates, Devil Rays, Tigers, Brewers, and Royals failed to earn any incentives based on their three-year track record. Yet, the money is clearly there to make it worth their while to improve. Given these kinds of financial incentives, teams who otherwise believe they can't compete will still be driven to maximize their rewards.

Objections

The biggest objection to a plan like this is that, as a tax on payroll, it's an external salary restraint and anathema to the MLBPA. Still, the union has previously agreed to a luxury tax, and there is no salary cap (or floor, for that matter). Nor is there a punitive large tax rate for exceeding an arbitrary payroll level, so if some plan is to be accepted, this one may be a more attractive option.

It is possible to construct a contribution model that is based totally on market size without tying it to payroll. The one problem is that to a large-market team, it would be treated as a fixed cost (i.e., the Yankees contribute $15MM/year to revenue sharing regardless of payroll). This has no impact on whether the Yankees maximize profit at a $90MM payroll or a $120MM payroll, since the marginal cost of talent is the same. With a system that includes both payroll and market size, you are affecting the marginal cost of winning. This method would, it must be said, be a drag on salaries.

Another objection takes the exact opposite tack, which is that this "solves" a problem that only the Yankees have created, and as such is basically targeting them for being successful. This gets back to a common sabermetric position that there is no economic problem here to solve. To be sure, the Yankees play in a large market, but they also combine that with a smart management team that knows how to exploit it. I have an underlying belief that the Yankees have shown the way for other large markets to follow, if they get the right management and marketing teams in place.

The rest of the teams are capable of addressing one of those advantages directly—quality of management—but that doesn't eliminate the other. I don't want to rely on continued poor management from other large-market clubs to keep a semblance of competitive balance. The Yankees have shown that smart management can exploit market advantages. Addressing half the problem is better than addressing none of it.

Another response is that the plan ignores costs. To use the example presented earlier, if a small market has a maximum revenue potential of $100 million, and a large market has a maximum revenue potential of $180 million, the latter is going to be willing to invest more to tap the market to the greatest possible extent. It will also have a larger initial investment and possibly larger operating costs, hampering its ability to do these things, which will level the playing field so that a larger-revenue potential market presents less of an advantage.

However, once the initial investment is made, it's a sunk cost as far as future decisions, unless there is debt service or some other ongoing cost related to the purchase price. It's not obvious that operating costs would be higher in a large market, and it is likely more related to the stadium deal the team negotiated (or whether the team owns the stadium), and the age of the venue itself. Some labor costs might be higher for staffing, and in some cases there may be city taxes to deal with, but in lieu of actual numbers (perhaps Doug Pappas or the Forbes study will shed some light on this subject), I'm inclined to think this is a small effect.

There is a public-relations angle to this plan as well. The "outrage" among baseball fans is mostly about large-market teams—usually the Yankees—being able to afford payroll expenditures that other teams can't. Tying the contribution to both market size and payroll causes the revenue-sharing contribution to be levied in greater amounts when a large-market team exploits its inherent market advantage. When your product's marketability is based on the perception of competitiveness, I can certainly believe that an owner would be motivated to fix a perception problem. However, it would help if the owners weren't demeaning their own product so loudly in public. It's a peculiar marketing strategy—telling everyone what bad shape your product is in.

The all-or-nothing threshold of the bottom 12 teams in market size qualifying for incentives could easily create an incentive for teams just outside the revenue-sharing pool to relocate to a bottom-12 market or to game the system by lobbying for a particular market-sizing scheme. I tried to address this by having the amount of revenue sharing start at a very low percentage for those just above the threshold, but there's still a discontinuity: if the cutoff is the smallest 10 teams get to participate in the shared pool, then the #10 team could get millions of dollars in reward for a good season, while the #11 team isn't eligible for anything and in fact pays a small amount to the pool.

A modification of the system that included some kind of scaled reward system, rather than an absolute cutoff where you're either a small-market team or not, would help. I strongly believe that a cutoff or a tapering to zero at some point should be part of the plan, because I don't think the Yankees, Mets, Dodgers, et al should be eligible for a fund set up to help small-market teams.

Conclusions

If revenue sharing is to be implemented correctly, teams that receive the money must have incentives to use it to field a more competitive team, or else the exercise is futile. By linking on-field success to their share of the available pool of money, yet guaranteeing that all of it will go to small-market teams, a secondary competition within the overall structure of MLB is created. This structure will motivate decision-makers for small-market teams to make the investments in free agents and player development because the risk/reward balance has shifted.

The plan I've presented may not be the best one, or even agreeable to all of the parties, who would certainly have to negotiate the specifics. But it demonstrates how such a plan might be constructed, how much each team would be affected by it, and how the money can be distributed in a way that rewards success among small-market teams.

Part 9
EXTRA INNINGS
Introduction by Ken Funck

"That is the entire difference between sabermetrics and traditional sportswriting. It isn't the use of statistics. It isn't the use of formulas. It is merely the habit of beginning with a question, rather than beginning with an answer." —Bill James

To most observers, the home was completely unexceptional—a small, yellow ranch house set back an indiscreet distance from a stretch of crumbling blacktop, huddled alongside similarly cramped and aging ranch houses of a style realtors would describe as "tidy" and "charming." It was trash day, and empty bins were scattered along the curb like mournful penitents denied forgiveness for another week of consumer excess. Birds chirped fitfully. A light breeze toyed with a few stray grass clippings on the sidewalk until, overcome with Tuesday morning ennui, it decided to laze around before having a more strenuous go at whatever plastic bins remained unclaimed that afternoon. An elderly man lobbed plastic balls towards his granddaughter, who occasionally launched them back at him with a dull plastic thwack.

Most observers would not have imagined that such an unexceptional house on such an unexceptional morning could have hidden a threat so insidious as to draw the attention of The Agent.

The Agent, however, wasn't just any observer. Crouching incompletely behind a row of peonies across the street from the yellow house, his presence there was unobtrusive in exactly the way a neon pink stegosaurus wasn't—not that it mattered much, The Agent thought, as the odds of someone in the house actually glancing in his direction and blowing his cover were quite remote. His quarry, though dangerous, was sure to be oblivious to its physical surroundings. It was this willingness to engage in first-hand observation, a willingness to trust his own eyes, which separated The Agent from the lethal threat currently festering uncontained in the yellow house, and in others like it across the nation. He knew what to revile when he saw it, just as he knew what to celebrate, and as he failed to conceal himself behind the peonies and waited for the other Agents to arrive, he reviewed the observations that led him to this neighborhood, to this house.

#

It was the pizza boxes that first tipped him off.

On Monday night, as The Agent happened to drive past the yellow house on his way home, he noticed a middle-aged woman dragging two plastic garbage bins to the curb, one of which was stuffed with empty pizza boxes. Unleashing his uncanny observational talent honed through years of experience—the only way to gain such insight, he reminded himself—The Agent realized the woman wore a bitter expression that usually meant only one thing: she had a child whose job it was to take out the garbage but once again forgot. Taking a sudden interest, The Agent noticed that the pizza boxes were the remnants of delivered pizza, not frozen, and the woman was staring at them with obvious disgust as she left them at the end of the driveway and trudged back towards her small garage.

Klaxons going off in his head, The Agent executed a skilled Y-turn and sped back to the yellow house, stopped across the street and peered into the garage before the automatic door ground shut. There were no sporting goods visible, further raising his alarm. After a quick call home to his wife to tell her he'd be late—something she'd grown accustomed to as the danger had grown and his off-hours surveillance had become more frequent—The Agent pulled out his battered notebook and jotted down his observations. He had once kept a small digital camera in his car, but discarded it when he realized the pictures the camera took sometimes contradicted what he remembered seeing with his own eyes, proving the camera's unreliability. He was obviously better off trusting his own observations, or those of his fellow Agents, an approach that had been good enough for generations before him.

As The Agent watched, the woman entered the kitchen from the garage and made herself supper, eating it alone at the kitchen counter. Meanwhile, there was a light gleaming through the basement's tiny hopper windows, and The Agent was sure he could discern a slight flicker in the light, less than you would get from a television, which his keen insight had come to associate with a computer monitor. The woman had eventually gone to bed without going downstairs, but the basement windows of the yellow house still flickered with a sickly, narcissistic light that failed to illuminate anything but itself. Typical. It was clear from the evidence—the basement light still burning, too many pizza boxes, the look of betrayal on her face as she dragged them to the curb—that the woman did not live alone. She had a son.

He was sure she had a son.

The Agent turned his attention to the yard, which was somewhat unkempt and in need of a mow. There was a raised bed of heavy stones, poorly laid, showcasing the husks of last year's annuals. This year's quack grass and creeping charlie had grown through an insufficiently thick spread of wood chips—not the nice cedar chips The Agent's wife used in their garden, but the stuff you could pick up for free from the city's yard-waste site after running their spring pick-up through the chipper. This unsightliness stood in contrast to the deftly edged and pruned neighboring yards, which The Agent (a man not known to be shy with his opinions) assumed were tended by elderly couples who had decided to commit more time and care to their gardens than they had to their children, hoping for better results.

THE LINEUP

Why Edgar Allan Poe Couldn't Play Fantasy Baseball
  by Keith Woolner..................................370

Casey's Random Batting Trial
  by Keith Woolner..................................374

Bug Selig's Successful Testing Program
  by Will Carroll....................................377

Dr. X2
  by Will Carroll....................................380

An Open Letter to Murray Chass
  by Nate Silver.....................................387

When the Rains Come
  by Rany Jazayerli..................................389

The Decline and Fall of Yankee Stadium
  by Jay Jaffe.......................................394

Redecorating Your Glass House
  by Gary Huckabay...................................399

Take Me Out of the Hall Game
  by Jay Jaffe.......................................402

Fernando Perez
  by David Laurila...................................408

Joe Maddon, Part One
  by David Laurila...................................415

Joe Maddon, Part Two
  by David Laurila...................................420

Ozzie Guillen
  by David Laurila...................................424

Jack Zduriencik
  by David Laurila...................................431

Learning the Game
  by Rany Jazayerli..................................437

The Doctor is...Gone
  by Rany Jazayerli..................................443

When he closed his eyes, The Agent could hear the arguments between the mother and the son, pleas to mow the lawn or weed the flower bed, or to fix up the mess he had made of laying the stones on the one occasion she had badgered him into doing some work she couldn't handle herself. They were large stones that required a certain amount of strength to carry and a certain commitment to lay them properly. The son apparently possessed one of those properties, but not the other.

It had to be an adult son, The Agent surmised, old enough to carry those stones. An adult son who disappointed his mother, neglected to take out the garbage or help with the yard. A son who spent all his time in the basement, refused to come up for a well-cooked meal, required no sporting goods, and continually ordered pizza they could not afford. A son who had leached the joy out of his mother's life and, if The Agent didn't intervene quickly, would try his hardest to leach the joy out of everyone's lives. A son whose properties were the exact opposite of those you would hope for in an American youth, a sort-of Tom Sawyer in reverse. And, come to think of it, hadn't there been a white picket fence at the back of the yard, badly in need of whitewash? It had grown too dark for The Agent to see, but he added it to his notes anyway. It had to be there, since it fit his expectations perfectly.

###

Now it was Tuesday morning, and The Agent waited in his half-hearted crouch behind the peonies, anticipating the arrival of his fellow Agents with growing excitement. He listened to the sounds of the little girl and her grandfather playing Wiffle Ball, wondering if they were aware of the creeping menace only a few houses away. It was for their protection that he did this, finding people like the boy across the street and making sure their views didn't ruin things for everyone. He wanted the girl to love the game she was now learning to play, love it the same way he did, with the complete joy and unquestioning faith and commitment to whole numbers his father had taught him.

He and his fellow Agents were part of the thin blue line that protected the next generation of baseball fans from twisted views and crooked numbers, from VORPs and WARPs and DIPS and the secret, profane numerical codes that sucked the joy out of the game's sacred beliefs. The Agent had spoken to several practitioners of those dark arts as he and his team hauled them away, and they sometimes claimed to be digging for some Universal Truth.

"Sure," The Agent said, "but when you dig, don't you know you leave a hole? You're hollowing out the game for everyone else, and we're here to stop you before there's nothing left."

He smiled at the memory, and smiled again at the irony that the yellow house across the street was 406 Exeter Way. Great number, 406. A whole number. No one would ever say Teddy Ballgame hit "Point-Four-Oh-Six," even though everyone knew it was a percentage. Baseball stories are told in whole numbers, and always will be. When we drag that kid out of 406 Exeter, the Agent thought, we should be sure to get a picture with the address in the background, while holding up his sabermetric screeds and copy of *Moneyball*.

A thought bubbled up: what about Earned Run Average? The Agent paused momentarily, then shook his head like a snow globe to clear his mind, just as another voice behind him rasped "What are you doing in my yard?"

The Agent turned to face the raspy voice, which belonged to a trim, solid woman in her sixties, belonged to her much as the Louisville Slugger she clasped clearly belonged to her. She struck everyone who met her as a woman who kept track of her belongings, and who was spending time near them.

The Agent smiled a quick smile, and brought a finger up to his lips. "I'm on a stakeout. Duck down here, before they see you!"

"Not in my yard, you're not," the woman said in an even tone. This was clearly meant as a statement of fact.

"You don't understand," the Agent protested. "There's a young man living across the street who's very dangerous, very un-American. We're going to get rid of him for you before he causes you any more trouble."

"No, there isn't," the woman said. Again, this was a plain statement of fact. "My neighbor lady lives there by herself. If somebody else was living in that house, I'd know about it. We keep track of things in this neighborhood."

"Well, ma'am, I think you're mistaken. Couldn't someone be living there you don't know about? Every time we do this, we find out from the neighbors that these people are always quiet and keep to themselves. People don't know them. Maybe the guy we're dealing with here is like Boo Radley. They're always pale like that. Isn't that at least possible? We're quite sure he lives in that house."

"No, it's not possible. I know the woman who lives there, and she lives there alone. Believe me. And unless you have some sort of badge to show me, I'm dialing 911 right now." The woman reached into the pocket of her denim jacket and pulled out a phone.

The Agent didn't have any sort of a badge, since his Agency was more of a loose affiliation than an official body. He looked at the woman, whose posture evoked the flexibility of a concrete embankment, looked back at the yellow house, and decided the best move was to believe her. "Nice, solid number, 911," he said. "No need to call it, though. Sorry to trouble you." The Agent walked slowly to his car, dreading the call he would have to make to his fellow Agents, and the ribbing he'd take for getting things so wrong. Again. For a fleeting moment as he drove off, The Agent considered whether he should stop trusting his eyes so much and do a little more research before fitting his observations to his conclusions. Then, with another quick shake of the head, the thought was gone, and he drove off sporting a quizzical smile.

The woman walked around her house to the back fence, still grasping the Louisville Slugger. She watched her neighbor's granddaughter take a big swing at the Wiffle ball, and with a crack send it soaring into the left field lilac bushes.

"Nice swing, Iris," the woman said. "Keep that up, and someday you'll be a five-win player."

Despite what you may have heard elsewhere, the most compelling products of Baseball Prospectus aren't advanced statistics or forecasting systems or fantasy baseball value calculators, though all those things are wicked cool. For me, the things that I love about BP are embodied by the pieces in this chapter: insight and wit, coupled with an infectious love of baseball. Between David Laurila's varied and insightful interviews, Will Carroll's coverage of the past and future of PEDs, and the always-engaging voices of Gary Huckabay, Rany Jazayerli, and Jay Jaffe, there's sure to be something here for you. I challenge any true baseball fan to read Keith Woolner's re-working of Edgar Allan Poe without sporting a face-wide grin; if you can manage it, you and I are very different people. Enjoy.

A POEM
Why Edgar Allan Poe Couldn't Play Fantasy Baseball
Keith Woolner

Keith Woolner made many important statistical contributions to Baseball Prospectus and our understanding of baseball, but as his reimagining of "The Raven" proved, he also had a talent for poetry.

With apologies to Edgar Allan Poe.

Once upon a midnight dreary, while I waited, weak and weary
For the ballgames to be finished on the distant western shore.
While I started nearly dozing, with my eyes so slightly closing
I flicked on the tube, supposing to catch the highlights, one or more
Grabbed the clicker, settled in, and tuned to channel thirty-four,
A certain channel I adore.

Ah, distinctly I remember, it was in the young September
Of that fantasy pennant horserace, which I would win, for this I swore.
From the first time I did enter, I most eagerly watched SportsCenter
And its erudite presenter, whose sage wisdom I did store
For the rare and radiant anchor whom the angels brought to fore
And named him "Berman" evermore.

He covered every highlight, whether day or night or twilight
My trusty, husky white knight always covered every score.
Every player, every stat line. Be still my heart! I just might flat line!
I felt as if on cloud nine, when Herr Berman took the floor.

Presently my soul grew stronger; hesitating then no longer,
And turning to the ghostly image on the tube I did implore.

"Sir, the fact is I've been waiting, now so long my teeth are grating.
I beg you! Please! Start stating my roto team results galore.
My team the Rally Ravens I must have the answers for.
Tell me whom they did outscore?"

Deep into the small screen peering, long I stood there, wondering, fearing,
Doubting, dreaming dreams that every batter on my team went 4-for-4.
But not a word was spoken, and the stillness gave no token.
Was the television broken? My trusty box was now done for?
Then it flickered and it crackled showing scenes of home décor.
Just a commercial, and nothing more.

Then there he was appearing, while my eye was slightly tearing,
The screen with Berman's visage, just as I had pleaded for.
And as he starting talking, of hits and runs and walks and balking
Still all the while he's hawking that brilliant shtick he's famous for,
Those clever clever nicknames, used a thousand times before,
Kept me waiting nevermore.

The rundown had now started; the ups and downs were swiftly charted
And players of my heart did on the screen begin to pour.
Here now is Jason Kendall, who will not a pitch mishandle
And once saved us all from Grendel, with his bat forever sure.
Rolled the game film of his at-bats, gathered from the sports press corps
Quoth the Berman: "0-for-4"

Stunned I sat to hear so plainly that my catcher so ungainly
Swung his bat so very vainly, and could not hit no more.
Crestfallen, seeking haven, I turned next to Johnny Damon
With beard and locks unshaven, abandoned razors at the store.
Surely Johnny's bat and ball had since developed some rapport.
Quoth the Berman: "0-for-4"

Ensconced, I was so puzzled, and so a beer I guzzled.
Why was my lumber muzzled? Were my troops not set for war?
I checked out my PECOTA, for Silver's wisdom rivals Yoda.
And while I sipped a soda, I checked every SUM() and CORR()

No! Everything was perfect, duly mined from data ore.
I do swear on Davenport.

Bah! These other books and journals (not Prospectus but external)
Did contain but not a kernel of the truth I had asked for.
I shall do no more relying, on a source forever lying,
And so I sent them flying: Shandler, Sickels, Waggoner.
Defiled and torn asunder, flitted past both desk and door
As they settled on the floor.

But Berman was now speaking, yet his voice was merely squeaking
Of sports I was not seeking, and mostly wanted to ignore.
Strange games these men were playing, so bizarre it was dismaying.
It could have been crocheting, so odd these games they opted for.
Some on ice, or bowls, or clay, or even on a parquet floor.
Speak of them nevermore!

Behold returns the diamond, they were merely putting time in,
I forgave them of their crime in showing other sports galore.
They told of Mike Matheny, O! My precious catching genie!
Though his bat is but a weenie, his game-calling I adore.
Yet my soul was left unguarded, mauled, forsaken, bruised and sore
When quoth the Berman: "0-for-4"

Thus I sat so still repressing, but no syllable expressing
The rage I felt distressing, as it chilled me to the core.
My face was so contorted, to see my hopes so quickly thwarted
While the TV set reported another outcome of my corps:
The fate of Julio Franco, ancient, eldritch king of yore.
Quoth the Berman: "0-for-4"

Ever faithful Tony Womack! Speed and grace you never will lack!
I will buy you a new spice rack, if even once today you score!
But once again disaster, like fabled John LeMaster.
Those hurlers must be faster, for every time his bat did snore.
On whose sinking ship my heart did plunge unto the ocean floor.
Quoth the Berman: "0-for-4"

Rey Ordonez! Great Defender! Web gem highlights never-ender!
In your comely saintly splendor, please save a fan hardcore!
Though your skills may show some rusting, in the clutch it's you I'm trusting
And though I smell disgusting, I humbly truly do implore!
And with quiet desperation, I turned to face the tube once more.
Quoth the Berman: "0-for-4"

"Be that word our sign of parting, evil fiend!" I shrieked upstarting
"I'd prefer some John Kruk farting than your vicious lies, you whore!"
I ripped the TV from the cable; threw it down off from the table
Though you think me so unstable, please consider this was war!
It crashed and broke while spewing sparks and smoke and glass and more
And it died upon the floor.

My anger grew much hotter; my brow would need a blotter
Was I the victim of a plotter, scheming from some distant shore?
I could picture them just sneering! Did they fear my team was nearing?
My room would need a clearing of every piece of baseball lore.
Every cooked-up, bogus scribbling could not be trusted anymore.
I cast them down upon the floor.

In glee I set the fire, like a giant funeral pyre
How I wish I had a lyre, so I could dance across the floor!
But just then amidst my caper, right before it turned to vapor
I thought I glimpsed a paper, the Ravens roster I adore.
The names of all my players across the burning sheet it wore
And "HACKING MASS" the title bore.

"Fool!" said I, while groaning. The players I was owning
Were supposed to stir such moaning, when perusing the box score!
And as I watched the burning of the fruits my whole life earning
Seems the lesson I was learning, was a bitter painful chore.
For the truth lies scorched both in my mind as well as on the floor
I must play this, nevermore.

A POEM
Casey's Random Batting Trial
Keith Woolner

Keith Woolner also demonstrated his poetry skills with a modernized, sabermetric take on "Casey at the Bat."

With apologies to Ernest L. Thayer.

The win probability was epsilon for the Mudville nine that day
With a minus-two run differential, and just three outs left to play

Then when Cooney lowered his OBP, and Barrows did the same
They took the last-ups advantage and the home crowd from the game.

The Dodger fans began to leave, the Expos fan did too
Just Red Sox fans did cling to hope which springs forever new

They thought, if only one at-bat, Casey he could get
Egad! Pete Rose could take those odds, and make a hefty bet.

But Flynn and Blake preceded him. Who made this lineup card?
For both were mere slap hitters, for whom patience was too hard.

So upon the stricken statheads, grim melancholy sat;
Just an infinitesimal probability of getting Casey to the bat

But Flynn singled off the closer, to the wonderment of all
Blake caused the fielder's UZR to drop, when he let the line drive fall.

And when the fielders finally stopped giving the ball a chase
Blake had doubled, while Flynn had failed to take the extra base.

Then from fifty thousand estimated arose a lusty yell
It rumbled through the concrete valley, and I think it crashed my Dell.

It pounded through the TV speakers, enhanced and amplified by FOX.
For Casey, mighty Casey, was advancing to the box.

There was ease in Casey's manner, and a smile was on his face.
Did his endless bat-touch ritual and then stepped into his place

When responding to the cheers, he flipped off the roaring crowd
No one doubted it was Casey, high-and-mighty and so proud.

All eyes were on Casey as the pitcher got the sign
All throats groaned and sighed when he stepped out one more time.

The manager debated the I-B-B, and then said with a sneer
"I've pitched to Barry Bonds before; I'll pitch to this jerk here."

At last he hurled the spheroid, sent a-whizzing toward the plate.
The FOX gun it read 95, but 'twas really 88.

Far too close the batsman stood, so the pitch came towards his head.
Casey dove, fell to the ground. "Strike one!", the umpire said.

From the stands, black with people, there went up a muffled roar.
"Is Enrico Pallazzo umping?" they yelled, plus a few "choice" words more.

"Kill the ump!" Don Zimmer shouted, and from the dugout he bound
And it's likely he would have killed, had not Casey thrown him to the ground.

Casey knew the state transition matrix, and should have showed concern.
But knew from the hurler's pitch count, his right arm was likely burned.

He stepped back in the box, and once more the dun sphere flew.
But this ump calls the high strike, and Casey took it for strike two.

"Fraud!" cried the maddened thousands, when they saw the Jumbotron.
The screen operator was ejected, and only then the game went on.

Pitcher and batter faced off as foes, and each refused to bend
Yet only one would increase his VORP when this day comes to an end.

"Walk-off homer" Casey thought, avoid the extra innings he did hate.
He pounds, with steroid muscles, his mighty bat upon the plate.

From the stretch to a full stop, so deliberate it's absurd.
Pitch in the dirt! The swing is checked! Catcher appeals to third...

Oh somewhere in this land, the Red Sox are champions of the day.
Steinbrenner's firing someone, and Rickey still wants to play.
Gaylord Perry and Joe Niekro are finally playing fair.

But there is no joy in Mudville
Casey cost them three Win Shares.

UTK SPECIAL
Bug Selig's Successful Testing Program
Will Carroll

Major League Baseball may have done some poor public relations work, but Will Carroll argued in 2007 that the game's drug testing program was superior to any other major sport's.

Bud Selig is right. The drug testing program in Major League Baseball is second to none. I'll include not only the other major American professional sports, but all sports. Pro or amateur, US or foreign, MLB has it right.

What MLB doesn't have right is the public relations angle. It came too late to the party—far too late—and has gotten knocked around for the puritanical sin of making us believe. The cardinal sin in modern America is truly Baum's rule: never let us see behind the curtain. While the NFL talks about undersized 300-pounders and men the size of Frank Thomas playing quarterback, no one's questioning the lack of a prominent drug suspension since the rug-swept Winstrol-fed Pro Bowl season of Shawne Merriman.

Instead, it's easier to hit the guy who's easy to hit, and Bud Selig is easy pickings on the pro sports playground. NBA commissioner David Stern and former NFL commissioner Paul Tagliabue live to challenge the media and have stared down Congress on several issues. Selig and his minions—aside from Rob Manfred, who was alone in standing up to Henry Waxman at the 2005 hearings—seem to have "hit me again" stamped on them. However, easily hit doesn't mean Selig's the right target, and on this issue Congress has been dead wrong. It's not just the U.S. Congress, to be sure—Florida funded a statewide high school testing program with the laughable sum of $100,000—but they've been good at grandstanding while doing little.

So when Selig, Senator Mitchell, and others sit in front of Congress this time, hearing calls for blood testing, independent testing programs, increasing the number of substances on the banned list, and an abandonment of due process, I hope Selig stands up and says, "I'd be glad to improve my program once every other sport catches up to us, including the Olympics." Baseball's testing program has taken a problem not easily quantified and reduced it from nearly 100 in 2003 to two in 2007. I'll hold my breath waiting for the Beijing Olympics to have a similar reduction, but no one expects there to be anything other than similar numbers. The NFL has done nothing to its testing program despite having its faces rubbed in the HGH issue by the Super Bowl steroid scandal involving the Carolina Panthers. The NBA, NHL, even NASCAR and PGA have nothing compared to MLB.

If the problem is one of role models, as many say, then why is Myles Brand, the President of the NCAA, not called on the carpet? The NCAA's testing program is an underfunded joke, with the result that it hasn't caught a single Division I football player this season. Why? "We weren't tested," I was told by a Division I player recently. "I never saw them come in once." I asked him when the last time he saw an NCAA tester was. "I helped out at a swimming meet last spring and I saw them testing there." The NCAA's policy for most sports is to test the winners; silver medals are fine for cheaters, but not gold. Add in that the NCAA's banned list is significantly shorter than any professional list, and you have a twofold problem of efficacy on top of credibility. Call it cost if you will, but I don't see the Bowl Committees chipping in nearly as much for steroid testing as it does for flower arrangements, logos, or corporate skyboxes.

I'll ignore the research, saying that a urine test for HGH is unlikely ever to be found, and I'll ignore the privacy issues that overlay the calls for blood testing. Perhaps no one read pages 9-10 or skipped past page 144, or even skipped past Sally Jenkins' phenomenal piece in the *Washington Post* regarding the use and effectiveness of HGH. Jim Bouton called amphetamines a "performance enabler" in his recent BPR interview, a commonly held position (or justification) stating that "greenies" just get people awake enough to perform up to their abilities. If many of us buy this argument, can't we do the same for HGH? Over and over, the overwhelming evidence—anecdotal and scientific—shows that the strength-building application of HGH delivers mixed results at best, but that its value in rebuilding, especially from injury, holds some promise.

Imagine Chris Carpenter coming out on Opening Day, nine months after Tommy John surgery, throwing like the ace that the Cardinals paid for. It's possible, if you believe that Jason Grimsley's recovery was aided by his use of HGH. No one said that Grimsley came out of surgery a better pitcher, just that he came back incredibly quickly while getting back to the same level. It's pretty clear to me that that's enabling, rather than enhancing. Check the list of pitchers who have been caught—either by testing or the Mitchell Report—and the same theme comes up again and again: pitchers trying to recover from injury using HGH or steroids. Andy Pettitte? Juan Salas? Juan Rincon? Rafael Betancourt? Maybe even Roger Clemens? All simply seeking to get back on the field to throw the ball. I'm not saying they were right, and I certainly believe they made the wrong choice, but the arguments about what they did and why don't always hold.

Nor does an increased or independent testing program stop this. Ignore that MLB uses a WADA-certified Montreal lab that would likely also administer the results if WADA took over the testing. Ignore that MLB uses a contractor to collect its samples, much the same way that WADA does for its out-of-competition testing. Ignore for a moment that baseball players have moved past the ineffective and expensive HGH treatments and on to designer steroids that are undectectable, such as Havoc, or to more advanced drugs like IGF-1 and insulin that are not tested for (or, like HGH, could not be tested for). Ignore that genetic doping is on the horizon. Ignore that no sport in the world has had better, faster, or more effective results than MLB. Ignore all that if you wish, but that doesn't solve problems.

Baseball could do more, especially with education and research, but the money that Congress wants spent on blood tests and testers could be used right now to fund those education programs. Joe Sheehan had this right in mid-2006. Bud Selig has it right in late 2007. Stand strong, Mr. Selig. You picked the right issue to be right on.

FEBRUARY 5, 2009

http://bbp.cx/a/8470

UNDER THE KNIFE
Dr. X2
Will Carroll

After the institution of Major League Baseball's steroid testing program, Will Carroll met with a member of the steroid underground and discovered that the next big performance-enhancer had already arrived.

I walked into the restaurant and sat at the bar, figuring it wouldn't be long until the person I was waiting for showed. Since leaving my hotel, I'd been feeling a sense of dread, excitement, and deja vu. Five years ago, I met with a man I called "Dr. X," one of the leading figures in the steroid underground. Tonight, I'd be doing the same. Last time, I had to jump through hoops, seeing meetings canceled and conditions changed, and when we finally did meet face to face, he was wearing a disguise. There were no such concerns this time, as if men like Dr. X had undergone the same transformation as their drugs. Things were more advanced, clearer (no pun intended), and done much more out in the open.

Since I last sat down with one of these men, baseball had come a long way, having instituted a testing program that had driven out most of the steroid users, and had pushed that percentage of hardcore users to more advanced products. In driving out deca-durabolin and boldenone, baseball had ushered in an era where the low end picked up things at the local GNC, hoping that the unregulated, hype-driven industry wouldn't spike their latest creation to get results, while the upper end—those with the money, knowledge, and connections—would deal with the underground. Drug usage on the whole was, I believe, down, but the idea that baseball was drug-free was simply fiction. Some had moved on to whatever this month's "clear" was, staying one step ahead of the testing regime, or using undetectable substances, like HGH, insulin, and now, something new.

But this time, I was meeting with another figure from the steroid underground, and—to use Mark McGwire's famous phrase—we weren't here to talk about the past. He had something new, something powerful, and something that he said could make testosterone obsolete. As he joined me in a booth, he didn't appear nervous, didn't worry about who was sitting near us, and he wasn't disguised in any way. His only guarantee was my promise of anonymity, though I think his ego might not care if his name were to leak out. We'll call him "X2." He's a master at putting together performance-enhancing programs built around legal and extra-legal methods, and he's one of the best because his programs are both effective and undetectable. In previous conversations, he had hinted that he had the next big thing, and that's what I wanted to learn more about.

As he sat down, the talk naturally started with baseball. I began taking notes. "So here we are," I said, looking at the menu and glancing around at the room. "We're five years into the testing era. Positives are down, home runs are down... so it's working, right?"

X2 smiled. "Well, home runs are down, but I don't think that drug use is down. People point to positives being down, but that's because the ante has been upped. Players can't just use whatever they want any more. It was the Wild West just a few years ago, but guys are just being smarter about it now."

I nodded. "I'd agree. All the statistical studies showed there wasn't a big effect, but that's neither here nor there. So what are the smarter guys doing now? What's the next THG?"

"Probably SARMs, which aren't even on the legitimate market yet, but you can find on the black market. They're a nightmare for testing officials."

I'd heard a bit about SARMs (Selective Androgen Receptor Modulators). The word on the street was that they had a powerful anabolic effect, but that it came from a completely different mechanism. "What do they do? I mean, how do they work and how effective are they?"

"Chemically, they bind to the androgen receptor, just like testosterone, and signal the body to build more muscle and strength. It's like testosterone without the testosterone. Actually, the testosterone analogy is apt, because they're every bit as effective as [testosterone]."

That was a big claim to be making. "Sure, but that's the goal of every steroid or supplement, isn't it? How close to testosterone is it? If testosterone is 100, what's this SARM? Even the various testosterone injectable forms aren't 100."

X2 jotted a few things down on a napkin. Just numbers. "Testosterone has an anabolic rating of 100, and the anabolic rating for SARMs is reported in medical studies to be between 97-103. Testosterone is 100 because it's the gold standard, and all steroids are measured against it on that scale."

"Firsthand?" I asked. In answer, he set a small bottle on the table. It was your basic tinted glass bottle, a dark blue with a medicine dropper top. It sat on the table with the salt and pepper, next to my iced tea. "You've used it?"

He nodded, as if I'd asked a stupid question. "Yes. On an ethical level, I wouldn't be telling athletes to use it if I hadn't already."

"That's both some big confidence and, for many people, strange ethics."

He laughed. "If I ask you to jump off a bridge, you can be sure that I've jumped off. Plus, you know all your friends are doing it."

I jumped in. "Let me pause you there. The worry about steroids has always been that people, especially teenagers, thought everyone was doing it and that they had to to keep up. Bonds supposedly started because he thought McGwire and Sosa already were. but we both know the numbers were never that high. Canseco said 80 percent, but I don't even believe 50 percent is accurate."

He shook his head. "I think the number in baseball is high. Not Canseco, but high."

"I won't disagree, but I think it's like marijuana use in high school. A lot experiment, but a few use."

He jotted something on the napkin I couldn't quite see. "The numbers—and I'm talking correlative figures here—don't support the idea that teenagers are emulating professional athletes in terms of steroid use. If the 'steroid era' in baseball could be counted as an upswing in steroid use, you can look at those years in teen use, and there isn't a corresponding upward trend. Kids nowadays love their MySpace and Facebook. Both of those sites have had active steroid busts on them, where members were selling to other members."

Good, now Congress can blame a series of tubes, cables, and wires for the problem. "Back to the SARMs. Your athletes are already using this?" I knew this was the case, but I needed to hear how he was setting up programs. "And if you're telling your athletes to use it, that means of course that athletes are already using this, something that most people haven't heard of."

He paused and took a sip of his water. "Yes, it has been in the literature for several years, well before this last Olympic games, though it became readily available in the United States last winter. December, I believe." Just in time for Christmas giving... or baseball's offseason. "At that point, we started using it for my athletes that needed to beat tests. I have an athlete who is coming off a two-year suspension, and they're playing a big role in his drug use. He was suspended for steroids, but that was before me."

I smiled. "Nice to see recidivism is at least educated. What have been the results?" Instead of answering, he took out his phone, showing me a picture on his Blackberry of a giant of a man. Clearly a bodybuilder, this guy was massive. "OK, no question about that. Now, if you're saying that in some cases its better than testosterone, why wouldn't you use it more broadly, even in an untested situation?"

"Practical reasons, actually. It isn't widely available, and since there are limited places to get it, I typically don't use it in place of testosterone. A low dose of testosterone is still undetectable. For example, 100 milligrams of testosterone propionate, administered every other day, will keep my test/epi ratio under 4:1, which is the accepted range, and my total testosterone gets to 958. 1000 is the accepted normal range."

"Sounds like more self-experimentation."

He nodded. "I've already jumped off the bridge. Some might call that a very apt analogy."

"What about side effects?" I asked. "Would George Costanza be worried about shrinkage?"

He laughed. "It doesn't convert to estrogen or dihydrotestosterone, and it doesn't affect natural hormones. I can tell you first-hand that there's no shrinkage," he said, eyeing the server.

The supply question really interested me. THG was effective because few places knew of it, let alone had the ability to synthesize it. With a bit more complicated chemistry at its heart, SARMs might be held back for a while by supply. X2 agreed, noting "We go through SARM droughts. There's none for sale right now in the States, but a shipment will arrive in 11 days. Don't get any ideas, because it's reserved!"

So it was perhaps self-limited. "We have a limited supply and presumably high cost. That should keep it limited to a very specific population."

He paused before agreeing. "It's more expensive than testosterone, but not prohibitively expensive for professional athletes. It's far cheaper than growth hormones. It's about as expensive as Lr3-IGF1, another undetectable performance enhancer." Lr3, the latest form of IGF-1 (insulin growth factor) had been around for a while, with most athletes abandoning it for the cheaper and more available insulin. WADA has been hinting about an IGF-1 test, though they've been talking about an HGH test for far longer, and it's still not widely available or even broadly accepted.

"Tell me, what kind of cost are we talking about? Most people have no idea what any of this costs."

He reached out and held the bluish bottle up. He unscrewed the top, drew some into the dropper and put some on his fingertip. The drop sat there, looking all the world like flaxseed oil. That wasn't going to help things. "This bottle? It will run you about seventy-five, maybe a hundred bucks."

"That's nothing," I said, stunned. "I could afford that, if I was ready to jump off that bridge."

"It's not expensive," he said, wiping his finger off and putting the bottle back in his pocket. If he was carrying it around like this, it wasn't just to show it to me. It had to be clear of the refrigeration issue that made HGH and IGF so tough to carry. "It's just more than testosterone. That's a concern for bodybuilders, people who aren't making the baseball or NFL money and need to megadose. It's expensive to be undetectable. Thousands for hormones, hundreds for SARMs, more hundreds for IGF-1, and I like to keep costs low. Barry Bonds was a notorious cheapskate. Athletes, even the very rich ones, balk at three grand a month on a drug bill."

"Cost and availability is why we're seeing minor leaguers and Latins go 'old-school' and get busted for Winstrol. I mean, I saw a bottle of Winstrol at the pharmacia when I was in the Dominican Republic last month, and that was at a resort!" He nodded, so I continued. "The one I've seen most inside of baseball has been insulin, and that wasn't even noted on the drug report that MLB made public recently. We have economic incentive, plus opportunity, to do it without being detected. Thousands of dollars in drug bills—and your consulting fee, of course—can lead to potential millions."

"Yes," he said, pointing at me. "We're really talking about incremental gains here. Added up over several seasons, that can create superstars. You don't go from Little Mac to Big Mac in a year, but look at the progress he made yearly, and those incremental gains were worthwhile, and hardly the gains you get from andro!"

McGwire may not be here to talk about the past, and while we may never know about his usage, theories abound. I wanted to test one of mine. "I've always been convinced that McGwire started using not to get big, and certainly not as early as what Canseco said, but to try to recover from the plantar fasciitis."

He didn't hesitate. "Wouldn't you? People want athletes to be noble and fall on their swords instead of taking drugs and getting over injuries, yet they take their Lipitor and Viagra to get over whatever ails them. Sports is the only job in the world where you're denied access to medication that can help you recover from job-related injuries. Yet somehow, cortisone shots are noble. Schilling gets a cortisone shot, plays through the pain, and is a hero."

I pointed to his pocket. "Limited supply. Reasonable cost. We'll see this in baseball this year, won't we?"

"No doubt." Looking into his eyes, I could see that he had none. It wouldn't surprise me if he knew names. "Everyone knows a guy who knows a guy. They're new and sexy and becoming a buzz word with the strength guys. McNamee or Alejo would know SARMs if they were still doing this." (I guess he didn't realize Bobby Alejo was back in the game, recently hired by Oakland.)

"But if it's a guy that knows a guy, like it was with steroids, isn't this just setting things up for another BALCO?" I asked.

"Not a BALCO, but smaller BALCOs. A couple rogue chemists and performance specialists working together with a select few athletes. We'll see cells like this popping up. We have already. The East German doping program was too big, and that's why it got busted. BALCO was too big and too loud, but little clusters of coaches and athletes teaming up with chemists... that's the future."

"Sure," I said. "We saw it before, but everyone treated BALCO like it was a singularity. Conte didn't get that he should keep his head down. Is this SARM thing the intermediate step between the steroid era and the genetic doping era? I thought Beijing was going to be where we had the freak step out and look like that cow."

He smiled. "I don't know if we necessarily need to go that far. You've seen those gene-doped rats and the Belgian bulls. They're not very athletic. It's crude at this stage, so we need another step. Something before that level, but above what we have now. That's SARMs."

"But what if your guy doesn't know the right guy or right cell with the right stuff?" I asked. "I mean, GNC is already selling something called 'SARM Extreme.' Beyond that, there's a shelf life for undetectable, since you can't market something and keep it a secret. How long is it before Don Catlin has a test for SARMs the way he did for THG?"

"Yeah, SARMX by MHP. That's nothing but a waste of money. The testing? Catlin? I like that guy a lot, actually. He realizes that he isn't there to catch every cheater, but rather a few here and there, and put up a good show that sports are clean. Clean-ish. How long? They're already trying to figure one out, and some studies have identified metabolites. Just remember, the side of the street I work on, we're usually a step ahead. If they come up with a test they're comfortable using, then a molecule here or there and we'll be OK again. I'm not convinced they're particularly close, either. They've said they're close on an HGH test since Bush was President. The first one, I mean. The real problem is that now, anyone who is good is suspected of drug use. If you put together a 75 home run season, that would mean you'd have to come correct and make sure 100 percent of your drugs are undetectable. Usain Bolt was suspected of doping as soon as he set a world record, and that's the new trend."

The meal was over, and neither of us were dawdlers. I had covered everything I'd hoped to and more in the hour I had. "So let me sum this up: you've got a drug that's as effective as anything you've ever had in your arsenal. It's undetectable, has no side effects, and only a few people have access to it."

He nodded and smiled. "Yes, and you know that insulin and IGF are in that arsenal too. IGF has been available on the black market for over a decade. Insulin is available at Walgreens."

"In other words, it's going to be a good year for the black hats?"

He laughed again. "The black hats always have a good year!"

With that, X2 got up to leave. As the waitress came with the check, she watched him leave, as I could tell many people were doing. She turned to me and asked, "Is he a football player?" I just sighed. "Something like that."

UNFILTERED
An Open Letter to Murray Chass
Nate Silver

When writer Murray Chass accused statheads of undermining "most fans' enjoyment of baseball," Nate Silver jumped to BP's defense.

Hi, Murray.

I write to you as one baseball fan to another. There are only a few of us who are fortunate enough to have turned our love for baseball into a career. We are both in that lucky group. That's why I was disappointed to read the following in your column today.

> I suppose that if stats mongers want to sit at their computers and play with these things all day long, that's their prerogative. But their attempt to introduce these new-age statistics into the game threatens to undermine most fans' enjoyment of baseball and the human factor therein.

Fans today have a lot of choices about how they consume baseball in general, and their baseball media in particular. Baseball Prospectus' mission is to provide them with an informed and independent perspective that helps to accentuate their enjoyment of the game.

I am not sure whether you have made a habit of clicking on those links in our daily newsletter, but if you do, you will find that we are talking about many of the same things that you are. We're talking about how the Oakland A's can win the World Series, how the Veterans' Committee is doing a poor job of recognizing the contributions of players like Ron Santo, and how recent moves in the baseball industry are shoving baseball's most devoted fans aside.

Sometimes, our arguments involve statistical analysis, and sometimes they do not. To the extent that we use statistics, we look at them as part of the puzzle rather than the whole picture. We do, however, try to ensure that where statistics are used, they are used correctly. We have argued, for example, that the writers who selected Justin Morneau over Derek Jeter in the American League MVP balloting made a mistake not because they didn't use statistics, but because they used statistics in the wrong way. They focused on Morneau's RBI total, while ignoring that Jeter did a far superior job of getting on base, plays a much more difficult defensive position—and actually did a better job than Morneau of knocking runners in from scoring position when he had the opportunities.

We have found that millions of baseball fans appreciate our perspective on issues like these. At worst, we hope to offer them a choice. At best, we hope to increase the caliber of baseball discussion, and to give them another way to love and enjoy the game.

I would personally invite you to attend one of the events on our book tour, to appear on Baseball Prospectus Radio, or to participate in a Baseball Prospectus chat. I think you will be pleasantly surprised by how much you have in common with our readers. We are all baseball fans first, and we come carrying neither agendas nor pocket protectors. Alternatively, I am in New York frequently, and would invite you to attend a Yankees or Mets game with me. You have done a lot for the game of baseball and it would be a pleasure to meet you. I hope that your comments today reflected nothing more than a lack of familiarity with our people and our product.

Sincerely,

Nate Silver
Executive Vice President
Baseball Prospectus

🕗 MAY 1, 2006   💻 http://bbp.cx/a/5026

DOCTORING THE NUMBERS
When the Rains Come
Rany Jazayerli

A 2006 game between the Royals and A's that was wiped away by water prompted Rany Jazayerli to take apart one of the game's silliest rules.

On Saturday night, the Kansas City Royals and the Oakland A's played a baseball game at Kauffman Stadium. The two teams elected to swap roles for the evening: the A's played the role of doormat, as starter Esteban Loaiza was assaulted for five runs in the first inning and was knocked out in the second. The Royals did their best impression of an offensive juggernaut, drawing seven walks against just one strikeout, and scoring six times, four of them on a grand slam from Reggie Sanders. Kerry Robinson, called up from Triple-A that morning, became the first Royal in two years to garner two hits in a single inning. Jeremy Affeldt had his third straight impressive start, allowing a single run and fanning five hitters in three innings of work.

But you can be forgiven for being skeptical that such an event ever took place. You will find no box score listing the above events at ESPN.com. A click on the box score at MLB.com renders a blank page. What actually transpired on Saturday night is destined to become a rumor, a myth, one eventually completely forgotten. Thousands of witnesses notwithstanding, history will tell us that no baseball game was ever played on this date, at this place.

Because, you see, it started to rain.

As predicted well before gametime, the Kansas City skies opened up and pelted the stadium with something fierce. The rains started almost as soon as the game got underway, steadily coming down heavier and heavier until, with two out in the bottom of the third, the umpires pulled everyone off the field. After a two-hour delay, when it became clear that the downpour would continue through most of the night, the game was officially postponed. And everything that had occurred up to that point ceased to exist, became null and void, was given a mulligan.

And I, for one, find this stupid beyond words. The rule that places major-league teams in a position of playing a "do-over" like they were six-year-olds on a sandlot might be the single dumbest, most offensive rule in all of professional sports.

(Quick tangent here: the specific details of this game have nothing to do with my outrage. My Royals fandom notwithstanding, I didn't particularly want the Royals to win, and I certainly didn't want the A's to lose. As far as my baseball loyalties lie, I am perfectly happy to see this game struck from the books.)

As the rules of baseball are written—rules which have not changed since the 19th century—no major-league game is considered "official" until five innings have been played, or four-and-a-half if the home team is winning. It is a rule so fundamental to the game that no one ever gives any thought to how absurd it is.

Because as the rule stands, any game that you attend as a fan has the potential to be meaningless. Until the magical bottom of the fifth inning rolls around, anything that occurs (Felix Hernandez strikes out the first 12 batters in a game, Albert Pujols hits three grand slams in his first three at-bats) does not officially exist. Once-in-a-lifetime events—an unassisted triple play, a pitcher who gets five strikeouts in an inning—are not officially sanctioned as "events" until the game itself is sanctioned as "official."

This isn't a theoretical concern. The story of Roger Maris is fairly well known, that he hit a home run in 1961 (July 17th, at Baltimore) that was rained out of existence with the Yankees up 4-1 in the middle of the fifth. His final tally of 61 would have been 62; more importantly, the grounds for an asterisk (or "distinctive mark") would have been so spurious that even Ford Frick might not have tried to add one to the record books. On June 1st, 1958, Al Kaline homered to lead off the bottom of the second inning, but the game was rained out in the fourth. (Thank you, Retrosheet!) Kaline finished his career with 399 homers; you do the math.

George Brett holds the Royals' franchise record with 317 home runs. I watched on TV as he hit another one in the top of the first off of Ben McDonald in Baltimore on August 5th, 1990. The game was halted in the middle of the first, which is why his record isn't 318 home runs.

Baseball is fairly unique among American team sports in that inclement weather can force games to be delayed or postponed quite commonly. But let's compare baseball to tennis and golf, two sports whose rulebooks are at least as hidebound in tradition as baseball's is. Golfers are not forced to replay an entire round because they were pulled off the course after six holes. When matches are delayed at Wimbledon, they resume from the point at which play was postponed. Yes, sometimes golf tournaments are shortened from four rounds to three on account of heavy rains throughout the tournament, but those decisions are made before anyone has teed off for the fourth time—the results of holes that have been played are sacrosanct.

In baseball, nothing is sacrosanct for the first four innings. On September 6th, 1995, Cal Ripken played in his 2,131st consecutive game, breaking Lou Gehrig's record. Desperate for good publicity in the wake of the strike that had just ended five months prior, Major League Baseball pulled out all the stops in celebrating the event, delaying the game for 22 minutes while Ripken took a celebratory lap around the field and shook hands with fans in the stands. When did this celebration occur? In the middle of the fifth inning, when the game became "official."

At least Mother Nature cooperated, and no harm was done to fans who had bought their tickets for that game months in advance. But what about the fans who ponied up the dollars for tickets to the Cubs game on August 8th, 1988—the first night game in the history of Wrigley Field? That game was rained out after three innings; the "official" first Wrigley Field night game came the following night. The fans who attended the August 8th game got a rain check and a Screw You sandwich.

Then there is the the utter absurdity of baseball's rules as they apply to a game that is stopped by rain after five innings. According to Rule 4.11 of the Official Rules of Major League Baseball:

> If the game is called while an inning is in progress and before it is completed, the game becomes a SUSPENDED game in each of the following situations: (1) The visiting team has scored one or more runs to tie the score and the home team has not scored; (2) The visiting team has scored one or more runs to take the lead and the home team has not tied the score or retaken the lead.

Assuming I have parsed the language of the rule book accurately—it appears to have been written in early-20th-century lawyerese—then there are four possible scenarios that can occur to a game that is stopped with two outs in the top of the seventh:

1. If the home team is winning, the game is considered complete, and all stats count.
2. If the visiting team has tied the game or taken the lead in the top of the seventh, then the game is suspended and will be resumed from that point.
3. If the visiting team was already ahead after six innings, then the game is considered complete, but anything that occurred in the top of the seventh inning is struck from the record.
4. If the game was tied at the end of six innings, then the game has to be replayed from the beginning, but the game is considered a tie and therefore all the statistics from the game are counted.

This is insane.

This is a rule that was concocted at a time when the rulebook also stipulated that a walk required nine balls, a pitcher had to stay inside a box fifty feet from home plate when he threw the ball, and games on Sunday were both illegal and a crime against God. The other rules have changed; this one has survived.

We haven't even considered the nightmare scenario here, which is a game postponed by rain in the postseason. (There may be a rule which allows for the suspension of games in the playoffs, but if there is, I can't find it.) While (to the best of my knowledge) no team has ever had an easy victory taken away from them in the playoffs by Mother Nature, there have been a number of close calls. As Rob Neyer discusses in his excellent new book, the deciding game of the 1925 World Series was played in weather that can only be described as unplayable, in large part because Commissioner Landis had already taken heat after Game Two of the 1922 World Series had ended in a tie because of "darkness" 45 minutes before sunset. After Game Six of the 1986 World Series —you might recall there was a bit of drama in that series—rain postponed Game Seven by a day. And while it may be in poor taste to point out, what if the Bay Area earthquake had hit an hour or two later, with the Giants well on their way to winning their first game of the Series in the fourth inning?

I can't be the only one to envision a scenario that has the Cubs beating the Cardinals 10-0 in Game Seven of the NLCS, when Wrigley Field is suddenly deluged with a rainstorm in the fourth inning, and the game is called off. If you think Cubs fans treated Steve Bartman cruelly—they'll probably drag weatherman Tom Skilling out of his house and toss him into a vat of boiling oil.

The solution here is so obvious that it's almost not worth describing. All games that are postponed will be considered "suspended games," and will be resumed from the exact point that the game was stopped. If the score is 14-0 in the top of the ninth, or if the game is scoreless in the bottom of the first, the game needs to be completed.

It would eliminate shenanigans like a team winning in the top of the fifth purposely making outs to get to the bottom of the inning before the rains came, or a team that's losing in the bottom of the fifth taking its sweet time between pitches while the rains come down.

The solution is so obvious that it already exists—at the minor-league level. From Rule 4.11:

> National Association Leagues may also adopt the following rules for suspended games in addition to 4.11 (d) (1) & (2) above: (3) The game has not become a regulation game (4 1/2 innings with the home team ahead, or 5 innings with the visiting club ahead or tied). (4) Any regulation game tied at the point play is stopped because of weather, curfew or other reason.

In other words, for National Assocation (i.e. minor-league) teams, games which are tied, or games which are not "regulation" because they haven't finished five innings, are allowed to be "suspended" and continued from the point of stoppage at the earliest convenient moment.

So why haven't major-league teams caught on? Simple: money. By allowing games to be considered complete as early as the fifth inning, major-league teams don't have to accommodate fans who bought tickets to a game they were unable to see to its completion.

Aside from being an exercise in selfishness, the unintended consequences of this decision are such that it may create as many problems as it solves. Because of the pressure to complete a game in one setting, umpires frequently will have the fans (and players) sit through hours upon hours of rain delays in the hopes of getting in enough innings for the game to count. Games that have to be replayed in their entirety require complete, 18-inning doubleheaders at a future date, which either cost a team a coveted home gate or lead to the dreaded day/night doubleheader.

Bud Selig likes to think of himself as "The People's Commissioner," bringing innovations to the game that the fans are clamoring for, or at least innovations that he thinks they're clamoring for: the wild card, three divisions, three rounds of playoffs, interleague play. How about fixing something that's actually broken, Bud? How about fixing a rule that is actively hostile to the fans? How about fixing a rule that one October day may well become the center of the biggest controversy in sports?

As it is, on the Royals' pre-game show Saturday, the announcers discussed the weather situation for several minutes, pointing out that the huge blip on the radar that was headed for the stadium, and they made the point that the teams would be lucky to get five innings in. In other words, the game started without any expectation from anyone that it would actually count. That is psychotic.

So the next time you go to a game, try not to dwell on the fact that everything you're watching on the field is just an illusion. At least until the fifth inning.

| SEPTEMBER 22, 2008 | http://bbp.cx/a/8108 |

PROSPECTUS HIT AND RUN
The Decline and Fall of Yankee Stadium
Jay Jaffe

After viewing the final game held in the Yankee Stadium situated at the ballpark's original site, Jay Jaffe reflected on the way the House That Ruth Built went out.

Back on September 13, a week ago last Saturday, I attended my final game at Yankee Stadium, the last of over 130 contests I've witnessed there over the course of 13 seasons. Like the Yankees' doomed run of consecutive postseason berths, like the team's residence in the House That Ruth Built, like so much else this season, my stay at the ballpark ended not with a bang but a whimper, as a listless lineup appeared barely able to summon the energy to go through the motions of losing to the Tampa Bay Rays, 7-1. The Yanks didn't score until the ninth inning, or even draw a walk on the afternoon. Who were those pinstriped zombies?

With little to engage me regarding the desultory affair beyond the sharp performance of Rays hurler James Shields, the return to the field of Rookie of the Year candidate Evan Longoria, and the friendly banter of my companion for the game, I made a futile effort to soak up my final hours in the ballpark. From my perch in Section 626, a Tier Box on the upper deck near third base, I attempted to drink in the familiar sights and hear the familiar sounds, but every time I tried to summon the requisite emotion regarding my last lap, I came up empty. It was an emptiness that had nothing to do with ballclub's current standing, either. Like many a Yankees fan, I accepted their October-less fate a while back; the moment when I reached for my emotional parachute arrived when the team's trainers ushered Joba Chamberlain off the mound on a steamy August night in Texas, the victim of a shoulder strain. Rather, the empty feeling came from the recognition that for as much as I once loved the venerable venue, my relationship with the place—and by extension, the organization—has been in an accelerated decline over the past several years, one that sadly robbed me of a bit of my passion for attending games in the Bronx.

As such, I had a hard time investing in the nostalgia surrounding Sunday's long-anticipated swan song at Yankee Stadium. All season long, with increasing frequency as the date approached, tributes to the most storied venue in sports history this side of the Colosseum in Rome could be found in every medium, as everyone from legendary writers to grizzled former players to fresh-faced bloggers offered their perspectives regarding what made the stadium special to them. I wrote one myself (it's pending at Bronx Banter), but only after spending months procrastinating the task. Deep down I knew I couldn't share my selected slice of history without serving a few stinging reminders regarding the ugly truth about the Yankee Stadium I've experienced over the last eight seasons. The encomiums may continue beyond the grand farewell, but I'm left with a bad aftertaste, and I'm sure I'm not the only one.

One of the ironies of my life was being the holder of a ticket to the Yankees-Red Sox game scheduled for Monday, September 10, 2001. A hard rain fell that evening, but with information regarding the game's status impossible to come by, my friend Nick and I had gone to the stadium, hoping the bad weather would subside. We snarfed down soggy hot dogs from under a rickety umbrella as the rain fell, and as we ate we watched a young woman in a Nomar Garciaparra jersey dance in the six inches of water which had accumulated in the front row of Yankee Stadium's upper deck. Full of nitrates, we went home, little knowing that the cataclysmic events of the following day would change our ballpark experience along with the rest of our world.

The Yankee Stadium which emerged in the immediate wake of September 11 was a defiant symbol of national unity in a time of crisis, and I had the honor of attending a few of the games there, including Game Three of the World Series, when President Bush threw out the first pitch of what *Sports Illustrated* writer Tom Verducci called "the ceremonial first pitch to America's recovery" (alas, stadium security was so heavy that night that I couldn't gain entry until the second inning, after Bush had departed). The problems began when the Yankee organization, from owner George Steinbrenner on down, couldn't let go of that symbolism. "God Bless America" became a permanent staple of the seventh-inning stretch, devolving from the spectacular pomp of Irish tenor Ronan Tynan's delivery during home playoff games to the banality of the canned recording of Kate Smith and the US Army Band's version. More on that in a moment.

Accompanying the regular renditions of "God Bless America" were heightened security procedures that subjected patrons to no small litany of hassles while doing little to make them more secure. Given the cursory frisking procedures and lack of metal detection capabilities, it would have been possible to gain entry with a 9mm handgun jammed down the back of one's pants and a Bowie knife sheathed in one's sock, but without those, the organization simply inflicted its increasing paranoia and greed upon paying customers. Backpacks and briefcases were immediately banned from the ballpark after September 11, as though any potential ticketholder might be a terrorist smuggling in a tactical nuclear weapon swiped from the imagination of some z-grade thriller. Not even Shea Stadium—located only two miles from LaGuardia Airport—stooped to such extremes. Anyone coming to the park while porting one of the banned bag types—from work, perhaps—was forced to check it for a fee at one of the bars or restaurants across River Avenue. Anyone wishing to schlep a bagful of items into the stadium—say, a scorebook, a jacket, and reading material for the long subway ride home—was forced to place those items in a flimsy, clear plastic grocery-type bag available outside the turnstiles. No other types of bags, such as ones with reinforced handles, were allowed, first for vague "security purposes," and then, once fans began pressing Yankee security to explain these increasingly irrational and seemingly arbitrary requests, "because you're not allowed to bring bags with logos inside." As you may have divined, I had many a terse confrontation over this policy.

Umbrellas were banned as well, subjecting patrons to a true soaking at the stadium's souvenir stands, where they could shell out $5 for a flimsy poncho. Confiscated umbrellas were consigned to giant heaps near the turnstiles, where aggrieved fans departing a game were granted the opportunity to choose a replacement vastly inferior to the one they'd brought. But perhaps the reductio ad absurdum was the stadium's ban on sunscreen—yes, really—thus creating another opportunity for profiteering inside the ballpark.

All of those were petty annoyances of a type not unfamiliar to any New Yorker; one basically signs up for a host of such inconveniences upon taking residence here with the hope that they'll be outweighed by the advantages of city dwelling. Far more ominous were the crowd-related issues that exacerbated over the past few years. To appreciate them, one need understand the trend of rapid attendance growth that occurred during the Joe Torre era:

Year	W-L	Attendance	Per Gm	Growth	Won
1995	79-65	1,705,263	23,521	---	Wild Card (under manager Buck Showalter)
1996	92-70	2,250,877	27,789	18.1%	Division, World Series
1997	96-66	2,580,325	31,856	14.6%	Wild Card
1998	114-48	2,955,193	36,484	14.5%	Division, World Series
1999	98-64	3,292,736	40,651	11.4%	Division, World Series
2000	87-74	3,055,435	37,956	-6.6%	Division, World Series
2001	95-65	3,264,907	40,558	6.9%	Division, Pennant
2002	103-58	3,465,807	43,054	6.2%	Division
2003	101-61	3,465,600	42,523	-1.2%	Division, Pennant
2004	101-61	3,775,292	46,609	9.6%	Division
2005	95-67	4,090,696	50,502	8.4%	Division
2006	97-65	4,248,067	52,445	3.8%	Division
2007	94-68	4,271,083	52,729	0.5%	Wild Card
2008	85-71*	4,298,655	53,070	0.6%	Nothing

Winning four world championships in the five years from 1996 through 2000 helped to drive per-game attendance in the Bronx up 61.4 percent, even given a millennial slump. Attendance leveled off from 2000 through 2003, but the combination of the team's dramatic return to the World Series via Aaron Boone's home run and the arrival of Alex Rodriguez the following spring helped push the Yankees towards and then over the four million mark, becoming just the third team ever to clear it. Growth slowed as Yankee Stadium approached its theoretical maximum, its narrow concourses and spartan amenities overwhelmed by the teeming masses; at that point, the ballpark became a hazard.

For me, the final straw came on April 30, 2007, after attending a tense Saturday game against the Red Sox in which the Yankees prevailed. A very bipartisan, alcohol-fueled crowd had been at each other's throats all game; the cheap seats in Tier Reserved had featured numerous fights and ejections. An irrational security force nonetheless sealed off several of the stadium's ramps, slowing the exits of legions of emotionally overheated fans. It took 40 minutes to crawl from the upper deck to the subway platform, and while I'm no claustrophobe, all I could think about on my painfully protracted way out was the deadly human crush of English soccer riots. The limiting of the exits apparently became standard operating procedure, and if the consequences didn't turn tragic the way I kept envisioning, they nonetheless added an unnecessary, dangerous level of discomfort to the experience of attending a game in the Bronx.

Then there was the "God Bless America" flap. Shortly after my uncomfortable exit experience, an odious policy regarding the playing of the song came to light in the local media. Stadium security forces had apparently been ordered to restrict fans from moving during the song as "an expression of patriotism." According to Howard Rubenstein, the spokesman for the Boss, "Mr. Steinbrenner wanted to do all games to remind the fans about how important it is to honor our nation, our service members, those that died on September 11 and those fighting for our nation." That's a noble gesture, but unfortunately, using security forces to coerce a crowd to participate is completely un-American, almost certainly illegal, and unconstitutional. That's not patriotism, that's fascism.

The policy returned to the public eye last month, when a fan alleged that he had been harassed and assaulted by New York City police before being ejected from the park for his failure to comply. The NYPD has refuted the man's story, but at least one witness account backs up his version of events.

The incident, which may result in a lawsuit, kicked off a wave of negative publicity surrounding the stadium's final days. The public was reminded of the fuzzy math of the park's $1.9 billion replacement on the other side of 161st Street, long a matter of some dispute at this site. Fans were forced to reckon with the the ugly reality that the new park is built not for them but for the corporate class. Inevitably, an increasing number of fans will be priced out of the ritual of regular attendance.

Even as the Yankees have made a show of maintaining stability in their low-end ticket prices as they move across the street, the truth is that fans are being forced to less desirable locations, with fewer choices. As the longtime member of a ticket plan, I can attest to this firsthand. Eleven seasons ago, my friends and I banded together to buy two seats for a flex plan allowing us to pick 15 games from the schedule, plus another pair for a guaranteed game in each round of the postseason. We chose the Tier Boxes, the lower portion of the upper deck, a terrific vantage point because of the seats' close proximity to the action. Our timing was ideal; we joined the party just in time to watch an ample portion of the 1998 Yankees' roll, right up through Game Two of their World Series sweep. The plan eventually increased to 26 games (one for each Yankee world championship) over the course of our tenure, and we maintained rights to post-season tickets even as those of later flex plan members were downgraded to "if necessary" games. As our seniority increased, a higher percentage of our seats wound up in the wedge between the imaginary extensions of the first- and third-base lines behind home plate, increasingly desirable seats that took some of the sting out of rise of our ticket prices from $20 per game back in 1998 to $60 per game this year, and the way the industry-wide trend towards a tiered pricing structure involving "premium games" (primarily those against the Red Sox and interleague opponents) took hold, limiting some of our choices.

Unfortunately, the team's relocation program is every bit as foreboding as it sounds. In the new park, our 26-game flex plan becomes a 20-game "unflexibility plan," with the choice of dates restricted to an every-fourth-home-game cycle beginning with either the second or fourth home game of the year. Instead of those tickets being located in the wedge behind home plate, we are limited to an option of paying either $75 per game for seats between home and first or third bases, or $65 from beyond the bases to the foul poles. Our shot at post-season tickets is reduced to the opportunity to partake in a Ticketmaster pre-sale Charlie Foxtrot. Futhermore, those Tier Box (now Terrace) seats are recessed 30 feet further from the field of play. I believe each ticket plan comes with a coupon entitling the bearer to be beaten with a truncheon across a kidney of stadium security's choosing, but that may just be a rumor.

So you can forgive me for being a little peeved about the run-up to Sunday night's finale. I couldn't avoid watching the game, but neither could I summon the will or the cash to attempt securing a ticket; instead, I viewed the festivities from the comforts of my couch. Despite the Yankees being more or less eliminated from post-season play, the event was a festive occasion, full of moments of genuine emotion amid contrivances which turned the game into something akin to the All-Star pageant which took place there back in July, such as the mid-inning removals of Andy Pettitte and Derek Jeter to elicit ovations from the capacity crowd, and the plan for Mariano Rivera to pitch the ninth inning no matter the score. I'll leave a description of the festivities to those lucky enough to attend, and simply concede that it took a heart much harder than mine to prevent being moved by the night's events.

Nonetheless, the spectacle wasn't enough to wash away the bad aftertaste over the way things ended at the House That Ruth Built, and I strongly suspect that I won't be the only fan voicing that sentiment in the years to come. As Yankee captain Derek Jeter told the assembled crowd last night, it was Yankee fans' legendary fervor that made the ballpark such a special place. It remains to be seen how much a more upscale crowd will have to cheer about in the team's new home.

SIX-FOUR-THREE
Redecorating Your Glass House
Gary Huckabay

After the BALCO scandal broke, Gary Huckabay cut through the self-righteous outcry uttered by most of the media with a dose of reality.

Over the last few days, the shrapnel from the BALCO explosion has started to find some flesh. In a staggeringly stupid move, someone—I'm presuming from the federal government—leaked grand jury testimony about specific MLB players and the drugs they received from people like Greg Anderson, Victor Conte, Charlie Callas, or anyone else working out of a strip mall or light industrial office in Burlingame, Calif.

Anyone with access to a keyboard, microphone, or telephone has weighed in on this. Local and national talk show hosts are more than happy to point out any number of things that may or may not be true, may or may not be relevant, but sure as hell serve to put the speaker in a position of perceived moral superiority, whether or not said position was earned.

There's enough decrepitude and childishness on this issue to go around, but let's start at the beginning, before the rules, before the ridiculous cries of "Who will save the children?"—a laughable cry from media outlets who sell half their ad inventory to beer companies looking to attract new, young customers under the age of majority. At the beginning is one simple question: Do steroids, human growth hormone and other "performance enhancing" drugs really enhance baseball performance? I assume that they do, but if asked for evidence, I couldn't supply any. There is significant evidence that anabolic steroids, used in a particular fashion, cause a number of deleterious physiological effects, but I've not seen any hard evidence that any of the drugs in question really do improve baseball performance. And if they do, do they help more than the amphetamines that ballplayers have been using for more than 30 years? I'm not a physiology guy, but I'm guessing a little meth would help a hitter more than the marginal muscle mass gain of say, Dianabol.

But let's assume there is a gain in performance due to "the cream," "the clear," HGH, THG, or other various and sundry chemicals. Do you really think this is something new, and falls disproportionately on the shoulders of Jason Giambi and Barry Bonds?

The idea that performance-enhancing drugs are something new in baseball is mammothly Pollyannaish. Americans on the whole tend to mythologize the past. The '50s weren't like "Leave it to Beaver," as much as a sizable chunk of the citizenry would like to believe that they were. Similarly, baseball has had players looking for a chemical edge as long as there have been games to win or lose or, more to the point, money to be made. West Coast Turnarounds, greenies, and all sorts of other chemicals have been used by ballplayers since before I was born. This isn't anything particularly novel.

I'm not going to defend anyone who's chosen to take performance-enhancing drugs to excel on the field. The drugs may or may not have specifically been against MLB's rules, but I don't think anyone can make a case based on ignorance; if you're trying to hide an activity, you've probably got a good idea that people wouldn't approve if they knew you were doing it. But I don't think this is a cut-and-dried issue of a few athletes using illicit substances. Instead, I believe the bigger concern here is one of hypocrisy, the symbolic trumping the substantive, and misplaced moralism.

The headlines are about Bonds and Giambi, but I'm struck by two other things that seem to me much more important and headline-worthy:

- A member of federal law enforcement appears to have broken federal law by leaking grand jury testimony. And to what end? To create a PR event and magically summon athletes' attorneys to ESPNews? On the scale of despicable crimes, I find that considerably worse than an athlete taking drugs, and hence risking their own health, to perhaps hit a little better.
- We have federal agents hanging out in Burlingame trying to track down people like Bill Romanowski and other athletes for acquiring or using drugs that really only represent a threat to themselves? Are you f***ing kidding me? Did we catch Osama Bin Laden over the weekend? Have these agents already finished working with the chemical and energy industries to harden soft terrorist targets like refineries and chemical plants? My tax dollars are being spent to go after people like Victor Conte, rather than building new schools or paying down the debt? Again, I'm forced to ask, are you f%^&ing kidding me?

This whole phenomenon has become a Rorschach test for everyone concerned. If you didn't like someone before, you'll use this as further evidence to support your position as logical and righteous. If you're a selective enforcer of morals, like most of us, you can scream from the rooftops that athletes are setting a bad example for our kids by using these drugs, which of course have been available and prevalent in high school at least since I graduated back in '83, before the press covered anyone in MLB using them. If you're one of the sepia-toned fans, you can cling to your illusions that today's players aren't as talented/tough/dedicated as players were in the past.

There's a lot of ugliness in our collective hearts and minds that gets reinforced and hardened by this, and the boys at ESPN have continued to move away from actual sport and towards melodrama in their coverage of it. Reality check: this is a story about a few athletes who may or may not have used drugs to improve their performance, at the risk of their own health. The drugs may or may not have been effective, but what's certain is that your tax dollars have been chasing a guy who gave a ballplayer a cream that may have resulted in a few extra hits, instead of enforcing other federal laws that actually make a positive difference in our lives.

Maybe the agents on this case could have been taking courses in Arabic, or learning about forensic accounting and how to detect white-collar crime, or putting together a program to increase security at ports. Instead, they've given us an Ionesco-esque set of press conferences and news stories as the lead-in to "3," next weekend on ESPN.

PROSPECTUS HIT AND RUN
Take Me Out of the Hall Game
Jay Jaffe

As Jay Jaffe reported, baseball labor pioneer Marvin Miller's desire *not* to be elected to the Hall of Fame made perfect sense.

The Hall of Fame was in the headlines last week, and not just because the retirement of Mike Piazza kindled the inevitable debate over the catcher's Cooperstown credentials. No, an even more deserving honoree made waves via what was almost certainly a first: a request to the voters not to be elected.

The unusual appeal came from Marvin Miller, who served as the executive director of the Major League Baseball Players Association from 1966 to 1982, overseeing baseball's biggest change since integration via the dismantling of the Reserve Clause and the dawn of free agency. Snubbed by an ever-changing electoral process three times in the past five years, the 91-year-old Miller is not only tired of his hopes being dashed, but disillusioned with the institution itself. "As I began to do more research on the Hall, it seemed a lot less desirable a place to be than a lot of people think," said Miller in a recent interview with Baseball Prospectus. "Some of the early people inducted in the Hall were members of the Ku Klux Klan: Tris Speaker, Cap Anson, and some people suspect Ty Cobb as well. When I look at that, and I looked at the more current Hall, it was about as anti-union as anything could be," he continues, citing recently ousted Hall president Dale Petroskey's past service in the union-busting Reagan White House. "I think that by and large, the players, and certainly the ones I knew, are good people. But the Hall is full of villains."

Thus Miller's sharp and unprecedented statement, which was sent in a letter to the Baseball Writers Association of America, a body that actually bears only a small share of the responsibility when it comes to the VC:

> Paradoxically, I'm writing to thank you and your associates for your part in nominating me for Hall of Fame consideration, and, at the same time, to ask that you not do this again... The anti-union bias of the powers who control the Hall has consistently prevented recognition of the historic significance of the changes to baseball brought about by collective bargaining.

> As former executive director of the players' union that negotiated these changes, I find myself unwilling to contemplate one more rigged Veterans Committee whose members are handpicked to reach a particular outcome while offering a pretense of a democratic vote. It is an insult to baseball fans, historians, sports writers, and especially to those baseball players who sacrificed and brought the game into the 21st century. At the age of 91 I can do without a farce.

Miller's odd request isn't exactly timely. The 2008 induction ceremony is two months away, and the VC isn't due to vote on the next slate of non-playing candidates for another 18 months. But at his age, there's little reason to wait, and when asked about the curious timing, Miller deflects the question, emphasizing the two decades between his retirement and ballot debut.

Miller was instrumental in shifting the game's century-old balance of power from the owners to the players, creating an impact that induced former Dodger announcer Red Barber to place him alongside Babe Ruth and Jackie Robinson as "one of the three most important men in baseball history." In addition to securing the right to free agency via the destruction of what was effectively a system of indentured servitude, Miller's leadership brought the average annual salary of a major-league player up from less than $20,000 to over $250,000, while establishing a salary arbitration system, substantially increased pensions, the right to impartial arbitration of grievances, the right to hire an agent to negotiate on the player's behalf, and the right to veto a trade after achieving enough experience. There's room for debate as to whether opening this Pandora's box was a uniformly good thing; nobody likes a labor stoppage, or to see a star player price his way out of town, but the talents of professional ballplayers don't mean that they should be deprived of basic workplace rights, and their skyrocketing salaries have gone hand in hand with ever-increasing attendance levels and revenue growth.

There should be little doubt that Miller deserves a place among the small handful of movers and shakers honored with a bronze plaque in Cooperstown, however. The various Veterans Committees charged with overseeing such elections have done a shoddy job in failing to reach this conclusion. From his retirement in 1982 to the VC's reconstitution in 2001, Miller never even appeared on a ballot, as even the most venerable members of the old committee, such as sportswriters Leonard Koppett and Jerome Holtzman disagreed on his eligibility, bogging down in the fine print of rule 6(b) of the "Rules for Election to the National Baseball Hall of Fame." To Miller's former constituents, the rule was clear. Said one former player on the committee: "The rule says 'baseball executive,' not 'executive employed by Major League Baseball.' Marvin Miller was the executive director for all the players in baseball, not just the players of just one team. The players are baseball. If Marvin Miller isn't a real baseball executive, who is?"

Heavy hitters concurred. Hank Aaron wrote, "Miller should be in the Hall of Fame if the players have to break down the doors to get him in." Tom Seaver called Miller's exclusion from the Hall "a national disgrace." Brooks Robinson, a member of the Hall's Board of Directors, promised, "This year, we're going to ask the right questions and find the right answer to get it done."

That was eight years ago. Since then, the reconstituted VC at least has solved the issue of Miller's eligibility, but they bypassed him on the 2003, 2007, and 2008 ballots. In the first two votes, the electorate consisted of all living Hall of Fame players, plus the Frick and Spink award winners (broadcasters and writers), plus members of the old VC. Each voter could list 10 candidates on his ballot, with a 75 percent threshold required for election. On the composite ballot with executives, umpires, and managers, Miller got just 43 percent of the vote (35 out of 81 votes) in 2003, as even the players whose careers he helped the most couldn't be bothered to return the favor. Reggie Jackson, one of the first big beneficiaries of free agency, struck out in spectacular fashion, failing to connect the dots between his own wealth and privilege and Miller's tireless work on baseball's labor front: Reggie sent in a blank ballot while telling reporters of the entire slate, "I looked at those ballots, and there was no one to put in."

Miller sees additional irony in Jackson's actions. "What he doesn't seem to understand when he says the Hall should be just for players is that it's not," he notes. "The first commissioner, Judge Landis, is in the Hall of Fame, and if he had lived long enough, not only would Reggie Jackson not be in the Hall of Fame, he never would have had even one at-bat in the major leagues, because Landis campaigned far and wide among the owners against breaking the color line."

Jackson's remarks helped stir some awareness among the Hall of Fame's rank and file. The slugger realized the error of his ways, and Miller fared somewhat better in 2007, when he received 63 percent of the vote (51 out of 84 votes) on the composite ballot, higher than any other candidate except umpire Doug Harvey. The increased support was of little consolation; indeed, Miller was already braced for the bad news, telling the *New York Times*' Murray Chass (a Spink honoree who made his mark by pioneering the coverage of the business side of the game), "It would be nice, but when you're my age, 89 going on 90, questions of mortality have a greater priority than a promised immortality."

Miller's candidacy wasn't due for reevaluation until the 2011 ballot, but the VC's string of oh-fers prompted another yet another reconstitution and a vote conducted at last December's Winter Meetings. Prior to the vote, even commissioner Bud Selig, a man who waged war against Miller's successor Donald Fehr, went to bat for him, stating that the "criteria for non-playing personnel is the impact they made on the sport. Therefore Marvin Miller should be in the Hall of Fame, on that basis... Maybe there are not a lot of my predecessors who would agree with that, but if you're looking for people who make an impact on the sport, yes, you would have to say that."

For the 2008 election, a pair of small, separate committees considered the managers and umpires on one ballot, and the executives and pioneers on another. A 12-member electorate which could vote for no more than four candidates gave Miller just three votes while electing former owners Barney Dreyfuss and Walter O'Malley, as well as Miller's bitter adversary, former commissioner Bowie Kuhn.

That last result is a travesty. "They might as well have elected Marge Schott," says Alex Belth, a student of baseball's labor history who authored *Stepping Up: the Story of Curt Flood and his Fight for Baseball Players' Rights*, a biography of the man whose challenge to the Reserve Clause was overseen by Miller. Kuhn served as commissioner during the bulk of Miller's tenure, and his propensity for playing chicken with the union led the owners to a series of high-profile defeats, including labor stoppages in 1972 and 1981 as well as the landmark Messersmith-McNally ruling by independent arbitrator Peter Seitz. Belth points out that while those victories over the owners are easily recognized, Miller's success in using collective bargaining to secure from management such rights as the impartial arbitration of grievances (the mechanism for the Messersmith-McNally case) and salary arbitration played a key part in reshaping baseball's landscape.

Candidate	2007	2008
Barney Dreyfuss	----	83.3%*
Bowie Kuhn	17.3%	83.3%*
Walter O'Malley	44.4%	75.0%*
Ewing Kauffman	----	41.7%
John Fetzer	----	33.3%
Marvin Miller	63.0%	25.0%
Bob Howsam	----	25.0%
Buzzie Bavasi	37.0%	<25.0%
Gabe Paul	12.3%	<25.0%
John McHale	----	<25.0%
Bill White	29.6%	----
August Busch Jr.	16.0%	----
Charley O. Finley	12.3%	----
Phil Wrigley	11.1%	----

In the 2007 election, Kuhn had garnered just 14 out of 84 votes, well behind not only Miller but six other candidates. In fact, of the elected, only O'Malley had received significant support beforehand.

The stunning reversal came about via a deck stacked significantly in favor of Kuhn and against Miller. Of the committee's 12 members, only Monte Irvin, Bobby Brown, and Harmon Killebrew ever played in the majors, and none played a single game in the post-Reserve Clause era. Along with three writers—Paul Hagen (*Philadelphia Daily News*), Rick Hummel (*St. Louis Post-Dispatch*) and Hal McCoy (*Dayton Daily News*)—the committee contained no less than seven owners or executives: Brown (American League president), John Harrington (Red Sox), Jerry Bell (Twins), Bill DeWitt Jr., (Cardinals), Bill Giles (Phillies), David Glass (Royals), and Andy MacPhail (Orioles). If anyone needed further evidence of the vote's reliance on the old boy network, it's worth noting that DeWitt, Giles, and MacPhail are legacies whose fathers (and in MacPhail's case, a grandfather) were on the management side during the Reserve Clause era. Worse, Giles, Harrington, and MacPhail were part of management during baseball's disgraceful collusion saga in the late-'80s.

"Now I took one look at that committee and I didn't have to have any help. I couldn't possibly get nine votes out of that committee," says Miller, noting not only the taint of collusion amid the voters but also more subtle links to management. "Just take Monte Irvin. Fine player, et cetera, but after he was a player, he worked for Bowie Kuhn for more than 10 years. Would you expect him to vote for me?"

Were this a jury, Miller could have demanded a mistrial due to the slate's bias, but Hall candidates have no such recourse. Jim Bouton succinctly summarized the shafting: "Essentially, the decision for putting a union leader in the Hall of Fame was handed over to a bunch of executives and former executives. Marvin Miller kicked their butts and took power away from the baseball establishment—do you really think those people are going to vote him in? It's a joke."

Still, a one-shot committee larded with management flunkies isn't solely responsible for Miller's plight. "The players have f—-ed this up time after time, year after year," says Allen Barra, who helped Miller write *A Whole Different Ballgame*. He's emphatic that the lion's share of the responsibility for Miller's plight lies with his former charges: "To a man they've all said that something needs to be done. Why didn't they do something?" That's a question Barra has been asking for at least the better part of the past decade. "If they were still part of the players union they might have gotten something done, but they're afraid of not being asked back for a ceremony. The players are the Hall of Fame. It's their bats, their balls, their memorabilia. All it really takes is leadership and the desire to buck the system."

Such leadership is apparently in short supply. According to an MLB.com article by Barry Bloom, three players who were key members of the union during Miller's heyday declined a spot on the voting committee: Seaver, Robinson, and Robin Roberts, the latter of whom served on the original committee that hired Miller in the first place. With friends like those, who needs enemies?

Asked how he accounts for this failure of support, Miller blames the process and the logistics of assembling the committee as much as the players. "I don't account for it... I've talked with some of those players, who have called me from time to time, and at least one has said that that was a mistake on the part of the players. He confessed that. He said they all are relatively busy people, that many of them don't like traveling to Cooperstown for meetings of committees and so on; including someone on the board of directors. It's just not considered a high-priority item, that's all."

It's unclear whether the Hall will honor Miller's wishes. Hall President Jeff Idelson—who took over in late March after Petroskey resigned—believes the VC will again be reconstituted before the next vote. He says that the institution plans to discuss the matter with Miller, and that while his request will be communicated to the screening committee, there's no guarantee his wish will be heeded; Miller will be nominated if the committee so decides. That reaction suggests Miller's statement may work as a bit of reverse psychology—if he's daring the electorate not to tab him, what better way to piss the man off?

Miller is hardly waiting for the Hall's overtures. He sounds genuinely at peace with his own intractability on the matter, invoking an unlikely pair of historical figures, Civil War General William Tecumseh Sherman and comedian Groucho Marx. "[Sherman] basically said, 'I don't want to be president. If I'm nominated I will not campaign for the presidency. If despite that I'm elected, I will not serve.' Without comparing myself to General Sherman, that's my feeling. If considered and elected, I will not appear for the induction if I'm alive. If they proceed to try to do this posthumously, my family is prepared to deal with that."

The mention of Marx adds a final bit of levity to Miller's request. "What [Marx] said was words to the effect of, 'I don't want to be part of any organization that would have me as a member.' Between a great comedian and a great general, you have my sentiments."

PROSPECTUS Q&A
Fernando Perez
David Laurila

Few ballplayers majored in creative writing, quote Bob Dylan, and express their fondness for Robert Creeley, but Fernando Perez was one such athletic intellectual, as David Laurila discovered.

Fernando Perez is not your run-of-the-mill professional athlete. A speedy outfielder who made his big-league debut in early September, the 25-year-old New Yorker is not only a big part of the Rays' future, he also holds a degree in American Studies and Creative Writing from Columbia University. Perez went into the last weekend of the season hitting .273/.344/.473 with three home runs and five stolen bases in 55 at-bats. He sat down with David in mid-September to talk about his views on both baseball and life.

David Laurila: How would you describe Fernando Perez?

Fernando Perez: As a baseball player, I'm a very high-energy guy; I'm sort of pesky. From talking to a lot of pitchers I've met—I think it's really cool, especially in pro ball, where you get the camaraderie between teams and you have guys talking before and after the game—I've been told that I'm a pretty tough out and very unpredictable. If I'm doing my job, I'm usually a problem out there for the other team. I play hard and love to run fast; it never gets old to me to make a ground ball to the second baseman a close play, no matter how many times I've been consecutively retired on the 4-3 groundout.

DL: How about away from the field?

FP: Off the field, I think I'm kind of the opposite, at least in terms of peskiness. That's not exactly a great quality to have socially. In baseball, you're just kind of what everybody says you are. On a team you get pegged, and then you're thoroughly reminded about what you are as much as possible. All we do is make fun of each other. I'm the eccentric. I'm a ridiculous person, a clown that doesn't take himself very seriously as a way forward socially. I'm the New Yorker—just about anyone who knows me well would agree that I'm sort of tirelessly anti-academic and way too cynical to own up to, or even be proud of, being the Ivy League guy—which is the subject of half the interviews I do. I'm also too self-deprecating. I would own up to being a New Yorker because it entails a number of characteristics I'm very proud to have acquired, like the many facets of tolerance, and maybe an ease and interest in modernity as it encroaches and alienates most of the rest of the population. I'm a bit of everything, because I think that's a good idea; I'm much more concerned with wellness, say, than politics, and hope to be a good man someday, not a rich one or a famous one.

DL: Getting back to baseball, do you pay much attention to statistics?

FP: I really try not to. Once I got into pro ball, I had a very clearly defined role, which I had really never had before. Especially playing in the northeast, where the baseball isn't very good; had I grown up in Florida or California, I probably would have always been a leadoff guy. I probably would have been a much more polished product coming into pro ball, but once I kind of understood my role as a leadoff guy—getting on base and being a table-setter—I really began to prize on-base percentage. And I did a pretty good job of that, really up until this year. This year is the first time I wasn't up close to the top of the league or where I thought it should be. But I'm not really a stat guy. I'm more big on how your teammates feel you did, and what they feel about what you can do and will do, let's say in the playoffs. A lot of guys gauge that by talking to their teammates about how they feel about certain guys as a player. To me, that's everything, because it's what your teammates and manager think of you; it's the feeling you leave when you leave a stadium. Those things are pretty important.

DL: A number of people who study statistical analysis argue that there is no such a thing as a clutch hitter. What do you think?

FP: I don't know. It seems like there are, but I don't think there is such a thing as a clutch hitter so much as there are guys who aren't as good when there's less on the table. For instance, if it's a 5-0 game in the eighth inning, you might not get the same out of that guy as you would if it was 1-1 in the eighth inning. It's funny, you'll have these guys who end up hitting .275, but with runners in scoring position they're hitting .350. Duly, there are a lot of players who are fantastic in lopsided affairs—again, it's a feel thing. Right now I'm hitting .240 in the big leagues and people in Tampa seem to be thrilled with my play because of the timing of the hits, although it's still feels very .240 to me. What makes the clutch hitter might be the chances he has to hit which do nothing but make his stats better—the not-clutch at-bats in lopsided games in which maybe his focus isn't quite as heightened, and he doesn't do as well.

DL: In an interview with *Baseball America* earlier this year, you said that you saw some very surprising pitch sequences in Triple-A. Should a hitter ever be completely surprised by how he's being pitched?

FP: That's a good question, and I think it's probably part of the reason why I struggled at the beginning of the season. Really, it's just from what you've seen before and how guys perceive you. Usually, if you're struggling a little bit, you're going to get a lot of fastballs because they want to dispatch you quickly, but once you're giving a team trouble they have to do whatever they can to throw you off your game mentally. I led off the game a couple of times where I saw off-speed pitches the first pitch of the game. Anything that can get you thinking that this situation is a little bit different from another situation pulls you out of your routine in baseball. Baseball players are creatures of habit, so that sort of stuff works. That's why guys throw up and in, to wake guys up and say, 'This isn't just an at-bat; watch yourself.' Those sorts of things work. But I think the surprising-pitch-sequences thing was kind of just something to get over; if guys can throw a pitch you're not expecting, and get it over for a strike, they're going to do it. It's similar to how guys have been very surprised when I've bunted in hitting counts—a guy moved back and I took advantage of it. In upper-level baseball, it is tougher to start rallies, so you have to take any advantage that you can get.

DL: In that same interview, you cited Dave Stewart as having been your favorite player growing up. Notably, you added that one of the reasons is that Stewart is black. From my observations, players typically cite people of their same race or ethnicity as their favorites or as being the best at what they do. What are your thoughts on that?

FP: My answer was a little tongue-in-cheek, but it was also based on real life. It wasn't so much that I was an Oakland fan, but they had my Little League colors, I was a pitcher and Dave Stewart was a pitcher, so he was someone I could look up to. Short players often like short players, and tall guys like tall guys. I think it's very simple kid stuff, but I think that any time, especially as a minority—if you see another minority that is there and is having success, it becomes sort of like an attainable thing for you. For me, Dave Stewart was a figure that affirmed that it was possible. So while idolizing Stewart wasn't really a serious thing, and my answer was mainly tongue-in-cheek, it was grounded in a true experience.

DL: With that in mind, do players, especially players of color, have a responsibility to be role models?

FP: Yes and no. I understand it. Years ago Charles Barkley made the comment, "I'm not your role model; your parents are your role models." And I really do believe that, but as a player it would be a little bit of an oversight to say that what you do, and how you represent yourself and the city and franchise you play for, or how you represent a race doesn't mean anything. It always means something. Let's say you have curly red hair, and you're out making trouble. If you are, you're making it rougher on guys with curly red hair. People watch too much TV and consciously or subconsciously take what they see as gospel, and brown-skinned folks these days understand that more than anyone. A few times a month I disappoint someone Caucasian by not speaking like a rapper. I don't know what's going on in the NFL, but the trouble they're having is a big deal, as you hear people discuss all the players going to jail, and I'm sure it affects young black scholar-athletes. Someone said to me at a bar once "all you guys have to do is behave." I don't think I have to explain how unfortunate that is. It is the less-adept parents that count on athletes, but you become a role model as soon as your image is reproduced in print or on TV, whether you care to acknowledge it or not—whether that's appropriate or fair or not, it has already happened.

I'm 100 percent Latin American, but I'm Afro-Caribbean, so I belong, really and truly, to the large umbrella of minorities that includes the African-American people. I understand the responsibility I've taken on; it comes with the territory of being an athlete. If you want to play baseball, there are going to be tons of kids looking up to you and heeding what you're doing. And there are going to be a ton of American citizens who are going to be holding you up to the light and making brash, sweeping assertions about your race and people who look like you, based on the way that you represent yourself. So, to me it's a responsibility, and I'm comfortable with it, but I do truly believe that the role model really falls with the parents. A lot of times the parents are really expecting too much from athletes, and many athletes are reluctant. So I'm kind of in the middle. I understand the power of an image on television, and let's say I get a chance to play in the big leagues for four years and my image was always on television—and people watch too much TV—there's a certain power that carries. So even though I don't think it's necessarily my responsibility, I'll always try to use that power in a positive way. It's really an opportunity to do good, or not to do anything, and I seek to do better as opposed to worse.

DL: What impact does being a Cuban-American have on your life?

FP: I'm second-generation, so I've really had all the experiences of being an immigrant, although for me they're mostly anecdotal; they're not completely mine, but they've always been very close to me in the way that I view things. I view myself as being extraordinarily fortunate. That's from my upbringing, from being at dinner tables at Thanksgiving or Christmas where people are just so happy to be in a free country. What always struck me at those dinner tables—what was always so striking is how grateful everybody was for this here and now. It's a thing where, if I didn't have those experiences, I might totally take some things for granted, as do many of my friends who grew up with me in that middle-class American experience. It has helped to shape my sense of being grateful for so many of the opportunities I've had. My parents and grandparents did all this work for me to have what is, for me, a very easy American middle-class life. I think it's something that most people don't have: a very strong collection of anecdotal history to draw upon. I'm a very grateful person. I felt lucky to be in Double-A; I felt extraordinarily grateful to be a Durham Bull. Now, to have this, is really, really amazing.

DL: I understand that one of your professors at Columbia once told you to "Let go of existentialism and write about baseball."

FP: Yeah, I did the writing program at Columbia; I wrote short prose. I had a teacher—her name is Leslie Sharp—and she has actually written quite a few personal essays about baseball published in fancy magazines and journals. And ever since high school, I've always fancied myself as a writer; I've had this real passion. And like any writer, I was just struggling to find my medium just as much as my voice, and my medium was somewhere in between short prose and personal essay. A really interesting thing that she said was that the best writers are real people having extraordinary experiences, not just "writers" trying to create something extraordinary out of nothing—that's the best writing. I had been sort of stuck in the world of fiction, and she and others told me that I have this incredible opportunity to use my skills to tell a real story, and slowly I'm submitting. But I'm in no rush, because the experience hasn't completely settled. To me, the most interesting story is the minor leagues. That experience, for a lot of guys, is like joining the army and not knowing quite what to do with life in these years of our physical prime and mental adolescence. To me, that's the story; the characters are richer. In the major leagues, the baseball is obviously incredible, but the other circumstances are so cushy it is almost like a country club. The drama isn't really there; it's in the really minor leagues with all the so much more authentic characters, many of whom are playing in less-than-favorable circumstances. There are guys with wives, and sometimes children at home, and they're not making any money. They're wondering, 'Will I ever be able to hit the slider?' or 'Will I ever be able to get good hitters out?' or 'Do I love her?' or 'Should I stop playing?' That, to me, is the story.

DL: How about the "existentialism" part of the comment?

FP: I'm using existentialism in the most general, almost inauthentic sense; to put a general tap on what I was most concerned with in my writing, which was self-discovery, and say, the life of the mind. A lot of people in the writing program were thoroughly into the social sphere, writing about things like relationships and politics; I was just very, very concerned with what you could probably call existentialism—natural for someone my age. I was writing in circles, tracing the meaning of life, and I think they wanted me to grow up and get on with a plan that would probably work! But I had never fancied writing a bestseller; it's more about what suits me and what I'm interested in. I write, and have always written, to organize complex emotions and to take my pulse. For nothing more, and for nothing less. It's a private art.

DL: You're a big fan of Robert Creeley's work. Why?

FP: He's amazing. I love how he's able to take these broad aural sensations and condense them into skinny, semi-linear poems that hit it right on the head. I love how accessible and undaunting he can be. I love his casual American masculine voice and the funny way he reads. But baseball really robs your attention sometimes. Right now I'm not reading at all. Like Bob Dylan said, "Right now I can't read too good; don't send me no letters." That's how I feel right now. I'm so vested in the team that I can't really give myself to a book. But Creeley is a guy that there's always time for; it's so easy; it's so simple, yet really satisfying.

DL: You started switch-hitting two years ago, which has me thinking about right-brain and left-brain, and if a person can teach himself to better utilize the non-dominant side of his brain, much like a hitter can learn to swing from the other side.

FP: That is stuff that is so interesting to me. I have learned a little about that, because I had a varied education in college—that's what American Studies is, really; I took everything from gender studies to jazz. But that was something I really began to wonder about. There's definitely a different feel from each side, so it's really a chapter in my minor-league experience. The experience of doing it was more than just an athletic quest, it was, as a person, knowing that you can do something pretty well one way, and to try it another way. And you're doing it in front of a lot of people; you're doing it for score, to be judged on. It was a really incredible experience, and I think it worked out pretty well. Had it not worked out, it would still have been a great experience.

DL: Are you left-brained or right-brained? Or are you a switch-hitter?

FP: I'm a switch-hitter. That's a great way to put it: I'm a switch-hitter. What's funny is that to balance myself I kind of have to employ some of the characteristics I use on the other side. From my right side, where I feel really strong, I have to often think with the simplicity that I approach everything with from the left side. From the left side I'm purely thinking about contact, about simple, fluid mechanics. That's what I need to bring to the right side to kind of square myself. And from my non-dominant side, my left side, I kind of have to bring grit and brute force to kind of square that side off. When I'm doing well, that's how I'm succeeding. I'm definitely right-brained though; I'm messy and a fan of intuition.

DL: Any final thoughts?

FP: I should maybe mention music, because it's such an important part of my life; it's probably my favorite thing. At my funeral I don't want them to talk: I just want them to play a few records. It kind of swallows all of my time. I don't really watch TV—I'd rather sit and let a record play. I didn't really give any modern stuff a shake until probably college, and now I've kind of heard so many different things, like guitar-playing stuff from the 1940s and old blues stuff. What I'm most interested in now is anything experimental and new, stuff that is kind of reaching for things, like a lot of experimental electronica and ambient music. Music is really, really interesting to me now. There was a while where they were saying that pop was so bad that music was dead, and I think the indie labels have saved music—labels that are capable of putting a certain type of music out there consistently. There are tons and tons of labels, which is really good because there's a lot of interesting music that gets out there and gets a chance to sustain itself by creating at least a small buzz.

DL: How many all-star teams do you think you'll have to make before your teammates let you pick the music in the clubhouse?

FP: Hah! Never, but I have a good way about it. I'll play the right sort of marginal thing that some guys like; usually I can find a way to play stuff that people like but they don't know that they like. But I'd probably have to make two or three all-star teams before I could hit shuffle.

PROSPECTUS Q&A
Joe Maddon, Part One
David Laurila

David Laurila's interview with Joe Maddon revealed the Rays' skipper to be a statistically-savvy hybrid of the old and new schools of managing.

When the Devil Rays hired Joe Maddon to replace Lou Piniella following the 2005 season, they replaced an old-school manager with someone who wakes up in the morning and pores over statistical information on his computer. The former Angels' bench coach is more than just a stat geek, though. Maddon may be a card-carrying member of the statistical analysis crowd, but he's also a strong believer in fundamentals and something called "good old baseball common sense."

David talked to Maddon about analyzing matchups, interviewing for the Boston and Tampa Bay managerial positions, and more.

David Laurila: In 2005, prior to you replacing him as manager, Lou Piniella criticized Devil Rays ownership for being more concerned with the future than the present. What are your thoughts on that?

Joe Maddon: I'm concerned with both. We do attack everything on a day-by-day basis—we go out and play and expect to win every night—but we know that we're fighting through some disadvantages. There are obviously some nights where, pitching-wise, the matchup isn't in our favor. On the field, we have some great skilled players, but the experience level isn't in our favor. But that doesn't bother me, because I know that what we're doing is proper. That's the present. The future is that I can see, in my mind's eye, what these guys will look like two to three years from now. I also believe that when these guys develop, and we figure out exactly what we do have—when the appropriate moment comes—we'll augment with the right guys from free agency or from trades. As an example, when you look at Edwin Jackson this year, and how he started out, it would be easy to say that in most places he'd be long gone by now. But we're developing him into what he's going to be in the future, which is a power pitcher who can throw his 99th pitch at 99 miles per hour. Of course you want to win every game, but we're not expecting to win the American League East this year, but we'd sure as heck like to be in a position to do that in 2009 and 2010.

DL: When you interviewed for the job, you reportedly presented a detailed plan of how you could turn the team around. To what extent can you tell us what that plan was?

JM: What we're doing on the field now, specifically, is—I'm really into fundamentalism. We have not been a fundamentally sound team, whether it's been on offense, or defense, or in general execution. For me, it's really about putting out the right concepts. I talk about concepts a lot. Even this year, during the course of the season, we'll come out once or twice during a home stand and make sure we go over things like cut-offs and relays; review bunt plays, etc. Offensively speaking, this spring training we had a big drive on seeing more pitches per plate appearance and on working on two-strike batting averages. We also put a big emphasis on getting runners in from third base with less than two out. What I did when I was with the Angels was try to break the game down into little compartments and create the concepts we need to attack them. What I've found here, with our group being so inexperienced, is that when you put out good information it takes time for them to mentally take it in and perform at a major league-level in the heat of a major-league game. But, going back to the plan, it was pretty much detailed, not just on the field, but off the field in regards to interaction with the coaching staff, front office, and scouts—just a variety of different topics. It was about analyzing the American League East and what it would take to beat those guys. It's what I used to do with the Angels, which is to try to cover every topic in trying to figure out what we need to do to get better, and then using our imagination to create concepts, or drills, or ideas, to get better in that area.

DL: You also interviewed for the Red Sox managerial job a few years ago. How did that interview differ from the one you had with the Devil Rays?

JM: The interviews with the Red Sox, with Theo [Epstein] and Josh [Byrnes], they kind of had it scripted a little more. They had specific exercises to perform, like rating things on a scale of one to five. As an example, some of the topics they wanted me to rate in importance were: the most important factors in empowering a coaching staff, how to handle a bullpen, and how to handle the media. There were five or six questions like that, and they asked about how I'd handle certain situations if they came up. With the Devil Rays, it was kind of like that, but it wasn't necessarily drawn up on a sheet of paper as specific exercises. It was more of a question-and-answer thing, like my thoughts on how to run an offense, how to put together a bullpen, how I handled a coaching staff, interaction with players; what my thoughts were on the communication process. So I think it was similar, yet different. The Red Sox were more specific, and exercise-oriented, while the Devil Rays asked many of the same things but presented them in a different way.

DL: Were there a lot of similarities in how the use of statistical analysis is viewed?

JM: Yes. The Red Sox, with Theo—they didn't really present to me that much, but I knew where they were coming from based on having played against them. With the Devil Rays, Andrew

[Friedman] and Matthew [Silverman] were both there, and they were interested in certain elements, but it was more of wanting to know what I thought. It wasn't them posing questions in such a way that I'd try to tell them what I thought they wanted to hear. That was something I appreciated. Listen, I'm really—I don't want to say I'm opinionated, but I feel strongly about what I believe. That said, I think it's also very important to be open-minded, and I'm always searching for new items of information and for new sources. If you can give me a compelling argument of why you think something, and it makes sense, I'm really open to it.

DL: How do you approach the use of statistics?

JM: Andrew and James Click supply me with a lot. I get the regular packet on a daily basis, and I go to ESPN.com and look at what's presented there. Then, Clicker presents me with this analysis based on groundball and flyball percentages, like, is this guy a groundball or flyball pitcher, and do hitters with a bit of an uppercut maybe have a better opportunity to hit against him than someone who is more of a flat-swinger. This is the kind of stuff I've paid attention to in the past, but now the information is there to look at, and it's backed up by numbers. So I might make a decision of who to play based on whether someone appears (on the printout) in blue, or if they appear in red, which is a negative, or in black, which is more neutral. Then I'll try to read into it deeper to see if there's anything I can use to exploit a match-up. Another thing I'll do is look at the opposing pitcher to see how he's been doing recently, and sometimes I'll look at box scores to see how he did in right-on-right, or right-on-left, match-ups against certain hitters I'm pretty knowledgeable about. I'm telling you man, when I'm trying to set this thing up on a daily basis, I'm looking at a variety of sources of information. I'm always looking for an edge. My mind never really shuts off.

DL: Does where your team is competitively, within the division, impact your decision process?

JM: If we were in the playoff hunt right now, I'd be even more extreme with what I'm analyzing on a daily basis. But because we are where we are, there are certain guys who are going to play regardless, and that's because we need to get a good look at them. I want to create the best matchups that I can, but a lot of what we're doing now is giving players an opportunity. It's what I talked about earlier—we need to know what we have as we look toward getting to the next level as a team. But overall, I can't even tell you how many places I look for information. Sometimes I get up in the morning and go right to the computer to pore over reports.

DL: Can you give us an example of something you might look at?

JM: I'll look at the opposing pitcher's breakdown, so I can see his batting-average-against in certain counts, in order to pick the best hit-and-run counts. And I always look at how often teams pitch out, and on what counts. When the other team is hitting, I look at how often, and when, their guys run. Some are negative-count guys, while others are almost always positive-count guys.

What that trend is will help dictate when we pitch-out. We have this tremendous report, that has so many different items in it, and I try to work it out early in the day, and then, about 15-20 minutes before the game, I like to lie down on the couch and go over it one more time, to make sure I've absorbed everything.

DL: Do you want your players to be statistically knowledgeable?

JM: No. They just need to go out and play. There are certain guys I might be able to give certain items to, but I've always handled players on an individual basis. If I think a guy can handle the information, I'll feed it to him. If I don't feel that he can handle it, I won't. There are some guys where you know it just won't matter to him—it's not going to make a difference—because he won't react to it one way or the other. To my mind, most of this information is for the coaches and the manager. Now, if you want to make a point, that can be different. An example would be Akinori Iwamura—his batting average has been slipping recently, and when he's hit fly balls he's been 9-for-62. We told "Ak" that those were his numbers when he put the ball in the air, and if he hit more balls on a line, or on the ground, he'll get on more and give us scoring opportunities. Another example is Josh Wilson, who has been doing a nice job for us—we'd like to see him do a better job hitting with two strikes. We showed him the numbers, and said, "this is your batting average with two strikes. Why not do something different, because if you continue on this pace it's going to be harder to hit around .300 or better, because you're killing yourself with two strikes." That's the kind of esoteric little information we keep, and I utilize it when it's appropriate to do so.

DL: If you have data that indicates you should go in one direction, and your gut instinct tells you that you should go in another, how do you reconcile that decision?

JM: For me—let's say that a hitter is hot; he's been swinging the bat well. On the other hand, the numbers show that he should have no success against a certain pitcher. Or maybe one of my pitchers has horrible numbers against somebody, but he's been pitching well recently. In those cases, I'll probably let the numbers go and put them out there. The other night, we were facing [Jeremy] Accardo, of Toronto, and I'd been studying his numbers. It wasn't a huge sample-size, but his numbers are so much better against left-handed hitters than they are against right-handed hitters. So we had two outs in the ninth inning, and I sent Josh Wilson up to hit for Ben Zobrist, which was right-on-right. He got a solid base hit, and we went on to win that game. That's an example of something that was according to statistics, but nevertheless against the book. A lot depends on where your players are. It's like whether you let one of your guys swing 3-0 or not. It might be someone who is perceived as one of your better hitters, but he hasn't been swinging well, so you don't let him fly. Or it's one of your lesser hitters, but he's been hot as hell, so you do let him fly. So, for me, it's a combination of the written information you have, your mind, your gut, and your heart.

DL: When you talk to old-school baseball guys, like a Don Zimmer, just how much of a difference do you find in how they approach the game compared to younger, more statistically-savvy, guys?

JM: The notion of the 'old school'—it's very difficult to get someone from that genre to want to study stats and analyze them as a method of making decisions. Instead, it's going to be primarily based on previous history, gut reaction, and whatever the book says. That's where the old school differs, and I'm not saying it's wrong, but that group just wasn't used to having all of this information available to make a decision. Of course, that group will make fun of this group, because in their minds the decisions are being made by a computer as opposed to good old baseball common sense. That always makes me laugh, because to me the best way to make decisions is to combine that good old baseball common sense with the information that is available—then you morph into this even better baseball mind. Somebody mentioned to me that they think I'm a pretty good combination of the old and new school, and I think that's the highest compliment I've been given as a manager and an instructor.

PROSPECTUS Q&A
Joe Maddon, Part Two
David Laurila

In the second part of his interview with Joe Maddon, David Laurila quizzed the Rays' manager on many of his unorthodox strategies.

DL: Your team, offensively, leads the American League in strikeouts right now. How concerned are you with that?

JM: I don't like it at all. Now, I know that some of the numbers guys might say that's OK, but strikeouts come into play in a lot of situations. You look at what we're doing with runners on third base and less than two outs—we're the worst team in all of baseball. That goes for American League, National League, and I believe all of Triple-A and Double-A. A lot of that is strikeouts, because we expand our zones too easily. I think if you can change your two-strike approach and put more balls in play, you're going to have an opportunity to score more runs.

DL: How much does the specific game-situation matter to you when you look at the impact of strikeouts?

JM: Sometimes I think the numbers are skewed a bit, because there's the first three innings, the fourth through the sixth, and the seventh through the ninth. There are so many different segments to the game, and they include times when you might want to bunt. You can't just blanketly take all of this information and say that it covers innings one through nine. I think you have to segment the game, according to what's going on, including your hitters versus their pitcher and who is on deck—what could possibly happen if we move the runner up here. Regardless, for me, the strikeout is the most useless out there is. I'd like to maintain a higher on-base percentage, and slugging percentage, and still do a better job of not striking out, because that contributes to better offensive production. I have specific ideas on how we can achieve that within the organization.

DL: Can you make those changes, which presumably include hitters cutting down on their swings, without sacrificing slugging percentage?

JM: I think you can, I really do. What I'm talking about is that when you get to two strikes, you go to what I call "The B-hack." For me, what that means is making a mental alteration as opposed to a distinct physical one. The "B-hack" consists of maybe choking up a little bit, looking away first, and thinking fastball first. I think that too many guys, by staying at the end of the bat, lose control of the head of the bat. I think that by not looking fastball, and thinking soft instead, when you get something hard you basically have no chance. I also think that when you're looking middle/in, and the pitcher goes away, you basically have no chance. However, when you're looking away, and he throws it in, you do. So, I'd like to set these parameters for hitters to work with. Something I want to do is a study on the number of doubles and home runs we've hit with two strikes, as opposed to what happened when we simply put the ball in play with two strikes. There are a lot of different ways to score runs, so where was there more benefit?

DL: Curtis Granderson was recently quoted as saying that he feels it's important to catch the ball out front rather than stay back and let it get deep. What are your thoughts on that?

JM: I agree and disagree, and I'll tell you why. When he says, "catch the ball out front," I think there's a bit of a misconception and you don't want your body to leak to catch it out front. To me, the closer the ball is to your body, the longer your swing is, and the farther the ball is away from your body, the shorter your swing is. Because of that, the farther the ball is from your body, the deeper you want to let it get. Conversely, you can't let it get deep if it's close to your body. For everybody, when you're hitting, your strike zone is basically a diagonal.

DL: Is there such a thing as a closer's mentality?

JM: Yes. To me, that's a guy who is good at that moment, and he enjoys that moment. He is able to maintain his "slowness" despite all of the stuff that's going on around him. Of course, a closer has to have at least one better-than-average pitch. It's also important that he has a short memory.

DL: Does that same mentality apply to hitters?

JM: The better hitters for me—yeah, they have short memories. It is one at-bat at a time, and an 0-for-4 doesn't bother them. Furthermore, they have this mental ability to grind out each at-bat. Chad Curtis and I used to talk about a mental batting average, and our goal, when he was in the minor leagues, was to have it be at least 90 percent—that he was fully prepared for at least nine out of ten at-bats. When he got closer to the major leagues, we wanted it to be closer to 100 percent. When you're talking about a minor-league hitter—God bless—if you're talking even 70 percent you're doing good. If a kid is doing well, he's going up there with a good awareness of everything that's going on, plus a good thought-process, including the team situation and his personal situation. There are a lot of things that go into an at-bat, and for me your mental batting average should be at least 95 percent at the major-league level.

DL: If the front office sends you a player and you find that he's closer to 70 percent than the 90-plus that you expect, how can you fix that problem?

JM: You sit him down. It's the old Dante Bichette theory, and we're actually doing it now with Dioner Navarro. When I had Dante down in Double-A, for about five minutes before the game I'd ask him how he was going to beat this pitcher: what did he know about him, how does he attack hitters, what is his go-to pitch? I got him thinking about his game plan. Right now, with Dioner, who is a catcher, we're sitting him down to talk about that night's pitcher, or maybe about one mechanical thing. Or it might be something like how we're going to attack David Ortiz that night. It's about five minutes—just a short burst of information—and it can make all the difference in the world for some guys.

DL: What can you tell us about the "Ortiz shift" that you've employed?

JM: Well, last year we employed it—this year we're not. He's changed dramatically since last year, and we based it on information. Last year we employed four outfielders against him, because there was nothing on the ground to the left side; nothing. There were no pop-ups either. But he was able to go down the line, and up the gaps, so we defended against that.

DL: Why don't you do it with more hitters?

JM: We have done it with Jim Thome and Travis Hafner. We did it for a while with Jason Giambi too, but we don't anymore. It just depends on where they're at, and we always have updated stuff to tell us that. Going back to Ortiz, he has a lot more ground balls to shortstop this year, and we've actually turned a couple of double-plays against him in those spots. It's a matter of what a player is trying to do, and that shifts yearly, if not monthly. The numbers help us determine that. Of course, part of it was visual, too—we wanted him to see something.

DL: So, it wasn't just based on spray chart information—there was also psychology involved?

JM: Absolutely.

DL: B.J. Upton struggled at shortstop last year, both offensively and defensively. Just how important was it to for you to get him settled, position-wise, especially from a mental standpoint?

JM: Last offseason, when we were trying to figure out how to do that, my suggestion was to make him a super-utility player. I wanted to de-emphasize his defense, because I felt that a lot of what we were seeing offensively was a result of him coming to the ballpark concerned about making errors. I told him to not worry about what happens on defense; I just don't care. I wanted him to bear down and concentrate on his hitting, and by doing that I thought he'd end up making fewer mistakes on defense. We started him out at second base, right field, and center field in spring training, and while he initially made some errors at second, he settled down after that. I think that he can still be a second baseman in the future.

DL: Do you feel that the pressure he felt at shortstop was primarily responsible for his struggles?

JM: Absolutely. The throw from shortstop is more difficult, and there isn't as much room for error as there is at second base. At second, you can bobble the ball for an instant and still have time to make the play. That extra leeway is like a little mental cushion. If you watch B.J. throw in the outfield, he has a great arm. He is like dead accurate from the outfield, because he knows that from that distance, if he's not accurate, it's OK. At shortstop, he felt he had to be accurate all the time, which made him inaccurate. Then, at second base, it's a shorter throw, so all he has to do is make the short flip over to Carlos [Pena] and not worry about it. I think with all players, you can work with them on all of the physical things that go into making plays, but until someone is comfortable between the ears, none of that stuff is going to matter.

DL: You majored in economics in college. What role do economics play in the baseball world of Joe Maddon?

JM: Honestly, I was not a very good student. With economics, "ubiquitous" was probably my favorite term. I guess that the number-crunching is something I liked. I've always been into that. I've always like analyzing statistical information, even before it was fashionable. When I was back in the minor leagues, as a roving hitting instructor back in the mid- to late-'80s, I probably had a more simplistic perspective, but nevertheless I saw the value in it. But my economics days at Lafayette College were probably a case of having to declare a major more than anything.

DL: Last one: How would you describe Joe Maddon?

JM: How would I describe myself? How about if we just say that self-definition is really boring?

PROSPECTUS Q&A
Ozzie Guillen
David Laurila

David Laurila spoke to Ozzie Guillen in an attempt to pierce the colorful skipper's public façade and ask him about his private personality, his in-game tactics, and the importance of his Latin-American lineage.

Ozzie Guillen is his own man. Outspoken and sometimes misunderstood, the mercurial White Sox skipper is not only colorful, he is also smart as a fox. Considered one of the most cerebral players in the game during his playing days, the 44-year-old native of Venezuela has shown himself to be no less wise as a manager, having led the South Siders to a World Series title in 2005. Now he has his charges—considered second-division fodder by most prognosticators when the season began—atop the AL Central as the pennant race enters its home stretch. A big-league shortstop for 16 seasons and a third-base coach for three more, Guillen took over as the White Sox manager in November, 2003.

David Laurila: When you signed your first professional contract in 1980, and someone had told you that you would someday manage in the big leagues, what would your reaction have been?

Ozzie Guillen: Well, I was only 16 years old, and it's hard for a kid at that age to go that far and think about it. But I've always liked to teach—I've always liked to coach—even at that time. From an early age, I always liked to be around baseball, and I liked to be around people, but there was no way that I was thinking about being a manager at that particular time.

DL: When did you first start thinking about managing?

OG: When I was playing, I was thinking about staying as a coach and staying in the game. Everything happens so quickly, and I am lucky to be able to say that I went from playing time to coaching right away, and not too many people have that opportunity—to finish your career as a player and all of a sudden you're a big-league coach, and a couple of years later you're a big-league manager. It happened so quickly. When I started to be a backup player with the Braves, Bobby Cox gave me the opportunity to start learning from him about situations and how to handle a staff. But when I was coaching, I never thought as a manager thought. Some guys, when they're coaching, they'll say, 'If I was the manager, I would do this, I would do that.' That would never go through my mind, because I had enough problems coaching and enjoying it. I never started thinking as a manager until after I got hired by the White Sox. I wanted the opportunity, but didn't have any experience; I didn't think as a manager, I didn't have any clue. I went to the meeting with Kenny [Williams] and I didn't even know what he was going to ask me. I never asked any of my managers what they were going to ask me, what the expectations would be, what I should do. I just went straight to the meeting and I guess that I responded the right way to the questions, which is why I have the job.

DL: How would you describe yourself as a manager?

OG: I'm fun to play for, there's no doubt. But it's not easy. I have a few rules that my players have to go by, and I think I'm kind of old-school. I think I'm more old-school than new-school; I'm an old-school type of guy. I like the little things, I like respect, I like discipline; it's 25 peoples' way, it's not only one guy's way. But I'm not going to say that I'm a good manager on the field, because the players will dictate how good you are. I treat my players like my brothers; I treat my players with a lot of love and a lot of respect, and I expect them to treat me the same way. The players know they have this friend for real, but I have a title and that title has to be respected. So it's not easy, but it's fun. It's not easy because I demand a lot of things.

DL: How much does the public perception of you differ from what you are?

OG: One hundred percent. I don't think the public knows who I am or what I do. I think that people see a different kind of personality than who I really am. A lot of people on the street, or around the ballpark, and a lot of media members that aren't from Chicago, they perceive me like I'm the tough guy, crazy, real bad, a troublemaker. But it's the complete, complete opposite of what the people perceive me as. I'm easygoing and have dinner with my players; I'm going out with the PR department guys and the clubbies. I don't want to say 90 percent different; I'm 100 percent different than what people look at me—the way I talk to my players; the way people think that I hate my players and that my players hate me. They think I'm walking around cursing people. I'm different than that, totally different.

DL: Casey Stengel provided reporters with a lot of quotable material, often to draw attention away from his players. Are you like Stengel in that regard?

OG: No. I never do that. Every time I say something to the media, I think that people think I'm pushing the button to take away the heat from my players. No, I say what I feel; I say what I should be saying; I say what I need to be saying. My players aren't about it. It never even crosses my mind to say something to give a distraction away from the players. No, I never will.

DL: How has what you experienced as a player impacted what you do as a manager?

OG: One thing about it is that they can't tell me something I don't know. They should respect, because I played a lot of years in the big leagues and always showed up. There are a few managers in this game right now managing because—I manage because I love the job. It's not because I need the money or need the fame. I manage because I love the passion of the game and I love to compete. But it's not about economy. That's why I say f*ck it. I say what I say and do what I do, and if people like it they like it, and if they don't there's one thing to do: they can fire me. And that would be fine with me, because I always say that managers have a job, and they have a job just to get fired. I don't worry about those situations. I don't want to say that I do this for fun, because this isn't a fun job. This is a pretty hard job, and I do it because I love it. I do it because I like to be around my players and so many different things. But I'm not losing sleep because I might lose my job. I don't need the money.

DL: You played for both Tony La Russa and Jim Fregosi early in your career. What did you learn from each of them?

OG: Well, with Tony I was a baby. And to me, I don't think there is a better manager than Tony when he has a rookie player under his wing. Tony prepares you unbelievably well to compete; he gives you the best chance. And I learned that; I learned to give the rookie guys the best chance to compete and have success. I think Fregosi changed my whole style of play and helped me to grow up in baseball. I think they're two different types of guys. You have to manage according to the type of ballclub that you have. But they are two people I admired a lot, because they helped me when I needed to be helped.

DL: How similar are you and Lou Piniella as managers?

OG: I don't know. I wish I could be half of Lou Piniella when I look at his career as a manager. I wish I had his experience; I wish I had the respect he has. But Lou, he can get away with a lot of things I can't. Lou can tell the media, "I don't want to talk to you guys today," or "Nobody ask any questions," and that will be fine. If I'm the same way with the media, I'm a piece of shit. I see that a lot. We walk in the same places, and I tell the Chicago media, "Two days ago, Lou walked away from the media room and you guys don't say anything." If I don't show up to the media room one day, I think I'd be blasted. But I like that Lou is aggressive. He's an old-school manager; he will protect his players the most he can. But I try to be my way. I love the way he manages, but like I say, the attitude is the same because of the way they taught us to play the game. We expect people to play the game the way we played the game, and that's not easy to do. We played the game different.

DL: What does the term Ozzieball mean to you?

OG: Ozzieball is baseball. Move the guy over, run the bases hard, break up a double play, pinch hit, hustle. A home run now in baseball is the big thing—'I hope I drive in 140 runs and hit 200 home runs.' I think baseball has forgotten about bunting and base stealing, putting on a pickoff play. There are so many things that can help you win baseball games, and I don't think that's Ozzieball, it's the way people should be playing baseball.

DL: Your team is currently second from the bottom in the American League in both stolen bases and sacrifice hits. Is that less your philosophy than it is roster-driven?

OG: I have a team, and I try to do the best I can with the guys I have. But I think that pretty soon in baseball—baseball is going to go back to the 1980s and the 1970s, where you have to do it. Now there are so many powerful players, and powerful lineups, that you have to try to compete against those guys in the raw power. But to me, I don't care what kind of lineup I have, I still believe that you have to play defense and you have to pitch. If you don't do those things, combined, I don't care how much power and how good a lineup you have, you're not going to win.

DL: What are your views on pitch counts and pitcher usage?

OG: Pitch counts are important when the game is not on the line. But if the game is on the line and I see that the guy is throwing the ball well, that's a guy I'm going to leave in. In the minor-league system they don't let the guys pitch very much, and then all of a sudden they're in the big leagues and they can only pitch six innings; that's it. You can't ask them for any more. But I always go with my gut feeling. One thing, my priority as a manager is to make sure I keep those pitchers healthy for as long as I can—don't overuse them. I want to make sure that the guys pitching on my ballclub are there in September and October, that they're ready to complete the last month of the season. To me, that's important.

DL: How much does your pitching coach, Don Cooper, influence your decisions when it comes to pitcher usage?

OG: I pull the trigger. It's easy for me, because he's been my pitching coach for five years. If I want a lefty warming up, I don't even have to tell him that I want this guy or that guy; he knows exactly what I want. That makes it easy for me.

DL: Are you concerned with how much your relievers are working in the bullpen, regardless of whether they come into the game?

OG: You have to be careful, and that's Don Cooper's job, to make sure to tell me that we didn't bring this guy into the game, but he was hot the last two games. Then we have to take into consideration that we may not use him the next day.

DL: Your 2005 championship team had Scott Podsednik in the leadoff position despite his not being known as a high on-base percentage guy. Why?

OG: Because he's the only guy we had who could run, and the key to the ballclub was when Podsednik was playing well. I think that the first two hitters were the key to that team. It was Podsednik and Tadahito Iguchi, and I think the big reason we won was because those two guys were unbelievable; they did a tremendous job. Now I've got [Orlando] Cabrera leading off. Right now there are maybe one or two guys in the league who are a legit leadoff hitter—the one you're really looking for to get on base and steal bases. I think you always try to put the guy with more speed on top, just in case for the big boys coming up. Getting on base is important, but if you get on base and are going to need three or four hits to score, that doesn't show me anything. I like the action, I like the action. I like to see some speed on the bases.

DL: To what extent do you identify yourself as a Latin-American manager?

OG: One-hundred percent, because I am. Nobody is going to take that away from me. I'm Latino and proud to be Latino. I'm proud to represent Latin America, and my hope is that every day that I step out on that field, I make sure that I do good because it will open the doors for a lot of different men. It depends how I do my job. I know that a lot of general managers will look at someone similar to me, someone from Latin America, and that's very important for me and our countries. The sooner you have the reputation as being a good manager in baseball—I guarantee they're going to be looking for people around Latin America to do their job. It's not easy to do, but I feel privileged to be myself, to have a job to open a lot of doors for a lot of people. And it can go either way. I can open a lot of doors for people or I can close a lot of doors for a lot of people. My job is to make sure I keep it [open]. Felipe [Alou] opened it for us, and we have a couple of managers keeping it open for us. I think that the worst thing that can happen is that we haven't managed for Latin America.

DL: That ties into the first question I asked, which was if you envisioned yourself as a manager when you broke into pro ball. How differently do you feel that Latin-American players are perceived, and treated, compared to 20 and 30 years ago?

OG: Before, we only had one guy on the team. Now we have three, four, five, six, seven Latin-American guys on the same ballclub. Before, you wouldn't even think about having a Latin coach. You wouldn't think about how many Latinos there are now. The game has changed. Now you have people here in the big leagues who speak the language. And that helps, having a coach or a manager who speaks the language. I think it also helps American managers if they can speak Spanish, because the communication would be better and you know when they say stuff about you. But there was no way I was thinking about it. I always wished that I'd be a manager one day in my life, but you have to think about how you get that shot.

DL: What was it like for you to sign out of Latin America in 1980?

OG: It was easy. Now is different than it was in the past. In the past, you'd see 30 kids for one scout; now you see 30 scouts there to see one kid. If you want to see somebody in Venezuela—if you go to Venezuela and you're a scout, they don't do shit. In my time, in the '80s, if you're a scout and go to Venezuela, everybody was kissing your balls and saying, 'Can you sign my kid?' Now, if you're a scout you're just another guy in the ballpark; now it's a different scenario. If the scout wants to sign you, he'll say, 'Here, take the money and sign with us.' Now, the players will say, 'Manny, I want $500,000; how much am I going to make? How much are you going to pay me?' Before, you were just happy to sign. I don't think that anybody in my era signed for more than a thousand dollars, maybe two thousand dollars. Now you don't sign nobody—I don't care who you are—if you don't give them at least 50, or hundreds. They're just not going to get signed.

DL: Should there be an international draft?

OG: No. No way. I think that hurt Puerto Rico; it hurt Puerto Rico bad. Now all the Puerto Rican guys have to go through the draft, and if they don't get picked they have to compete with the United States. To me, and this is my opinion, that's why you don't see too many Puerto Rican players like in the '80s when you had Rodriguez and Sierra, the Alomars—my god, just name them—Benito Santiago. Now you don't have those types of players; now there are just a couple of Puerto Rican players out there. I think that hurt Puerto Rico; that's my opinion.

DL: Any final thoughts?

OG: I think that, as a manager, a lot of people say that baseball has changed. Baseball hasn't changed. The people running this game have changed the game. Everybody, from managers to minor-league offices to coaches to trainers to scouts—they've changed it. Now it's a different ballgame; now you sign and you have an agent. That's one thing people ought to know: we need the media more than we need agents. Agents are there only to make money; the media can help you in your career. They can also destroy you, yes. But the agents? They can only destroy you. A lot of people think there are good agents, but there are no good agents in baseball. There are good players in baseball. A lot of people talk about the agents. "Look at this guy making 250 million dollars, Alex. Wow." I say, yeah, that's Alex Rodriguez. Why doesn't the same agent go find Pablo Ozuna the same amount of money? Before, I could count the agents; there were maybe four or five guys who were agents in baseball. Now, even my kids have f*cking agents. Everybody has an agent. That's why I think that baseball has changed. And maybe that's the owners' fault? Maybe they don't trust. I have an accountant to count my money. I have my kid, who is 16 years old, and I already have agents calling him, or calling me about helping him. That's changed a lot. At 16 years old I was worried about getting three hits every day. Now, at 16 years old, they worry about how much money you're going to get as a first-round pick. That's changed all this shit.

PROSPECTUS Q&A
Jack Zduriencik
David Laurila

Jack Zduriencik quickly became a sabermetric darling after taking over the Seattle Mariners' GM job, and BP's David Laurila sat down with him to discuss the busy start to his tenure.

He has only recently become a household name, but people within the game have known Jack Zduriencik for quite some time. Long regarded as one of baseball's best talent evaluators, the personable "Jack Z" started out as an area scout in 1983 and since that time has worn multiple hats for five different organizations, most notably the Brewers from 1999-2008. Named as the eighth general manager in Seattle Mariners' history in October, 2008, the 59-year-old native of New Castle, Pennsylvania has wasted little time in turning a seemingly backwards-thinking franchise into one that deftly melds old-school scouting and statistical analysis. From rebuilding the organization's infrastructure to executing an array of trades and free-agent signings, Zduriencik has been more than a little busy. The result is music to the ears of Mariners fans: in just 15 months, Jack Z has built a contender.

David Laurila: Is it fun being a big-league general manager?

Jack Zduriencik: Well, I don't know if I look at it quite like that, but I enjoy my job. I've always enjoyed my jobs, so I've been fortunate in that respect. Whether it was as an area scout, when I started out, or as a national crosschecker or a farm director or a scouting director or even an international director, I've enjoyed every position that I've had. When you're in this game, you go where it takes you, but you're always curious about this position. You have faith in your abilities, and when you're given a new job it's, "OK, here is the next challenge." So, I'm enjoying it and I'm very happy to be here in Seattle.

DL: Prior to getting the job, did you ever think to yourself, 'If I ever become a general manager, I'm going to earn a reputation as a real wheeler and dealer?'

JZ: No, I never looked at it like that. I think that you just do the job the best that you know how to do the job. When I was a minor-league director, years ago with the Mets, we did a lot of things in a short period of time, a lot of significant things that helped the major-league club. I think there was a two-year span where 11 guys we signed, or traded for at the minor-league level, got to the big leagues. Rick Reed and Brian Bohanon were two of them, and at one point in time they were two-fifths of the rotation. And there were other guys. We traded for Matt Franco. We signed Andy Tomberlin. We brought in Todd Pratt, who hit one of the remarkable home runs in Mets history, a historic home run that got us into (the National League Championship Series). So really, you just think about doing your job and about what you can do to get better.

DL: You're not in any way surprised at how active you've been since taking over?

JZ: Once again, I don't look at my job that way. I don't sit and evaluate myself and think about what I have to do to be effective in terms of wheeling and dealing, as you put it. I just come to work every day with the idea of, 'How do we get better?' 'How do we make our ball club better?' 'What are our options?' 'What are our opportunities?' We go forward from that with any deal that we make, or with any free agent-signing. And with any trade, I always hope that it helps both clubs. I hope that the guy on the other end is getting a deal that helps his club, just as it helps ours, so that we've met each other's needs. I've never tried to be in a position where I "won" a deal. I don't like that, and when I deal with people who have that approach I think that it's self-serving.

At the end of the day, we're all professionals, and when you sit and talk to someone, your credibility is on the line. You obviously may see things differently, and that's OK, but when we're making a deal it's because the other team has a certain need and we have a certain need. And sometimes clubs go in different directions, and that makes things come together. Take the deal we just made with Philadelphia. We think that we probably gave them three very nice young players who are going to be big leaguers for a long time. That serves what they were looking to do, and we, in turn, got a pretty good pitcher (Cliff Lee) that fits nicely in our rotation. So, at the end of the day when I sit down with Ruben (Amaro), we can say that we met each other's needs and let's talk again in the future. I think that is how deals come together.

DL: You've obviously made some attention-grabbing deals. What about moves that have mostly flown under the radar but you see as having a notable impact on your ball club? Do any stand out?

JZ: So much gets written about a deal at the major-league level, but there are other things, such as the people that you bring in to work with you, including at the minor-league level. I think that we've made some significant moves in the minor leagues this year, which no one talks about. We hired Carl Willis as our pitching coordinator. This guy has seven years as a big-league pitching coach and had CC Sabathia and Cliff Lee under his tutelage in Cleveland. We brought in Tim Laker as our Double-A manager. And we've done some things in other areas. We've brought statistical analysis to life here in Seattle, if you will. I'm sure that other people have done it here in the past, but I think that we've taken it to a different level, at least in terms of meeting our needs, with someone like Tony Blengino. Things like that sometimes fly under the radar. We hired Andy Stankiewicz as our minor-league field coordinator and I think he's going to be terrific. Moves like those go unstated because people don't really know them, but we think they're big moves. And hiring a guy like Don Wakamatsu—as far as any moves, that might be at the top of the charts because of what Don did last year. He was simply a good fit, and at the end of the day, you're just trying to have the best fit for your organization, for your city, for your club. There are a lot of nice pieces that are helping us a lot, and those would be some of the top ones.

DL: One of your recent hires was Jeff Kingston, who replaced Lee Pelekoudas as assistant general manager. Can you talk a little about that?

JZ: Lee is very qualified and had a tremendous amount of experience. He had been here forever. But with Jeff—every time you're in this chair, you want to make sure that everything around you meets your comfort level. With Jeff, there was a real bonding, if you will. I've known him for awhile, and when the position became available, I interviewed a bunch of guys, a great group of guys, and Jeff was someone who just really fit the criteria I was looking for. He's young, he's smart, and he's done a lot of things in a short period of time. There was simply a great comfort level, and I think that's important. And that's nothing against anybody. We made a lot of changes when I came in. We changed the farm director. We changed the scouting director. There is just a natural progression, when new people come in, where you're going to have changes. That's just how baseball works.

DL: One year ago, your statistical analysis department consisted of Tony Blengino and a handful of consultants. What does it look like now?

JZ: We've brought in a couple of people. Jeff has a good background in that. Andrew Percival, who does a lot of advance work for us, helps in that regard. We've kept Tom Tango on board, which is good. We have another gentleman on board whom we brought in. Matt Olkin is no longer with us; he was a consultant for us a year ago. We've also hired a few of our interns, who are some pretty bright people. We brought them on board, and they're kind of getting their feet wet doing some leg work for Tony. So, it's expanding a little bit, and we're real happy. We've also hired Dave Lawson to work with us. He's done that work in the past. It's ongoing, it's very informational, and it's helped us a lot.

DL: When he talked to Baseball Prospectus last winter, Blengino said, "defense is kind of the final frontier, with a few teams coming at it from different perspectives." How would you define the Mariners' perspective?

JZ: Well, we've emphasized it. I don't think there's any question about that. And I think the one thing you always need to look at is the availability of what is out there when you're making a move. And when you do make a move, how does it fit your ball club, and how does it fit your ballpark, and how does it fit your philosophy? What kind of product are you trying to put on the field? And when you're looking at defense, which has obviously been an emphasis this winter for a few clubs—Boston being one that has really stretched out to improve its defense—it does come down to pretty simple things. If you're really good in center field, and you're really good at shortstop, and you can be really good behind the plate, there's one defensive statistic that gets overlooked. What is the No. 1 defensive position on the field? It's pitching. I mean, that guy holds the ball and controls everything that goes on in the course of a ballgame.

But, we talk about defensive zone ratings and all those things, and they're very important, and what I think they do is solidify and put credence to a lot of your thoughts and philosophies. You now have, as opposed to just an opinion, something that will verify your thoughts. Take Ryan Langerhans. I give Tony a lot of credit on Ryan Langerhans. Now, that was one that was under the radar. Here is someone who was sitting in Triple-A and nowhere in sight in terms of their radar screen, but we lost Endy Chavez, who we had been very happy with defensively, and we were looking for someone to come in and not only be a big-league player but also help us defensively. Tony came up with Ryan Langerhans. He walked into my office and said, "This guy fits our needs," and in the course of a couple of phone calls we ended up with Ryan Langerhans. He wasn't a huge piece, but he was certainly a guy who did a very nice job for us, playing very solid defense. As a general manager, it's my job to interpret information and fit it into what we're trying to do. Our pitching was successful last year, in large part, because we had good defense. We had really good defense, and that became a theme. The more we went along, the more we realized that if we can catch the ball and prevent runs, the more it will help us. Outside of Russell Branyan, we didn't have any 30-home-run guys on our ball club, so what are you going to do? You prevent runs, and that's what we did.

DL: Talking about the advancement of defensive metrics, Bill James recently said, "The only difference between our ability to evaluate defense and offense, at this point, is confidence." Do you agree with that?

JZ: Well, Bill James is a hell of a lot smarter than I am, and he's got an enormous amount more experience than I do, but I'd have to read the entire context of how he said that in order to be able to interpret it exactly. I know we have confidence in our own information. We have confidence in what we're doing, and it goes hand-in-hand with how we'll try to solidify something through defensive metrics or whatever type of form we're looking at. We also try to have a scout in the ballpark to see what he thinks. It's checks and balances, because I like to have a lot of information before we make a call. Using Ryan Langerhans as an example, we made calls to scouts. Can he play center field? Can he play left field? Can he play right field? But as far as (defensive metrics) go, yeah, it is a new frontier, and I think that's what (James) was probably referring to. People haven't all jumped out there and said, "This is what we're going to do because we believe in these numbers," but we've taken steps. Any decision we've made in terms of addressing our club, in regards to defense, was made with a lot of information, and we're continuing to go that route.

DL: Scouting is generally accepted to be an inexact science. That being said, are there elite scouts?

JZ: Oh, yeah. I tell our guys this a lot. I've always been amazed, over the course of the years, when somebody makes an acquisition, and you'll end up sitting with people and saying, "How did that guy become Comeback Player of the Year?" or "How did you know this guy was going to do that?" There is so much said about the understanding of the swing of a hitter or the understanding of a hitter's confidence, and there are also the instincts of a scout who really gets it. He sees the body type, and he sees the things that the player does, like how he hits in certain counts. He sees pitchers' deliveries and how they use the stuff they have.

What is the difference between a really good pitcher and one that should be a really good pitcher but isn't there yet? What is it? Is it adjustments? Is it the ability to use his stuff? I mean, I can sit here with Carmen Fusco, who I have a great deal of respect for, and he can tell me about the swing, he can tell me about the approach to hitting, he can tell me a lot of things. And this is why you go out and hire quality pitching coaches and quality hitting instructors. They understand it. They get it, and really good scouts see it. And once they tell it to you—sometimes you're going to make a decision based on a particular person's gut feel, and that says a lot about people who have had a lot of success. They have confidence, they believe in what they see, and they have a track record of being right. They've done their homework, so it's not a shot in the dark. There's a definite reason why they're making the assessment they make.

DL: How seriously did your organization look into Aroldis Chapman?

JZ: Well, he's a tremendous talent, and I tip my hat to Cincinnati for securing that type of player. We were there. We saw him. And we've seen him pitch for awhile. Bob Engle had a history with him. He knew him. We sent our guys in to watch him work out, but at the end of the day Cincinnati put the best deal on the table, apparently.

DL: If you were given information that showed Barry Bonds could help your ball club, would you consider signing him?

JZ: I think that we're open to doing a lot of things. I don't think we've ever closed a door to anything. So, if anybody walked in today and said, "We need to consider this player," we would have to look into a lot of factors. Finances would be one issue. In this case, how long the guy has been away from the game would be another. There are many factors that go into any decision, but we would certainly keep our door open to anybody who wants to come and play in Seattle.

DL: Mariners fans are getting pretty excited about the team you're putting together. Knowing that, would you be willing to make a deal that resulted in the team's taking one step back in 2010 in order to take two steps forward in 2011?

JZ: I wanted to win last year, so I don't think that anybody's expectations for this ball club are ever going to be any higher than my expectations. I expect us to be competitive. I expect us to be a ball club that goes out and plays day in and day out. That said, the message I hope to send out there is that we want to build this organization and sustain it for a long period of time. I've never been one to look for instant success. Or maybe how I should put it is that I've never looked to have success for just a short period of time. That's not what we're trying to do. What we're trying to do is, through the draft and through the acquisition of players... an interesting note on this club is that every position player on this club will be back next year. Ichiro is signed. Gutierrez is signed. Bradley is signed. And any of the young players that will play left field, whether it is Saunders—he's a young kid who will be back. Figgins is locked in. We've got Jack Wilson coming back, who will be a part of this organization. We've got Kotchman. We've got the catching back. If we're going to be a good club, stability is going to be an important factor as we move forward. And if we're going to be an elite organization, we're going to have to do it with the players in our system, like your Carlos Triunfels and your Alex Liddis and your Nick Hills, with guys like that emerging through the system and becoming forces at the major-league level. That's how you build and establish a good major-league ball club.

We've done a lot of things this year because we had to do a lot of things. We did things last year because we had lost 101 ballgames (in 2008), so we couldn't exactly run that same club out on the field. As we move forward in this whole process, I hope that our best players are players that we drafted, signed and developed. And when you acquire players, you acquire players who will be with you for awhile. Sometimes you need to go out and add a piece here or there, and we have done that, but again, if we're going to become elite it's because we developed our good players and maybe added here or there to put the finishing touches on it. By 'it' I mean a championship ball club here in Seattle.

DOCTORING THE NUMBERS
Learning the Game
Rany Jazayerli

Rany Jazayerli wasn't the only BP author who had a love affair with Strat-O-Matic, but he was the one who wrote the following ode to the game's utility as a teaching tool.

I'll never forget where I was 10 years ago this Monday.

It was not the kind of earth-shattering, life-changing moment that would forever alter the world in which we live, like the moment I heard about the Challenger disaster, or watching the horrors unfold six weeks ago. But like the first time I saw my future wife, it was a day that would change the course of my life.

On October 22, 1991, I saw a Strat-O-Matic card for the first time. My life as a baseball fan has never been the same.

I had just begun my freshman year of college at Johns Hopkins University. Even then, my passion for baseball was all-encompassing, but having spent the previous seven years living overseas my relationship with the game was a lonely one. My first days of college were no different; hard-core baseball fans who had read Bill James were in short supply, and that September I went to a half-dozen games at old Memorial Stadium, just a few blocks from the university, mostly on my own.

So when I saw a flyer advertising for a "simulation baseball league" that would be drafted the following day, I tore off a stub and quickly called the contact number to learn more. At the time, I had never heard of Strat-O-Matic. I was familiar with Rotisserie-style fantasy leagues, but the concept of simulation gaming was completely foreign. Every player's performance is re-created on a card? Dice are used to reproduce at-bats?

But it was baseball, and it was a group of guys who loved the game. When you're a college freshman, one of your top priorities is to fit in. This was a group in which I would. So with a ticket to the Friday night game on Memorial Stadium's final weekend already in my possession, I passed up the real thing for an imitation. Nearly a dozen guys showed up, and about half were as new to the game as I was. The Strat veterans in the room went over the ground rules, and by the time we finished the 26-round draft (25 players and a ballpark) around midnight, I was hooked.

Ten years later, the relationship shows no sign of ending. Along the way I started my own league, participated in tournaments all over the country, and met people of every different stripe, bonded only by their love of the game.

Along the way, something completely unexpected happened: the more I played Strat-O-Matic baseball, the more I learned about the real thing. The following truths about baseball were burned into my brain:

- The heart of the game lies in the matchup between the pitcher and the batter. The importance of that statement cannot be overestimated. The result of every at-bat is determined by how these two players stack up. In Strat-O-Matic, each at-bat's result is selected from one of six columns: three of these columns exist solely on the hitter's card, and three on the pitcher's card. The result is a natural 50/50 balance between offense and defense.

    This 50/50 balance has been proven correct by study after study—teams with good offenses but poor pitching staffs do just as well as teams with great pitching but an impotent lineup—but a strong sentiment that pitching is somehow more important still lingers in baseball. In Strat, as in real baseball, good hitting can beat good pitching. And vice versa.

- Performance is independent of context. Strat-O-Matic devises each playing card to perform as closely as possible to the player's real-life performance, but in doing so the game company assumes that the context for each player remains the same as in real life.

    For example, in 1990, Joe Carter had one of the great fluke RBI seasons of all time for the Padres: despite a .232 average and just 24 home runs in more than 600 at-bats, he amassed 115 RBIs and cemented his reputation as a run producer. Those naive enough to fall for this failed to notice that batting ahead of Carter were Bip Roberts, Tony Gwynn, and Roberto Alomar, all of whom got on-base at a terrific clip, were pretty fast, and rarely cleared the bases with a homer themselves.

    Strat-O-Matic correctly figured that in creating Joe Carter's card, there was no need to make a drastic adjustment to his RBI total. Used in the same role as he was used in the majors, batting fourth and fifth, Carter would be likely to drive in close to 115 runs even with his terrible performance. But taken out of that context—in a draft league—Carter's RBI total would be more in line with the rest of his numbers: unacceptable.

This wasn't true just with RBIs. Bobby Thigpen wasn't anything special because he had 57 saves; his Strat card mimicked his performance in real life. If he was used as the closer for the White Sox in a replay of the 1990 season, he no doubt would have racked up tons of saves, pitching for a team that had lots of small leads to protect in the ninth inning. Taken out of that context and evaluated on his own merits, he was no better than any other closer with a similar ERA and peripheral numbers. Bob Welch might very well have won 27 games in a Strat league had he pitched in front of the A's offense all season, but taken out of that context, he couldn't hold a candle to Roger Clemens's better ERA and baserunners-allowed totals.

- On-base is king. Strat made a change to the visual appearance of the cards beginning with the 1990 card set, which was the first one I saw. All results in which the batter reached base safely were in bold print and all caps. All outs were left unbolded and in lower case. You can't play Strat for long before realizing that, in essence, only two things can happen in an at-bat: either the batter reaches base or he makes an out. Nothing drives home the point like seeing WALK on a card with the same rousing font as HOMERUN: reaching base safely, regardless of how, is ultimately a victory for the hitter. Making an out, no matter how many times you move a runner from second base over to third, is ultimately a failure.

I learned other things as well. I almost instantly became more knowledgeable about individual players. Before I played Strat for the first time, I would have been hard-pressed to tell you whether Barry Bonds batted from the left side or right side. I had no idea about lesser players who didn't appear regularly on ESPN's first season of *Baseball Tonight*. I knew that Eddie Murray was a switch-hitter, but Mark Lemke?

By playing Strat, I learned that Cal Ripken grounded into an enormous number of double plays, and that John Wetteland was easy to steal bases on. Because every card is separated into performance versus left-handers and right-handers, I learned that Shane Mack was a lefty-killer of the highest order, that Roberto Alomar hit better from the left side than from the right, and that the right-handed Gregg Olson was actually much tougher on lefties than on right-handed hitters.

I already knew that Wrigley Field was a great hitters' park and that Dodger Stadium was a pitcher's dream. But because Strat incorporated ballpark effects on homers and singles into the game, I learned that Riverfront Stadium was one of the most underrated home-run parks in baseball, while Jack Murphy Stadium was a terrible place to hit for average.

I learned to test my own theories about the game. Having watched numerous managers devise their own cockamamie lineups, the ones with Darren Lewis leading off and George Bell batting cleanup, I had the chance to create my own. I started by selecting the best leadoff hitter and then moving down the lineup, and suffered through years of dysfunctional lineups until I learned that you have to start with your #3 and #4 hitters, and then build the lineup outward from there. I learned that I would have a tactical advantage by alternating left- and right-handed hitters as much as possible. The first time I played in a Strat tournament (where they eschewed the DH), I was completely intimidated by the art of the double-switch. Eventually I became not only comfortable with the move, but by learning to slot an outfielder in the #6 or #7 spot and stash a good fourth outfielder on the bench, I learned to anticipate it before the game even began.

Bill James once wrote—in all seriousness—that every prospective new manager should be forced to play a simulation game like Strat-O-Matic or APBA until he mastered it. As silly as that may sound, the fact is that too many managers get wrapped up in the personal relations of the job (keeping 25 personalities in check, talking to the media, staying on the GM's good side) and overlook the personnel relations, continuing to put Joe Hacker and his .280 OBP in the leadoff spot. A few hundred games of Strat might help managers take a step back and coldly evaluate their players as resources. They might come to see the importance of high OBPs at the top of the lineup, the futility of using a "contact hitter" with no other redeeming features in the #2 hole, or that the costs of trying to steal with anyone other than the best base-stealers outweigh the benefits.

Once I had learned things playing simulation baseball on a hardwood table, I found that this new knowledge made the experience of watching the real thing more intense. Before, I could watch Tommy Lasorda bring in a lefty to face Andy Van Slyke and have no idea how that move altered the game. Now, knowing that Duane Ward didn't hold runners well, I could see the added importance of Harold Reynolds working a full count against him. During the playoffs, I could look at the Braves' assortment of bench players and figure out for myself that Bobby Cox, whatever his strengths, was tactically unprepared for a close game.

A year after I picked up the game, I started my own play-by-mail (now play-by-Internet) Strat league. Now, instead of drafting cards which were merely representations of how a player performed, I was drafting the players themselves; the league was a perennial one, and as in the era of the reserve clause, once you acquired a player you owned his rights permanently. I was GM of a franchise, scouting the best minor-league talent, scouring major-league rosters for overlooked ability, reading the injury reports on sore-armed pitchers.

In this role, Strat-O-Matic is no different than any other fantasy baseball league that carries players over from year to year. Except it is. In a Rotisserie league, the strict salary cap means that the relative value of a player is as dependent on his salary as on his talent. You might argue that the lack of salary considerations in a Strat league is hardly a realistic model of modern baseball economics, but it helps to keep the focus on two things: how to spot talent, and how to mold that talent into the framework of a winning baseball team.

Strat players have known for years what major-league teams are only beginning to discover for themselves: you're either contending or rebuilding. If you're not going to win this year, the best way to win next year is to move every aging veteran, lock, stock, and barrel, to a contending team for the best collection of young talent you can extort. There is no glory in third place, while a pennant flies forever. Better to win 50 games this year and win 95 games the next than to finish at .500 in each season.

Strat-O-Matic's greatest weakness is that, unlike Rotisserie or other fantasy leagues (and unlike Scoresheet Baseball, the premier in-season simulation game on the market), Strat is not played in real time. The game company releases the cards during the winter, after the season is complete and the statistics are all known. When you sit down to play, you know what your players can do; you know if you've got the .350-hitting Darin Erstad or the .250-hitting version. This is, of course, completely unrealistic, and strips the game of one of baseball's greatest treasures, its unpredictability.

The saving grace is that, by displaying all the numbers in plain sight and baring the inner workings of the game, Strat creates a transparency which gives someone who plays the game the illusion that he is in control of his own fortune. In real life, it is impossible to know the exact odds of any given move, because you can never track every single variable that can affect the outcome: wind speed, the glare of the sun off the third-deck facade, whether the opposing pitcher has a tweak in his shoulder which he only feels when he throws his slider, whether the home-plate umpire decides to expand his strike zone an inch so he can get home early to watch *ER*... In Strat, it is theoretically possible to determine the costs and benefits of any particular decision. You really do know if pinch-hitting Dave Magadan for Damian Jackson will increase your chances of tying the game with a single. You know the exact probability that Eric Young will steal a base successfully.

While on the surface this seems like a flaw in the game's design, the result is that by allowing managers to make an informed decision, the consequences of those decisions provide powerful and instant feedback. It's easy for Don Baylor to give Young the green light with Sammy Sosa at the plate and the wind blowing out at Wrigley, or for Bobby Valentine to let Rey Ordonez hit with the Mets down by a run in the eighth. There's no accountability, because there's no way to know that Young had a 40 percent chance of being thrown out, or that Lenny Harris would have tied the game with a double.

In Strat, there is. Once you've played enough games and had enough baserunners thrown out trying to steal when they had a 60 percent chance of success, you learn to be more conservative. Once you've had your light-hitting shortstop come to bat in the middle of enough ninth-inning rallies, you learn to pinch-hit aggressively in order to maximize run-scoring opportunities. More importantly, you learn to stock your bench with players whose strengths coincide with your starters' weaknesses, so that you might have an attractive pinch-hitter candidate to call on.

My suspicion is that this transparency is the reason why so many people continue to play Strat instead of another simulation game like Diamond Mind, which is a more realistic game run by people who understand sabermetrics. For all its advantages, when Diamond Mind stopped printing cards in order to focus exclusively on its computer game, it lost any chance of convincing longtime Strat players to switch. (Strat-O-Matic's computer game, while it adds an impressive array of bells and whistles, is at its heart simply a faithful re-creation of the card game.) When every conceivable outcome is printed before you on a three-by-five piece of card stock, it's easy to think that you're in control. When the results are generated behind the curtain of a computer program, the illusion of control is lost.

In the end, though, it is just an illusion. Perhaps the most important lesson to be learned from Strat is this: no matter how well you prepare, no matter how much the odds are in your favor, Chance can sweep in at any moment and trump your best-laid plans. Not everyone accepts this gracefully—I've lost count of the number of 20-sided dice I've seen hurled out of windows from a great height—but eventually you have no choice but to accept that there is only so much you can control. Randomness lurks behind every corner, ready to ambush your team at a moment's notice.

And this, too, is like real baseball, for in baseball, more than in any other major sport, the best team doesn't always win, even against the worst team in the league. In 2000, every team in the majors won between 40 percent and 60 percent of its games. The Chicago Cubs (with the worst record in baseball) faced the Atlanta Braves (who were tied for the second-best record in the game) nine times—and won five of the matchups. In a sport where the margin between greatness and mediocrity is so slim, where the winningest team of all time can lose in the World Series in six games, talent will take you only so far.

DOCTORING THE NUMBERS
The Doctor is... Gone
Rany Jazayerli

In 2000, Rany Jazayerli used the term "the Three True Outcomes" to describe offensive events that were not dependent on defense, in the process spawning a long-running series on the TTO leaders at BP. Once Vörös McCracken found that batting average on balls in play against a pitcher in one season is not very predictive of his future performance, compared to his strikeout, walk, and home run rates, TTO assumed additional importance as an analytical tool.

For this week's article, I'd like to look at the amazing hot streak of Johnny Damon, who is hitting .477 since th-...hey, who let you guys in here? And what's with the funny-looking helmets? Hey! Put me down! STOP THA...

Do not adjust your computer screen. We are in control now. Do not be alarmed. Do not panic.

But do not ignore us.

My identity is not important. What is important is that, if you ever want to see The Good Doctor again, you will listen to what we have to say.

We are members of the Rob Deer Fan Club. And we are here to tell you that the Revolution has begun. The Revolution that will spread the Gospel of the Three True Outcomes to every man, woman and child on Earth.

What are the Three True Outcomes, you ask? They are:

- The Home Run, the weapon with which we fight the evil legions of Little Ball.
- The Strikeout, a symbol of our refusal to compromise.
- The Base on Balls, which brings balance to our cause.

Together, the Three True Outcomes distill the game to its essence, the battle of pitcher against hitter, free from the distractions of the defense, the distortion of foot speed or the corruption of managerial tactics like the bunt and his wicked brother, the hit-and-run.

(Some in our ranks claim that the hit-by-pitch meets the spirit of the Three True Outcomes and should be included in their ranks. The issue is to be decided at the Council of Oakland later this year.)

Still skeptical of our cause? Consider that the highest single-season Three True Outcome (TTO) average (defined as (HR+BB+K)/(AB+BB)) by a batting qualifier in history, 57.7 percent, belongs to Mark McGwire in his record-setting season of 1998. Feel our power.

If the Three True Outcomes are sacred, those who practice their art are our prophets, brave men who dare to lead mankind down a brave new path. The position players who have the highest career average of TTO (min: 1000 PA):

Name	Career	AB	HR	BB	K	TTO%
Dave Nicholson	1960-67	1,419	61	219	573	52.1%
Melvin Nieves	1992-98	1,228	63	136	483	50.0%
Rob Deer	1984-96	3,881	230	575	1409	49.7%
Jim Thome	1991-	3,077	196	646	882	46.3%
Bo Jackson	1986-94	2,393	141	200	841	45.6%
Mark McGwire	1986-	5,652	522	1185	1400	45.4%
Mickey Tettleton	1984-97	4,698	245	949	1307	44.3%
Sam Horn	1987-95	1,040	62	132	323	44.1%
Jay Buhner	1987-	4,604	282	725	1299	43.3%
Gorman Thomas	1973-86	4,677	268	697	1339	42.9%

Dave Nicholson may be forgotten today, but to members of the RDFC his name is still spoken in reverential tones. The first great leader of the TTO movement, Nicholson's message fell on deaf ears in an era of Maury Wills and Walter Alston, but his efforts paved the way for the all-or-nothing sluggers of today.

After breaking in with the Orioles in 1960, striking out 55 times in 113 at-bats, he was tortured with a return to the minor leagues for all of 1961 but returned in 1962 unrepentant. Nicholson finally got a chance to start for the White Sox in 1963 and fanned 175 times in just 126 games. Prior to 1963, no player in history had struck out more than 142 times in a season; Nicholson brushed that aside by the fantastic margin of 33 whiffs. Even today, Nicholson's season still ranks eighth on the all-time single season strikeout list. And every player in the Top 40 played in more games than Nicholson did that season. In fact, he still holds the all-time record with 1.39 Ks per game played.

(Yes, we know that the strike zone was expanded prior to the 1963 season, but every player that season had the same benefit. Only the greatest of men know how to seize such an opportunity to do something truly magnificent.)

While Nicholson's efforts went for naught, his cause was taken up by a new generation of heroes. Men like Gorman Thomas, Gene Tenace (40.6 percent career TTO), Reggie Jackson (40.4 percent) and Mike Schmidt (39.9 percent) paved the way for the modern era. An era defined by no one better than Robert George Deer.

During his heyday, 1986-93, Rob Deer led the AL in strikeouts four times and set the AL record with 186 Ks in one season, while averaging 27 home runs and 66 walks per year. In his most glorious season, 1991, Prophet Deer hit .179...and still managed a .252 Equivalent Average on the strength of 25 home runs and 89 walks.

After being banished from the majors for two seasons, Deer returned for one final farewell in 1996. In 50 at-bats, he struck out 30 times, hit four homers, and drew 14 walks. His TTO percentage that season was an unfathomable 75.0 percentage. The student had finally become the master: the record Deer had broken (minimum: 50 at-bats) had been set by Dave Nicholson in 1960.

But Deer's career ended that season, and the RDFC has been looking for a new leader, another great man willing to take upon himself the mantle (not Mickey Mantle, another early practitioner) of the TTO. We turned to men like McGwire and Jim Thome, but despite their obvious talent for the TTO, they were reluctant to actively proselytize the cause. Like Schmidt before them, they had received too much media attention as superstars to be seen for what they really are—great leaders of the TTO movement.

But just as we were giving up hope that we could one day find someone worthy of succeeding Rob Deer, a great man has emerged to lead us once again. We have held out hope since 1996 that he could be The One; that year, he struck out 166 times, with 40 home runs and 62 walks, in 130 games for Columbus of the South Atlantic League. His prodigious TTO abilities were not affected as he moved up the ladder; he drew 80 walks, hit 39 homers, and posted 150 strikeouts in 124 games in 1997. An injury felled him for much of 1998, but not before he had converted the entire Eastern League to his cause, hitting 16 homers, striking out 58 times and drawing 35 walks, all in just 43 games. His TTO percentage that season was an impressive 54.8 percent. He made his major-league debut that season, and he whetted our appetites when he went 0-for-4 with two strikeouts.

Last year, serious doubts emerged whether his strict adherence to TTO policy would make him nothing more than a martyr for our cause. Despite 30 home runs and 187 strikeouts for Triple-A Buffalo and a 56.1 TTO percentage in a late-season callup, major-league exceutives got bent out of shape over some perceived "weaknesses," like his .208 batting average in Buffalo.

But just as the darkest hour is followed by the dawn, so has the deep despair of last season been followed by the true breakthrough for our hero, Russell Branyan. In his first extended opportunity to play in the major leagues, Branyan has answered the call. In 122 at-bats, Prophet Branyan has hit 13 homers, drawn 17 walks, and struck out 55 times. His TTO percentage this season is 61.2. The greatest single-season TTO percentages of all time (minimum: 100 at-bats) are:

Name	Year	AB	HR	BB	K	TTO%
Russ Branyan	2000	122	13	17	55	61.2%
Dave Nicholson	1960	113	5	20	55	60.2%
Tony Phillips	1996	104	7	11	51	60.0%
Mark McGwire	1998	509	70	162	155	57.8%
Billy Ashley	1996	110	9	21	44	56.5%
Dave Duncan	1967	101	5	4	50	56.2%
Dave Nicholson	1962	173	9	27	76	56.0%
Jack Clark	1987	419	35	136	139	55.9%
Dave Nicholson	1964	294	13	52	126	55.2%
Rob Deer	1985	162	8	23	71	55.1%

For his career, Branyan has a TTO percentage of 59.8 in 164 at-bats. No position player is even close; the next-highest career TTO (minimum: 150 at-bats) rate is 53.4 by Rob Nelson, who as all members of the RDFC know, was the man who started at first base for the Oakland Athletics on Opening Day 1987—ahead of Mark McGwire. Maybe the A's had a reason to start Nelson after all.

Prophet Branyan has again been exiled to Triple-A Buffalo by an intolerant regime in Cleveland, which is why we have had to take such desperate measures. We will hold Dr. Jazayerli hostage until our demand is met: Russ Branyan must be allowed to practice his beliefs freely. He must be allowed to spread the Gospel of the Three True Outcomes to fans at major-league parks everywhere. He must be granted the privilege of rendering the opposing defense utterly irrelevant more than half the time. We will not rest until this is so.

We leave with a message for all loyal members of the RDFC: a great and glorious new era is upon us. Rejoice! A great man is here to lead us, and a new movement has been born.

The Russ Branyan Fan Club lives!

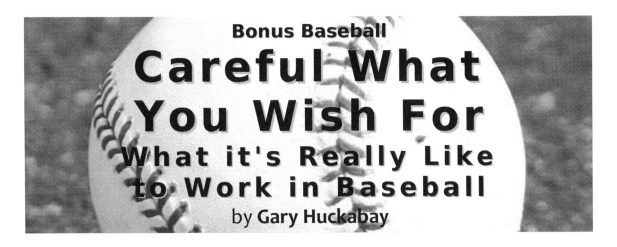

HR, But not the HR You're Thinking Of

I have a relative who's been an employee at Microsoft for a very long time. He also travels a great deal. One thing he's gotten pretty tired of hearing over the years is, "Hey, you know what I really hate about Windows?" So, for self-preservation purposes, he's developed a kind of canned faux identity, so he won't have to either hear unsolicited market research on the perceived shortcomings of products he's not involved with or get pelted by endless questions about ODBC drivers in Windows 7.

I have a similar problem.

About six or seven years ago, we at BP created a new logo and ordered some very nice polo shirts with the BP logo and the script "Baseball Prospectus." We ordered quite a few of these shirts. They're wonderfully comfortable pima cotton, jet black, with white logo and script. They're also numerous. I'm not much of a fashion plate most days, so the surplus shirts have been in my wardrobe ever since. Which leads, about once a month, to an unsolicited conversation, since I commute to San Francisco on BART every day. The conversation usually starts like this:

"Excuse me, do you work for Baseball Prospectus?"

Invariably, the person approaching me is a guy in one of two distinct demographic groups—both male, one older than 50, the other under 25. The conversation can go any number of directions, but it invariably ends with some version of "I think I should be working in baseball analysis. Can you help me get a job?" A smarter and more self-aware guy than myself would donate the shirts somewhere and purchase some new shirts. Instead, my brain went to exactly one place—do these people really have any idea what they're signing up for?

Certainly, baseball is cool. And I understand the increasing pressure and uncomfortable mendacity of many of the jobs in San Francisco's Financial District. But the really surprising thing is how little these people—fans and geeks enough to approach a perfect stranger on a train because he's wearing a website logo that they recognize—know about what it's actually like to work in analytics in baseball. I don't know why this surprises me; there's no reason they should.

I made the case many years ago that the real challenges in baseball analysis weren't really in the data anymore—they were in education, persuasion, and in championing the use of the best analysis available. So what are analysts and research groups and personnel doing in front offices today, and what are some of the implications of their work?

For this piece, I went back through my own research, deliverables, and notes from over the years and spoke with people who work as analysts or have a team of analytic types that work for them. Most work for major-league organizations, a couple work for player representation firms, and one works as an independent consultant.

I ran into an unexpected issue while going through the interviews. Most of the clubs and interviewees had no problem with my quoting them in this book. Unfortunately, a few of them really didn't want to discuss anything where they'd be identified by name. But when I wrote up the initial draft, you could so easily tell who the people were who didn't want to be identified that I might as well have provided their home addresses, Twitter feeds, and STD workups. So I've gone to simply making everyone anonymous; many of these folks have agreed to have some conversations with me for the BP website in the future, so I expect their anonymity will be short-lived anyway, much like their careers when they're outed as the wretched, unloyal leakers they are.

Sweet Leisure
The general public has a large number of misconceptions about working in the game. Usually, they're healthy misconceptions. Tony Bennett busts his butt working on scales so he can hit those notes, and the audience perceives it as effortless. This is a healthy misconception. With a few freakish exceptions, people don't go to concerts, or come to baseball games, to focus on the operational tedium that requires a huge amount of planning, execution, and repetition. They're not interested in how many reps Albert Pujols has to take to retain and refine that swing—they want to see him hit the ball with bad intentions. But the distance between observer knowledge and reality might be even longer when it comes to the "statheads lucky enough to land a job in MLB." One sentence really brought this home when talking with interviewees for this article. "We had touched base through email, and when I told him what I do, he said, 'So what do you do in the offseason?'"

Naturally, there's some variability in the amount of actual work time put in by different people in different places, but by and large, positions within clubs have high time demands. The work cycle, and the nature of the work, is often driven by events, most notably the June amateur draft. "It's pretty much living here as we get closer to the draft. Probably a quarter of the time is spent on putting together all the data, then there's putting together all the reports, adjusting, modifying, and then lots of communication and meetings." Other events, deadlines, and drivers of work? "As the trade deadlines get close, there's an assumption of availability; if the GM calls with a potential deal, it's time for in-depth research right now, and right now might be 11:30 pm on a Saturday night, with no slack time."

As you move towards the end of the season, clubs want to look at all their likely roster and team requirements for the upcoming season. "First, there's some broad reporting on pretty much everyone in the league or available to us. After that, we narrow down the focus to a smaller set of players which we evaluate in depth." What kind of metrics are used to perform these in-depth assessments? "I can only speak for us, but we don't end up with a single number like VORP or anything similar. They are competitive assessments, but it's not a quick-and-dirty situation. We might print out all the stuff from BP, FanGraphs, etc., and include those as part of a report, but only as a first cut."

Is there any part of the year where things do, realistically, slow down? It can't all be peaks—that'd be a flat line. "Pre-draft is the big peak. If there is a slowdown, I guess it would be more towards the end of the season, but the truth is that we never have enough people to do what we want to do."

Handcrafted

Have you ever read your own job description? How high was the correlation between the job as written on paper, and what you actually spend your time doing? Personally, my job heavily leans on the phrase that's probably in your job description as well: "...and other duties and responsibilities as required." No matter the industry, for most white collar workers, a large part of any position is what you carve it out to be, based on the needs of the company and the demands of the marketplace. The story is the same for statheads working in baseball. "When I first came on board, we needed to build the infrastructure to even support any analysis. So I was in IT and reported up that line. Then, once that was kind of in place, I started working on developing reports and simple applications. Over time, I got more involved with the actual stats, metrics, and presentation. Now I report up through Baseball Ops."

A second analyst became more and more involved in finance. The basic analysis of running iterative models—a player's contribution is worth X many additional wins above baseline, which could reasonably be expected to translate into more ticket sales, more listeners and viewers, etc. "It really was more on the revenue side, but that's changing. Revenues are decoupling from direct on-field performance somewhat." How are performances decoupling from revenue? It is happening to some extent in specific markets. As clubs move away from over-the-air free broadcasts and instead join sports networks like Comcast SportsNet, the revenue is driven more and more through subscriber fees, rather than through advertising sales. Depending on the specifics of a given contract or broadcasting situation, the rightsholder may view the package of baseball games as part of a portfolio of shows, rather than as a vehicle for selling ad impressions. "A lot of what we do in terms of player comparison and evaluation was originally driven by team need. Now, the team need may not be as clearly defined. it's not clear yet what's going to happen to calculation of a player's value. I think reevaluating how we think about that is going to be the biggest part of the next wave of analytic development."

Defining the questions to be answered is the biggest part of defining what the jobs will entail.

It's Just Some Combo of Ketchup, Mayo, and Relish, Right?
The biggest change in front-office analytics in recent years has been the introduction, use, and integration of more and more data. Instead of everyone working off a few databases that were pretty much available to anyone with a computer, clubs are now integrating scouting data, detailed positional information from the field, and a bunch of stuff I'm not allowed to mention into their quantitative assessment of players.

"The internet and web really drove the last generation of analysis. That's just not going to be the case with the next advancements." Why not? Because the next generation of analysis is going to take place in a competitive environment, not a largely academic one. "The web and the associated noise are largely a peer-reviewed model. And every club can spend $500 a year and get very good player evaluation. You can't have a competitive edge based on publicly available data anymore."

It's an interesting premise. One possible interpretation of this is that analytics can't really be the source of a competitive edge anymore. This is obviously not the opinion of the vast majority of clubs. If they didn't think generation and maintenance of a competitive edge through analytics was possible, they wouldn't be spending large amounts of time, engagement, and money to augment their analytics departments. "We've carefully investigated a bunch of new data sources and methods to determine which ones are valuable and which ones aren't. And of course I'm not going to tell you the results of our work; I just told you that it was a major undertaking, and we're not in the business of sharing the return on our investment."

So the time has apparently arrived for the clubs to turn the tables on the public. Where the public sphere once used advanced techniques on publicly available data to improve baseball management techniques, the private sphere has co-opted the best practices and best people to use on data that's not available to the public.

Even Pornographers Need Bookkeepers

There's a difference between intellectually understanding something and really internalizing it. In my specific case, I knew I wasn't going to be fielding groundballs at third base. I knew that I'd be working largely with data and would have to spend more time than I'd like persuading, cajoling, and educating in order for my contributions to get traction. There'd be people in the office who were tools. I had no doubts that there'd be at least one person who wore Axe Body Spray. It would still be an office. But after a bit of time, you're still working with SAS, still staring at a screen, still dealing with bureaucratic and administrative crap, and you're doing it for a heck of a lot less money than you could make somewhere else.

"If there really is any glamour, it wears off pretty quickly." No matter what, it's still a job. There's still the reputational pressure that comes with any job. Your name is on your work, and it's got to be done, and there's never enough time, resources, money, or people to do it. Your Microsoft Outlook still bombs out, or takes forever, or loses your email when you have to migrate machines. In short, it is a career, and for some, there are some perverse risks. "I don't work for my favorite team. Or, I guess I do now, but you kind of lose some of your personal attachment to a team. It's about the only way I can think of to 'lose' your personal favorite baseball team. And that's a strange feeling."

As for the money? "The money sucks. The free market works. There are thousands of people who would take my job in a heartbeat, most of them with way better qualifications than I have. And they'd do it for 1/3 the money they could make in another field. And my salary reflects that hard reality." But hey, you can usually eat off leftovers from the spread.

If you're in it for the money, you might be too dumb to do the job well, so you probably should stick with your first love, dentistry.

Everyone Wants A Buick Regal!

If you've ever worked at a company that wasn't the market leader and didn't have something else going for it, like cool products or engaged employees, I feel your pain. But think about this for a second—it could be worse. Someone, somewhere, was Alfredo Griffin's agent. Think of the sheer personal satisfaction of being part of those joyous conversations. "Like Alan Trammell, 'Fredo's a biped and enjoys significant vertical symmetry! His carbon dioxide expulsion rate is also right in line with Mr. Trammell's!!"

Such is often the lot of analysts who are in positions at player representation firms. Like clubs, agencies, particularly larger ones, have adopted and embraced statistical analysis techniques as part of what they do. The main difference, of course, is that their goals are different. Where clubs use statistical analysis to drive decisions, deploy resources, and try to maximize performance as best they can, the job of the agent is, of course, advocacy. The agent isn't in the business of optimizing the spend for a particular club—far from it. In the short term, the agent is looking to get the best possible outcome for his client—the player. That usually includes getting as much compensation for their client as possible, provided other criteria are satisfied.

So how does that flow down to an analyst working for an agency? I know it's hard for many traditional Baseball Prospectus readers, but imagine yourself bright-eyed, energetic, and ridiculously well-educated. A seeker of knowledge, and yes, even truth. Your favorite childhood ballplayer was Dwight Evans, and by God, he was dramatically underrated—the media didn't pay attention to his superlative defense, his propensity to draw walks, and his ability to take the field. Jim Rice did draw walks, had less ground to cover, and while being a great player, wasn't Dewey.

Now, go into your job as a player advocate and put together 40 pages on why the Milwaukee Brewers should sign Kei Igawa. It's not exactly seeking a higher truth.

"It takes a particular way of thinking, pretty much like a defense lawyer," said a junior analyst for a representation firm. "Everyone's really entitled to the best job advocating them as they can get. So we kind of try to find our guy's strengths and support the narrative and marketing that the agents are out there doing. In some cases, it's actually more fun than working the club side."

The Problem With Low-Hanging Fruit Is Some Other Bastard Has More Trees

There actually have been a large number of people and organizations that have gotten a lot of credit for development and adoption of advanced analysis techniques—Bill James, the Red Sox, Billy Beane, and Branch Rickey, just to name a few. By the 1990s, baseball was really in a position where its combination of loyalty over merit, conservative culture, and official status as "The Ultimate Old Boy Network" had effectively stunted its growth as an enterprise. Almost every other industry had been forced to modernize and improve, but not baseball. Even the most basic concepts in serious analysis, like ballparks having an effect on raw performance metrics, weren't really in heavy use.

The result was that there were a bunch of gains that clubs could make through early adoption of analysis. On-base percentage is something we should use more in player assessment? Okay. We shouldn't let Dallas Green and his pitcher-mangling usage patterns anywhere near a ballclub? Okay. Minor-league statistics really are valuable, when properly interpreted? Excellent. Early, big findings were capitalized on by early adopters, who could often find and exploit little glitches in the market for big gains. Pretty quickly, though, clubs saw that other teams were seeing real gains from this kind of high-minded stuff and started copying them. And it worked, by reducing the gains that could be easily seized by cutting-edge clubs and making it progressively harder to actually be "cutting-edge."

And that's where the nature of analytics jobs has landed. Much like investing in infrastructure and young players, teams (and, to a lesser extent, agencies) are now investing in an arms race where the battlefield is the backroom and decision-making, not hitting a baseball 500 feet or throwing a great fastball. As the field becomes more and more mature, and possibly less transparent, the importance of having the resources to perform great analysis might just amplify the importance of revenue. Where just a few short years ago, the limited number of statheads in the game may have served to level the playing field for the have-nots, they may now serve as a powerful mechanism to reinforce the leverage of the game's monied elite.

Which, of course, may dramatically change how I have to answer questions from potential job-seekers on the morning train.

Biographies

Mark Armour is the author of three baseball books, including *Joe Cronin: A Life in Baseball* (University of Nebraska, 2010), and his work has been featured in many journals and web sites. He is also the founder and director of SABR's Baseball Biography Project. He writes from his home in Corvallis, Oregon.

Tommy Bennett is a law student in New York. He has written various columns for Baseball Prospectus and was formerly editor of Beyond the Box Score. He believes the best way to judge a baseball city is by the number of people who keep score at the games. His interests include statutes, administrative law, and Mickey Morandini's unassisted triple play.

Russell A. Carleton is a life-long fan of and currently a consultant to the Cleveland Indians. He earned a Ph.D. in child clinical psychology from DePaul University, where he developed an unrequited crush on the Cubs. He currently lives in his mother's basement... erm, Atlanta, Georgia with his wife and two daughters, works for a research consulting firm specializing in mental health evaluation, and constantly has to endure reminders of the 1995 World Series.

Will Carroll wrote for Baseball Prospectus for several years and left in 2010.

James Click is currently the Director of Baseball Research and Development for the Tampa Bay Rays.

Bradford Doolittle is freelance sports journalist who writes for Basketball Prospectus, Baseball Prospectus, MLB.com, and the Associated Press, and has written for Slate, ESPN, *Sports Illustrated*, *The Kansas City Star*, Deadspin, *The Hardball Times*, and numerous other outlets. He is a member of the Pro Basketball Writers Association, SABR, and the Baseball Writers' Association of America. Bradford is based in the Uptown/ Edgewater area of Chicago, where he lives with his wife, Amy. You can follow him on Twitter under the handle of @bbdoolittle.

Jeff Euston writes the "Contractual Matters" column at Baseball Prospectus and maintains BP's Compensation Pages, an extensive online database of contracts and salaries dating back to 2000. In 2005, he founded Cot's Baseball Contracts, a web site tracking players, agents, salaries, and payrolls for each of the 30 major-league clubs. He lives near Kansas City, where he practices commercial real estate law and fixes his own speeding tickets.

Ken Funck has contributed his "Changing Speeds" column to BaseballProspectus.com, focusing on issues both absurd and sublime, and written for the annual each year since winning the inaugural Prospectus Idol competition in 2009. Ken lives outside Madison, Wisconsin (America's greatest small city) with his ever-supportive wife Stephanie, their children Max and Abby, two cats, two dogs, and a half-complete shrine to Rick Reuschel and the 1977 Cubs.

Kevin Goldstein is a national writer on scouting and player development for Baseball Prospectus. His work also appears at ESPN and other national outlets. He is the host and producer of Up and In: The Baseball Prospectus Podcast. He speaks to scouts and front office personnel on a daily basis, and his annual Top 11 prospects and overall Top 101 lists are must-reads throughout the industry. He lives in DeKalb, IL with the love of his life, Margaret, her kids Cameron and Xander, and a menagerie of animals with names like Otto, Underpants, Pickles and Neko-Chan.

Shawn Hoffman wrote for Baseball Prospectus from 2009 through 2010. He is now a research analyst with the Tampa Bay Rays.

Gary Huckabay is the Founder of Baseball Prospectus. He has served in a consulting capacity for several MLB clubs and player representation firms. His areas of focus are performance forecasting and valuation. Mr. Huckabay currently works in small business lending for a large financial services firm and serves on the Board of Directors of the Epilepsy Foundation of Northern California. He lives in the NorCal East Bay with his wife Kathryn and son Charlie. Gary is a frequent speaker at universities, charitable fundraisers, and corporate events.

Jay Jaffe is the founder of the 11-year-old Futility Infielder website (www.futilityinfielder.com), one of the oldest baseball blogs. He's been a part of Baseball Prospectus since 2004, writing the "Prospectus Hit and Run" column, covering the annual Hall of Fame ballot, and contributing to seven BP annuals as well as *It Ain't Over 'Til it's Over* and *Mind Game*. Elsewhere, he has written regularly for Fantasy Baseball Index and the YES Network's Pinstriped Bible. He once came in third in the famous Milwaukee Brewers sausage race, and in December 2010, he became a member of the Baseball Writers' Association of America.

Rany Jazayerli was a first-year medical student when he co-founded Baseball Prospectus in 1996. He's now a dermatologist in private practice in the western suburbs of Chicago, where he lives with his wife and three daughters. He writes regularly about the Kansas City Royals at ranyontheroyals.com and hosts a weekly radio show on the Royals in Kansas City. He also writes regular baseball columns for Grantland.com. He still contributes to Baseball Prospectus when time allows. As you can guess from the rest of this paragraph, that isn't very often.

Christina Kahrl is one of the five founders of Baseball Prospectus. Like many of her colleagues, that led to an unexpected career in sports, sparing her from a life spent studying 19th-century Europe and trying to come up with witty jokes about *junkers*. She has participated as a contributor to or editor of every edition of the annual, as well as *Mind Game* and *It Ain't Over 'Til it's Over*. She has contributed columns to *Playboy*, Salon, Slate, the *New York Sun*, SportsIllustrated.com, and ESPN.com and is also an associate editor of *The ESPN Pro Football Encyclopedia*. She's now a member of the BBWAA and an editor at ESPN.com and lives in Chicago with her partner, dog, cat, fish, and an everlasting sense of curiosity.

Jonah Keri is the lead baseball writer for Grantland. He is the author of the *New York Times* national bestseller *The Extra 2%: How Wall Street Strategies Took a Major League Baseball Team From Worst to First*. A Baseball Prospectus alum (2002-2006), he contributed to multiple BP publications, including *Baseball Between the Numbers*, *Mind Game*, and several BP annuals. His next project is a book about the comprehensive history of the Montreal Expos (due out spring 2014).

David Laurila grew up in Michigan's Upper Peninsula and now writes about baseball from his home in Cambridge, Massachusetts. Formerly with Baseball Prospectus, he now authors the Q&A series at FanGraphs.com and is a regular contributor to several other publications, including *Red Sox Magazine* and *New England Baseball Journal*. A co-chair of SABR-Boston, he is the author of the book "Interviews From Red Sox Nation" and has similar projects in the works.

Ben Lindbergh is an author and editor of BaseballProspectus.com. He has contributed to three BP annuals, ESPN Insider, and *Yankees Magazine*, and he served as assistant editor of *BP2011* and editor of the two-volume *Best of Baseball Prospectus* collection. He daylights as a baseball analyst for Bloomberg Sports, has interned for multiple MLB teams, and was inducted into the Baseball Writers' Association of America in December. A recent graduate of Georgetown University, Ben makes his home on the western shore of his native Manhattan, where he fancies himself the first line of defense against New Jersey.

Jason Parks joined the Baseball Prospectus roster in 2011, having spent the previous three years covering the Texas Rangers minor-league system for Baseball Time in Arlington (BBTiA), while also moonlighting as a pro scout in Mexico and the New York-Penn League. In addition to his regular writing duties, you can listen to Jason on the ever-popular "Up and In: The Baseball Prospectus Podcast," which he co-hosts with Kevin Goldstein. A native Texan, Jason now calls Brooklyn his home, living in the Bushwick neighborhood with his lovely wife Arden, their three cats, and his three personalities.

Dayn Perry is a regular contributor to FanGraphs, FOXSports.com, and ESPN Insider. He's the author of two books, *Winners: How Good Teams Become Great Ones* and *Reggie Jackson: The Life and Thunderous Career of Baseball's Mr. October*. He lives in Chicago with his wife, son, and dog.

Joe Sheehan was a founding member of Baseball Prospectus in 1996. He now writes for *Sports Illustrated* and contributes regularly to the MLB Network.

Keith Woolner joined the Cleveland Indians in 2007 and currently holds the position of Director of Baseball Analytics. He is the inventor of VORP, a well-known sabermetric statistic, and has published seminal research on many topics, including catcher defense, replacement level theory, pitcher workload management, bullpen strategies, and win expectation. He was a longtime analyst for Baseball Prospectus, contributing to several editions of the BP annual, as well as *Baseball Between the Numbers* and *Mind Game*. His Column "Aim for the Head" ran for many years on the BP website, where he answered statistical questions from readers. He also worked behind the scenes at BP developing much of the technical infrastructure and statistical databases that powered the website. He holds dual Bachelor's degrees from MIT in Mathematics with Computer Science and in Management Science and has a Master's degree from Stanford University in Decision Analysis.

Colin Wyers is the Director of Statistical Operations for Baseball Prospectus, which means he does a fair amount of math and logical thinking. He writes the "Manufactured Runs" column, which also entails a fair amount of math and logical thinking. When doing neither of these things, he can frequently be found rooting for the Cubs, which requires him to ignore most of the math and logical thinking from the previous two items.